D1095830

Lock, Stock and Barrel

THE STORY OF COLLECTING

THIS EDITION IS LIMITED TO FIVE
HUNDRED FIFTY NUMBERED COPIES,
FIVE HUNDRED OF WHICH ARE FOR
SALE. THIS IS COPY

NO. 84

The Pennsylvania Academy of the Fine Arts, Philadelphia

"The Artist in His Museum." *Self-portrait by Charles Willson Peale, pioneer American collector (p. 268).*

Lock, Stock and Barrel

THE STORY OF COLLECTING

By Douglas and Elizabeth Rigby

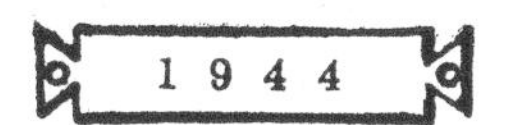

1944

J. B. LIPPINCOTT COMPANY

PHILADELPHIA · NEW YORK · LONDON

FIRST EDITION

❧

Under Government regulations for saving metal and paper during the war, the size and thickness of this book have been reduced below the customary peacetime standards. Only the format has been affected. This text is complete and unabridged.

Printed in the U. S. A. by H. Wolff, New York. Designed by Stefan Salter.

TO THE ENLIGHTENED AMATEUR, PRESERVER OF SO MANY GOOD THINGS OF THE EARTH, WHOSE CONTRIBUTION TO SOCIETY, ALTHOUGH GREAT, HAS BEEN LITTLE ACKNOWLEDGED.

"Collecting is a world habit. Collectors practise it consciously and with a definite, recognized aim. The rest of us practise it more or less unconsciously."

ARNOLD BENNETT

CONTENTS

A GUIDE TO THE ILLUSTRATIONS

(*Italic entries indicate titles of books and works of art*)

FACING PAGE

A WORD TO THE READER

WITH MANKIND'S CHANGING FORTUNES, there is to be found over the years a series of rising and falling cycles in collecting, and we of the twentieth century, even through the teeth of war, have been living in a period of great collecting ascendancy. There is overwhelming evidence to attest that the first half of this century in the West has witnessed more extensive collecting than ever seen before, and the evidence continues to promise for the future a still wider spread of the activity.

Should we measure collecting as a game, the question might well arise, has there ever been another that could compete with it or even fall within its shadow? It would be difficult to name a pastime which could muster over the centuries and the millennia a similar mass of devotees from children to graybeards, including athlete and cripple, king and commoner, intellectual and moron, the poor and the wealthy. As an international language collecting is not far behind love, as the *amateurs* at international clubs and exhibitions often demonstrate.

It is in the astonishing possibilities of collecting, which can accommodate so many kinds of humans, that much of its appeal is to be found. The hero of our time, the scientist, stems directly from collecting, and from the collecting bulk depends much of the continuity of cultures.

When Arnold Bennett wrote of collecting that it is a "world habit," practiced more or less unconsciously even by the non-collectors, he expressed an opinion that is today shared by many. Quite naturally, particularly over the last century, a habit so widespread has prompted a considerable literature. Yet, almost without exception, the hundreds of books on the subject have dealt solely with one or another of the collector specialties. This volume represents, apparently, the first attempt in any language to present a reasonably comprehensive picture of the general field.

Why and what is a collector? What makes him tick and to what purpose? For society at large and for the collector himself, what have been the outstanding contributions of this activity? These are among the questions considered. The reader is asked to remember, however, that on this subject a book of less bulk than a Shetland pony cannot have an encyclopedic completeness; for, as it has been wisely enough written, a true encyclopedia of collecting could be no less than a Britannica and would require the knowledge of many sages rolled into one. Regrettably but inevitably, then, certain details and phases of collecting must be omitted in these pages, which span the collecting gamut from rudimentary to highly selective forms and include an exploration of the psychology, history and techniques of the field.

There is nothing puzzling about the fact that collectors have limited their descriptions of the vast house of collecting to the single rooms enclosing their own favorite specialties. On the other hand, in exploring that house, it must strike the investigator as increasingly strange that its domain should have been so sparingly reported by anthropologists, sociologists and psychologists; for the roots of the phenomenon of collecting are of the roots of man himself, and they nourish many millions of us today through the practice of this ancient pastime. How many millions? No one knows. Never has there been a general census. Yet for the single field of stamp collecting the professional average estimate is seven and a half million followers in the United States alone.

We know that in this country and Canada there are dozens of periodicals and scores of special magazine and newspaper sections published solely for the benefit of various kinds of collectors; more than fourteen thousand art and antique dealers who cater largely to collectors; thousands of collectors' clubs, large and small, local and state-wide, national and international; while in purchasing power collecting is equivalent to a major industry.

It should be unnecessary to add that the conclusions submitted in the following pages are by no means offered as dogma; but rather with the conviction that, even within the limitations of authorship and space, a generalized interpretation and accounting of this prodigy which claims so large a share of humanity's affections and energies should in the aggregate be of positive value.

Granted that it is practically impossible to discern with accuracy every "why" behind George's impulse to collect books, Joe's to gather furniture, Tom's predilection for old witch balls, and Harry's apparent lack of interest in collecting anything; yet many of the answers yield to scrutiny and provide necessary pigmentation for the panorama. In approaching the story of collecting as we see it, the basic and primitive background is important and no less absorbing than the more familiar foreground; hence we search the lower branches of the collector's family tree before reaching the mature contemporary who is ensconced, like the silver star on the Christmas tree, at the top.

When the collector reads this book, as we hope he will, he will be reading about the long line of his ancestors, about history and the part he plays in making it. He may sometimes have wondered about that rowdy gang, the souvenir-snatchers, who pass themselves off as collectors. He may have wagged his head over the "magpie" and "warehouse" collectors, his backward brothers. They are here; but so are the great collectors, men and women to whom the world owes an infinite debt of gratitude. So, too, are the vast numbers of everyday collectors, not only of this age but of ages that have gone before.

Although *The Story of Collecting* will not instruct a man how to collect in his special field, the reader will find on display collecting techniques and practices common to all fields, the collector's relationship to museums and other public institutions, the parts played by wars, by social changes, by science, and a view of the cultural significance of the activity as a whole. In short, the collector will find his own likeness, his background and a glimpse of the future; and though it may not all be flattering, we believe it to be a fair presentation of a valuable member of the community, a fellow of deep ardor and unquenchable persistence who is able to take the composite picture in his stride.

Part One

THE COLLECTION AS A MEANS TO PHYSICAL SECURITY

> *"This is the way the sap-river ran*
> *From the root to the top of the tree—*
> *Silent and dark,*
> *Under the bark,*
> *Working a wonderful plan*
> *That the leaves never know*
> *And the branches that grow*
> *On the brink of the tide never see."*
>
> JOHN BANISTER TABB

TO UNDERSTAND the collector who, in today's world, is busy gathering up assortments of precious, beautiful or instructive things, it is not enough to think of him merely as an accumulator, a man of more than average energy, finding in his own way remarkable satisfactions.

The true collector is neither odd nor ordinary; his collecting is at once an art and a response to impulses of great depth. As an art, collecting has its history and its traditions. As an impulse, it is related to life earlier than man's. And in the aggregate, the form of its development may be likened to the unfolding roots and the branching of a great tree which, like some Burbankian masterpiece, bears a variety of fruits.

The first prodding in the evolving drama of collecting appears in that characteristic common to all organic life—the instinct to live; and while Man the Collector becomes the hero, he is far from being the only actor in the cast.

Using the word in its broadest sense, it can be said that there are three general types of collecting. The simplest form is to be found in the gathering and storing of food and other elements essential to survival, by and within the structure of a living thing. The body—of plant and animal alike—collects in this fashion, automatically.

This organic type of collecting parallels, in certain important respects, man's conscious effort in the forming of a true collection, since the organism brings together related matter selected for a definite purpose, and true collecting may be briefly defined as the intentional and selective gathering of related objects which, when assembled, form a unified and meaningful entity. The parallel becomes more significant when we examine the basic causes for collecting. The organism gathers and stores food in order to survive; and we shall soon see that much of man's impulse to collect also springs from factors originally related to his security needs.

In contrast to this process, wherein collecting is confined starkly within physical bounds, there appears another basic type that might be called external collecting. There are beasts, birds and insects which bring home and stow away food that may be needed in times of scarcity; some go further and store much more than they could ever use; others, reaching an even closer approximation of man's highly varied collecting activity, gather and hoard many useless objects, things to them apparently attractive, curious, strange. Moreover, these lower-life "amateurs" sometimes betray such collector-like attitudes as possessiveness and rivalry in ownership.

Man's reasoned method of forming a collection represents a far more intricate web of motives and techniques than either of these. For man has found multiple uses for the originally simple activity of accumulation; and the ultimate direction taken by human collecting in its various aspects is influenced by complex psychological mechanisms, by emotional urgencies and by racial and individual culture-differences, as well as by basic impulses.

Among all living things—plant, insect, bird, beast, human—food is the first material collected; and it will be found again and again, as the dominant theme, that the most significant single factor in all collecting is the search for security. Even the most enlightened collector is not excepted from this influence. Yet humanity's vast accumulations—the gatherings of stuffs and ideas into piles or collections, by individuals, communities, peoples—have been garnered not alone to serve the primal needs, but also to add to man's knowledge and spiritual well-being.

Man the Collector scales the heights and turns up the earth itself to bring home, not only the bacon, but the whole hog, the lock, the stock, the barrel, and the Lord's Prayer on a grain of rice.

Life, like the gods of the Egyptians, assumes many and various forms, and in nature each of these is deadly enemy to some other. There is a purpose in this counterbalance, in this NO opposed to the YES of life. The individual, however, doggedly ignores nature's intention. Rather does he exert himself, constantly and strenuously, to overcome the forces of opposition in the difficult business of remaining alive.

With many living things, the collecting of individuals into groups for mutual protection and service is a phase of this struggle against the NO in nature, with nature herself directing the "collecting." How much group activity may do to promote life requirements has been proven, chemically and biologically, even for quite simple organisms. As gregarious, and as aggressively protective of their essential property rights as any collecting human are some of the plants that grow in clusters or colonies; and when we turn to the animal kingdom we can find every form of "collection," from the rudimentary to the highly organized.

The flock and the herd, created by nature's plan rather than by their own volition, are nevertheless true collections in the sense that they consist of many individual "items" gathered together in one place for a definite purpose. They differ from collections of objects only in so far as no one individual asserts ownership over the lot; and at times—as when the stag gathers his does about him—even this difference disappears.

The purpose, as well as the degree of organization, varies in animal aggregations. Sometimes they occur for breeding purposes, sometimes to defeat collectively the dangers of darkness and cold. Sometimes they are created to provide a solid defensive front against attack. Or it may be to serve a more positive and creative purpose, as with the social insects whose whole life cycle is built on a base of co-operation. Always, however, collections of the living are in some fashion directed toward survival-insurance, and man has effectively woven protective gregariousness into the entire fabric of his life.

The tribe, the clan, the "large family" which included all relatives by blood or marriage—these were, and are, protective units, collections of individuals who feel themselves safer together than alone. Early man was afraid of solitude even in death, and practiced collective burial by placing several bodies in a single grave. The nomad traveled with a group of his fellows; and when he settled down, the cave he selected for his home had to be capacious enough to shelter the many rather than the few. This need for "sticking together" determined the communal character and the round shape of man's first true house, built when the group emerged from under the guardian rock; and it influenced the way in which he dug his graves, for early burial customs reflected the living habits of the people.

In later periods, with the large family split into many small families separately domiciled, man continued, nevertheless, to collect himself into well-defined groups—villages, towns, cities, nations, and even federations of nations—for convenience as well as for protection. Moreover, within these groups, founded upon a comparatively broad racial, religious, or geographical mutuality, smaller and more specialized groups collected about the idea of some specific co-operative service—burial societies, "fraternal" societies, mercantile and craft guilds, trade and labor unions, social clubs, cultural organizations, and so on.

Not even in our own "individualistic" society can the individual stand alone. He must still act, in most aspects of his life, as a component part of some ordered whole (in other words, within the structure of a true collection), if he is either to survive or to progress. The interdependence of all peoples is, indeed, increasing rather than decreasing, and despite the periodic setbacks of war (in which the primitive struggles for food and dominance still assert themselves collectively), we are fumbling toward an era of local, regional and world planning.

Not morality but necessity, necessity of the old imperious sort, is forcing us to this. Man, the collector of men and goods, will have to incorporate into his collections the three cardinal factors of form, order and value, or perish under the disorganized weight of his accumulations.

Of the many enemies which living things must hold at bay if they are to survive, starvation is the chief; and hunger is probably the taproot of the collector's family tree. "Granary, bin and cellar," as Lewis Mumford aptly puts it, "are village prototypes of library, archive, museum and vault." After food-hunger, other hungers follow—the hunger for power and prestige, the hunger for understanding and the higher pleasures—but since the primitive fear of physical insecurity, still strong among us, motivates many forms of collecting in the modern world, it must be dealt with first.

Before man learned how to cultivate the soil, he was a "food-gatherer." He hunted and fished and garnered his fruit and nuts and roots wherever he could find them. Even today there are some primitive tribes that have never advanced beyond this stage of development. But those peoples who were destined to march forward into civilization soon learned that mere gathering was not enough.

The first progressive step was taken when man ceased to rely upon the chances of the hunt, when he no longer counted upon finding grains and berries as he needed them, but, meeting the challenge of necessity with increasing forethought and prudence, began to construct places of storage. When drought came and the wild grains shriveled on the stalk, frightened man discovered how to make baskets and pots to hold reserve supplies, how to build granaries that would defeat the ever-lurking enemy, scarcity. When the caribou herds of the far north moved on to new grazing grounds, the northern man, who depended upon the caribou for his meat, evolved the use of the cache. And when long marches over waterless reaches became necessary, man alone among all creatures solved for himself the problem of storing water externally and portably.

In the animal kingdom there are numerous examples of external food collecting and storing. The grain-collecting ants, for instance, have been a source of human wonder since the days of King Solomon, and moralizers from Aesop onward have drawn lessons of prudence and foresight from these busy creatures. The bee stores her honey in combs, and the spider sometimes sews up a reserve supply of moths, flies and caterpillars, in neat little bundles hung on her web.

But often in the life cycle we find effect overstepping cause, so that an instinct which was, originally, absolutely necessary for the preservation of a species, may persist far beyond the limits of true usefulness. Our exemplary, grain-storing ants go right on putting by a supply of food, long after they have accumulated all and more than they would ever be able to use under any conceivable circumstance; and in the case of the bee, it has been proven, according to Rivers, that "the strength of the impulse to hoard stands in no true relation to the size of the hoard already accumulated."

Among birds, too, there are prudent collectors, and others, seemingly prudent, who are actually following a collecting pattern that no longer serves its original purpose.

Certain North American woodpeckers gather acorns and store them in holes that have been painstakingly pecked out of the trunks of trees. In the early spring, when these birds return from their winter travels, food is still scarce in the homeland, but the stored nuts—as convenient as canned goods from the corner grocery—are there to spread the tables of the wanderers. On the other hand, a species of woodpecker found in British Honduras makes similar food collections, despite the fact that the tropical climate renders any such foresight superfluous.

Like the Canadian Indian and the Eskimo, the bear sometimes stores his surplus food in pits which he covers up and camouflages. Leopards hang the unconsumed flesh of their prey on the branches of trees and bushes until such time as it may be needed. Even the lowly earthworm, so carefully observed by Darwin, stores in the underground passages of his home such a varied collection of objects as half decayed or partially dried leaves, twigs, pieces of paper, feathers, tufts of wool, horsehair, and even pebbles.

Among animals the rodents are the most extraordinary collectors. The squirrel's habit of collecting and storing food for possible future need has been the occasion of almost as much moralizing as has that of the ant. Beavers chew up wood and straw, and deposit hoards of this silage in their co-operatively damned-up homes. Rats have been known to make off with such delicacies as bags of sugar, whole puddings, heaps of potatoes, bunches of carrots and turnips, and so on, piling up the lot near their nests, much as we might lay in an extra supply before an expected blizzard. Field mice, piping hares and hamsters are also assiduous storage-room collectors of food.

Recently we watched a dog in a New York City apartment make a valiant attempt to bury an imitation bone in an overstuffed armchair. In the same way, a pet squirrel has been observed trying with passion to accomplish the impossible feat of burying nuts in a carpet; while a park squirrel will, despite the continuing bounty of its human guests, persist in hiding food to which it often fails to return. One writer has compared this "maladaptive instinct survival" to the physical survival of the appendix in the human body, an organ which persists in making its appearance although it no longer has any useful function to perform. And in much the same way, man's "collecting instinct" in its lowest terms is, in part at least, a survival of the methods of meeting primitive nutritive needs, and represents a no longer entirely required persistence of those methods. What, for example, would be the comment of a reasoning goat, upon seeing already well-fattened humans trying, in various ways, to store more and more and still more money?

Yet man's case is a bit complicated, for in him the initial impulse has been multifariously transformed, and has been turned toward the accomplishment of numerous ends which, bearing little resemblance to the original, have become in themselves the servitors of new and more complex requirements—as we should insist upon explaining to that hypothetical and presumably cynical goat.

Behind this transformation lies man's gift of imagination, his capacity for feeling and emotion. To the mind of man, things are not always what they seem. The commonest objects become transfigured, by a long and devious process of association, into symbols of more comprehensive significance, and more often than not the old meaning is thereafter completely submerged in the new.

The gregariousness of early men afforded individuals a measure of mutual protection; but later man finds something equally compelling in the ideal of friendship divorced from all thought of service. So, too, early man's craving for a physical security that should endure beyond the requirements of the moment expressed itself in the amassing of surplus supplies; but later man creates out of the security thus achieved the symbol of further goads and further satisfactions.

To be admired by one's fellows and to have influence and power among them is a desire almost as deeply rooted in man's nature as the desire to eat, and many a man has cooled his belly in order to warm his ego.

He may, if he be a New Guinea Trobriander, collect and display food, less out of necessity than for the prestige value of such a collection and display. If the primitive belongs to a cattle-herding people, he may want a larger herd than he needs, simply because he knows he will be admired and looked up to in his community, if he can accumulate more cattle than his fellows. Or, if he be a Bolongole savage, he may work the iron ingots which serve for money in his part of the world into thin spearheads, curiously shaped according to the whim of the maker. In this form, the spears are utterly useless for physical combat, but they serve as competitive symbols of wealth and originality. Every ambitious native wants to own as many as possible, and, at the great dancing feasts, will "delight in showing off his own" quite like any stamp-collector at a hobby show.

The entrance of the symbol and complex motive, however, does not always result in the elimination of the physical-security motif. It is obvious that either a full granary or a large herd of cattle signifies primarily a sufficiency of food and other material essentials. In many societies a collection of wives or of slaves may also have security value, because such a collection represents an adequate labor supply, directed, perhaps, toward the harvesting of food.

Moreover, wives, slaves and livestock frequently assume an additional security value through being used as mediums of exchange. A Fiji Islander can sell his wife for a musket, or use her as collateral with a creditor; and in Homeric Greece, slaves were negotiable commodities and might represent a profitable investment, while surplus livestock was gathered for the same reason. The interplay of exchange values is here neatly shown by the fact that an average female could be had for four oxen (there is no such stability in our market), while an exceptionally desirable one might command a price of as many as twenty of the beasts.

When man created money, it, too, became a symbol, a symbol but one step removed from the food he could purchase with it; and interestingly enough, the early import of cattle as money as well as a source of food carries over to our own language in at least two words of monetary significance. Thus, our word "fee" first meant cattle specifically; then property in general; and finally came to mean a sum of money awarded as compensation for services. Its German cognate, *Vieh,* still means cattle. And the English word "pecuniary"—relating to money—went through exactly the same evolutionary process starting with the Old Latin word, *pecus,* meaning cattle, followed by *pecunia,* which first signified property-in-cattle, then any kind of property, and finally, money.

Many of the things which civilized man collects—in the special sense of "forming a collection"—have definite commercial value. Books, paintings, antiques, stamps, coins and the rest—these things can be sold, often at a considerable profit. Hence purchase of them may represent an investment, a potential source of future security.

The amateur (the man who truly loves his collection and its subject) sometimes bitterly—and sincerely—resents the imputation that he is in any way swayed by material considerations in forming his collection. "The prices of old writings and paintings should not be discussed," declared Mi Fei, an eleventh-century Chinese amateur and connoisseur, and in so saying he spoke for a whole class of serious collectors. Many an amateur, far from improving his fortunes by gathering together a fine lot of artistic treasure, has actually maneuvered himself into comparative poverty in the process.

In strong contrast are those collectors for whom intrinsic value is actually the paramount consideration. The jewel collections of the Indian rajahs, for example, represent accumulated wealth first and foremost, even though certain of the jewels may also be prized for beauty or for historic association. And under special circumstances whole societies tend to collect only those things possessed of intrinsic or utilitarian worth—precious stones, armor inlaid with gold, gold and silver plate, or such books, for instance, as are required for a particular purpose. Whatever artistic worth things collected under such conditions happen to possess may appear more important to the outside observer than it actually did to the collector himself.

Between these two extremes—the amateur who refuses to consider or even to discuss the price of his treasures, and the collector who is only interested in the intrinsic value of his—many gradations of type are to be found. Moreover, there are certain facts of which every modern collector is well aware, and which must, unless he be of the fanatic variety, affect his attitude in this regard to greater or less degree. For example, he knows that *any* sort of object collected by a sufficient number of people may, through any one of the factors which affect the value of a collectible, at some time happen to command a price well worthy of consideration. Thus a single matchbox label—than which nothing could seem more valueless to the non-collector of matchbox labels—once brought the solid sum of eight hundred dollars, merely because a particular collector of labels needed that one specimen to "fill in a series."

Any good collector knows that if he creates an excellent collection, one not too greatly based upon a momentary fad or fashion, he is likely to have something that will retain much of its value even in bad times. It may even prove a safer investment than the more usual stocks and bonds. So one famous collection of books that cost its maker, Robert Hoe, about five hundred thousand dollars brought his heirs nearly two million. And a case closer to our own day was the stamp collection of Arthur Hind, the Utica manufacturer whose distinction it was to own, among other treasures, the most expensive single postage stamp in the world. Hind was a multimillionaire during the boom days of the nineteen-twenties. But when he died, during the depths of the subsequent economic depression, it was his stamp collection, *alone among all his holdings,* that retained its value, brought its original purchase price at auction, and gave his wife an inheritance. On a lesser scale, there are thousands of examples of this sort of thing which most collectors can hardly ignore.

Of course the informed collector realizes how greatly the value of an object of a sort generally desired by collectors may increase with the passage of time. Currier and Ives prints, to take a familiar example, were originally a form of American popular art, and they sold for from six cents to four dollars apiece, largely according to their size. Yet since these nineteenth-century prints have become twentieth-century collector's items, as much as thirty-six hundred dollars has been paid for a particularly rare example.

Few price rises can equal the record of Shakespeare First Folios, which sold originally for one guinea in 1623; brought thirty pounds in 1792; one hundred and twenty-one pounds in 1818; twenty thousand dollars early in the twentieth century; and for which, in the fabulous nineteen-twenties, fifty thousand dollars was paid not once but several times, while one price of sixty-two thousand dollars was recorded, and another of eighty-five thousand is thought to have been paid—all by private collectors. Rises in price very nearly as spectacular have been known to occur even within the span of a single collector's lifetime. A certain fine tapestry group, *The Months of Lucas,* which was sold out of the effects of King Louis-Philippe in 1852 for twelve thousand dollars, commanded a price of a hundred thousand, less than three-quarters of a century later; and Jerome Kern once paid four thousand dollars for a copy of the eighteenth-century English novel, *Tom Jones,* which, when his library was put up at auction four years later, brought him thirty-nine thousand.

It is significant that many of the greatest collectors of Europe and America, not only in recent times but ever since the rise of the capi-

Museum of Modern Art, New York

AMERICAN "PRIMITIVE" (*c.* 1790)

Anonymous and without intrinsic worth, the disarming appeal of "primitive" art such as this meets a warm response today—a refinement in collectors' values.

talistic system, have been bankers, businessmen and industrialists—hard-headed men of affairs who have realized that intelligent collecting of such things as books and *objets d'art* may represent a fruitful and comparatively secure form of saving and investment, an additional method of diversifying, and hence of protecting, wealth. This is not to say that shrewd prudence is the only motive which has turned such men to collecting, but it is true that they, above all others, have recognized this particular value of collecting and have usually taken it into consideration.

Years ago a dealer, George S. Hellman, hopefully brought J. P. Morgan, the Elder, a painting by Vermeer. At that time there were not four paintings by Vermeer in the United States, and the great Dutchman's name was strange to the Morgan ear. So—tactful and shrewd, after the manner of his kind—the dealer proceeded to deliver himself of some essential information. He discussed Vermeer's importance as an artist, and concluded with the statement that, since only twenty-eight examples of this painter's work were recorded in all the private and public collections of Europe, Vermeers were practically unobtainable.

Morgan gazed at the picture; abruptly asked the price.

"One hundred thousand dollars," said the dealer.

"I'll take it," snapped Morgan, and the deal was concluded.

Remembering that Morgan, although sincerely moved by beautifully wrought objects, was no authority on art, it seems more than likely that the banker's belief in the potentially increasing value of such a rarity was one important factor in producing his quick decision. (In 1927, according to the experts, the painting for which he had paid a hundred thousand dollars was worth a quarter of a million.)

Even nations have profited, in hard times, by the security value, the cash value, of collections. When old Egypt needed wood, she successfully exported well-wrought vases and jewelry, and in modern times, when nations are pressed for ready funds they often put on the market portions of their collections of art. The Russian and German governments have, in recent years, sold paintings and other art objects on the open market for this purpose.

By more indirect methods, the French government formerly brought huge amounts into its money coffers, for, shrewdly emphasizing its artistic leadership, France for years drew hordes of art students, art lovers, and art buyers to its shores, and these foreigners converted a steady stream of foreign money into French francs—which remained in France.

Collecting as a pursuit is ideally part of a world at peace, but when the collector is hurried along on the tide of war, he must pick up a few lessons in "realism," or sink.

In wartime, life itself, seeking escape, sometimes hangs in the balance for a little cash; and for the individual, as well as for many nations, the security value of collections may be forced into high relief by military upheaval. Successful collectors, often men of considerable acumen, are well aware that a neat bundle of fine art, of valuable books, of jewels or postage stamps can, in times of world stress, be the means to a new life if the old one should be ruined; and they realize, too, how relatively easy it is to take out this form of insurance. In some wars—World War I, the French Revolution, and the Napoleonic debacle are examples—buyers swarm to the impoverished: Americans rushed to Europe in the nineteen-twenties, as the British had overrun France a century before, hot on the trail of collected treasure at bargain prices.

Other wars produce hordes of refugees, and then salvation lies in taking one's possessions with one, if possible. Compared to his fellows, the collector often finds himself in a relatively favorable position under such circumstances. Homes cannot be shipped abroad, neither can industrial investments be abruptly torn out after the storm has broken; but collections of worth may be moved in ample time without disrupting a man's entire mode of living. And that is why, long before World War II had become a certainty, many collectors in every European nation (even in those traditionally neutral) began sending their valued possessions to America, either as "loans" to museums, or, more frankly, to be stored in the warehouses of dealers for safekeeping.

Of the items "temporarily" stored in this fashion, most are fated to remain in America, under new ownership. After every great war or revolution, many an amateur finds himself forced to acknowledge, ruefully enough, that his collection is all that remains to him of once numerous assets. Actually, no matter how disinterestedly he may have loved that collection, no matter how tenaciously he may have held out, collector-fashion, against relinquishing it, the realization of its potential value in a time of ultimate emergency has long been in the back of his mind; and when that time comes, he finds the will-to-live overcoming even his collector's scruples.

Moreover, in wartime, realism extends beyond the mere salvage of existing collections. Although one might expect "luxury objects" to be a drug on the market in wartime, collectors continue to buy—and then, more than ever, are purchases keyed to investment. Up to the Spring of 1940, for example, international art dealers were still doing a big business in France and England. Even before there was intensive bombing to account for the fact, rare books had become rarer than ever in the London market. Rare stamps were still bringing high prices. Jewels, valuable ornaments and other *easily portable objects* were noticeably at a premium, while more ponderous items fell in favor. The fabulously wealthy Rothschilds, emigrating from France after her defeat, carried a million dollars' worth of jewels in an oversized portfolio: prime collateral, these could be used as security, or disposed of if necessary. But if that portfolio had been crammed with French currency, and if all the family's hopes had been in it, hope had soon died.

Even in America, collectors, seeing the writing on the wall, were hastening to lay by a supply which, they felt sure, could be counted on for longer than any other sort of investment. In the art world, many minor dealers, it is true, suffered from the effects of war-inspired caution on the part of their clients; but others—who, perhaps, stocked wares of more certain value—reaped a harvest in 1940 that topped by fifty per cent the sales of the previous year. One New York gallery disposed of nearly two hundred and fifty thousand dollars worth of Old Masters in less than a month, while other establishments sold large numbers of the popular French Impressionist paintings, and even certain American contemporaries changed hands for impressive sums. During 1941, the season before America's entry into the war, the *entire year's sales* of the Parke-Bernet galleries in New York City (auction clearing house for many of the country's most important collections of paintings and *objets d'art*) amounted to three million six hundred thousand dollars; but in *six months following the attack on Pearl Harbor*—months to be counted as among the most jittery in modern American history—these same galleries moved out three million nine hundred and forty-six thousand dollars worth of art merchandise and commanded an audience, at seventy-nine sales, of one hundred thousand people.

Wealthy European refugees were, interestingly enough, among the heaviest buyers during these war years (some of the Rothschild diamonds, for example, were reconverted into paintings to replace the collections lost in Europe). More accustomed to wartime upheavals than most Americans, they swarmed like prudent ants to one of the few sure granaries left. In August, 1940, the highest priced stamp in the world (the same stamp which figured so importantly in the Hind collection) was sold by cable for forty thousand dollars to a foreigner who kept his name a secret and ordered his purchase locked in an American bank vault—for the duration. Unique, and with a vouched-for pedigree, the morsel of paper should always find a market not seriously affected even by the gyrations of Wall Street, for there are always people in various parts of the world, citizens of still solvent countries, who are able and eager to pay fat prices for the rare and famous items of the collecting world.

The time may come when, with changing economic and social conditions, collections will no longer have this particular kind of security value. Even now high inheritance taxes have changed the pattern somewhat with regard to the wealthy collector, and a valuable collection which represented, in part at least, a safe reserve to its creator, easily becomes a serious liability to his heirs. More and more great collections are being dispersed, or are being made over to the public before death can call that headsman of wealth, the tax collector, into action.

This process affects both bad and good collections, so long as they are expensive. William Randolph Hearst's costly miscellany, while its creator still lives, is rapidly consigned to the limbo whence he extracted it. Andrew Mellon, who bequeathed his truly magnificent collection of paintings to the people of the United States, is said to have been more than a little anxious until the government had accepted his proffered gift, for had he been forced to pass it on to his children at a time when values in less stable fields were abnormally depreciated, the inheritance tax (payable in cash) would have amounted to more than thirty-two million dollars on an evaluation of fifty million for the collection.

Cases such as these, though extraordinary, forecast future events. Should wealth one day cease to play the security role for the individual which it now pre-empts in our social scheme, the security motif as a valid feature of the contemporary collecting pattern might sink further and further into the obscurity of primal causes. Yet collecting will not disappear, since the search for physical security is only one of its several roots.

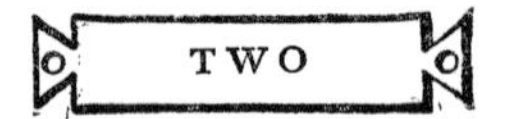

THE COLLECTION AS A MEANS TO DISTINCTION

"Possession means to sit astride of the world,
Instead of having it astride of you."

CHARLES KINGSLEY

After the first battle against nature had been won, man slowly settled down in the lull of comparative peace and surveyed his accomplishments. He had fought off the leopard and the tiger and, where he had stopped the jungle, he had sown seed and had gathered and stored his small harvest. Shelter and raiment were now his. The wild dog acknowledged his bidding. Cattle submitted to him. He was to live—and was well on the road to world mastery. Yet the war of life was to continue, for man would not remain unchallenged even by himself. The urgency which had sent him forth to beat recalcitrant nature into acceptance of his puny existence continued strong within him, seeking new adversaries, forcing him into new efforts.

Unlike the bear and the garden grub, man has not been content with mere physical survival; and even though so far he has shown little more ability than they truly to control the direction of his life, even though the predatory competitive thrust which is so deeply a part of him often constitutes a lively threat to his continued existence, it is through meeting the demands of that same competitive urge that such valuable human instruments as imagination, intelligence and will have been developed.

All this is flesh and bone of our collector, since everywhere in the higher forms of collecting competition and the desire for recognition are boldly apparent.

Success in the struggle for recognition is attained in numerous ways, and the direction taken in each case is largely determined by the individual's own background and environment. Where one man may lay greatest stress upon proving himself physically unbeatable, another may prefer to demonstrate the superiority of his intellect.

Thus where cultural attainments are admired, he may, if he be a money-prince, form a thunderous collection of art objects (discreetly assembled by experts). Where bargaining skill commands respect, he may try to prove his superiority in that regard, whether by acquiring more and better wives than his fellows, or by outsmarting his rivals in the rarity market; and when distinction is to be earned by the exhibition of physical strength even primitive man after the kill often saves some material token of his prowess. The African hunter wears about his neck the tusks of wild boars, the teeth of lions and leopards he has slain; and the more he can exhibit, the prouder and happier he is.

This pride in hunting skill survives lustily among men in civilized societies and the modern "sportsman," though only pleasure bound, still keeps his animal heads, horns or skins, or has his prize fish stuffed and mounted for exhibition. We may be amused by the African chieftain who gathers together his subjects' trophies in order to boast of them; but the collective prowess of a civilized nation's Nimrods can, even today, be a source of great national pride. In November, 1937, the Third Reich staged a huge international competitive display of hunting trophies to which almost every country in Europe sent exhibits and which sportsmen from all over the world attended. Interestingly enough, this particular event was utilized for political ends, since it was made the occasion for an exploratory visit to Berlin by Lord Halifax, who came in his unofficial role as a Master of Foxhounds.

As a hunting creature, man has seldom confined himself to battling the beasts. Through the entire course of history he has fought against other men, been proud of victory when it was his, and—to signify success—has collected the most gruesome of human trophies: heads, complete with hair and skin; skulls; scalps; locks of hair; ears; hands; even phalli.

In widely separated places and far down into "civilized" periods, this form of trophy-gathering has been far more prevalent than we generally realize or admit. After each great battle, the ancient Egyptians, for example, were in the habit of cutting off the right hands of the circumcised, the phalli of the uncircumcised among their fallen enemies and, when recorded in the papyri, this practice has been of value to modern historians, helping them to establish the identity of the peoples against whom the Egyptians fought.

Among the pre-Confucian Chinese it was the custom to punish a rebel by cutting off his ear. The avowed purpose of this was to make possible the future identification of such recalcitrants, who—if they were fortunate enough to be common soldiers and not leaders of the revolt—were set free after the ordeal. But these amputated ears also assumed the aspect of trophies and were collected as such, if we are to judge by the account of one great battle as given in the ancient *Book of Odes*. After this particular combat, the soldiers of the victorious army proudly presented their prince with hundreds of such prizes—which they had preserved as mementoes of the occasion.

As late as the sixteenth century of our era, the Japanese soldiery celebrated their Korean victories by collecting and burying at Nara thirty-eight thousand pairs of ears and as many smitten noses, then pridefully erected a special monument, known as the Mimidzuka or "Ear Mound," above the spot.

Materially suited to more permanent collections, human skulls have also been a popular item in the trophy collector's harvest. The early Chinese, the Huns, the Gauls and many other peoples preserved these souvenirs of vanquished chieftains. Converted into drinking cups, such skulls were so highly valued that they became the personal property of the victorious kings, or were accorded the even greater honor of being turned over to the high priests for use in the temples. Perforated human skulls and jaw bones—still bearing the marks of the stone knives with which they were cleaned—have frequently been found buried with male skeletons in the graves of the North American Mound Builders. Presumably once worn—as ancestral relics, as trophies of war, or as both—by the men with whom they were buried, these had obviously been highly treasured possessions. Among the Toltecs of Mexico, a religious variation of this theme occurred; for these people, when sacrifices of human victims had been completed, collected the skulls of the dead and strung them around the sacred burial grounds for fences.

Shrine in a Urama clubhouse, New Guinea. The skulls are trophies, the shields represent ancestral spirits. Our collections of portraits and other relics of our forebears are a modified form of ancestor worship.

Photo by Captain Frank Hurley
American Museum of Natural History

BELOW: *Grand-scale display of hunting trophies, an exhibit at an international competitive show staged in 1937 by Hermann Goering.*

Press Association, Inc.

Sometimes the valued trophy is the hair of the enemy. Among certain of the Bornean tribes a warrior inserts in the sheath of his knife a lock of human hair for every person he has decapitated, and these convenient tokens of successful valor he carries about with him wherever he goes. Since Colonial days every American child has been raised on the stories of Indians who, to the understandable horror of the white man, collected scalp-lock trophies; but it is not so widely known that some of our own colorful and honored frontiersmen also played the game of scalp-lifting, while more of them notched their guns for each killing—exhibiting thus a similar pride in the number of victims, but with taste and neatness, as befits civilized people.

Central Africa, Malaysia, Melanesia, the Philippines and South America produce first-class head-hunters whose activities show clearly the evolution of a true collecting pattern. Like many early peoples, including the Egyptians, most of the head-hunting tribes believe in a life after death that is really only a modification of the life they know on earth; and this is an important factor in determining the nature of their collecting activity. For example, they may feel sure that a wealthy man will need slaves to serve him in the next world, that his very rank in spirit-land will depend upon a plenitude of servants. They may also believe that the original owner of each head captured on earth will, if the head is dealt with in accordance with a certain ceremony, be forced to follow the spirit of his conqueror when the latter dies. It is quite natural, therefore, that a successful tribesman with a position to maintain should be concerned to acquire a goodly collection of slave heads while he is alive, so that after death he may be properly provided.

Among other tribes, a collection of "souls for the departed" is taken up in a single bloody inning: before the funeral the dead tribesman's relatives, lying in wait near a neighboring village, will sweep off as many victims as they can; for, like the ancient Egyptians, the early Chinese, the Japanese and many others, these people believe that the spirits of the ancestors must be propitiated, kept happy, fed, and cared for—else they will return malevolently to plague their ungrateful descendants. The security motif is also responsible for the practice in operation among certain tribes of gathering and preserving the skulls of their own ancestors; for this represents an attempt to keep the protecting spirits of departed kinsmen in the vicinity of the village, and derives from the belief that the head is the home of the soul, just as, among many civilized people, the heart is spoken of as the seat of the affections.

Out of this idea differently directed grows the complicated behavior of the Jibaro Indian head-hunter of South America. Believing that the soul of a slaughtered enemy will naturally thirst for revenge, these Indians have devised a ritual which, they feel certain, gives them complete control over the victim's spirit and thereby eliminates the threat of retaliation. By this ritual the trophy-head is turned into a fetish, or *Tsanta,* charged with supernatural powers, and it then becomes a source of protection rather than of danger to the new owner. And because the Jibaro also believes that all animals were once head-hunting humans, he will often make similar trophy-fetishes of the heads of jaguars, of the harmless sloth, or of other creatures thought to be Indians of a foreign tribe who have assumed new shape in the process of reincarnation.

Yet slowly, even in the presence of such complex religious-security notions as these, an involved change of purpose comes about among certain tribes in their head-collecting practices. Then it is that the hunt for personal distinction appears in crystalline example, disarmingly, nakedly, accompanied by the predatory killer urge and topped off by the wish to collect heads mainly as tokens of prowess. Thus the Dyaks, masters of ambush, practiced their art soberly enough in the beginning; but gradually, as rivalry among head-hunters grew up, butchery of men for their heads began to take on the aspect of a "national sport." There followed, says Thomas, "an intense preoccupation with head-hunting for the sake of individual and group distinction," and heads were no longer taken primarily for religious reasons but "for the glory and prestige which the trophies bring their owners."

Even farther afield from the motive of self-protection is the custom of stealing out at night to rob a nearby village cemetery of its freshly buried corpses. When the marauding tribesmen have smoked these stolen heads in proper manner, they will march home in triumph to tell vainglorious tales of how they were surprised by a powerful enemy band, and how they themselves, great warriors, subdued all the intruders —in proof of which they brandish the newly smoked heads of the "vanquished."

The extent to which individual rivalry in gore can whip on the actors is succinctly illustrated by the following tale. One day a missionary chanced to overhear a conversation between two Bornean natives.

"I have cut off four heads already," boasted the first.

"I have cut off seven," was his companion's swift retort.

Not long after this the second man disappeared from the village; and when eventually his friends fished the body out of the river, it was seen to be headless. Then they knew, and the missionary knew, that the first man now had five heads (besides his own) and need fear no immediate challenger of his record. "Thus grows the rage for collections," comments Frobenius in reporting the incident.

Some tribes substitute gold earrings or bracelets, shell or feather ornaments or a special form of tattooing, in token of heads successfully severed but not preserved. Occasionally the privilege of wearing garments of particular colors takes the place of trophy collecting, each color denoting a given number of heads captured. So, as a Bagobo, if the reader had achieved six decapitations he might not, like the Bornean, feel impelled to keep the six heads on display; yet he would give equal notice of his success by parading about in a blood-red suit, knowing that this distinctive garment would henceforth mark him as a man of prominence among his people—a fit candidate for the Bagobo equivalent of a Union League Club or Master of the Hounds.

When, from invaded lands in ancient days, military leaders sent home the sculptured images of gods and kings, they were impelled originally by much the same motives as guide the head-hunter. For just as the head-hunter continues to believe that the head is the seat of the enemy's soul, so in those days of anthropomorphic religion, when gods were "but men writ large," those sculptured images were thought essential to the well-being of the state. And, conversely, as in the case of the primitive who believes that a dead enemy still threatens him so long as that enemy's spirit is at large, in ancient times no national adversary was felt to be truly defeated until its gods had been brought captive into the temple of the victorious nation's own divine protector. It is for this reason that old records in the cradle of civilization are so full of lamentations over holy images carried away by conquerors. While the statues of the gods remained, hope lived; but once these were lost, the defeated peoples felt bereft of their own souls and of all help from heaven.

Founded partly on this desire for war trophies as abettors and symbols of victory, and partly on the desire to add to the wealth and hence to the material security of the conquering leader or his nation, war plunder was a very important ancestor of early collecting. For although religious motives were at first responsible for the gathering of trophies on a national scale, more personal desires made themselves felt as well.

Among aborigines some head trophies may be more highly regarded than others—the preference being determined chiefly by the relative importance of former "owners." The head-hunter can hardly extend his standards of value beyond such ideas—since there is not much room in his field for emphasis on intrinsic worth or for the development of esthetic discrimination. When, however, a richer and more varied harvest is available to the warrior, both these factors come to play an important part in the plunder picture and exert a significant influence over the looter himself; so that in time, with the slow awakening to beauty, he who came to pillage indiscriminately may remain to admire —and even, perhaps, to purchase.

Even in very early times we see some of the great generals robbing vanquished peoples of nonreligious art objects, not only of prestige-bearing relics but also of charming trivia, not only of gold and valuable gems but also of books, handsome vases and intricately decorated boxes, the finest furnishings of homes and palaces. A few of these looters, caught up in the toils of such softer enchantments, in days of peace became genuine collectors.

In the third millennium before Christ, one Rimush, son of Sargon of Akkad, brought back an Elamite vase from the sack of Susa and had it inscribed with his own name along with the prideful legend of how he had taken it. Found in his grave by excavators more than four thousand years later, this vase bears mute testimony to an ancient prince's theft of a victory trophy (which was also an object of *virtu*) from the ashes of a conquered city.

It was in pride of conquest that Thutmose III of Egypt (1501–1447 B.C.), the diminutive monarch with the "conquering nose" who founded a far-flung empire, published—after his campaign in the Lebanon Tripolis, Megiddo and elsewhere—an impressive "*List of that which was afterward taken by the king, of the household goods of that foe . . . together with all the goods of those cities.*" The plunder as he listed it included, in part:

". . . flat dishes of costly stone and gold; a large two-handled vase of the work of Kharu; various drinking vessels; three large kettles; eighty-seven knives; a silver statue in beaten work; six chairs of that foe, of ivory, ebon and carob wood; six foot-stools belonging to them; six large tables of ivory and carob wood; a staff of carob wood, wrought with gold and all costly stones in the fashion of a scepter, belonging to that foe; a statue of that foe, of ebony wrought with gold, the head of which was (inlaid) with lapis lazuli; vessels of bronze; and much clothing of that foe."

But Thutmose, who significantly beguiled his spare time designing exquisite vases, was not content merely to bring back victory trophies of intrinsic or symbolic value. He imported Syrian artists and craftsmen as well, so that objects of equal beauty might henceforth be fashioned in his own country.

When Shishak, another Egyptian, defeated King Rehoboam of Jerusalem in the tenth century before Christ, it was remembered of him in the stricken land that he

"took away the treasures of the house of the Lord, and the treasures of the king's house; he even took away all: and he took away all the shields of gold which Solomon had made."

This is a story that can be repeated indefinitely in man's past; nor has any one part of the world had an option on it. The Chinese, far to the east, have an endless scroll of similar recording. There was, for example, the fourth-century rebel, Huan Hsüan, who, when he came into power, "took hold of all the various objects of the Chin court," all the "beautiful and rare things"—the paintings and calligraphies for which, in particular, "he had a great passion." And when Huan Hsüan himself was vanquished, the next victor again took all. Change name, date and locale, and this cycle becomes an old familiar; and herein, incidentally, lies a curious paradox.

Plunder is undoubtedly a dismal technique of collecting, and yet innumerable conquerors, even though inadvertently, have managed thus to contribute much to the dissemination of cultures, and have been instrumental in preserving numerous works of art and objects of historical value which, because they were once swept up by some vigorous if ruthless hand, live on for today and tomorrow as the sole bridge to distant peoples. Those Roman generals who initiated one of the greatest collecting eras of all time found their original impetus in plunder, and in plunder alone; yet in the course of some hundreds of years of association with the conquered Greeks, the marauders learned to savor the great art of their victims, and by gathering up all of it they could find, and by preserving and copying it with care, they performed an incalculable service to all of us who are their inheritors. The torch of enlightenment, we perceive, is sometimes carried forward in mysterious ways by strange hands.

The harsh carnival of plunder has marched through tens of centuries; and although, for a time—in the century that elapsed between Napoleon and Hitler—the Western world, at least, seemed to have succeeded in curbing its most blatant demonstrations, there is no reason to believe that we shall see the last of it. There are still three main types of booty being seized today, as they were yesterday. There is loot of intrinsic and hence of security value, such as gold, food and other useful things. There are the direct trophies of military victory such as captured flags and weapons. And there are the so-called cultural objects—books and archives, art, and historic relics—possession of which symbolizes to the modern mind a high degree of superiority, and hence of prestige.

Napoleon, the ambitious, is an excellent example of the sophisticated looter who consciously appreciates the national prestige values: he hauled cultural swag from the whole of Europe and dumped it at the feet of Paris—for the glory of France and his own aggrandizement. His booty was restored to its rightful owners by the Second Treaty of Paris, and subsequent European conflicts saw, until recently, no revival of his ruthless rape of museums, libraries and private collections.

It has never been properly underscored that the Allies, in drawing up their victory treaties after World War I, exercised a laudable restraint with regard to cultural "reparations," and by absolutely refusing to seize upon spoils of this nature seemed finally to have established a civilized anti-plunder precedent new to all history. But Hitler—driven by material necessity on the one hand, and, on the other, by a craving for prestige more obsessed than Bonaparte's—shattered this hopeful young precedent in his crash through Europe, the loot bag scooping hungrily, near and far, greedy for every manner of trophy, as well as for oil and butter.

Where orderly freedom rules, however, brutish plunder and murder for prestige give way to the implements of the mind, to imagination,

THE ADORATION OF THE LAMB *by Hubert and Jan van Eyck*

This jewel-like altarpiece, painted 1424-32, has more than once tempted national looter and civilian thief. Its rightful home is the Church of St. Bavon, Ghent.

resourcefulness, skill and creative energy; and in primitive as well as in civilized societies a formula of living appears which creates of accumulated property, peacefully acquired, a symbol of prowess having little to do with mere animal strength.

In some societies the possession of many wives connotes distinction. A goodly collection may be a sign of valor or it may denote superior skill in some specific respect. Among agricultural and cattle-raising groups it gives evidence of wealth. Such a group are the African Bantus and with them the wife-collection is particularly important since it plays a vital role in the attainment of wealth, authority and social importance—all part and parcel of the tribal ideal of success. Here each of a man's many wives must every evening prepare and carry to him a pot of food; and she will do this regardless of the number of her rivals. The man who has been able to acquire a large number of cooks will, so Thomas tells us, "become large and stout, quite shining, which in South Africa is a sure sign of wealth and nobility, and the stouter he gets the more he will be respected." In fact among these people the words for "rich" and "fat" are almost identical.

Often, however, the fortunate man cannot consume all that his wives make ready, and so he invites his neighbors to share the feast. In this way he gains the desired reputation for good fellowship, and other men hoping to emulate his success listen with respect to all he says. No wonder men in such communities set about collecting women with even more than the usual ardor, sometimes reaching such heights as the reputed seven thousand wives of King Mtessa of Uganda whose black glory dimmed Solomon's to a modest flicker.

By contrast with the primitive, the civilized collector may be said to incline toward conservatism, a conservatism based upon restrictions which tend to block him from the direct approach. No longer does he eye the neighborhood heads appraisingly; and he is, as a rule, resigned to the possession of one wife at a time (although there still exists the biologic man of parts who continues to collect women and to halloo his success).

In many fields the civilized collector need not have wealth to achieve distinction in modest but palatable degree; and sometimes, through collecting, he may reach distinction when all else has failed. By creating a fine or unique collection, a man may win to an eminence beyond all previous expectancy, and may create out of an originally simple hobby a successful life-work that brings him rich returns in recognition and distinction plus numerous other satisfactions.

In a small Pennsylvania town, there once lived an eleven-year-old newsboy named Farran Zerbe. While sorting his change one day, this lad happened upon a small coin about the size of a dime. It was stamped "50 Cent.", and, thinking it was an unusual fifty-cent piece, he took it to a bank to exchange it. There, however, he learned to his astonishment that there are in the world thousands of different kinds of money—and was told that his find (a fifty-*centime* coin) was worth almost nothing in America. Although he was momentarily disappointed, his discovery awakened the collecting genie in him, and he began to study numismatics. Unlike most youngsters who start collections and then pass on to something else, Zerbe persisted in his until, years later, he had assembled over fifty thousand items covering a period of five thousand years—the most comprehensive collection of moneys and mediums of exchange in the world. Of course this achievement required long and undeviating effort; but, starting with no money and depending entirely upon a conventional job at first, out of his slowly growing collection he carved, eventually, his ideal career.

Before Zerbe was thirty, he was earning his livelihood exclusively by means of his hobby. He became, in time, one of the most distinguished numismatists in America, holding, among other offices of honor, the presidency of the American Numismatic Association. As a writer, a lecturer, an editor of numismatic magazines and the director of coin displays at great national expositions, he was able to devote all his time to the subject that interested him most; and when, toward the end of his long life, the Chase National Bank transformed the Zerbe collection into a numismatic museum, the former newsboy, happy that his collection was to be permanently preserved, was named curator.

The desire to excel offers inviting targets to the caustically inclined. Yet who entirely escapes the power of this universal human wish to be First in something, or as nearly first as possible? If our efforts in this direction seem at times ridiculous, we may take heart in recalling that without this persistent goad man would, in all probability, still be a furtive jungle creature. And before a social commentator can drop a wrench into this paragraph, let us add that collecting, which can be a formidably competitive pursuit, offers many different kinds of opportunity to satisfy this desire in ways essentially beneficial to the community as well as to the individual.

For the individual collector one of the most benign forms of distinction—and one of the simplest to attain—comes through possession of superior knowledge in some one field, the distinction of being justly considered an "authority" or an "expert." Like our ex-newsboy, the head of a nation or a Croesus is delighted when respect is paid him as a collecting authority; for by attaining eminence in this extracurricular field he has succeeded in demonstrating his own catholicity. That is all to the individual's good, of course; but a similar success may be far more important (and equally attainable) for one of the "forgotten men" who, because he has failed in business or vocation (perhaps through no basic fault of his own), is weighted down by frustration. Let such a man become a good collector, a master of his subject, and the members of at least one group will make him feel that he has, after all, a place of importance in his world.

Although his field may seem entirely trivial to the non-collector like Dr. Johnson, who commented rather peevishly on ". . . that desire of accumulating trifles, which distinguishes many by whom no other distinction could ever have been obtained," any specializing collector will recognize the "very rare and very keen pleasure" which, in the words of the more sympathetic Arnold Bennett, becomes his when he approaches his goal of "knowing all there is to be known about something." The desire to excel may be gratified in this comparatively subjective way, while on the competitive scale, as the distinguished connoisseur, Duffield Osborne, promises, there is also much for the specialist "in the rich harvest that springs from knowing more than one's neighbors." This is a harvest which has its petty side, undoubtedly; but in so far as it may contribute to a man's emotional security, it is an extremely valuable one.

Most collectors derive considerable pleasure from being, in one way or another, unique. Men generally share this desire, but the collector more often does something about it. In this he may be likened to all individuals who try for exclusive distinction—from epic explorers to record-seekers in absurd regions. The flagpole sitter, the marathon dancer, the man who waits all night in the cold so that he may be the first to drive over a new bridge, these are related to the collector who yearns for prestige in the matter of finding a unique pinnacle; yet compared to theirs, the true collector's resources are rich indeed, since they extend far beyond mere novelty and originality for its own sake.

There are some collectors who seek to form entire collections which cannot be duplicated in any respect. Others find ample satisfaction in the possession of one or two unique items among a store of more commonplace objects. The wish to own unique items is, of course, more complicated than a simple desire to achieve prestige; but there is an unmistakable elation—often quite frankly admitted to by collectors—in knowing one's self to be the only person in the world who possesses some treasure that is highly prized in the community and vainly coveted by one's competitors.

> "It is the dream of every fisher of books to have at least one item in his collection that no other fellow has or may ever possess,"

declared Barton Currie.

> "To own some one thing that has no duplicate in the world, made by an artist who put his soul and all his love into this object . . . on such there is no money value!"

wrote the late George Dexter of New England. And, continuing with the description of one of his own unique treasures, he added,

> "The miser may hoard his money. What is it after all—so much silver and gold. Any man can work and accumulate money; but where is the man with another string of Persian enamel beads such as these?"

A. S. W. Rosenbach, the rare-book dealer who has turned the collecting instincts of others into a highly profitable business for himself, nevertheless gives strong evidence of being a true collector in his own right, for he has built up a famous and valuable pile from which, it is said, he refuses to sell, no matter how great the profit at stake. Speaking in his role of collector rather than dealer, he admits that he takes a "perverse delight" in adding to his private collection "books so rare that they have survived only in a single example."

Had George Dexter sold his string of Persian beads for the large sum he was offered, he might have continued to see them in a museum; but no longer would they have been his. And that is the important point. For since a man is inclined to identify his possessions with himself, his own importance is enhanced when those possessions are important; to relinquish them is like relinquishing something of one's personal stature.

Naturally there are exceptions to this attitude, exceptions in themselves as uncommon, and as luminous, as perfect emeralds. There was a fourteenth-century Chinese, generously named Hsieh Huan, tzŭ t'inhsün, who owned a truly wondrous collection of writings and paintings by T'ang and Sung masters. These were, even in his time, exceedingly rare, and many of them, being unique, were irreplaceable. Now Hsieh Huan—the trusted adviser to two Emperors in matters concerning their collections—was prosperous, and he lived in a large house, suitable for the display of his treasures. Being an amiable man, he entertained many visitors, and when, as sometimes happened, a guest admired a picture to the point of murmuring aloud his wish to possess it—lo, it was his. This amateur, Hsieh Huan, demonstrated enlightenment in the great art of living. He believed in, and *lived,* the ancient saying of his country, "One should find pleasure in objects yet be not tied to them." It might be said that freedom from slavery, whether physical or spiritual, is a mystical concept; but the Chinese's attainment could easily be named the higher realism—true maturity.

The ideal has been presented to the West in the form of the crucifix—for "God gave up His only son for man." But man finds it hard indeed to give up that which he identifies with himself, even though he longingly seeks peace and is urged, at the gates of most world religions and philosophies, that it is better to give than to receive. Stubbornly heedless of sweet reason, his inner self plods on, clutching what security it can. In contrast to our Chinese gentleman, there is another sort of amateur who would give up his own life rather than part with a single cherished item out of his collection. Both represent extremes in attitude. But there are those—true amateurs also—who, though lacking the completely impersonal approach, are nevertheless able to relinquish rare and valuable possessions for broadly valid reasons, men like the American John Gribbel, who, generously and with a sense of true fitness, presented to the people of Scotland his unique "Glenriddell" manuscript collection of the works of their national poet, Robert Burns.*

---

* The Glenriddell Manuscripts, so-called because they were presented by Burns to his friend Robert Riddell of Glenriddell, consist of one volume of unpublished poems and one of letters, the former partly, the latter wholly, in the poet's own hand. Sold to a dealer by the Liverpool Athenaeum, they were purchased by the American

It is hard enough to find one or two unique items, but the "exclusive" collector is an even more determined individualist, for he is content only when completely alone. One entire field must exclusively be his, and choosing it for that reason, he faces a difficult task indeed. No matter how trivial or abstruse a subject may be, people have an annoying habit of thinking of the same things when least expected to do so. A writer, working on an "original" plot, often discovers that a play or a story using the identical theme has just been published. Highly complex scientific theories or revolutionary inventions have been produced simultaneously in widely separated places by men working in complete independence and in ignorance of each other's efforts. The chagrin is the same for the man who collects razors, or fleas, or letter-form twigs, if he hopes that he is alone in the field, for should he trouble to investigate, he would almost certainly find other collectors similarly occupied.

So long, however, as he is unaware that rivals exist, he solidly enjoys the distinction of his exclusiveness. That such collectors lay great stress on this aspect of their pursuit is proved by the fact that they usually have more than a touch of the *prima donna* about them. Dealers who seek to satisfy them must step softly in conversation with other collectors and carefully guard against divulging the nature of the more temperamental client's activities. From bitter experience the vendor knows such buyers to be brittle and dangerous, and the game has often been abandoned the moment a poacher appeared on the "exclusive" preserve.

Almost any collector will admit to an intense pleasure in outmaneuvering his rivals for the possession of some mutually desired treasure. The reason for this, in the words of the amateur, Duffield Osborne, is that the inclination to collect is itself partially based

"on the desire to possess competitively, that is, to gather objects which, by their degree of rarity or difficulty of attainment, represent readily *comparative achievements.*"

As compared to the primitive's hunting techniques, the civilized collector's weapons of competition include the keen eye, backed by a comprehensive knowledge of his subject, and superior bargaining skill. Often enough in his desire to prove himself the clever hunter and the

---

collector for the express purpose of being returned to Scotland where, he considered, they truly belonged.

As this Collection almost wholly consists of pieces local or unfinished, fragments the effusion of a poetical moment & bagatelles strung in rhyme simply pour passer le temps, the Author trusts that nobody into whose hands it may come will without his permission give or allow to be taken, copies of any thing here contained; much less to give it to the world at large, what he never meant should see the light.— At the Gentleman's request, whose from this time it shall be, the Collection was made; and to him, & I will add, to his amiable Lady, it is presented, as a sincere though small tribute of gratitude for the many many happy hours the Author has spent under their roof.— There, what Poverty even though accompanied with Genius must seldom expect to meet with at the tables & in the circles of Fashionable Life, his welcome has ever been, The cordiality of Kindness, & the warmth of Friendship.— As from the situation in which it is now placed, this M.S.S. may be preserved, & this Preface read, when the hand that now writes & the heart that now dictates it may be mouldering in the dust; let these be regarded as the genuine sentiments of a man who seldom flattered any, & never those he loved. —

27th April 1791 Robt Burns

ROBERT BURNS' PREFACE TO THE GLENRIDDELL MANUSCRIPTS

John Gribbel's gift to Scotland (p. 31) was a fine gesture of generosity. This page is from the volume of poems and bears the stamp of the Liverpool Athenæum, which sold these prime association items.

shrewd fighter, he has been known to stoop to practices which he would heartily condemn, in other fields, as unethical.

But if the collector relishes the demonstration of skill in negotiation, he also glories in the evidence that his taste and discernment are of the highest order. If he has been first in the field, or if others have failed to detect the beauty or the potential value of some battered old rocking chair or a piece of smudged glassware, the amateur who succeeds in making the treasure his own will ever afterward love to boast of his especial wisdom in having appreciated the find at first glance.

Pride in one's discrimination as a collector can be so strong that a public demonstration of failure is nothing short of tragedy. Such was the case of the French amateur, Didier-Petit, whose untarnished reputation as a connoisseur was the mainstay of his enjoyment of life. This unfortunate man once paid a substantial price for an antique shield of *repoussé* work. Of course he thought his purchase genuinely old, but in due time it was discovered—and publicly revealed—that this shield was one of three identical imitations excellently wrought by a master copyist. The fact that it was so competently faked, easily fooling other experts as well, did not soften the blow. They wrote "apoplexy" on this collector's death certificate, but to those who knew Didier-Petit intimately, it was a case of fatal shock.

Rivalry among collectors is often of an unbelievable intensity, and the envy of competitors is, almost always, something devoutly to be sought. About this many collectors are refreshingly frank.

"There is one evil about the otherwise harmless habit of autograph collecting," declared Adrian H. Joline, one of the most disarming of the many writers on this subject. "It fosters envy, hatred, malice and all uncharitableness. When I glance over the other man's collection and find that he has so much better specimens than mine, and even several which I have sought for in vain . . . I proceed to break that commandment recently appended to the decalogue, 'Thou shalt not covet thy neighbor's autographs.' Yet when I go home and think over it, I reflect that perhaps I may excite that neighbor's ire if I choose, but I will be magnanimous and gloat secretly over my possessions."

Having had occasion to reflect on this and other perverse qualities of collectors, Edmond Bonnaffé, first curator of the Louvre's department of applied arts, was moved to revise an old Latin proverb in the following manner: *"Man against man is like a wolf; woman against woman is worse; but worst of all is collector against collector.*" However, although collectors may be both malicious and ruthless at times, they are more inclined to turn rivalry into a sporting affair. Their "malice" is often of a whimsical nature. They enjoy competition, just as the tennis player enjoys it, and the pitting of skill against skill is a large part of their pleasure. Moreover, the resentment of a temporary setback at the hands of an adversary is usually soon offset by the admiration, however grudging, accorded the victor, and by the knowledge that, since the game is never ended, one's own turn may come next.

Distinction achieved through owning something unique, through learning more or being more clever or more discerning than one's neighbor, is largely a matter of ingenuity, ability, and, occasionally, luck. It has little to do with wealth, although adequate means undoubtedly give the collector a definite advantage.

However, when the lords of wealth, accustomed to homage in the material world, turn, as they often do, to seek fresh victories in the rarefied atmosphere of Culture through collecting, they may use their wealth as a token of power and find their chief satisfaction in this form of distinction. No more vivid example could be entered here than J. P. Morgan, the Elder. His weapon lay in the possession of almost unlimited means, and governments themselves could not successfully contest his will when he had set his mind upon possession.

When the famous Garland Collection of Chinese porcelains, then the greatest grouping of its type in the world, fell into his hands, Morgan remarked to the dealer who acted for him, "I understand that Mr. Garland did not complete the collection." Henry Duveen replied that this was so.

"Then," said Morgan, "I shall be glad if you will complete it for me." *

This short edict was loaded with an awareness of power, for Chinese porcelains can be among the most expensive and illusive of all objects of *virtu*. By his "request" Morgan gave his dealer *carte blanche* to buy up, through sheer weight of reserves if necessary, those missing portions which, by the way, are always the most difficult to obtain. If one is a collector, one wishes to be pre-eminent in the field, no matter what dis-

---

* This collection, which had long been on loan at the Metropolitan Museum of Art and which Morgan left there under a similar arrangement, was dispersed during the early days of World War I, some time after Morgan's death, and no longer exists as a unit.

tinctions one may already have attained elsewhere: the Garland porcelains had long been the most famous in existence, and the Morgan porcelains must, therefore, surpass them. As for the rest of us, it is just a matter of degree.

Although it is said that Morgan always carefully refrained from bidding against the British Museum if he knew that this institution of his adopted land wanted a particular item, he exhibited a considerably smaller concern for public causes farther from the reach of his own sentiment. While his collection of miniatures was under construction, he was advised that an exceptionally desirable group by the French master, Augustin, was about to be thrown on the market. Unique of its kind, this group included, in addition to a long series of the artist's works which had come down in direct inheritance from his wife, many of Augustin's own notes on the methods and materials he had employed. By every possible means the French government tried to obtain this important collection—but lost it in the end to the American. It is only fair to say that Morgan, the mountain, was affectionately disposed toward miniatures, a circumstance which influenced his decision in this case; but the fact that he could shoulder out of his way a great nation must also have been a source of mild satisfaction. As a postscript to this incident, it is illuminating to learn that by way of friendly gesture (at the suggestion of his curator, Dr. George Williamson), Morgan ordered a perfect replica made of one of the miniatures which the French Republic had most desired—an unfinished sketch of Napoleon—and then presented the *replica,* not the original, to the people of France.

In every form of collecting, from the simplest to the most complex, ownership is an essential part of the pattern. All the desires and interests which contribute toward making any sort of individual into a collector are given focus by the fact of personal possession. From the small boy to the great connoisseur, the joy of standing before one's accumulated pile and being able to say, "This belongs to me!" is the culmination of that feeling which begins with the ownership of the first item.

Over our possessions we exercise a definite control; and when we "love" them, it is in part because they are fallen to us and become of us. Since the ego demands that whatever has become a part of itself should be as important as possible, there arises out of this a kind of protective proprietorship—as in the case of the "beloved," possessed of the lover

—which tends to magnify the virtues of the possessed. The game of conquest, the sense of triumph in victory, also plays its part; driving men on to seek ever more and more possessions, more conquests, which, once attained, enhance by just that much more the importance of the victor, the possessor. For the collector, the case has been most simply stated by Arnold Bennett when he says:

"The collector has a museum of his own and he is the curator."

In other words, where his gathered possessions are concerned, if nowhere else, he is supreme master. And whatever other value his collection may have in the eyes of the collector, and there are usually many and more obvious ones, this extension of the "dominant and triumphant self" contributes the vivifying spark.

Even plants may stage actual battles for their own living space. Insects, birds and beasts all claim for themselves particular ranges of territory and useful forms of property; and we can assume that early man was no less possessively inclined. There are grounds for believing that certain incision "decorations" found on very ancient prehistoric weapons were actually marks of proprietorship, the claiming "signatures" of individual owners; and a similar conclusion has been drawn (in cases such as that of the predynastic Egyptians) when all vessels placed in the grave of any one individual have generally been found to be marked with identical signs.

It would be difficult to prove at just what stage of human development the simple survival aspect of possessiveness gave way to more complex, more subjective factors. The small boy, glowing with pride and pleasure, returns home from an afternoon's excursion, his pockets crammed with "finds" from, perhaps, the town dump. But he has not just picked these up. He has discovered them, chosen certain ones and rejected others, for reasons close to him. Now he brings his "collection" home to show his parents (if he feels he can trust them with his confidence), or else he gloats over the trove in secret, until such time as he may be able to display his prizes to his friends. Certainly he expects his audience to be duly impressed and to admire him for his cleverness in finding and recognizing so much wealth. If, instead, those others should laugh, he would probably be deeply hurt; and so, in a limited way, he feels and behaves much as would any true collector. To the satisfactions of possession, however, the latter most often adds personification, love, and an abiding interest; and in these qualities there works that constant magnet which binds so many people so ardently to their more delicately wrought collections.

A true collection is not casual; it is a gathering that has been made at the expense of much thought and effort; often in successful competition with others. What one values most in skill and understanding is included in it. It is the visible embodiment as well as the extension of the aspiring, successful self. And that is why it is so resolutely protected: no mother of the wilderness fights more resolutely for her young than the collector, with word or deed, fights for his "children." Still strong enough to be heard today is the echo of the fierce curse upon library thieves that Assyrian Ashurbanipal sent ringing down the ages when he sought to safeguard his palace collection, assembled in the seventh century before our era:

"Whosoever shall carry off this tablet, or shall inscribe his name upon it side by side with my own, may Ashur and Belit overthrow him in wrath and anger, and may they destroy his name and prosperity in the land!"

Like Madame Geoffrin, that still famous holder of a famous eighteenth-century Paris *salon,* some people attempt to "collect" celebrities, perhaps hoping thereby to become known as birds of the same feather. So of Louise Chandler Moulton, a nineteenth-century Bostonian, Van Wyck Brooks has this to say: ". . . she collected poets as others collected old masters; and she passed from Mallarmé's circle to Lord Houghton's in London, discovering, acclaiming, acquiring and sharing her treasures."

The hostess who achieves a reputation for gathering about herself, at teas or dinners or at weekly "at-homes," the socially "very best people," bigwig politicos, noted painters or writers of the hour, wits, *prima donnas,* entertainment stars, feels that her guests belong to her, and that by her ability to assemble a group of distinction, she partakes vicariously of their success. Although most celebrity collectors are content to get what they can in the current market of "accepted" personalities, some may, like other true collectors, become specialists, concentrating, perhaps, on the formation of a "straight series," say of theater people, of men of adventure, of learned folk, or even of freaks.

The collecting of important people, of successful people, is a direct shoot from the competitive urge; but it goes without saying that here, as in other forms of collecting, a genuine interest frequently supplements that urge—a love of good company and good conversation, a desire to benefit from association with capable minds, a true enthusiasm for the subject in which one is specializing. And if the collection happens to be successful for all concerned, it may, like any other good collection, have a value of its own and reflect true credit upon its creator.

There is, however, another way, more acceptable to the true brotherhood of collectors, of identifying one's self with the great and admirable, and that is through assembling so-called "association items."

Few phases of collecting hold more fascinating grounds for speculation than this one. Certainly a vast portion of the population is held helpless for a moment by hypnotic attraction when gazing upon some relic of a hero; and of the several factors involved in this wide appeal, the much-discussed human worship of "success" is, of course, basic. It is not altogether surprising, therefore, that a large number of people should collect such relics, or at least wish to include a few of them among other items in their collections. Nor, as we noted in the case of the head-hunter, is the wish to own objects associated with success exclusively a civilized attribute. Indeed, this wish has been extensively observed among primitive peoples, but a single rich example, that of the Trobriand Islanders of New Guinea, should suffice to show how great a stress may be put upon the association item even in societies far less complex than our own.

The Trobrianders have an institution known as the *kula* exchange which combines, in closely interwoven fashion, the functions of trade and of social ceremonial in the community, and it is in the social aspect of this institution as described by Malinowski that we find a close counterpart to the civilized "association" collector.

Chief among the things which the Trobrianders exchange as ceremonial gifts, in a never-ending cycle of tradition-ruled transactions, are axheads, necklaces of red spondylus shell-discs, and bracelets made of the white conus shell. According to the custom, certain men become "partners"—that is, are entitled to exchange gifts or *vaygu'a* with each other—and the gifts thus received must, after a time, be again passed on to other partners. The exchanges are governed by definite rules of direction and date, so that the *vaygu'a* are only temporarily owned by any one man, and necessarily pass through a great many hands in the course of time. In this way, each necklace or armshell eventually acquires a history of its own. Each becomes known and is recognized in the communities through which it passes, and, like a person, is given an individual name. It is here that we come to the important similarity to our own attitude—for among the Trobrianders, as among ourselves, *the items held in highest esteem are those once possessed by famous chieftains or those which have figured in historically important events.*

To form a permanent collection is impossible under such a system, but the Trobriander reacts to even temporary ownership in a manner extraordinarily like that of the civilized collector. As the latter raises his bid again and again when competing for a particularly coveted item at auction, so among the islanders a form of the auction may be noted, when all the partners of one man compete intensely for the favor of receiving one of the association items at the next exchange, and heap added gifts upon the owner in a heated attempt to gain the desired object. Moreover, he who comes into possession of one of these finer *vaygu'a* becomes, to his fellows, a subject of envy—just as the "other man" was envied for finer autographs by Joline. As a collector among his colleagues, the Trobriander, too, achieves prestige and renown through the circumstance of possession; and so long as the admired object belongs to him, he makes the most of his opportunities to display it to his companions, to tell them how he managed to come by it, and hugely enjoys their respectful comments.

In partial explanation of the association item's appeal, it must be admitted that there appears to be, inherent in such objects, a peculiarly *dæmonic* quality. Examine your own reaction to, let us say, a letter or manuscript in the handwriting of some distinguished man now dead whom you esteem highly, your feeling when confronted with the very brush once used by an admired artist, or your sensation when you hold in your hand the gavel with which a great statesman rapped for order upon an historic occasion. Unless you are rather exceptional, you will see how strong that *dæmonic* quality can be. It is as if, in some mysterious way, you yourself had established contact with the illustrious one; as if something of the man himself and of his spirit were being conveyed to you through the channel of this *thing* which had once been his.

There is, then, a mystical side of the desire to possess objects associated with the great. Its origins rest partly in animism—the belief, anciently embedded, that even inanimate objects are possessed of spirit. It is from this fruitful seed that the root of belief in the power-for-good of religious relics also springs, and therein lies another fascinating side of collecting that we must, with regret, leave for later accounting.

From the souvenir fiend to the venerator of saintly bones, from the awe-struck child who collects soldiers' trophies to the most intelligent bibliophile, it would seem that the animistic conception, despite all intellectual denial, lives on among us, hale and hearty. Nathaniel Hawthorne is only one of many cultivated men who have written on the evocative power of the autograph manuscript as compared to impersonal print. The numerous beds in which George Washington may have slept take on a significance in the eyes of many of his admirers that is quite apart from ordinary antique-furniture values. And although J. P. Marquand's description of a family bitterly quarreling over the disputed possession of "a badly worn square of carpet upon which General Lafayette inadvertently spilled a glass of Madeira during his visit to Boston" may be purely fictional, the stain of irony is authentic.

Collecting contemporary relics or souvenirs can become something very like a mania, producing many undesirable results. The undisciplined or naïve hero-worshiper, the autograph hound who joins with his fellows in mobbing popular entertainers, authors or statesmen, the seeker of personal celebrity trophies, can become a gadfly of a pest, even a petty thief. So, sending his shirts to the laundry used to be a hopeless business for Charles A. Lindbergh until he solved the problem by sailing for England.

While one shirt does not make a collection, it must be admitted that a similar technique is widely practiced by a type of souvenir collector whose harvest is usually characterized by extreme triviality. What, then, is the dividing line between trivial souvenir hunter and true collector? Perhaps the answer lies partly in standards of intrinsic significance as applied to the harvest. Yet it will be seen continuously—and emphatically is this true here—that it is extremely difficult to locate the borderlines between various collector types, for the gradations leading from one to another are interwoven with changing cross factors which appear only infinitesimally at variance as they progress. A collector who combs Hollywood barber shops for movie-star hair might be worlds apart from the English collector who once paid nearly three thousand dollars for one of Sir Isaac Newton's teeth. And, on the other hand, disregarding the difference in their financial resources, one might find that the two actually approximated the same level of interest.

It would be unfair to pigeonhole the personal-relic collector as "queer," since whole peoples, the state as well as individuals, take pride in the possession of such things. On behalf of his native city, Lorenzo de' Medici once tried hard to acquire the body of the late illustrious Florentine painter, Fra Filippo Lippi, which had been buried elsewhere, but he found the citizens of Spoleto unwilling to give it up. The by now somewhat tattered body of Francisco Pizarro, conqueror of Peru, is still displayed under glass in the cathedral at Lima. The skull of composer Haydn was the cause of an international feud lasting more than a century and a quarter. Lenin's body, carefully mummified, is exposed to the view of all, in Russia's national shrine. And in 1919, the makers of the Treaty of Versailles took time out from apparently more important matters of state to demand that Germany hand over to the British Government the skull of the Sultan Mkwawa, which had been removed from German East Africa and taken to the Reich.

More orthodox and more broadly significant association items than shirts and skulls are, however, the usual concern of most collectors, who often find in objects of associative value a perfectly valid historical interest. Most amateurs can succumb to the appeal of association occasionally without stressing it to the exclusion of all else. And an association item has added collector value in that it is likely to be unique as well as significant: a "Queen Anne" chair may be just one of many fine examples of the style so named, but if it is known to be the very chair upon which the Queen herself customarily perched to drink her tea, it becomes not only mystically evocative, a transmitter of prestige, and an historic "document," but also quite different from every other chair of its type.

There is nothing either small or mean in the recompense to the community, as well as to the individual collector, when men gather and preserve evidence in "association," collecting the sort of objects which, because of that highly personal relationship, help to inspire the present and keep young the face of the past. Let us step softly, then, as we pass a collector in communion with some autographed "presentation" volume, or another who raptly contemplates the very stick that a tempestuous Voltaire brandished before the nose of the world.

The satisfactions that attend the display or exhibition of his garnered treasure may be said to comprise, for the average collector, one of the richest rewards of his pursuit. Some collectors are bold exhibitionists, blaring like brass. Others disclose the quieter pride of an unassuming parent in his lovely and gifted child. There are the completely secretive, hermit-like ones whose lips are sealed—they are generally the rarities of repression or those fewest of men who need no approbation from their fellows. Far more numerous are the collectors who take circuitous paths to collect an audience.

How long ago did man first begin seeking acknowledgment for his collections of odd or beautiful things? The French authority, Luquet, speaking of the brightly colored stones and curiously shaped shells sometimes worn by prehistoric peoples, suggests that it was "owing to lack of cabinets" in which to display them that these trinkets were turned into bracelets and necklaces, and that they belong "rather to luxury than to decoration properly called." Of the dozens of silver buttons attached to a Menominee Indian woman's garment, perhaps five or six will perform the useful function of fastening. The rest are decorative, but they also represent wealth and are worn chiefly because the garment offers the best possible means of exhibiting the amount of silver, the number of buttons, owned. On behalf of the wearer, they seem to say: "See how much I have, how successful my husband has been." Societies past and present are honeycombed with obvious parallels.

When food is regularly plentiful, even this prime necessity of life, becoming an equivalent of wealth, may be "accumulated for purposes of display as well as for consumption," may, in other words, be collected and so exhibited as to impress one's social competitors. Kitchen-gardens, among the Trobrianders, assume an importance out of all semblance to their actual usefulness, and become, in a sense, both galleries of art and exhibition cabinets. At harvest time each man piles his yams (the chief crop of the region) into conical heaps under shelters made of the vines (as in Italy and southern France the farmers heap their handsomest gourds and squashes at the doorways of their homes for all to see). Then the Trobriand neighbors promenade from garden to garden, "admiring, comparing, praising the best."

The urge which spurs the ego to compete for superiority and applause is, in itself, a useful thing. As the kitchen-garden of the Trobriander becomes a show-place of crops, new competitions arise in the development of farming techniques; and it is not too far a cry to point out that through similar processes the jackdaw collector became a scientist.

Even in the Orient, where certain human frailties seem better controlled than elsewhere, a conventional display of collections is not considered unseemly. In happier times than our own, a Chinese host for the entertainment of his guests might show some of his finest fabrics, exhibit porcelains from his collection, or unroll his favorite scrolls.

Obviously, parade of this sort can be something much more than a mere manifestation of pride. It can also be a laudable attempt to share with other initiates one's pleasure in beautiful or interesting objects; and this element enters largely into collectors' display everywhere. Yet it would be unrealistic to deny the satisfaction attending the display itself. When one wishes to view a private collection in Japan, a special appointment is mandatory, and the occasion itself is made one of extravagant ceremony. Ordinarily, all but one or two items in a collection remain packed away in chests or boxes, or are kept in a fireproof building somewhat apart from the flimsy dwelling; but if a visitor is expected, a few more are selected and brought into the house for the pleasure of the guest. With ceremonious gravity, perhaps a clap of the hands, each of these is produced in turn, taken out of its wrappings and displayed, then carefully rewrapped before the next is disclosed. And with each successive vision, the onlooker is expected to make quite audible his delighted and approving surprise.

Repose is innate in Oriental art and decoration, and it is, therefore, consistent that the time, the company, and the items to be shown should be as carefully considered as might be the revelation of a great relic by the Catholic Church. This attitude permits of restraint, and, in its implicit self-discipline, is a typical characteristic of Japanese culture. Yet these Children of the Sun were not always so subtle, nor so restrained.

In the sixteenth century, a man named Hideyoshi rose from the peasantry to supreme regency of the land, and became, thereafter, a great but ostentatious collector. In the fourth year of his power, this General-turned-dilettante erected the castle of Osaka, flamboyantly decorated and filled with costly works of art. His greatest pleasure was in showing off these treasures to his guests, one of whom recorded, with pardonable amazement:

". . . the very privies were decorated with gold and silver, and paintings in fine colors. All these precious things as if they were dirt. Ah! Ah!"

But not content with the opportunities for display offered by private or even state visits to his castle, Hideyoshi used to give immense special entertainments, during which he could parade his objects of *virtu* before the admiring eyes of an even greater multitude.

In our own society we have often met face to face with a collector-propensity for thrusting the collection before the eyes and ears of any potential audience; and although this procedure is often directed toward the evocation of praise, sometimes it seems to miss the mark, since of all the characteristics by which the collector is to be known, his exhibitionism is the one that has most frequently furnished a target for satire, from the days of Lucian to our own. Martial and Juvenal, Molière and La Bruyère, Samuel Johnson and Oliver Goldsmith, these are but a squad from the regiment of barb-tongued writers who have launched such sallies through the centuries. Yet the good collector, perhaps wisely, is content to laugh with the audience, for he knows what he knows about his own harvest of pleasure, and ridicule cannot destroy the tree of his delight.

THE COLLECTION AS A MEANS TO IMMORTALITY

> *"For there is hope of a tree, if it be cut down, that it will sprout again, and that the tender branch thereof will not cease."*
>
> BOOK OF JOB

MAN, COMBATING with fair measure of success the dangers that threaten the outer and the inner self, must still face the ultimate battle forever lost. The body need not decline in hunger, and the spirit can be revived often. Yet before the finality of death, man is still powerless—and this fact Western man in particular can seldom face with equanimity. Of all difficult goals man has set for himself, that of immortality has ever been the most passionate quest, and here, with his fellows, the collector strides along, seeking a rift in the fog.

For some men there is consolation in leaving children to carry on the name, the heritage, and yes, in some mysterious way, the personal identity. But one's children may die or turn out badly. They cannot be surely counted on to perpetuate the line and desired reputation. The important collector's "family," on the other hand, is made of more certain stuff. A collection can be left to bear its founder's name. It will constitute a lasting monument to his predilections and achievements. And because the collector has identified his creation so closely with himself (a very strengthening bond for some men), he sometimes feels that, like a strong boat, it will bear him through the centuries after his body has gone to the earth again.

In the last will and testament of Samuel Pepys, diarist and impassioned collector of books, there lies a suitable text. When Mr. Pepys went to bed never to rise again, he provided that, in due season, his library should become the property of Magdalene College, Cambridge; but the dead hand, not quite buried, still reached for its possessions from beyond the grave, in that testament which commanded that not an iota of change should ever alter the exact form of the Pepys collection as it had existed when its creator's eyes last looked upon it: except in so far as certain instructions were given for the completion of the collection, no book might be added, subtracted, or set in another place on the shelves, then and forever.

Now it so happened that the system of arrangement devised by Pepys was one peculiarly his own. Based entirely upon size rather than subject, it was both inconvenient and illogical for scholarly use. The temptation to break the will and ignore the gentleman's instructions, once he was safely out of the way, must, therefore, have been great. But Pepys himself had foreseen such a contingency; and to guard against it, he evolved an eternal spy system, in the hope that jealousy would live so long. Hot or cold, posterity would have to take his blemishes along with the rest of him, as he had, leniently. And so he decreed that once a year a delegation from Trinity College must visit the Pepys library at Magdalene, and there conduct a thorough investigation. As long as the vigilants from the rival school could uncover nothing unseemly, Magdalene was to keep the collection. But should the Trinity men ever find that so much as a single book had been moved from its proper place, or that any intruders had been foisted in among the original three thousand chosen volumes, then the entire library was immediately to be transferred to them!

The desire to prevent dispersal or alteration of a collection, and the hope of controlling its fate from beyond the grave, are not uncommon. There is a further example in Dr. Thomas Addis Emmet, whose priceless collection of American historical autographs (including a copy of the Declaration of Independence in Jefferson's own hand) is in the New York Public Library. Believing himself, at one time, to be afflicted with a mortal illness, Dr. Emmet sold his collection—the work of a lifetime—to one of the trustees of what was then the Lenox Library, in order to insure its future inviolate. It was to be known as the "Emmet Collection," and, like the Pepys library, was to be left just as he had arranged it (which, since Emmet's arrangement had meaning in itself and added to the interest of the collection, was reasonable enough). Rather than either of these conditions, however, it was the manner in which this collector endeavored to see that his wishes should be carried out that was unusual and revealing. Into each of the volumes containing his mounted items, Emmet had bound his own photograph so that it might plead his cause for him when he was gone; and he added the following admonition for the benefit of any man who might be tempted to lay careless hands upon this child of his heart. Notice the personal identity with which he endows his collection, the close association he makes between it and himself when he writes of it:

"In the same spirit that Shakespeare wished his bones might remain at rest, I would ask that these relics of mine be kept together. I commenced this collection at twelve years of age, and some portion of it has been my companion through a long life. But there will come a time, in the near future, when we must separate, and dear to me is the wish that the labor of years, collected in all these volumes of historical matter, may not be lost and scattered through the destructive spirit of some new owner. A happy conscience will certainly be the reward for respecting so charitable a request; *and in the spirit hereafter, so far as may lie with me, I will invoke it, as I would burden the conscience of the vandal who disregarded my wishes.*[*]

"I place my portrait here, as my representative, that it may remain in the years to come a silent pleader, and selfish indeed must be the person who does not respect the appeal."

A man's desire to preserve his collection can, of course, be more than a wish for a monument to his own achievements. It may, as in this case and so many others, again be likened to that emotion of protective love which could only envisage with acute distress the separation or mistreatment of the members of one's own family.

Often, however, the desire for personal perpetuation is undeniably a strong factor. And for this purpose certain men have long favored museums—permanent repositories which the community regards with awe, public places having the build and atmosphere of glorified vaults —there to plant their possessions. Perhaps a room or a wing can be ticketed with the donor's name, and more than one entire museum wears the label of some man who bid thus against the mortality of his fame. Until fairly recently, indeed, it was the highly exceptional col-

---

[*] Italics ours. Compare with Ashurbanipal's bookplate-curse, above, p. 37.

lector who, if he bequeathed his collection to public use, did not endeavor to make of it a personal monument. When Andrew Mellon, in 1937, stipulated that his great art collection, a gift to the people of America, was *not* to bear his name so that other collectors might be moved to add to it later, he evoked a furor of delighted—and surprised—gratitude.

To meet the requirements of donors, museums were once forced to accept bad with good. Scientific collections and other specialized types given by their creators to a single institution often duplicate each other in part, or the original arrangement of such collections may become outmoded in the light of later educational developments. It is then in the public interest, for purposes of intelligent use, to combine a number of different collections in appropriate centers, eliminating duplications and second-rate items, and rearranging the remainder in such a way as to form a new and consecutive whole. Yet to do this it becomes necessary to forfeit the identity of each individual collection; and many donors—quite often including scholars and scientists who are intellectually aware of these facts and yet who, as collectors, are unable to avoid the emotional approach of the amateur—provide as absolute conditions of their bequests that no such changes shall ever be made. Today, however, such restrictions sometimes defeat their own ends, for museums, growing more independent and more selective, frequently turn down encumbered gifts, even at the sacrifice of outstanding items. Both the Metropolitan Museum of Art and Columbia University reputedly refused the gift of the two-million-dollar Wiggin Collection because of the donor's insistence that the collection be kept intact. The Cleveland Museum of Art allows no strings attached to its donated collections. Any gift collection—and this museum has a number of important ones—can, therefore, be broken up and displayed in whatever way seems most logical. The ideal of the modern museum is to exhibit only the finest examples under the best possible circumstances, and it is highly dubious whether Mr. Pepys' strictly qualified gift would be accepted by most institutions if offered in the same fashion today. The collector of the future, while still able to memorialize himself to some extent, will have to make more and more concessions in the way he goes about it.

This question of the collection as a monument occasionally has curious repercussions. It was, for example, supposed by everyone that the elder J. P. Morgan would leave his sixty-million-dollar collection to the

Photo copyright Horydczak

EAST END OF READING ROOM, FOLGER SHAKESPEARE LIBRARY

THE COLLECTION AS A MONUMENT. *The ashes of Emily and Henry Clay Folger, at their wish, are immured where Shakespeare presides. Their portraits and name identify them with a monument lovingly built* (*p. 300*).

nation, presumably to the Metropolitan Museum of Art, where large portions of it had been on loan during his lifetime and to which he had made a number of very generous gifts. In articles written immediately after Morgan's death in 1913, and in the relevant chapter of Royal Cortissoz's *Art and Common Sense,* it was taken for granted that the treasures would be concentrated in one place and given to the public. The great loan exhibition then being arranged for the Metropolitan was considered the preparatory step; and somewhat prematurely as it turned out, the American public was felicitated by art authorities for its good fortune in being the great man's heir!

While in his will Morgan declared that it had been his "desire and intention" to make his art collections "permanently available for the instruction and pleasure of the American people," lack of time, so he said, had prevented his carrying out this plan. Nevertheless he spoke of the sort of monument (his own word) that he had had in mind, and expressed the hope that his son and heir would eventually find it possible to make a permanent disposition of the kind. Since the elder Morgan was seventy-six years of age when he died, lack of time hardly seems an adequate explanation for his failure to realize his original intention. Some writers believe that the financier's annoyance over the Washington trial was at the bottom of his withholding so important a gift from a public which had offended him in its judgment of his business career. Some even accept in explanation the later plea of financial necessity offered by the younger Morgan when he disposed of such incomparable sections of his father's collection as the Chinese porcelains, the miniatures, the tapestries, and the Fragonard panels which, now in the Frick Collection in New York City, were sold to Mr. Frick in 1915 for one million four hundred twenty-five thousand dollars. Morgan had paid three hundred fifty thousand dollars for them in 1898.

Even after the contents of the will were known, however, the art world apparently continued to believe that the Morgan treasures would eventually be given to the Metropolitan. When the dispersal occurred, the trustees of the museum, writing their annual report, had great difficulty in concealing their disappointment; while others, in a position to exercise more frankness, quite openly declared that, in their opinion, violence had been done to the collector's real wishes.

One other explanation of Morgan's failure to make the expected bequest was advanced by Hellman, and it is of particular relevance here.

This theory assumes that if the City of New York had offered to provide the relatively insignificant sum needed for the addition of a special wing to the Metropolitan—a wing bearing the collector's name and reserved for the Morgan Collection alone—the bequest would have been promptly made, but that Morgan, "who was a man of intense personal dignity," was unwilling to take this particular step himself. If this theory is correct, the great man did indeed want a monument, but was not prepared to make public admission of the fact. Nevertheless, he may have cherished the hope that the tribute would be paid him in the future; and something of the sort did come about, for in 1917, when his son finally presented the Metropolitan with some three thousand items (in addition to the previous gifts), a part of the building which had formerly been known as the Wing of Decorative Arts, or as the Hoentschel Wing, was renamed the Pierpont Morgan Wing, and many though not all the Morgan items owned by the museum were placed in it.

There have been collectors in all times, however, who, upon approaching the final door, have conceived of their collections as a means to a far broader sort of immortality. There are amateurs willing to submerge their own names in the interests of society, allowing public institutions full authority in the use of their collections, while still others hope, through the dispersal of beloved possessions, to live on in the sympathy of kindred spirits.

The American book collector, A. E. Newton, often declared that he wanted his library sold at auction so that other collectors might share the fun of competing for its prizes. And Edmond de Goncourt wrote of his collection:

"My wish is that my drawings, my prints, my curiosities, my books—in a word, these things of art which have been the joy of my life—shall not be consigned to the cold tomb of a museum, and subjected to the stupid glance of the careless passer-by, but I require that they shall all be dispersed under the hammer of the auctioneer, *so that the pleasure which the acquiring of each one of them has given me shall be given again, in each case, to some inheritor of my own tastes.*" *

Here is a fine example of the old type of collector from the inner circle—an amateur's amateur. Goncourt wished his treasures to go to those who

* Italics ours.

would best understand and love them; these objects he had preserved for a little while, and he wanted others to find in them what he had found. In this, he and his kind are fortunate in being less troubled, less anxious, in a way, about their status among men, than those who take steps to leave more concrete monuments.

Yet the monument often builds itself. Of men who *write* books, an ancient Egyptian once declared:

> "A man hath perished and his corpse become dirt. All his kindred have crumbled to dust. But writings cause him to be remembered in the mouth of the reciter."

And much the same thing can be said of many of those who have *preserved* the works of others, books or paintings or humbler craft, by collecting and cherishing them. In this lies the true collector's real immortality. There are, in public museums today, numerous treasures the histories of which can be traced back through generations of devoted collectors—some, it is thought, as far back as Caesar and Cicero —and many men today accord a deep and sincere gratitude to those early curators. Caesar and Cicero would, of course, have been remembered without benefit of a single Greek statue preserved; but there are other men whose names are known and venerated today solely because they were once great and generous amateurs.

In sixteenth-century France there lived a man whose reputation in his own time was secure, his position enviable. He was, successively, an army contractor, director of the public revenues, ambassador to Rome, and a minister of finance under Charles IX. There are such men in every generation, in every country, who are quickly forgotten, often in their own lifetimes. But this man was more than a *cliché* of success. To him, in 1518, the scholar Erasmus wrote:

> "You owe nothing to books, but books will ensure your immortality."

And Erasmus was right. Few people now remember Grolier the ambassador, nor Grolier the finance minister; but Jean Grolier, collector and bibliophile, is known to lovers of books the world over; and that cordial device—"For Grolier and His Friends"—emblazoned upon each of the fine bindings of which he was so justly proud, ensures to his memory more honoring friends than any man could hope to gather in a single life-span. Societies of book-lovers are often named for this collector even today; and for generations after his death, it was the ambition of every bibliophile to own at least one volume that had been in Grolier's library.

Impassioned amateurs like Newton and Goncourt may eschew the public monument in favor of other enthusiasts like themselves. Other men, less purely inspired, less completely intoxicated, perhaps, by the pursuit itself, are likely to place their emphasis somewhat differently. For them, the collection as a unit—as a commendable creation—must always be important of itself; wherefore, if they wish to be remembered as collectors at all, they will choose the direct, not the subtler, path. And despite Goncourt's distrust of "the cold tomb of the museum"—which now tends to be less "cold"—despite the mistakes so often made in the past, such collectors today can, with reason and generosity, turn to these institutions for an honorable perpetuation of their names and works. A collection intelligently bequeathed to public use and enjoyment can be a monument more vivid, and, in its effects, far more comprehensive and enduring, than the toughest stone; and citizens of the world, mature in outlook, care more about the lasting effect of their work than for the mere remembrance of a name.

Many collections are now being passed on with few or no restrictive provisions; and collectors today, aware that a man is often and justly honored for some constructive gift to the community, long after his obscurely successful career in business or industry has been lost to limbo, are more and more given to planning their collections from the outset in such a way that these may, in the end, be acceptable for a larger use. The desire, once so prevalent, to freeze a collection into its original form, together with the old idea that the collection's life, its period of growth, must halt with the life of its creator if it is to be a fitting memorial, is rapidly giving way to the conception that the surest road to immortality for the collector lies in the continued expansion of the work he began; and donors now frequently make provisions for future additions as well as for the upkeep of their bequeathed collections.

Under such circumstances the mere inclusion of a man's name need in no way detract from the usefulness of his gift. The fact that Morgan's library—housed, by the way, in a building of its own that is not tomb-

Courtesy, The Grolier Club of New York

IMMORTALITY WITHOUT MONUMENT. *One of the rarest of the Aldine editions, printed in Venice in 1515, this copy of Erasmus'* The Praise of Folly *was once owned by Jean Grolier and bears his famous motto, "For Grolier and His Friends." As Erasmus himself predicted, Grolier's books have preserved the collector's memory over the centuries.*

like but soothing to the eye—still bears his name does not in the least impair its very real value; and that library continues to function as a growing collection, which students and bibliophiles may enter.*

The Field Museum of Natural History in Chicago is no less great and useful an institution because it memorializes the merchant whose gifts made its establishment possible. No one could reasonably begrudge to that excellent collector, Henry Clay Folger, the posthumous glory of having his name coupled with Shakespeare's over the memorial library in Washington, D. C., since he had lavished a lifetime's devotion upon that library's contents, and spent a lifetime's effort in assembling it. Charles Lang Freer's notable collection of Oriental art loses not an iota of its notability from being housed in a building called after him. The "Altman" paintings in the Metropolitan Museum of Art are no less great, and give no less pleasure, for being so designated, quite inconspicuously. And much the same thing can be said of countless institutions, collections, and single items, which, having become public property, continue to bear the names of former collectors.

As time passes, those names lose much of their personal meaning for the public—being then used purely as descriptives, as one might say the "South Wing" or the "Blue Room" by way of identifying or locating certain exhibits. Yet the benefaction to an immense number of heirs remains.

It was an American industrialist, Henry E. Huntington, who said:

"The ownership of a fine library is the surest and swiftest way to immortality."

And if we may assume, judging by the course he himself took, that by "ownership" he meant creation and temporary possession followed by intelligent donation, then we can agree with him heartily. Surely Huntington's own enduring fame will rest, not on the fact that he was a fabulously wealthy owner of real estate, nor probably on the huge railway empire he helped to build, but on the magnificently planned collection of books and pictures which now, in accordance with his wishes, belongs to the people of California and has become a mecca for students from all over the world.

* Differently dealt with than the other Morgan collections, the library was turned over to the public, in trust, by J. P. Morgan, 2nd, in 1924, with the condition that it should not be dispersed before 2013, one hundred years after the elder Morgan's death.

When the desire for immortality is broadened to include not only the individual but the race as well, it exercises an equally important, though somewhat different, influence over collectors.

From this root stem all "historic sentimentalisms"—the collecting of ancestors and of those ancestral relics which we call heirlooms; out of it grows the familiar worship of the old which is one of the commonest marks of a large class of collectors; and here belongs that seeker of substantial contact with the human past who is antiquarian, archaeologist, or historian. This man, gathering and preserving wherever possible the tangible evidence of our ancestors and their works, is responsible for much of the knowledge whereby we enrich and guide our own short lives. And to him the collector is first cousin, although the relationship is not always willingly admitted.

The book-collector who seeks old volumes rather than new first editions—volumes whose chief appeal often lies in their battered leather bindings and their worm-eaten pages—the collector who disregards esthetic standards, or standards of condition, in favor of mere antiquity, in selecting his items—whether those items be coins, furniture, or bric-a-brac—is largely attracted by the endurance-quality displayed by these things in having survived for so long in the face of so many obstacles. Here is a relative immortality for man's works, if not for man himself. And if he can find any similarity between his own achievements and those of his forebears (bath tubs in ancient Rome, for example) or, better still, any signs of notable progress (as in tracing the development of the easy-chair from the hard and utilitarian chest), such a collector finds himself strengthened and encouraged by this tangible evidence of continuity and improvement.

Intense interest in the past exists, in part, because man is ever curious about himself. He is absorbed in his history because he is his own favorite subject. And why not? No other subject has ever been heard of that was half so diverting. But man, as an individual, is never quite robust enough to stand alone; so he turns to that common pastime of the world, old and new—the collecting of famous or prideworthy ancestors.

There is no need here to trace the history of this curious occupation, since two or three examples, selected from widely divergent periods and places, will do to underline its universality. Glotz tells us, of the Homeric Greek, that:

"To assert his importance a man displays his family tree as well as the list of his goods."

The renaissance Italians collected real or imaginary imperial Roman forebears for themselves in an effort to show themselves descendant from a long and honorable line. In the genealogy departments of our own libraries, in the archive rooms of our county courthouses, one can usually find numbers of nice old ladies and gentlemen burrowing into formidable tomes, anxious to discover whence they and their families came, compiling the records of names and dates with the persistent intensity of the true student of history. Catering to this desire, profitable businesses exist today (and have existed in older times) for the sole purpose of refuting the unsatisfactory answer—"Out of the everywhere into the here"; and so strong can the desire to improve upon this explanation of our origin be that, when no suitably impressive ancestors are to be found, fictitious ones are commonly invented.

The coarse stuff from which our own important-ancestor hunt is spun is to be found among primitive head-hunters, too. Among the sea tribes of Sarawak, where, so Thomas tells us, "the family is of distinction according to the number of heads in its possession," baskets full of these trophies are displayed in every household of any pretensions, and "are handed down from father to son as the most valuable property"; while the Philippine Ifugao who lives, significantly, in a highly competitive society under a system of definite class distinctions, also takes pains to save his prestige-bearing hunting trophies and passes them on as family heirlooms. Forming, as they do in the terms of the country, a continuing monument to a family's prowess, these head-collections are a source of great pride. So we cherish the family silver not only because of its beauty and intrinsic value, but also because it attests that we come of older, not a new, stock of successful, respectable people.

Modern archaeologists continue to make discoveries that move the "dawn of history" ever farther back; and as this path unfolds, we become increasingly aware that, in those very times which once we called "earliest," there lived men whose forebears were historical characters, preceding them by as much time as now intervenes between ourselves and our Greek and Roman heritage. The Egyptians, the Assyrians, the Babylonians, even the Sumerians, all had long and rich histories of their own to investigate, all had heroes of a bygone age whose memories they delighted to honor, and all themselves engaged in antiquarian research and collected the relics of their own past.

Gudea, priest-king of Lagash in Mesopotamia, in the twenty-fifth century before Christ—he whose own handsome statues have been, in our own day, among the ornaments of the Louvre—"promoted the study of classical antiquity in the spirit of the expeditions that (have since) unearthed him."

In another and greater Sumerian city—that mighty Ur whose name survived in men's memories long after that of its founding people had been obscured—there were men of the third millennium B.C. who copied and collected, from the even then ancient brick and stone, those inscriptions which illumined the past history of their city. To the labors of these scholarly ancient collectors we owe, in the words of Woolley, the modern archaeologist, "most of what we have learned concerning the life and thought of their time." Today we know that this city of many vicissitudes, spoken of in the Bible as "Ur of the Chaldees," was, in reality, a Sumerian stronghold, with a history going back at least as far as 3500 B.C., whereas the Chaldeans were a new race in the land as late as the eighth century before Christ. Located south of the Euphrates, in territory later dominated by the Chaldeans, Ur received its misnomer from the Jews of this later day—men who had never heard of Sumer, although their own ancestor, Abraham, had emigrated, perhaps in the year 2000 B.C., from this most important city in the final period of Sumerian ascendancy.

It is as though Rome, falling to the Nazis, should have gone down in nistory as a German city! Even to the Assyrians and Babylonians, who all unwittingly inherited a generous share of such culture as they possessed from the great predecessor race, the once glorious name of Sumer represented but a hazy legend. It might seem ironical in this connection to speak of immortality, were it not for the fact that Sumerian fame has been resurrected in our time for men to marvel at once more. But to us it is particularly significant that, to make this resurrection possible, the lively collecting interest in that far-distant age should ultimately have combined with a similar interest some four thousands of years later.

The collecting picture is rather less clear in ancient Egypt, whose civilization developed contemporaneously with that of Sumeria, Babylonia and Assyria. Yet no men ever laid more stress on immortality than did the ancient Egyptians. In them, the desire for physical and spiritual survival was so strong that an adequate preparation for death became one of the foremost activities in life, and at times the personal concern of the individual to create lasting monuments to himself seems to have beclouded the more impersonal veneration for past glories of the race. A Pharaoh, in his anxiety to do himself honor in the eyes of the gods (and perhaps in those of the people as well), might vandalize a temple or an obelisk erected by his grandfather, so that he should have better materials for his own memorial than would otherwise have been available. In contrast to this, there were other periods during which the damaged monuments of antiquity were piously restored.

Obviously, one cannot generalize from facts as contradictory as these. But if the surviving evidences of antiquarian and heirloom collecting are rarer and less conclusive in Egypt than in Mesopotamia, it is nevertheless true that fragments of the oldest surviving libraries found in the world so far have been discovered in Egypt; that in those libraries were preserved the "sayings and doings of ancient kings, together with the number of the years of their lives and the exact duration of their reigns"; and that in the temples, and on the walls of tombs and obelisks were collected the records of a long and prideful history, in a form which must have seemed likely to last forever.

Occasional heirlooms have been discovered in Egyptian tombs, notably in that of Tutankhamen, one of the few such repositories to come down to us relatively intact; and it is quite possible that further evidence of this sort of collecting—evidence as indisputable as that in Bel-Shalti-Nannar's museum* so recently brought to light in the remains of Chaldean Ur—may some day be unearthed in Egypt, too.

After Egypt, the Greeks and Romans preserved historical relics in their temples long before they were interested in making private collections. In ancient China, archaeology early became a special branch of scholarly study, and private collectors of antique objects existed there in considerable numbers. Among ourselves as collectors, the question of antiquity will be seen to be one of the chief criteria of value.

When later in this book we pause for a view of the collector's march through history, we shall see that some form of preoccupation with the

---

* This was a museum of archaeological relics, the earliest yet discovered. See below, p. 103.

past has been characteristic of all peoples. There may be several reasons for this, but surely not the least of them lies in the fact that man, by identifying his perishable self with such durable objects as he may collect, by gathering and preserving the remains of a proud past, can sometimes feel that he is putting Death itself out of countenance.

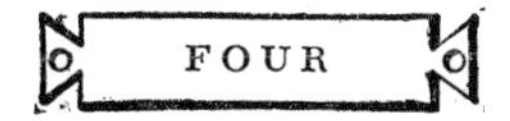

THE COLLECTION AS A MEANS TO KNOWLEDGE AND ESTHETIC SATISFACTION

"All our progress is an unfolding, like the vegetable bud. You have first an instinct, then an opinion, then a knowledge."

RALPH WALDO EMERSON

IT IS COMMON human experience that an end finally achieved is soon taken for granted; that success, no matter how urgently sought, more or less quickly loses its power to satisfy. Such adages as "the oats in the next pasture are always fatter" are significantly universal. Phantom oats of this sort are the grist that keep the human mill turning; when reasonable security has been attained, man finds himself urged on to reach for rarer goals—for beauty, knowledge and understanding, for order, harmony and form—demanding, in the process, an ever more selective excellence. In these fertile fields, he may, without chance of exhausting the possibilities, find a continuing outlet for his aspiration. Here his noblest crops are harvested; and when, in his maturity, the collector reaches this place, he tastes of the golden fruit.

The search for beauty and the search for knowledge are, in some ways, only differing aspects of the desire to find and understand essential form. Man's experience of beauty consists mainly in a sensory and emotional response to form, to the rhythmic and orderly arrangement of parts in a whole; while knowledge without orderly arrangement is largely valueless. Intellectual understanding intensifies the experience of beauty, as it lends meaning to knowledge; and balance, pattern and reason are searched out equally in science and in art.

These are the elements with which the "true" collector—the aspiring amateur, the thoughtful gatherer—is deeply concerned. His mind disciplined to purpose, he uses order and reason in assembling his collection, and strives to build of its various parts one unified and significant structure. If it so happen that his eye can grasp the scale of beauty, he will also, despite the emotional quality of his original response, be critical and selective; and if his interest lies in some purely technical subject, he will, even so, apply a degree of creative imagination to his pursuit. The scientist essays to determine truth through the interpretation as well as through the methodical accumulation of knowledge; the artist strives to create beauty through a selective use of forms, colors, tones, rhythms and meanings available within the confines of chosen materials; and the highly developed collector, also methodical, steadily adds to his capacity for perceiving beauty and truth, within the pattern of his traditional culture.

By his restlessness, driving him on to conquer new worlds without end, man is distinguished from the lesser creatures, content to satisfy elementary needs; and it is by his effort to bring order into his own world to match the larger order of nature that the true collector may be recognized, for to him system is an essential of method. It might seem that no true foreshadowing of those higher forms of human collecting which emphasize order and are rooted in the search for beauty and knowledge could be found outside man's own province. Yet in the evolutionary scale there seems to be a beginning for everything.

Among lower forms of life, order, in a limited and utilitarian sense (for direct purposes of survival) is attained through instinctive action, although we find no signs that a generalized conception of the value of order here exists, and we assume that subhuman creatures are even less capable of arriving at such a conception than are those primitive peoples whose vocabularies even to this day are without words for abstract ideas. On the other hand, curiosity, which has been called the impulse to knowledge and which has played a vital role in the stimulation of human collecting, is found to a marked degree in much of the lower world; and at least the rudiments of an esthetic reaction can be discerned in the response to sense-stimulating qualities such as color, sparkle, texture and shape.

It is sometimes difficult, particularly in the earliest stages, to distinguish between curiosity and sensory response. The two may go hand in hand and produce an identical result; an instinctive need or apparent desire to maintain contact with the provocative object. The tropisms of plant and animal life—the innate tendency of the organism to react in a certain manner to external stimuli—are well known: ordinarily beneficial stimuli attract and harmful ones repel. Wherever consciousness may be said to exist, the essentially beneficial stimuli may be presumed to be pleasurable; and it is significant that certain creatures make that active effort to acquire pleasure-giving or curiosity-arousing objects and to hold them in possession which is the basic act of collecting. There are some birds, in particular, whose behavior in regard to strange, bright objects is so suggestive of the human reaction that they have been called "museum collectors." Most famous of these are the jackdaw and the magpie, whose very names have come to symbolize a certain low order of the collecting tendency in civilized man.

How explain such behavior? It has been suggested that it is related to the nest-building instinct; but although this idea may have some foundation (similarly, the pebbles collected by certain kinds of fish are used for the construction of a nest within which to deposit the eggs), it certainly does not tell the whole story. In the first place, comparatively few birds are attracted to bright or strange objects in particular, although most of them construct homes. Furthermore, items of a nature not useful as nest material are not discarded by bird "collectors" when their ineffectiveness is discovered. They are kept and often used as decoration. Moreover, not all members of a species behave alike in this regard, for some individuals decorate their nests abundantly, others very little, still others not at all. So some men collect art objects and curios, others do not.

An interesting point is that those bird species most noted for the non-utilitarian collecting tendency are regarded by some students as the more social and, by implication, the more intelligent of their kind. The strength of this tendency among them is in itself taken as indicating "greater curiosity and interest as well as a capacity to distinguish and enjoy" which is superior to the simpler reactions of birds whose collecting activities are limited to the purely utilitarian. In the same way, although with a greater possibility for accuracy of judgment, Dr. Walter Nelson Durost, who conducted an extensive and controlled survey of the collecting activities of children, concluded that the more intelligent youngsters were also the ones who made the most frequent and best collections.

Ravens, who have been watched collecting such bright portable objects as colored marbles, yellow pencils, tin lids, pieces of broken china, pretty leaves and whitened bones, will, in the presence of other ravens, attempt to hide their treasures, and will steal them from each other if possible. When alone, the birds are far less secretive, so that their behavior in this respect would seem prompted by a definite feeling of ownership and competition. The fact also suggests that the raven's hoarding is not on the same blind level as that of the dog who tries to hide his bone regardless of necessity or condition. That the bird sometimes forgets his accumulation once it is out of sight does not alter the significance of his previous behavior: it merely indicates a limited capacity for remembering.

Certain animals also seem to be so strongly attracted by bright or strange objects as to be impelled to collect them. Various writers, confronted by the wall of mystery which so largely separates us from a sure understanding of the animal "mind," have interpreted the observed facts in quite different ways and probably will continue to do so, agreeing only as to the facts themselves.

One of the greatest puzzlers to confront observers has been the "trader" rat, who, briskly carrying on his affairs oblivious to human brow-wrinkling, will take for himself anything portable, from buttons to a stick of dynamite. Distinguished by his habit of always leaving something in the place of the objects appropriated, he has been known to exchange toadstools for a bunch of silver spoons, a rabbit's skull for a kitchen clock. With what appears to be sweet hope for a reformed world, some men have attributed this habit to a highly developed "moral sense." Others have declared that it must represent a "carrying mania." But even without explanation, the results must be rather startling to the homesteader who, upon returning to his cabin in the evening, finds a stone where he had left his soap, and a handful of acorns in a case that had been full of cartridges when he went out in the morning!

In one instance, reported by William James, a trader rat made off with a bundle of nails and proceeded to arrange them along the edges of its nest in a symmetrical, fortress-like pattern, the points protruding menacingly outward as though to protect the miscellaneous hoard of other objects within the nest itself. The temptation to anthropomorphize such an example is almost (but not quite) irresistible. Seton believed that the trader rat—whose harvest has included such oddly assorted objects as false teeth, boxes of matches, bright neckties, silk socks, broken buckles, bits of china, and perfectly good perfume bottles—is motivated by an esthetic instinct of sorts. It was his idea that the rat "enjoys seeing, handling and owning strange and attractive things, much like the human collector." And even Beaglehole, who inclines to the theory that the nest-building instinct is at work here, manages to agree that the animal's attention is at least focused by bright portable objects, just as is the case with some birds and most young children.

Although not similarly inclined to make amends for his thefts, the house rat also shows a proclivity to gather and hoard things other than food. One managed to assemble three towels, two napkins, five dustcloths, two pairs of linen knickerbockers, one silk and six linen handkerchiefs. Another, a clever fellow, profoundly obsessed by a napkin specialty, made his home in the wall of a restaurant and had accumulated one thousand seven hundred twenty-eight napkins before he was discovered and brought to justice! Until this arrant collector had been collared, the restaurant's prodigious loss of linen was probably charged off against those human souvenir hunters who make such constant raids on all public eating places.

Possessive behavior has been observed in the howler, the baboon, and the chimpanzee. The apes upon whom Koehler conducted his experiments were attracted by a diverse variety—sticks, stones, tin cans, pieces of wire, rope, wood, or bits of rag. The wire, the rope and the colored rags they would place around their necks or elsewhere on their bodies, and their reaction to the result seemed very like vanity. They did not often attempt to accumulate more objects than they could play with or wear at one time, but as soon as anyone—another ape or one of the human observers—exhibited the slightest interest in any article which was the property of one ape, tension in the cage visibly increased. Such an object might be hidden protectively; each creature seemed to feel a definite sense of proprietorship over his own claimed possessions, and competition only served to augment his desire to keep these for himself.

Alverdes further points out that certain objects were, "in fashion" at particular moments. This is not unlike the case of the human collector who, if he have no true focus of interest, is influenced to shift frequently from one subject to another.

Although curiosity is indeed the impulse to knowledge, if followed for its own sake without purposive direction it may lead one into a *cul-de-sac.* The man or monkey who picks up one thing, examines it casually, then discards it to go on to something else, is hardly to be compared with the sort of collector who searches out the origin and meaning of his "curios" and preserves his items according to a well-conceived plan.

Nevertheless, there is an innate response to things out of the ordinary (which stimulate the mind), and to things highly pitched in tone or color (which stimulate the senses), and that response, deep-rooted in man, may be said to lie at the base of much human collecting activity.

In varying degrees of intensity, aborigines and many of our contemporaries, young and old, seem irresistibly impelled to pick up and keep certain kinds of oddities—a few suggestively shaped or brightly colored stones from a woodland path, sea shells or dried starfish from the beach. Many a drawer or mantelpiece has been cluttered with accumulations of such strange or beautiful objects of nature, a useless but inexplicably fascinating miscellany.* The average person who brings home curious "finds" of this sort is usually a collector only so long as his curiosity is piqued. He soon grows indifferent and the exhibits are then thrown out or relegated to the attic. On the other hand, the "born" collector often takes his first dive from the same springboard. As the first flush of curiosity merges into collectorship, the field of attraction narrows perceptibly until the once casual attention focuses with growing intensity upon one particular type of object: the man who began by thoughtlessly accumulating every intriguing natural oddity may become a gatherer of falcon eggs or of brightly colored tree snails, as serious in his methods as a naturalist; or he may turn to some completely different field as his changing interests direct, the collector in him roused by these early, haphazard encounters.

This development is most often observed in children. Like the raven

* Sea shell collecting, a popular hobby in Victorian days, was scorned as "childish" by succeeding generations. Today it has once more attained the status of a "serious" and flourishing pursuit; but regardless of such shifts in collecting fashion, most of us have, at one time or another, succumbed to the charms of these infinitely variegated and provocative curios of the sea.

and the ape, the young human desires to have and to hold anything which arouses his interest or curiosity. Naturally acquisitive, he, too, likes to store up such articles for future inspection or play, and is rendered all the more possessive by competition. And although this is but a rudimentary forerunner of his later behavior when he has acquired discrimination and a sense of values, it is significant in view of the theory that in the development of the child the evolutionary steps of the race cycle are repeated.

When we separate the sophisticated experience of beauty from the instinctive reaction to a pleasure-giving stimulus, it seems likely that the search for knowledge came somewhat before the conscious search for beauty. Curiosity develops at least partially from security needs, and where it continues to function vitally, intelligence is potential; or to put it another way, without a high degree of curiosity, intelligence is not reached. Therefore, when we are tempted to censure or deride the "curious" collector (who is interested mainly in the odd or unusual), we should remember, with Samuel Johnson, that

"Curiosity is, in great and generous minds, the first passion and the last."

Our "curious" collectors are on the right track, at least.

And what of esthetic appreciation? Its foundations have been in us and of us since the beginning. But there is an important difference between the first instinctive reaction to sensory stimulation and the more highly developed perception of beauty in form. Young children, like savages and certain beasts and birds, react spontaneously to the most brilliant colors: it would be the home-polished small boy who preferred a Gobelin tapestry to a circus poster; and in the sense in which the term is commonly used, this primal reaction to things like simple color would not be considered true "esthetic appreciation." Actually, the development of conscious appreciation can hardly occur, in individuals or in societies, before the development of intelligence has made possible some degree of critical evaluation.

So much for chronology. As for relative values, it is possible for a man with a first-rate mind to have little esthetic sense, and it is likewise possible for one of equal intellect to be concerned above all else with the experience of beauty and its transmission. The point is of interest here only because, in sophisticated collecting, the line which divides accumulation for the sake of esthetic pleasure and that which is grounded in mental inquisitiveness may determine the difference between, say, the art collector and the collector of scientifically interesting specimens. Even as between two stamp collectors, or two numismatists, this variation in basic interest will probably decide the particular emphasis which each man puts upon his collecting. It will decide for him whether he is to gather chiefly those stamps or coins which seem to him good to look upon or whether he will concentrate instead on the technical or historically significant aspects of his hobby.

Curiosity and superstition often work in conjunction with each other to stimulate rudimentary forms of collecting, just as do curiosity and sensory response. In early Egypt anything in the shape of a baboon was conceived of as having talismanic properties; and it was among a collection of man-made baboon amulets, on the site of the prehistoric temple at Abydos, that Flinders Petrie found two unworked flint nodules bearing a distinct resemblance to that venerated ape. Nature, not human hands, had created the shape of these particular stones, but some ancient man, happening upon them, had been struck by the curiosity of their form, and had valued the stones sufficiently to pick them up, save them, and carry them a mile or more from the desert to deposit them with the amulets they had suggested to his mind.

English and European peasants still do much the same sort of thing with the prehistoric flint axheads and arrowheads they come across in their fields. These "elf arrows" or "thunderbolts," as they are variously called, may be hung in the cow barns to keep away the fairies, or placed as curatives in the water which is given sick cattle to drink. Sometimes the "finds" are mounted as jewelry and worn by their finders as charms or mascots.

Wherever such beliefs exist, it is obvious that superstition is in part responsible for the desire to accumulate certain types of objects. Yet superstition is not all that is involved, nor need we assume that it is always present. The interest that attaches to the strange or unusual, the response that man makes to what pleases his vision, are both of importance in accounting for his wish to possess such things.

Glotz tells us, for example, that the early Cretans, while still living in primitive huts (a period which succeeded cave-dwelling), preserved such objects as elephants' tusks or the vertebrae of whales which could serve no useful purpose but to which they attached great value. Later men called items of this sort "natural curiosities."

In the homes of the Basketmakers, the first Americans of whom we have any appreciable knowledge, F. Martin Brown reports the discovery of strings of beads or of acorn cups and others of small snail shells or bits of bone and stone. Piled up accumulations of fossils and small, brightly colored stones have also been found. These, according to N. C. Nelson, could only have been rudimentary collections of the sort made by children and animals.

On the Mongolian desert in modern times, beside the tombs of high religious dignitaries near the lamaseries, numbers of prehistoric stone implements have been seen heaped around the base of the monuments. These, we are told by Dr. Nelson, the paleontologist who found them, had been picked up and collected as curiosities by modern natives who had, of course, not the slightest conception of the historic interest of their finds. There is little reason to believe that superstition plays any but a modest part in such kinds of rudimentary collecting.

It has been suggested that early or simple peoples may wear their "collections"—of odd, pretty, or valuable things—because they have no cabinets in which to display them. Here, again, a number of motives can be discerned, often inextricably intermingled. There is first the simple delight in wearing things pleasing to the eye. Adornment as a gadget of sex is of course important (if you were an old-time Freudian you might say it was all-important, but there are few absolutists left). Security may be sought in wearing ornaments believed to be endowed with magical properties. And it is apparent how the desire for prestige may assert itself through the wearing of collected trophies or of objects having an accepted value such as wampum, iron rings or diamonds set in platinum.

The impulse to turn certain kinds of collections into something wearable can be found in many places under many different guises, nor need we look exclusively to simple peoples for examples. Even those who might have cabinets if they wished sometimes prefer to decorate themselves with their items. Thus, in April, 1939, an American child wrote to the hobby club of the magazine *Woman's Day:*

"I collect anything that has to do with nature—plants, bugs, bones. I have fourteen skulls, including fox, sheep, cow, horse and dog, and eleven kinds of joints of a sheep. I am going to make a chain of different kinds of animal teeth."

Also reminiscent of earlier times were the bracelets, popular only a few years ago, which consisted of miniature oddments or "charms" that a girl might assemble, one by one, until she had collected enough to go around her wrist. The goal was primarily adornment, but the fun of hunting down and acquiring the individual pieces—so important a feature of collecting—also played its part.

When such things evolve naturally—that is, when no commercial fostering enters—the collecting impulse may come first, the assembled ornament an afterthought. Here is one example with apparently modern overtones. Daily visiting a Riviera beach, Ruth Thompson Grandin one day discovered that certain small and attractive green "stones" were not stones at all but bits of glass (probably from old Provençal wine bottles) polished smooth by the sea. Casually, at first, she began to save the choicer finds until, happening upon a particularly beautiful specimen, the idea came that these luminous fragments, properly selected, might be made into an unusual bracelet. It was then that she started collecting in earnest, discarding the imperfect pieces, choosing others for variation in color and some for their grace of form. The bracelet finally created in this fashion, with the help and guidance of a local jeweler who loved his craft, had a personal meaning seldom attached to the ready-made.

A beauty of one's own choosing—therein lies a double key to a deep, most satisfactory pleasure; and from very early times man has reached out for this experience.

Fifty thousand, possibly a hundred thousand years ago, men of the Old Stone Age had already begun to shape their primitive fist hatchets in search of symmetry and grace. Certainly such frivolous work did nothing to improve the usefulness of the instruments, but it was practiced nonetheless to feed an appetite for rhythm, for a more personal expression of inner forces: the craving for "art" fashioned by hands of men is easier for those hands to express than for the mind to define.

In time, as man learned to carve stone and ivory and bone, this hunger grew. Not content, then, with mere decoration, he began to fashion crude statues, and some, surviving, bear an astonishing resemblance to "modernist" sculpture. The precedence that beauty, as expressed in fine material and exquisite workmanship, may assume over such utilitarian considerations as economy and speed is shown among peoples like the Imerina of Madagascar: they make their spade handles of fine cabinet woods, although such handles are no better, practically speaking, than those of ordinary wood, cost more, and are harder to obtain. Objects thus distinguished from the merely useful may be prized all the more for the pleasure they give, and the "savage" collects them for this reason, even as you and I. Pride in display plays its part, it is true, but it is a pride conditioned by a value set on beauty. In such cases, says Malinowski:

"It is not rarity within utility which creates value, but a rarity sought out by human skill within workable materials."

We can watch this very transition take place within our own society. Although objects once useful may become obsolete or altered in value, they often remain of importance to the community—as decoration. Things long useless are rediscovered, not to utilitarian purposes but as "significant art," and this whether or not esthetic considerations were consciously present at the time of their creation. Thus certain rugs, fashioned as ordinary floor-coverings or, perhaps, for religious purposes, are often divorced from utility entirely and hung upon the walls like paintings. The plebeian oil jar or pickle crock, its original function completely outdated, becomes a prized ornament when we find some quality of beauty in its shape, color, or design.

Today many esthetes consciously search for beauty in fields generally supposed to be as far removed from art as possible. Witness the exhibitions held in museums and galleries, here and in Europe, in recent years, in which humble machinery and machine parts, for example, became the current Cinderellas, shown, and reviewed by critics with uncertain respect.* Such awareness, peculiar to our era, anticipates the time when these tools of ours will also be obsolete: in them essential beauty, suddenly discovered, exists because men, building things for a definite need, were forced to simplify, thus dealing with basic forms that are

* It so happens that the awareness of museum and gallery people responsible for such exhibitions was first aroused by the work of certain contemporary sculptors and painters (notably the painter, Léger) who used machine forms in their own work. This new emphasis on beauty in utilitarian objects has resulted in a conscious endeavor to improve the esthetic quality of all such objects equally with their efficiency, so that we now have "streamlined" refrigerators and railroad engines designed in form, color and contrasting materials by artist-engineers.

inevitably sound artistically. The beauty of much "early" or "primitive" craftsmanship derives from this same principle.

For beauty no satisfactory definition exists, since beauty lies not in any objective quality but in the personal response which such a quality may evoke, and each individual, each group, responds in a fashion individually determined: standards of esthetic value peculiar to the background of each are evolved.

If, in spite of this variation, there is one point common to all experiences of beauty, it might consist in part of a pleasurable response to innate form—a response to that rhythm and proportion which we sense underlying all life and all life-processes, and which we seek to match through our own efforts. The work of the first artists is thought, by some, to have been man's earliest attempt to bring order from apparent chaos by synthesizing observation, experience and feeling. And although this thought, behind its cool façade of weighed wordage, may be quite romantic, it is as plausible as any interpretation of genesis.

We experience beauty of one sort or another (higher or lower, as we may choose to call it) in the contemplation of any thoroughly satisfactory object or effort. Thus, one man is entranced by that colossal masterpiece of nature, the Grand Canyon at dawn or with sunset included; another can turn his back on such thunder and be swept by kindred emotions as he bends over a particular postage stamp; and in the same manner, the ecstatic scientist exclaims with delight when he holds up a beautiful (his term) example of diseased tissue from his pickled collection.

We might say that one or more of these gentlemen had missed the point of beauty; but it seems more likely that beauty actually burns brightest for a man in that activity or special object which holds his most ardent interest, for that which becomes greatly important to a person is endowed for him with qualities that others are likely to dismiss shortly. Truly a specialist, man often has difficulty in admiring another's child in the same warm light reserved for his own.

In addition to purely personal responses of this sort, some values are traditionally determined for us. A woman who is "beautiful" in one land may actually seem grotesque in another: svelte Egyptians laughed scornfully at the buxom, big-bottomed Nubians—and expressed that amusement effectively in art. Our fashion, too, changing more easily than a conditioned preference for blue or brown eyes, has its word to say in this regard: we admire hothouse pallor or healthy tan by turns; seek tiny waists, fulsome curves or poker-straight lines according to the temper of the day. Similarly, in purely esthetic fields, moods and standards of beauty have varied continuously down the centuries—the grace and grandeur of Egyptian art; the ferocity of the Assyrian; the noble realism of the Greek; the eloquent simplicity of the Chinese; the decorative Persian; the complex symbolism of the East Indian; Medieval contemplation; Renaissance exuberance; baroque and rococo extravagance; and, in our own day, earthbound academicism, nostalgic primitivism, intellectualized abstractionism—changing, intermingling, each contributing something individual and something eclectic to art forms.

However, and here is the rub, in the prized stuffs and materials of their times, created objects much sought after are often arbitrarily endowed with "beauty" following the old curious law of supply and demand: thus the rarest too often becomes the "best," and antique things in most ages are indiscriminately invested with superior attributes.

The average man found no beauty in dull ancestral pewter, hidden away in the attic, saw nothing to admire in old-fashioned H-and-L hinges, until the news arrived that such stuff was considered "good" enough to bring real money. Thereafter, though he may have remained dubious, he no longer felt quite as free to express his true opinion, and this quite apart from the economic factor involved. Wishing to measure up to contemporarily accepted standards of criticism and social judgment, the majority find it difficult in the extreme to rely solely upon their own reactions in the field of art and are reluctant to admit to reactions which may differ radically from current fashion. Often such people are no longer truly conscious of their personal responses. Their standards, not of their own making, are evolved through a series of compromises from mind to eye, and borrowed standards thus become inherited standards.

In our time, we tend to believe in a "basic" art—in forms that are built out of undying "truth"—but this is a standard of limited use, since in practice it is difficult to reach an agreement as to its meaning. Today, the flower of Greece, the "ideal" art of the Apollo Belvedere or the Venus of Milo, seems less of timeless stuff to the advance guard of connoisseurship than the work of earlier Greece, heretofore considered "crude." We now admire Egyptian art, though not all phases of it. Primitive art appeals to us, while highly polished realism is in large measure discarded, and so on. However, we must remember that we ourselves are in a "phase," a phase of appreciation or response, and it will not be known in our lifetimes how timeless or passing our own tastes may be.

We know, however, that man, when he allows himself so to be, is inevitably moved by a beauty that touches him, and that this experience, whether it follow the dictates of fashion or not, is nourishment to an inner craving. It seems impossible to prove, for example, that calendar art is not good art; and what answer is there to the farmer's skepticism of a man who shuts himself up in a somber room to pore over landscape prints while the sun lavishes life on the countryside? Here, it might be said, life is read in translation and in the original. Which is better? Why not both? Either can be profound, and, when suspicion and preciousness are forgotten, these two attitudes can meet on common ground. Moreover, if taste changes, it also tends to run in cycles (romanticism to realism, for example); and although the cycles may never duplicate each other exactly, there are art lovers in each generation (including those who would never think to wrap themselves in such a name) who are affected by qualities not recognized by the accepted tastes of their times.

The individual who would truly experience beauty—through his collection, in museums, in nature, in life itself—should, then, conduct his own quest, uninterrupted by scorn or praise from the mouths of professional interpreters. Let him worship where he will.

Men whose concern with beauty is largely philosophical sometimes refuse to admit the collector into the charmed inner circle inhabited by the so-called true art lover. These purists, says Mather, tend to

"deprecate the collector's desire for actual possession as impairing that ideal possession which is appreciation."

But surely such generalizations are foolish, for man has complex, not "pure" experiences—and this is as true where beauty is concerned as in any other direction. Simply because a collector might infuse the objects he owns with a personal glow of affection and esteem of the sort reserved by other men for their own dependable and accomplished offspring, because our collector is in this fashion quite human and inclined to magnify the virtues of his possessions, it would be folly to dismiss him with a smile, dubbing his antics peculiar. Actually, although possession

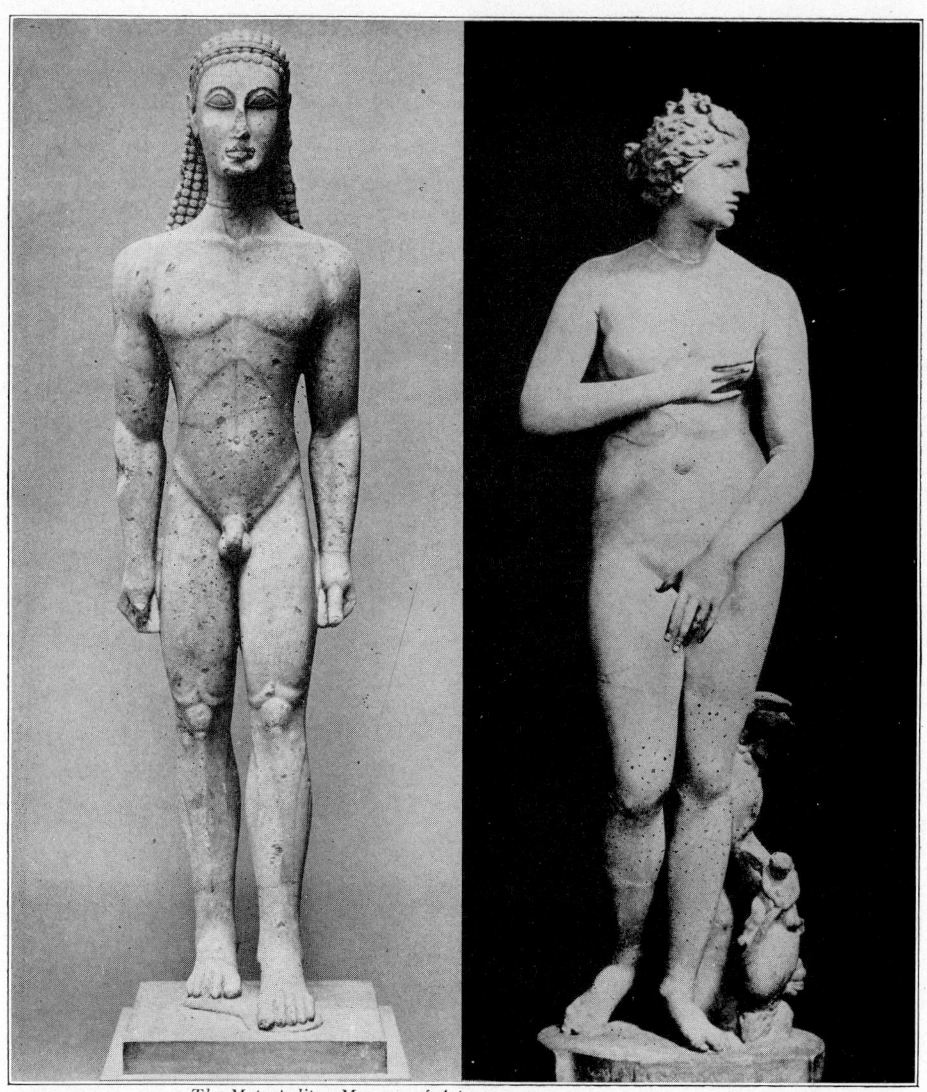

The Metropolitan Museum of Art

ATHENIAN APOLLO, *7th or 6th century* B.C.

VENUS DE' MEDICI, *4th century* B.C. *or later, now in the Uffizi Gallery, Florence.*

TASTES CHANGE. *The power and simplicity of archaic Greek sculpture was brushed aside for more than twenty centuries, with rare exceptions, in favor of the "perfect finish" of the classic and neo-classic periods. Formerly adored by poets and critics, today this modest Venus is less esteemed by connoisseurs than the direct and impersonal young man.*

may impair the quality of discrimination or use of taste, it does not necessarily do so. If we tend to identify ourselves with the things we own, and to feel elevated in proportion as those things are elevating, there is nothing to decry in that. Moreover, one type of collector, neither run-of-the-mill nor a curiosity,

"looks as austerely at his treasures as the true artist looks at his own works."

Such a man does not consider an object beautiful merely because it is his. Rather, he wants to own it because he considers it beautiful. And if, as he lives with it and learns to know it better, he comes to admire it less (which can easily happen if his perceptions are acute and knowing), he will not fear to discard it just because he had once put upon it his stamp of approval.

It is, furthermore, all very well to say of the man who collects paintings that he might see and enjoy the same pictures just as well on the walls of a museum. But could he? Beauty is all around us, potentially, in the stone, in the tree, in natural relationships in space, in any object carefully observed or deeply felt—but it is called into being only by our participation. The more we have to contribute, from the highly developed facets of our minds and spirits, of sensitivity, of awareness, of understanding, the more intense will be our pleasure. Now paintings in a museum (and paintings are, of course, only one of many possible examples) can be seen only at specified times, under conditions far from ideal so far as unhurried contemplation is concerned. The art lover who owns paintings can look at them whenever he wants to, for as long or as short a time as he likes, under conditions which permit of concentration, absorption, and, upon occasion, ecstasy. No one jostles his elbow. No one stands between him and the picture. No one distracts him with irritating or irrelevant remarks. When he is concerned with certain fine points (whereby he may widen his capacity for appreciation) he can take the picture off the wall, place it in the most favorable light, look at it as closely as he needs to, and even, with a touch of his finger, experience the texture of its paint. The more he is able to indulge in this sort of observation, and in that other sort of intimate contemplation, the more the picture becomes a part of his own being.

Professional estheticians notwithstanding, such a result is as near to true appreciation as most men would hope to come.

In the beginning, man saw, wondered about, and attempted to explain things that were strange to his understanding. He picked up such objects because their oddity attracted his attention. Keeping them, speculating as to their origin, he decided for himself what they were, what meaning and purpose they possessed, and if he did not always decide correctly, neither was he always wrong.

There were fossils, for example. These are the major concern of that recently born scientist whom we call paleontologist; but even in the Old Stone Age, according to the French authorities Boule and Piveteau, men noticed and collected these petrified remains of still more ancient epochs. From such relics, so these modern scientists suggest, the first collectors probably evolved theories of their own to explain the beginnings of the world and its inhabitants, theories which may have survived in "racial memory" or tradition, to be passed on, in constantly modified form, to the makers of the earliest civilizations. From this distant source, if the supposition is justified, stems some of our greatest epic literature.

It is an exciting vision, this glimpse of the first struggle of the human mind to find intelligibility in the world around it. We cannot prove how the mind worked at so early a date, of course; we can only surmise. But we have some actual collections to ponder upon, and if our early men accumulated their fossils as alert children gather similar things today and thought about them only afterward, investing them with meaning different from our present conception, the process was at least a beginning of the search for understanding.

In later but still quite early times—as in ancient Greece, where fossils and prehistoric implements were collected—we know that definite theories as to the origin and significance of such things were being formulated; and that these theories were often in error, according to our present light, is again beside the point.

The Greek temples contained many collections of natural curiosities, and although these were then more valued for their rarity or peculiarity than as specimens to be studied, there was, nevertheless, some attempt to explain their origin. The prehistoric stone implements, for example, were believed to be thunderbolts or "thunderstones" which had fallen from the sky during storms; and our condescending smile at this ancient naïveté should turn to humility when we are reminded that exactly the same belief was everywhere prevalent until well into the nineteenth century, and was even then with difficulty dislodged from the minds of European savants.

Side by side with more or less haphazard "curiosity" collecting, scientific collecting had already taken form among the Greeks. Dr. Barnum Brown, American paleontologist, investigating the ruins of the famous Greek medical school where Hippocrates worked, came upon a fossil elephant tooth of the Pliocene Age some millions of years old. It had been brought to the Asklepion for study in the earliest days of that institution's existence and was, it is legitimate to assume, only one of many specimens gathered there for examination.

It is significant that the earliest true or well-developed collections we know of were libraries, the repositories of information, and that the first true museum yet to be unearthed was a collection of antiquities assembled in the interests of history. From collections such as these, knowledge could be regimented and subjected to interpretation; and an orderly conception of racial or national development could be drawn up out of the hitherto helter-skelter remnants of the past.

"A collection," according to Webster, "usually implies some order, arrangement, or unity of effort"; and, in the strictest sense of the word, nothing is really a collection which does not partake of these elements. Hence the importance of classification to a good collection. The impulse to classify is primarily the evidence of an active intelligence, since classification is, after all, nothing more nor less than a tool for creating order, a means for arriving at valid interpretation.

Similarly, that striving for an order and unity which we sometimes call "form" manifests itself in the tendency of the modern collector to specialize, first in one general subject, then progressively in smaller and smaller divisions of that subject, so that by limiting his scope he may, in one field at least, approach the ideal of order and completion. This procedure is familiar also to the scientist. However, specialization, in collecting as in science, is a relatively late development. Even a century or so ago a collector might consider the whole world his oyster, but today the most eclectic gatherers set certain broad limits within which they confine their collecting scope.

The striving for form also manifests itself in the tendency of modern collectors to follow a specific sequence in forming and arranging collections, as well as in the desire to complete definite "sets" or series of exhibits. The nature of these sequences will vary according to the subject of the collection itself. They may be historical or geographical; they may have to do with size, or with material, or with any of the special classifications evolved by collectors; and in this connection an entire array of rules and regulations develops in each collecting field, an array which will be examined in a later chapter.

The collector, in common with other men, may sometimes carry an originally valuable attitude to what seems the point of absurdity. So Samuel Pepys, who arranged and rearranged his library, finally classified his books according to size. In double rows on the shelves the larger volumes were placed behind the smaller so that the lettering on all could be seen; and in order that the tops might be even with each other, this neat collector built wooden stilts where necessary and, placing these under the shorter books, gilded them to match the bindings! Subject and reference-convenience were secondary in this arrangement, except in so far as the sacrosanct diary was concerned, and this, which had been written in notebooks of varying size, Mr. Pepys, reverting to reason, had bound uniformly so that its parts might be kept together without disturbing the library's general arrangement-scheme.

Carried to these extremes, the desire to classify can be compared to the "maladaptive instinct survival" and to the anatomical appendix. Wholly unreasonable in intelligent usage, it has become a passion in itself—a passion toward order from which the desire for intelligibility has been lost.

Such wanderings of adult "reason" are in part responsible for the antagonism which many scientists feel toward lay collectors, and help to account for the frequent unwillingness of the scholar to admit kinship with men whom he considers dilettanti or worse. Yet in at least two respects—in his desire to know all that can be learned about one subject, and in the value he places upon systematization—the true collector is related to men of the laboratory and the study, and may even, lest we forget, lay just claim to ancestorship of the whole breed.

While science is based essentially upon accumulated knowledge that has been organized and formulated with reference to the understanding of truth, collections, too, are ordered accumulations which frequently, though certainly not always, contribute to knowledge and interpretation. In a sense, science is actually a form of socialized collecting: the scientist's gatherings are usually added, not to a personal collection, but to mankind's collection of wisdom, and in this way science uses the highest and most useful forms of the collecting impulse.

To attain an impersonal approach to life has long been the aim of thoughtful men: the ideal of impersonal living—forgetfulness of self—has been the key to many great religious philosophies from the early East Indian to Christian teachings, and the man who can approximate that ideal finds in it the most tolerable way of life. For the achievement of this end, the ordinary emotion-ridden collector is at an obvious disadvantage, while the scientist appears to have the inside track. The very nature of the latter's work demands that he strive to attain an objective attitude, that he reject the individual self until, adding himself to a thousand or so, he becomes a statistic; and theoretically he does accomplish a self-effacement equal to that of the true religionist, since he has on the whole disciplined the collecting impulse (with its overtones of possessiveness and prestige-seeking) to serve a broader purpose. Yet the scientific attitude is also available to the intelligent collector: there is such a thing as the code of the amateur for those who aspire to it.

Scientists or scholars—when we consider them individually we find that they often fall short of the ideal of their calling and betray certain nonobjective attitudes—good, bad, or indifferent—which make them, under scrutiny, indistinguishable from human beings. The scholar, like the collector, is inclined to be proud of his own field *as a personal possession* and jealous of its reputation. So anthropologists and archaeologists wrangle over priority of man's cultural development in Egypt and Sumeria, and each will defend his "own" land with clannish passion. Does the scientist a-hunting take less pride than the collector in bagging his prey? Of course not. Indeed, so far is the scholar from a uniform objectivity that, for the glory of being first, he often rushes forth, not quite fully dressed in preparation, to beat his colleagues to "publication." Yet, aside from such peccadillos, the scientist-scholar holds an enviable place in the community, for it is possible for him to fulfill his larger mission with ample skill and still to partake of much of the amateur's personal joy. Such a man experiences the same incomparable excitement in uncovering an unsuspected custom of an extinct tribe, or in finding and describing some unknown flower, as would the manuscript collector in coming upon a letter written in Shakespeare's own hand. Or, conversely, as a scholar-collector, James Westfall Thompson, once put it:

"The bouquineur's thrill when he discovers some rare volume he prizes is akin to the sensation of the astronomer 'when a new planet swims into his ken.' "

In essential human quality, there is little to choose between a man who spends years of his life in deciphering a single puzzling inscription and the one who ruins his eyes over a microscope to establish the original "plate position" of a stamp. Each is a specialist, obsessed by his specialty and finding a kind of personal exaltation in the unraveling of its mysteries, in the conquest of a difficult problem. There are chapters in books on stamp collecting so scientific in attitude and terminology as to stupefy the layman, who may be amused to find in such writings the same pedantic hair-splitting as appears in the scholar's treatise. Deciphering the Rosetta Stone is unquestionably of greater communal importance than establishing the plate position of a postage stamp; yet many estimable men could be found who would judge both as being of equal futility.

In certain places and times, the conflict between collector and scientist has been marked by much thunder and lightning. The archaeologist, in particular, holds it against the collector that in the early years of his science's life the acquisitiveness and ignorance of the private collector or antiquarian sometimes worked irreparable damage to the cause of accumulating scientific knowledge. Yet some of the greatest of the early archaeologists made mistakes identical with those perpetrated by the blistered collectors. Moreover, from the days of Nabonidus, King of Babylon, to the nineteenth century and the industrial revolution, collecting by lay antiquarian and professional archaeologist have always developed side by side. In renaissance Italy, for example, the "revival of learning" brought with it an enormous interest in all the physical survivals of antiquity and produced a tremendous number of private collectors in this field. Not only were the most learned men of the time also the most ardent antiquarians, but popes, princes and diplomats, bankers and merchants, all participated in the search for classic relics. In order to make collections for themselves, they promoted vast excavations on ancient sites, and unearthed such a quantity of marbles, bronzes, inscribed stones and other valuable monuments of the past as would make any modern collector's eyes pop out of his head with envy. But much was lost in the process, and from one point of view the treasures might better have remained underground to await the birth of scientific methods now available.* This is a nice afterthought, yet surely such a considered delay, even had it been possible, would not have been wholly desirable.

Geology as we know it and modern archaeology were both born as a result of the industrial revolution in the nineteenth century, and collecting was given fresh impetus by the same phenomenon that produced the flowering of these two sciences. It was then that the beginnings of mechanization caused the frantic digging of railway cuts, tunnels and mines deep in earth and rock that had been untouched for centuries and millennia; and in those diggings were discovered, by chance at first, remains of earlier forms of life and survivals of man's work that had long been consigned to oblivion. At the same time, and also as a result of the growth of industry, a new class of men came into being. These were the merchant princes who were rapidly acquiring more money than they could use, and much uneasy leisure. More curious than enlightened, many turned to collecting fossils, curios or buried antiquities, and since their approach was unscientific and frequently hoggish, it is quite true that they interfered seriously with those who wished to assemble the available data with every specimen before removing it and to make the finds accessible to all.

The same thing happened in many places at once, for the collecting rage is highly contagious. Excavating soon became a private pastime, quite divorced from the haphazard chances of mechanically required "diggings." In England, in Etruria, in Egypt, and later in China, the private collector was for a long time the victorious enemy of the scientist who, more often than not, was impeded in the chase by lack of funds. Today, the danger, though limited, still exists when the natives of some lands (such as Persia, where the archaeologist has begun to explore only recently) learn of the profitable market for antiquities and take to injurious rifling of ancient sites; but the collector himself is now usually aware of proper methods and quite willing to respect them.

---

* Actually, however, much of the loss was due, not to unwise collectors, but to other "civic-minded" men who, wishing to rebuild old cities (particularly Rome), used the antique marbles for this purpose, while collectors like Farnese, on the other hand, were rescuing many treasures from the lime-kiln.

Egypt, after Napoleon's expedition, was invaded by collectors, and James Baikie says of their kind that they were men who

"wrangled like shrews, cheated like horse-copers, and fought like brigands over mummies, papyri, statues and inscribed stones. . . . No doubt Messrs. Drovetti, Passalacqua, Belzoni and the rest of them were, in ordinary life, most estimable members of society; but put them in the presence of an interesting mummy or statue, and forthwith morality fell from them like an outworn garment, and they lied, cheated and stole."

Yet it was not always the private collector who indulged in this Klondike rush after culture, and great nations were not above condoning the same questionable characteristics and methods in the persons of their representatives. Drovetti was the French consul in Egypt. Salt, who was equally active, was the British consul-general, and Belzoni, a former circus giant, was his agent.

"Many men," Baikie continues, "let us say 'conveyed' the plunder of ancient Egypt to various capitals with such energy that over a good deal of the material which is the pride of some of the greatest museums there might be written with perfect truth 'stolen goods.' "

But what were the scientists doing all this while? Were their own methods letter-perfect? It seems not, for in any modern work on the history of archaeology you can find the plaints of latter-day scholars deploring the fatal errors made by even the most eminent of their predecessors.

In those pioneer days, archaeological excavations were often discarded before operations had been properly completed, leaving, perhaps, an ancient mud structure in Mesopotamia exposed to the weather from which it had long been protected by accumulated debris—with the result that half a century later, when a more experienced excavator resumed the work, much valuable evidence had disappeared. Certain objects—tablets containing cuneiform writing, for instance, for which the modern scientist would fervently bow thrice to the East—were discarded as valueless because their meaning was not then understood. Often they were thrown back into the rubbish heaps, and although some of these have since been rediscovered, others were so badly broken as to be rendered forever useless for research. The list of such unwitting sins might be stretched out for pages. They must be charged in part to unavoidable ignorance, shared at the time even by the scientists who were apparently unaware that structures which had survived for thousands of years when protected by outer layers of dirt would be destroyed in a few decades once they had been exposed. Also in part responsible were external circumstances peculiar to the period. The early archaeologists needed funds, and in order to obtain them they had to produce startling and showy discoveries, easily understood, that would impress wealthy patrons back home. Practical necessity, therefore, often forced the excavators to neglect such things as the still mysterious cuneiform tablets, the painstaking gathering of which, although conceivably useful for the future, could have produced no immediately sensational results.

Today the picture is radically changed. The scientist now has things pretty much under control. He is busily engaged in field expeditions that are handsomely financed by museums, privately or governmentally. When he discovers an Egyptian tomb, he can, if it seems advisable to do so, seal it up and wait for an entire year before he makes known the spectacular nature of his find. He can labor for ten or fifteen seasons in a single area and know that support will continue to be forthcoming, no matter how esoteric his results. The private collector, also, is more enlightened and inclined to co-operate. He, too, understands the value of a careful approach. And unless he be subject to some idiosyncrasy, he takes pride in making of his collection a workmanlike unit, available to scholars and students. Even among scientists, therefore, he now stands a reasonable chance of being considered a gentleman.

The bibliophile also has received from the learned a measure of contempt, and the charge against him is usually that he is grossly ignorant of the true significance of his treasures, or, at the very least, pitifully superficial in his appreciation.

Lucian, the second-century Greek satirist, expressed his opinion of the book collector of his day with devastating scorn:

"You may have collected the works of Demosthenes, including one of the eight copies of 'Thucydides' which he wrote with his own hand," he declared, "or all the books which Sulla, when he made himself master of Athens, seized and sent to Italy; yet how could that avail you? If you made your bed on the best copies of the great authors, or were decked in manuscripts from head to foot, would you be less ignorant than you are now? There is a proverb that says, 'An ape is still an ape though adorned with jewels and gold!' "

Thirteen centuries after Lucian, Sebastian Brandt castigated the bibliomaniac in words somewhat gentler in tone but identical in intent when, in the *Ship of Fools*, he put these words into a collector's mouth:

> *"Still am I busy bookes assemblynge,*
> *For to have plentie it is a pleasaunt thynge*
> *In my conceyt and to have them ay in hande,*
> *But what they mene do I not understande."*

It is quite true that not all book collectors read every volume they own, but neither are they in a class with the man who fills his library with dummies so that he may appear "cultured," or with that other amorphous sort of person who so mistakes the nature and function of a book as to choose volumes for the colors of their bindings in order to carry out the decorative scheme of a room. The impassioned collector loves books, books for themselves, and would rather smell books than ambrosia. While he may not study the contents of each of his possessions in detail, and despite the thick screen of extraneous values which at times apparently govern his selections, he reads some and dips into many, else he could never understand the intricacies of his pursuit or seek books out with such genuine devotion.

For the defense, Rosenbach gives another and curious slant when he declares, with some justification:

> "Had [all collectors] pawed their books about, wearing them to shreds in the scholastic manner, few rare volumes would have been saved for us today."

In that fact lies the essence of the book collector's contribution to society, for he has discovered an endless number of treasures that otherwise would have been lost, and has treated these with such tender care that their chances of being well-preserved have been greatly increased. The very scholar who most appreciates the value of certain rare books as sources of information and data is sometimes inclined to shrug off the debt he owes the collector. Yet it is a fact worthy of homage that most of the great libraries in the world, and most of the museums, were born in the homes of private collectors or have battened at the same source.

HOW THE COLLECTION IS BORN

"Thy moist clay is pliant to command,
Unwrought, and easy to the potter's hand:
Now take the mould; now bend thy mind to feel
The first sharp motions of the forming wheel."

JOHN DRYDEN

RARELY DOES A MAN ARISE upon a certain morning and announce abruptly, over his breakfast coffee, "Today I shall begin a collection!" It is far more common to waken to the sudden realization that one has, without intent, already become a collector. And if the average person is asked why he collects, he will probably say that he does so because he "wants to," or because he finds it amusing, or interesting, absorbing, relaxing, or exciting. For his purpose such an answer is sufficient, and we can respect his attitude; but actually he is explaining how he feels about collecting after—not before—he is fully embarked upon the pursuit. On the other hand, he can usually cite some specific incident apparently responsible for his first step in this direction; and it is quite possible that without that incident he might never have become a member of the great collecting fraternity, for the processes leading up to the birth of a collector are often slow and inconspicuous. There is boring from within and nudging from without—and behold! a combination of events has finally roused the hidden daemon.

Take the case of James Hart and Henry Gant. Henry is a book collector, while James, although he likes books, has always maintained that collecting them is not for him. Yet for a long time James has been stimulated, perhaps unconsciously, by his association with his collector-friend. There is within him a growing ferment, composed in part of interest and in part of some well-hidden competitive element. Then, on a fatal day, Henry is calling on him. The conversation veers to books, as Henry, the collector, browses as usual in his host's library. (Even though he knows that it consists of a commonplace lot of volumes, he can no more resist looking at books than he can help talking about them.) Suddenly there is a startled yelp, a book is whisked off its shelf, examined closely; and James, poor unsuspecting fellow, is treated to the information that he, of all people, owns a fairly unusual first edition.

Very nice. So the thing has some value, has it? A week or so later, James "happens" into an old-book store and, with beginner's luck, stumbles upon something that looks good. Is it, or isn't it? Impulsively he makes a purchase. His thoughts run to Henry's reaction—if the affair should turn out well. And that evening, breathing a bit more quickly than usual, he announces himself at his friend's house. Barely is he over the threshold when he pulls out his package, but his voice is elaborately casual as he remarks, "By the way, Henry, here's a little thing I picked up today. Thought it might interest you."

Dubiously, then with growing attention, the connoisseur examines the acquisition. At last he solemnly notifies his novice friend of his decision. "You have something of exceptional value in this," he says, then adds, with a condescension he does not bother to conceal, "you'd better sell it to me at market price. It will only go to waste, otherwise."

James grits his teeth. "Oh, you think so, do you? Well, we'll see about that!" And he strides home clutching the book in triumph, a weird bright look in his eye that knowing people say is peculiar to collectors.

It may not be as simple as that. Occasionally a very personal note is indicated, of a sort that suggests or permits of the centering of a collection in the identity of the person making it. There is a well-known citizen who, since childhood, has had to endure the uncomplimentary nickname, "Piggy." He makes up for this, good-naturedly and effectively, by collecting all sorts of porcine ornaments and toys—porcelain pigs, silver pigs, wooden pigs, pig banks and pig paperweights—in short, anything in the form of a pig that he can lay hands on. Then there is the very real lady whose initials were L. E., until, by her marriage to a Mr. Fant, she acquired for herself the poignant label of L. E. Fant. Naturally this was all too obvious for her punning friends to let slide, and they began presenting her with toy elephants of every size and description. Soon Mrs. L. E. Fant succumbed to the fascination of her new distinction and entered the arena herself. Her collection now includes everything except an authentic specimen. She has pachyderms of soap, wood, iron, felt, silver and celluloid, from all over the world, elephants standing up, sitting down, trumpeting, charging, sleeping, doing tricks and playing the piano. Although this may be a case of collecting in self-defense, it probably indicates a collector whose industry lay dormant until the self-coincidence.

A dental student once received the routine assignment of carving in ivory the model of a tooth. Thereupon his mind fixed on the subject of ivory carving in general. He found himself attracted by the miniatures so often executed in this material. Soon he was spending all his spare cash for carved ivory trinkets. Years later he became prominent not only as a dentist but also as the amateur-owner of more than four hundred and fifty fine examples of carved ivory.

A man's desire to bolster his own arguments with "authoritative" facts and figures was solely responsible for the initiation of one valuable contemporary collection. No one would have been more astonished than its founder had he known in 1915, when he first started clipping newspaper and magazine articles on the World War, that, twenty-six years later, he would be receiving letters from the secretary to the President of the United States, from the Secretary of State and the Secretary of the Navy, as well as from the presidents of a dozen universities and colleges, on his subject, which had become a fifty-ton war library. Dr. Joseph Broadman was studying medicine in Germany at the outbreak of World War I, and upon his return to this country he got into endless, heated discussions. As armament for these he began to carry a few casual clippings in his pockets. They grew into a scrapbook, then a drawerful, and when the tide flowed on he decided to create a complete record of the war as seen by its contemporaries. He realized that hundreds of people had similar projects sketchily under way, but he felt (quite justifiably) that most of these would be abandoned incomplete. Today among his files of five hundred thousand items are many records which cannot be duplicated anywhere else in the world, and on the basis of the material assembled with scholarly pains over the years, Dr. Broadman has been able, during World War II, to publish a number of research bulletins which have been effectively used throughout the country by editorial and other writers. Destined eventually for some university library, the collection occupies forty thousand cubic feet and has cost the inquiring physician about five dollars per cubic foot—a far cry from the few clippings originally made in the interests of discussion.

Sometimes an accidental discovery will turn the trick. A resident of New York City, digging in his backyard garden, chanced to unearth some strange buttons and buckles which aroused his curiosity. Investigating, he discovered that these were survivals from Revolutionary War uniforms; and although the subject of war-coat buttons had never before entered his head, he was already on his way to the formation of a famous collection.

Frequently the "accident" is a matter of gift or inheritance. A legacy of an old spinning wheel may be accepted with reluctance because there is no convenient place to put it, or because it does not fit in with the rest of one's furniture. But should it become an object of interest, beware! That might easily be the "awake" signal to the slumbering collector. First he will look, rather casually, into his wheel's history, expecting that step to be the last of a foray into the field of antiques. But in the process there will probably be unearthed some unusually provocative facts about spinning wheels in general; other examples of the period will be examined; and before the treacherous footing has been realized, the heavenly bog has embraced our adventurer, who, almost unaccountably, has become a full-fledged collector of spinning wheels, or, if his mind has slipped in that direction, of books on spinning wheels, pictures of spinning wheels, even of all sorts of early American antiques. When called upon to explain how a single item casually or fortuitously acquired grew into several hundred, many a collector has been genuinely puzzled but seldom regretful in his answer: "Really, I don't know. I never meant it to happen!"

Among children, the nature of a collecting hobby may supply the first indication of what is to be a lifelong preoccupation. Thus, while still a youngster, Charles Darwin was already a passionate gatherer of shells, seals, coins and minerals. Later, he dropped coins and seals by the wayside to become a scientific specialist in the natural history branch of his early hobby; and this procedure is far from uncommon among both scientists and amateurs.

Conversely, the collecting proclivities of adults are frequently given focus by the professional occupation already chosen; and from this sequence emerge, besides many of the most logical hobbies, an occa-

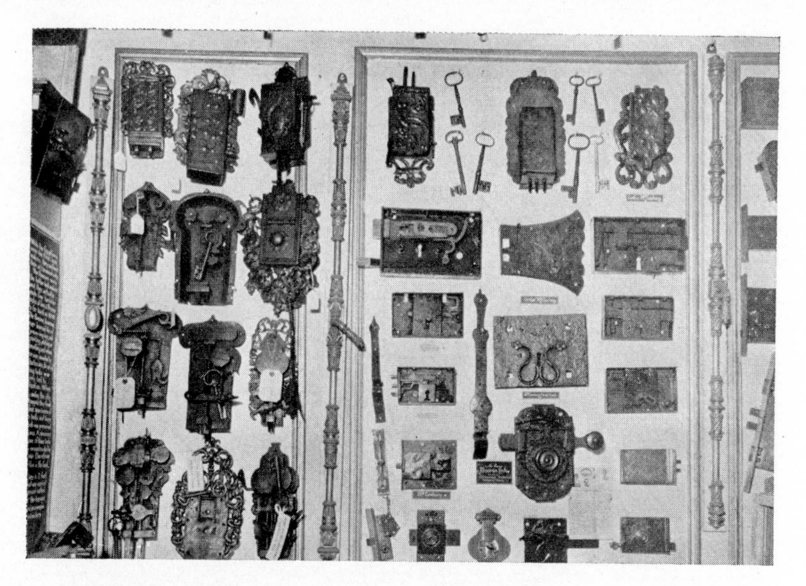

Section of the Courtney Collection, which includes "locks from the world's most famous palaces, castles, cathedrals, harems and dungeons . . . safeguarding the wealth and treasures of the world since 400 B.C."

Antique bronze mirror, Hellenistic; American 19-century barber bottles and occupational shaving cups from the De Zemler Collection.

sional startler. There is, at a western American university, an entomologist who collects lice, and we have his word that this is purely for his own amusement. There is more than one surgeon who, quite without humor or fear of the psychoanalysts, collects instruments of torture. Charles Sanson, seventeenth-century Paris hangman, spent his spare time dawdling over paintings of torture and death. Charles Courtney, president of the International Locksmiths' Association and the man who can "outwit any lock ever created," owned ten thousand keys and two thousand locks, including many antiques and association items. Seversky's designer, Kartveli, collects ten-cent comic books featuring super-space rocket ships. There are many bankers who collect toy banks, and some who specialize in ancient account books and ledgers. An American engineer collects old Italian and Latin books on engineering, and a famous American Cardinal used to gather up the "autograph-letters-signed" of saints.

Charles De Zemler, New York barbershop proprietor, has formed an extraordinary collection of items relating to the history of hairdressing. As barber to Lord Kitchener in Egypt, the collector within him stirred when he saw ancient tomb depictions of his calling.

Shampoo—Ancient Egypt

Since then he has assembled hundreds of items dating from antiquity, including material from Egypt, Greece, Rome and the Orient. Ancient mirrors, rare barber tools, instruments of sixteenth-century barber-surgeons and barber-dentists, ancient and medieval combs and razors, prints, paintings and old books, barber bottles, shaving bowls and mugs, mustache cups and old barber chairs, even a Chinese ambulatory barbershop, are in the De Zemler Collection. His specialty-within-a-specialty is gathering those American shaving mugs which bear pictures illustrating the occupations of former owners, and he has written an authoritative volume on the history of his calling.

When collecting follows a man's profession or business, it seems reasonable to deduce that he enjoys his work. Collections which bear a definite relationship to a man's vocation may be merely amusing, but frequently they serve to supplement the work itself, and such a collector, because he approaches his hobby already well-instructed, is likely to create something of permanent value in this use of leisure hours. Collections made by scientists furnish an obvious illustration, but they are not alone. We can go to the amusement field and consider, as an example, the collection of books brought together by Houdini, the magician. Those books, blanketing the fields of magic, legerdemain, spiritualism, occultism, witchcraft, demonology and the theater—more than five thousand items—are now in the Library of Congress. Valued at five hundred thousand dollars, they are sternly guarded by the might and main of the United States government, which makes them available only to serious students.

But what of the uncounted thousands of individuals who are unhappy in their daily occupations? Here collecting supplies a means of satisfaction that is, perhaps, even more valuable, since through it men can often express interests that are otherwise completely shut off, and the hobby proves to be a bombproof solace, or the one staunch anchor against the storm.

THE FASCINATION OF FIRES *for the small boy does not die when the boy grows up; and while few men can collect real fire engines, Harold V. Smith of New York has gone further and has assembled a complete museum of items connected with fire fighting and insurance. His business is fire insurance. 1) Early fireman's parade hat. 2) Lead fire mark, Philadelphia, 1784. In the old days each insurance company had its own fire-fighting brigade whose members often stood around admiring the blaze, unless their company's emblem adorned the burning building. 3) Silver-plated lamp. 4) Cast-iron fire mark, Cincinnati, 1845. 5) Lead fire mark, London, 1696. 6) Cast-iron fire mark, Poughkeepsie, 1814.*

The Home Insurance Company

A PRIVATE COLLECTION BUILT AROUND VOCATIONAL INTEREST BECOMES A COMPANY MUSEUM OF HISTORICAL VALUE. (*See facing page.*)

Part Two

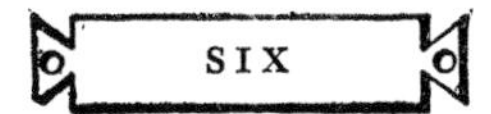

THE OLD MEN: COLLECTORS IN THE ANCIENT WORLD

"This—all this—was in the olden
Time long ago."

EDGAR ALLAN POE

EPOCH AFTER EPOCH up to the moment these words are read, collectors have trudged through all the reaches of history, fiercely clutching their possessions or lightly holding them. Figures tragic or serene, drab or noble, assuming all shapes and guises of which man is capable, they thread the human tapestry completely, disappearing into the woof from time to time, only to reappear once more; and indeed there is no valid reason to suppose that this colorful pageant will ever end unless man, in some improbable laboratory of the future, should learn to eliminate personality variations and in the process strip away the collecting motives.

The whims of chance, accidents of climate or of materials, have had much to do with determining the nature of such glimpses of the distant past as remain available to us. It is significant, for instance, to recall that potsherds survive where baskets perish; that stone and baked clay will outlast paper, cloth or wood; that desert and frozen tundra will preserve things that would be lost in fields constantly turned; and yet that it is from such variably perishable materials, at the mercy of quite dissimilar conditions, that our story must in large measure be fashioned.

Early burial practices have transfixed certain ritual objects and material remnants of daily life from long-vanished homes and places of worship, but these relics, useful as they are, at best are fragmentary.* Violence and bloody revolution as well as death are on the side of archaeology and history, as opposed to the gradual decline of a nation at peace.

"Nothing helps an excavator like violent destruction," writes Woolley. "If a building has fallen into decay, one can be sure that the impoverished inhabitants have removed everything of value. The best thing that can happen is a volcanic eruption which buries a place so deeply that nobody goes back to salve his belongings. . . . If an enemy sacks a temple or town, he is sure to overlook some objects at least which were of small intrinsic value for him, but may be very precious for the archaeologist; and if he was so considerate as to set fire to the place and overthrow its walls, there is the further probability that his search was hurried and that no one else troubled to look for what he left behind."

Yet even the sudden catastrophe of earthquake, fire, or war-tumbled walls may bring us a deceptively unbalanced version of history, as when it holds in anomalous suspension for the critical examination of latter-day students the tattered remnants of an insignificant provincial town like Pompeii rather than those of a more important metropolis.

Certain gaps in our knowledge will never be filled, and so inference must sometimes take the place of materially provable fact. For this reason, a single clue often assumes exceptional significance in solving the mystery of the distant past. If there was a great collection of books in the palace at Nineveh which we have by chance dug out of the debris of succeeding centuries, the fact that dozens of similar collections have not been discovered in other Assyrian cities is no proof that they never existed. Rather, it might be presumed that one such collection was an example, possibly pre-eminent, of a custom widely prevalent at the

---

* Fortunately for historians of the human race, there have been many peoples in all parts of the world whose religious beliefs led them to bury with the dead a representative array of those objects requisite to the business of living. Some of these things were purely utilitarian. Some have had special ritualistic significance. Some, however, have been luxuries pure and simple—the symbols of a lifetime's felicity which could no more be relinquished in the presence of death (as these people conceived of death) than could food, drink, or propitiatory offerings to the gods. Many of these buried objects have survived the ravages of time—protected as they were by the sanctity of the grave and by their coverings of earth or stone—which would otherwise have disappeared forever from the view of succeeding generations. Therefore, it is to the cemetery that we must turn for much of our early evidence.

time, and to this conclusion the few lesser libraries that have been unearthed lend timely emphasis. When a Hindu chronicle of the third century B.C. (the *Vinaya Pitaka*) refers to King Pasenada's palace as containing picture galleries, we should not assume that this king was a biological sport among Indian princes of his day; in the presence of an established culture we are justified in believing that he was typical of his kind.

Positive collecting data is at this date scarce in the remains of the early civilizations—Chinese, Indian, Sumerian, Egyptian, Cretan, Assyrian, Babylonian, Persian—yet there are good indications that many forms of the pursuit existed within them all. Each of these peoples rose to its period of greatest power when princes snatched territorial possessions beyond earlier limits; and those very rulers who were the most insatiable collectors of other peoples' land were usually the ones who brought back foreign works of art, who gathered and catalogued botanical and zoological specimens, or established libraries so that the glories of their own race might not be forgotten. Each of the ancient races produced a body of literature and objects of art and adornment, treasured and carefully preserved. Each was proud of its history and venerated the monuments and relics of the past. Even the early Greeks who, for various reasons, had no great passion for private collecting, accumulated and displayed quantities of statuary in their public meeting places, and, feeling "much as we do, the sanctity of antique quaintness," preserved the weapons of Homeric heroes in their temples.

In all of these cultures, distinction was measured to a large degree by wealth and number of material possessions. These people engaged in trade with the outside world, importing and exporting luxuries as well as necessities; and since, to this day, collecting thrives most extensively in periods of prosperity, and frequently feeds upon foreign goods, we may expect the existence of collecting wherever a considerable commercial activity is in evidence.

So deceptive is time in relationship to human progress that we are commonly inclined to claim as our own many things that are actually hoary with age and very nearly universal. Yet the most casual inquiry will reveal that man's thought has struck similar or identical notes over all the world from the earliest cultures to the latest, no matter how far removed in time and space these cultures may be from each other. Indeed it is true that many things are not new under the sun. This very statement, far from being modern, was voiced by Khakheperrensenb, the Egyptian, who wrote in 2000 B.C.:

"Would I had phrases that are not known, utterances that are strange, in new language that hath not been used, free from repetition, not an utterance which hath grown stale, which men of old have spoken."

And it was voiced also by that Hebrew preacher who wrote in *Ecclesiastes,* sometime between 250 and 168 B.C., the passage which has given us our way of phrasing it:

". . . the thing that hath been, it is that which shall be; and that which is done is that which shall be done; and there is nothing new under the sun. Is there anything whereof it may be said, See, this is new? It hath been already of old time, which was before us."

There are some things, of course, whereof it may be said, "See, this is new." Such innovations exist in the field of practical endeavor, in invention as applied to physical manifestations, and in utilitarian objects made by man. Bronze weapons were new when man first learned to work metal—and there was, obviously, a first time. There is no reason to believe that we are duplicating past performance in the plastics and alloys of our machine age, or in understanding of some of the principles employed in creating them. And, so far as we know, such things as the science of long-distance communication by electrical means are new, although distance communication had its early counterpart in the jungle drums. The science of aeronautics is new, although the idea that finally led to its successful evolution is probably older than the Grecian myth of Daedalus. And so it is with collecting—the impulse from which it springs is primitive, and the conscious, thoughtful development of the pursuit into a pleasurable art, while younger than the original impulse, is still very old.

But it does not follow that men have always collected the same things for all purposes in all places. The most creative races have not always furnished the greatest art collectors. During their greatest periods, everything the Egyptians touched was endowed with beauty, and they were a people familiar with luxury; yet there is available more evidence of their interest in collecting plants and animals than of accumulations of art objects among them. This may be pure archaeological chance (the royal tombs supply a hint of other forms of collecting, and the full story is unknown). Or it may actually mean that their collecting impulses were focused mainly by other powerful factors such as the forces which determined the kind of houses they lived in, the social customs peculiarly theirs, and their strong predilection for spending as much time as possible outdoors.

By contrast, throughout their long history the equally artistic Chinese have been a nation of collectors, numbering many practicing painters among their most famous amateurs and connoisseurs. In renaissance Italy a magnificently creative period existed side by side with enthusiastic art collecting; and although there were artists among the collectors it was largely true that the most impressive gatherers of painting and sculpture were not the artists themselves but the princes and merchant-princes, the worldly churchmen, and the scholars, men whose desire to seem great in the eyes of their fellows or whose search for long-buried sources of knowledge helped to lead them into collecting paths. Far from confining themselves to a single field, however, Italian collectors of this period evinced an equal enthusiasm for books, coins and many other things, including the creation of beautiful gardens filled with exotic flowers, and the establishment of menageries that were really collections of strange animals.

It is obvious that each group or nation answers to its own conditioning and environment for its habits in collecting. The gathering of botanical and zoological specimens aroused the Persians in their day of empire as it did the Mogul monarchs of India, collectors also of books and of art. The Mesopotamians seem to have had a passion for history, since the collections which survive from their time are largely archaeological or archival in nature. Yet the Greeks, who lived and breathed art (and also managed to attend profitably to commerce) became private art collectors only after their own civilization had been mixed with influences from artistically less developed peoples.

In striking contrast, the Assyrians and Babylonians, the imperial Romans, and the Japanese—all peoples whose cultures were to a certain extent derivative—foreshadowed, in the intensity of their collecting spirit, the modern enthusiasm for this pursuit. Of this group the most numerous records are available of the Romans and the early Japanese, and we know that they were, like the modern Americans, eclectic collectors with activities extending into many different fields.

Not men but gods, however, were the greatest of the early collectors. Through their servants, the priests and the priest-kings, it was they who took toll of all the products of the land. The ancient temples, like the churches and monasteries of our own middle ages, were repositories for great accumulations of wealth, of art and literature; and the temple treasuries were the forerunners of our banks, our libraries, our museums. Even these divine collectors began, as nearly as we can judge, with the collection of food and wealth, graduating soon to the collecting of books and records, of art objects and antiques, of curiosities and relics.

The gods shared in the plunder of war as well as in the natural wealth of the state, and the king was the first to pay them tribute out of his own hard-won loot—partly because in all theocracies such a course was mandatory, and partly because it redounded to his personal credit to do so.

The Egyptian and Mesopotamian temple communities eventually became large and powerful organizations in themselves with vast holdings in land, slaves and livestock. Schools and industries grew up within their precincts, and a goodly portion of the land's resources were needed to support them. Since coinage had not yet been invented, these temple communities required a constant revenue not only of precious stones and metals, but of food, drink, clothing and the implements of temple service. On the other hand a certain proportion of the more durable wealth, including the plundered or imported weapons, furniture, vases and other richly decorated objects, was not consumed in the business of daily living but was preserved in special rooms of the treasury and catalogued forever on its walls. These rooms were the earliest prototypes of the modern museum.

The temples, like the tombs of Egypt, bore a definite relationship to the homes of men. In order to appreciate this an important aspect of the Egyptian religion should be remembered. These people believed that every human being was composed of two distinct parts—the body, and its "double," the soul.* The gods also had doubles, but they were, of course, more resourceful: gods possessed the power of dividing each double into many separate doubles. Close behind strode the king—for the royal soul was considered such an holy "double" detached from

* Similar beliefs are a feature of many religions, and the various developments of this conception are related to such things as ancestor-worship and a belief in ghosts.

a god. When a king ascended the throne it was thought that the divine soul awoke in him, rendering him a divinity incarnate. Since the divine king was sometimes also the high priest of the god he represented, he seems to have had a majority control in the temple property, and it is likely that he himself drew no very sharp distinction between the "mine" and the "thine" of it. As the kings grew stronger they demanded ever a little more godhead; and in time they struck up a kind of partnership with the divinities, perhaps even finding it a part of the *cameraderie* of good business to make gifts to the temples and then to be rewarded by the gods with an affectionate wink.

Under these circumstances it seems not unlikely that some of the Pharaohs, at least, experienced a collector's pride and joy in the great accumulations of beautiful and valuable things gathered and catalogued in the houses of the gods, accumulations to which they themselves were at such pains to add. And did none of them gather similar treasures in their own homes? Capart tells us that:

"The god lives in his temple like the king in his palace, and the temple itself is nothing but a replica, constructed for eternity, of the ephemeral palace in which the Pharaoh resides."

From this we might conclude that trophies of war and works of native and foreign art were gathered in the palaces as they were in the temples; and this was probably also true, on a lesser scale, in the homes of wealthy citizens, for what the king does his people try to imitate.

We know that the Egyptians had many of the characteristics of collectors, and we have definite proof that they collected certain types of things—books, plants, animals, and perhaps relics. They might even be said to have collected gods, and in speaking of the vast Egyptian pantheon, Mayer and Prideaux make this illuminating comment:

"If we are dumbfounded that a few people along a river-bank could have produced such a multitude of deities, and given each deity a multitude of names, let us remember that these gods represent the accumulation of over four thousand years, and that the Egyptians never threw anything away."

An unwillingness ever to throw anything away, while in itself not enough to make a collector, is certainly a characteristic directly related to collecting. Capart gives a hint of a more concrete sort in speaking of a particular Egyptian.

"Amenophis III," he says, "had a passion for jewels and vessels of blue or polychrome enamel. It is from the ruins of his villa that for years have come forth these specimens which excite the imagination—cups, drinking bowls, pots for eye-salve, ampullas, flower vases, amulets, beads, bracelets, plain rings, rings with gems. . . ."

Each of these objects might have served an utilitarian purpose, but the quantity of them found, and the fact that all of them were of similar material (although other materials were plentiful) suggests that here was a connoisseur, a collector who specialized in jewelry and in blue and polychrome enamelware, much as one of us might specialize in milk-glass or celadon porcelain. Had these objects been examined on the spot by an archaeologist, we might have had in them incontrovertible proof of a true collection. Unfortunately the native peasants were first to discover the ruins of the villa, and, following their age-old custom, took out the treasures gradually, selling one now and then to the highest bidder. This method effectively disguises the fact that the finds all come from a single trove; so that by the time the source is discovered by experts much valuable evidence has been destroyed or dispersed beyond possibility of reconstruction.

It has often been said of the early Egyptians that, although they sought to beautify even the commonest objects of daily life, they were chiefly concerned with utility, and were "not inclined to make a beautiful thing solely for its beauty"; that their purpose in creating statues from diorite or granite was "to make permanent the benefit to the dead, and not to cause wonder in the living." Yet it would be preposterous to assume that such supreme art could have been won and held without definite esthetic convictions. How literally, then, should we apply the notion that these people were unconscious of their art in terms of art values and appreciation removed from religious impulse? How generally effective a force did the basic religious beliefs actually remain through three or four thousand years of history, including periods of obvious luxuriousness?

Take note, for example, of the vast number of amulets with which every Egyptian was bedecked in death as in life. Did these always retain the same intensity of religious value as surrounded them in early centuries, or did the motive behind this custom undergo a change to such an extent that the original significance was buried under new interpretations or formalized by the single virtue of habit? Will some scholar, five thousand years from now, upon learning that we (to draw a plausible parallel) were in the habit of throwing handfuls of rice after newly wedded couples, conclude that we did so because we still believed implicitly in the pagan fertility rite which gave this custom birth, or will he realize that most of us were no longer even aware of the original significance of the act? Accumulating amulets, when one believes them to be imbued with supernatural powers, is related to other early forms of collecting for security; but collecting such objects after they have lost a good deal of their superstitious meaning may conceivably continue as a matter of tradition, and then other more sophisticated elements may direct the process, with true collecting as a possible result.

Again, what ideas of our own conduct would that future historian develop who might try to visualize our lives from a literal interpretation of the precepts of the New Testament? And may we not arrive at a similarly distorted or idealized version of the Egyptian of the Empire period if, judging him by his Bible, the *Book of the Dead,* we feel that he had little interest in the objects about him except in so far as they might be of use to him in the afterworld? Nor should we forget the important fact that the Egyptian tombs (from whose inscriptions, wall-paintings, and massive sarcophagi we have derived much of what we know of the people who built them) were frequently rifled in antiquity; while the cities of the living, the very houses to which the plunder was taken, survive only in some architectural diagrams, in the wall-paintings of the tombs, and in a few silent foundations.

What is perhaps the most concrete evidence of private and royal-family collecting yet to be uncovered in Egypt comes from the sepulcher of an inconsiderable king who reigned briefly toward the middle of the fourteenth century B.C. Tutankhamen's once obscure name has become famous in our day chiefly because his tomb, being one of the few to be recovered practically intact, provided archaeologists with such a rich haul that many hitherto moot questions could be settled on its basis.

Here Howard Carter found certain objects of which he remarked, with true scholarly caution, that they were "in all probability pieces of personal property that had been in the family," in other words, heirlooms. Among them was a solid gold statuette of King Amenhotep III, and a tiny mummy-form coffin containing a carefully preserved lock of hair which, according to the inscription on the lid of the container, had come from the regal head of Queen Tyi. Also found in the tomb were other objects already antique in the young king's lifetime, including a pair of ornate Babylonian couches and an ornamental footstool that was about a hundred years old at the time of its interment. Some of the oil jars and vessels went as far back as Thutmose III and some showed traces of old breakages and repair. Some "seem to have contained family oils from famous presses"; and in view of the Egyptian uses of oils and unguents (much more various and personal than our use of such things) and their epicurean attitude toward them, this appears to be a collection corresponding in type to a modern collection of famous and rare vintages.

Shortly after the tomb's discovery, James Baikie advanced the theory that, for political reasons, this particular mausoleum had been made the repository for what was actually

"a collection of the art of various periods, and even of different nations—in short, a collection of the palace heirlooms gathered by Pharaoh after Pharaoh over a considerable period."

Carter rejected this idea, but he concluded that the young king himself was something of a collector, for in the tomb were found not only relics of Tutankhamen's ancestors, but also a number of mementoes of his own boyhood including a toy chest in which were samples of minerals which the prince had evidently gathered after the fashion of youngsters everywhere. Growing up, he seems to have acquired quite a different specialty, for buried with him were walking sticks of every size and description, concerning which Carter comments:

"The young Tutankhamen must have been an amateur collector of walking sticks and staves, for here [in the room of the tomb now called the Annex], as in the Antechamber and the Burial Chamber, we found a great number."

It is worthy of note that here, as elsewhere, when we find a person who gives evidence of being a collector, he often reveals the tendency in more than one fashion. Tutankhamen apparently was sentimentally attached to relics of the past and equally so to the souvenirs of his own youth. As a boy he collected geologic specimens, and as a young man he collected canes. Amenhotep III collected the count of the lions he

Photo, courtesy of The Metropolitan Museum of Art

WHIPS AND WALKING STICKS FROM TUTANKHAMEN'S COLLECTION, NOW IN THE CAIRO MUSEUM

Note the extraordinary freshness and vitality of the carved heads on the inverted handles of the two lower ceremonial walking sticks. The materials are gold, gold-foil, ivory and ebony.

killed and had a passion for blue enamel. And Thutmose III, Egypt's Little Napoleon, not only imported foreign art but also "paused between battles to gather botanical specimens," and "ordered carved on stone [in the botanical chamber of the temple at Karnak] the catalogue of specimens collected."

Part of Karnak Temple Botanical Catalogue

Always a nature lover, the Egyptian made much of the sports of hunting and fishing and would often exert great effort to take alive specimens for the menageries and outdoor aquariums which were the pride and extravagance of his estates. His garden was his especial delight, and he stocked it with foreign plants and rare trees. These people had a lively curiosity which prompted them to bring home new things, and natural history collecting persisted among them down to the time of the Ptolemies. Ptolemy Philadelphus sent expeditions into distant parts of Africa and Arabia in search of rare plants and animals, and the Museum at Alexandria had, in addition to its famous library, botanical and zoological collections of note.

It was not only as a result of providence and conquest that the ancient temples (and perhaps the palaces) became the most magnificent art museums the world has known—piety and respect for the past also played a part.

It was once the custom for kings and citizens of high estate to make dedicatory and votive offerings to the gods—statues, vases, jewels, or symbolic objects of various sorts. Once made, the offerings became holy in themselves and were never destroyed. As centuries passed they took on the significance of temple heirlooms. The great Egyptian temple of Karnak, for example, once owned eighty-six thousand statues.

In other lands a comparable situation existed. Scientists continue to find new evidence which shows that antique objects were cherished five or six thousand years ago much as they are today. At Warka in Mesopotamia, for instance, on the site of ancient Uruk (the Biblical Erech), Woolley tells how there was found in 1933, beneath the temple or *ziggurat,* a room of a Jamdat Nasr building (*c.* 4000 B.C.). Here, under a packing of later bricks, lay a great accumulation of temple vases and ornaments "which had outlasted the fashion." Much older than the building in which they were found, the archaeologist believes they might even have stemmed from the still earlier Uruk or post-diluvian period; and he points out that "the best of them had been broken and mended in antiquity"—a sure sign that they had been highly valued.

Included in this temple collection, which six thousand years ago had reached such proportions that a part of it had to be stored away, were small figures of animals, stone vases decorated in relief, vases of dark steatite inlaid with red limestone, lapis lazuli and shell, and a quantity of cylinder seals. Many such examples could be given, and in most cases the objects collected in each temple are known to have originated at widely separated periods, indicating that "modern" statues, vases and so on were constantly being added to accumulations which contained objects generations and centuries old. Since we have much evidence to show that the Mesopotamians, during at least twenty-five hundred years of their history, were intensely preoccupied with the study of their own past and were constantly seeking out and preserving its surviving relics, it seems likely that they came to consider the temple collections, too, from an antiquarian as well as from a religious point of view.

Quite outside of the *ex votos* it is sometimes possible to trace the Mesopotamian Odyssey of an antique "association piece" for centuries, here and there recapturing the identity of a few of its successive owners. One such example is to be found in a stone cup, once in the possession of King Naram-Sin of Akkad (2678–41 B.C.), which was treasured by collectors for a thousand or more years after his time. Naram-Sin had inscribed this vessel with his own name, a fact which undoubtedly augmented its value in the eyes of future owners (in the same way Thomas Jefferson's signature would today greatly increase the value of a book which had once formed a part of his personal library).* Three hundred years after Naram-Sin's death, this cup was the cherished private possession of a royal princess who happened also to be high priestess of the Moon God at Ur. To the king's inscription she added her own (as the modern book collector sometimes writes his name beneath the autograph of a former owner). The temple of the Moon God, within the precincts of which the princess lived, was burned by the Babylonians in 1885 B.C., but a local antiquarian must have retrieved the historic cup from the ruins, for when found by modern excavators it was reposing in the remains of a house that had been built about 1400 B.C., the possession, perhaps, of some anonymous collector of Babylonia's Kassite Middle Ages.

The preservation of one such piece by different individuals over such a long period suggests that other antiquities were similarly treasured, and indeed several collections of the sort have been discovered. For example, in one private house, probably the residence of a priest of the seventh century B.C., was found a quantity of antiques, including two gypsum figures and some pottery of the style of the First Dynasty of Ur (a period nearly twenty-five hundred years earlier than that of the house in which they were gathered), a large collection of beads in lapis lazuli, carnelian and crystal, some small gold pendants in the form of vases, some silver pendants set with lapis, and a number of copper and stone bowls. All were relics of the past when brought together, although the collector had not specialized in antiquities of any one period.

Most interesting of all is the story of Nabonidus (555–539 B.C.) and his daughter, Bel-Shalti-Nannar. Last of the Chaldean kings of Babylon, Nabonidus was also father to Belshazzar, who according to our Bible saw on the walls of his banquet hall that ghostly writing which foreshadowed the disastrous approach of the Medes and Persians. The Persian danger had been growing even in the days of Nebuchadnezzar, but Nabonidus was more bemused by the past than aware of the present; and, too busy reconstructing the historic monuments of his country to pay much attention to the enemy at the gates, he enjoyed his life immensely, while it lasted, then lost both life and country to the invader. When this history-minded king restored the local *ziggurat,*

* Woolley attributed this inscription to the venerated Sargon of Akkad (*c.* 2750–2695 B.C.), but this attribution has been altered by more recent studies.

writes Woolley, "he was careful to give full credit for its founding to Ur-Nammu and his son Dungi, and he has left on record the delight he felt when, deep in the foundations of an ancient temple which he was repairing, he unearthed the foundation-tablet of Naram-Sin, son of Sargon of Akkad, and looked upon that 'which for three thousand years no human eye had seen.'" The quality of this delight, experienced twenty-five hundred years ago, will be as unwithered as spring to any contemporary antiquarian.

Following a time-honored tradition, Nabonidus appointed his daughter high priestess to the Moon God at Ur, and stated, in characteristically antiquarian fashion, that in doing so he was following a precedent set by Kudur-Mabug, one of the Larsa kings who had reigned in the land some fifteen hundred years before. Like her father, and like that other royal priestess who had treasured Naram-Sin's inscribed cup, Bel-Shalti-Nannar was also of the inner circle of collectors. In one of the buildings restored by Nabonidus (the old sanctuary of the temple at Ur, which probably served as a private chapel for the priestesses) modern excavators have found two probable items from her collection. One is a limestone relief from the ancient city of Eridu, "a product of the great art of the Third Dynasty" (2278–2170 B.C.). It was sixteen or seventeen hundred years old by the time it reached the reconstructed nunnery of the Chaldean princess. The other is an ivory toilet box, the work of some Phoenician craftsman of Sidon or Tyre, and though it had once been broken, it had been carefully repaired as only a cherished possession would be.

From the chapel these excavators proceeded to another room, and it was there that the best find of all was made. So that you may sense the collector-like excitement that an archaeologist experiences when he comes upon something unique, here is Woolley's own description of the discovery, at Ur of the Chaldees, of the earliest museum of antiquities yet to be unearthed anywhere:

"In one of the rooms, suddenly the workmen brought to light a large oval-topped black stone whose top was covered with carvings in relief and its side with inscriptions; it was a boundary stone recording the position and the outlines of a landed property, with a statement as to how it came legally into the owner's hand and a terrific curse on whosoever should remove his neighbor's landmark or deface or destroy the record. Now this stone belonged to the Kassite period of about 1400 B.C. Almost touching it was a fragment of a

From collections in The University Museum, Philadelphi

TWO GREAT LINKS TO COLLECTING IN ANTIQUITY. *The earliest museum label known, this 7th-century* B.C. *clay drum pedestal* (ABOVE) *was found in Bel-Shalti-Nannar's museum at Ur.* BELOW: *The remains of a Phoenician ivory* pyxis *from the same 6th-century* B.C. *collection.*

diorite statue, a bit of the arm of a human figure on which was an inscription, and the fragment had been carefully trimmed so as to make it look neat and to preserve the writing; and the name on the statue was that of Dungi, who was king of Ur in 2280 B.C. Then came a clay foundation-cone of a Larsa king of about 2000 B.C., then a few clay tablets of about the same date and a large votive stone mace-head which was uninscribed but may well have been more ancient by five hundred years."

All of these things, Woolley continues, were

"lying on an unbroken brick pavement of the sixth century B.C.—the newest seven hundred years older than the pavement and the earliest perhaps two thousand: the evidence was altogether against their having got there by accident, and the trimming of the statue inscription had a curious air of purpose. Then we found the key. A little way apart lay a small drum-shaped clay object on which were four columns of writing; the first three columns were in the old Sumerian language, and the contents of one at least were familiar to us, for we had found it on bricks of Bur-Sin, king of Ur in 2220 B.C., and the other two were fairly similar; the fourth column was in the late Semitic speech. 'These,' it said, 'are copies from bricks found in the ruins of Ur, the work of Bur-Sin, king of Ur, which while searching for the ground plan [of the temple] the governor of Ur found, and I saw and wrote out for the marvel of beholders.' "

The Sumerian language is apparently better understood by modern scholars than it was by the ordinary Babylonian scribe, and it is amusingly incongruous to hear Woolley's mild rebuke to the old-time underling who did not know his business as well as he should have:

"The scribe, alas! was not so learned as he wished to appear, for his copies are so full of blunders as to be almost unintelligible, but he had doubtless done his best, and he certainly had given us what we wanted. *The room was a museum of local antiquities maintained by the princess Bel-Shalti-Nannar, and in the collection was this clay drum, the earliest museum label known,** drawn up a hundred years before and kept, presumably together with the original bricks, as a record of the first scientific excavations at Ur."

It is perhaps only a coincidence that the majority of such collections seem to have been made by people connected with the temples—a coincidence brought about partly by the accidents of excavation, partly determined by the fact that the temples were centers of education as

* Italics ours.

well as of religion and, aside from questions of heritage, probably attracted to their ministry those individuals most given to cultural pursuits, as was the case with religious communities during the medieval period in Europe. At least one collection has been discovered, however, that was undeniably the creation and valued possession of an individual who had nothing whatsoever to do with temple life. This, too, was at Ur, and was found in an ordinary coffin that had been placed in the earth some time in the late fifth or early fourth century B.C., when the city had lost its last vestige of importance and was gradually being deserted. The coffin, when discovered, had been plundered of everything intrinsically valuable, but it still contained something upon which its one-time owner had apparently set the greatest value, since it was upon this collection that his body lay in final sleep—a collection of nearly two hundred seal impressions on clay. Of them Woolley has this to say:

"That these were really a collection was evident, for the lumps of soft clay had been pressed against the gems (the finger-marks were plain on the backs and there was no hole in any of them through which a string could have been passed) and had afterwards been baked so as to make the record permanent."

The group contained Greek, Egyptian, Babylonian, Assyrian and Persian pieces, as well as a cast from an Athenian coin of *c.* 450 B.C., and would have corresponded in its day approximately to our own collections of stamps, coins, autographs or inscription rubbings.

Wherever books have existed they have hypnotized collectors, and they were among the first items gathered by civilized peoples. The earliest writing was the tool of commerce rather than of literature *; yet it was because of this very fact that books were first created and accumulated in the places of worship. As the temples grew to be the chief repositories of communal wealth, and as the gods became more and more active in business, the priests, in order to administer their affairs, were forced to keep permanent records. So were born the temple archives, and from there it was a logical step to the writing down and preservation of ritual, of the magic formulas, the sacred legends, prayers and hymns, and to the recording of the names, dates and deeds of kings. Of this nature were the "books" in the earliest

* Even before this, of course, came primitive picture-writing used to ward off evil spirits and as a means of simple warning and directional communication between men.

AN EARLY ASSOCIATION ITEM. *Sometimes known as "Sargon's Cup," this relic, highly treasured in antiquity, bears two inscriptions, one* (left) *the name of King Naram-Sin of Akkad* (2678-41 B.C.), *the other a dedication by the daughter of King Dungi of Ur who ruled some three hundred years later. Modern excavators found the cup in a house at Ur dating from about 1400* B.C.

From collections in The University Museum, Philadelphia

AN EARLY PRIVATE COLLECTION. *Items from a collection of nearly two hundred seal-impressions found in a Persian coffin at Ur. Dating from the 5th or 4th century* B.C., *the collection contains Greek, Egyptian, Babylonian, Assyrian and Persian pieces and one cast of an Athenian coin of c. 450* B.C. *Interred beneath the body of their owner, the seal-impressions had escaped the raids of ancient tomb robbers.*

By permission of the Director of The British Museum

libraries, and such they remained for centuries, until the legends were at last transformed into epics and tales of adventure, the hymns into secular poems, the magic prescriptions into medical treatises, and the date-lists into flowing historical chronicles.

Temple libraries have been discovered in the ruins of many an ancient city, and no one land is unique in this. The earliest of the forty thousand clay tablets of the temple at Nippur (in what had once been the land of Sumer) date from the third millennium B.C. while the latest had been inscribed in the Persian period—truly an enviable record of continuity. The Aryan Persians had a library in the temple at Susa, the Medes had one at Ecbatana, and so on.

But if the priests were the first book collectors the kings and nobles were not far behind. An Egyptian inscription speaks of "the land of the collected works of Khufu (Cheops)." Another refers to the library of Khafra (Chefren). Khufu and Khafra were two of the Pharaohs who built the great pyramids at Gizeh, and while theirs may still have been temple libraries—for which the all-powerful monarchs took the credit—they were no longer mere accumulations of archives and accounts; for literature was already honored in the time of the pyramid builders of the Old Kingdom * and special deities presided over books and libraries. There was Thoth, the possessor of all knowledge and the inventor of writing, the scribe of the gods and the inspirer of human scribes. There was Safekh, goddess of books, who was venerated at Memphis, capital of the Old Kingdom. And there was Selk, whose generous province included libraries.

The qualities that relate peoples removed from each other by oceans and continents of space and time are often difficult to find, and antique

---

* Early Egyptian dates, like early dates elsewhere, remain a subject for scholarly dispute. A "long" and a "short" chronology exist and each has its defenders. The short chronology, which seems to be preferred, places the Old Kingdom between 2980–2475 B.C., dates King Khufu at about 2898–2875 B.C. and King Khafra at about 2867–2811 B.C. The long chronology places these Fourth Dynasty rulers as early as 3098–3075 and 3067–3011 B.C. respectively.

This is a good place also to note that the spelling of Egyptian names is as variable as are the dates given by different authorities. There is no definitely correct way of transliterating the sounds from this ancient language, any more than there is a way to be sure of the "correct" English rendition of Chinese or Arabic names. However, modern scholars have arrived at certain forms which are presumably closer to the originals than those traditional forms which have come down to us through Biblical or Greek sources. For an amusing commentary on a similar problem, T. E. Lawrence's introduction to the *Seven Pillars of Wisdom* is recommended.

Egypt has been held up as an example of such difficulty; but the character, the living likeness of the collecting habit, brings even the Egyptians well within range of our sympathetic understanding. Take their method of arranging and classifying books. Special chambers or "houses" were set apart in palaces as well as in temples, and in private homes as well as in palaces, as repositories for the papyrus rolls.* Such a room was known as "The House of Books," or sometimes as "The Dispensary of the Soul." Jars or wooden book boxes, neatly labeled, served to protect the rolls and were kept in rows on the library shelves. Included in Egyptian libraries were the oldest story books in the world and the oldest dramas, the oldest examples of social thinking and the most ancient scientific treatises.

Even more extensive remains of book collections have survived in the land of the twin rivers, where clay tablets rather than the more perishable papyri were in general use. Not only at Nippur but at Tello, also, on the site of ancient Lagash, a library of more than thirty thousand tablets has been found, contemporary with the cultured priest-king, Gudea (2500 B.C. or earlier). In Mesopotamia, as in Egypt, the private collector in modest comparison followed the temple and the palace. In evidence of this are some few smaller libraries preserved at Ur in typical houses of the time of Abraham.

Four thousand years ago, while Sumeria was gradually being ground to dust, men in Mesopotamia were busy saving her letters and books. In that very era when the remarkable Sumerian race was disappearing as a world power it touched its highest point of literary and scholarly activity. As if forewarned of the imminent downfall, scribes were feverishly collecting and recording the old legends, the traditional rituals, the documents of their long history. In the private libraries of the next generations were kept not only the usual business documents and land plans but fairly varied reference and literary collections as well. Hymn-books were included, and grammars, and works on mathematics; texts concerning the mythical heroes, Gilgamesh and Lugal-banda; copies of ancient inscriptions; date-lists of the last Larsa dynasty; and, in one case, letters of Rim-Sin, that Elamite king of Larsa who, in 2094 B.C., had lost all of Sumeria to the house of Babylon under Hammurabi.

Many of these were libraries of the sort that any modern patriot

* This was the commonest form of Egyptian book, but stone, wood and occasionally parchment were also used.

collector in a conquered nation would cherish as a means of keeping alive a beloved national tradition, as Eve Curie has testified the Polish people did during the years of their pre-Hitler enslavements. Sumeria, already old as a political body, never lifted her head again after the Babylonian conquest, but her laws (as codified by Hammurabi, to whom history long gave all the credit) ruled the land for centuries more; her language became the classic tongue in a territory far more extensive than her own domain had ever been, even when she waxed fullest; and her legendary progenitor, Gilgamesh, was transformed into the hero of Babylonia's greatest epic—all this chiefly because Sumeria's scribes had become collectors in her declining years.

The peoples who rose to power in Mesopotamia in the following centuries were all makers of libraries or collectors of archives. In a house at ancient Nuzi, inhabited during the fifteenth and fourteenth centuries B.C., archives of one family have been found *collected through four or five generations.* In another, more than a thousand tablets have survived.

The heavy collectors, however, were still the gods and the kings. Sargon of Akkad, venerated by the Assyrian race as its greatest forebear, was traditionally supposed to have formed a library as impressive as the empire he created, and that tradition may some day be substantiated. No longer legendary is the library of Sargon of Assyria who lived some two thousand years later (rg. 722–705 B.C.), for it was retrieved at Khorsabad in 1933.

The most notable of these old-time libraries, however, was one that came to light nearly a century ago on the site of ancient Nineveh—the books collected by Ashurbanipal (669–626 B.C.) or Sardanapalus, as he was called by the Greeks. Most formidable of all the Assyrian rulers, Ashurbanipal was long known to history chiefly as a ruthless conqueror who, at the cost of much human suffering, extended the domain of Assyrian power to the farthest limits it ever reached; and it is an ironical commentary on the nature of "greatness" that fourteen years after the empire-builder's death Assyria as a world power was no more, while the warrior's library, surviving for over fourteen centuries, served at last to render his name more blessed than cursed because, perhaps more than any other single discovery, it helped modern scholars to reconstruct some thousand obscure years of history.

What motives could have caused this dictator, like those other grandiose collectors of territory, Thutmose III of Egypt, Caesar of Rome, Napoleon of France, to take time from political accumulation in order to gather instruments of culture? As an individual he may have had much the same incentives as they. Conquerors are energetic, aggressive and predatory above the run of common men, and these qualities constitute effective implements for grand-scale collecting. Moreover, such men are likely to be ambitious to climb more than a single peak. Thutmose and Caesar were both men of considerable culture. Even Napoleon, who plundered art treasures chiefly because of their prestige-value to his nation, was a sincere lover of books. And perhaps—if we could get to the man himself behind the anguished cries of his political victims, cries still so vivid over the centuries—we should find Ashurbanipal the bibliophile. As a statesman, however, the Assyrian was influenced to collect books, in part at least, by needs peculiar to his own times. An illuminating explanation of the political aspects of early library-making is suggested by Edward Chiera in the following passage from *They Wrote On Clay:*

"In Babylonia, as in other ancient countries, political power was closely associated with religion. . . . And yet long ago in Babylonian times political power gradually began to rid itself of church control . . . and with the increase of royal prestige, it was thought wise by some of the more intelligent kings to restrict the influence of the church in education. If the church had libraries, then the kings also could have them. We thus find some of the later Assyrian kings, the very same personages who are generally depicted as ruthless destroyers, taking the lead in encouraging and reviving art and science. We see them also sending their own scribes throughout the land for the purpose of collecting all the important works gathered in the temples."

Whatever inspired Ashurbanipal, he was certainly a most thorough collector. There remains a letter, unsigned but almost without doubt written by him, in which he instructs one of his many agents how to proceed. To insure success, the royal collector sends his book hunter three assistants:

"Word of the king to Shadunu," the letter begins. "It is well with me; mayest thou be happy. When thou receivest this letter, take with thee these three men . . . and the learned men of Borsippa [where there was an important temple library] and seek out all the tablets, all those that are in their houses, and all those that are deposited in the temple of Ezida. . . ."

After naming specifically those books which he most particularly wants the king concludes:

"Hunt for the valuable tablets which are in your archives and which do not exist in Assyria and send them to me. I have written to the officials and the overseers . . . and no one shall withhold a tablet from thee, and when thou seest any tablet or ritual about which I have not written to thee, but which thou perceivest may be profitable for my palace, seek it out, pick it up, and send it to me."

Here, then, in a sweepingly ideal position, is the picture of the ambitious collector. He is endowed with unlimited power—power beyond millions in gold, beyond any law but his own appetite. And as we see him, he is stroking his curly black beard in anticipation, and exclaiming, "Oh, Boy!"—in Assyrian, of course.

As efficient as men of the Nazi Gestapo were the agent-scribes of Ashurbanipal, for when his library was unearthed in the nineteenth century of our era it was found to contain over thirty thousand tablets covering the entire range of Mesopotamian literature, history, science and religion. Although this number of tablets does not represent the modern equivalent of thirty thousand volumes, it was a most impressive accomplishment in its day. Here were copies of texts in the ancient Sumerian tongue, to the Assyrians a dead but classic language, as Greek and Latin are for us. Here were copies of the great temple archives, collections of birth omens, of moral precepts, of incantation texts, medical texts, legal documents, myths and legendary literature, school books, dictionaries, grammars, everything, in short, that a great national library of the period should have contained.

There is reason to believe that this library was sometimes open to the public. It was certainly available to scholars. Here, as in other Mesopotamian libraries, large and small, the books were catalogued and consecutively arranged on shelves. Sometimes, for protection, boxes or rectangular baskets were used, and these served the additional purpose of keeping the books in proper order. The tablets were too small to contain the full context of a long work, and so several were required to make the equivalent of a modern book. To prevent confusion the scribes would number each tablet and put at the bottom the first line of the following installment, as it is our custom to print, in newspapers or magazines, "continued on page 58." In fact, after allowing for the variation in materials employed, we find little difference between ancient libraries and our own, even to the use of bookplates.

Although archaeology has progressed farthest and with richest rewards, in its study of Egypt and Mesopotamia, a great quantity of book or archive tablets are known to have been stored in coffers of gypsum in the palace of King Minos at Knossos, while elsewhere on the island of Crete wooden chests held similar collections. The Cretans, or "the people from the back of beyond" as the Egyptians called them, also had parchment or papyrus rolls as well as tablet books, but here an unfavorable climate long ago destroyed these more perishable materials.

What do the surviving tablets contain—the literature of this highly cultured race, perhaps, or, when the Cretan script has finally been deciphered, will there be only archives and business documents for the translator to work over? Here, awaiting future penetration, is but one of many unknown stories of ancient peoples. Nevertheless, there are at Knossos certain definite suggestions of the collecting temperament among its one-time inhabitants; and where the king "owned workshops which had to supply him with objects of art and luxury which were envied by all, and bore witness to his glory, all the world over," it seems unlikely that his library consisted wholly of dull and unimaginative records.

That these were an artistic people is everywhere attested by the exquisite decorations they left behind them, fragments of an art as original in its way as that of Egypt. Close by the Knossos library was the royal porcelain factory, including a studio for the sculptors who turned out those graceful statuettes and handsome vases for which Crete became famous. There was even a workshop for His Majesty's jeweler, whose specialty was mounting gems and other rare substances in settings of precious metal and marquetry.

"A whole staff of workmen and perhaps of slaves was employed in these establishments under the order of eminent masters," writes Glotz. "With the corps of builders and the officials in charge of them, they composed a kind of rudimentary Department of Fine Arts."

The earliest Cretans gathered and kept natural curiosities. Later, the chieftains amassed quantities of jewelry which they carried with them, in one great final display, to the grave, along with gold and silver plate, handsome weapons, imported faïence, and such luxury articles

The Metropolitan Museum of Art

CRETAN WOMAN CARRYING CASKET IN A PROCESSION.
From a wall painting at Tiryns, 1350-1100 B.C.

No finer decorations are known than those produced by the ancient Cretans, who traded fineries with the collectors of Egypt and Babylonia.

as ostrich eggs mounted as precious vases. At the height of their civilization, these people traded fineries with Egypt and Babylonia, while certain costly imported things were carefully copied for the average customers in Cretan workshops, for the seafaring men of Crete were long active in commerce and enjoyed periods of great prosperity which must have intensified urban interest in collecting *objets d'art.*

Eastward from this "cradle world" lived the early Hindus who wrote on pages of bark strung into volumes by means of cord, and who collected their books into libraries reminiscent of the Egyptian, libraries which they called "Treasure Houses of the Goddess of Speech." Still further East, in China, where bamboo leaves were in use until the invention of paper at the beginning of our era, the imperial palace included treasuries for the preservation of imperial archives, historical documents, jewelry and other precious belongings, perhaps as early as the twelfth century B.C.

An indication that books in particular were highly valued in the Land of the Dragon is given in the ancient custom of burying manuscripts with their deceased owners. A copy of one of the oldest extant sources for early Chinese history—the *Annals of the Bamboo Books*—was thus immured in the tomb of a prince of Chou, to be rediscovered in 280 B.C. nearly six hundred years after its burial. In this manner was a collector once again responsible for the preservation of an invaluable document; for although authorities were long skeptical of the reliability of this and other ancient repositories of traditional history, recent excavations (begun in 1928 at An Yang) have provided striking testimony to the accuracy of certain phases of the tradition—so much so that, in the words of one Sinologist, that tradition must now "be treated with more respect than scholars were wont to accord it."

One of these traditions, which asserts that so prominent a leader as Lao-tze, founder of Taoism in the sixth century B.C., assumed curatorship of the Royal Library of Chou, supplies an indication of the importance accorded book collections in ancient China.

When, three hundred years later, the great destroyer and equally great builder, Shih Huang-ti, swept over the land, he was forced to acknowledge the power that lay dormant in those collections. For Shih Huang-ti, having made himself first emperor of all the Chinese states, was confounded in his despotic practices by scholarly quotations and thwarted in his reforms by the citation of tradition. It was then that he decided to destroy all cultural monuments of the wrangling, feudal past. Owners were commanded on pain of death to deliver their books for burning, and all such cherished relics as the precious bronze vessels from the Shang and Chou* periods were to be handed over. Some collectors complied, but many scurried frantically to hide their treasures as best they might. Bronzes were dug into the ground, and books were hidden in hastily constructed secret chambers in the walls of buildings or tombs. Despite these efforts, Shih Huang-ti attained his objective to a certain extent—yet for his pains he has ever since been hated, and in China his very name has been submerged under the epithet, *Burner of the Books.*†

In that dismal time, four hundred and sixty scholars paid with their lives for evading the emperor's command; yet could they have looked into the future they might have felt that the sacrifice was a worthy one. Because of their efforts, and because of the excellent memories of certain survivors who, years later, were able to repeat with at least partial accuracy whole volumes of the destroyed literature, much was eventually saved from the holocaust. Under the Han dynasty which followed immediately many of the hidden books and relics were recovered. In the days of Wu Ti (140–87 B.C.) the Imperial Library again contained eleven thousand five hundred seventy-two volumes, including works on the classics, philosophy, poetry, mathematics, medicine and war; while under another Han emperor, Ming Ti (A.D. 59–75) we first hear of collections of silk-paintings being brought together in the imperial palace.

The greatest single collection created in ancient times was not the product of one culture, but resulted from that cosmopolitan marriage of civilizations which was Egyptian Alexandria under the Greek Ptolemaic rulers. At the height of their own cultural supremacy the Greeks themselves had produced few important private collections of any sort.

---

* Shang (1766–1122 B.C.); Chou (1122–249 B.C.). All dates before 842 B.C. are considered semihistorical.

† The burning of the books and the destruction of relics, carried out on the advice of Shih Huang-ti's prime minister, was actually only a part of the emperor's otherwise laudable effort to unify the country, an effort which included the building of the Great Wall, the eradication of a feudal aristocracy which had split China into many mutually hostile states and had prevented the common man from taking any part in political life, the construction of uniform roads to facilitate communication, and a standardization of the varying scripts. These innovations did much to ensure China's amazingly long survival as a national entity.

There had been, it is true, some private book collections—the property of scholars, philosophers, and occasionally of "tyrants"—but these seem to have been exceptional.

The art collections, far more numerous, were in effect public property, displayed where all could see and enjoy them in the temples or in the *agorae,* in the *pinacothecae** or in the gymnasiums. The Greek citizen spent much of his time out-of-doors, and the peculiar construction of his dwelling in the early days did not make it a suitable place for housing works of art. Wherefore even family monuments and portraits of obscure individuals were set up in public meeting places or along the public thoroughfares. And the gathering of relics, antiquities, association pieces and natural history collections were, like the art collections, assembled and exhibited in the temples.

At first, the Greek temple collections were much like the early temple collections of Egypt and Mesopotamia, being composed largely of votive offerings and of objects having some definitely religious significance; but as time passed, they came to include not only objects which might be venerated, but also those which were of secular interest *because of their rarity or strangeness.* Exhibited were such things as are today included in anthropological or zoological displays or in a museum of the decorative arts, with the single difference that specialization was lacking. Piles of ivory, either natural or carved into curious and beautiful objects, barbarian costumes, Indian jewelry, snake skins, bear hides, elephant skulls, whale skeletons, gorilla skins (thought to be those of "hairy, savage women"), reeds as thick as tree trunks, coconuts, distorting mirrors, antique musical instruments, foreign weapons, curious vessels of all sorts—these were a few of the things harbored.

In fact Greek temple exhibitions bore a striking resemblance to the helter-skelter "curiosity museums" of the European baroque and rococo periods; and in time Roman citizens would visit them as part of the traditional "grand tour," being taken through the temples by prattling guides who were as annoying in their rapid-fire, parrot-like rote as the European museum guide long has been to the intelligent modern tourist.

Since they constituted the nearest approach to the religious relic and

---

* In the changing connotation of this word the evolution of art museums from temple collections is succinctly expressed. Originally signifying "hall of tablets" (from *pinakes,* or votive tablets), *pinakotheka* eventually came to mean "picture gallery" in exactly the modern sense.

were doubly venerable, *association* pieces came first in these displays; appealing both to man's awe before antiquity and to his desire to come close to the great and the sanctified. Thus the Temple of Apollo at Sicyon owned, among many treasures of this sort, such items as the shield and sword of Agamemnon, the cloak and armor of Odysseus, the bow and arrows of Teucer, Penelope's web, and the garment worn by one of this lady's swains. Even the helm of the Argonauts' ship and one of the rowing poles they had used were there, to say nothing of such gruesome souvenirs as the skin of Marsyas and the kettle in which old Pelias had been boiled.

It was only when Alexander of Macedon had conquered a great slice of the known world for Hellas, putting the riches of Persia into circulation and initiating a period of fabulous prosperity, that the Greeks as individuals were to become passionate collectors.

Alexander himself is said to have followed in the footsteps of other great conquerors by gathering animals and other natural history specimens in all the lands he invaded. These he sent back to his beloved and illustrious teacher, Aristotle, who used them in the preparation of his monumental *Natural History*—an interesting example of curiosity and method, using collecting technique to the scientific result.

With the influx of precious plate, pottery, fine carpets and hangings from the East that accompanied this era of conquest, display in the Greek home became more common than hitherto, and the physical standard of living was raised appreciably. Even the Achaeans and the Aetolians, those inhabitants of the scrubby, infertile sections of Greece who had always perforce been army mercenaries, were affected by the spirit of the new age. The nature of their traditional profession afforded them a rare opportunity when the sumptuous world of the Eastern empires was first revealed, and they returned home laden with treasures with which they proceeded to enrich their homes as well as their public buildings. Rude soldiers though they were, they now, writes Mahaffy,

". . . sought ornaments, treasures from tombs and temples, and works of art in a captured town in preference to mere money, and carried this plunder back to their capital city of Thermus, which, being in time sacked and ruined itself by Philip V of Macedon, was found to be full of such treasures . . . not only the buildings immediately around the temple . . . but the homesteads on the outskirts also."

History seems never to tire of this cycle, as the twentieth century now reaffirms.

In our time it is commonly believed that the Romans were the first people to collect in the grand manner. But in this, as in so much else, the Greeks of the Hellenistic age clearly preceded them. In fact, it was the growth of a vogue for collecting in this period that was partly responsible for certain radical changes in the form of Greek art itself.

As the number of private collectors increased, their convenience and taste had to be considered by the artist, and now easel paintings (on wooden panels) began to take the place of the earlier frescoes that had been suitable for public buildings, and these were destined to become even more popular than statues. Secular portraiture began to supplant religious subjects in both sculpture and painting, and realism came into fashion. Gradually the temples became art galleries in quite a different sense than before, for now the pictures shown had frequently no religious significance whatsoever.* In the home, life in Hellenistic Greece was far more luxurious than it had been in the days of plain living and high thinking that had prevailed under the old republics; and even the members of the Doric aristocracy, conservatively wedded to ancestral ideals though they were, filled their houses with rich plate, elaborate furniture and collections of paintings and statues.

It was now that the city of Sicyon came to be known as a world-center for the study of painting and sculpture, a "sort of Hellenistic Florence," and, according to Mahaffy, in this

"age of art-collecting, when rich kings and satraps liked to obtain the *chefs d'oeuvre* of renowned artists, and paid large prices for them, such a reputation meant power and wealth."

Sicyon's strategic cultural position was even of political benefit to her, in one case, as a direct result of a royal collector's passion for her artistic products. The incident, related by Plutarch, concerns the soldier-statesman, Aratus (271–213 B.C.), and King Ptolemy of Egypt. Aratus devoted his life to an almost hopeless attempt to unite the several Greek states so that they might be strong enough to combat the dangers threatening them from Macedon and Rome, and it was an important part of

* The Christian art era, starting again from scratch, would move forward into the renaissance before most of these changes reappeared. Similarly in India under the Moguls the patronage of the royal collectors, Akbar and Jahangir, fostered the development of a school of secular portrait painting.

his plan to bring the powerful Ptolemy into a military alliance. His efforts in this direction, however, met with lukewarm response until, as a final masterly stroke, he sent into Egypt a superlative selection of those Sicyonian works of art then so greatly in fashion. Ptolemy could not resist, and he forthwith agreed to enter the alliance.

At this time a taste in articles of *virtu* was expected of educated men, much as it is in our own day. Exhibitions of the new portable panel-paintings were frequently held, and publicity stunts were developed to promote the sales. Theon of Samos, for example, painted a figure of an armed warrior rushing into battle, and when he wished to put the panel up for sale he first veiled it, then hired a trumpeter to blow an alarum throughout the city. The populace, thinking that the city had been surprised by some enemy, congregated in great excitement, whereat Theon unveiled his painting before their astounded and admiring eyes!

Even Athens, now gradually losing her political importance, developed her schools for the express purpose of attracting wealthy students and tourists, a phenomenon not unheard of in a beloved Paris. Under the new system, sculptors, painters, musicians, even philosophers became, not the honorable yet unpretentious tradesmen they had been in the old days, but celebrities more in the manner of our day, and as such they, too, were collected by the wealthy dilettanti while, long before the time of Lytton Strachey, the juiciest anecdotes of their private lives were gathered up and retailed for the delectation of the populace.

Fashion held the reins, and—ah, familiar bone of contention!—a work of art signed with a famous name could command a higher price than an anonymous piece of equal quality. The minor arts also were increasing in popularity. People now began to collect engraved gems, fine pottery and embroidered textiles; and when a new hobby was born—collecting or copying the letters of famous men—we find our first Greek autograph hounds.

And what of the book collectors? Aristocrats of Greek amateurs, they were connoisseurs long before the existence of the Hellenistic *nouveaux riches* dilettanti. Peisistratus, brilliant ruler of Athens in the sixth century, is said to have been the first to indulge this passion on a considerable scale. Plato and Euripides are known to have been bibliophiles, as one might expect, but the most famous of all Greek book collections was Aristotle's library, marked by a dramatic history.

Bequeathed by the great scholar to his disciple, Theophrastus, Aristotle's books passed on into the possession of Neleus at a time when the sharpy kings of Pergamum were busy assembling an impressive library of their own. In order to prevent these semiforeign monarchs from laying hands upon his precious and historic collection, Neleus carried the books to the town of Scepsis, where he secreted them in a cellar—so the tale is told by Strabo. And there they moldered. Their glory was forgotten or obscured until Apellicon of Teos, another eager collector, discovered them and carried them back to Athens. Later, when the Roman general, Sulla, plundered Greece of her treasures, the library of Apellicon did not escape, and it has been said that "the transference of this important collection to Rome is noted as a special moment in the higher education of that city."

Aristotle's library and the Greek "Museum," founded in his honor by Theophrastus, are credited with having inspired the foundation of the extraordinary collections at Alexandria, largest of their kind in the ancient world. In this cosmopolitan city, built on Egyptian soil by the conqueror whose name it bore, the first Ptolemy, Soter,* established that royal "Museum" which later, in the days of its fullest splendor, is said to have housed from four to seven hundred thousand books. Although the book rolls, like the tablet books of Mesopotamia, contained much less matter than a modern volume, the library was one of the wonders of its time. The second Ptolemy, Philadelphus, whose reign (285–246 B.C.) was inaugurated with a festival of almost incredible magnificence, took enormous pride in the library and stinted not in making it the greatest collection of its kind the world had ever seen.

According to Josephus, a Jewish historian of the first century A.D., Ptolemy's ambition was to assemble "all the books that were in the habitable earth." The king is said once to have inquired of his library-keeper, one Demetrius Phalerius, how many ten thousands of books he had gathered together; and when Phalerius replied that he already had twenty times ten thousand but that he would soon have fifty times ten thousand, Ptolemy was greatly pleased and praised him for being so "zealous to procure him an abundance of books." As Ashurbanipal had

* Alexander's former general and eventually his successor in the valley of the Nile; reigned 305–285 B.C. The exact date of the founding of the Museum is not known.

sent his agents into every part of Mesopotamia, so now the Greco-Egyptian ruler dispatched book hunters into Greece and Asia in search of literary treasures. And with equal zeal his successor, Ptolemy Euergetes, is said to have seized for the library all the books brought into Egypt by foreigners, who had no choice but to accept the inferior copies supplied them in partial restitution.

Although we have come to think of them as the predecessors of the great public educational institutions of a later day, actually the library, the zoological collections, and the rest of the Alexandrian Museum remained always in royal possession and under royal patronage. Seneca declared that the library itself was chiefly an occasion for royal ostentation, and although it attracted students from the entire Hellenistic world, there is some question how many were independent thinkers engaged in true research, how many were pedants or subservient bureaucrats.

As it grew in fame, the library at Alexandria began to excite the envy of ambitious rulers elsewhere. The kings of Pergamum especially—rulers of that Greek city-state in Asia Minor which was becoming, in the beauty of its architecture and the wealth of its cultural life, a new Athens—took note of the prestige that Alexandria and her rulers derived from their possession of the great collections in the Museum. Strong and able Attalus I (241–197 B.C.) devoted much of his long life to the encouragement of art and literature, and his ambition was to make his capital the cultural rival of the Egyptian metropolis. He imported antique works of art from Aegina—an island which he had purchased, it is thought, for the sole reason that it was full of examples of archaic Greek sculpture which the natives were now neglecting in favor of the newer *objets d'art* brought in from the East—and almost certainly by this action Attalus preserved those valuable pieces from ultimate destruction.

In this king was also strong the collector instinct for keeping an orderly record: each statue he acquired was carefully labeled with the name of the artist and its place of origin. Meanwhile the assemblage of an important library was begun, and, when eventually transported to Egypt at a later date, the collection had reached the impressive total of nearly two hundred thousand volumes.

The motives behind the building of two such great libraries may have been matters of personal rivalry and of royal display indulged in by two predatory creatures, but the results of that rivalry are now more important. Although the Alexandrian library declined greatly in its later years, the memory of it has remained an inspiration to students and collectors to this day; and, directly or indirectly, it rescued from oblivion much of our own fine heritage of Greek literature and thought.

The malignant fate that overtook all the great collections of the ancient world finally swallowed this library, too. In a roar of destroying flame the valuable collecting of nearly a thousand years was largely undone; but before that last day, many of the volumes, consulted and copied by scholars and pedants during the centuries of the Museum's existence, had been circulated in distant lands and so were saved.

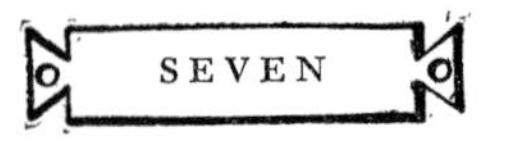

A ROMAN HOLIDAY

"All things at Rome have their price."

JUVENAL

AMONG ALL ancient peoples the Roman approximates most closely the American collector, so closely, indeed, that as the comparison is made two thousand years melt away. Patently, the Romans themselves created the ornament of their own connoisseurship from gems of vanquished and absorbed civilizations. Yet more than any of the other Old Men, they have left us a relatively clear and detailed vision of their daily lives, so that in the history of Rome, from the later days of the expanding Republic, through the gorgeous stride of the Imperial Age with its full music of unbridled desire, the entire collecting pattern can be traced easily and consecutively. Where in earlier history that pattern was implicit but often vague, here it is substantiated by an impressive body of concrete evidence.

One gift, great and badly needed, Rome gave to the lands she invaded —her genius for organization, epitomized by good government. But although the ability to organize is of inestimable value to genuine collecting, the Roman collector took far more than he gave in things both real and of the spirit, for most of his own art values and attitudes were built upon the accomplishments of his victims.

The peoples whom the Romans met and conquered were the cosmopolite collectors of the Hellenistic world. In Sicily and in the Greek colonies of southern Italy, in Greece proper and in Macedonia, in Egypt and in Asia Minor, wherever Roman generals marched, they found temples, palaces and homes crowded with the treasures of old cultures; and Rome's collecting era, which took root simultaneously with her era of world domination, was fed almost entirely by the importation of these treasures.

Importation as a word is, of course, too polite for what really happened in the beginning. Long before purchase, came plunder—largely dedicated at first to religion or to the state. When Marcellus, in 212 B.C., robbed the cultivated Greek city of Syracuse in Sicily of her finest statues and pictures, he exhibited these at Rome in the temple of Honor and Virtue! From then on the procession of artistic booty was virtually unending. In 209 B.C., Fabius brought home similar spoil from another Greek colonial city, Tarentum on the coast of southern Italy; and Flaminius, after Cynoscephalae in 197 B.C., carried to Rome most of the collection which Philip V of Macedon had gathered partly through plunder, partly by inheritance. Ten years later, M. Fulvius Nobilior made off with the marvelous treasures of the cities of Thermus (itself full of earlier loot) and Ambracia (once the capital of ambitious Pyrrhus). To house the five hundred and fifteen bronze and marble statues which comprised a part of his booty, he erected a special temple and named it the Hercules Musarum. This procedure, which was quite typical, shows how closely these "temples," built for the exhibition of artistic plunder, approximated the nature and intent of true art museums.

Despite a tendency to segregate the statues and pictures from the rest of the plunder, however, it was the exceptional Roman who, at this period, had any innate appreciation of the treasures that fell into his hands. At the sack of Corinth in 145 B.C., for example, the consul Mummius seized that beautiful city's art objects for the Roman state, but despite his greed he neglected some of the best pieces and, by the crass ignorance of his instructions to his soldiers, earned for himself the scorn of future generations: should the men damage any of the statues, he declared, they would have to replace them themselves. Mummius may have been a boor even among Romans, but he was scarcely alone, for, as the modern scholar, Friedländer, expressed it:

"The accumulation of ancient works of art was only a form of the Roman love of splendor. . . . The lords of the world aimed at possessing and enjoying . . . all the precious things of the world . . . but their appropriation of these treasures was only material."

Even the first libraries came to Rome as spoils of war, for we hear of none until the last century of the Republic. Again it was the unusual citizen who valued the seizures as anything more than victory trophies. Aemilius Paulus, an upright man by the light of his times, with no great interest in personal aggrandizement, was to some extent such an exception. When, in 168 B.C., he defeated the wealthy Perseus of Macedon at Pydna, he turned most of the booty over to the state, but reserved the king's books for his sons who, according to Plutarch, were great lovers of learning. Yet strangely enough, when one of those sons, Scipio Africanus Minor, commanded the Roman forces at the razing of Carthage twenty years later, he and his men cared so little for the books they found in this ancient Phoenician city that, despite the fact that they were well able to read the language, they turned over all but a few useful volumes on agriculture to the local African kinglets; and more than eighty years were yet to pass before the next important milestone in Roman library history was reached with the bringing in, by Sulla, of Aristotle's great collection.

After the battle of Pydna the Romans were determined to teach the rebellious Greeks a lesson. More than a hundred and fifty thousand people were enslaved at this time, and seventy cities were sacked, after giving up their treasures. Quite unlike the generals of later generations, Aemilius kept little of the loot for himself, but the Roman state was so greatly enriched that never thereafter did the Republic tax its citizens! Aemilius did make one small personal gift, however, a gift which should be mentioned because it serves to point up the contrast between the relatively simple Roman life of this period and that of the luxurious Rome that was to follow. The gift was a gold bowl weighing five pounds, which Aemilius presented to his son-in-law, Aelius Tubero, as a reward for extraordinary valor, and this bowl was reputedly the first plate of precious metal that Aelius' family had ever owned.

Aemilius' "triumph" took three days to pass through the streets of Rome on its way to the temple of Jupiter on the Capitoline. On the first day, which, according to Plutarch, was scarcely long enough for the sight, there were to be seen:

> "the statues, pictures and colossal images which were taken from the enemy, drawn upon two hundred and fifty chariots."

The armor and standards of the defeated cities were displayed on the second day, followed by three thousand men carrying the looted silver coin in seven hundred and fifty vessels. These vessels were so heavy

PLUNDER FED THE COLLECTIONS OF IMPERIAL ROME. *Relief from the Arch of Titus, in Rome. Titus* (A.D. *48-81*) *shared with his father, Vespasian, the Triumph which followed the capture of Jerusalem in* A.D. *70.*

Photo, courtesy of The Metropolitan Museum of Art

Silver cup, probably of the Augustan period, now in the Pierpont Morgan Library, New York. Intrinsic value, as well as beauty, interested the realistic Roman collector.

that four men were required to lift each one, and they were succeeded by others bearing bowls, goblets, and cups of silver "large and embossed." On the third day, after the one hundred and twenty oxen destined for sacrifice, came more men carrying seventy-seven vessels of coined gold; others bearing cups which had belonged to Antigonus and Seleucus, the great Alexander's generals, and all the gold plate, once Alexander's, from Perseus' own table. After this, still more men appeared with four hundred crowns of gold from the vanquished cities. Countless slaves, Perseus' unfortunate children, and, *pièce de résistance,* the wretched king himself, brought up the rear of the procession.

Here was state collecting on the grand scale, and this was but the first of many such victory parades, for although Rome was now rich enough, although she was no longer a "have-not" nation, plunder continued to flourish.

It was inevitable that the constantly available foreign treasure should eventually damage a selfless spirit of public service which contented the earlier generals; and this evolution from necessity to cupidity played an important part in determining the early course taken by Roman collecting. However, it was something of quite a different nature which, perhaps more than anything else, first turned the face of collecting toward a new direction. In 133 B.C., Attalus III, King of Pergamum, died without issue and willed his entire realm to the people of Rome, with whom he had long been allied.

Thus, in peace, did the Imperial City gain her first foothold on Greek Asia, a hold which she was soon to extend by more conventional means.

Many Romans migrated to the new province at this time, and some of them were charged with the administration of its cultural treasures, for it will be remembered that Pergamum had been second only to Alexandria in the wealth of its artistic and literary collections. Here, exposed more intimately than before to the Hellenistic culture, observing just what sort of things were most valued by the local nabobs, the Romans began slowly to develop their own taste; and, as had happened among the Greeks under Alexander when they were confronted with the novelty of Asiatic art, a change in attitude was soon to be noticed: the Romans were now in the process of becoming, in the true sense of the phrase, a nation of ardent collectors.

Even Mummius, the insensitive plunderer of lovely Corinth, had been stopped short when, during the sale of some of the spoil, he had heard King Attalus offer a staggering sum for a painting by Aristides of Thebes. Surprised, "and suspecting that there might be some merit in the picture of which he himself was unaware," the consul had suddenly refused to sell. No doubt he looked at the painting more carefully thereafter—and perhaps he absorbed something of art values. It was from such material shocks as this that a part, at least, of Roman connoisseurship eventually sprang, and neither the attitude nor its effects are entirely strange to recent history.

As the conquest of the East proceeded, more and more Romans were thrown into contact with the major and minor arts of the Greek world, and also with the Greek collectors. Gradually the Latins came to value the things they saw, not only as potential plunder, but in much the same way as the Hellenes valued them—as objects of *virtu* offering pleasure to the potential owner. Particularly was this true during Lucius Cornelius Sulla's campaigns in the middle eighties, when Roman troops camped in Greek cities through the long, inactive winters; and Sulla himself (138–78 B.C.), hard soldier though he was, acquired a sure eye and is accredited as the first great private collector of Rome.

When Sulla, returning to Italy after four years of highly successful operations in Greece and Asia Minor, defeated the Martian faction and made himself dictator, he instituted proscription lists for the purpose of extirpating the political opposition. But as events generally prove, following the use of such dictatorial weapons, the lists far exceeded their political intent in effect, and became, rather, tools for satisfying personal grudges and cupidities. A man's sole crime, in Sulla's later days, might be that he owned something which the dictator or one of his friends wanted.

Supplementing proscription at home and outright looting abroad, bribery was often used as a clinching argument for the "rights" of such conduct. One collector of the next generation, Caius Verres (d. 43 B.C.), is known to every school child as that governor of Sicily who, according to Cicero, brazenly admitted that a three-year term of provincial governorship was quite sufficient for his purpose:

"In the first year he could secure plunder for himself; in the second for his friends; in the third for his judges."

Like Sulla, Verres carried the plunder system into private life, and invited to a dinner party, he would not hesitate to make off with the silver bas-relief plates if he happened to like them. This rapacious fellow, having gone to a good school, became one of Rome's best connoisseurs of art.

The Sicilian cities—by this time united into a Roman province—contained some of the finest examples of Greek art then extant. Their temples owned many famous statues which, having once been plundered by the Carthaginians, had been restored to their owners in the previous century by Scipio Africanus Minor, a Roman more just than Verres. And not only the temples but the homes of the Sicilians were full of artistic treasure. Wealthy collectors, proud of their historic possessions, gladly exhibited these to their Roman visitors, one of whom, at least, repaid such hospitality by seizing whatever pleased his fancy. Statues, paintings, ivories (Verres' particular passion), vases, gold and silver plate, gems, medallions, tapestries, all were grist to Verres' mill; and though he developed critical pretensions as a result of his unparalleled opportunities, he always retained two Greek "experts" to help him "revise his judgments on art."

Verres owned a beautiful bronze statuette of Hercules, by Lysippus; and the long history of this figure's famous but unfortunate owners added considerably to its value. The statuette had been, originally, a gift from the sculptor to Alexander the Great, who cherished it above all his artistic possessions and is said to have died with it in his hands. Later it passed into the possession of the Carthaginian general, Hannibal, an amateur of antique bronzes who must have valued this particular piece especially for its close association with the great conqueror. Hannibal carried it with him into exile at the court of Bithynia; and when in despair he finally took poison there, his host, the king, claimed the little masterpiece for his own. In the royal Bithynian family it then remained, until the invading Sulla in turn seized it and brought it to Rome.

Another Asiatic collector of antique art was Mithridates the Great, King of Pontus, who specialized in engraved gems. When Pompey, also called the Great, defeated this monarch at Nicopolis in 66 B.C., he made off with Mithridates' collection, only to lose it, together with the rest of his artistic treasure, sixteen years later to Marc Antony, after the battle of Pharsalia. Antony himself was a veritable prince among plunderers. His fine library was assembled at the cost of many lives, and in his day the proscription lists were again wide open to the owners of such rare gems or handsome bronzes as he or his partner, Octavian, desired. Not even the wishes of Antony's great friend, Julius Caesar, had final claim against the former's passion for ownership. Caesar was an enlightened man and one of Rome's most enthusiastic collectors. It was his plan to bequeath his artistic treasures to the people of Rome, a note strangely ahead of his time; but he was no sooner dead than Antony promptly took possession of all that had not been previously and publicly donated.*

In the days of the early empire, markedly in contrast to the early republican period, everyone who could possibly manage to do so was collecting something. The Roman remained always more deeply interested in historical association than in pure artistic merit, and he was particularly susceptible to external standards of value as represented by rarity or expensiveness of material, but within these limitations he developed every degree and every kind of collectionitis.

In the city, an entire group of new activities sprang up in the wake of this fashion. Dealing in art objects became a highly profitable business, as it has been today. Antique and bric-a-brac shops, grouped together in certain neighborhoods, were established in great numbers.

Auction sales, with pre-sale exhibitions of the sort familiar to us, became a commonplace of city life, and the methods of conducting transactions were much like our own. Any modern auction-goer knows how carefully he must guard against inadvertently raising his hand or nodding his head during a sale, since these gestures increase the bid. Suetonius tells a story about the Emperor Caligula (rg. 37–41) which shows that exactly the same system prevailed at Rome. Needing money, Caligula organized an auction of old palace furniture. During the sale, which he himself attended and supervised, the emperor noticed that

---

* Arthur Weigall, in his *The Life and Times of Marc Antony,* takes issue with the usual accounts of Antony's predatory collecting activity. This fine biographer pictures Antony as an impetuous but large-hearted man of action, with little of Sulla's connoisseurship or scholarly tastes. According to Weigall's theory, Antony's frequent seizures of other people's treasures (including Caesar's) was due to his constant and desperate need of funds to be used for political purposes, while his seizure of Pompey's mansion with all it contained had been a gesture of defiance to Caesar, with whom he was temporarily at odds. Weigall discounts Antony's reputation for ruthlessness as having come down to us either from his bitterest enemies, such as Cicero, or from the gossiping pens of minor historians, such as Dion Cassius, writing more than two hundred and fifty years after Antony's time.

Aponius Saturninus, a former praetor, had fallen asleep on his bench. Whereupon Caligula told the auctioneer to watch the sleeper. Every time the old man's head nodded, the emperor instructed, it was to be taken as a bid; and when the unfortunate Aponius finally awoke, he discovered that he had purchased, sight unseen, some three hundred forty-seven thousand four hundred dollars' worth of royal furniture.

Roman collecting fads rushed in and out again, one upon the heels of the other; and among the collectors who followed each were the usual modicum of connoisseurs and the inevitable hangers-on who were concerned only with "doing the right thing." The names of purchasers of this or that famous piece were bandied about in the gossip of the day, while wealthy lute players or prosperous freedmen competed with senators and consuls for the possession of coveted items. Fantastic prices were asked, and paid, for whatever archaic or curious objects of *virtu* happened to be in vogue at the moment, and although it is difficult to translate ancient prices into modern values, one authority declares that many of the high sums paid in Rome for collectors' pieces have never since been equaled.

As always when collecting prices go up on the basis of rarity and fashionable demand, faking and forging became richly worth-while occupations for the unscrupulous, while frank copyists and skillful restorers also found a plentiful market for their talents. The prevalence of forgeries necessitated the use of "experts" to pass judgment on the genuineness of collectibles, and so another familiar profession was born. Such experts in the Roman world were usually Greeks who, by this time, were much older hands at the game of collecting than were their Latin employers, and were possessed of a far better background for understanding those imported works of art which the Romans (like Americans) so often preferred.

The Roman collector's harvest was nearly as various as our own. Books and autograph manuscripts (those inscribed by the author himself and not by some professional copyist), found many enthusiasts, and whereas libraries had been scarce indeed in former days, it now became the pride of emperors to establish them, while for the ordinary citizen possession of an expensive collection of books "became a normal badge of personal achievement."

One of Julius Caesar's pet projects—a plan cut short by death—had been to make "as large a collection as possible of literary productions,

Greek and Latin," for public use; and he had assigned Marcus Varro, "most learned of the Romans," to the task of assembling and classifying these books. After Caesar's death, Varro prevailed upon Asinius Pollio (76 B.C.–A.D. 5) to carry out the plan; and this first public library in Rome, which was also an art gallery, is thought to have contained as its nucleus both Varro's and Sulla's private collections.

Augustus founded two more libraries, the Octavian in 33 B.C. and the Biblioteca Palatina in 26 B.C., and other such institutions soon followed throughout the empire. Most of them remained in the temples, to which wealthy private citizens often left their books, as well as their collections of art, rarities and natural curiosities. It had now become "fashionable for rich men to furnish their libraries well"; but it was not entirely a matter of *bon ton*, for there were genuine bibliophiles among the Romans. Both Cicero and Pliny collected autographs, and Cicero in particular was an impassioned book collector. He had libraries in each of his numerous villas and was constantly on the trail of old Greek works and handsome editions. He employed a Greek library adviser, Tyrannion, who was later in Sulla's employ in the same capacity; and his letters to his friend and agent, Atticus, show him to have been quite at the mercy of this hobby. Writing of his books, he once declared:

> "I cannot express the delight they give me, not only when I am among them, but even when I think about them." And again, "Don't think of selling your books to anyone else; I am saving every little bit I can to make the purchase . . . I want them so badly that everything else disgusts me."

Sculpture and painting, both antique and modern, were among the first things to be collected in Rome, and they never went out of vogue. By the close of the republic, the *pinacotheca,* like the library, was becoming a feature required of every fashionable home. Greek works were at all times extravagantly admired and were in far greater demand than the products of native artists: no unusual discrimination was needed by the Roman connoisseur to note that the Roman artist was seldom the equal of the Greek; while the Roman snob pursued foreign works for the reasons which have ever dictated snobbish tastes.

For those who could not afford to buy originals it was common practice to make copies, and although these were sometimes passed off as the real thing, more often than not they were frankly accepted as replicas. Many masterpieces of Greek sculpture are familiar to us today solely through this channel.

Stone and bronze were far more widely collected in Rome than they are today, for the architectural scheme of ancient times made vast use of sculpture, and the layman was accustomed to thinking of the products of this art as an essential adornment to his private estate—just as we consider paintings and etchings a natural embellishment of the home. Thus Pliny writes of a certain Tullus:

"He was so great a collector that the very day he purchased a huge garden he was able to adorn it completely with antique statues drawn from his store of art treasures."

Of the true connoisseurs in Rome, one of the first was Lucius Licinius Lucullus (*c.* 114–57 B.C.), general, consul, and epicure. His villa (on the site where a Medici home was to be built more than a thousand years later) contained a fine library and a collection of Greek paintings ordered direct from Athens. Lucullus' home became a rendezvous for artists and writers, and when his guests wearied of discussion they could visit the zoological and botanical gardens which their host had stocked with imported specimens.

Brutus, Cassius and Cicero, Julius Caesar and Caesar Augustus, Agrippa and Maecenas were others among the famous Roman collectors of painting and sculpture. Cicero, to serve a particular purpose (as in the speech against the looter, Verres) could play down to the mass belief that such niceties as a concern for art were not occupations suitable for real men. Nevertheless, in his desire to climb upward socially, he himself made great efforts to amass a "suitable" collection of art. Maecenas was another snob-patron of artists and writers: he seems to have been influenced both by political considerations and by a desire to achieve immortality through the praises of those whom he sponsored with lavish generosity, and in this he was indeed successful, for his name is still used as the dictionary equivalent of the all-out patron.

As an example of a sincere and impassioned amateur, the figure of Julius Caesar commands the light. Collector of both the modern and the antique, he would, declares Suetonius, "purchase at any cost gems, carved works and pictures, executed by the eminent masters of antiquity"; and some of the most renowned pieces of Greek and Roman sculpture extant today, including the *Meleager* of the Vatican and the

Venus of the Hermitage, are said to have been in his collection. As he had considered the common weal in his library project, so he built a temporary portico at the Capitol for a public exhibition of works of art, and opened to the people his own gardens on the Tiber, where he had installed a gallery of paintings and sculpture.

Augustus, too, was a patron of literature and art. As a young man he himself collected art objects and was accused, along with Antony, of being so fond of fine furniture and Greek antiques that he would proscribe a man for his collection. His tastes, however, changed with the years, and he came to prefer curiosities and antiques of another sort. It was then that he found amusement, during dinner parties, in selling to his guests "tickets" or lots composed of things of very unequal value, or pictures faced away from the company. In this sophisticated Jack-Horner-Pie game, everyone was obliged to bid for and buy at least one lot, and the suspense among collectors present must have been high indeed.

In the days of Augustus, most of the important art collections were being removed to the country villas of the nobles, and this state of affairs drew fire from Agrippa, the emperor's great minister, who was himself an enthusiastic connoisseur. Foreshadowing, as Julius had, the evolutionary tendencies of latter-day collecting, Agrippa felt that the public should derive some benefit from the accumulations, and he accomplished much toward beautifying the city by installing statues in public places.

The minor and applied arts also came in for an important share of the Roman collector's attention. Ceramics, engraved silverware, engraved gems, fine furniture, Maltese tapestries, Babylonian carpets and oriental embroideries were all part of the general harvest. There were successive vogues for each of these, as we have had vogues for collecting Americana, early pewter, or Sheffield plate, and the Roman's hand was at least as free with coin as the modern enthusiast.

At one time it was tables made of the rare citrus wood that were in especial demand, and for one of these Cathegus is said to have paid the equivalent of fifty-eight thousand dollars—a price that would silence any auction room today. Even Cicero, who was not adjudged wealthy, paid more than twenty-one thousand three hundred dollars (five hundred thousand sesterces) for such a table. Caesar had in his collection some precious mosaic tables to which he was so devoted that he always

Bronze tripod table, Greek style, found at Herculaneum. From the Museo Nazionale, Naples.

Museum of Fine Arts, Boston

Corinthian bronze oinochoe *or pitcher of 5th century* B.C.

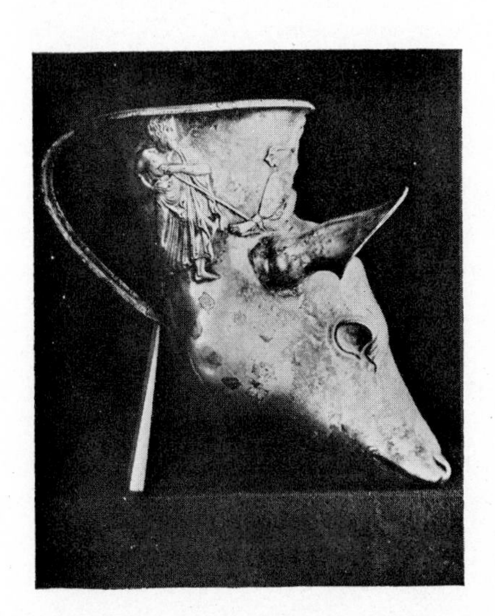

Greek silver rhyton *or drinking horn of 5th century* B.C. *From the Museo Civico, Trieste.*

Greek silver bowl, APOTHEOSIS OF HERACLES, *of 3rd century* B.C., *found near Nice. Now in the British Museum.*

ROMAN COLLECTORS FAVORED OBJECTS OF BRONZE AND SILVER, AND IF THESE WERE ANCIENT AND GREEK, SO MUCH THE BETTER.

carried a few of them on his campaigns; and Seneca, who owned five hundred fine tripod-like tables with ivory feet, must have knit his brows over the storage problem much as the modern collector of antique beds.

Antique wrought silver, at another period, was all the rage. Some of the greatest artists had worked in this ware which was, therefore, an attraction comparable for collectors to the goldsmiths' work of the renaissance, plus an additional rarity-factor due to the circumstance that the working of silver had become almost a lost art by the time of the empire. In the days when Verres stole such ware, prices paid by more scrupulous collectors were often twenty to thirty times the worth of the metal itself. Chrysogon, Sulla's wealthy freedman, for example, offered so large a sum for a silver plate-warmer at one auction that, according to Cicero, people outside, hearing the bid, thought he must be buying a farm!

One hundred and fifty thousand sesterces was not considered an unusual price to pay for a single rock crystal cup, if it happened to be an excellent specimen; and the popular *murra* ware (cups, bowls and vases made of a material not surely identifiable today) commanded even more fantastic sums. More than one collector is known to have paid three hundred thousand sesterces for a single example. Nero had a drinking cup of this valuable stuff which cost him a million sesterces. And Petronius is supposed to have given three hundred talents, or nearly three hundred thirty thousand dollars, for the superlative specimen which eventually cost him his life. Vases of Corinthian bronze vied with the *murrhines* as *pièces de résistance,* and every virtuoso was bound to have at least one. These were Marc Antony's particular passion, and Verres was not the only collector proscribed for the extraordinary offense of owning examples that Antony desired.

Less expensive but equally popular were the engraved gems or signets which corresponded to the cylinder seals of the ancient Mesopotamians. The collecting of engraved gems was an especially satisfactory pursuit, for in many of these stones one could find beautiful workmanship, historic association, and intrinsic value, all encompassed in a single small and convenient object. Perhaps for this reason such gems have been favorites among collectors from the time of Mithridates to our own. Scaurus, stepson of Sulla, was one of the first Romans to specialize in this field. This was Pompey's hobby, and it was one of the many that attracted Julius Caesar's interest. Caesar had six distinct collections of cameos and cut stones which eventually he consecrated in the temple of Venus Genetrix; while Marcellus, nephew of Augustus, presented another such collection to the temple of Apollo.

Coin collecting was another widely practiced art, and Augustus was a practitioner of royal gesture who sometimes distributed "coins of all sorts, even of the ancient kings of Rome and of other nations" among his fortunate guests. Augustus also furnishes us with the prototype of the Roman collector of fossils and natural curiosities. According to Suetonius, the emperor

". . . had a particular aversion to large and sumptuous palaces. . . . Those of his own, which were far from being spacious, he adorned not so much with statues and pictures, as with walks and groves, and things which were curious either for their antiquity or rarity; such as at Capreae [Capri], the huge limbs of sea-monsters and wild beasts, which some affect to call the bones of giants, and the arms [weapons(?)] of old heroes."

Then as now, however, the majority of curiosity collectors were either those who, liking to collect, lacked the true amateur's intensity, or were obscure citizens who could not afford the more expensive and fashionable hobbies. Martial reports one man who made a collection of pieces of amber containing fossilized insects, and Seneca tells of another whose hobby was the gathering of rusty fragments of metal. Collectors who were forced to satisfy their urge in such modest manner were, as a rule, mentioned only in ridicule, although probably they enjoyed themselves as much as the wealthier and more pompous.

The paradox of the proud Roman's humility toward all things Greek was not unlike the American veneration for the products of Europe's older civilization. The Roman collector, like his modern brother, enjoyed talking about his collection and loved to show it to anyone who could be induced to look. "Isn't Euctus a bore with his historical silver?" asks Martial, much as we might say, "How George does go on about his Wedgwood!" The Roman collector, too, liked to be thought of as an expert in his field, and delighted in parading his superior knowledge before an admiring audience. In his anxiety to get his hands on certain treasures, he was as heartless as most of the tribe in all ages, a heartlessness which appears quite clearly in one of Pliny's letters to Rufinus:

"You have now all the town gossip—nothing but talk about Tullus. We look forward to the auction sale of his effects."

For a parallel to this, the candid joking of the modern bibliophile, Rosenbach, springs to mind:

"Book collectors, I make no exceptions, are buzzards who stretch their wings in anticipation as they wait patiently for a colleague's demise; then they swoop down and ghoulishly grab some long-coveted treasure from the dear departed's trove."

There are even modern parallels to those cases of Roman collectors who, like Petronius, loved their collections better than life itself. Petronius, author of that *Satyricon* which so bitingly caricatures the boorish parvenu of his day, made the mistake of living under the Emperor Nero's benevolent rule. Both men were collectors, Petronius of bowls and drinking cups, Nero of anything he could lay hands on, including musical instruments and the five hundred bronze statues which he had taken into "protective custody" from the oracular temple at Delphi. Petronius, be it remembered, owned a particularly valuable *murrhine,* and this Nero wanted. Suspecting that the writer would never be shaken from the prize, Nero did not even ask for it. Instead he sent a messenger bearing, not a message, but a draught of hemlock. Petronius knew quite well what the messenger would take for his master, once the poison had done its work. Equally aware of the futility of resistance, he solved the problem neatly and in his own ironic manner. From the *murrhine* itself, we are told, he drank the proffered brew, then dashed the bowl to bits.

Every type of collector was present on the Roman scene; and among the contemporary writers who described the members of this variegated family, painting them in all gradations from true amateur to foolish faddist, were Cicero and Pliny, Horace, Seneca, Martial, Juvenal, Quintilian and Statius, several of whom were collectors themselves.

No imagination is required to find the modern counterpart of each of these Roman types. There was Codrus, the impecunious amateur depicted by Juvenal, who could afford only a few books, a few cups, and one or two pieces of sculpture. There was Paullus, the vulgar show-off of whom Martial speaks. His sole purpose in collecting, whether paintings, antiques, or famous people were at stake, was to make a great display. There was Licinus, the wealthy noble who, according to Juvenal, was so afraid that something would happen to his statues, his figures in amber, his furniture inlaid with ivory and tortoise shell, that he kept slaves on continuous guard to protect them.

Seneca tells of a man who, specializing in small vases of Corinthian bronze, used to spend his days handling his treasures, arranging and rearranging them, as the American Joline refers to his autographs. Another writer describes the secretive collector who hoarded his objects of *virtu* and would not show them to anyone: he is unusual, but we shall meet him again.

Many a modern dealer will recognize Martial's Mamurra, the shopping collector, who, in Rome, used to go to a different store each day, forcing the dealer to show him everything on the premises. He would spend the entire day there, asking to see articles that were placed out of reach. He would measure this or that piece of furniture as though he were thinking of placing it in a particular spot at home, then find each one to be the wrong size. He would smell a Corinthian bronze and find fault with the odor, or examine a rock crystal cup and declare it to be cloudy. He would try the weight of an antique bowl and be displeased with that also. In the end he would ask the dealer to reserve a dozen valuable *murrhines* for him—then leave, after buying one plate for a trifling sum.

Nouveau riche Trimalchio, reported by Petronius, wanting the biggest and best of everything, suggests the familiar undiscriminating and ostentatious collector, a William Randolph Hearst, for example. Sulla brings J. P. Morgan to mind, to the extent that both were keen-eyed collectors who knew what they wanted and had the power to get it despite hell and high water. The connoisseurs Lucullus, Caesar and Agrippa recall another branch of the family, men like Henry C. Folger, Henry E. Huntington, and Harry Elkins Widener in whom innate good taste and a generous social outlook held sway over those ruthless and more primitive qualities latent in the collector's make-up. Even in Rome and in the America of the early twentieth century there were a few men of this sort.

DARK AGE IN THE WEST

"Out of the dusk a shadow,
Then a spark . . ."

JOHN BANISTER TABB

WHEN THE CYCLE fell dying, when the tides of vigor and the fire receded from the old world, then darkness came to Europe. At the vast base of Western tradition, the first great surge of man's aspiring had been spent. Wide flowering of intellect and living art declined; and so, as Greece had died, disintegration now devoured Rome, and the entire West slithered backward into an era of chaos.

Warfare was as common to that day as security was absent. There was little leisure for pursuit of the cultural arts, and it was small wonder that for the mere amenities of life enthusiasm waned. If there had been hours of freedom they would have availed little; for outside Italy few even of the landed noblemen could read or write, many of the simplest crafts were lost, and the fine arts were completely submerged. There were, in short, few things to collect and fewer men to see or appreciate what did exist.

A nobleman who possessed three leathern garments qualified as a rich man. A bed was a luxury. How then could one bother with such pleasant *divertissements* as books or antiques? And if one did bother, the full measure of one's reward was quite likely to be robbery, with, perhaps, one's own murder thrown in. Possessions, therefore, were often more of a liability than an asset, from any point of view—that is, if you were a common man who could not hope to rise above the class of your birth.

Certain types of rare and precious objects were accumulated by members of the upper classes, but even kings were more concerned with the intrinsic value of these treasures than with their artistic or sentimental merits. The costly gems, the cups of chased silver and the gold caskets studded with precious stones, the gem-encrusted ornaments and bejeweled weapons gathered by the Merovingian rulers, Clovis, Chilperic, Dagobert—these represented a form of rapidly convertible wealth easy of transport and concealment in time of necessity.

Centuries would roll by before such fair omens as the "Carolingian Renaissance" and the "Twelfth-Century Renaissance" appeared; before the true Renaissance could finally free the European collector from the fetters of medievalism and allow him to reach, in some respects even to overreach, the collecting monument created by the ancient Romans.

During these dark ages, the quest for mere security again became paramount in the minds and hearts of men. In an age when the entire social pattern was largely determined by a universal need for protection against innumerable adversaries, we find men collecting themselves into defensive groups in much the same way as they had done in the ancient days of the "large family." Eventually the medieval city—made up of individuals collected within a strongbox of walls—was developed as a successful attempt to meet the common problem of insecurity. The church, the manor, and later the guilds, furnished similar expressions of collective solution. But under such conditions the individual ceased to be important, ceased even to wish to be an individual. "Individualism" was too risky to be attractive.

Religion, although not identical with the state as it had been in the theocracies, reassumed political and social dominance, furnishing the ruling theme for every aspect of life; and so it was again the church which became the pre-eminent collector, its treasuries the greatest storehouses of precious things, of books and art, of curiosities and relics.

As had been the case in ancient Greece and elsewhere, it often happened that the wealth of an entire city might be stored within the church building for safekeeping, since only here could one be sure of sanctuary from violence. And as the early temples and houses of the priesthoods had once been school, library and museum in their communities, so now it was the cathedrals and convents that fulfilled these functions. Chiefly within the religious institutions, and largely for their benefit, again the art and literature of a period was created; only now it was the monks who, taking the place that had once been filled by priests and scribes, with painstaking labor succeeded in preventing the written word from being sucked into oblivion in the whirlpool of a prevailing political disorder.

Because they fitted well into the monastic scheme, books eventually became the most fruitful harvest of such medieval collectors as there were, but it was a harvest slow to reach maturity. Christianity had become the state religion of the Roman Empire in the fourth century. Most of the public libraries of Rome had been housed within the pagan temples, and when, in A.D. 392, these were officially closed, the libraries, too, were destroyed or so neglected that they disappeared, even to the recollection of their existence. Most Christians regarded the classic literature as hostile to their religion, and this attitude toward books in general was fostered by the asceticism of the early church. That certain classic manuscripts survived in monastic libraries until a later date was largely a matter of accident. Nevertheless, even in this murkiest period of the dark age, there was here and there a book collector whose passion for things of the mind enabled him to reconcile his acquisitive desires with the church doctrines. To the scholar-collector, if not to the common monk, it was obvious that all the threatened enlightenment of the ancient world was contained in books, and books became the main concern of these men.

Some of the early Christian leaders possessed small working libraries of Christian literature; and in the post-apostolic age, the church itself, says Ramona Bressie, exhibited:

". . . a simple impulse to collect and preserve literary material concerning the faith."

There were a few men like Cassiodorus (480–575), a Roman noble and great landowner, who held an official position at the court of Theodoric the Great. Despite his impeccable Christianity, Cassiodorus was unable to restrain his enthusiasm for the ancient writings, which he considered complemental, not hostile, to Christian literature. And so, on one of his estates in Calabria, where he had founded a monastery aspiringly named the *Vivarium,* he set about establishing the first medieval library, the presses of which, he declared, should properly contain, not only the Scriptures and the writings of the Church Fathers, but classic works on cosmography, geography, rhetoric and literature, as well. To this end, Cassiodorus became an energetic book hunter, and he inspired his associates with a like enthusiasm. The books in the nine presses of his library were carefully catalogued and arranged, and—unmistakable sign of the bibliophile—Cassiodorus paid marked attention to the appearance of his items, to their bindings and decorations.

Another book collector of the period was Isidore of Seville (*c.* 570–636), whose library of four to five hundred volumes was not to be surpassed for size, at least, until the far-off days of the Italian renaissance. It is Isidore who, in his *Soliloquia,* tells us that even in his day, unfavorable as it was to the sport of collecting, there existed a few enthusiasts who

> ". . . wish to have many books with fine and attractive bindings, and keep them in closed bookcases, never reading them nor letting others benefit from them."

In general, the puny book collections of the time were created under the auspices of cathedrals and monasteries, and were of a nature suitable to their habitat. The cathedral of S. Martino at Lucca could boast, in the ninth century, of no more than nineteen volumes, all abridgments from ecclesiastical commentaries. Nor was this an unusual paucity, since for centuries even the greatest of the religious institutions are said to have possessed ". . . far fewer books than many farmers of the present age."

Every monastery had its *scriptorium* for the copying of manuscripts, it is true, but the basic principle behind this was moralistic in character: the *scriptorium* provided work for the monks and kept them out of mischief. The production and collection of books was a secondary consideration, so much so, indeed, that older works were often destroyed in order to provide material for the manufacture of new ones. It was only the individual abbot of scholarly tastes who treasured and preserved books for the sake of the books themselves, men such as Lupus of Ferrières (805–860) who concerned himself chiefly with nonreligious works and who was constantly writing to Rome, to England, and to Germany for manuscripts of all sorts to add to his library: his surviving letters indicate not only the scholar but also the true amateur of possessive passion, with a typical enthusiasm for "variations."

The ninth century, when Lupus lived, witnessed a temporary revival of interest in book multiplication and collection, and such of the earlier

Latin works as are extant today have come down to us mainly in the form of copies made from fourth-, fifth- and sixth-century manuscripts (also copies) during this so-called Carolingian renaissance.* Named for Charlemagne, the period is dedicated to this king's effort in the revival of culture. Patronizing native crafts because he hoped to create among the Germanic tribes a cultural unity hitherto lacking among them in contrast to the binding unity of the Roman Empire, the Frankish monarch, first of a long line of collecting princes, showed himself in this, as in so much else, centuries ahead of his time.

For his day a man of rare education, Charlemagne pondered the general ignorance of his court and people, and to his capital at Aachen he summoned Alcuin, the English theologian and scholar. Under Alcuin's direction both a court library and a royal private collection were begun. Book hunters were despatched to Italy, and the Academy at Aachen soon became a mecca for scholars and copyists, the first of its kind in the north. Upon Charlemagne's death, however, the monarch's own books were, in accordance with his will, sold for the benefit of the poor. The small libraries gathered by his two successors, Louis the Pious and Charles the Bald, have also disappeared; for the ways of the Caesars had been forgotten, and there was no inkling of the latter-day sentiment that a royal collection should be passed on to the nation for the public benefit and the greater glory of the people.

During the Carolingian renaissance, the cathedral and monastic libraries grew apace; but from the end of the ninth century until the middle of the thirteenth, private collections practically disappeared, while in this period the number of books in the church libraries actually decreased. War, loans, fire, theft, and the intellectual decline of the monasteries all contributed to this retrogression. Italy, with her inherited store of old books, proved somewhat of an exception, for some of the collections in religious institutions in that country were guarded by competent librarians. There were Italian abbots who thought of book collecting first and of their other duties afterward, to the benefit of posterity. In Sicily and in southern Italy some private lay libraries continued to exist, and Italy was to remain the book mart of western Europe for a long time to come. In Germany and the north, however, the great

---

* The Carolingian renaissance is usually dated from 782 to the end of the ninth century.

monastic libraries lay fallow, waiting for the humanists of the Italian renaissance to rediscover their riches.

Meanwhile, throughout Europe another sort of collector was laying the base rocks for future museums and future science. As churches and monasteries became repositories for the finds of traveler, pilgrim, and later crusader, accumulations of religiously significant art objects, of relics and marvels and natural curiosities were forming in a way to recall the ancients with their pious gifts to the gods, or to prefigure latter-day amateurs and their donations to public museums.

The religious preoccupation of the age obviously determined the goal of this sort of collecting; but varying collector interests and individual temperament found some leeway to assert themselves even so. One type of traveler or crusader might bring home association pieces which also happened to be works of art—a rock crystal goblet that had once reposed in King Solomon's temple, a gold and jeweled cup that had belonged to the great king himself, or a cameo bearing the likeness of the Queen of Sheba. Pilgrims of an antiquarian turn of mind busied themselves, when they went to Rome, copying old Christian inscriptions; and because Rome was the holy city of the West, collections of these transcripts were deemed worthy of presentation to the abbeys. Men who were fascinated by natural curiosities, on the other hand, would bring back "thunderstones," "giant" bones and "giant" teeth (supposed to have survived from antediluvian days), "griffin" eggs, ostrich eggs, or tortoise shells.

The medieval church preserved these "marvels," just as the Greek and Roman temples had preserved them; and as the Greeks had attached an historical or mythological significance to similar objects,* so now many of the oddities were infused with a "relic" meaning, becoming, in the minds of their collectors, the bones of saints or the material survivals of miraculous happenings. Frequently, however, the attraction lay as much in the quality of rarity or oddity as it did in any superimposed religious significance, and the all-wise Church was shrewd enough to recognize

---

* Bronze Age weapons, for example, were thought by the Greeks to have been the arms of Homeric heroes—as some of them actually may have been. Other examples are numerous. The "bones of the monster to which Andromeda had been exposed" were to be seen at Joppa, and were later brought to Rome for exhibition. The Romans called such things *miracula*.

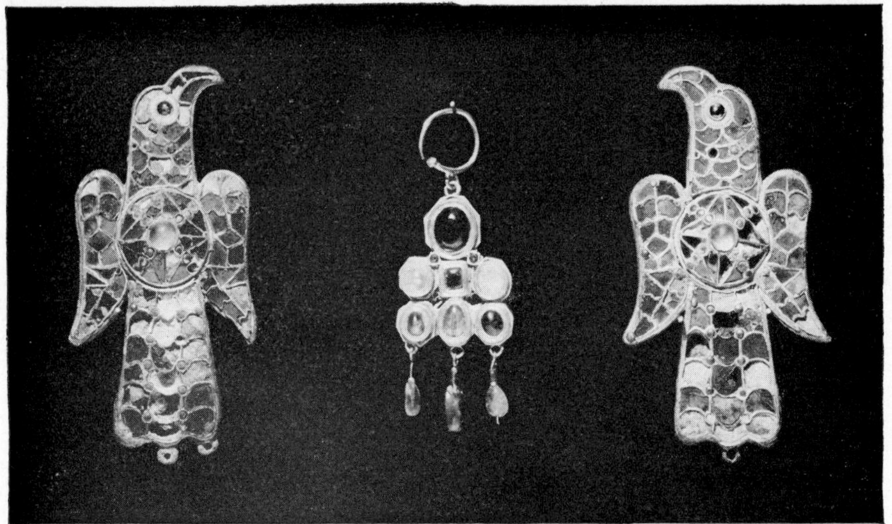

Walters Art Gallery, Baltimore

Early 6th-century Visigothic FIBULÆ *or buckles, and gold and jeweled earring, found at Estremadura, Spain; all thought to be part of same treasure.*

Walters Art Gallery, Baltimore

Reliquary CHASSE, *North French, c. 1180; low reliefs added in 13th century; once contained the relics of St. Amandus of 6th-century Flanders.*

OCCASIONAL LIBRARIES, RELIGIOUS RELICS, AND OBJECTS POSSESSING INTRINSIC VALUE CONSTITUTED THE CHIEF HARVEST OF SUCH MEDIEVAL EUROPEAN COLLECTORS AS THERE WERE.

this fact and to capitalize upon it. One medieval writer quoted by Murray tells how in his day, in certain churches, a variety of objects

". . . which cause admiration, and which are rarely seen, are accustomed to be suspended, that by their means the people may be drawn to the church and have their minds more affected."

Nevertheless, it was the true relic collection that was most highly prized, both by individuals and institutions, in this superstition-ridden age when all men, from the highest to the lowest, believed in the miraculous efficacy of such things. Among individuals, writes Murray,

". . . princes and ecclesiastics had collections of the relics of saints which they carried about from place to place in a reliquary, chest or cabinet."

There existed a trade in relics as extensive, and as ruthless, as the modern trade in art, while every church and monastery tried to outdo its rivals in the fame and extent of its own relic collection. Surprisingly un-Christian activities accompanied this collector-like competition among institutions bidding for fame and prestige. Violent quarrels flared between monasteries over the acquisition of certain highly coveted relics, and in extreme cases thievery and murder were not strangers to the pursuit of victory.

It made little difference that many of the relics were completely fantastic, like the "hair from the beard of Noah," which was exhibited at Corbie in the ninth century. The authenticity of such objects was seldom questioned except in the case of duplication, and faking of relics to supply the demand continued to exist through the early days of the renaissance.

In some places there was a tendency to specialize, to center the collection about specific personalities: thus the Abbey of St. Denis, which owned Solomon's cup and the Queen of Sheba cameo, also possessed what were supposed to be the king's actual foot and no less a trophy than the queen's arm.

Even in this field there was room for some display of individual taste, since included among the things venerated as "relics" were items ranging in character all the way from some beautifully wrought carving or handsome bit of craftsmanship that happened to have a religious association, to the thumb of St. Bartholomew, the shift of the Virgin, or a phial of sand or water brought from the Holy Land.

So deeply had the church dye saturated all medieval activity that no matter what inherent interest might stimulate the tentative collector, whether love of beauty, reverence for the past, or curiosity about natural phenomena, all collecting of nonreligious objects was deviously conducted in a manner calculated not only to fool the carping observer but even to disguise his true motive from the collector himself.

A curious story illustrates this. It is recorded of Henry, twelfth-century Bishop of Winchester, that, having had some trouble with the Pope, he journeyed to Rome to see whether he might not be able to patch up matters with his superior. While in the holy city, Henry was seen buying a considerable quantity of antique sculpture and since there had been, as yet, no church-sanctioned pagan revival, such goings-on seemed less than fitting a bishop. The irregularity was so striking, in fact, that it caused one irreverent and amused grammarian to confront the long-bearded English churchman with Horace's classic quip: "Damasippus is a madman for purchasing antique statues." Even the relatively enlightened twelfth century demanded from Henry a better answer than a shrug, and so that he might continue with his "sacrilegious" behavior he stood squarely in the light of piety: he was buying the statues, so he said, to protect the money-loving people of the city from their own weakness, for it appeared to him that these modern Romans were showing signs of worshiping pagan idols in more ways than one!

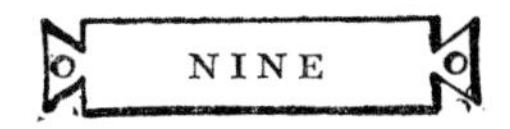

LIGHT FROM THE EAST

"Beautiful things from all over the country were gathered together thick as clouds."

CHANG YEN-YÜAN

WHILE THE BENIGHTED Europeans were searching miserably through the age of darkness, there lay, immeasurably beyond their ken, another world wherein a race of collectors, enlightened and tranquil, were already making a fine art of their pursuit.

That land was China, to whose ancient fount the men of young Japan came eagerly to drink, learning the intoxicating pleasure of collecting. Not until much later, when the "Age of Discovery" revealed to a startled Europe the fabulous and unsuspected riches of the Orient, were western collectors to know anything about their eastern brothers. But at last, when the time came for these two worlds to meet, western men would find on the shores of the Orient a fascinating treasure store to which they would ceaselessly return with delight.

Even in the first century of our era, some five hundred years before the date traditionally assigned to the founding of the Japanese Empire, Chinese influence had reached Japan through Korea; and the Japanese even then were showing themselves eager to obtain the products of Chinese wealth and skill—such things as swords, mirrors, jewels, golden ornaments, silken textiles. By the seventh century, the little people of the islands, always the good imitators, had taken over Chinese culture wholesale (including the Chinaman's passion for collecting) and were adapting it to their own ends. Because of the rigid Japanese class system, however, and because of the extreme poverty of the mass of the people, collecting on any notable scale became in Japan an exclusively royal and aristocratic privilege (temple collections excepted) and so it was to remain for more than a thousand years, until the rise of a wealthy bourgeoisie under the Tokugawa Shogunate, in the seventeenth century, altered the picture and produced a group of everyday collectors much like those of our own society.

Extensive art and *virtu* collections were already being formed in the eighth century, a period which has been called "the blossom time of Japanese civilization." Of the treasures then assembled, many passed into the Buddhist temples and monasteries as gifts, the repetition of an already familiar phenomenon, but the mansions of great families were also being filled with Chinese importations—books, pictures, ornaments of all sorts—which were regarded not so much for their intrinsic value as for luxurious and pleasure-giving qualities.

It was in this century that the Emperor Shōmu (724–749) formed that marvelous collection which is housed today, still intact, in a repository known as Shōsōin. Dedicated to the Buddha of the Tōdaiji by Shōmu's widow in 756, the collection includes such a wealth of variety that enumeration of its contents might sound like the Hearst catalogue. Manuscripts and paintings, weapons and musical instruments, lacquer and textiles, pottery, metal work and vessels of glass, of both native and foreign origin, had all been assembled in quantity by this early emperor. Many of his importations came from as far away as Greece, Persia and Central Asia, and there were even native reproductions of some of the more exotic objects.

Shōmu was but the first of many ambitious Nipponese collectors. Throughout the subsequent Heian period (794–1185) the Japanese aristocracy remained a luxury-loving, art-patronizing group; literary collections were formed under imperial auspices; while the Buddhist monasteries acquired an ever-increasing store of artistic treasure, so that later, during Japan's turbulent early feudal period, the church, here as in the West, would keep alive the arts through social chaos and transition.

As in Europe, the Japanese feudal period grew out of a weakened central power and the increasing strength of local families and leaders. Eventually, the elimination contest fought between rival houses resulted in a return of national unification and centralized power under former military generals, the *shoguns;* and these dictators set up heredi-

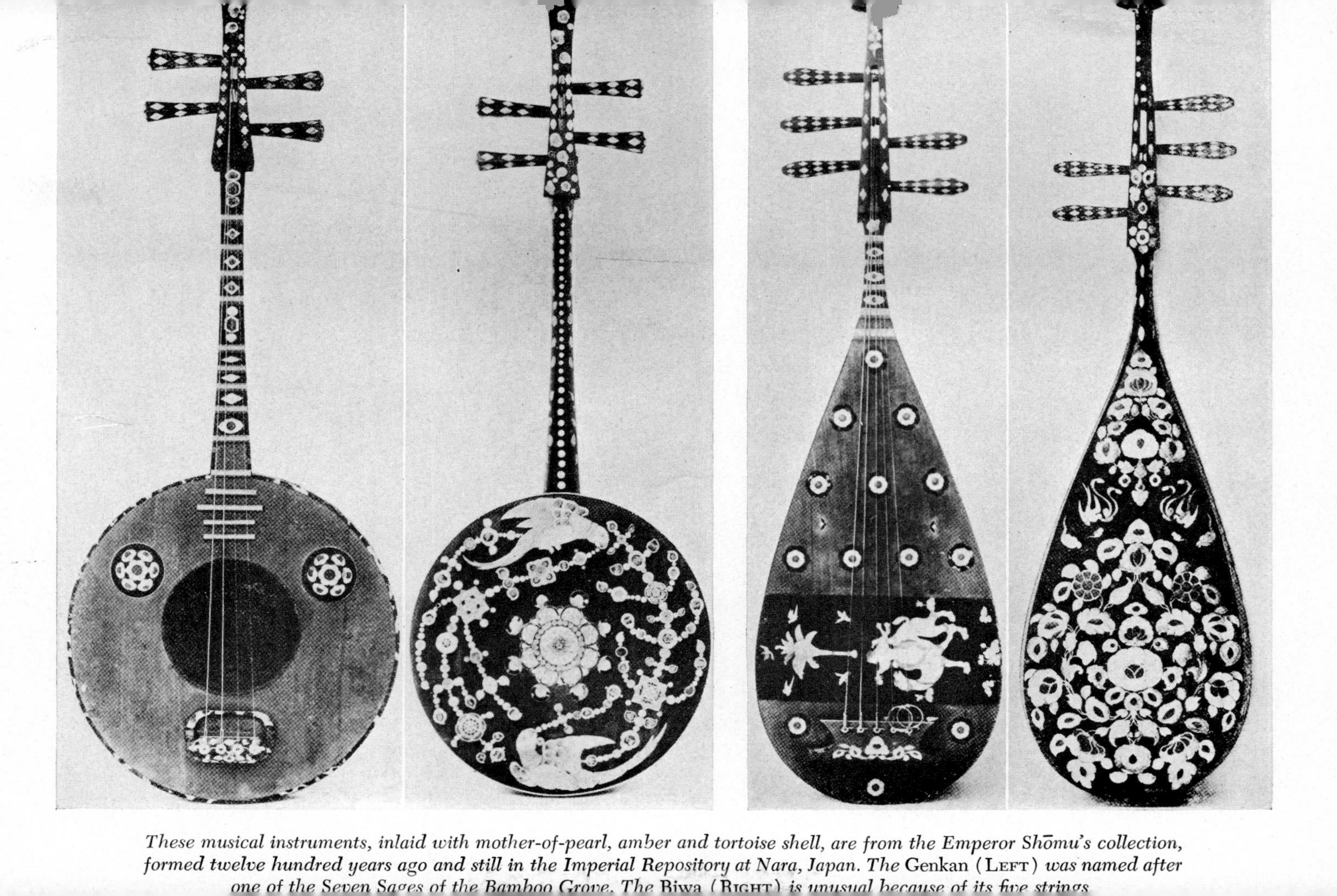

These musical instruments, inlaid with mother-of-pearl, amber and tortoise shell, are from the Emperor Shōmu's collection, formed twelve hundred years ago and still in the Imperial Repository at Nara, Japan. The Genkan (LEFT) *was named after one of the Seven Sages of the Bamboo Grove. The* Biwa (RIGHT) *is unusual because of its five strings.*

tary lines of their own which were to become ruling houses in everything but name and religious significance.

Among the founders of this new regime we again encounter collecting directed toward the attainment of prestige. Lacking the steadying bulwark of inherited right, these upstarts felt, in the beginning at least, a need to prove themselves in every way worthy of the high position they had usurped by arms or political genius. They desired to own fine things, particularly those of a cultural nature, because, as Sansom says, such things furnished "the symbols of success, the means of ostentation needed to satisfy the pride of men newly risen to power and riches."

Yet here, as elsewhere, the turn which accumulation and display might take depended somewhat on the temperament of the individual, becoming, in the hands of the mediocre, a senseless sort of self-indulgence, for the more intelligent and sensitive, a way toward personal attainment and social conscience.

Exemplifying the first type there was Takatoki, one of the Hojo regents (*c.* 1333), who collected some four to five thousand dogs, developing such a predilection for them that he would accept them in payment of taxes. He fed them on fish and fowl, had them carried in palanquins on their daily outings, and provided for their accommodation kennels with gold and silver decorations. We shall encounter his fatuous prototype more than once among princes of the Italian renaissance.

On the other hand there was Yoshimasa (1438–1480), the Ashikaga shogun, who patronized all the arts and who, according to Lafcadio Hearn, "grew into so refined a connoisseur that the pieces selected by him and his associates are the most coveted prizes of collectors today." His kind, too, is richly represented among renaissance rulers. Yoshimasa gathered about him a group of experts (including the Zen monk, Shukō, who, in matters of taste and judgment, was regarded as an unrivaled connoisseur) to assist in forming a splendid collection of porcelain and paintings. To house his treasures, Yoshimasa built the famous Silver Pavilion; and many generations of Japanese collectors have since jealously guarded the inheritance, being careful from one generation to the next that each item descended from it be vouched for by "solemn certificate," and, in times of political disturbance, giving first thought to the protection of those precious masterpieces.

It was Shukō, the monk, who was the accredited author of the "tea ceremony." Although based on an almost ascetic worship of beauty, this gentle rite from its inception fostered collecting by the very nature of its requirements. Sansom describes it thus:

"In a small room bare of all but a few beautiful things, tea is prepared and drunk according to a strict rule, and the guests discuss gravely the merits of some object of art, perhaps one of the utensils they are using, a bowl of which the glaze harbors rich lights, or an effortless-seeming picture on the wall, or a poem or an arrangement of flowers."

Despite the simplicity inherent in this idea, rivalry inevitably developed around it among many of the early Japanese hosts. Each man took pride in having something more beautiful or more rare to display at his session than any of his predecessors had had; and among its wealthier practitioners the ceremony became an excuse for extravagance and overelaboration. It seemed more important to own pots, cups, vases, that were unique or uncommon than to possess the merely fine esthetic examples; more desirable to impress the guest with one's acumen or superior purchasing power than to afford pleasure to mind and vision—and once more we see the snob collector rearing his head beside the true amateur.*

In China, meanwhile, a mature and more varied set of collecting pursuits had already evolved.

Even in the first century B.C., a hundred or so years after the great burning of the books, the Imperial Library had contained more than eleven thousand volumes, and for paintings and calligraphies the Han emperors built special halls.

The fall of the Han dynasty in A.D. 221 was followed by long years of partition and strife, but five hundred years later under Ming Huang, the "Brilliant Emperor" of China's Golden Age (the T'ang dynasty, 618–907), the library increased five-fold. During the following three centuries China enjoyed unparalleled prosperity and culture, and her merchants and Buddhist pilgrims habitually carried home Sanskrit books and Buddhist relics in much the same spirit as the men of the European renaissance were later to comb their own continent and the lands of the Near East for the remains of Greece and Rome.

The good face of Chinese collecting has borne many wounds. It was

---

* Nevertheless, the amateur also survived; and later the possibilities of this Japanese invention were eagerly taken up by thousands of European and American collectors.

not plain sailing for the early collectors, and the great collections of no other land have undergone so many heartbreaking vicissitudes. There was more than one book-burning episode in Chinese history, and war, flood and fire periodically added to the havoc. Chang Yen-yüan, in his *Records of Paintings in Various Ages,* gave a condensed account of the numerous disasters which had, even in his day, resulted in the disappearance of most of the early masterpieces. He speaks chiefly of the imperial collections because they had contained many of the best pictures; but there were numerous Chinese amateurs besides emperors, and Chang himself came of a noted family of collectors.

The characteristic traits of collectors in other lands and other walks of life were exhibited by many of the royal Chinese amateurs. Kao Ti (479–483) of the Southern Ch'i dynasty had his most valuable treasures recorded and classified, not by periods but according to merit,

". . . and when he was free from affairs of state in the mornings and evenings, he took them out and enjoyed them."

Liang Wu Ti (502–547), who added many rare and valuable things to the imperial store of art,

". . . was always trying to complete the collection."

And the sacrificial ardor of the fanatical extremist flamed in the person of Yuan-ti (522–555) who, when forced to abdicate, brought together all the most famous pictures, calligraphies and classical books (a thousand cartloads, we are told, comprising some two hundred forty thousand pieces in all) and ordered them burned to thwart the grasping hands of his successor. According to the story, Yuan-ti wanted to add himself to the flames and was proceeding with this plan when, at the last moment, he was hauled out by the protesting ladies of his court.

When the Sui conquered Ch'ên (589), restoring a semblance of political order to the land, two official recorders were appointed to take care of such ancient paintings as remained, and they succeeded in assembling more than eight hundred items. Sui Yang-ti (606–616) built two repositories at the Eastern Capital, one, "The Excellent Model Tower," for the conservation of old writings, and another, "The Tower of Treasured Relics," for the storing of old pictures. Yet even as the tower waited, destruction ran to meet the treasures, which were being moved by boat this time; one of the vessels sank, and only a fraction of the precious cargo could be rescued.

Thus it was that at the beginning of the T'ang period there were only some three hundred pieces left in the imperial collection. And did malignant fate at this point go home satisfied? Not at all. The Empress Wu-hou (684–705) was induced to have some of the masterpieces "restored." Instead of restoration, however, excellent copies were made by some scoundrel who made off with the originals. These found their way into the hands of a certain prince who, in a sudden access of panic, burned them all, lest he be discovered in his misappropriation! Another T'ang ruler, unlike his predecessors, cared so little for art that he gave away his paintings to his favorite court ladies, who straightway proceeded to sell them. Since some of these masterpieces came to rest in the collections of private connoisseurs, however, this was far less calamitous than the previous events.

The emperors of the succeeding dynasty, the Northern Sung (960–1127), were patrons as well as collectors of art. Greatest collector of them all was Hui Tsung, who, like Nabonidus of Babylon, could not match his superlative collectorship with an equal political ability and so lost his empire to the fierce invader. Hui Tsung's magnificent collection—the most extensive that China had ever seen, and one that has not since been surpassed—was almost entirely destroyed by the Chin Tartars who sacked the emperor's capital and forced the house of Sung to flee into the south.

Yet despite the irreparable loss of the collection itself, we know, ironically enough, what it contained, for the catalogue, describing six thousand three hundred and ninety-six paintings by two hundred and thirty-one masters, miraculously survived the Tartar holocaust.

The Chinese had long been interested in collecting those survivals of the past which might cast light on their own history. It was in the tenth and eleventh centuries, however, under the Sung dynasty, that archaeology became a special branch of study in China and the favored concern of Chinese collectors. Although at the beginning of this period there existed a collection of antiquities in the imperial treasury, the widespread fashion seems to have been launched by private individuals, scores of whom are mentioned by name in contemporary works on "ancient objects." One illustrated volume of the time even places beside the picture or description of each item discussed the name of the respective owners. The harvest in this field included antique bronzes,

Photo, courtesy Fogg Museum of Art, Cambridge

Detail from a landscape scroll, said to be the most famous work of the painter-collector-Emperor, Hui Tsung. From the Imperial Palace Collection at Peiping.

stones, bells, tripods, ancient ritual vessels, ancient household utensils, ancient furniture, pottery, wooden tablets, and rubbings from ancient bronze or stone inscriptions.

Hui Tsung was inspired to create his own extraordinary collection of antiquities, and with that scholarly approach typical of the age, the emperor appointed an eminent archaeologist, Wang Fu, to the task of cataloguing the imperial collection. A thirty-volume work, *Illustrations of the Ancient Objects in Hsüan-Ho Hall,* was the colossal result of this savant's five-year labor. In a short time, the collection had sprung from five hundred items to more than six thousand; and when all the paintings, calligraphies, ancient jades,* public and private seals, tripods, stone drums, and so on, were brought together and recorded again between the years 1119 and 1125, it is said that the entire collection included more than ten thousand pieces.

If these figures are, as is sometimes suspected, slightly exaggerated, there can be no doubt of the remarkable wealth and variety of the material. Wang Fu himself ascribed one hundred and forty-eight of the bronze vessels to the Shang period (1766–1122 B.C.), making them over two thousand years old at the time they came into Hui Tsung's possession. The oldest items were the ones most highly prized, and articles as recent as those of the Ch'in (221–206 B.C.) and Han (206 B.C.–A.D. 221) periods were not even included in the catalogue unless distinguished by some particularly unusual feature! Indeed, this was one of the finest collections ever drawn together, and when it was torn to pieces human culture lost some of its richest blood.

The irrepressible Chinese amateurs, however, were not long dismayed even by so major a catastrophe as the Tartar invasion. Under the Southern Sung dynasty (1127–1280), in the new capital of Lin-an (now Hangchow), "inspiring collections" of bronzes, paintings, manuscripts and jades were again created, great libraries were formed anew, and the Emperor Shao-Hsing succeeded in acquiring imperial treasures that almost rivaled Hui Tsung's. For, be it remembered, China's art was long

---

* To the ancient Chinese, Fitzgerald tells us, jade had been "the most precious of stones—a sacred material containing the quintessence of virtue—its use confined to ritual objects or to ornaments having a religious (protective) significance." Long after this exclusive significance had disappeared, Chinese collectors valued jade objects so highly that they might spend years searching for a single piece, and would sometimes pay as much as $100,000 for a necklace made of the precious and beautiful stuff.

and it was virile; no matter what befell, there was hidden in town or in distant province always more treasure for the searching hand.

In this period, China was once more split into two parts, with the Chin or Kin Tartars ruling in the north and the Chinese Sung in the south; yet after the initial war was concluded, this resulted in so peaceable an arrangement that the rival kingdoms and the two royal houses were quite willing to carry on trade with each other. In the north it soon became known to the semibarbaric invaders that both rulers and officials of the southern kingdom were soft in the head about certain kinds of old rubbish and would pay fantastic prices for such things. The shrewd ruffians were glad to accommodate their former victims, and in this way many of the treasures rifled from Hui Tsung's great Hsüan-Ho Hall or from the homes of private connoisseurs eventually found their way back into Chinese collections.

It was in 1260 that an heroic Chinese general, Lu Hsiu-fu, rather than surrender to the newest spring tide of Mongols then pouring irresistibly over China, jumped to his death in the sea, bearing upon his back the boy emperor, last of the Sungs.

Thirty-five years later, three merchants of Venice forced their way over the long reaches of two continents, back to their native city. They were ragged and weary from as many years of difficult travel, but they carried bundles of precious stones that were to keep them all the rest of their lives in comfort. Maffeo, Nicolo, and Marco Polo soon made themselves notorious in Venice by their insistence upon tales of the fabulous wealth and advanced culture of a people over whom, they said, the

---

IN THE FORERANK of Collectordom Count the Chinese Collectors of the Sung Dynasty (A.D. 960–1279), Scholarly Amateurs of Ancient Objects Such as These. *1) Bronze* ting *or ceremonial vessel of the Shang Dynasty (1766–1122* B.C.*), formerly in the Tuan Fang Collection. An unusually fine example, this antiquarian's prize shows evidence of having been carefully hand polished for generations. 2) Dried lacquer head of the T'ang Dynasty (*A.D. *618–907), China's "Golden Age"; gift of The Orientals to the Art Institute. 3) Bronze mirror of the Later Han Dynasty (*A.D. *25–220), with good luck inscription; in the Nickerson Collection. 4) Pottery Pilgrim Bottle of the T'ang Dynasty. Its decoration, purely Greek and probably copied from a repoussé silver flask of the Antioch type, is illustrative of the constant intercourse between Orient and Occident which prevailed at this time. 5) Covered bronze jar with silver and gold inlay, middle 5th to 3rd cent.* B.C.*; like the* ting, *in the Lucy Maud Buckingham Collection.*

1 2 3

4 5

From collections in The Art Institute, Chicago

(*For legend, see facing page.*)

great Mongol, Kublai Khan, now ruled,* and among whom they themselves claimed to have spent the better part of the past quarter century. Such vaporings amused the home folk greatly, for to them it was unthinkable that any land could possibly boast of greater prosperity, of more progressive institutions, of cleverer practical inventions than those possessed by the Venetian Republic, and if there were indeed such a land, it certainly could not be far-off half-mythical Cathay.

Wherefore it came about that Marco, the youngest of the Polos, when he went so far as to describe the wonders of the East in a lengthy book "full of numbers large and marvelous," was scornfully nicknamed "Marco Millions," and that, after his death in 1323, his co-citizens created a new carnival-figure which, dressed like a clown and bearing the same derisive name, was destined to entertain *hoi polloi* of Venice with tales that were obviously, ridiculously tall. More than two centuries had yet to pass before Portuguese navigators were really to open the eyes of the Western world to the glories, and exploitable possibilities, of the East. In that space of time the Mongol dynasty (1260–1368) would already have gone the way of all alien conquerors of China, and another native house, the Ming (1368–1644), would be firmly established upon the throne of the Flowery Kingdom.

If the Venetians of Marco Polo's time could laugh heartily at the possibility of a civilized China, it was equally true that the Chinese considered all Europeans barbarians. In their eyes, even the developments of the next two hundred years in Europe—the period between the tentative and the final discoveries of East by West—were of no significance whatsoever. Yet it was this period that forged the true connecting link between the modern and the ancient worlds, and which before its close created both material and intellectual bonds between Europe and Asia, as well as between those continents and new America.

Swept along in the general cycle of European rebirth, collecting also was to achieve astonishing proportions: out of the renaissance, particularly as it took shape in Italy, would stem all important western collecting activities up to the present day.

---

* The Polos were the bearers of greetings from the Great Khan to the Pope; but by the time they reached Italy, three and a half years after their departure from China, both Kublai and the Pope were dead.

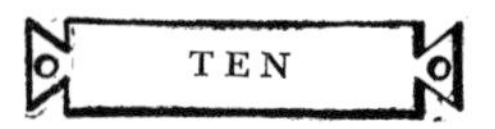

THE ITALIAN RENAISSANCE: REBIRTH OF WESTERN COLLECTING

". . . the all-sided man."

Early in the fourteenth century, Richard de Bury gave unconscious voice to a changing attitude when, as a churchman, he permitted himself to write:

"Man is naturally fond of two things, freedom from control and some pleasure in his activity."

Such a statement of individualism would have been almost unthinkable in the depths of the Middle Ages.

A dawning social equality, in an era of merchant princes and a well-to-do middle class, gave many men means whereby they might hope to gratify in possession certain newly awakened desires. From the very beginning of the fourteenth century, the rich burghers of Cologne, for example, began collecting such objects of art as would increase the comfort and luxury of their own homes—woven tapestries, stained glass, heraldic signs, and reliefs which were immured above their fireplaces, and toward the end of the fifteenth century they were ordering portraits of themselves for the further adornment of their rooms. As the church declined as an all-dominating and convincing influence, curiosity, individual and unhampered, rose like Jack's beanstalk; and objective inquiry and subjective enjoyment, flower and fruit of this rushing growth, pushed forth mightily.

All these changes bid collecting be bold again, while the true glory of the period, a certain large spirit that characterized it, tended to develop a type of collector particularly sympathetic. For although we encounter as much ruthless reaching for power in the renaissance as we did in ancient Rome, we find also sincere first enthusiasm, youthful and aspiring search for knowledge and personal development, and a genuine love of beauty unadulterated by overrefinement and snobbish imitativeness.

Renaissance collectors were closer to the sources of creativeness than the Romans had been: they were more like the Greeks, in that a love of beauty and a vivid mental alertness were innate in their very natures. In so far as ambition existed among them as collectors (it was, of course, quite otherwise in politics) it was usually an intellectual rather than a social ambition, representing a desire to possess the tangible evidences of a newly discovered and high ideal, not only because possession of such things might reflect glory upon the owner, but also because through possession the evidence could be better observed, studied and enjoyed. It is this leaven which explains the paradoxical lack of parvenu spirit among renaissance collectors, a lack that is the more surprising because the period, particularly in Italy, was itself full of actual parvenus in a political and social sense.

Overtones of the extraordinary renaissance approach to collecting often make themselves heard where least expected. Even the corrupt and egotistical Galeazzo Maria Sforza, Duke of Milan (1466–76), was "sufficiently the child of his time" that, after visiting the Medici collections he could say, "In comparison with these, gold and silver lose their value." And King Christian of Denmark, who, visiting the Medici collections at about the same time (1471), was particularly interested in the manuscripts, gave perfect expression to the wholly sincere spirit of the age when he declared: "These are the true treasures of princes!"

As soon as literature ceased to be created exclusively in the service of the divine and began to concern itself somewhat with the earthly scene and with human problems, more and more people found themselves interested in it. Libraries began to emerge from the monasteries and were soon being re-established in private homes.

Early in the fourteenth century, in England, Guy, Earl of Warwick, formed a rather frivolous collection of French novels; a certain John of London left a legacy of eighty books, of which only three were theological; and a simple monk, named Thomas Arnold, was specializing in light literature and in works having to do with the history of books.

In France, the great university of the Sorbonne was founded when Robert de Sorbonne established, in 1257, a house for poor theological students and left his possessions, including his books, to the masters and students. His collection was chiefly of the old-fashioned kind, scriptures and works of the church fathers, but his friends, and the scholars and students who soon afterward followed his generous example—increasing the Sorbonne library to more than a thousand volumes by the end of the century—added works on law, medicine and philosophy. One of these donors, Gérard of Abbeville, gave almost three hundred volumes; more than most religious institutions could have claimed in medieval days.

Now kings and nobles of England and queens of France were rediscovering the joys of book collecting, and their small but carefully chosen libraries contained exquisitely decorated and illuminated manuscripts, works on history and astronomy, romances and books of chivalry, as well as the more familiar religious fare.

The greatest bibliophile of this early period, however, was still a churchman, and, like the antique-collecting Bishop of Winchester, he was an Englishman. Richard Aungerville de Bury (1287–1345) was the emergent modern—or better, the universal—collector, surprisingly full-fledged, having quite cast aside the medieval disguise of ecclesiastic motivation. His well-rounded life, based both in the church and in statecraft, richly served his natural collecting proclivities. Successively this man was tutor to Edward III, Treasurer Royal, Lord Privy Seal, Ambassador to Rome, and Bishop of Durham. Widely traveled, the list of men he knew on the continent ran a remarkable gamut, and he numbered such notables as Petrarch among his personal friends. Wherever he went, on whatever mission, he found time to search for books, books and ever more books. They fascinated him, and fortunately he found it unnecessary to hide this fact, for he would have encountered considerable difficulty in doing so: it was said that he owned more volumes than all the other bishops of England together, that five wagons could hardly hold all the books he insisted on taking with him when he went on a journey, and that his private rooms were always so full of books lying about that it was difficult to move without stepping on one of them and thereby incurring the bibliophile's not uncertain displeasure.

Richard de Bury knew and dealt with booksellers in France, Germany and Italy as well as in England. He obtained books through private individuals "of both sexes and of every rank and position," as he himself tells us; and in his capacity as an influential churchman, he exchanged favors for books with members of the mendicant orders. His own house harbored a staff of copyists and illuminators, and there a careful catalogue of his collection was compiled, a catalogue which shows that his preference for old volumes did not exclude contemporary works.

From his own writings it is obvious that his love of books found the scholar second to the collector; comparatively speaking he was not a great scholar at all, yet he cherished books with that personal intensity which no one familiar with collectors can fail to recognize. Urging that all books should be well cared for, it hurt this man of the world with an almost physical violence to see some thoughtless lout of a student forcing bindings for convenience, dropping crumbs and worse on the pages, or trimming the margins in order to obtain writing parchment; and against such abuses he inveighed passionately in one of the most picturesque and graphic chapters of his own work, *Philobiblon.* And would this amateur lend his books? Yes, but his theories on this ponderous question were keyed to the surety that a borrowed book be returned. He counted price as nothing in the face of a volume desired, and the gift of a book was admitted by him to be a sure way to his favor. Before the bookstalls of Paris he went into rapt ecstasies, and he counted that city a veritable heaven on earth because one could find so many books there. Indeed, in spirit his *Philobiblon* might have been written by any modern bibliomaniac, and it still makes appealing reading to one who has a feeling either for books or for collecting.

Richard de Bury was, however, unusual both for his time and his place. For several centuries there would be more men like him in any one Italian city than in all of England: it was in Italy that book and art collecting became, from the fourteenth century on, the major preoccupation or the pleasant hobby of scores of men in widely varying walks of life; and there princes and popes, prelates and poets, doctors and lawyers, wool merchants and bankers and many obscure citizens gave themselves over to this passion, often devoting most of their energies and their entire fortunes to its demands.

In speaking of renaissance collectors we have confined ourselves chiefly to Italy, the country in which the "rebirth" took on its most characteristic and highly developed form. From this period on, because collecting now becomes increasingly prevalent and complex throughout much of the western world, a single country has been selected as the main prototype of each period. After Italy comes France, followed by England, then America, each representing a major development in the modern cycle of collecting.

It is, of course, understood that there were many collectors of similar types in countries which have been almost entirely omitted, among them Spain, the Netherlands, Russia, and the German and central European states. Germany, the Low Countries and the nations of central Europe followed roughly the pattern that will be traced in the collecting activities of Italy, France, England and the United States. In Spain, because the people as a whole remained at a very low economic ebb and never entirely emerged from the medieval pattern of church and state control in which they were wed, there was little general collecting, although there were great collections in the hands of royalty, the nobility and a few institutions. Actually, for generations Spain has sold to the collecting field, buying little. As for Russia, there were, in pre-Soviet days, a few great collections. The Soviet Union has sold some of them, and presumably its own collecting era lies ahead.

Perhaps because book hunting had never been as completely eclipsed as had other forms of collecting, it was the first to be revived in force. The new individualism, the new interest in learning, classic learning in particular, all played a part in its restoration, while special circumstances of the times required that any renaissance book lover be a true collector if he were to collect at all. During the period which preceded the invention of printing it was not enough that a man who wished to form a library, whether for use or for show, should possess sufficient funds with which to make purchases. He must also have had a definite plan of action, boundless enthusiasm, enduring perseverance. From the moment that he gave serious entertainment to such a project he embarked, of necessity, upon a treasure hunt, for books were not then to be bought in bookstores at a ducat or two. They had to be hunted out, and more often than not the hunt was as full of drama, difficulty and suspense as the most fantastic piece of fiction.

Manuscripts had to be obtained from the Near East, from the north, from obscure monasteries or from great ones fallen into decay, and long, sometimes perilous journeys were entailed. An elaborate system of agents and literary spies filled the scene, for it was not only the known works which were sought, but the hitherto unknown ones as well—Latin or Greek classics the very names of which had been forgotten for a thousand years, only to be revealed now through a hint here or a mention there in other recently rediscovered works. For such lost or forgotten books the religious institutions of Europe were ransacked, and when some forlorn, dusty manuscript was unearthed the triumph was as great as in the discovery of any treasure in gems.

Sometimes the find could be purchased. Not infrequently it was stolen. Little it mattered to the finder, so long as he obtained the prize. Some of the quests, like the search for the lost books of Livy, endured for generations and spread into distant lands without success, now raising, now dashing the hopes of one book hunter after another.

Many of these men, the poets and scholars especially, sought books so ardently in part because they intended to make practical use of them; but even where the formation of a working library was the ultimate objective, the peculiar considerations of sentiment and conduct which govern the collector were easily discernible. Boccaccio (1313–75) did not scruple to rummage through a neglected monastery in search of manuscript prizes. Petrarch (1304–74), who sought books definitely in order to use them, wanted to own copies of Homer and Plato in the Greek, although he could not read a word of that language; and he liked the volumes he acquired to be in the most beautiful format available.

The humanist scholars themselves devoted months and years to the arduous search and excelled not only as detectives but as shrewd bargainers as well. One of the most successful collectors among them was Poggio Bracciolini (1380–1459). Befriended and treated as a son by the great collector, Niccolò Niccoli, Poggio was later aided in his literary ferreting by the bibliophilic Pope Nicholas V. Long in the papal service, he had access to many of the northern convents and was one of the few Italians of his day to visit England. Rare manuscripts were constantly brought to light by his efforts, which were so tireless that:

"Nothing prevents him," wrote a contemporary, in classical vein, "from obtaining the masterpieces of literature, neither the cold or snow of winter, nor the length and inconvenience of the journey."

He was among the many who seemed for a while to have caught the scent of Livy's elusive works, and although here he too failed, among his finds were the texts of Lucretius, Columella, Vitruvius, and one of Cicero's lost orations.

Probably because Latin had so long been the language of the church, Latin works were at first more widely sought than Greek, but with the growth of the humanist movement the latter came rapidly into their own. One of the scholars to study the older language was Filelfo (1398–1481), and nothing less would content him than a sojourn in Byzantium (Constantinople) itself. Starting out in 1419, he journeyed for five months to reach his goal, and after eight years in the East he returned with an impressive collection of Greek books, including the works of such men as Aristotle, Strabo, Herodotus, Thucydides, Demosthenes, Hesiod and Euripides.

A quarter of a century later, the threat of Mohammedan Turkish invasion quickened the search for Greek books, and there was then a lively scramble to the territories of the Eastern Empire for the sake of invaluable literary treasure. One diligent book hunter, Giovanni Aurispa (*c.* 1370–1459), who had been Apostolic Secretary under Pope Eugene IV, at this time saved many precious classical texts from destruction; and Cardinal Bessarion (*c.* 1395–1472), a Greek prelate in whom "patriotism was mingled with a zeal for letters," managed to collect, at great personal sacrifice, hundreds of old manuscripts, both pagan and Christian. It was the aim of Bessarion to preserve these until Greece should once more be freed from bondage, and with this in view he succeeded in inducing the Venetian government to erect a special building for his collection, much of which is still in the *Biblioteca Marciana.*

Not even the dread plague could make these renaissance enthusiasts forget their passion for books, and when the scourge temporarily forced prince or pope from a pest-ridden city, it was not uncommon for translators and copyists to be included in the party, for such men were invaluable.

It was in the nature of things that book collecting, until and even long after the invention of printing, should have consisted as much in hiring copyists to make more books as in finding or buying manuscripts already in existence. For this reason the translating of texts and the transcribing of manuscripts, particularly of Greek works, had become in itself a highly paid profession to which needy scholars were, on occasion, glad to turn. The renaissance *scrittori* * were honored only to a somewhat less degree than had been the scribes in Egypt and the calligraphers in China. Copyists * formed an important part of the staff of every vendor of manuscripts, and book dealing prospered again as a business just as it had in late Greek and Roman days.

Of the renaissance book dealers, the most famous, Vespasiano da Bisticci, the Florentine (1421–98) brings to mind such internationally famous figures of our own day as Bernard Quaritch, the Rosenbachs, and, in the art world, Vollard and the Duveens. Vespasiano, who had correspondents and purchasing agents stationed throughout Europe, and who received orders from collectors in Germany, Hungary, France, Spain and England, catered to most of the famous amateurs of his generation. His good friend, Pope Nicholas V, was only one of the pontiffs who made use of this broker's services, and he was employed by both Cosimo de' Medici and Federigo of Urbino, owners of two of the finest libraries in Italy.

Like his successors of a later time, Vespasiano greatly enjoyed his contacts with celebrities and wrote down his observations so fully that we owe much of our knowledge of collecting methods and attitudes in fifteenth-century Italy to him. The following passage which paraphrases certain information proudly retailed by Vespasiano himself, casts an illuminating light on the problems confronting even the wealthiest bibliophiles of that time, and it also reveals how the dealer made an "honest penny" when asked to be of assistance:

"When Cosimo de' Medici was in a hurry to form a library for his favorite foundation, the Badia below Fiesole," writes Jacob Burckhardt, "he sent for Vespasiano, and received from him the advice to give up all thoughts of purchasing books, since those which were worth getting could not be had easily, but rather to make use of the copyists; whereupon Cosimo bargained to pay him so much a day, and Vespasiano, with forty-five writers under him, delivered two hundred volumes in twenty-two months. The catalogue of the

---

* As between the *scrittori* and the *copisti, scrittore* was the more honorable title, being usually reserved for those copyists who understood Greek.

works to be copied was sent to Cosimo by Nicholas V, who wrote it with his own hand."

Under such conditions of production, the gathering of two hundred volumes in twenty-two months would, even in the eyes of a modern tycoon, appear as a very respectable venture. The difficulties encountered by the book hunters, and the laboriousness of the copying process, meant that even the greatest of renaissance manuscript collections were small indeed if judged solely by modern numbers. Niccolò Niccoli, who had spent his entire fortune and a considerable amount of the Medici funds upon antiquities and manuscripts, and who had, in his day, the largest library in Florence, possessed but eight hundred volumes. The Visconti family at Pavia had nine hundred and eighty-eight, Cardinal Bessarion six hundred, and even the Laurentian Library of the Medici in 1494 is thought to have contained only somewhat over a thousand.

When, in 1431, Pope Eugene IV brought the papal library back to Rome after the "Babylonish Captivity" in Avignon, there were but three hundred and forty volumes to transport; and even Nicholas V, inspired book collector though he was, did not succeed in expanding the papal collection to the proportions of an ordinary American municipal library of our time. (In 1929, there was an average of thirty-three books to every twenty-five persons in public, society and school libraries in the United States.) Estimates of the number of books which the Vatican collection contained after the efforts of this great bibliophile are variously given as one thousand, five thousand, and nine thousand; but an inventory drawn up immediately after his death shows that the actual number was one thousand and twenty-nine volumes, a figure which, small as it may seem, represented an almost threefold increase in the eight years of Nicholas' incumbency.

Offsetting the numerical weakness of the renaissance collections, however, there was quality of content, clarity of script, beauty of illuminations or of decorative adjuncts, fineness of parchment, of velvet binding and silver clasp, and all these considerations contributed, in the collectors' eyes, to the value of a book. The importation of the printing press into Italy (*c.* 1472) was greeted with small enthusiasm by such distinguished amateurs as Lorenzo de' Medici and Federigo of Urbino, for the crass products of this grimy gadget seemed to them

From a manuscript copy of MIRACLES DE NOTRE DAME, *1456, showing Jean Mielot, the monk-scribe, at work. In the Bodleian Library.*

The Bettmann Archive

Page from a rare copy of Servius' COMMENTARY ON VIRGIL, *printed at Florence, 1471-72, by Bernardo Cennini and his son, Domenico. The Cenninis were first to bring printing to the city of the Medicis.*

The hand production of books in the SCRIPTORIUM *continued for some time after the invention of printing. Although modern collectors prize fine* incunabula *equally with illuminated manuscripts, many Renaissance bibliophiles were inclined to be scornful of the "vulgar" early printed books.*

BVCOLICA VT FERVNT DICTA SVNT A CV-
STODIA BOVM IDEST PRECIPVA
ENIM SVNT ANIMALIA APVD RVSTICOS BO
ues. Huius autem carminis origo uaria é. Nam alii dicunt e
o tépore quo Xerxes psaꝝ rex iuasit graeciam: cũ omnes intra
murum laterét & nec possent more solito dianæ sacra psolui: p-
uenisse ad mótes laconas rusticos & in eius honorem hymnos
dixisse. Vnde natu carmen bucolicum ætas posterior celebrauit. Alii dicunt ho-
restem cum dianæ fascelidis simulacrú raptum ex scythia aduexer&: & ad siciliam
esset tempestate delatus: completo anno dianæ festú celebrasse hymnis collectis
nautis suis & aliquibus pastoribus conuocatis: & exinde pmansisse apud rusticos
cõsuetudinem. Alii non dianæ sed apollini nomio cõsecratú carmen hoc uolunt:
quo tempore admeti regis pauit arméta. Alii rusticis numinibus a pastoribus di
catum hoc asserunt carmen: ut pani, faunis, ac satyris. Et hic est huius carminis ti-
tulus. Qualitas autem hæc est scilic& humilis caracter. Tres enim sunt. humilis.
medius. grádiloquus: quos omnes in hoc inuenimus poeta. Nam in æneide gran-
diloquú habet. In georgicis mediú. In bucolicis humilem pro qualitate negocioꝝ
& pṡonaꝝ. Nam pṡonæ hic rusticæ sunt simplicitate gaudétes. Scilic& a quibus
nihil altum deb& requiri. Adhibétur hæc ad carmé bucolicú: q deb& quarto pe-
de terminare parté orationis: qui pes si sit dactylus meliorem efficit uersum. ut
Nos patriæ fines & dulcia. Primus etiam pes secúdú Donatum dactylus esse de-
b&: & terminare partem orationis. ut Tityre. Quam legem Theocritus uehemé-
ter obseruat: Virgilius non adeo. Ille enĩ in paucis uersibus ab ista ratione deui
auit: hic eum in paucis secutus est. Terentianus cum de hoc metro diceret Plu-
rimus hoc pollet siculæ telluris alumnus. Noster rarus eo pastor maro. Intétio
poetæ hæc est: ut imitetur theocritum syracusanú meliorem Moscho & cæteris: q
bucolica scripserunt. Vnde est prima syracusio dignata est ludere uersu Nostra
nec erubuit siluas habitare thalia. Et aliquibus Locis per allegoriam agit gratias
Augusto uel aliis nobilibus: quoꝝ fauore amissum agrú recepit. In qua re tantú
dissentit a Theocrito. Ille enim ubiq; simplex est: hic necessitate compulsus ali-
bus locis miscet figuras: quas perite plerúq; etiã ex theocriti uersibus facit: quos
ab illo dictatos constat esse simpliciter. Hoc autem fit poetica urbanitate: Sic Iu
uenalis Actoris arúci spolium. Nam uirgilii uersum de hasta dictum figurate ad
speculum transtulit. Et causa scribendoꝝ bucolicorum hæc est. Cum post occisú
.iii. iduum martiaꝝ die in senatu Cæsarem Augustus eius filius cótra percussores
patris & Antonií ciuilia bella mouisset: uictoria potitus cremonésiú agros qui
cótra eum senserant: militibus suis dedit: Qui cum nó sufficerent etiã mátuanoꝝ
iussit distribui: non propter culpam sed propter uicinitatem. Vnde est. Mantua uæ
miseræ nimiú uicina cremonæ. Perdito ergo agro Virgilius Romã uenit: & po
tentium fauore meruit: ut agrum suú solus recip&. Ad quem accipiendú profectus

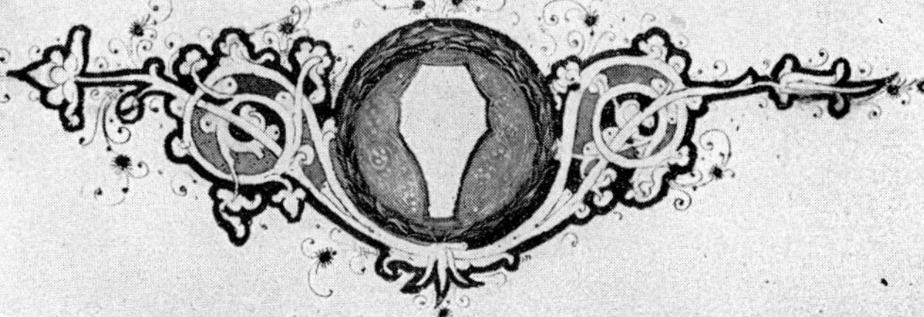

The Pierpont Morgan Library

paragons of ugliness in comparison to their elegant and proud hand-wrought volumes.

The fact that the spread of printing must eventually result in the reduction of prices was for them no particular attraction, and if they considered this possibility at all, it may have been with some misgiving that their own treasures might depreciate in value as books became more common. And it must be said on their behalf that it was probably beyond the predictive powers, even of such able and public-spirited citizens as these two, to realize how this vulgar invention would make possible wide diffusion of learning and culture.

If the rare spirits of the renaissance enjoyed display, as undoubtedly many of them did, it was in the manner of youthful and generous exuberance. Their pride of possession was tempered by a true love of the things collected, and often resulted in a form of encouragement to contemporary creative effort which has set these men apart from many of their would-be modern imitators.

There was Niccolò (1363–1437) of whom his scholar-protégé, Poggio, wrote:

> "No one who knows anything can come to Florence without thinking he should see Niccolò's house and books."

The famous collector's home was not meanly opened to visitors.

> "With noble confidence," writes Burckhardt, "he lent his books to those who asked for them, allowed all comers to study them in his own house, and was ready to converse with the students on what they had read."

Nor can it be forgotten that Niccolò's magnificent collection had itself been made possible in large measure by the generosity of that banker-prince, Cosimo de' Medici, who, when the scholar's own fortune had been completely expended, placed the resources of the Medici bank at his disposal.

After Niccolò's death, when Cosimo came into possession of his friend's precious books, he gave half of them, as Niccolò had suggested, to the Florentine monastery of San Marco, accompanied by this eloquent inscription: *Ex hereditate doctissimi viri Nicolai.*

Actually, the learned Niccolò, despite his relatively self-abnegatory qualities, had had sufficient collector-pride in his own collecting achievement to make provision in his will for just such posthumous acknowledgment, albeit couched in more modest terms.

Cosimo himself, although an extraordinarily busy man of affairs, was genuinely interested and active in the cause of collectors and collecting. As he aided Niccolò in the latter's time of need, so he redeemed the treasures which Giovanni Aurispa, upon his return from Greece, had been forced to pawn. During his own exile in Venice in the year 1433–44, he built the library of San Giorgio Maggiore, although in all probability he did not expect to stay the rest of his life in that alien state.

The first public library in Italy, the Library of San Marco at Florence, was also Cosimo's creation, as well as the library of the abbey at Fiesole; while for himself and his family he founded the Medicean Library, which the Florentine Pope, Nicholas V, later used as model for the Vatican collection, and which, when added to by Cosimo's successors, formed the nucleus of what was to become one of the world's most famous libraries, the Laurentian.

Cosimo's two sons, Giovanni and Piero, although less known in the annals of collecting than Piero's son, Lorenzo, nevertheless shared the family passion for book collecting, and between the years 1450 and 1460 their competition became a contest to determine who could form the better library.

But the Magnificent Lorenzo was the greatest collector of them all, greater even than had been his grandfather. In the formation of his library he had the help of the Greek scholar and collector, Johannes Lascaris, much as Cosimo had had that of Vespasiano. And as with Cosimo, his interest roamed beyond his own collection, for he could grow equally enthusiastic over any superlative library. While on his deathbed he is said to have murmured to his friend, Pico della Mirandola, the noble and handsome young scholar who was then gathering a fine collection of his own, "I wish death had spared me until your library had been complete!"

It was at the end too that he cautioned his son Giovanni, who was later to become Pope Leo X, against excess of worldly show:

"Your taste will be better shown in the acquisition of a few elegant remains of antiquity or in the collecting of handsome books," said Lorenzo.

Compare this advice, with its emphasis on taste and beauty, to the tone of one of "George Apley's" letters to his son John. Although this letter is fictional, it is historically sound and well represents the humorless and juiceless puritan, conscientious, but far from the rich vein of the renaissance collector to whom American collectors of the late nineteenth and early twentieth century are often likened:

> "There are certain definite obligations for one in my position and one in yours," wrote Apley. "When one is steward of a large fortune one should not dissipate it by useless spending . . . As you know, for a number of years I have been making a collection of Chinese bronzes. I have tried to inform myself fully about these things . . . I have made the collection out of duty rather than out of predilection, from the conviction that everyone in a certain position owes it to the community to collect something."

As the result of such an injunction John Apley might well have looked sourly on collecting, but Giovanni must have heeded his father with spirit, for later on as collector and patron he fostered learning and the arts so fully that the years of his pontificacy came to be known as the Golden Age of Italian literature.

Of all the princely libraries existing in Italy at this time, only one approached the Medicean in importance. The library at Urbino differed from the Medicean in being wholly the creation of a single collector, Duke Federigo da Montefeltro (1424–82). As the Medici had achieved political leadership by means of commercial power wisely and cleverly exercised, so Federigo, starting out as a soldier of fortune, had catapulted himself into high position by military means. In the typical fashion of the period—a period in which self-made men were almost as common as they are in modern America—what amounted to hereditary monarchies resulted in both cases; but unlike many other Italian states, Florence and Urbino were fortunate, for a few generations at least, in the characters of rulers whom their people could not help but love, honor, and trust.

Under Cosimo, Piero and Lorenzo de' Medici, Florence remained nominally a republic; but Urbino, as a duchy, might well have been subjected to those horrifying, despotic abuses which existed in so many of the petty states in which power had been violently seized by *condottieri*. Urbino, however, during the lifetime of the great Federigo and his immediate successors, was a happy, prosperous and contented place. Federigo could go about alone and unarmed in a day when other, less scrupulous rulers were forced to place bars of iron as well as hordes of spies and bodyguards between themselves and their subjects.

Federigo had begun to collect manuscripts while still a boy, and though a man of much smaller means than the Medici, he employed thirty or forty *scrittori* in various places, and spent some thirty thousand ducats on his collection with great selectivity. This collection, now a part of the Vatican library at Rome and one of the richest and most nearly "complete" of its own time, contained, in addition to a great number of theological and medieval works, every book on medicine which was then available, many Greek manuscripts (including a complete Sophocles, a complete Pindar and a complete Menander), the works of twenty-five humanists both in Latin and in Italian with all their translations, and an important modern section in which the complete works of Dante and Boccaccio were given a prominent place. Here was an ideal library for its period, and Federigo himself was an example of the ideal type of collector, a cultured man, always eager to increase his own learning, one who loved his books and used them, who gathered them intelligently and preserved them with care. When he said that he would be ashamed to tolerate a printed volume in his library, it was because he valued and honored the beauty of the manuscripts, not because he was either mercenary or a snob.

The renaissance was characterized by a great awakening of historical consciousness, and Rome became the destination of a multitude of pilgrims less for the old reason that it was the Holy City than because it was an important site of historic ruins. The road to holiness had not been completely deserted; there were still many people who, continuing to believe in the efficacy of religious relics, sought them in Rome and elsewhere. Giangaleazzo, the tyrannical Duke of Milan (d. 1402), was one who, for all his grandiose worldliness, placed great faith in the relics of saints and assembled a large collection of them, which he housed in his magnificent palace at Pavia. The people in certain towns, notably Padua, Milan and Venice, were reverential and at times even fanatical in their devotion to sacred relics of all sorts.

Yet seeds of doubt had been sown in the minds of the more intelligent, for in religion, if not in other fields, renaissance man was becoming, perforce, sophisticated; and in most places the religious feeling about things such as relics was gradually being transmuted into another and more contemporary sentiment—concern with historical tradition and the sense of reflected glory that comes from association with or possession of famous remains.

The popes themselves, whose collecting influence was strong, did not escape this change of attitude. The literary Pius II was popularly acclaimed for acquiring the Apostle Andrew's head for the Church of St. Peter; but in his own account of the affair he intimates how little interest he himself had in even such an outstanding relic as this one, which had been brought all the way from Greece. He was impelled to the purchase, apparently, chiefly from a sense of shame: so many secular princes were competing for the head that he, as pope, could not permit the church to be outdone in its enthusiasm.

The gradual weakening of medieval faith, combined with the simultaneous growth of the "conception of fame"—which was fostered by the new individualism and fanned to intensity by constant study of Roman writers who themselves had been "saturated" with the fame idea—produced a new cult of relics, however, far more like our own than had been the medieval cult. For now it became a point of honor for cities to own the bones of *celebrities.*

Sometimes a single set of bones might conveniently fulfil in their original owner's home towns both secular and religious requirements. Most often, however, there was a complete switch from saints and holy men to lay figures of fame.

The custom, so familiar to us, grew to prominence then as the birthplaces and graves of writers, artists, philosophers and statesmen were honored, and now for the first time the individual so admired could even be a pagan with no possible claim on Christian piety, as in the case of Virgil. What distinguished this development from similar manifestations today was a curiously intense interest in the *physical* remains of the honored person, a link which survived from the medieval world. Thus, although the realistic and cultured Florentines had less reverence for sacred relics than had any other Italians, *il Magnifico* himself urged the people of Spoleto to yield up, for his home-town cathedral, the corpse of the Florentine painter, Fra Filippo Lippi, a request which the Spoletans politely but firmly refused, asserting that they had few enough such treasures as it was!

As the religious "don'ts" fell before renaissance vigor, those highly instructive inscriptions waiting to be rediscovered on the many half-buried stones and ruins of antiquity were, after the classical manuscripts, among the first items to claim the attention of antiquarian collectors. Like most renaissance collecting, the work of such men in gathering together for study numerous transcriptions of these words carved on stone had a definite influence upon the life and thought of the time. For even as this form of collecting was a tangible manifestation of the new appreciation of history, so it in turn produced constructive tendencies growing out of an increased understanding of past events. The Roman Tribune, Cola Rienzi (1313–54), for example, was an ardent collector of antique inscriptions. And it was his long study of the records and monuments of the ancient Roman Republic that led him (by birth, a man of the people) to conceive his magnificently patriotic dream of delivering modern Rome from the misrule of her nobles, and of restoring the once-proud city to her former position as head of a united Italy.

Scholars, of course, were pre-eminent among the inscription collectors, and often they combined this pursuit with book collecting, since the two were closely allied. Poggio, in his walks through the city of seven hills, scraped the moss and obscuring vegetation off scores of valuable inscriptions, and he was the first definitely to correlate the information thus obtained with the works of old authors, which he also collected.

Although in Rome alone there were more than enough inscriptions to occupy several generations of students, many of the inscription collectors, like the book hunters, undertook long and arduous journeys. Ciriaco Pizzicolli of Ancona (*c.* 1391–1457), who, under Pope Eugene IV, had been responsible for bringing the papal library back from Avignon, in order to collect manuscripts, antique art and inscriptions visited Greece and other countries of the Near East, under the patronage of Pope Nicholas V. It was Ciriaco who, when asked why he took so much trouble over musty remains, replied tersely, "To wake the dead!" And the dead were indeed awakened when the urgent collectors of the Italian renaissance had done with them.

Even artists, in this contradictory period, became collectors of antiquities; and the influence that the prevailing admiration for classic survivals exercised over their work is obvious. The sculptor, Donatello (1386–1466), copied from antique gems the relief medallions which he designed for Cosimo's *Casa Medici,* restored a great number of antique heads, and had much to do with interesting his powerful patron in the treasures of ancient art with which Cosimo filled his new home.

Lorenzo Ghiberti (1378–1455) formed his own collection of Greek sculpture, which he imported at considerable expense. At least one of his items was an association piece—a bed that had reputedly belonged to the Greek sculptor, Polycletus (*fl. c.* 430 B.C.); and while this supposedly eighteen-hundred-year-old couch may possibly have been genuine, it is even more likely that Ghiberti, man of wide culture though he was, was as wishfully gullible as many an amateur since his day. Michelangelo (1475–1564), who had his own reasons for resenting the worship of antique sculpture, nevertheless collected antique gems with enthusiasm, and Benvenuto Cellini (1500–71) was another fancier of these eternal favorites.

Coins, too, were popular as significant relics of antiquity. Benedetto Dandolo, member of one of the most illustrious patrician families of Venice, is supposed to have been the first to form a "cabinet" of them. Time was taken away from books by Petrarch to collect coins, and they were also a specialty of Cardinal Pietro Barbo, afterwards Pope Paul II. By the middle of the sixteenth century there were over three hundred and eighty recorded cabinets of coins and medals in Italy, in the Netherlands two hundred, two hundred in France, and in the combined German states one hundred and seventy-five.

The verve, the warm desire to possess the fruit of the ancients resulted in a sudden spurt of excavation on ancient sites. Toward this movement, local pride and a new desire to live amidst pleasant and beautiful surroundings also contributed, particularly in Rome, which was, as the fresh eye of the renaissance first rose over the scene, a degenerated, unkempt and filthy city where pigs and cattle wandered.

At first there was little discrimination shown in depositing the finds. Many of the old ruins were stripped of their marble coatings and other decorations for the embellishment of newly erected palaces and villas; or, worse, antique marbles, transformed in the stonecutter's shed or the builder's kiln (it is the antiquarian's misfortune that marble may so easily be burned into lime) lost their original form altogether in being utilized as building material for the new constructions. Nevertheless, there was a vast number of antiquities which collectors rescued from such fate, and, by such men as Cardinal Alessandro Farnese, many of the excavations were initiated and financed for the sole purpose of recovering the art of the past.

In the neighborhood of Rome alone it is said that from sixty thousand to one hundred and seventy thousand statues were thus unearthed in the years 1450 to 1550, and Rome, although the most important, was but one of many localities to witness such activities. The homes of wealthy nobles and cardinals now were increasingly filled with bronze and marble figures, or with fragments of such figures, which had not seen the light of day since the Imperial Age; and as time went on there developed a more thoughtful approach to the study and preservation of antiquities which eventually was to become the definite science of archaeology.

Even the briefest review of treasures recovered during this period impresses one vividly with the excitement and exultation which must have animated all collectors. The rewards of the hunt were still infinite, happy accident paid large dividends, and the immensity of the trove which lay but a short distance underground is today all but inconceivable. One could never tell when some chance thrust of hoe or spade might lay bare an unsuspected golden vein.

When Alfonsina Orsini, widow of Piero de' Medici and mother of Lorenzo, was having a new wing built for a monastery under her patronage, her workmen came across five exquisite marble figures, copies of those famous bronzes which, more than twelve hundred years before, Attalus of Pergamum had presented to the people of Athens. The *Apollo Belvedere* was found in the time of Pope Alexander VI, and shortly afterward such treasures as the *Laocoön,* the *Venus of the Vatican,* and the *Torso of Cleopatra* appeared under the shovels of the excavators. The Baths of Caracalla, whereon, says Lanciani, "all the Roman emperors of the third century had lavished all the art treasures they could lay hands on," were uncovered between 1546 and 1549. And so, after sleeping for centuries, the great past was wakened fittingly enough by people of comparable genius.

To obtain as many of these treasures as possible was, even to the greatest and most powerful of the collectors, often as important as any political triumph, another illustration of how irrevocably men of this age had become exponents of the gentle art. When Lorenzo visited Pope Sixtus IV, just after the latter's elevation, to seek a cardinalship for his eighteen-year-old brother Guiliano (intended eventually to bring the papacy itself into Medici hands), the unwilling pontiff could put off his powerful and usually adamant guest with vague promises, merely because he was astute enough to make Lorenzo a present of a pair of antique marble busts and to allow him to purchase, at bargain prices, a quantity of artistic treasure from the papal storehouses, whereat "Lorenzo returned home exulting."

Another renaissance innovation—education stressed as important and desirable for everyone—created an extensive and intelligent audience for the arts. This, in turn, engendered a correspondingly larger group of people desirous of possessing books and art objects in their homes, where, as a rule and typically enough, they arranged such things not in the mausoleum-like galleries of a later day, but in such a manner as to enhance everyday living.

Even the ladies were benefited by this facet of the new freedom; and the renaissance, famous for its brilliant and capable women, produced a number of distinguished feminine collectors. Outstanding in Italy was Isabella d'Este (1474–1539), wife of the Marquis Francesco Gonzaga, who was himself a collector of fine armor. Regardless of sex, Isabella was one of the wisest and most discerning of all the Italian amateurs, notable as many of them were for their discrimination. A woman of wit, charm and determination, impeccable in her taste, insatiable in her desire to possess beautiful things, collecting was to her the very breath and substance of life itself. Hampered as she was by a comparatively limited fortune, her assemblage of ancient and modern books and works of art was necessarily small, but so carefully and knowledgeably had it been chosen that, years after her death, portions of it were to be snatched up in all eagerness by such powerful amateurs as Charles I of England and France's Cardinal Richelieu, while the reputation of the original, unlike that of many once "great" collections, still endures, secure in its fame.

Isabella's desire to obtain the best examples in her field was so strong that often, reaching for a painting, a piece of sculpture, or an object of *virtu* upon which she had set her determined little heart, she forgot all about being ladylike. When her funds ran low, she was not above asking an artist to give her a painting or a statue, and if this failed, she could haggle over prices with the best of them. When Mantegna, whose works were the glory of her precious *Grotta Studio*, was himself in urgent need of money for the doctoring of his ailing daughter, Isabella helped him out, but at the price of tearing from him, without hesitancy or scruple, his beloved antique figure, *Faustina,* the one ornament from which the aged court painter had sworn never to part—and this although Mantegna had worked long and hard for his patroness, and though she was well aware of the old man's passion for this statue.

In order to obtain Michelangelo's famous Cupid (now lost), the lady could intrigue with Cesar Borgia, although Cesar, under circumstances that made such intrigue look particularly shameful, had just betrayed her own brother-in-law, Duke Guidobaldo of Urbino. Borgia had given the statue to the duke as a mark of special friendship, but when, in treachery, he marched upon Urbino and plundered its palace, he took back his gift as part of the booty. Nine days later, even while giving Guidobaldo sanctuary at Mantua, Isabella wrote to her brother in Rome and begged him to do what he could to get hold of the Cupid, not for Guidobaldo but for herself! Three weeks after that, she received it triumphantly into her possession. Later still, when Borgia had fallen from power and Guidobaldo, restored to his duchy, was in the act of reassembling his stolen treasures, Isabella rejoiced with him in his good fortune—but would she return her own prize? Emphatically, she would not!

Except in the broadest sense of the word, renaissance collectors were seldom specialists. There were too many exciting new things surrounding them of the past and present to permit of settling down immediately to detailism.

As early as 1335, Oliver Forza, a citizen of Treviso, had made a collection of manuscripts, goldsmiths' work, medals, crystals, bronzes, marble statues and other objects of *virtu:* then, a collection such as this could have been labeled "complete." One hundred years later, in Paris, there lived a wealthy bourgeois named Jacques Duchié who collected "because he liked to collect," and without reference to increase in value or the exigencies of social position, an impressive variety of art objects and curios, books, musical instruments, precious stones, games, furniture, armor, flags, and birds. Poggio collected not only manuscripts and antique inscriptions but coins and portrait busts as well. Besides the books, paintings and statues, the Medici collection included cameos, engraved precious stones, coins, medals, jewels,

Etruscan vases, agate cups, tapestries, armor, ivories, embroideries, and natural curiosities. In Rome, the Farnese Palace, begun for Pope Paul III and completed by his grandson, Cardinal Alessandro Farnese, contained, in addition to the museum of statuary (formed partly by purchase and partly from contemporary excavations), a great number of paintings, books, objects of *virtu,* and simple curiosities, the whole comprising, according to Lanciani, one of the rarest and best collections ever formed by a private individual. Then there was the collection of enamels and pottery formed by that Huguenot potter, Bernard Palissy (1510–90), whose own works are now among the most prized of collectors' items; he also had a museum of natural objects—shells, fossils, minerals—to which, as he records with gratitude, many of his friends contributed.

We shall in time see this catholicity of interest breaking down into a number of smaller and more specialized fields, just as science was later to undergo such a transformation, with the number of specialties growing ever more numerous in proportion to the extension of factual knowledge. The seed of specialization, however, was already discernible in certain phases of renaissance life; and of course there existed some cases of specialized collecting.

In Italy one of the fields in which such a concentration of interest was gradually making itself felt was music. The exploratory bent of renaissance man here sent him off in search of new instruments capable of creating an ever wider gamut of sound, and as new developments made their appearance more and more musicians began to devote their talents to specific instruments. Inevitably this activity attracted collectors whose ears were charmed by fresh possibilities, and examples of available instruments were soon being gathered by men whose interest in them, far from being purely musical, often leaned definitely in the direction of the historical or associational values of such items.

The fact that an instrument collector, when entertaining professional musicians, might pass his items around among his guests so that the latter could provide an impromptu concert was merely a typical assertion of the renaissance urge to make a living use of everything, and did not alter the nonutilitarian values that such an amateur set upon his instruments as components of a true collection.

Many renaissance instruments were decorated by famous artists, and one might, therefore, find examples of them in general art collections.

Isabella d'Este's collection, although primarily one of art and books, also included viols, organs, and lutes of inlaid ivory and bronze. In Lorenzo's palace there were five organs; and his son, Giovanni, both as Cardinal and as Pope, patronized all the arts and collected in several different fields, although he loved above all his possessions his rare and beautiful instruments, some of which had been imported at great expense.

One might suppose that natural history would have been another field in which specialization appeared early. This was so, however, only in the most limited sense. The "all-sided" humanist, for example, might make collections of natural objects to illuminate his study of Pliny, but this would be only one of several collecting subjects to claim his interest. Even collectors whose interests were primarily scientific almost always included, with their natural history specimens, "artificial curiosities" (a classification which embraced art objects, among other things), just as antiquarian and art collectors included "natural curiosities" in their collections. The terms "artificial" and "natural curiosity" stretched over anything collectible under the sun; and up to the nineteenth century, the majority of so-called scientific collections were of this sort.

If there were any "specialists" in natural history at this time, they were to be found among those princes and other wealthy men who, in laying out their estates, endeavored to collect specimens of as wide a variety of plants and animals as possible, chiefly as a method of display and an assertion of power-symbolism. Collections of wild beasts or domesticated hunting birds and animals have been favorite symbols of power among rulers in many periods and places; and on this subject, Matarazzo wrote of the renaissance: "It belongs to the position of the great to keep horses, dogs, mules, falcons and other birds." Undoubtedly it was this that many of the petty rulers had in mind when they set about accumulating lions, leopards, bears, elephants or wild boar, all creatures symbolizing great strength, or, as in the case of Filippo Maria Visconti, when they concentrated on adjuncts of the chase and collected, at fabulous expense, hunting birds from the countries of northern Europe, valuable English dogs, and blooded steeds.

By virtue of their own limitations, men of this sort were likely to be specialists of the least admirable variety. On the other hand, there were those who derived genuine esthetic pleasure or intellectual satis-

Tuscan majolica jar, early 15th century, blue and manganese on creamy white; in the Mortimer L. Schiff Collection. ~ Palissy, the famous potter, collected natural history specimens and often used the theme, as in this faïence plate ascribed to his workshop; ex. coll. Dean Garnier, now in Walters Art Gallery.

faction from their accumulations of rare and beautiful plants, their pools of exotic fish, their peacocks and Indian fowl, their porcupines, ostriches, and long-eared Syrian goats.

Whatever the motives of the individual collector, the foundations for the future development of scientific botany and zoology here lay inherent in two conditions: first, in the widespread practice of making such collections at all; and second, in the new opportunities for study which the collected specimens afforded scholars.

In this fact there may be some historical compensation for the circumstance that the worst side of renaissance man frequently asserted itself among the animal collectors and their ilk. It is not the least unusual characteristic of this remarkable age—at its best so highly civilized, at its worst suspicious, cynical or superstitious and unbelievably savage—that the princely houses, many of which had been founded on violence and could only be preserved by ever-increasing doses of the same medicine, should have produced human monsters as extraordinary as, in their way, were the geniuses.

The collecting mania, degenerated to its lowest possible terms, found fertile ground in the mind of the lowest-grade renaissance man, for whom also no stretch of the imagination was too great, running the gamut from the revolting to the bizarre. Thus, "even human menageries were not wanting"—gathered along the same principles as were the zoological ones, with emphasis placed on the variety, quality and rarity of the exhibits. For example, Cardinal Ippolito Medici (1511–35), so Burckhardt tells us, ". . . kept at his strange court a troop of barbarians who talked no less than twenty different languages, and who were all of them perfect specimens of their races."

The collection formed by the brutal Ferrante, King of Naples (1423–94) was undoubtedly one of the most appalling ever to be recorded in all the history of collecting. Ferrante was supposedly the bastard son of Alfonso the Great of Spain, but history has judged that he was "not improbably the son of a half-caste Moor of Valencia." Certainly he betrayed all the grimmest traits of both races, and after he succeeded to the throne of Naples his unparalleled ferocity was the cause of numerous plots against his life. These he always succeeded in foiling; and it became his delight, after executing his defeated enemies, to have them carefully embalmed, dressed again in their best clothing, and collected in a special room in his palace, there triumphantly displayed, making, in effect, a museum of contemporary mummies whose faces were still poignantly familiar to whatever audience might be forced to look upon them.

In the activities at the Vatican for a hundred years, beginning with the early part of the fifteenth century, all the salient characteristics of renaissance collecting are clearly mirrored. In the most literal sense they were princes temporal as well as spiritual, these popes who, in regard to collecting, partook of the best and the worst qualities of the age. Some of them were born poor, but upon reaching the highest office most of them had vast sums at their disposal. Several were flamboyantly fond of worldly show in all its forms; a few made themselves notorious for all time by the unscrupulous means they used to augment their powers; and yet, as a group, the renaissance popes maintained a continuous tradition of fine scholarship, even fostering the resurrection and study of pagan antiquity, whose relics many of them collected. At least one, Aeneas Sylvius Piccolomini (Pius II (1458–64)), was a distinguished and prolific writer. With but one or two exceptions, all were liberal patrons of contemporary art and literature. And most were collectors on the grand scale. To Rome, the popes now became what the Medici had been to Florence; and because of them the Eternal City was to regain its position as the center of the cultural world.

Nowhere is the contrast more striking than here between the rich and varied manifestations of renaissance collecting and the collecting poverty of the preceding period. We have seen how, immediately after the exile at Avignon, the papal library, for example, numbered but three hundred and forty volumes. It was to be thirty years after the unity of the church had been restored before any important effort would be made to extend the Vatican collections. When, however, the Florentine scholar, Tommaso Parentucelli di Sarzana, became Pope Nicholas V (1447–55), papal collecting received an impetus which was to sweep on vigorously for nearly a century, until the northern Reformation had created problems which would force the popes to curb somewhat their "pagan" pursuits and worldly prodigalities.

The best of the renaissance popes, Nicholas, was a man of learning, intelligence, enlightened appreciation and wide interests. True collector, he gathered every sort of art object from all parts of Europe, and his private collection was praised for its fine tapestries, goldsmiths' work and majolica. One of the first to stress the desirability of restoring and beautifying the city of Rome, he himself was responsible for the founding of the Capitoline Museum. But books were his first love. As a young man he had joined the humanists in combing the convents of the north for hidden treasure, and it was common knowledge that, while still an impecunious monk, he had been in the habit of paying more than he could afford for beautifully written and well-bound manuscripts. The great collector, Niccolò, had been his friend, and to him Tommaso had presented a rare copy of Tertullian's work, one of the many valuable discoveries he had made on his journeys through France and Germany.

Popehood did not shake Nicholas from the humanists. He patronized and encouraged them, and he employed an army of book hunters in every part of the known world, even sending one such agent to Scandinavia to look for a "perfect copy" of the phantom Livy which, he had heard, was to be found either in Denmark or in Norway. At home he kept a hive of copyists busy making more books, and he himself directed not only the collecting but also the editing and arranging of his manuscripts. His fingers knew the collector's passion for handling treasures, and his eye appraised volumes for their rarity or excellence of workmanship almost as much as for their text. He loved to walk through his library, stopping before this or that special item; and, because there were biblioklepts even among the humanists in the papal employ, he kept the most precious manuscripts for greater safety in his own bedroom. He was, withal, exceedingly public-spirited; and it had been his intention to use his library—which he considered to be the greatest of his achievements—as the base for an even more splendid collection which he hoped to create for the especial use of scholars. This collection

". . . was to be preserved in the palace itself, as its noblest ornament, like the library of Ptolemy Philadelphus at Alexandria."

And although death cut short this project, as it had Caesar's, his books nevertheless form the nucleus of today's magnificent Vatican library.

Had the popes who came after Nicholas followed in his steps, they would need no apologists today. As collectors several have been compared to him—but always in the sense of his having furnished the ultimate criterion. Paul II, who was a devotee of worldly pleasure as well as of art, specialized in ancient vases, statues and coins, yet despite his zeal he did not even approximate Nicholas' stature as a collector. Sixtus IV, on the other hand, under whose brutal cynicism simony and nepotism grew to hitherto unheard of proportions, nevertheless gathered about him many of the greatest painters of the age and was responsible for the creation of the Sistine Chapel. A learned if not an admirable man, he was the first pope after Nicholas to take an interest in the Vatican library. The new building which he erected to house it was opened in 1475. In the course of the next ten years, under his patronage, a thousand volumes in Greek and Latin were added to the collection, which was now for the first time made available to the public. Sixtus also provided a special revenue for the maintenance and expansion of the library, and the effect of this was such that Vespasiano, the Florentine bookdealer, could write enthusiastically of Sixtus' pontificacy as "marking a new epoch in the book trade."

Of all the papal collectors the greatest, after Nicholas V, was Leo X (1513–21)—like Nicholas, a Florentine, and a Medici to boot. Giovanni de' Medici was Lorenzo's second son, and he had been groomed since childhood for the papacy. He was far more capable than his elder brother, Pietro, and had the government of Florence fallen into Giovanni's hands after the death of *il Magnifico,* the subsequent history of that great city would undoubtedly have taken a different and happier course than it did. Instead, it was Rome that benefited under his expansive and tolerant rule, and during this pontificacy the papal capital reached the height of its renaissance glory. Although, to Leo's taste, music was without peer, he patronized all the arts, like his father and great-grandfather before him; and during his incumbency, painters, sculptors, writers and scholars flocked to Rome in even greater numbers than before. As a young man he had collected manuscripts in the best humanist tradition, and had made many valuable contributions to his father's library. After the disastrous sack of Florence in 1494,* he made it his business to seek out and buy back as many of the Medicean books as he could locate, and he succeeded in obtaining the entire library of San Marco, which had fallen into the hands of strangers during the dismal period of the invasion.

In the fashion of several of his predecessors, Pope Leo kept his pri-

* In that year, Charles VIII of France entered Florence upon the invitation of Lorenzo's weakling son, Pietro, and sacked the city, dispersing many of the Medici treasures.

Marble Relief of Cosimo de' Medici, the Elder, *attributed to Verrocchio. In the Kaiser Friedrich Museum, Berlin.*

Spinelli Medal of Lorenzo, the Magnificent. *In the Museo Nazionale, Florence.*

Four Members of a Great Collecting Dynasty.

Pope Leo X with One of the Volumes from His Library. *Note the elaborately chased bell. Giulio de' Medici, who later became Pope Clement VII* (left), *and Cardinal de' Rossi are the other figures in this detail from a painting by Raphael from the Pitti Palace, Florence.*

vate library separate from the Vatican's, and eventually his books were returned to Florence. Because of its curious history, marking the wanderings to which so many collector's items have been fated, one of these books—the original copy of the Emperor Justinian's *Pandects*—may be cited in particular. In 1137, when the Pisan fleet had captured Amalfi, the *Pandects*, found in the vanquished city, had been carried off by the victors. When Pisa itself was conquered by the Florentines, in 1406, this valuable manuscript came into possession of the Medici. Inheriting it, Leo X took it to Rome with him; and three centuries after his time, after God knows what adventures, it found its way back to Florence, stripped of its handsome binding.

In expanding the collections of the Vatican itself, Leo was a man who followed worthily in the footsteps of Nicholas V. He employed agents to seek out the rarest and best manuscripts, and even advertised publicly for certain items, offering rewards for their discovery. In a way strangely reminiscent of dictator Ashurbanipal, he demanded that his book hunters be given free access to all libraries; and his agents, like those of Ptolemy Euergetes, were "instructed to appropriate such rare copies as could not be bought or borrowed." This was done, according to Pope Leo, "for the good of scholarship"; and as Ptolemy had supplied the bereaved owners with inferior copies of their valued originals, so Leo made some restitution by replacing manuscripts with printed editions.

The Leonine days of Rome, prodigal in the joy and brilliance of life, were destined to gain immortal fame, no less because Luther had already appeared upon the scene in the north and the great renaissance was soon to feel the effects of a new, crusading asceticism. Wars would again fall upon Europe—wars of religion, wars for power among the slowly forming northerly nations—the birth pangs of yet another era; and Italy, which had never bothered to mold herself into a single nation, would become first a helpless pawn and then a victim in the struggle. Humanists and princely popes, grand gestures and lavish thoughtlessness of living—the good old days would be no more. The French invaders, intoxicated for a time, would create a renaissance of their own from seeds gathered in Italy, and as this grew and changed it would become a new age, the modern age, our own.

The eyes of collectors in this new age would ever turn, through nostalgia and for inspiration, back toward the renaissance; but the conditions of their lives would inevitably carry them on into other worlds. The full blast of life would grow less, the field of multicolored genius dwindle. And in their place, a new and more purposeful symmetry would develop, wherein collecting would eventually earn a new laurel called usefulness.

FRENCH COLLECTORS TAKE UP THE TORCH

"*. . . this Valois king riding, lance on thigh, across the Alps to conquer Italy, had been conquered by Italy.*" GRACE HART SEELY

SELDOM IN WORLD HISTORY have seemingly isolated events produced results so far-reaching as did the discoveries, toward the end of the fifteenth century, of ocean routes from Europe to the Far East and to the "new world" of the West. The ferment created by those geographical revelations set in motion a progressive development in political, social and economic life which is still far from spent, and the trends fathered by the adventurous voyagers have influenced every Western collector since that time.

The opening of rich markets and new territories for exploitation gave impetus to the consolidation of national states, and as nations extended their domains, international capitalism developed and came to play a vital role in the new imperialism. Then efficiency demanded concentration of political power, so that the princely courts that survived became stronger than before, while the church lost the major portion of its political and social leadership, until once again the palace had supplanted the temple as the center of the social scheme. Of this courtly world, "power and pleasure . . . were the two poles," its symbol the amassing of material splendors. Soon splendor itself set forth in prodigal display became the primary goal, and then followed inevitable decadence in the evolution of a cult of "exquisite uselessness."

As trade and finance grew in national importance, money became the valued premium set upon newly recognized forms of ability. The premium was available to anyone strong or shrewd enough to go fetch it, and so from personal ambition the old shackles began to crack and fall away. The middle class grew in strength, until the houses of merchants rivaled princes' castles, and in them many of the greatest collections, such as those of the still renowned banking Fuggers of Germany, were to be found.

The mass of the people, however, were still living in misery, largely cut off from the cultural amenities until, as a natural consequence of all that had gone before there appeared upon the scene the three sister revolutions, political, industrial and social. Contributing heavily to these were the sciences, which flowered toward the end of the baroque period and whose valuable fruit collectors helped to cultivate.

Out of scientific knowledge and understanding, out of the growing clamor against too uneven a division of the instruments of life, out of a more comprehensive sense of social responsibility, there were now to appear the modern achievements of public museums, art galleries, and libraries, of the community-owned botanical garden and zoological park, all evolutionary developments from the great private collections of an earlier day. In the currently increasing trend toward an ultimate social use of important collections, the whole collecting cycle seems to swerve back toward its beginning when the greatest gatherings of cultural treasure were to be found in the open temples. There is, however, one important difference. In the old days such collections were formed largely at the behest of superstition and at the cost of oppression, whereas today they have become a symbol of enlightenment, consciously created for the good of the community.

When the vigor of French militancy swept into a weak and disunited Italy, the collecting initiative, along with a great deal else, was carried off by the French people; and thereafter, for three rich centuries, these zestful Latins were truly a nation of collectors, the leaders and cynosure of all Europe.

Of course, this phenomenon did not spring suddenly into being the day after Charles VIII implemented his dynastic claims to the kingdom of Naples with invasion. Long before this there had been royal collectors in France; and the late medieval princely collections (first of books, later of art objects), even though minuscular and gathered purely as personal luxuries, were true foundation stones of the great national libraries and museums so familiar to the modern era. Wherefore, before describing some of the great collectors of a later day, let us pay fleeting tribute to the venerable bones of such trail blazers as Philip the Fair (1268–1314), Louis X (1289–1316), and John the Good (rg. 1350–64).

Because he was first to take political issue with the church, and first to try to bend the feudal nobles to a central will, Philip the Fair is known in France as "the first of the modern kings." He had a library which, though exceedingly small (it consisted of perhaps a dozen manuscripts), was for its time a respectable holding. New goals were reached by his successor, Louis X, who, before his early death, owned about thirty-five volumes, notable because they were almost all in French—and it will be remembered that one of the signs which marked the emergence from medievalism was this recession of Latin works in favor of the vernacular. Not to Philip or to Louis, however, but to John the Good we must turn for the direct lineage of achievement.

This monarch beguiled long hours of captivity in England by acquiring books; and the origins of the great *Bibliothèque Nationale* can be traced to his collecting activity and to his encouragement of his sons in similar endeavors. Those sons—John, Duke of Berry; Philip the Bold, Duke of Burgundy; and Charles V of France, known as the Wise—were the most eminent French bibliophiles of their day, and the extent and nature of their collections show how far library making had advanced even in the fifty short years following the death of Philip the Fair. The influence of Italy was already discernible in their collecting methods; but the distinctive national taste was also in evidence, since, as has generally been the case with French book lovers, it was the physical beauty of a volume which made the greatest appeal to these princes. The Duke of Berry hired the most skillful copyists and illuminators to increase his fine library. His avidity for books became famous, and from favor-seekers he received many as gifts (once, at the New Year, four of his secretaries, quite modern-wise, banded together to foot the cost of such a gift). Yet, like certain of the renaissance princes, this medieval amateur himself made generous donations to the libraries of his favorite religious institutions. A prodigal figure, unusual for his time, he did not quibble over enormous prices when desirable items were at stake, and at his death many of his books had to be sold to pay the piper.

The most important milestone of this early period, however, was the library of Charles V (1337–80), who, despite the smallness of such collections even in cathedrals, monasteries, and universities, was able to muster some nine hundred and ten volumes, including works on astronomy and astrology, history and literature, as well as a wide selection of romances in prose and verse, all of which were carefully catalogued by a large staff of copyists and translators. When this king remodeled the Louvre, which before his day had been little more than a fortress, he placed his books in the *Tour de la Fauconnerie,* where they occupied three rooms one above the other, with a librarian in charge. Here was a true collector doing a good pioneer job; but he was considerably ahead of his times, and his immediate successors gave little thought to such matters.

A hundred odd years after the death of Charles the Wise, Charles VIII (1470–98) marched into Italy and brought back with him the seeds of the French renaissance—and it might be mentioned in passing that this Charles had the first collection of artillery of which there is any record.

The beauties and pleasures of the southern peninsula had quite enchanted the ugly little king, so short of wit and long of nose; and though his campaign proved to be somewhat of a fiasco from a military point of view, it nevertheless yielded him an abundance of booty for the remodeling and refurbishing of his medieval château at Amboise. There were exquisite Italian manuscripts for the hitherto meager library. Tapestries and paintings, marbles and carved alabasters helped to brighten the once gloomy chambers. Imported Neapolitan stonemasons were put to work on the castle's forbidding exterior, while Neapolitan gardeners planted and tended the groves of newly acquired orange and peach trees. So it came about that, at the behest of the last prince in the elder line of John the Good, France was taking her first definitive step out of medieval darkness into the light of the renaissance.

Charles' contribution to this metamorphosis was cut short by a blow on the noggin, when he forgot to duck a low door at a tennis match. But as Charles stepped down, up stepped Louis XII (1462–1515) of the House of Orléans. The continuing Italian wars, plus his attempts to consolidate the realm at home, were taxing; yet the twelfth Louis found ample time for collecting. And small wonder, for collecting was literally in the blood of this monarch, who enjoyed nothing better than driving a bargain over a work of art. A great-grandson of Charles V, and, on the maternal side, a descendant of the Visconti of Milan, he had inherited the libraries of his grandfather, his father and his mother—bibliophiles all. In his case we see for the first time the operation of that cumulative process which was eventually to transform royal into national collections. Yet James Westfall Thompson's remark that with Louis XII "the private library of the kings became that of France" is true only in this broad sense, since actually royal collections remained private collections in his day and for long after.

It was with Louis' young cousin and successor, Francis I (1494–1547) that the great French collecting era took off under its own power. Italian blood flowed in Louis' veins, and he himself spent some time in Italy; yet he always preferred the old French ways, and in him the true renaissance prince had not completely emerged. Francis was a man of different vintage. To the end of his days it would remain his ambition to make the French court as much like the courts of the Italian renaissance as he could; and an integral part of that transformation was to be the collecting of Italian art, in the Italian manner. Had not renaissance Italians always referred to members of the French nobility as "barbarians"? Francis would change that in short order.

He began by collecting Italian artists in person—Cellini, Andrea del Sarto, Primaticcio, even the great Leonardo. Back to France he brought them, and set them to work on commissions, like a hive of captive bees. But all the Italian art Francis wanted could not be made to order. He acquired Michelangelo's *Leda* and Raphael's *Holy Family,* now known as *La Belle Jardinière.* He borrowed from the Pope the famous *Laocoön,* rediscovered at Rome sixty years previously, and bought from Leonardo those three paintings—the *Mona Lisa,* the *Saint John,* and the *Virgin of the Rocks*—which have ever since been so highly regarded by the French. (In 1939, after France had fallen before the Nazi armies, Italy's Mussolini laid claim to the *Mona Lisa,* declaring falsely, through the official publication of the University of Rome, that the painting had been stolen by Napoleon.)

Francis had inherited not only the library at Blois (made up of the collections formed by the House of Orléans over several generations, and enlarged by the Visconti-Sforza library and other acquisitions of Louis XII), but also the books which his own ancestors of the House of Angoulême had been gathering for some time. All these, together with his art treasures, he now moved to his newly built palace at Fontainebleau, the while he dispatched Italian agents to search the archives of Europe for more. He had a plan for establishing a library of ancient manuscripts near Fontainebleau; and John Lascaris—the Greek scholar who had once been Lorenzo's adviser, and who, invited to France by Charles VIII, had remained to work on Louis' library—was still on hand to give invaluable assistance to Francis. The king's eagerness to gather up books and works of art became so well known that even Isabella d'Este, most jealous of amateurs, could see the political wisdom of sending him gifts from her famous *Grotta* at Mantua.

Besides his art gallery and library, Francis owned a collection of armor, a cabinet of curiosities, and another of medals and engraved gems. Nor were the majority of these items perfunctorily selected, as royal brides so often were. He loved his possessions, and so active was his pride in them that he was eternally organizing exhibition excursions among his courtiers and guests, who, if they did not all equally enjoy such enforced culture feeding, at least made merry on other refreshments.

At least one member of these gala occasions, however, shared to the hilt Francis' enthusiasm. She was lovely Diane de Poitiers, upon whose person the king, now and then forgetting his paintings, was wont to cast an admiring and covetous eye—with exactly what results historians disagree. For her and other members of her sex, a special section of this chapter has been reserved, since women played an extraordinarily important part in this era.

Under Francis, the palace of Fontainebleau became "a greater museum than Versailles ever was"; and although as man and king the gentleman was far from faultless, he performed an inestimable service for his people by providing them with "an abiding stimulus for the acquisition of the national wealth in arts." Mark Francis, then, as the first notable prince among French collectors.

None that followed, not even Louis XIV, matched the pioneer achievement of this zealous royal amateur, although most of his successors at least dabbled in collecting. One who may be mentioned here, however, is Henry IV (1553–1610), first of the Bourbons. His interest lay chiefly in those engraved gems and antique coins on which princes had long recorded their glorious doings, and he purchased several private coin and gem collections, adding them to what was left of the royal

Portrait of Francis I by Clouet, *from the Louvre.*
This monarch's collecting vigor was never surpassed by his successors.

cabinet after the havoc wrought by the wars of religion. His eldest son and successor, Louis XIII (1601–43), had no great interest in collecting, although, as was still the aristocratic fashion, he did assemble a hall of armor; but a younger son, Gaston, Duke of Orléans (1608–60), carried on Henry's work and became one of the greatest coin collectors of all times. To him natural history also made a strong appeal, and he established a private botanical garden of some importance. Upon the duke's death, the coins passed to the crown, eventually to be added to the bulk of the national collection; while a portion of the natural history collection was purchased by the minister Colbert, and, greatly augmented by subsequent additions, became in time the Museum of Natural History of Paris.

The age which, in France, extended in unbroken progression from the renaissance to the revolution, was marked by a number of distinctive collecting characteristics, and of these one of the most striking was the growth of a strong vogue for Oriental products. As a fashion this derived directly from the Age of Discovery, but it has endured into our own time, and in this a genuine esthetic appreciation has since become the dominant factor.

It is noteworthy that such enthusiasm has been little reciprocated by Oriental connoisseurs. To this there have been temporary exceptions, one during the eighteenth century when the Chinese, intrigued by merchandise supplied them by the Jesuits, appear to have collected English and French clocks, watches, enamels, miniatures and mechanical toys in considerable quantities; and another, briefly, toward the end of the nineteenth century, when the Japanese, undergoing a process of Westernization in many phases of their life, rejected their traditional standards of art in favor of Occidental importations.

With occasional exceptions in favor of religion, the Orientals have fought off most aspects of European culture, and have adopted only utilitarian phases which could no longer be avoided in an industrial, imperialistic, and closely interlocked world. For example, although the Japanese, after World War I, assembled an ambitious collection of Occidental art both ancient and modern, intending to install it in a museum in Tokyo designed by a well-known Western architect, they themselves admitted that this was solely for the purpose of educating Japanese designers and workmen to the psychology and tastes of those

Western peoples whose markets they hoped to capture, and not because of any admiration for Western culture.

Although the wares of the Orient had not been completely unknown to Europe prior to the Age of Discovery, they had been extremely rare. Lorenzo de' Medici had owned some examples of the highly prized Chinese celadon porcelains, obtained indirectly as a gift from the Sultan of Egypt, but in his day few if any similar pieces could have been seen elsewhere in Europe. Two centuries later, however, any collector of moderate means might have purchased quantities of both Chinese and Japanese ceramics and curios, and most of them did. As the navigators and traders of the sixteenth and seventeenth centuries unlocked the knowing world of the Far East, with its Golconda of strange and beautiful artistry, the imaginations of these later collectors were inevitably fired, and at first, no doubt, the sense of adventure made an even more urgent appeal than the esthetic, since to own some rarity or curiosity which had traveled all the way from India, China or Japan was then, in some measure, to participate in the discoveries, to move in the new lands of splendor.

With the growth of the East India companies and the establishment of religious missions in the Orient, an increasing number of Eastern products were imported into Europe, and the effect of this in altering the character of the Western collector's harvest was comparable to the situation which had prevailed in ancient Greece on the heels of Alexander's Eastern campaigns, or during the late middle ages in Europe, when the crusades had been responsible for a similar influx of new materials. The Jesuit missionaries of the seventeenth century made collections (of natural objects as well as of objects of *virtu*) in all the countries to which they were sent, and shipped these collections back to Europe, particularly to Paris. And from the proceeds of their own importations, European merchants of this period lived well indeed. In 1664, for example, the Dutch alone shipped forty-four thousand nine hundred and forty-three pieces of Japanese pottery to Holland, and Holland was but one of the nations active in this trade. The spreading demand for Oriental ware exerted an important influence not only upon the tastes of the Westerners, but upon European ceramists as well; and the very word *china*, which we now apply indiscriminately to any form of crockery, bears lasting witness to the extent of this influence.

Soft-paste porcelain, of the sort in which the Chinese had so long excelled, could not be produced in Europe at all until five years before the close of the seventeenth century, when it was first made at St. Cloud in France, and soon thereafter at Dresden in Saxony. Even then, the slow, stubby ships came in from the East laden with cargoes of blank porcelains for the factories of Holland and other countries, where they were painted and refired; and the custom persisted of sending European models and designs to China, to be made up in the superior porcelain of that country. This latter was the famous "Oriental Lowestoft" ware, which received its name posthumously through a scholar's error.

The origin of "Oriental Lowestoft" constitutes a note on the conflicting interests of fashion and practicality—for much as Europeans (and later Americans) admire Chinese porcelain, the Westerners often found Oriental shapes inconvenient, Oriental patterns too puzzling to enjoy, wherefore they shipped their own silver vessels to be copied in porcelain, and even supplied the Chinese craftsmen with European armorial and other designs, including Biblical subjects! About a million pieces of this hybrid ware left Canton for Europe on English, French, Danish and Dutch ships, in the year 1735.

During the courtly age, no collection was deemed worthy of the name which did not boast of some specimens of Oriental work, and it will be noted that almost every important collection hereafter described includes numerous items of the sort. By the eighteenth century—the "age of the dilettanti"—the spirit of adventure was dead, but the collecting forms it had begotten remained. Then it was that a "porcelain room" was indispensable to a gentleman's house (as an art gallery and a library had been in Imperial Rome); and for visiting courtiers even the paltry collectors of corals and sea shells would dress up in Chinese costumes to do the honors of their collections.

Often, in the early days of this period, it would seem more important that an object, in order to claim the place of honor in a collection, should be new and different than that it should be beautiful or intrinsically interesting. Even serious collectors were temporarily overwhelmed by the wealth of novel material, their judgments for a while beclouded, and understandably so, for time must pass before the unusual can, with fair vision, be evaluated.

As a corollary to this attitude, skill used in novelty came to be intensely admired in native works of art and craftsmanship. Today, the patience and ingenuity of a man who carves the Lord's Prayer on the head of a pin or builds in miniature an intricate piece of furniture of matchsticks may command fleeting notice, but his work is considered freakish and is not much valued. In the post-renaissance era, however, the most discriminating collectors were proud to acquire such *tour de force* items, and seldom hesitated to welcome them into the society of more orthodox masterpieces.

Expressive of these standards of value were some of the words common to the collector's language in the sixteenth, seventeenth and eighteenth centuries, adjectives such as *extravagant, curious, outlandish,* nouns like *marvel* and *wonder.* An "outlandish" item was one of foreign derivation and became, by that very fact, of extreme interest. An "extravagant" object was one varying widely from the usual—something abnormal or strange—and the more "extravagant" it was, the more it was likely to be admired. A butterfly that looked like a bird, or a bird that resembled a rhinoceros, were the ultimate in desirability.

Among seventeenth-century collectors, the word *curious* in all its forms enjoyed great popularity. Its connotations were somewhat different than in modern usage. When used with reference to a person, it usually meant one who was interested in science or art; hence the later *curioso,* an admirer or collector of curiosities, a connoisseur, a virtuoso. A "curious" object was one of the sort to interest the curioso or the connoisseur. Nevertheless, an overtone of its modern significance was also present, since the phrase was often used to indicate that the object in question was skillfully or elaborately wrought under difficult conditions, with emphasis on the elaboration and the difficulty.

Interchangeably employed, either for the room in which a collection of any sort was displayed or for the collection itself, were the words *cabinet, closet, museum.* Cabinet collectors were much given to such fantasies as that of having masterpieces of painting reproduced in miniature on rare stones or some other precious material, or of assembling such futile but wonder-evoking works as cherry stones hollowed out to contain ten dozen miniature tortoise-shell combs.

A similar interest was extended to natural objects. One of the principal divisions to be found in collections of minerals and stones consisted of "formed" stones—that is, stones the shapes of which were such as to make them resemble things ordinarily found only in the vegetable or animal kingdoms. In the seventeenth century, one scientifically-inclined French collector described by John Evelyn arranged his specimen butterflies to represent a beautiful piece of tapestry. By the eighteenth century the very gardens in France were laid out to be copies of Aubusson carpets, a process which was typically reversed by the Dutch collector, Levinus Vincent, when he arranged his corals to suggest a park of shrubs and trees.

It was inevitable that the prevalence of interests and conceptions so much at variance with those of our period should have produced a system of arrangement and classification that was also very different. The first goal in arranging a collection was to display it impressively, a purpose quite in harmony with the spirit of the courtly age. Collectors were no longer content simply to disperse their art and objects of *virtu* throughout their homes. Concentration obviously made for greater show—and so it became increasingly frequent to set aside, in mansion or palace, special galleries and halls for exhibition purposes. About the walls would be niches, shelves, or console tables backed by mirrors to increase the effect, while in the center of the room were more tables, together with pedestals and cases, all arranged so as to show off the items to maximum advantage.

Out of this segregation of the private collection within the home would eventually spring—in a development as natural as that in which the cells of certain organisms separate from the parent body—the nineteenth-century conception of the completely autonomous museum. Educational intent, however, was almost completely lacking from these earlier displays. For example, collections of weapons, costumes and the artifacts of primitive peoples were frequently assembled, but their chief interest lay, not in their informative significance, but in the fact that they were strange, surprisingly rude and clumsy, or unexpectedly finished and elegant, and in their display no attention was paid to logical classification.

In the case of the so-called "natural curiosities" there was some attempt to achieve such classification, but it was an attempt limited by the embryonic state of science itself. "Natural curiosities" included animal, vegetable and mineral (often known as "fossil") substances, and all the ethnographical exhibits came under the head of "animal." Under "artificial rarities" were grouped works in wood, glass and ivory; pictures; gold and silver work; works of art in marble, wax and other substances; antiquities and coins. At the end of the seventeenth century, when Addison visited the Medicean Museum, the articles of ivory and amber and crystal, the *Venus de' Medici* and other statues, the precious stones and the archaeological exhibits were, according to his description, all displayed under the head of "artificial curiosities"; and as late as 1791 the British Museum was described as containing "an exhibition of a great variety of antiquities and natural curiosities."

Within these two broad divisions, any of a number of arbitrary (and today meaningless) systems of arrangement were commonly employed. In some collections, the items were placed according to graduated size. In others they were grouped according to substance—bronze, silver, gold, ivory, amber, stone, coral, and so on—with the result that natural history specimens and works of art and craftsmanship were often exhibited side by side in pell-mell confusion, and that it was practically impossible to obtain a constructive picture of any single subject.

Scientists of this period betrayed the same interest in the bizarre and the marvelous as did lay collectors:

"Ordinary phenomena," says Murray, "were passed by by the older naturalists as of no importance, or as too familiar to deserve notice or to require explanation."

In 1663, John Ray, a fellow of the Royal Society, wrote an account of his travels in which he described many of the collections he had visited. Among these was that of the Duke of Modena, which, although as miscellaneous in content as a pawn shop and full of mere oddities, nevertheless proved of great interest to this scientific observer:

"What we most minded," wrote Ray, "was the cabinet or *museaeum,* furnished with choice of natural rarities, jewels, ancient and modern coins and medals, ancient and modern entaglias, curious turn'd works, dried plants pasted upon smooth boards, whiten'd with ceruss, which may be put in frames and hung about a room like pictures; and a great collection of designs of the best painters. Among other things we took notice of a human head petrified; a hen's egg having on one side the signature of the sun* . . . moss included in a piece of crystal, silver in another. A fly plainly discernible in a piece of amber. A Chinese calendar written on wooden leaves. . . ."

---

* That is, the impression of the sun. Objects bearing this mark were much valued. To some extent comparable is the modern specialty—followed by certain very serious rock collectors—of gathering only rocks which bear the marks of wind, water, or storm.

Since the medieval belief in the miraculous had not yet completely disappeared, no collection was considered complete without one or more specimens of the supposedly magical horn of the unicorn. In the middle ages such horn had been considered the symbol of virginity and purity, and was thought to possess properties whereby it could reveal treason or the existence of poison. Even as late as the seventeenth century, unicorn horn was believed to have similar virtues and was much used in medicine, as, incidentally, were also pieces of mummy! The existence of the horn was accepted as proof that such an animal as the unicorn existed, and although none was ever brought to Europe, alive or stuffed, many travelers claimed to have seen them in foreign lands.

To this day there are those who, believing that where there was so much smoke there must have been some fire, still search for the unicorn in remote places; and in 1939, Sir Thomas Comyn-Platt advanced the theory that the one-horned moufflon of Cyprus, long thought to be extinct but recently seen by him, was the original of this fabled creature. It is now believed that the "unicorn" horns in old collections were really narwhal tusks or horns of the rhinoceros. Even in the old days it was recognized that not all specimens so attributed were genuine unicorn. Horns recognized as deriving from the narwhal or the rhinoceros were considered less potent than true unicorn horn, and although these were also sought, a lesser value was set upon them, "experts" being often employed to detect the difference between true and spurious specimens.

Nevertheless, and despite the strangeness of its methods in our eyes, the courtly age possessed many true amateurs. Outstanding were those powerful ministers of church and state, who, throughout most of the seventeenth century, were the true rulers of France, in practice if not in name. Richelieu, Mazarin, Colbert—each was a great collector. Typical of their period, they were universal types also; and, like those of royalty, the collections they formed were eventually to make abundant contribution to the nation's heritage.

Physically a sickly little man, but a blazing hound in the pursuit of power for his king, and of books and art for himself, was Armand-Jean du Plessis, Cardinal-Duc de Richelieu (1585–1642). Born into the nobility in impecunity, he died one of the wealthiest men in the land—this churchman who governed France for years in the name of Louis

XIII, and who, perhaps more than any other, determined the course of his country's destiny by welding it into political unity.

In collecting, too, Richelieu was ambitious, brilliantly shrewd, and relentlessly persistent. Here, as in statecraft, he availed himself of any and every means to achieve his ends and one of his personal objectives was to assemble treasures that would rival, and, if possible, surpass the king's in magnificence.

One, two, three palaces were required to house his assembled items, and the *Palais Cardinal*, built for him between 1629 and 1636, became so obviously the show place of Paris that his noble enemies tried to use it as a weapon with which to arouse the jealousy of the king. With characteristic suavity, Richelieu parried the charge by declaring that he had built the palace and gathered its magnificent contents with the sole intention of doing his master honor; and indeed before his death he did turn over to Louis this treasure-house, which thereafter became the *Palais Royal*, though only a wing and part of a gallery of the original building now remain. The key to his true purpose, however, was to be found in his will, which contained the significant request that this property should be made inalienable from the crown:

". . . the intention of the Cardinal being that it shall serve as a residence for his majesty and his successors, or for heirs of the Crown, having built this palace at such expense with this design."

So Richelieu had hoped that his home would become his monument, to be lived in only by kings after him. Unfortunately for his ambition, this request was disregarded. Louis died shortly after Richelieu himself, and though Anne of Austria continued to occupy the *Palais Royal* during her regency, it was afterwards put to other uses.

Richelieu also remodeled his ancestral château, taking pains to see that plenty of shelves were built into the walls of the rooms *"pour mettre des raretez"*; and then, still not content, he purchased another at Ruel, near Paris, which became his favorite residence. It was there that he created the famous park, notable for its collection of pedigreed dogs and fine birds, for its enormous flower bed, the grottoes, statues and fountains.

Each of these châteaux was magnificently furnished and adorned, but it was the future *Palais Royal* which housed the most prized items. Tapestries, oriental rugs and costly furniture filled its salons. There was a library—the largest and best in the world—and a picture gallery containing five hundred paintings, including works of such masters as Rubens, Veronese, Correggio, Titian and Raphael. Five of the paintings, acquired after the sack of Mantua in 1630, had once belonged to Isabella d'Este. There were a hundred sculptured heads and busts, most of them antique, and about fifty statues. There were more than four hundred pieces of Chinese porcelain, and a whole collection of perfumed sachets! There was jewelry, too, but Richelieu was particularly enamored of gold and silversmiths' work, of which he possessed a great store. Nor were the typical seventeenth-century curiosities lacking, for the Cardinal owned, among other less startling items, the petrified body of a boy, who, according to the testimony of the donor, had recently been turned to stone by the judgment of God.

First and foremost a statesman, it is not surprising that one of Richelieu's hobbies should have been the collecting of portraits of historically notable figures. In his palace, there was, in addition to the gallery of miscellaneous paintings, a hall of fame—a special "Gallery of Famous Men"—which contained twenty-six portraits of celebrated Frenchmen ranging from Sugèr, the Cardinal's twelfth-century predecessor in government reform, to Louis XIII; and fifty-eight additional portraits of the same kind hung in the library.

Occupying an entire wing, it was this library which represented the Cardinal's deepest collecting interest. As an accumulator of art, Richelieu may well have been more ambitious than truly appreciative, and those who scoffed at his love of the magnificent gave him the malicious sobriquet of *Eminentissimus.* But his love of books was without pretense. Engaging learned emissaries to visit Germany and Italy in search of rare items, he was not above plunder in this field: after the fall of the Huguenot stronghold, La Rochelle, he topped off the victory by seizing the town's books for himself; yet with other collectors of gentle tradition, he often swapped items like a lamb.

Richelieu, although pleased to be compared with Maecenas, did not always play the role of lavish patron felicitously. He quarreled with Corneille, whom he had sponsored for a time, and had the great dramatist attacked by the Academy. His own writing ambitions seem to have caused him to prefer those men who would agree with him in literary matters, and it was perhaps because of this that most of those whom he patronized were second-rate authors. Yet the *Académie Française,* first unit of the *Institut de France,* owes its foundation to this knife-sharp man; and his books, which he left to a nephew, upon the latter's death came by bequest into possession of the Sorbonne, thus marking the beginning of a long tradition of non-regal gifts to the public collections.

Early in Richelieu's career, a young Italian churchman succeeded in meeting the great minister; and thereby was determined the course of French history for another generation. The Italian was one Giulio Mazarini, who, since he was later to become a naturalized Frenchman, is better known to history as Jules Mazarin (1602–61).

At the time of the momentous meeting, Mazarin was a nuncio in the papal service, constantly plying between Rome and Paris. Needing funds for his career, the canny young man was in the habit of bringing with him, on each northward journey, a variety of pictures, books, ebony tables, tables of Chinese wood, German cabinets, and objects of *virtu,* to sell to the French, for Paris was rapidly becoming the best market in the world for such things. In Paris, Mazarin lived with a family by the name of Chavigny; and to Madame Chavigny, who was somewhat of an amateur herself, he often brought minor works of art, in addition to soap from Naples and gloves from Rome. The prize pieces he reserved to present to the powerful Cardinal, his acquaintanceship with whom was rapidly ripening into a relationship based upon mutual respect and friendship. Mazarin was a courtier as well as a churchman, and his talent was instinctive for the gift deftly placed. He was well rewarded in after years for his astute study of character, for Richelieu, recognizing in the young Italian a kindred spirit as well as a man of extraordinary ability, accepted him completely and trained him to be his successor.

In 1641, two years after having become a French subject, Mazarin was elevated to a cardinalship. Two years after that, upon the deaths of Richelieu and Louis XIII, he was appointed to the presidency of the French Council. Louis XIV was then only four years old; and though Anne of Austria, the Queen Mother, had been named regent in her husband's will, Mazarin remained, almost to the year of his death, the virtual ruler of France. Even Richelieu's power had been less than his —and opportunities for indulging a passion for collecting were correspondingly available. Mazarin's taste for the pursuit had long been evident, but now he was master of the hunt, and for the rest of his exceedingly active life nothing could deflect him from becoming one of the greatest amateurs of modern times.

Actually, Mazarin's was a series of collections, a true museum, and he employed a special agent for every section. Agents sent him shipments of antique and modern statues and busts from Rome; furniture inlaid with ivory and semiprecious stones from Florence and Milan; rugs from the Levant; laces from Haarlem, Genoa and Venice; porcelains from China; tapestries from Flanders and Portugal; paintings from Italy; and books from everywhere.

Like Richelieu, Mazarin was a bit grandiose in his love of display, and like Richelieu he paid full tribute to the value of money; but his collectomania went far beyond mere ostentation and ambition. The strong fiber of his personality was soaked in the friendly mead of the amateur. Amateur he was completely, and there was no man more so. He employed experts, yes, as well as agents, so that he might have quality as well as quantity; but, not always content to leave his men to their own devices, he was constantly urging them on to bigger and better acquisitions.

Even when the revolting nobles of the Fronde twice threatened bodily violence, Mazarin's concern was for the safety of his collections, which had by that time grown to imposing proportions. Forced to flee the country in January, 1651, he immediately wrote to Jabach, his banker, and to Bernardin, his curator, about precautions to be taken "in case of accident." That dreaded accident occurred nearly a year later, when the Cardinal's enemies ordered that all his effects be put up for sale.

There followed for him a hard period, since the members of the Fronde, temporarily in control of the government, did indeed initiate the sale, all royal decrees to the contrary notwithstanding. Gabriel Naudé, who had been Richelieu's librarian and was now Mazarin's, made an impassioned but fruitless plea before parliament in an attempt to save at least the books; and Mazarin himself, unable to interfere, must have presented a pitiable figure when he learned that all the treasures which he had brought from the ends of the earth were being methodically dispersed. For several months, with occasional interruptions, the sale went on; and not until the weakened political position of the nobles made it advisable at last to heed the constantly reiterated royal command to cease was there an end to it. Yet as soon as the Cardinal returned to Paris, like a retriever he set about hunting his scattered covey, and sycophants were not slow to use the old favor-currying trick, hastening up to him with objects that had been sold, or presenting new items in place of the vanished.

Unlike many early collections, Mazarin's was catalogued before his death, and he considered this volume one of his finest items. The catalogue was compiled by Jean Baptiste Colbert, later finance minister under Louis XIV, but at this time Mazarin's secretary. Extant today, it shows that the Cardinal owned, even after the catastrophe of the dispersal, a library of fifty thousand volumes and four hundred manuscripts; some five hundred and forty-six paintings, including Leonardo's *Saint Ann, the Virgin and Infant Jesus;* three hundred and fifty statues; twenty-one cabinets; four hundred and eleven tapestries—considered among the chief glories of the collection; forty-two Persian rugs; a large quantity of marble tables, Venetian glass, and rock crystal chandeliers; precious stones of great price; and numerous other items.

Richelieu planned to found a library for students, but Mazarin was the first in France actually to open his own book collection to scholars and to the general public. He went even further, for he supplied his guests with chairs and writing materials, and provided attendants to assist them in finding the books. In his will, the Cardinal left his treasures to Louis XIV, but the young king, refusing the splendid bequest, would accept as a gift only those eighteen large diamonds which, two hundred years later, were still reputed to be among those in the French crown.

UNIVERSAL FAVORITES. *Even the Orientals, who have spurned most products of the Occident, have collected Western timepieces, and clocks and watches have long been favorites of European and American collectors. 1) One of the earliest watches known, bronze gilt table watch, Nuremberg,* c. *1560. 2) Silver death's head watch by Isaac Penard,* c. *1600. 3) 17th-cent. rock crystal watch set in cross with enameled case, by Charles Bobinet,* c. *1650. 4) Gold and enamel watch by Daniel Vauchez, commemorating one of the ascents of the Montgolfier balloon, probably 1783 or 1784. 5) Late 18th-cent. French gold, enamel and jeweled watch in form of mandolin, with monogram of Marie Antoinette. 6) Enamel watch with engraved gold back,* c. *1800, said to have been presented by Napoleon to Murat as a gift on the fête day of the Emperor after the Battle of Marengo; contains a mechanism for playing tune at beginning of each hour. 7) Early 19th-cent. French or Swiss gold repeating watch; kitchen scene in varicolored metal and enamel on open back, with mechanical spit, wheel and figure.*

The Metropolitan Museum of Art
(1–6, from The Pierpont Morgan Collection; 7, from The Hearn Collection)

(For legend, see facing page.)

The rest of the collection was, by Louis' command, divided among Mazarin's legitimate heirs, from whom the king then purchased the finest of the statues and paintings. Many of these, including a hundred of the paintings, now belong to the Louvre, while thirty thousand of the books were to become the nucleus of the *Bibliothèque Mazarine.* So Mazarin's name joins that of other immortals, for the world remembers the great collectors, particularly men of the early days, who might well be called curators of culture.

One might not expect hard-headed men of affairs to become true connoisseurs, yet a surprising number, particularly in France, earned the name. The great book collector, Jean Grolier, was one of the earliest of this type. Another was Florimond Robertet, a financier who became Minister of the Treasury under Charles VIII and continued to serve in that capacity under both Louis XII and Francis I. Sincerely devoted to the arts, Robertet used his fortune and influence to build a collection of rarities so extraordinary for its time that it became a legend in the neighborhood of his Château de Bury. There were the first Chinese porcelains to be seen in France, and many masterpieces imported from Italy.

Both these men were strongly marked in attitude by the renaissance, but they were also the spiritual ancestors of the great bourgeois collectors of modern times. It has been noted that when the Age of Discovery brought commerce into its own, it also initiated that new aristocracy which was to march down the highroad of power proudly wagging the scepter of Money. The new people, as important collectors, were soon rivaling kings and ministers. One of the first and greatest was a man names Evrard Jabach (d. 1695), an ancestor of the famous art-dealing Duveen family of modern times. Like Mazarin, Jabach (pronounced *Shabah*) was a Frenchman by adoption only, although he lived in France for some sixty years. The renaissance had had its Medici banker-princes, it is true, but they had been exceptional, and despite the financial basis of their power, their careers had been built into the princely fabric of the times. But in this new era, the Jabachs were beginning to take over that theme of financial authority unadulterated which was to reach its climax in the "money barons" of nineteenth-century America; and Jabach's own career was aptly symbolic of the change and of the factors which brought it about.

Of German origin, probably a native of Cologne, he had come to Paris in 1635, attracted by the commercial opportunities in that now important city. There fortune, coaxed by his own remarkable business ability, smiled upon him. He became the first director of the French East India Company and was Mazarin's trusted banker, two positions which gave him ample means and opportunity for the exercise of his discriminating amateurism. Everything this rich merchant owned was reputedly of exceptional quality. His house was crowded with paintings, drawings, bronzes, marbles, and "the finest porcelains produced in China." Some of the latter were of such distinction that dealers and collectors still know them by his name, and the search for them is as ardent as once it was for "Grolier" books. Among his treasures were two Correggios, now the property of the Louvre, which he had purchased from the Charles I collection but was later forced to dispose of to Mazarin; two Giorgiones; Holbein's portrait of Erasmus; and a *Saint John* by Leonardo. His particular predilection, however, was for drawings: here was a man who owned better than five thousand five hundred "splendid examples" of these, and they too now belong to France's great national museum.

Jabach spent so much time and money on the arts, to which he also gave lavishly of himself, that he was called the "Maecenas of Cologne." During the height of his collecting career—from about 1650 to 1670—his house in the *rue Saint-Merry* was almost as famous a rendezvous for amateurs as had once been the Florentine Niccolò's.

Times had changed since Niccolò's day, however, and when, in 1671, Jabach suffered serious financial reverses, there was no Cosimo de' Medici to save his collection for him. Forced to part with his treasures in order to make good his losses, Jabach first sold some of the paintings to Mazarin and to the duc de Richelieu, Cardinal Richelieu's nephew. When this was not enough and he realized that he must liquidate the entire collection, he offered to sell it to Louis XIV. There followed months-long negotiations through Colbert, who, as finance minister, felt himself bound to obtain the treasures for the least possible amount.

Poor Jabach! It was bad enough to have to relinquish the collection at all, but to have it grossly undervalued by the king's representative was an almost unbearable insult, and the banker's letters on the subject display a change from proud assurance to desperate pleading, and finally to a bitter acceptance of the ridiculously small price offered. Yet despite this succession of hard blows, Jabach showed himself the irrepressible amateur, for as soon as circumstances permitted, he set about forming another collection; and it is good to know that he lived for twenty-five years after the loss of the first to enjoy the second.

A gargantuan bourgeois collector of the next generation was Pierre Crozat (1665–1740), a banker who, having made his fortune, did the first of many remarkable things in retiring at the age of forty to devote all his time to his hobby. Fortunate in having the three requirements—taste, time and money—for successful virtuosity on a large scale, Crozat amassed an enormous collection of artistic treasure, including the astounding number of nineteen thousand drawings (he came into possession of Jabach's entire second collection), four hundred paintings, one thousand four hundred engraved gems, and a distinguished group of ceramics.

His house in Paris (to which city he moved from Toulouse in 1704 in order to be nearer the collecting center) contained special galleries for the exhibition of his paintings and statues, and became a meeting place for amateurs from all Europe. Crozat bought many famous collections to add to his own (a practice common to the tycoons of our own day) and sent agents to every foreign sale of note, while he himself journeyed several times to Italy to purchase pictures.

Like many wealthy collectors of the modern era, Crozat loved to play at being a renaissance prince. Yet with him the game was no half-hearted pretense, since, to the best of his capacity, he retained the typical renaissance generosity in doing so, pensioning, in truly regal fashion, a considerable number of artists, and even going so far as to lodge some of them in his own house. One item in this human art collection was the painter, Lafosse, who, until he died a querulous octogenarian, had free run of the Crozat mansion. Another was the Italian artist, Rosalba Carriera, whom Crozat imported and took in together with her mother, two sisters, and one brother-in-law!

From the artist's point of view, however, there was a grave disadvantage to this apparently heaven-sent arrangement. For Crozat was one of those men who like to exhibit their protégés—and artists, obstinate fellows, could not always reconcile themselves to pleasing him in this respect. Watteau, for example, came at the height of his career to live with Crozat, hoping thus to escape the pursuit of other celebrity hunters. But he soon found that he was expected to keep the regular hours of a well-ordered bourgeois household and to attend the musical and artistic *soirées* which his host was forever staging. Before the year was out Watteau had fled back to his old Bohemian haunts, although he managed to do this apparently without offending the benevolent collector.

Side by side with the virtuosos of books and *objets d'art,* there existed throughout Europe in this period another group of collectors, fewer in number and comparatively colorless, who were making an even more important contribution toward the advancement of knowledge.

Even more than art and literature, scientific thought had suffered a setback during the Dark Age. Such remnants of ancient science as were known to the medieval world were contained only in the meager surviving fragments of Latin compilations, and it was not until the twelfth and thirteenth centuries that the rediscovery of many of the original Greek works, and of the Arabic commentaries on them, prepared the way for a scientific renaissance.

One of the few very early collectors to exhibit anything of the scientific spirit had been the German Frederick II (1194–1250), Holy Roman Emperor and King of the Two Sicilies; and though his time is behind the era that now concerns us, he is worth noting as a possible connecting link in the evolution of modern scientific collecting. An amateur in many fields, Frederick stood far in the vanguard of his own age. According to the modern scholar, Charles Homer Haskins,

"... it was well understood that the Emperor valued a book, a rare bird, or a cunning piece of workmanship more highly than mere objects of luxury."

His chief interest, however, lay in animals and birds. Not only did he collect these in great numbers, but he studied them meticulously. Typical of his attitude was the treatise he wrote on falconry, which, as we are told by Haskins, opened with

"... a systematic and careful discussion of the species, structure and habits of birds, for which the author utilized the *De Animalibus* of Aristotle, such previous treatises as he could find on the subject, and the results of his own observation and inquiry."

A fondness for the unusual and the exotic was a distinguishing characteristic of scientific collectors centuries after Frederick's time. And no more than the amateurs who collected purely for pleasure did these men confine themselves to specialized fields, so that, were it not for their trail-blazing accomplishments, the extent of their interests and activities would seem almost childish today.

Typical of the many sixteenth-century "fathers" of modern science was Georg Agricola (1494–1555) whose real name was Bauer, of which Agricola is the Latinized form. We know him as the "father of mineralogy," but in his own lifetime mineralogy was far from science, and Agricola's pursuit of the subject was little more than a hobby. He was a practicing physician who concerned himself with mathematics, theology, philology and history as well as medicine and mineralogy, and it was only because he lived in a mining section of Germany that he was able to indulge so fully in the collection and study of mineralogical specimens. For this work he is now best known, but he was also indirectly responsible for a communal benefaction of quite a different order, since his writings influenced the Elector Augustus I of Saxony to found the famous Green Vaults of Dresden in 1560, and these collections, later greatly expanded by the porcelain fancier, Augustus the Strong (1670–1733), became stepping stones to various museums which have crowned modern Dresden one of the cultural centers of the world.

Throughout the sixteenth and seventeenth centuries, the assembling of natural history specimens along with curiosities and wonders was widely practiced, by dilettanti as well as by more serious men; and the methods employed were such that it is not always easy to distinguish between the two types of collector. Of this confusion Nicolas-Claude Fabri de Peiresc (1580–1637) of Aix furnishes an excellent example. An antiquary and a scholar who spent his life in study and travel, Peiresc was an omnivorous collector. Natural history, archaeology, numismatics, literature and art all fell within his broad province.

Peiresc would give away any one of his treasures to a scholar who really required it for study, but there was an erratic quality here—he kept an army of cats to act as policemen for his library. For his day Peiresc was an intelligent and serious collector; but should a modern student be able to visit his house, he would find it the very epitome of disorder. Crowned by an observatory (Peiresc also studied astronomy) that house was filled from top to bottom with books, antiquities, and curiosities without any attempt at classified arrangement. The library could not hold all the books, and so there were manuscripts in among the statues, vases, coins, and engraved gems, while portraits were mixed up with rare animals, exotic plants, mummies, and mathematical instruments.

Letters formed an important part of this eclectic collection: there had been more than ten thousand of these at the time of Peiresc's death, but a small niece, not yet initiated into the mysteries of collecting, used a good many of them for fire-kindling before she was discovered in her crime. Of those that survived, some were purchased for Mazarin, and some now belong to the *Bibliothèque Nationale* and to the British Museum.

Peiresc was an outstanding but not unusual representative of the collector of his period. By the seventeenth century, collectors had become so numerous, among all groups but the most poverty-stricken lower classes, that several inventory-minded persons set about collecting collectors, so to speak, compiling long detailed lists of contemporary followers of the pursuit and listing their special interests.

Two of the earliest of these lists were published in France by men who were themselves confirmed collectors. In 1649, Maistre Pierre Borel (1620–71), a physician of Castres, published a book called *Antiquitez de la ville de Castres* in which he gave the names of the principal "curiosity cabinets" in the chief European cities. Maistre Borel's own collection was typical, and included such varied objects as books, medals, prints, engravings, armor, pottery and paintings, to say nothing of "human rarities," four-footed beasts, birds, fish, other marine exhibits, insects and serpents, plants, woods, roots, leaves, gums, seeds of grain, rare fruits, other fruits and grains, minerals, stones, and petrified objects.

Another of the list-compilers, Jacob Spon (1647–85) of Lyons, was somewhat more moderate, for he collected only coins, manuscripts, inscriptions, antiques, and rare plants. Spon was a physician, antiquarian and traveler who occasionally sold some of his items in order to raise funds for still another journey. In reference to his catalogue of collectors, published in 1673, he wrote:

"It is not surprising that I, too, am something of a collector, because I know almost all the collectors in Lyons, and it is well known that the disease is contagious even when it is not fatal!"

The "disease" was certainly contagious in his day, for although the population of France was at that time but a third of its present size,

Walters Art Gallery, Baltimore

THE "RUBENS" VASE

Carved from a single mass of agate more than seven inches high, this Byzantine piece is one of the most important gem carvings known. The painter, Rubens, bought it for his collection at the Paris "Flea Market" in 1619, and from it made a cast and a drawing for his friend, Peiresc. Ex. colls. Louis de France, Duke of Anjou (1339-84); French Royal Collection, Fontainebleau (1560); William Beckford (c. 1823); Duke of Hamilton (1882); and others.

one writer in 1693 was able to enumerate a hundred and thirty-four *fameux curieux* in Paris alone; and two centuries later a modern savant, compiling a biographical dictionary of seventeenth-century French collectors, found his work extending to three hundred and thirty-two pages and including nearly eleven hundred individuals, many of whose names had survived for two or three hundred years chiefly because they had been collectors.

Private collections were far more freely exhibited in those days than they are in our own. Spoken of as "museums," they actually did in some degree take the place now assumed by public institutions, and travelers in search of culture or amusement were in the habit of visiting them much as the modern tourist "takes in" the galleries and museums covered by his itinerary.

One collection mentioned by the English diarist, John Evelyn—that of a Monsieur Morine—is particularly noteworthy because of its similarity to another formed contemporaneously in England by the Tradescants. The British Tradescants, father and son, are generally credited with having founded the first true museum of modern times, although the chief difference between their collection and the ordinary ones of their period lay in the fact that it was regularly open to the general public (no invitation being required, as was usually the case) and that a catalogue to its contents was published. In both the Tradescant and Morine collections, the close relationship which existed between curiosity hunters and scientific collectors is clearly shown. Both had been formed by men whose chief interests lay in the field of natural history, yet both were general collections, containing the usual run of *objets d'art*, exotica, marvels, and simple curiosities, in addition to the specialized exhibits. Of the Morine collection, Evelyn wrote, on April 1, 1644:

"I was had by a friend to the garden of Monsieur Morine, who, from being an ordinary gardiner, is become one of the most skilful and curious persons in France for his rare collection of porcelain and coral, whereof one carved into a large crucifix is much esteemed. He has also books of prints by Albert, Van Leyden, Callot, etc. His collection of all sorts of insects, especially of butterflies, is most curious; these he spreads and so medicates, that no corruption invading them, he keeps them in drawers, so placed as to represent a beautiful piece of tapestry. He showed me the remarks he had made on their propagation, which he promised to publish. Some of these, as also of his best flowers, he had caused to be painted in miniature by rare hands, and some in oil."

Because of his own interest in natural history, Evelyn was particularly fascinated by this collection, and some years later he again visited it, recording, in an entry dated May 23, 1651:

"I visited Mr. Morine's garden, and his other rarities, especially corals, minerals, stones and natural curiosities: crabs of the Red Sea, the body no bigger than a small bird's egg, but flatter, and the two leggs or claws a foote in length. He had abundance of shells, at least a thousand sorts, which furnished a cabinet of great price; and had a curious collection of scarabees, and insects, of which he was compiling a natural history. He had also pictures of his choice flowers and plants in miniature. He told me there were ten thousand sorts of tulips only. He had *taille-douces* without number; the head of a Rhinoceros bird, which was very extravagant, and one butterfly resembling a perfect bird."

Mentioned in entries picked at random from Evelyn's diary are a gardener-scientist, a count, a former ambassador, a painter-curator, and several plain *monsieurs.* Everyman was coming into his own. Yet this was the height of the courtly age, whose most famous exhibit, Louis XIV (1638–1715), now sat upon the throne. And it was Louis who epitomized the true spirit of that age in collecting, much as Francis I had epitomized the spirit of the French renaissance.

Although surrounded by officials and wealthy citizens who put a tremendous enthusiasm into their own collecting activities, *le grand monarque* was not himself intrinsically an amateur. He was, however, perhaps the first to appreciate the prestige value of vast royal accumulations of cultural objects. Upon his accession, the *cabinet du roi,* as the royal collections were then known, consisted of some two hundred paintings, the coin and gem collections initiated by his predecessors, and a not inconsiderable group of objects of *virtu.* Louis determined to make it the most impressive set of collections on earth. Wherefore there was flung out over the world a large net of special agents, and in his later years his very ministers became *commissionaires* on his behalf. During his reign important purchases were negotiated, notably from the Mazarin and Jabach collections, and a short royal road to favor lay in making a substantial gift to the "cabinet." It is not surprising, therefore, that by 1710 the number of paintings owned by the crown (in a collection which included the work of contemporary artists as well as that of old masters) had increased from two hundred to two thousand three hundred and seventy-six.

Privately, Louis' eyes turned with the greatest enthusiasm to the coin and gem collections, and into this flowed the largest sums. It was his conception to use this part of the cabinet as a means of commemorating and passing on to posterity the record of his own military victories by adding modern coins and medals—specifically designed for this purpose—to the vast number of ancient specimens he was accumulating. As a corollary development, modern coins of a general nature, both French and foreign, were now collected for the first time, and the present *Cabinet National des Médailles et Antiques* contains this royal collection as its base.

In 1683, Louis had ordered the royal collections moved to Versailles, and there the coins and medals (with the exception of the most precious gems and some of the gold medals, kept in the king's own casket) were proudly displayed in seventeen cedar cabinets. Here was Louis' favorite retreat, to which he came almost every day after mass. To spare the medals from handling, he used special gold spatulas; and he himself took an active part in the compiling of a great catalogue of them, published, however, only after his own eyes were closed forever.

When Mazarin was with one hand directing the affairs of France and with the other so freely gathering up items for a magnificent private collection, Louis XIV was still too young to be a serious rival. Mazarin's successor in the councils of the king was less fortunate; for though Jean-Baptiste Colbert (1619–83) became extremely influential as one of the ablest finance ministers in French history, Louis saw to it that he never attained the almost absolute power that had been both Richelieu's and Mazarin's; as a virtuoso, Colbert had need to stand back while the royal collector took first choice.

Had it not been his fate successively to serve two masters whose acquisitive desires, as strong as his own, were backed by greater authority than his, Colbert, like Mazarin, might have been known as one of the great amateurs of his time. As it is, his reputation in this field rests securely on certain more disinterested services. In his younger days he had created Mazarin's much-prized catalogue, and now he devoted a large share of his energy to the formation of Louis' collections. Under his tutelage, French consuls in every European country were constantly on the lookout for every sort of collectible. Much of their garnering went, of necessity, into the king's hungry cabinets; yet even so a considerable allotment usually found its way into the hands of the minister amateur, who managed to secure for himself a typical, if not outstanding, collection of *objets d'art* and numismata. His library was considered the third most important in Europe, while his scientific leanings found expression in the collecting of mathematical instruments and natural history specimens.

Yet this was not enough for the energy and scope of the man. A genuine patron of art, literature and the sciences, Colbert founded the *Académie des Inscriptions et Belles Lettres* (1663) and the *Académie des Sciences* (1666), augmented the *Académie des Beaux-Arts* which had been organized by Mazarin, encouraged foreign artists and craftsmen to come to France, negotiated the purchase of the Gobelins tapestry factory for the state, and organized the royal collection of prints and engravings.

In the life of this successful realist, then, we see how an interest in collecting can supplement an interest in science and in art, and how, in a mind such as Colbert's, appreciation and understanding in these three fields can build worthily.

Seldom have women, as collectors, achieved such equality of reputation with men as was theirs among the French for several centuries. Even in late medieval times, France had produced a few women amateurs who could claim equal rank with their men, occasionally even surpassing them in a day when presumably such achievement was impossible. Thus Clemence of Hungary, second wife of Louis X (rg. 1314–16) formed a library richer than her husband's. Most of her books were acquired by another queen, Jeanne d'Evreux, third wife of Charles the Fair (rg. 1322–28), whose own collection was considered so important that the great bibliophile, Charles the Wise, reached eagerly for a portion of it. Jeanne of Burgundy and Blanche of Navarre, the two wives of Philip VI (rg. 1328–50), and Bonne of Luxembourg, first wife of the bibliophile, John II (rg. 1350–64), were all book lovers and book collectors. And another lady amateur of this early period, the Duchess of Bourbonnais, heiress of John, Duke of Berry, went so far in her enthusiasm for books as to renounce her claim to the succession

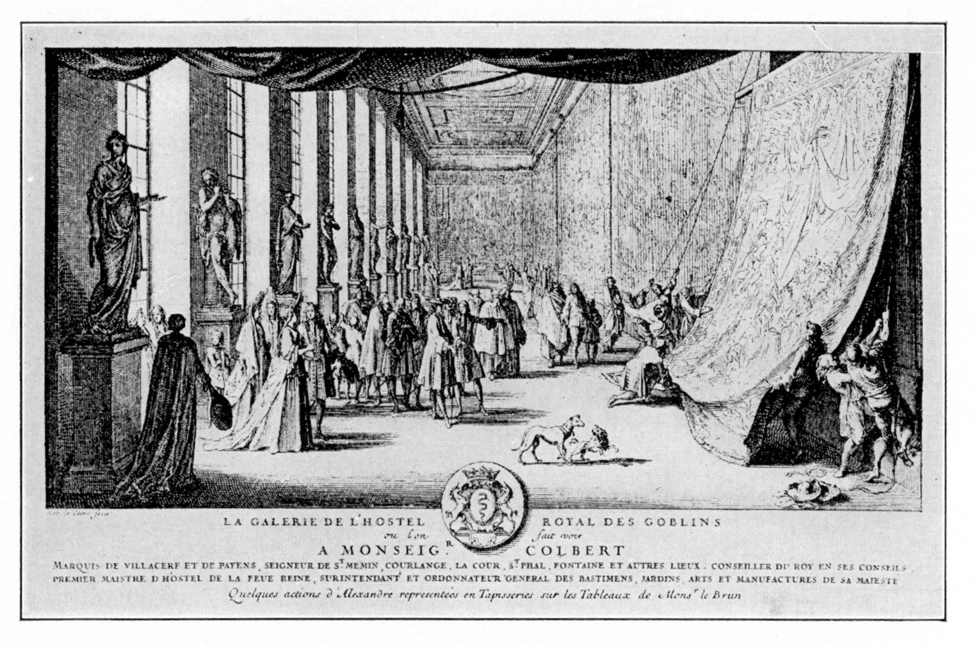

COLBERT PAYS A VISIT TO THE GOBELINS TAPESTRY FACTORY, *purchase of which he negotiated for the State. From the engraving by Sébastien Le Clerc (1673-1714).*

CARDINAL MAZARIN IN HIS GALLERY. *Note the globe, and the maps in his hand and on the wall behind him. From an engraving by Robert Nanteuil (1623-78); the very rare first state.*

AMONG THE GREATEST OF FRENCH PATRONS AND COLLECTORS WERE CHURCHMEN AND MINISTERS OF STATE.

in order to obtain forty-one of the most beautiful volumes from the duke's library.

It is in the more glamorous eras of the renaissance and the courtly age, however, that we encounter the truly brilliant feminine procession. Then, although there was no open suffrage, the masculine brain in women was increasingly accepted, and the prerogatives of meddling in politics and in that splendiferous collecting which had become the first fashion of the day were jointly embraced by the ladies. From the sixteenth through the eighteenth centuries, queens and queen mothers and the mistresses of kings, to say nothing of the holders of "salons," were frequently as active in political and social life as were the most powerful ministers. They had at their disposal, therefore, the same extraordinary opportunities for competitive collecting as the rulers themselves, and they entered this portal with all the charm of feminine grace—a grace which concealed masculine determination.

The first member of the scintillating coterie was Michelle Gaillard de Lonjumeau, wife of that Florimond Robertet who was minister of finance under Charles VIII, Louis XII, and Francis I. She must share the honors of a great collection with her husband, with whom she also shared a deep and sincere love of the arts. Yet she is outstanding in her own right for the fact that, after Robertet's death, it was she who compiled the catalogue of their paintings, bronzes, marbles, ivories and alabasters, the Chinese porcelains, goldsmiths' work, silverware and jewelry, the tapestries, Venetian glass, French *faïence,* Italian, German, Flemish, English and Spanish pottery, church ornaments and books.

To do this could have been no mean task, and it is the more noteworthy that Madame Robertet's catalogue, still extant, is far from being a mere inventory, but rather, in the words of Bonnaffé:

". . . a little masterpiece, drawn up lovingly, giving details of the provenance, use, form, location, and associations of most of the items, taking one into the Robertet family circle, showing a couple of lovers and amateurs."

This lady was, then, a good and a true collector, well equipped both in heart and in mind to excel in her chosen field, fortunate in her marriage to an amateur of equal caliber. Charming, and touching, is her note on one item of her own:

". . . twenty-three rings on a little gold chain, in each one of which there is a diamond worth two or three hundred francs. Their number is that of the years of my marriage, and I have taken pleasure in collecting them so that every time I look into my cabinet I may be reminded how long I enjoyed happiness."

Collecting is a habit which often runs in families, and he who was the greatest virtuoso of the French renaissance, King Francis I, came honestly enough by his fondness for the pursuit, as the son of an ardent lady bibliophile.

Born into the world twenty years after the invention of printing and six years after the installation of the first French press, Louise de Savoie, strong-willed Duchess of Angoulême (1476–1531), has, like Isabella d'Este, often been accused of penury, yet seldom did she spare expense where books were concerned. One of the first things she did after her marriage was to enlarge the library at Angoulême; and in 1497 she engaged the fashionable bookseller, Vérard, to assist her in expanding her own collection at Cognac.

Reputed to have possessed one of the most brilliant minds in France, Louise could be cold and ruthless when beating her direct way to a political goal, but she had a soft spot in her heart for artists and writers, often taking them under her protection in time of need; and not only to her son, but also to her lovely daughter, Marguerite d'Angoulême (1492–1549), Queen of Navarre, did she pass on her interest in cultural pursuits.

Marguerite, whom Francis fondly called his *mignonne,* and whom others named variously *"la Marguerite des marguerites,"* the "Fourth Charity," and "Queen of the Muses," was herself a distinguished writer, her most famous work being the still much-read *Heptameron.* Yet not content merely to be a creator in her own right, she became also a great collector and a great patroness. Although often pressed for funds, she was so generous that poets and scholars were moved to apply to her also the somewhat overworked name of "Maecenas," and her motto, *plus vous que moi,* spoke for itself in this regard. No doubt her collection—of sculpture and paintings, of Limosin enamels, Cellini gold plate and delicately wrought jewels—and her fine books bound in a rich brown leather sprinkled with marguerites, would speak equally well for her taste if they could now be reassembled.

Strangely, sadly intertwined were the lives of two other women of this period, two devoted collectors, forced to share between them the man they both loved.

One was Catherine de Médicis (1519–89), great-granddaughter of Lorenzo the Magnificent and wife of Henry II of France (1519–59). The other was Diane de Poitiers (1499–1566), who, though the senior by twenty years of both Catherine and Henry, commanded the king's love for nearly a quarter of a century, from his early youth to the day of his untimely death. Able and intelligent women both, Catherine and Diane were each descended from families long steeped in the collecting tradition, and both showed an especial bent for the pursuit.

Daughter of Jean de Poitiers, a well-known bibliophile, Diane had been brought up in an atmosphere of book lore, and during her early married life—to a man more than thirty-seven years older than herself—she turned more and more to the company of books, and horses. Four years after her husband's death, however, the friendship with young Prince Henry took root; and when, in 1547, Henry ascended the throne of France, Diane found herself suddenly transplanted into collector's heaven, for not only was she now in possession of the obvious advantages of her favored position, but her royal lover bestowed upon her the title of Duchess of Valentinois, which carried with it a great fortune and one of the loveliest castles in the land.

It was at Chenonceaux, gift of the king, and at Anet (her husband's ancestral château, which she replaced with a beautiful renaissance building) that Diane assembled her fine collection of Limosin enamels, Palissy pottery, tapestries, furniture, and, above all, books. Patronizing French artists and craftsmen, she made of Anet such a cultural center that the writers, painters, sculptors, architects and designers who flocked there were known as "the school of Anet." As Grace Hart Seely has aptly expressed it:

> "The Château d'Anet [became] the book of Diane de Poitiers' life carefully cut in stone, a casket to enshrine her treasures. First among these were her books . . . one of the best if not the first collection, outside of the Royal Library, in all Europe."

Truly French, Diane delighted in beautiful bindings, and Henry never tired of presenting her with superlative examples. Yet she did not permit him to neglect the royal collection, and it was largely due to her influence that there was passed, in 1558, a law requiring every

French publisher to present to the libraries at Blois and at Fontainebleau a copy of each book issued—an ordinance of obvious importance to the future of the French national collection.

This lady was the first of the so-called "cabinet-book collectors"—that is, collectors of small but elegant volumes—and long after her death, when, in 1723, the library at Anet was dispersed, a small case of these volumes came to light, all bound in red and citron morocco and decorated with the crescents of Diana, the huntress. For generations afterward to own even one of those exquisite books was the dearest hope of many a bibliophile.

Catherine, the Queen, was loser in the battle of love, but a cynical fate gave her the upper hand in the end, for shortly after Henry's death his wife became regent, and for thirty years thereafter during the lifetimes of her two sons, Charles IX and Henry III, Catherine de Médicis was to be the dominating figure in France. One of her first acts upon Henry's decease was to oust his mistress from that Château de Chenonceaux which she, his wife, had always coveted, and to change all the "H-Ds" with which the building had been decorated into "H-Cs."

Catherine's career as regent has been the subject of much historical controversy, and so also have been her motives as a collector, but no one can dispute the fact that she did amass an enormous and widely varied group of items. When, as a thirteen-year-old child, the future queen journeyed to France to be married, she brought with her as a nucleus for later accumulations several valuable manuscripts which had once belonged to the Eastern emperors, and which had been purchased long before by her ancestor, Cosimo de' Medici. During those unhappy days when Henry was held under Diane's spell, Catherine may have found some consolation in her growing collection, but even during her busiest years as regent she never ceased accumulating. Her tastes leaned toward luxury, and it has been said that she was more wealthy dilettante than true connoisseur. A Venetian ambassador once declared:

"The Queen Mother has this much of the temperament of her ancestors that she desires to leave behind her a memory attached to buildings, libraries, and collections of antiques. So she has made a beginning of every sort of artistic patronage and dropped it and turned to doing something else."

The Pierpont Morgan Library

French women bibliophiles were captivated by fine bindings. This book, a Camerarius, Paris, 1556, was bound for the library of Diane de Poitiers and her royal lover, Henri II. Note the royal crown, the crescents of Diana, the Huntress, and the entwined initials.

This charge is substantiated to some degree by a staggering inventory of her possessions, still extant. Yet there is evidence that she had taste, and even painters admitted that she could draw beautifully. Historical subjects comprised a good part of the three hundred and forty odd paintings in her possession, for Catherine, like Richelieu after her, was fascinated by people. An indication of her adventurous mind was her collection of thirty-three manuscript maps, by such great cartographers as Mercator and Ortelius, on which she continuously followed the exciting geographical developments of her day. When tired of the broad world, however, she might journey to a special and favorite room, built for the exhibition of her Limosin enamels, and these jewel-like beauties she loved without question.

It is true that Catherine followed every fad and fashion of her day, as her corals and sea shells, her miniature objects, and her array of costumed dolls (the collecting of which was a popular Italian vogue) bear witness. Yet beautifully appointed books attracted her genuinely, and her eclectic library, which contained four thousand five hundred volumes (including manuscripts of the tenth, eleventh, twelfth and thirteenth centuries) was impressive. Like so many others before and since, when she could obtain a volume in no other way she would steal it. And there was the case of *le maréchal* Strozzi, her own kinsman, who died in the French service. He possessed a fine library, and upon his death, according to one modern account, Catherine seized upon this with almost indecent haste:

"She made no secret of the fact that she had awaited his death with anticipation,"

runs this report, although the truth of the matter is that she did offer to pay Strozzi's heirs at some later date. Actually the payment was never made, but this may well have been a defection due rather to womanly procrastination than to intention, for extravagant Catherine was always in debt, and upon her own death, queen though she was, her treasures had to be sold to make good her obligations, which amounted to eight hundred thousand *écus*. The library, however, was saved, mainly through the efforts of another great bibliophile, Jacques-Auguste de Thou (1553–1617), and, added to the gradually expanding royal collection, it has since come into possession of the *Bibliothèque Nationale*.

Catherine's bookish tastes did not die, for they were inherited by her erratic daughter, Marguerite de Valois (1553–1615)—whose carefree way of life as first wife of King Henry of Navarre led her people to christen her, somewhat irreverently, *"la reine Margot."*

Known as the most learned woman of her day, Margot, like Marguerite d'Angoulême, that other intellectual Queen of Navarre, was a writer as well as a collector of books. Today her library is chiefly notable for an excellent scheme she concocted, whereby each classification in the collection was marked by the distinctive color of its bindings. Thus, the works on science and philosophy were bound in citron morocco, history and theology in red, and so on. The poets, with a single exception, were in green, although, strangely interesting twist, the writings of the brilliant but scurrilous and blackmailing poet-wit of the Italian renaissance, Pietro Aretino, were set apart in covers of immaculate white. What really gives Margot her permanent niche in the collector's Hall of Fame, however, is the fact that this arch-feminist was probably the first in history to employ a member of that now ubiquitous tribe, the lady librarian.

To name a royal lady or a royal mistress of the seventeenth and eighteenth centuries is almost equivalent to naming a collector. Clanswomen in this one respect were such varied characters as Mazarin's regal friend, Anne of Austria, and Madame de Montespan, Louis XIV's elegant mistress; the virtuous and rather dull Marquise de Maintenon and the dazzling Pompadour. Many others might be mentioned, all the way down to that unfortunate queen of revolution, the lightheaded Marie Antoinette. But let us speak here of another lady, who, although without royal connection by birth or amours, belonged to the same sisterhood.

The story of Jeanne-Baptiste d'Albert de Luynes, born at Paris in 1670, is one of those slightly tarnished glamour tales for which the courtly age is notorious. She came of excellent family, and the king's minister, Colbert, attended her baptism. So did the current royal mistress, Anne-Julie de Rohan, whose presence upon such an occasion, might, by those superstitiously inclined, have been held partly responsible for the wavering course traveled by the little girl's star in later years. Of such matters we know nothing, and can only report that, married at the tender age of thirteen to one Comte de Verrue, Jeanne was taken by her husband to Savoy, where her wit and beauty even-

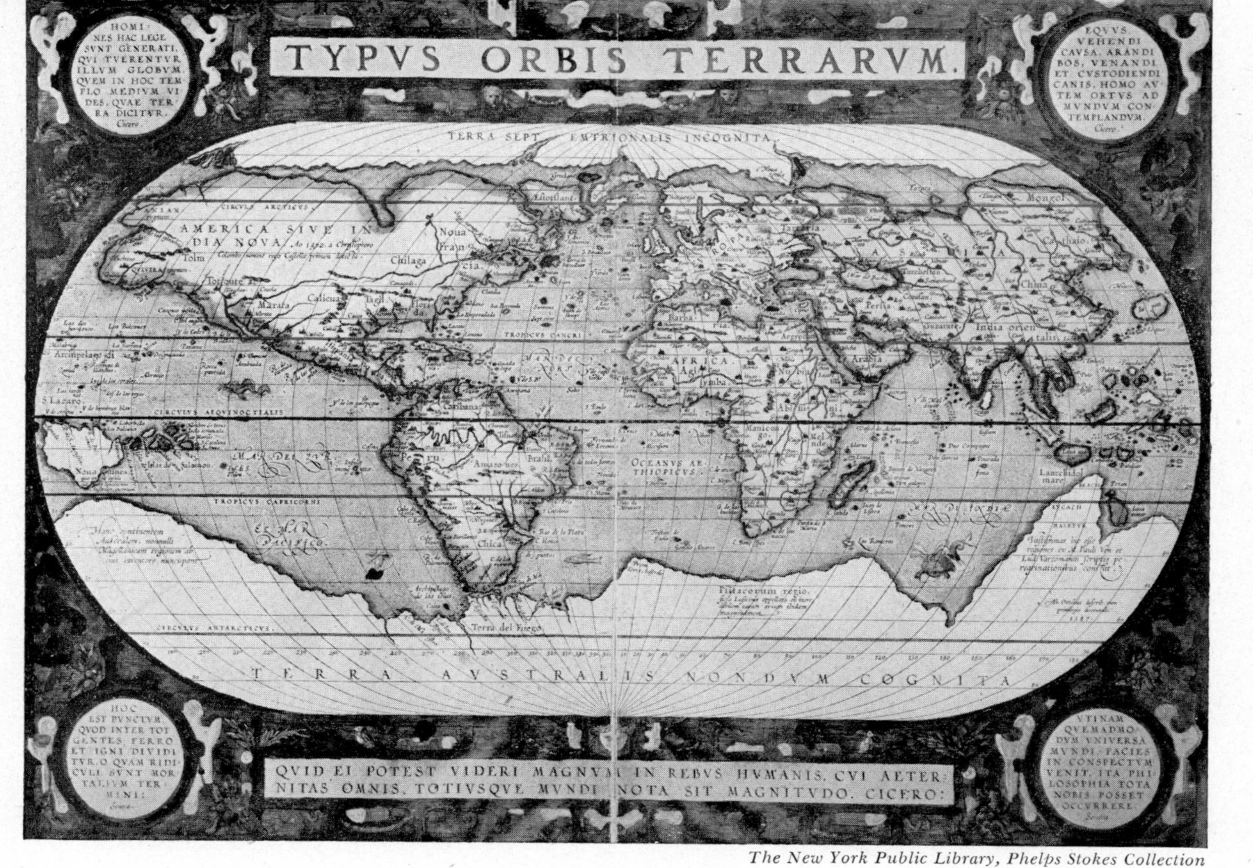

The New York Public Library, Phelps Stokes Collection

THE IMAGE OF THE LANDS OF THE EARTH *by Abraham Ortelius, from the atlas,* THEATRUM ORBIS TERRARUM, *first published in Antwerp, 1570. Catherine de Medicis pored over maps like this in her collections, tracing the exciting geographical developments of her day.*

tually attracted the more than casual attention of the reigning duke, Victor Amedèo. We are told that the young countess at first made every effort to avoid her wicked suitor; but gentle virtue received scant encouragement from either husband or mother-in-law, who, apparently far from being mortified, were delighted by the turn of events, since they stood to benefit politically from any sort of intimate connection with the Duke of Savoy. Thus trapped, the girl-wife took up the role of ducal mistress before she had turned twenty. Though her years were few, she had already become practiced in bearing children, and during the ten years that she remained in favor with the duke she continued the practice. Thus was she kept well enough occupied. The duke, however, was a jealous lover who guarded his favorite in virtual imprisonment; and it was this final detail which bored the high-spirited countess almost beyond endurance, until at last she sought refuge and distraction in collecting.

Like Catherine de Médicis, Jeanne's attention wandered restlessly from one hobby to another. For a while she collected coins, but her interest in these quickly waned. Then, in turn, she took up porcelains, Chinese knickknacks, fine furniture, and rare textiles; and when, in 1700, she escaped to France during the duke's absence, she took care to send her collections on ahead of her. She built a fine house in Paris, and since she was witty, gay and generous, she was soon the center of a distinguished circle of friends including, they say, a new lover now and then.

As for collecting, it appears that she had become a completely unreserved subject, and her nephew, the Duc de Luynes, writing of her in his memoirs, declared that she was always buying something (she spent about a hundred thousand *livres* a year), that she was, indeed, unable to exercise the least restraint over her acquisitive whims. Whenever she wanted anything, she was in the habit of purchasing six to ten times what she actually needed, with the result that when she died a year was required to compile the thousand-page inventory of her effects.

Everything from clothing to pigeons, from paintings to snuff, became a collectible to this redoubtable shopper. Even her wardrobe was swollen beyond measure in this manner: in it were found some sixty corsets, four hundred and eighty shirts, an unbelievable number of dresses, six dozen fans, and more than five hundred dozen handkerchiefs. In a more serious direction, she had a library of from fifteen to eighteen thousand books, particularly rich in the drama and in light novels, many of the volumes annotated in her own hand. Of her four hundred paintings, the majority were displayed in a special gallery; and she must have chosen them with discrimination, for it was said of her that her love affairs had given her fame for a day but that her books and paintings would win her immortality.

The most striking of her hobbies, to a latter-day observer, was her collection of snuffs. It was the custom, in the eighteenth century, for each individual to prepare his own snuff according to his personal taste. A mixture thus prepared retained the name of the fancier for whom it had been made, and might easily become a collector's association item. Madame de Verrue had more than sixty pots, urns, and boxes of famous snuffs—in themselves a veritable museum group—for among them were the snuffs of the East India Company, those used by the queen, by the Cardinal de Rohan, the Elector of Hanover, and so on, all carefully catalogued either according to vintage or "association."

Of all the collecting sisterhood, however, the greatest was probably that long-named girl, Jeanne Antoinette Poisson le Normant d'Etioles, who became Madame de Pompadour (1721–64). Sex aside, this lady was in many ways the *type par excellence* of the eighteenth-century virtuoso, and many facets of the age in which she lived were reflected in her career.

A member of the "middle section of the middle classes," 'Toinette was brought up among wealthy financiers and merchants, many of whom were enthusiastic collectors. Her father, vulgar, unattractive—a typical by-product of the more unsavory side of a commercialistic age—earned his living as *commissionaire* for a profiteering Paris firm, and was eventually forced to flee the country in order to avoid imprisonment for his shady dealings; but her mother, in significant contrast, was a woman of beauty and wit, intelligence and ambition—qualities to which the daughter fell heir in full measure.

'Toinette also had a guardian, Charles le Normant de Tournehem, who assumed the responsibility for her education. This gentleman, says Margaret Trouncer, was a "wealthy and intelligent bachelor . . . a kind of Lorenzo il Magnifico, friend of artists, lover of art, collector of beautiful objects"; and it was with him that Madame Poisson schemed for her offspring's advancement. 'Toinette was introduced to artists, writers and connoisseurs, among them the Comte de Caylus, one of the greatest antiquarians of the day; and when the whirlpool of intrigue at last drew her to the attention of that most susceptible monarch, Louis XV, she was no gauche and scratchy creature, but, like the talented young swan, could swim with the finest.

That she perform with ease all things required of her was essential, for la Pompadour was put to the severe social test of being the first bourgeoise to become acknowledged mistress of a French king. Though to do so in this small strange world was a breathless game, the young woman had both spirit and intelligence sufficient to overcome her most malicious opponents; and so firmly did she take hold that for nearly a quarter of a century she virtually ruled the intricate social life of Versailles. In this, the period of unbridled court luxury, it was Pompadour who set the pace. She had no less than a mania for rebuilding, redecorating, and refurnishing houses, and the châteaux of Bellevue, Choisy, Menars, la Celle, Montretout, and the Hermitage at Versailles all felt the touch of that airy, capable hand. The horde of sculptors, painters and builders, of gilders, smelters, workers in glass, carpenters and gardeners which she employed helped to bleed white the treasury of France, but artists and craftsmen profited richly by her patronage.

Although she had the eighteenth-century enthusiasm for *chinoiseries*, an enthusiasm which as a collector she fully indulged, it was Pompadour's aim to patronize and encourage French arts and crafts above all others. Some of the finest book bindings of the period were made for her library. She thought of completing the Louvre and converting it into a national museum. And it was she who, in 1756, transported the Vincennes china factory to Sèvres, and, by her subsequent patronage, set a fashion for this ware which has endured ever since. With a shrewd talent for promotion, she herself acted as saleswoman at the inaugural sale of Sèvres porcelain at Versailles; and one biographer, declaring that Pompadour had always been ambitious for immortal fame, concludes that she recognized one road toward that goal in the foundation of the national china factory.

In some matters Pompadour was unquestionably a dilettante, but in others she was as unquestionably the serious and intelligent amateur. A natural reservoir of good taste was underscored by a talent for music and drawing, and engravings from her own hand were sincerely praised by professionals. Boucher, the painter, was her friend, and shared with her, among other things, a delight in collecting small objects:

"Many a time he brought to her the latest treasures he had purchased," writes Margaret Trouncer, "—his amethysts and crystals full of strange fires, his Siberian malachites, his corals, his alabasters and his collection of beautiful sea shells. . . . Both of them loved the eighteenth-century land of caprice, China, with its jades and porcelains. He was blamed by all his contemporaries for making China, at the instigation of Pompadour, a province of Rococo."

Pompadour loved gardens and collected rare and imported plants, among which were fifty orange trees, one yellow jasmine of Judea, a sensitive plant and two oleanders. She had a fine library, notable for its valuable section on the theater. She formed collections of engravings, of Chinese porcelains and Chinese and Japanese lacquers, of Saxe porcelains, Sèvres ware, and Boulle marbles. On Oriental lacquers alone she is supposed to have spent one hundred and ten thousand *livres*, and the ultimate dispersal of her furniture took an entire year to accomplish. Small wonder that Mercier then wrote:

". . . the wealth of the four quarters of the world seemed to have been raked together to provide the objects of luxury, fantasy and magnificence found in this rare collection."

The eighteenth century was the "brilliant" period of French collecting, but it was a brilliancy which tended more and more to degenerate into mere dilettantism. Money had become almost as important as birth or valor as a means to position, and spending had grown competitive and exhibitionistic. The court, in its last splendid flare, popularized the ritual of conspicuous waste and ornamental idleness, so that even those who had newly garnered their riches in the market place tried to demonstrate the artistic tastes and the capacity for luxurious living which had so long been an aristocratic trademark. To follow the fashion of the moment was the common height of ambition—and so one collected, whether or not one had any real desire to do so.

Toward the end of this century, collections—with, of course, a few exceptions—changed and depreciated in character. To the incalculable loss of France, even interest in great paintings waned. Little pictures and little "curiosities" (miniatures, knickknacks, snuffboxes, bonbonnières, and other tinkly things) claimed attention instead. Other parts of Europe were enriched, as the older, finer French collections were broken up to make way for the current fads. And bringing up the tail of the procession were those fakers and forgers who always prey upon the unenlightened ambitious collector. Such men found business unusually good during these years of declining taste and became so brazen that at least one of them published his "confessions."

Meanwhile a suppressed earthquake was rumbling ominously—the earthquake of revolution. It broke forth at last; and then it was that the court's mad extravagance brought an accounting in the wanton destruction or theft of all it had held most dear—for the people's grotesque revenge in blood was inevitably paralleled in a contempt (born both of rage and of ignorance) for the priceless objects which had symbolized the life and values of the oppressors. It is true that the revolution finally resulted in the foundation of public museums in France, but havoc visited the private collections, for, in one way or another, most of the treasures of the nobility were dispersed.

Some members of the court had shown signs of prudence, hastily burying certain items against an all-clear signal that, for so many, was never to come; and even today such caches are occasionally unearthed during the course of builders' excavations. Considerable numbers of precious objects were successfully smuggled out of the country, and, if their owners succeeded in following them, served as precarious capital for a while. Many were given as bribes in the desperate barter for life, or were sold for anything they would bring—say a priceless snuffbox for a peasant's rags, or a carriage in which to escape. And after the hurricane had spent itself, remaining families still possessed of valuables were often forced by poverty to sell what was left.

In the days of the Bourbons in France, the royal collection had still been a possession of the crown exclusively, a monument to the glory of the king. Yet even then the shut door was occasionally to be found ajar; for while the palace exhibition rooms were not at the time officially open to the general public, parties of carefully selected sightseers were not infrequently permitted to gaze upon its dazzling spectacle. Moreover, beginning in 1750, exhibitions of paintings from the royal cabinet were, for the public benefit, staged twice weekly in the palace that afterward became the *Musée du Luxembourg.* Even as the revolution was gathering, a further plan for converting the palace of the Louvre also into a museum was being drawn up by the Comte d'Anigiviller, director of the king's buildings under Louis XVI.

Thus even at this time the *cabinet du roi* was well on its way toward becoming a public treasure. But revolt against the oppressive fripperies of the *ancien régime* was not to permit of any such painless evolution. Blood and tears hastened a process here which in other lands came about in the natural course of social development. The shock of flaming revolution suddenly crystallized the idea of concentrating and centralizing all great cultural collections for general use. The revolution actually turned that proud old palace, the Louvre, into a national museum with the motto, "Art for All"—and the contents of that palace were sifted and rearranged to eliminate most of the works considered symbolic of "decadent" court life. This fact accounts for the comparative poverty of the Louvre exhibits in its early days as a museum. Later, however, these items, discarded in the first fervor of reform, were restored to the collection. In France it was the revolution which created the first public natural history museums and similar institutions which in England had come into being considerably earlier.

Into the new museums—favored children of the new era, yet inheritors of an old and rich tradition—were poured selected items from all the royal palaces and many of the great private collections of the nobility, as well as from churches and suppressed monasteries throughout the land. And the bridgehead of princely and popular notions in the use of collections was to be the Corsican who, although having little personal interest in art, became, for his empire's prestige, one of the most voracious art plunderers the world has ever known.

Even before Bonaparte's day of power, soldiers of the Republic on the warpath had been spreading the booty nets. More than a hundred famous paintings had been taken from Belgium in 1794. The private art collection of William V of Holland swelled a caravan from The Hague in the following year. And now, sped by Napoleon's increasing enterprise, the national possessions of other states followed the road to the French capital. Rome reluctantly contributed the invaluable archives of the Vatican. From Vienna and Madrid came those of the Holy Roman Empire. Loretto gave up the Madonna and relics of her famous shrine. In 1806, Napoleon, who greatly admired Frederick the Great, struck a history-conscious pose by seizing for himself the former

Courtesy, Mitchell Samuels, New York

Louis XV Marquetry Boudoir Desk, 1771

On the eve of revolution Madame Du Barry arrived in London with many items from her collection. Among them was this exquisite piece which had been created especially for her by two master cabinetmakers, Hache and Cramer of Grenoble. She sold it in a vain attempt to aid the crown.

Prussian monarch's sword and sash. As early as 1797 he wrote home from his southern campaign: "We shall soon have every fine thing in Italy, except a few objects at Turin and Naples." In 1803 he had to order more ample quarters for his darling, the ten-year-old museum in the Louvre, which was growing alarmingly on its imported delicacies.

But still, from north, south and east, by barge and *camion,* the treasure kept pouring in—Rembrandts and Van Dycks, Raphaels and Titians, Holbeins and Cranachs, Rubens by the cartload, and, among the sculpture, the Vatican's *Apollo Belvedere,* the *Venus de' Medici,* beloved of Florence, and the bronze *Horses of St. Mark's,* lifted by the Venetians centuries before from Constantinople. The excitement which these shipments of artistic booty caused among the populace in Paris is a vivid index to the importance which, for centuries, the French have attached to the possession of beautiful objects. To the sound of martial music, great wagons, bearing the paintings and statues in plainly labeled crates, rolled through the streets of the city on their way to the Louvre, and about them swarmed wildly cheering crowds of people who waved flags and shouted a delighted welcome to each new acquisition.

In this manner did the Louvre (now renamed *le Musée Napoléon*) become almost overnight the greatest storehouse of artistic wealth in Europe. But the triumph was short-lived. In 1815 it came to an end, as Waterloo stopped the flow of booty, as the Second Treaty of Paris decreed that the stolen goods must be returned. The French protested this decision with such violence that it could be said of them they seemed to mourn the loss of *objets d'art* more than that of victory itself. In vain did the directors of the Louvre insist that most of their new possessions had been ceded to France by treaty and that, therefore, they belonged to her forever. And in vain these same desperate amateurs hid certain of the most sparkling items, declaring them lost, or secreted the records of provenance and then asserted that there was no way for a claimant nation to prove that the claimed objects ever had belonged to it. Some of the smaller, weaker cities and states victimized by Napoleon were forced to appeal to England's Duke of Wellington for satisfaction of their claims; but contrary to the popular modern belief nothing of importance was left to France out of Napoleon's immense artistic haul, with the exception of certain Italian "primitive" paintings now highly valued (which escaped notice because they were little thought of at the time) and a few large items considered too unwieldy to retransport and for which equivalent French possessions were handed over.

Yet though the French government was obliged to relinquish a huge number of paintings, statues, books and other objects at this time, nothing that rightfully belonged to her was taken; and the Louvre, building on the country's great past, became one of the world's most important museums, a central monument to the acquisitive accomplishments of a long line of collector kings, nobles and lesser Frenchmen.

ENGLAND CONTRIBUTES THE SCIENTIFIC IDEAL

"New times demand new measures and new men."

JAMES RUSSELL LOWELL

THOSE ENGLISH COLLECTORS who swarmed so eagerly into France after the Napoleonic debacle had behind them a not inconsiderable collecting history of their own. The full impact of the Dark Age failed at first to strike faraway England, so that the island retained important institutional libraries long after barbarian destruction wiped out similar Roman collections on the continent. For illustration of this one need only remember that when Charlemagne, in the latter half of the eighth century, wished to gather books for his court and school at Aachen he sent for Alcuin, the English scholar.

For several centuries thereafter, it is true, the island collectors lagged far behind their continental neighbors. And yet there were always some signs of vigorous collecting activity in England, signs which flamed in an individual here and there and then died out but which were none the less significant. Henry, Bishop of Winchester, the adventurous pioneer collector of antique sculpture in late medieval days, was an Englishman. Richard de Bury, one of the greatest of early bibliophiles, was English, and time has not yet dulled the words in which he expressed the fervor of his love for books. Chaucer's vaunted library of sixty volumes, mentioned in the *Legende of Good Women*, equaled in size and importance the libraries owned by some of the contemporary colleges of Oxford and Cambridge. And there were other Englishmen whose only claim to fame now rests upon the fact that they formed small private collections of books at a time and place generally arid of such pursuits.

These early English libraries consisted mostly of Bibles, chronicles and other works in the limited medieval category. By the end of the fourteenth century, however, private libraries were increasing not only in size but in variety of content as well, and by the end of the fifteenth century a growing intercourse with Italy had begun to influence the tastes of those English book-lovers who stood in the vanguard of an army of enthusiasts in this field. Latin works—the medieval favorites—still caught most eyes, and English collectors as yet paid scant attention to the significant Greek revival that was firing their Italian kinsmen, for the time-lag existed to some extent although most of the English amateurs were now sending to Florence for their manuscripts. Among them were some of Vespasiano da Bicci's best customers. Bishop Grey of Ely, for example, acquired over two hundred manuscripts from the Florentine book dealer, and one Andrew Hollis purchased so many items that he had to send them home by sea instead of overland to the channel as was customary.

The great royal collections of France, on the other hand, were not mirrored in England, although some of the early kings, Edward II, Henry IV, Henry V, and Edward IV, gathered libraries of minor importance. Most of these were typically medieval in scope, and the changing attitudes and tastes of the new era were better reflected in the libraries of two bibliophilic brothers, Humphrey, Duke of Gloucester, and John, Duke of Bedford. Gloucester, who eventually bequeathed his books to Oxford University, compiled his own lists of literary desiderata for the guidance of his agents on the continent, and was, in the true renaissance manner, a bountiful patron of scholars, both English and Italian. Bedford inclined more toward France and focused his attention chiefly upon handsomely decorated manuscripts and French translations. It was he who, in acquiring a major portion of the library of the French king, Charles V, most clearly foreshadowed a long history of exchanges between the collectors of the two nations.

One of the lighter forms of collecting to appear relatively soon in England was the gathering of souvenir autographs—a branch that would always remain vigorous—preceding the more scholarly collecting of signed holograph letters and documents of literary or historic significance.

At least one lady attached to the court of Henry VII is known to have had a blank page bound into her prayer book or "prymer" on which, at her request, members of the royal family wrote their names accompanied by appropriate sentiments. By the second half of the sixteenth century *alba amicorum*, as the small oblong pocket albums of this day were called, had achieved great popularity even among "men and women of quality and learning."

In a vogue which lasted well into the seventeenth century, students and members of university faculties everywhere amused themselves by corralling the signatures of their friends and acquaintances. Today serious autograph collectors can find no greater object for scorn than just such souvenir albums which, to their view, are fit only for the distraction of giggling school children or moronic celebrity chasers. Yet at least two of the extant signatures of John Milton were preserved in *alba amicorum*, and since it is customary now, as it was then, for the signer of such a book to add some motto, piece of verse or personal inscription, it is quite likely that among the densely populated contemporary autograph albums now reposing in obscure desk drawers a few at least conceal lines that will some day be as highly valued.

Though England, like France, had her courtly age, few English kings or queens ever ranked in collecting with their French compeers. Henry VII was the first English monarch to own a library of any considerable size. Henry VIII, specializing in wives and in tapestries, acquired six items in the first category and two thousand in the latter. Three of his wives, as well as both his daughters, collected books, and so did Mary, Queen of Scots, who brought back from her sojourn in France a taste for Gallic literary and artistic products. Not, however, until the Stuart monarch, Charles I (1600–49), came to the throne did Britain produce a royal amateur the equal of Francis I, and after Charles came no other worthy of the name of amateur.

Unlike Henry VIII, who, although he had been Holbein's patron, could hardly have been called a connoisseur, Charles possessed outstanding taste and discernment in art. He was buying Rembrandt paintings at a time when many of the local critics failed to understand the true quality of that contemporary Dutch genius, and, beginning with Raphael, all the important Italian painters were represented in his collection. Devoting the better part of twenty years to gathering those art treasures which so impressed his age, Charles combed the continent for the finest items available, and probably his greatest single *coup* was the purchase of much of the splendid collection formed a century before by Isabella d'Este. So that he might carry some of his favorites with him wherever he went, he commissioned miniaturist Peter Oliver to make copies of them, and one of those miniature copies is all that now lives to remind us of a lost Titian masterpiece which, so experts believe, was later destroyed in the burning of a Spanish castle.

If Charles' collection could be reassembled and exhibited today, a modern critic declares, it would still be found to surpass any other ever formed in England. But Charles was less fit to rule men than to gather great works, and for his ineptness in dealing with the burgeoning democratic instincts of the British people he eventually paid with his head. Following his execution, the new government, which was sorely in need of funds, did execution upon the king's life-work as well and initiated that history-making sale in which, at intervals from 1650 to 1653, some fourteen hundred paintings and four hundred statues were once more set at large.

Amateurs from every European country were drawn as by a lodestone to this unparalleled opportunity. Mazarin sent Jabach and later Monsieur de Bordeaux, the French ambassador, to buy for him. The King of Spain, the Queen of Sweden, the Governor of the Netherlands, and many others of almost equal note were among those who attended in person or who commissioned agents to make purchases for them, and even the dour Cromwell is said to have taken personal advantage of the sale. Many of the outstanding collections in modern Europe owe some of their finest items to an English collector whose misfortune it was to have been born a king, and occasionally even in recent years some treasure, catalogued during the Charles I sale but since lost to view, has reappeared upon the market accompanied by the hosannas of a choir of experts and amateurs.

As a sidelight on collectors at the mercy of political vicissitude, it may be interpolated here that the dispersal extended on a lesser but equally merciless scale to collections owned by followers of the late monarch.

In contrast to the paucity of great collectors among English royalty, there were some exceedingly great collectors among members of the

CHARLES I AT THE AGE OF TWENTY-ONE. *The collector-king as portrayed in Peter Oliver's miniature from the Ryks Museum, Amsterdam. Actual size of this portrait, which is hung in a gold filigree frame, is 2¼ x 1¾ inches.*

SIR HANS SLOANE, FOUNDER OF THE BRITISH MUSEUM, *from the Slaughter portrait in the National Portrait Gallery, London. Successful physician and scientist as well as inveterate collector, Sloane's vision of a great national museum bore lasting fruit.*

British nobility, from the close of the sixteenth century onward. Notable among them was Sir Robert Bruce Cotton (1570–1631) who formed the first English collection of manuscripts and antiquities to achieve a reputation throughout Europe.

Although Sir Robert was a highly personal collector, completely in love with his possessions, he was not amateur alone, for that serious purpose which was to be England's distinctive contribution to the collecting pattern was evident in him. An ardent researcher among ruins and old records, Cotton became a kind of walking encyclopedia often consulted by such notables as William Camden, author of the *Britannia,* and Sir Walter Raleigh, both of whom came to him for enlightenment on obscure historical problems; Ben Jonson, who sought guidance on points of Roman geography; our French friend, Peiresc, who consulted Cotton on numismatics; and the Earl of Arundel, who asked for the solution of certain genealogical questions. William Lisle consulted him about Anglo-Saxon language and literature, and others went to him with puzzlers on such varied subjects as legal precedent, parliamentary forms, and etiquette. Sir Robert always had the answer, derived from material in his collection or research done in connection with it.

His assemblage, which included coins, Roman inscriptions found in England, antiquarian curiosities, manuscripts, books, historical documents, and the letters of sovereigns and statesmen, has been called "one of the greatest collections of source material for English history ever made." To make it such had been the purpose in Sir Robert's mind from the time when, as a young man, he had begun collecting. Cotton took a leading part in the establishment of the first English Society of Antiquaries, and was one of those who begged Queen Elizabeth to establish a state library in which documents of national interest might be preserved. When this suggestion met with no response he did his best to make his own collections such a repository, with the result that he was accused of having stolen public records, which, it was said, properly belonged in the public record office and not in the hands of a private collector. The dissolution of the monasteries, which occurred during the reigns of Henry VIII and Edward VI, enabled him to acquire many of the treasures of those institutions, and, until his own downfall under Charles I, his political eminence gave him easy access to certain other important material. In 1700 Cotton's heirs turned the collection over to the nation, and eventually it formed one of the foundation collections of the British Museum.

Cotton loved nothing better than to show off his library and museum, and this amiable collector-quality once embroiled him in serious political difficulty. It happened when Gondomar, the shrewd Spanish ambassador, wished to get Cotton to work for the proposed match between Prince Charles and the Infanta of Spain. Presenting himself at Cotton House "in the guise of a virtuoso" and displaying his usual brilliant understanding of human nature, Gondomar first tackled his host in the latter's most vulnerable spot by asking with apparent eagerness whether he might not see the Cotton museum of antiquities. It was only when he had gotten Sir Robert into that mellow mood which follows upon the discussion of a pet hobby with a sympathetic listener that the Spaniard led the talk around to the subject which had really inspired his visit. In this manner did he succeed in inducing the unwary amateur to espouse a cause which, being deeply unpopular in England, was charged with dynamite for anyone who ventured openly to promote it.

Cotton's somewhat younger contemporary, Thomas Howard, Second Earl of Arundel (1586–1646) is most often mentioned as the first great English collector. Horace Walpole called him "the father of Vertu in England," and a contemporary declared that to him

"this angle of the world oweth its first sight of Greek and Roman statues."

Properly, Arundel should divide the pioneering honors with Sir Robert Cotton and King Charles, although it is true that his collection of inscribed marbles, antique statues, architectural fragments and vases, paintings, gems, coins, books, and manuscripts, was the most ambitious and varied of its day.

Like Cotton, his friend, the Earl of Arundel devoted much of his early life to public affairs. But unlike Cotton he escaped before the devious politics of his time had entangled him in disaster, and he was able to consecrate his last years entirely to his chosen pursuit of collecting. Of those several important collections which he formed in the course of his career, three in particular—the gems, the manuscripts, and the antique marbles—have won enduring fame.

The manuscripts which he began assembling at the age of twenty were given by his grandson to the newly founded Royal Society in

1666. For this gift John Evelyn, who had feared that the collection might be dispersed or damaged by neglect, was directly responsible. In 1831 the manuscripts were transferred to the British Museum, where they are still preserved under Arundel's name. The Arundel intaglios and cameos, a sumptuous gathering, eventually found their way into the Marlborough Collection and were then known as the Marlborough Gems. These are now widely dispersed.

One of the most dramatic stories in the history of collecting centers about the assembling of Arundel's great collection of Greek marbles. After the collector's death, in a succession of catastrophes comparable only to the disasters responsible for the loss of so many early Chinese paintings, over half of these were destroyed. Yet the indefatigable Evelyn was instrumental in retrieving some of the priceless carvings from the neglectful hands of an unworthy heir and succeeded in having them transferred to Oxford where, as the "Marmoria Arundeliana," they can still be seen. Earlier many had been lost during the civil wars. Some had been sold after Arundel's death. Others were broken or lost when being moved from Arundel House. As in ancient times, some, left carelessly on a vacant lot, were gradually covered with debris, and fragments of these were long afterward rediscovered when London workmen were digging the foundations for new houses. How horrified Arundel would have been could he have foreseen the fate of his hard-won treasures, for he had been quite conscious of their importance and had allowed scholars access to Arundel House during his own lifetime so that for some years it had served as a kind of "anticipatory British Museum."

A serious amateur, the Earl carried on a wide correspondence with continental (particularly Italian) artists and archaeologists, for here was a man built to the measure of the high renaissance; to him art was a living substance closely related to the rest of life. His agents roamed Germany and the Netherlands as well as Italy and Greece, and six months before his death he was still so enthusiastic over his undertakings that he requested his friend Evelyn to assist in expanding still further the enormous gatherings. His zeal as a collector, and the attention which his successes attracted, undoubtedly set a fashion and aroused the ambition of numerous contemporaries to emulate him. King Charles himself is said to have been started on the road to connoisseurship by his admiration for Arundel's achievements in the field of picture collecting, while the Earl's own brother-in-law, the Earl of Pembroke, as well as his political rival and enemy, the Duke of Buckingham, both tried hard to outdo him in antiquarian joustings.

Robert Harley, First Earl of Oxford (1661–1724), was more show-collector than genuine bibliophile. Nevertheless, he was considered the greatest book collector of his age, and because of his outstanding position was made a trustee of the Cottonian Library after its nationalization. Harley's own library, which contained a collection of choice engravings in addition to the ancient manuscripts and rare books, was made up, according to a contemporary account, of at least seven complete collections formed by earlier bibliophiles, as well as of "the flower of a hundred other libraries." Here then we find, perhaps for the first time, that "consolidation" approach to collecting that has been typical of modern big-business collectors.

In contrast to his father, the Earl's son, Edward Harley (1689–1741), was mesmerized. His ears sang with the music of book collecting. Even as a boy Edward was always spending more than he could afford in pursuit of this taste, and although constantly he resolved to mend his ways, he followed the pipes time and again over the cliffs into the financial bogs. When he died his widow was forced to sell the entire accumulation in formidable numbers—fifty thousand printed books, four hundred thousand pamphlets and other ephemera, forty thousand prints, and a large collection of coins, medals and portraits—except the eight thousand manuscript volumes, and these, for a slim matter of ten thousand pounds, she was invited on patriotic grounds to release to the British Museum in 1753.

Upon entering the Metropolitan Museum of Art or any similar institution, it is hard to believe that quite similar institutions have not always been a feature of highly developed civilizations. Yet the fact is that the museum, as we know it today, is in most respects essentially a modern invention, and the first museum to be opened to the public under that name in the Western world made its appearance as late as the seventeenth century.

To us that first museum would have seemed not unlike an earlier version of P. T. Barnum's notorious emporium. Yet despite its seeming resemblance to a conglomeration of side shows, or, in glorified form, the pocket collection of some small boy, it was something considerably more important, for it was born as the result of serious collecting on the part of two modest individuals who lived in England in the period when collecting and collections there first began to command widespread attention.

Although English collectors were long chiefly concerned with books, paintings and classical antiquities, from the seventeenth century on the subject of natural history assumed a position of increasing importance, and it was from this field that England's greatest contributions to the pattern of collecting, particularly in regard to museums, have sprung. Here the pioneer was the John Tradescant (d. 1637?) already mentioned as bearing a striking resemblance to Evelyn's French friend, Monsieur Morine. Both a naturalist and a professional gardener, Tradescant was also something of an adventurer, in his early years following the highroads of the sea as did so many men in that era of exploration. With this dual interest it was only natural that he should have become a collector, but in his collecting he became universal and attempted to gather and catalogue everything within the scope of a world that was still highly exciting because so much of it was newly discovered. He, and other men like him, became the advance guard of a new age that was to be typified by intellectual rather than by physical exploration and discovery.

In 1618 John Tradescant traveled as far as Russia in search of rare plants. Two years later, while serving as a "gentleman volunteer" in an expedition against Algerian corsairs, he found time even under such unfavorable conditions to gather additional botanical specimens. By 1625, however, the adventurer had settled down to gardening once more and was in the service of the Lord High Admiral, George Villiers, Duke of Buckingham. It was on behalf of his employer that Tradescant then wrote to one Edward Nicholas in Virginia stating it to be the Duke's pleasure that he, Tradescant, should

> ". . . deal with all merchants from all places, but especially from Virginia, Bermudas, Newfoundland, Guinea, Binney, the Amazon and the East Indies, for all manner of rare beasts, fowl and birds, shells and stones."

Still later Tradescant entered the service of King Charles and his queen, Henrietta Maria, and again his employers encouraged him to continue his collecting activities.

It was at this time, as nearly as can be determined, that John Tradescant established his famous museum and botanical garden at South Lambeth, a milestone in the history of collecting. Although remaining in private hands, both garden and museum were opened for general public inspection—a startling innovation—and many of the more prominent visitors became so much interested that they themselves made donations to the collections, hardly aware how in bearing their contributions they had become the first of a long line of museum donors stretching far into the future.

When his father died, young John (1608–62) carried on the work of expanding and cataloguing the Tradescant collections. Following his parent's ways he too was a gardener, and he spent much time in Virginia collecting specimens. Later he devoted most of his time to the museum, and chief of his accomplishments was the catalogue which he compiled and had printed "to be sold by Nathanael Brooke at the Angel in Cornhill" in 1656.

The first museum catalogue to appear in the English language, this list of the contents of the *Museum Tradescantium or a Collection of Rarities Preserved at South Lambeth neer London by John Tradescant of London* is worth quoting at some length because of the exact picture it gives of a typical seventeenth-century collection, along with methods of classification then in use. The foreword, "To the ingenious reader," tells how the collector's friends had urged him to list the rarities in the museum because these were "more for variety than any one place in Europe could afford." It may be noted that that very variety, which today would be considered more than a little confusing, represented then a matter deserving honest pride.

The system of classification was the same employed by most contemporary private "museums" or collections:

"Now for the *materialls* themselves I reduce them unto two sorts; one *Naturall,* of which some are more familiarly known and named amongst us, as divers sorts of Birds, foure-footed Beasts and Fishes . . . Others are less familiar . . . as the shell-Creatures, Insects, Minerals, Outlandish-Fruits and the like, which are part of *Materia Medica;* . . . The other sort is *Artificialls,* as Utensills, Householdstuffe, Habits, Instruments of Warre used by severall Nations, rare curiosities of Art, &c . . . *The Catalogue* of my *Garden* I have also added in the Conclusion . . ."

The table of contents shows that, far from being a mere natural history museum, the assemblage embraced practically every collectible subject known to man. Headed "A View of the Whole," it lists the following groups of exhibits:

"1. Birds with their eggs, beaks, feathers, clawes, spurres.
2. Fourfooted beasts with some of their hides, hornes, and hoofs.
3. Divers sorts of strange Fishes.
4. Shell-creatures, whereof some are called *Mollia,* some *Crustacea,* others *Testacea,* of these, are both *univalvia,* and *bivalvia.*
5. Severall sorts of Insects, terrestriall,— { anelytra, coleoptera, aptera, apoda }
6. Mineralls, and those of neare nature with them, as Earths, Coralls, Salts, Bitumens, Petrified things, choicer Stones, Gemmes.
7. Outlandish Fruits from both the *Indies,* with Seeds, Gemmes, Roots, Woods, and divers Ingredients Medicinall, and for the Art of Dying.
8. Mechanicks, choice pieces in Carvings, Turnings, Paintings.
9. Other Variety of Rarities.
10. Warlike Instruments, European, Indian, etc.
11. Garments, Habits, Vests, Ornaments.
12. Utensils, and Housholdstuffe.
13. *Numismata,* Coynes antient and modern, both gold, silver and copper, Hebrew, Greeke, Roman both— { Imperiall and Consular }
14. Medalls, gold, silver, copper, lead.

. . . . .

HORTUS TRADESCANTIUS

15. An enumeration of his Plants, Shrubs, and Trees both in English and Latine.
16. A Catalogue of his Benefactors."

The itemized inventory further illustrates the catholic interest in objects from near and far, as well as the special emphasis put upon curiosities, exotica, and items that savored of the miraculous. One exhibit, for example, was:

"Blood that rained in the Isle of Wight, attested by Sir J: Oglander."

Also present were relics and association pieces, including:

"A piece of Stone of Saint John Baptists Tombe;
A piece of the Stone of Sarrigo-Castle where Hellen of Greece was born;
Pohatan, King of Virginia's habit all embroidered with shells or Roanoke;
Henry the 8 his Stirrups, Haukes-hoods, gloves;
Effigies of divers Personages of honor, note and quality."

There were shoes and boots from all over the world, and "An Umbrella" —the only one in England at that time. There were endless miniature objects; musical instruments from various places; birds' nests from China; a bundle of Amazonian tobacco; idols from India, China and other pagan lands; Greek, Roman and Jewish antiquities; a circumcision knife of stone; and the following curiously assorted items:

"A Brazen-ball to warm the Nunnes hands;
Casava Bread 2 sorts;
Severall draughts and pieces of painting of sundry excellent Masters;
Mosaick work of divers sorts;
Several Heads cut on Agates;
Divers Figures cut on Shells;
A Variety of Figures cut in crystalls;
Divers sorts of Ambers with Flyes, Spiders, natural;
A Dodo bird;
A Bird sitting on a pearch naturall;
Divers things cut on Plum-stones;
Several curious paintings in little forms, very antient;
A little Box with 12 Apostles in it;
Divers sorts of Purses of Outlandish work in gold and silver;
Jupiter, Io and Mercury wrought in Tent-stitch;
Cloath spun of the down of yellow feathers;
Chirugeons Instruments framed upon the points of needles;
Halfe a Hasle-nut with 70 pieces of housholdstuffe in it;
A Deske of one entire piece of wood rarely carved."

And, by way of anticlimax:

"Two figures carved in stone by Hans Holben."

After the death of the younger Tradescant, the "Ark," as some contemporaries called the museum, had a checkered career, and although it came to a worthy end it did so only at the cost of losing its identity.

Exactly what happened is not completely clear, but certainly there is material in the case for a good novel.

It appears that sometime around the year 1652 Tradescant made the acquaintance of one Elias Ashmole, antiquary, Freemason, student of astrology and the occult, author of a *History of the Order of the Garter* and of a volume on the *History and Antiquities of Berkshire.* For a time Ashmole and his wife boarded with the Tradescants, and since Ashmole was also a collector of books, coins, antiquities, prints and paintings the two men became fast friends.

Ten years later when Tradescant died he left a will, dated May 4, 1661, bequeathing his museum to Hester, his wife. After her decease the collections were to go either to the University of Oxford or to the University of Cambridge, the choice to be hers. No mention was made of Ashmole in this will, but the antiquarian stepped forward with a claim that Tradescant actually had executed a deed of gift (to take effect upon the death of the donor) turning the museum over to him. Ashmole could not produce the deed, but he asserted that this was because Mrs. Tradescant had had it in her possession and had subsequently destroyed it. Perhaps more evidence existed on his side than remains today, for the court decided against the wife in favor of the claimant, whereupon began a bitter feud which raged sixteen full years. Ashmole tried to get hold of the collection and Mrs. Tradescant refused to relinquish it. There followed a series of public recriminations and fantastic name-callings, and the fact that the two were neighbors did not improve the situation. On November 26, 1674 (twelve years after Tradescant's death), Ashmole wrote in his diary:

"Mrs. Tradescant being unwilling to deliver up the rarities to me, I carried several of them to my own house."

And five days later he added:

"I began to remove the rest of the rarities to my house at South Lambeth."

Within two years, however, forced by what pressure we can only surmise, the unfortunate woman signed a surprising retraction of the many accusations she had previously made against Ashmole. In this curious document she declared that Ashmole had actually urged her to keep the rarities in the beginning; that it was she who had pressed them upon him; and that she had threatened to throw the collection on the street if he did not remove it! The contradictions between these statements and the entries in Ashmole's diary are all too obvious. There is, perhaps, an overtone of dark doings: remember that Ashmole was privy to the occult world.

In any case, the miserable affair came to an abrupt and equally miserable end on April 4, 1678, when, at eleven-thirty in the morning, Ashmole set down the following terse entry in his diary:

"My wife told me that Mrs. Tradescant was found drowned in her pond. She was drowned the day before about noon, as appeared by some circumstances."

And on April 22 this unswerving collector added flatly:

"I removed the pictures from Mrs. Tradescant's house to mine."

Hard as it might be to find excuses, on Ashmole's behalf one biographer, A. L. Humphreys, has written in attempted extenuation:

"The pleasures of acquisition and possession were great with him. He therefore considered always that the end justified whatever means he used . . . He loved old things, and was passionately anxious to save everything he could from destruction in a destroying age."

The year before Hester Tradescant's removal from the scene, Ashmole had offered his own collection—plus the Tradescant rarities—to Oxford University on condition that a suitable building be found to house it. Two years later the foundation stone of such a building was laid, and in 1683 the Ashmolean Museum was opened. Twelve carts were required to transport the Ashmolean treasures to the barge which was to carry them up the Thames; and on February 17, 1683, Ashmole made the following pathetic comment:

"The last load of my rarities was sent to the barge, and this afternoon I relapsed into the gout."

But we need not waste too much sympathy on this gentleman, for he had taken care to see that the collection which the two Tradescants had spent their entire lives in forming should be completely merged with his own. The man was a monument builder—for himself. No longer was the museum Tradescant's. It was Ashmole's, and under Ashmole's name it became, in the words of John Evelyn,

"the first public institution for the reception of Rarities in Art, or nature, established in England."

The subsequent history of the Ashmolean Museum constitutes an illuminating commentary on the progressive attitudes towards such institutions. In the eighteenth century the museum was presided over by a curator who had little conception of his responsibilities. He allowed visitors to handle the exhibits as roughly as they pleased, with the result that many were broken or stolen. In 1860 the items which remained, together with additions made during the intervening period, were redistributed and rearranged according to more modern standards. The manuscripts and books were then moved to the Bodleian Library where they now fill an entire room, and the botanical and zoological exhibits were placed in the New University Museum. In 1925 the old gallery was reopened and dedicated, appropriately, to the history of science. Today the long-neglected Tradescants have received their deserved recognition, and a section of the museum has been set aside for those items from the original collection which have survived. This section is now known as the "Tradescant Lobby."

Drawn together by a common passion, yet often tangled in a web of bitter rivalry, collectors may love or hate their confrères as the wind happens to blow. Moreover, since friendships between collectors are often formed upon a single premise, such friendships, judged by ordinary standards, can prove strangely assorted. On the basis of essential personality, surely few men could have had less in common than John Tradescant the gardener, Elias Ashmole the antiquary and mystic, Samuel Pepys, venal but capable Secretary of the Board of Admiralty, and John Evelyn, scholarly man of the world. Yet between the four there existed a strong bond forged by a common interest in collecting.

Of the four, three were diarists, and on their well-covered pages of record the names of the quartet constantly reappear. Each member of the group, albeit with highly varying degrees of awareness and intellectual approach, exerted some concrete influence on museum history in England, but of the four only John Evelyn truly foreshadowed the new era. How well he realized the historic value of accumulations of books, art objects and antiques is shown by the numerous and often at least partially successful efforts he made to prevent the dispersal of certain famous contemporary collections. In each case his efforts were directed toward preserving the treasures for public use. Yet he himself had been early smitten by a strong personal collectomania, a mania to which for many years his diary bore impassioned witness.

In 1641, when Evelyn was only twenty-one years old, he noted during a stay in Holland:

"Upon St. Bartholomew's day, I went amongst the booksellers, and visited the famous Honius and Bleaw's shop to buy some maps, atlasses, and other works of that kind. At another shop I furnished myself with some shells and Indian curiosities . . ."

Eleven years later in London, having grown considerably more ambitious, he recorded in an entry dated April 15, 1652:

"I wrote to the Dean, touching my buying his library, which was one of the choicest collections of any private person in England."

Although, like Tradescant, Evelyn was primarily a naturalist, he was by comparison to the founder of the famous "Ark" a man far advanced in knowledge and more truly cosmopolitan and sophisticated in interests. Author of *Sylva,* the first English work on forest conservation, and of *Terra,* the first attempt at a scientific study of agriculture, one of Evelyn's hobbies was landscape gardening. It is told of him how intensely he suffered when Peter the Great visited him and insisted upon being trundled in a wheelbarrow through the beds and borders of Evelyn's famous garden at Sayes Court, Deptford. Yet gardening was but one of his host of hobbies, and in his wanderings he became, so far as we know, the most detailed chronicler of collectors and collecting that any age has ever had.

Evelyn's diary is, in fact, one long record of seventeenth-century collections—his own and everybody else's—at home and abroad. For every contemporary development in this field one can find countless illustrations in his chatty and informal entries. "I went to see the collection of one Trean, a rich merchant, who had some good pictures," he wrote on February 15, 1649, and the multitude of Treans whom he visited for the sake of their collections shows us how prevalent the pursuit of collecting was becoming, and how men of the middle class like himself were succumbing in ever greater numbers to this new pastime. Most strongly reflected is the growing interchange between collectors in Paris and in London, now in full swing. "I was showed a collection of books and prints made for the Duke of York," is an entry dated September 28, 1651, from Paris. Yet by this time London had something to

The Bettmann Archive

PEARLS, PISTOLS, A BONNET AND SOME MINIATURE SKULLS. *Here is a hearty indication of 17th century virtuosity. From a rare painting of a curio cabinet by Georg Henz, in the* Schlossmuseum, *Berlin.*

offer even the greatest amateurs in Paris, and on March 25, 1653, Evelyn, back in England, received a visit from ". . . that rare graver in *taille-douce,* Monsieur Richelt, sent by Cardinal Mazarin to make a collection of pictures."

Of quite different dimension as a collector was Evelyn's fellow diarist, Samuel Pepys (1633–1703), who claims considerable space in this book because he stands as the perfect example of the collector who carries "system" and classification to extremes, of the ambitious man using collecting as a tool, of the poisonous effects of clutching a collection after death by means of a will.

Although he bought paintings, miniatures, engravings and objects of *virtu* as well as books, in no sense of the word could Pepys have been called a connoisseur. He is sometimes described as the first middle-class collector of objects of art in England, and his career in this field was curiously like Cicero's. Although he finally rose to a position of considerable importance, he began life as a tailor's son, and this humble origin he forever tried to live down. Like Cicero he was ambitious to "belong," and as one means toward that end seized upon the aristocratic fashion of his time, collecting. This social climber, whose diary has entertained so many, must have been near zero in esthetic perception. Yet even had his rating been high, it seems likely that he would have smothered individual preference in order to conform to patterns set by the socially prominent. In the manner of his day, he chose the unusual item rather than the merely beautiful, and acquired a typical collection of Indian and Chinese "curiosities." In painting his preference ran strongly to portraiture—particularly portraits of himself, and here he demanded that the canvas reflect him to the last hair.

He set especial store upon his collection of silver plate, the foundation piece in which (the first of many items procured in similar fashion) was "a silver can" given to him as a political bribe. As one should expect of a literary gentleman, however, Pepys' first and most constant love was his library, and upon this he lavished a lifetime of collecting effort.

From our contemporary point of view, the most valuable part of that library is the section on naval history, a subject on which Pepys himself was excellently qualified. Yet this constituted but one portion of the heterogeneous miscellany of manuscripts, books, pamphlets, prints and clippings amassed by the indefatigable collector. There were numerous association items, a whole collection of ballads, and another of handwriting specimens, many of the latter having been cut from valuable manuscripts with that ruthless thoughtlessness generally limited to childhood hobbyists. In addition, there were rows of scrapbooks in which Pepys pasted carefully labeled drawings, prints, and clippings descriptive of various customs, pastimes, costumes, scenic views, and so on, which, though comparable in a way to the scrapbooks or albums kept by the very young, have gathered considerable interest and value in the course of the years.

Torn between his natural thrift and his extravagant desires as a collector, Pepys hit upon that strange compromise which led him to concentrate his efforts so largely upon the arrangement and appearance of his library.

> "Whereas before my delight was in multitude of books, and spending money in that and buying alway of other things," he wrote on August 10, 1663, "now that I am become a better husband, and have left off buying, now my delight is in the neatness of everything, and so cannot be pleased with anything unless it be very neat which is a strange folly."

Carrying out his obsession for neatness and "order" he had all his volumes bound alike, and then arranged them symmetrically according to size—taking infinite pains to see that even the tops of the rows were level, without a single individualistic volume raising its head a fraction of an inch beyond the others.

In order that the library might be usable in spite of the exigencies of this scheme, Pepys evolved an elaborate cataloguing system whereby the presses were numbered consecutively around the room. Thus, the shelves were numbered from top to bottom (from one to five in each press, the fifth or bottom shelf containing a single row of the largest volumes); the front row in each of the four upper shelves was lettered "a," the back row "b"; and the books themselves were numbered consecutively from left to right, beginning at the lefthand end of the front row of Shelf Four in Press One, and continuing on that shelf around the twelve presses before beginning again in Press One on the front row of Shelf Three. A key-catalogue was then prepared, and by consulting this for the title desired one could locate the volume's position on the shelves by number: i.e., the first book in the front row on the shelf fourth from the top in Press One would be marked "1.4a.1." As a result of this extraordinary system, a single new acquisition often meant that a whole section of the collection had to be renumbered and recatalogued, and Pepys was busy rearranging and perfecting his system until the very day of his death.

Even death did not put a stop to the implacable proceedings—for Pepys' system took death into account too. On May 12, 1703, he had drawn up a paper bequeathing his library to a nephew, John Jackson, indicating that he wished to consider the best means

"for preserving the said Library entire in one body, undivided unsold and Secure against all manner of dimunition damages and embesselments."

Elsewhere in this document was

"a scheme . . . relating to the completion and Settlement of my Library."

This "scheme" was characteristically detailed and began by requesting the heir to see to it that the library be compared with the catalogue and

"outlying books be immediately lookt up and put into their places."

Then he asked that all sets in the library be completed; that room be provided for further volumes of Lord Clarendon's *History*, which was at that time "under press"; that Gronovius' *Sett of Greek Antiquities*, lately published, be forthwith bought and added to the collection; and that

"this being done my said library be closed and from thenceforward noe Additions made thereto."

Further requirements made of the heir had to do with the arrangement and appearance of the library, for with these, apparently, the meticulous Mr. Pepys was not quite satisfied even when he felt the hand of death upon his shoulder. So he instructed his nephew:

"That my Arms or Crest or Cypher be Stampt in Gold on the outsides of the Covers of every book admitting thereof; that their placing as to heighth be strictly reviewed and where found requiring it more nicely adjusted; that so soon as their order shall be thus fixed the whole be new numbered from the lowest to the highest; that the said new number be Stampt on a piece of Redd Leather fixt at the head of the back of every book where now the guilt paper is; that all the Additaments with their new numbers be then properly incerted in the bodies of the Catalogue and Alphabet and there elegantly and finally transcribed to remaine unalterable and for ever accompany the said Library; lastly that as farr as any room shall be left for further improvements or embellishments as to my books by Ruling, Elegant writing or Indexing the same be done at the discretion and convenience of my said Nephew."

Having elaborately drawn up his provisions and set them in *rigor mortis* to meet all eternity, the seventy-year-old collector went wearily to bed. He must have had bad dreams, however, for the next day it occurred to him that after all he could not be sure of a

"constant Succession of Heirs from my said Nephew qualified like himself for the use of such a Library."

Such being the case, and since he, Samuel Pepys, could not

"but be greatly Solicitous that all possible provision be made for its unalterable preservation and perpetual Security against the ordinary ffate of such collections,"

he felt himself constrained to add a second codicil to his will decreeing that after his nephew's own death the precious library should go to either of two Cambridge University colleges, Trinity or Magdalene—preferably to the latter, which had been his own school—and his provisions and method of choosing between the two colleges are probably unique in university annals.

First, he added still further instructions for the maintenance of his library. Perhaps he remembered his own occasional excursions into book-lifting, for one of the conditions of his final bequest had to do with the borrowing of books. No one but the Master of the college receiving the Pepys library was to be permitted to remove volumes from the repository room, and even the Master might not take more than ten at a time. Nor might he take them anywhere but to his own Lodge in the college. Furthermore, he must keep a strict record of the date and time of the borrowing and return, entering these in a book to be kept in the library "for that only purpose." Before either college might have the library, it must accept all the conditions in the will and express its willingness to submit to an eternal spy system—a yearly check to be made by members of the second institution.

Surprisingly enough the collector's scheme worked admirably for his purposes, and so scrupulously were his conditions observed that when, more than a hundred years after the receipt of the library, Magdalene College wished to move the books to a room other than the one that had been housing it, a letter was written to the Master and Seniors of Trinity asking permission! Surely the ultimate result of his painstaking arrangements would have made Mr. Pepys unutterably happy, for today there is no other collection of comparable age which still retains so nearly the form given it by its original maker.

Pepys, the eccentric, illustrates, though in exaggerated form, certain tendencies which have been far from uncommon among collectors of every age in many lands. A collector's career more characteristic of seventeenth-century England itself was that of one William Courten (1642–1702), fourth of that name, whose activities formed a binding link between the earlier age of discovery and the modern age to come.

Courten was the descendant of an enormously wealthy family whose riches had been gained, over several generations, in those East Indian trading pursuits and West Indian colonization projects which the age of discovery had fostered. Indeed Courten may have owned, as the foundation of his own great collection, some of the curiosities which his grandfather, Sir William (1571–1636), had brought back from these remote new lands. Young William, however, was more given to serious study than to grappling with business affairs, and when he found himself beset by endless lawsuits resulting from his inherited estate he changed his name to Charleton and fled to the continent.

From the first, this man's name was linked to collecting, for at the age of fourteen he was listed as one of the benefactors of the Tradescant Museum, and Edwards said of him that:

". . . the collection of a museum which should eclipse everything of its kind theretofore known in England became, from his attainment of manhood, the leading aim and object of William Courten's career."

During his years of foreign residence Courten made long tours through France, Germany and Italy, and always he collected more and more items for his cabinets and presses, studying assiduously meanwhile so that his collection of knowledge might keep pace with his material accumulations. At Montpelier, where he made his continental headquarters, he first met Dr. Hans Sloane, then a young man, whose collection was eventually destined to swallow Courten's and become the first great pillar of the British Museum. Both men were highly interested in the natural sciences, and when Sloane shortly after the meeting set sail for the West Indies, he promised to send back to Courten samples of such "curious" things as he might find. Other friends rendered similar services, but on the whole Courten made his own collection, which included miniatures, drawings, shells, insects, minerals, natural and artificial curiosities, and ancient and modern coins and medals.

When Courten finally moved back to England, in about the year 1684, his collection filled ten rooms of a large house. He was most generous about exhibiting it, and the ubiquitous Evelyn saw and described it in December, 1686, referring to his host as "Mr. Charlton of the Middle Temple."

The fashion for visiting collections, a fashion to which the Tradescant Museum earlier in the century had lent impetus, was now growing so fast that by the beginning of the eighteenth century "museums" had actually become a popular form of amusement. It was no longer merely a question of tourists coming to private homes to see collections which had gained repute among the well informed. Now enterprising proprietors of coffee houses, remembering the crowds that had flocked to South Lambeth, set up "repositories of curiosities" in their establishments as special attractions, much as modern restaurants employ orchestras and floor shows.

Similar "museums" were one of the chief extracurricular attractions of old-time American barbershops in seacoast towns, and it was a barber who was responsible for the best known of the English coffee-house collections. He was one James Salter, who went by the more picturesque name of "Don Saltero." Salter, who had once been in the employ of Hans Sloane, was aided in his project by contributions from his former employer, and his coffee house, opened in 1690, achieved such popularity that many other establishments, including the famous Chelsea Bun Shop, followed suit. Although Salter claimed descent from the Tradescants, and went so far as to have a catalogue of his collection compiled, his museum was largely side show. Among the exhibits, for instance, were "pieces of the true cross," lace made from human hair, and so forth. And yet Benjamin Franklin, when in London, considered it worth a special expedition. We have no record of the worthy doctor's opinion, but Richard Steele, who visited it in 1709, described Salter's museum as little more than "ten thousand gimcracks round the room and on the ceiling."

The widespread popularity of such exhibitions was a symptom of the increased general interest in collecting of all kinds, the last link in the evolutionary chain preceding the foundation of a great national museum. The setting prepared, the final stroke was reserved for the great collecting physician, Dr. Hans Sloane (1660–1753).

Like the Tradescants, Sloane's basic interest lay in the study and collection of natural history specimens. But he also roamed far afield, and his collection eventually included jewels, engraved gems, ancient and modern coins, several rooms filled with books, a room full of choice and valuable manuscripts, and antiquities of Egypt, Greece, Etruria, Rome, Britain and even America, as well as corals, crystals and "figured" stones, minerals, insects, shells, birds, fossils, horns and preserved animals.

At the age of twenty-seven Sloane had journeyed to the West Indies as physician to the Duke of Albemarle, Governor of Jamaica, and during his fifteen-month stay in the islands he collected over eight hundred species of plants which he brought back with him to London. This was but the shallow seepage of the full tide to come, for although Sloane attained exceptional eminence in his profession (he was physician to the royal family and in 1727 he succeeded Sir Isaac Newton as president of the Royal Society) his reputation as a collector soon bid fair to overshadow his name as a man of science. Courten made Sloane his residuary legatee, and at least four other great collections eventually came into his possession. True, there were many contemporaries who, failing to discern the physician's true purposes, looked upon his insatiable appetite for collecting as a rather ridiculous eccentricity, for this was an age when the study of physical sciences and the need for documentation were still regarded with considerable skepticism. Thus the poet Young saw in Sloane, the collector, only "the foremost toyman of his time," and other wits found him a convenient target for their gibes. Yet none of this bothered Sloane. With the "unweariable power of taking pains" that was his leading characteristic, he went on collecting until eventually he had amassed nearly two hundred thousand items.

Despite the miscellaneous nature of this collection, a great advance had been made since the days of the Tradescants, for the imposing mass of Sloane's exhibits was organized and displayed in systematic order on the several floors of his own house given over to it, while a painstaking catalogue—consisting of thirty-eight volumes in folio and eight in quarto—numbered and described each item, giving a short history of each. Always willing to show his museum to guests, Sloane soon discovered that curiosity, rather than scientific interest, impelled many of them to seek admission, and he once wrote:

"My collection of dried samples of some very strange plants excited the curiosity of people who loved things of that nature to see them, and who were welcome, until I observed some so curious as to desire to carry part of them privately home and injure what they left. This made me upon my guard."

Yet even this experience did not deter him from his main purpose, which was to make his great collection available to the nation as a whole, and in his final disposition of it he foreshadowed the generosity of many collectors who were to succeed him both in England and America.

In bequeathing his collection to the nation, Sloane stipulated only that his family should receive a small financial compensation, and the statement he made regarding his purpose in turning his life's work over to the people showed an attitude of public service and a belief in the educational value of collections that was revolutionary for its time. Since, he wrote, the items in his collection were things

"tending in many ways to the manifestation of the Glory of God, the Confutation of Atheism and its consequences, the Uses and Improvement of the Arts and Sciences, and benefit of Mankind,"

it was the donor's hope that those things might

"remain together and not be separated, and that chiefly in or about the City of London, whence they may by the great influence of people be of most use."

"CURIOSITIES" AND SCIENCE *were still on friendly terms late in the 18th century, when oddity was often valued above significance or beauty. The* Egyptian earthenware vessel *shown opposite, a gift from the Duke of Richmond to Sir Hans Sloane, was prized chiefly because of its porousness, which made it possible to grow "sallad herbs" in the furrows! The* Coral Hand *fell into the popular category of natural objects which resembled other objects. The* Scythian Lamb, *the shaggy rhizome of an Asian fern* (Cibotium Barometz), *had once been believed to be both plant and animal, having bones, blood and flesh; but the 1778 cataloguer explodes this theory in a long and learned footnote, declaring of the shoots which form the legs and ears, "These, I imagine, are cut by art to make them proportionable." Yet he holds tightly to the theory that "Stones do grow," and points for his proof to the* Glass-Tumbler *"the under part of which is incrustrated with a Limey or Stoney Substance, for to Show, and to convince that the Stone was once in a Liquid State, though some will have it to be made so by Fire."*

Two plates from British Museum Catalogue entitled, "Museum Britannicum: Being an Exhibition of a Great Variety of Antiquities and Natural Curiosities Belonging to that Noble and Magnificent Cabinet, The British Museum." John and Andrew van Rymsdyk, Pictors, London, 1778. *(See facing page.)*

Here was no Pepys, bent upon perpetuating his own name and works. Here was a man of vision who may have foreseen the day when collections of all sorts would become one of the chief visual aids to public education. And of such importance was his gift that Parliament, in 1753, passed a special act accepting it and providing for the purchase of a building suitable for its exhibition. To be included were the Cottonian Library (already a national possession) and the Harleian Collection of Manuscripts, provision for the purchase of which was made by the same act of Parliament. In 1757, George II presented the old Royal Library, and on January 15, 1759, the British Museum was formally opened. Until 1852 the museum was housed in old Montagu House, now torn down. The new building, begun in 1823, just behind Montagu House, was completed and added to at various subsequent dates.

In the early days a visit to the British Museum was made in much the same spirit as a trip to any other kind of show. For a long time admission was charged, and one went to "see the curiosities." Parties were escorted past the exhibits in groups of ten, with no more than an hour's time allotted to each group. Not to be caught napping, the first guardians of the British Museum took excessive care that no damage should be done to anything on display—such care, indeed, that visitors complained they could hardly see anything at all. Despite such disadvantages the institution attained rapid popularity. In the year 1776, for example, those who had applied for tickets in April were still waiting to get them in August, with the result that ticket-speculators as gouging as our own sprang up and did a flourishing business until, in 1808, the issuing of tickets was discontinued.

At first the museum was divided into three departments—manuscripts, printed books, and natural history exhibits—and the antiquities were "regarded as little more than a curious appendage to the Natural History collection." By 1807, however, a special department had been created for marbles, minor antiquities, prints, drawings, coins and medals. As the collections grew and more modern ideas of museum arrangement took root, more and more subdivisions were created in each department, until, between 1880 and 1883, the natural history collections, originally the nucleus of the entire institution, were set apart in a special museum at South Kensington, and the British Museum itself was given over to the library and antiquities.

One of the trustees of the new museum was Horace Walpole (1717–97), who seems to have been slightly dismayed by the nature of his duties. He wrote to his friend, Horace Mann, on February 14, 1753:

"You will scarce guess how I employ my time; chiefly at present in the guardianship of embryos and cockleshells. Sir Hans Sloane is dead, and has made me one of the trustees to his museum, which is to be offered for twenty thousand pound to the King, the Parliament, the Royal Academies of Petersburgh, Berlin, Paris, and Madrid. He valued it at fourscore thousand; and so would anybody who loves hippopotamuses, sharks with one ear, and spiders as big as geese! It is a rent-charge, to keep the foetuses in spirits! You may believe that those who think money the most valuable of all curiosities will not be purchasers. The King has excused himself saying he did not believe that there are twenty thousand pounds in the treasury. We are a charming wise set, all philosophers, botanists, antiquarians, and mathematicians . . . One of our number is a Moravian, who signs himself Henry XXVIII, Count de Reus. The Moravians have settled a colony at Chelsea, in Sir Hans's neighborhood, and I believe he intended to beg the Count Henry XXVIII's skeleton for his museum."

The bantering, unappreciative tone of this letter is deceptive, for in a different field Walpole himself was one of the most enthusiastic collectors of his time. He had been brought up in a collecting atmosphere, since his father, Sir Robert Walpole, First Earl of Orford (1676–1745), had been a great connoisseur, the collector of a fine library and of "a magnificent and almost unique collection of pictures." The collecting careers of this father and son, each of whom achieved great fame in his way, furnish a clear picture of the changes that were taking place at the time in collecting attitudes and methods.

The elder Walpole was of the old school, still savoring of the renaissance in collecting manner and choice. "For years a host of industrious foragers [his influential friends] sought out . . . treasures" for him, treasures which included splendid paintings by such masters as Rubens, Van Dyck, Murillo, Guido Reni, Teniers and Wouwerman. Yet there was relatively so little competition for father Walpole to contend with, even in the early part of the eighteenth century, that the highest price he ever paid for a picture would seem enviably small to the more numerous brotherhood of the next generation or two, and his entire collection, outstanding as it was, cost him no more than forty thousand pounds.

In 1753, Horace Walpole, serving out his collecting apprenticeship, assisted his father in cataloguing these important paintings, which, under a later and lesser member of the family, Horace's ne'er-do-well nephew, the third Lord Orford, were to be sold to Catherine of Russia. Horace himself was to develop more along the lines of those elegant and somewhat precious dilettanti which the eighteenth century produced in such profusion. It is true enough, as Austin Dobson has said, that

"As a virtuoso and amateur, his position is a mixed one. He was certainly widely different from that typical art connoisseur of his day—the butt of Goldsmith and of Reynolds—who travelled the Grand Tour to litter a gallery at home with broken-nosed busts and the rubbish of the Roman picture factories."

And yet, despite his background, despite the incipient elements of true connoisseurship that were surely a part of his own nature, Horace Walpole made of Strawberry Hill, his famous pseudo-Gothic castle, only "a memorable curiosity shop," and his library of about fifteen thousand volumes consisted principally of those works "which no gentleman's library should be without." Like all well-to-do young Englishmen of his time, Walpole did travel the Grand Tour, and, like most of them, he too fell under the romantic spell of the continent. Under the influence of that spell collecting became one of his chief preoccupations, to an extent clearly seen in this excerpt from a letter written in Rome:

"I am far gone in medals, lamps, idols, prints, and all the small commodities to the purchase of which I can attain. I would buy the Coliseum if I could."

This is not quite so fantastic as it was intended to sound. In a later day a clever charlatan once "sold" Trajan's Column to an ambitious and gullible American collector who got as far as assembling the workmen who were to take down the monument stone by stone, before he was halted by a puzzled and indignant Italian government.

Another of Walpole's comments shows to what dismal straits the Eternal City had been reduced since the glory years of its renaissance:

"I am persuaded," he wrote in 1740, "that in an hundred years Rome will not be worth seeing. All the public pictures are decayed or decaying; the few ruins cannot last long; and the statues and private collections must be sold, from the great poverty of the families."

In France, at this time, Louis XV was king, Jeanne Antoinette Poisson was but twenty years old, and the Paris which Horace visited in company with the poet, Thomas Gray, was, in striking contrast to the Italian city, gay and highly prosperous, at least in the upper circles. Though it would be said of Paris, too, in much less than a century, that "the statues and private collections must be sold, from the great poverty of the families," the future then was unsuspected. English collectors of Walpole's type, in Walpole's day, made much the same impression upon the sophisticated French as Americans of the late nineteenth century were to make upon both British and French, and for somewhat the same reasons. It is not without significance that the eighteenth century in England is still known as the "century of the dilettanti," even though the word *dilettante* originally meant "one who enjoys the fine arts" (an amateur as distinguished from the professional in such matters) and did not carry quite the connotation of "trifling" which now belongs to it.

Although Walpole knew a good deal about painting, and through his many friends on the continent had unusual opportunities to secure the best for his collection, he assembled, actually, an immense hodgepodge of items in which the great were mingled indiscriminately with the mediocre. Within the anachronistically crenellated walls of his "Gothic" castle—which itself was indicative of a precious and superficial approach—trivial curios and souvenirs jostled the books and paintings, the statuary, ceramics and engraved gems.

Among Horace Walpole's many friends was one Margaret Cavendish Holles Harley, Duchess of Portland (1714–85), whose background was thick with collectors including Robert and Edward Harley of library fame, and who was herself one of the most fanatic in an age of collectomaniacs. From her mother, Margaret inherited "a prodigious collection of portraits of her Ancestors . . . fine Miniatures, Enamels & Vases of crystal," and a taste for collecting which became the dominant interest in her life. In Walpole's account of this lady he tells us that at first the Duchess confined herself to gathering shells and old china chiefly, "a collection of odd pieces" in which she sought "one specimen of every pattern she could get." But soon she was including pictures (which, so Walpole declared, she did not understand), books, busts, coins, medals, miniatures and jewels, and, again in Walpole's words, "indulging her taste for Virtù, she spared no expence to gratify it for about thirty years."

The Bettmann Archive

VOLTAIRE'S BEDROOM AT FERNEY, *showing a part of his collection of portraits. From an engraving by J. N. Nee.*

The Bettmann Archive

THE IMPERIAL LIBRARY, VIENNA. *It is said that large birds, possibly pelicans, were employed to service the upper shelves. Note the museum exhibits on the wall, left background; Royalty, right foreground. After an engraving in Edward Brown's* Sonderbare Reisen, *1711.*

One of the Duchess' specialties was collecting prints by Hollar, and "to compleat his work, She bought at any price." As if all these subjects were not sufficient to fill her time and empty her purse, she "latterly went deeply into natural history [so deeply that she even acquired a menagerie], and her collection in that Walk was supposed to have cost her fifteen thousand pounds." To this part of her collection friend Horace contributed a scarlet spider, which he weaned away from Admiral Boscawen.

Towards the end of her life the formidable Duchess ceased piling up treasure to devote her energy to the cataloguing of her natural history specimens. Yet she could not resist temptation entirely, and it was only a few months before her death that she acquired the celebrated Barberini Vase, later known by her name. This invaluable piece, made of dark blue glass with figures cut in high relief from a layer of superimposed white glass, is the most famous example extant of the style of Egyptian glassmaking as that style was continued by Roman craftsmen. Although discovered at Rome in 1550, in a tomb of the third century B.C., the Portland Vase is thought to date from the first century. It was brought to England by Sir William Hamilton, from whom the Duchess purchased it, and in 1810 was deposited in the British Museum by the Duke of Portland, and there it remained for many years.

In England, it was not the collectors of books and art objects but rather the scientific collectors who initiated most of the significant collecting innovations. As John Tradescant first had the idea of publicly exhibiting collections of rarities, as Sir Hans Sloane had first expressed the conception of a great collection's being for "the use and improvement of the arts and sciences and benefit of mankind," so now another naturalist, Sir Joseph Banks (1743–1820), first formulated the ideal of intelligent specialization for collectors.

Banks saw that a collector who chose to pursue his hobby with discrimination might easily perform a specific service to any one of the branches of knowledge. In regard to the formation of libraries, for example, he wrote that in his opinion private collectors should renounce their former haphazard ways and

"confine their libraries to one individual branch of human knowledge, by which means a great number of particular collections, each complete in its kind, would quickly be brought forward, and the purposes of instruction be more easily attained than whilst the rage of indiscriminate collection subsisted, and the number of competitors for the same book precluded the possibility of completion."

To us this appears simply as good sense, but it was an idea that had presented itself to few minds up to this time.

Banks did not carry his principle to its ultimate conclusion of specialization within a specialty, but he did apply it in his own case to the extent of limiting himself to the field of natural history, with the result that finally he assembled one of the best libraries ever created on this subject. Although on his trip to Iceland, for example, he purchased a collection of Icelandic manuscripts and books, he presented these to the British Museum immediately upon his return, since they lay outside his chosen field. Eventually he bequeathed his entire library as well as his herbaria and other natural history collections to the same institution (of which he was trustee), after giving a prior life-interest in them to Robert Brown. They were transferred to the museum in 1827.

Always deeply interested in botany, it was his ambition to follow in the footsteps of Linnaeus, and he seized upon his inherited wealth to make numerous expeditions of genuine value into distant parts of the world which few scientists had studied. Newfoundland, Labrador, the South Seas, South America, Australia and Iceland were among the places he visited between 1763 and 1771, and from each he brought back rich collections of plants, insects, drawings, maps and charts. The grand goal, the advancement of science, to his mind was above all other considerations and he demonstrated this in a single act when, with extraordinary objectivity, he saw to it that certain natural history collections seized by British men-of-war during the Napoleonic conflict were sent on to their original destination, the *Jardin des Plantes* at Paris, remarking, "I have never heard of any declaration of war between the philosophers of England and the philosophers of France."

Although it would be unduly optimistic to say that Sir Joseph Banks typified the spirit and the conscience of the new age in collecting, he did, perhaps, represent the ideal toward which that age would strive consciously or unconsciously, willingly or unwillingly, and with varying degrees of success. The tempering of "curiosity" collections now began in earnest, and although the old tendencies may never completely die, the days of world knowledge under one hat had passed. Science was exploring, cataloguing, seeking exact evidence, and while collectors watched, the universe was expanding before their eyes. Before long it would be an inevitable choice between two courses only, specialization or "magpie-ism." And henceforth even a Morgan, although expansive, could ill afford to welcome into his sanctum, as did Lorenzo, a unicorn's horn, or a petrified body of the sort so gratefully accepted by Cardinal Richelieu.

The evolving scientific attitude, which had had its inception as early as the seventeenth century and was now rapidly becoming a dominant characteristic of the modern era, was important in the growth of specialization since it influenced thoughtful amateurs as well as scholars, and contributed much toward the growth of a more purposive approach toward every activity, even hobbies.

Still another factor—the swiftly approaching end of the courtly age, with its emphasis upon elegant uselessness—was to lead, as its logical conclusion, to another great modern variation on the age-old collecting pattern, the ultimate use of many private collections for public service.

Although Horace Walpole's house and collection had been open to the public by ticket of admission, few of the great art collections of eighteenth-century London were similarly unbent. Places like Spencer House and Lansdowne House, with their galleries of sculpture, fine libraries and magnificent and varied displays of artistic treasure, were still private palaces exclusively. Yet toward the turn of the century, gradually at first, a new sense of social responsibility made its appearance, and the owners of important collections increasingly understood that the cultural possessions which they had acquired might fittingly become a part of the national or common heritage. Political democracy had long been a reality in England, but the French Revolution forced the old nobility everywhere in Europe to take stock of its position in relation to the common people, and the epochal revolution in industry with its attendant social dislocations pushed into high relief the problems of human rights regardless of wealth or class. Here and there men more fortunate than their fellows began to question the justice of their franchise to the cream of the earth, and if they happened to be collectors they could look to leaders like Sir Joseph Banks to discover how, with a certain amount of intelligent direction, they could in this field render their own pleasurable activities potentially useful to the many.

During the eighteenth and early nineteenth centuries there were founded in England a number of literary, philosophical, antiquarian and natural history societies, the members of which made the assembling of specialized collections an important part of their program. Later many of these society collections were either converted into authentic museums or in other ways made available to the public. Of the five hundred and thirty museums in the British Isles today only four or five —all originally based upon private collections of "rarities and curiosities" —were founded before 1800. In the nineteenth century, on the other hand, nearly two hundred and fifty museums were established, and private donation made most of them possible. One example of a museum built upon a succession of private bequests is England's National Gallery. Founded in 1824 by the purchase, at George IV's insistence, of the Angerstein Collection, it was later enriched by the successive donations of such collections as the Beaumont in 1826, the Carr in 1831, the Olney in 1837, the Farnborough in 1838, the Vernon in 1847, and the Turner in 1856.

The process was a cumulative one and the old motive of pride-competition remained in full strength to reinforce an increasingly intelligent idealism. The collector mass did not suddenly become an angelic choir with eyes turned solely toward the public good. The industrial age produced a new oligarchy of wealth given to plunder and display. The dilettante did not disappear, nor did the antiquarian become immediately or wholly scientific in his approach.

Yet although the industrial age bred a prodigal horde of parvenus intent upon buying their way into culture and so into the upper classes, it also was responsible for that wave of archaeological excavation which, more irresistibly than anything since the humanist movement of the renaissance, gave impetus to serious antiquarian collecting.

This phenomenon was a direct corollary to the mechanical forces which brought the age itself into being. A revival of interest in classical antiquities had begun with the discoveries, in the second half of the eighteenth century, of the long-buried cities of Herculaneum and Pompeii. Napoleon's Egyptian campaign (1798–99) had opened up a whole new field of endeavor to collectors. But now the digging of railway cuts and the carrying out of other engineering operations were disclosing unexpected archaeologic and geologic wealth in field and ditch and under the very foundations of the houses close to home. Ambitious to outdo each other in the wealth of their cultural treasure, nations as well as individuals turned to collecting. High-pressure competition made its appearance, and though from this, assuredly, there rose up unpleasant fumes of materialism and bungling, out of it was developed a means of making more widely available the educational opportunities inherent in collections, of giving man the chance to see for himself the cultural achievements of his fellows throughout the ages.

An elegant example of the paradox involved is to be found in the collecting career of Thomas Bruce, Seventh Earl of Elgin (1766–1841), who, though known to history as the "despoiler of the Parthenon," actually represents the first gropings toward the new ideal, since he dedicated a large share of his life and fortune (no matter how misguided his course) to what he conceived to be the cultural enrichment of his country.

It began with his appointment as ambassador to the Porte (Constantinople) toward the turn of the century. Hearing of the appointment, Elgin's friend Thomas Harrison, the Scottish architect, suggested that a great public service might be performed if an extensive collection of casts and drawings made from Grecian antiquities could be assembled and brought back to England for the use of students, painters, sculptors, architects and historians. It had long been the custom for wealthy diplomats to attach draftsmen to their staffs, but Elgin, listening attentively to Harrison's suggestion, was stimulated to a particularly ambitious undertaking by his desire to rival both Napoleon's achievements in Egypt and those of the former French ambassador to the Porte, the count Choiseul-Gouffier (1752–1817), who had acquired an outstanding collection of Grecian antiquities.

Elgin's original idea was sufficiently grandiose, since he planned to obtain material for a complete artistic and architectural picture of ancient Greece, but once embarked upon the project he was seized in the grip of a genuine and unmistakable collectomania which was only increased by the physical and political difficulties which the task entailed. Not content with the casts and drawings first considered, his mounting appetite now demanded nothing less than the actual statues, the original columns, and such fragments of buildings and architectural decorations as his men could carry off. When later he was accused of wanton and unpardonable vandalism, he justified his conduct on the ground that the monuments were being gradually destroyed anyhow, whereas he, although removing them from Greece, was actually taking measures to preserve them—and to preserve them so that western students could observe and make use of them.

For at least the first part of this reasoning there was considerable justification. The Parthenon (blt. *c.* 447–*c.* 438 B.C.) had remained almost intact until 1687 when, during the course of the Venetians' siege of Athens, a powder-magazine exploding within the ancient building had destroyed one entire portion of it, and the fact that in Elgin's day the Acropolis had been converted into a Turkish fortress made the possibility of further destruction a strong likelihood. It is true that unless properly bribed the Turks were at all times reluctant to part with any portion of the antique Greek remains, but their reasons for this were fraught with added danger for the precious relics. Greek history had little significance to the Turks, and their religion forbade an interest in representations of the human figure. Only because they believed that removal of the monuments would bring bad luck did they cling to them, and for this reason they would often deface statues to prevent their being taken away. Often too, like the renaissance Romans, they pounded the ancient stones to mortar for building purposes and in many other ways damaged them irreparably.

The modern Greeks were as bad as their Turkish overlords. Ignorant and superstitious, one of their habits was to roll a sick person over and over on an inscribed stone in the belief that this would cure him of his ailment, and so many the sick and so strong the belief that numerous inscriptions were obliterated by constant repetition of this process. In addition, stones long buried were visibly deteriorating after being dug up and left exposed to the weather.

How the Elgin collection was actually assembled, at the cost of an almost incredible amount of labor, intrigue, and persistence, is told elsewhere. Here we are concerned chiefly with its disposition. As the marbles arrived in England, shipload after shipload of them, they were installed in the Elgin mansion, and there they were first exhibited in 1807. A year later the collection was opened to the public without charge on Saturdays and Sundays, and so many came to look that it became necessary to engage a curator. Elgin had always intended the nation to be the beneficiary of his labors, and before embarking for the East he had unsuccessfully solicited government financial aid for his project. Now, however, when the true significance of his collection grew every year more obvious, Parliament cast covetous eyes upon it and questioned the right of any individual to own such treasure. Elgin was subjected to severe questioning, and though it entered no one's head that the precious marbles might actually belong to Greece, it was suggested that the English government had the right to claim them. Now it was the collector's turn to be stubborn, and he demanded that before turning over the collection he should be reimbursed for a part of the enormous expenses incurred in assembling and transporting it. He eventually received thirty-five thousand pounds, half the cost, and in 1816 such of the Elgin Marbles as were then in England were transferred to the British Museum.

No one better exemplified certain characteristic trends of the transitional period than did Sir John Soane, architect of the Bank of England (1753–1837), whose extraordinary collection was on view in London at least until 1939 in very much the same state as its founder had left it.

Born in the year that Hans Sloane died, Soane presented, both in his methods and in his interests as a collector, something old and something new. Architecture was his ruling passion, as science had been that of Sloane and Banks, and he declared his collecting goal to be "the promotion of the study of art and architecture." Within this relatively broad territory he specialized, gathering an immense number of pictures, statues, books, furniture and *objets d'art,* antique and modern, of all schools and styles. Included in his collection were architectural fragments, thousands of architectural and topographical drawings, and many association items concerned with the great architects. His country home at Pitzhanger Manor and later his town house became museums in the truest sense of the word, and four years before he died he arranged that the latter should pass eventually to the nation on condition that it be kept always as he himself had arranged it. His purpose in making this condition, however, was different from that of Pepys'.

A man of originality and of strong personal opinions, Soane believed that a good collection in the field of art should be organized to show the close relationships between, say, painting, sculpture and architecture, or between painting and music, and having followed a purposive scheme in the arrangement of his museum he felt that his entire intent would be destroyed by any change in that arrangement. It is no reflection on the sincerity or seriousness of his motive that the system he followed produced what, when judged by modern standards, appears to be hodgepodge, and that the chief value of the Soane Museum today is one of historical documentation, illustrating, as it does, certain typical characteristics of the period in which the collection was formed.

Much under the influence of the medieval or Gothic "revival," this architect-amateur had, in his museum, rooms representing a monk's cell and oratory and a monk's parlor. From the window of the latter one could look out upon the synthetic "ruins" of a monastery and the "tomb" of the mythical monk. So far so good, for this scheme served excellently to illustrate the life of a bygone age. Yet within the monk's "parlor" were exhibited, in addition to certain quite suitable period items, such completely unrelated objects as seventeeth-century Dutch chairs, early eighteenth-century tables, and a case containing a collection of ancient Peruvian earthenware vases. The so-called Sepulchral Chamber had, as its main exhibit, the famous "Belzoni Sarcophagus," now known to have been that of the Egyptian Pharaoh, Seti I (*c.* 1300 B.C.). In Soane's day the identifying hieroglyphics had not yet been deciphered. This Egyptian relic was surrounded by casts of Roman and Greek architectural ornaments, fragments of antique sculpture, and a post-mortem mask of Parker, the English mutineer, which seems to have been remarkable chiefly for "its striking likeness to Oliver Cromwell." Such lapses in good collecting sense on the part of men disposed toward science are to be attributed to the lingering fascination of the merely "curious," a fascination which could still absolve a discipline and criticism to which later men have become more accustomed.

Although Soane was also a pioneer of the Greek revival in architecture, he apparently had little realization of the instructive possibilities inherent in the dawning science of archaeology. At Pitzhanger Manor, for example, he erected a colonnade leading to a court of sham Roman ruins composed of columns and other architectural relics gathered during his stay in Italy, but he declared that his object in creating this exhibit was

> "to ridicule those fanciful architects and antiquarians who, finding a few pieces of columns, and sometimes only a few single stones, proceed on these slender data to imagine magnificent buildings."

Yet Soane was definitely a man of the new age to the extent that he visualized an educational purpose in collecting. And in his original methods of display—including the use of movable planes, special lighting, and clever recesses designed to make the best possible use of limited space—he was well ahead of his time.

More characteristically reflective of the general nineteenth-century pattern is the history of the Wallace Collection, which was built up over three generations and has been public property only since 1900.

The founder was that Francis Charles Seymour-Conway, Third Marquess of Hertford (1777–1842), who figured as the Marquis of Steyne in Thackeray's novel, *Vanity Fair.* An enormously wealthy man, the Third Marquess accumulated houses as well as art objects, and at least three of his palatial homes were filled with special sections of the collection. The bronzes, marbles and furniture were at St. Dunstan's. Old Dorchester House contained, according to a contemporary account, the "vast collection of gold and silver coins, portraits, drawings, curious snuffboxes and watches." And in Manchester House (now renamed Hertford House and used to house the present collection) hung a collection of paintings particularly rich in examples of Dutch art. In 1940 Hertford House was struck by German bombs, but according to reports received in the United States, the paintings had been previously stored for safety.

This gentleman was in no way different from the many other wealthy collectors of his day who followed the fashion in gathering and displaying vast numbers of artistic possessions; but his son, Richard Conway, Fourth Marquess of Hertford (1800–1870), to whom he passed on those possessions, stands out in the annals as a collectomaniac of an unusually picturesque variety. Beginning life after the common fashion of the conservative upper-class Englishman, with a promising career in the army, diplomacy and politics, he soon withdrew from public life to take up art collecting on a full-time basis. Moving then to Paris he gradually became an eccentric recluse, never marrying, interested only in his growing collection, and in animals.

In addition to the many houses which Hertford already possessed in Britain in legacy from his father he bought several in Paris, and not only did he fill all these homes with his own accumulations, but he took great care to see that his inherited treasures should also be preserved. Able to pay top prices, he achieved fame as that English *milord* who could challenge all the crowned heads of Europe on the collecting battlefield, a reputation in which he took considerable pride. In this, as in a number of other ways, he resembled the American industrialist collectors who were his contemporaries.

His taste in art, if judged by critical standards, was somewhat dubious. He preferred the French school of the eighteenth century, and once defined his esthetic standard thus briefly, "I only like pleasing pictures," a dictum that was later to be echoed by the American, W. K. Vanderbilt. Like another American collector, Henry Walters of Baltimore, Hertford owned so many paintings that he often lost track of individual items. A famous Titian, for example, was forgotten for many years until finally it showed up in a bathroom. It is told of him that he once had an agent searching all over Europe for a picture which the Marquess described in great detail as one he particularly desired to own. The painting was eventually located behind a bundle of other pictures in one of the collector's own houses, where he himself had placed it, after purchasing it several years before.

Although the extent of his holdings was too much for an average memory, no one could have credited the Fourth Marquess of Hertford with having created his collection in the public interest. "Things were everything to him, people nothing," though he made an exception on behalf of artists and was most generous to those who needed financial assistance. In strong contrast was the attitude of his heir, Sir Richard Wallace (1818–90), who was so deeply interested in people that he was knighted for humanitarian work carried on in Paris during the Franco-Prussian War. It is generally thought that Sir Richard, born when the Fourth Marquess was but eighteen years of age, was Hertford's illegitimate son. No such relationship was ever acknowledged, however, and there are those who believe him to have been a late-born natural son of the Marquess' famous mother, "Mie-Mie." *Comme ci, comme ça,* Wallace was long associated with Hertford and, whether by inheritance or otherwise, he shared the older man's passion for collecting. As "Monsieur Richard" he assisted Hertford in the creation of his collection while forming an independent collection of his own which consisted chiefly of paintings, miniatures, ivories, bronzes, and antique armor.

After Lord Hertford's death there was dramatically discovered secreted in a desk drawer a will which gave all the Marquess' unentailed property, including the collections, to his younger "friend." About this will Wallace had apparently known nothing, and now, coming into his inheritance during the troubled period of the *Commune* in Paris, he felt himself faced with grave responsibility. Fearing for the safety of the treasures he decided to move them to London, and there, while Hertford House was being altered to receive them, the combined Wallace and Hertford collections were publicly exhibited, attracting, between 1872 and 1875, nearly five million people.

A systematic builder, unlike Hertford, Wallace continued to expand the collection, filling in many of its yawning gaps with the intention of presenting the finished effort to the people of England. Plans for a national art museum were considered, but ill health blocked the project, and upon Sir Richard's death the collection passed to Lady Wallace who, following her husband's wish, eventually bequeathed the larger part to the nation. In doing so, however, she stipulated that the Wallace must be kept a "closed" collection, a condition which tends to die in a maturing society. For newer trends, as developed out of the kaleidoscoped history of collecting in the United States, we may turn our eyes upon the rambunctious young offspring of the collecting world.

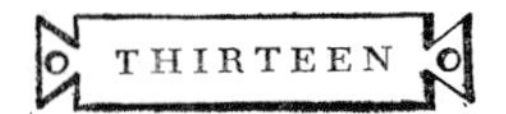

AMERICAN GROWTH

> *"Miniver loved the Medici,*
> *Albeit he had never seen one;*
> *He would have sinned incessantly*
> *Could he have been one."*
>
> E. A. ROBINSON

THE EARLIEST white inhabitants of America were far too busy to indulge greatly in hobbies. Doubtless some of them gathered and saved, as souvenirs of their struggles with the wilderness, hunting trophies, Indian arrowheads and similar relics; but the many objects in daily use which later were to be prized—the simple, homemade furniture, the humble pewter utensils, the hand-hewn farm implements and other tools—had, of course, little intrinsic value and less sentimental interest for their hard-pressed users, while books and luxury objects, all imported, were expensive and rare. In early colonial days, therefore, America fitted into the collecting scene chiefly as a source of exotic curiosities for the cabinets of European collectors.

It was only toward the end of the seventeenth century that this condition began slowly to change. Then the New World sprouted a few amateurs of its own, the sparse and lonely vanguard of a future army of enthusiasts which, for size at least, has never been matched.

As almost always happens, the procession was led off by book collectors. Marching staunchly at the head were members of the famous Mather "dynasty." Richard Mather, early in the century, embarked upon the difficult project of forming a modest library, and became one of the first true collectors in this country. For three generations after him, members of his family were to concentrate upon bettering Richard's pioneer achievement; and by 1683 Cotton Mather could proudly claim "a library exceeding any Man's, in all this land." Concurring with this opinion was John Dunton, the eccentric London bookseller who found it worth-while to ply the Atlantic several times, so considerably had the number of collectors increased. Of Mather's collection he wrote:

"I do think he has one of the best (for a Private Library) that I ever saw . . . Mr. Mather's Library is the Glory of New-England if not of all America."

That library, so auspiciously begun, had, by the eighteenth century, increased to some seven or eight thousand printed volumes (an enormous quantity for the period in America), and contained, in the words of Cotton Mather's son, Samuel, "a prodigious number of valuable manuscripts" as well.

Closely associated with the Mather family was Thomas Prince (1687–1758), theologian, scholar and bibliophile, of whom Edward H. Dewey writes:

"Outwardly a zealous patriot, ardent in his advocacy of civil and religious liberty, he was privately devoted to his library. It is undoubtedly as a bibliophile and student that he will be longest remembered."

Naturally enough the majority of colonial and early American collectors followed the conventional patterns set for them in Europe; but the more foresighted realized that a new and invaluable field lay closer at hand, and among these pioneers Thomas Prince was outstanding. From the moment he entered Harvard at sixteen he began acquiring every book, pamphlet and paper he could find which touched upon New England history. Especially he sought those original documents overlooked by his contemporaries because they were so new, so fresh that the ink was barely dry. These, he realized, would have exceptional value to future historians and scholars, and in his own words he collected them

"from a public view, and with the desire that the memory of many important transactions might be preserved which would otherwise be lost."

Like many others obsessed by a specific goal, Prince's conscience sat lightly upon him where other people's property was concerned, and from the Mather library, to which he had free access, he sometimes borrowed valuable documents which he failed to return. His intention had been to write a chronological history of New England based largely upon the source material in his own and the Mather collections, but work on this cherished project was interrupted by his appointment as minister to the Old South Church in Boston and thereafter official duties never permitted his taking it up again. It was then that he wrote, half in pride, half in sorrow:

"I could propose no other than to go on with my collections, and provide material for some other hand . . . Which I have been at no small expense to gather: having amassed above a thousand books, pamphlets, and papers of this kind in print; and a great number of papers in manuscript, so many indeed that I have never yet had leisure to read them."

The collection, now considered as important as its owner had foreseen it would be, comprised in all one thousand eight hundred and ninety volumes. Prince bequeathed it to the Old South Church in Boston, and there it remained until 1866 when it was transferred to the Boston Public Library.

Four out of five of the first presidents of the United States were book collectors, and the greatest of these was Thomas Jefferson. Over a period of fifty years he assembled between nine and ten thousand volumes, and though his was a "working" library, it also contained many fine, rare, old, or first editions of the sort that collectors prize, even from the shops and fairs of Germany. Jefferson's declaration that he longed to retire from public life so that he could return to his family, his farm and his books is famous, yet some of his best collecting opportunities came to him in the line of duty.

Jefferson classified his books according to "the faculties of the mind" to which he felt they might best be applied, i.e., memory, reason and imagination. A detailed description of the collection is contained in a gossipy little journal written by Francis Calley Gray who, in company with the historian, Ticknor, visited Jefferson in 1814 when the retired statesman was seventy-two years old. Here, in part, is the diarist's account:

"Mr. Jefferson gave us the catalogue of his books to examine and soon after conducted us to his library, and passed an hour there in pointing out to us its principal treasures. His collection of ancient classics was complete as to authors but very careless in the editions. They were generally interleaved with the best English Translations. The Ancient English authors were also all here and some very rare editions of them. A black letter Chaucer and the first of

National Gallery of Art, Washington, D. C.

A FINE SYMBOL OF AMERICAN MARITIME PROWESS *and of the great years of trade expansion, this early 19th-century figurehead of Benjamin Franklin is a fragment of the national heritage. Drawing by Malcolm Hackney, Index of American Design. Life-size original, by William Rush or his studio, is in Yale University Art Gallery.*

Wadsworth Atheneum, Hartford, Connecticut

OAK CRADLE OF PILGRIM FATHERS. *John Alden is said to have made this sturdy piece of furniture (c. 1650) which, according to an unbroken tradition, came down from Dr. Samuel Fuller of the Mayflower. From the Wallace Nutting Collection.*

Milton's Paradise Lost, divided into ten books, were the most remarkable. A considerable number of books valuable to the Biblical critic were here, and various ancient editions of all the genuine and apocryphal books, Erasmus' edition, etc. Many of the most valuable works on the civil and maritime law and on diplomacy, together with a complete collection of the laws of the different states, those of Virginia in manuscript, and all the old elementary writers and reporters of England formed the legal library. The ancient and most distinguished modern historians render this department nearly complete, and the histories and descriptions of the Kingdoms of Asia were remarkably numerous . . . Mr. Jefferson has also a fine collection of Saxon and Moeso Gothic books . . . Of all branches of learning, however, that relating to the history of North and South America is the most perfectly displayed in this library. The collection on this subject is without question the most valuable in the world. Here are the works of all the Spanish travellers in America and the great work of De Brie . . . finely printed and adorned with many plates . . ."

In 1814 when the Library of Congress was burned by the British, Jefferson, impoverished by the expenses incurred in public service and by his own excessive hospitality, offered to sell his library to the government to replace the one destroyed. This offer was gratefully accepted and the ex-president received a much-needed twenty-three thousand nine hundred and fifty dollars. Unhappily, more than half of the collection was destroyed by a second disastrous fire in 1851.

A man of wide interests, Jefferson was outstanding as a collector in scientific fields also. His personal concern for the advancement of scientific knowledge in America was one of the chief whips to the famous Lewis and Clark Expedition (1804–06) which was organized at his suggestion and in which the collecting of natural history specimens played at least as important a part as did the exploration of the hitherto undescribed country to the west. A year later Jefferson commissioned Captain Clark

". . . to cause the ground near the Salines, called the Bigbone Licks [in Kentucky] to be dug up; and the fossil relicks to be forwarded for him to Washington city."

Concerning this project, Samuel L. Mitchell wrote in 1826:

"This was so faithfully executed during 1807, that a consignment which arrived in the Potomac early in March, 1808 by the way of New Orleans, was charged with expences for transportation etc. to the amount of three hundred dollars. The collection was probably the most extensive that was ever seen together at one display. As they lay on the floor of one of the great saloons in the President's house, the present narrator surveyed them in company with the owner; and methodized them under the following heads . . ."

This collection, which consisted of some three hundred specimens of fossil bones, was later separated by Jefferson into three sets. One he kept for himself; one he sent to the American Philosophical Society, to which he had earlier (1797) presented a collection of bones gathered in Greenbrier County, Virginia; and the third he dispatched to Paris to supplement a collection he had previously presented to the great French zoologist, George Louis Leclerc, Comte de Buffon.

An amusing motive lay behind that earlier gift to the French scientist. Buffon had written a treatise claiming that the American climate had a degenerative effect upon all animal life, including man, and had advanced as proof of his theory the "fact" that beasts common both to Europe and the New World were found to be much smaller in the latter. To this idea Jefferson took strong exception, and in characteristically concrete and practical fashion he set about refuting it by sending to Buffon a collection of bones and skeletons of the beasts under discussion, with the request that the scientist measure them carefully and then reconsider the validity of a theory so damaging to America. Confronted with such evidence, the discomfited Buffon had, of course, no choice other than public retraction.

Jefferson's paleontological research was carried on during some of the most troublous years of United States history and at the time it occasioned more criticism than praise throughout the country, but today scientists speak with heartfelt reverence of his pioneer work in a field the future importance of which he was wise enough to foresee.

In scientific collecting doctors seem always to have been among the early birds, and one of the first botanical collections to be formed in America was that of Dr. Samuel Bard (1742–1821) of New York. As a lad of fourteen Bard had been sent to the country for his health, and there an accomplished lady botanist had initiated him into the fascinations of collecting plant specimens. From then on, in the later words of his son-in-law, John M'Vickar, this pursuit "ever remained in him a favorite amusement." As a young man Samuel Bard spent five years abroad traveling and studying medicine, but even then he made time for his "favorite amusement" and while at the University of Edinburgh was awarded a prize for preparing the best herbarium of indigenous Scottish vegetables.

All his life, so M'Vickar tells us, Samuel Bard betrayed

> ". . . an insatiable inquisitiveness of mind, which led him, wherever he was, to ransack and examine whatever came within his reach, whether of art or nature; minerals, plants, animals, man and his works, were rapidly and alternatively the object of his attention. Whatever was rare, or beautiful, or useful, immediately seized upon his imagination, and afforded matter for curious investigation."

Is there any doubt that a man so engaged is a man as nearly content as any? Toward the middle of the eighteenth century, Dr. John Bard, Samuel's father, had acquired some property near the Hudson River at Hyde Park, New York, and here he had begun planting specimen trees. Into this project the son entered with great enthusiasm. He himself imported trees from many European countries and in his own old age he was to devote almost his entire attention to orchard and garden. It was then that he

> "laid exactions on all his friends who could aid him in obtaining what was rare, beautiful or excellent in its kind . . . drawing from England its smaller fruits, the larger ones from France, melons from Italy, and vines from Madeira."

The special interest of this portion of his collection lies in the fact that much of it still exists. At one time Bard's partner, Dr. David Hosack, journeyed as far as Russia and Scandinavia to obtain additional specimens, and, as Stephen Early tells us, subsequent owners of the estate

> "took special pains to preserve the many interesting examples of trees and shrubs, replacing them with new ones when necessary. Thus, over nearly two hundred years, the place has acquired the character of an arboretum containing many mature species of trees from all over the world that can be found nowhere else in America."

The President of the United States gave his opinion of this property (near his own) in a letter written in 1939 to a prospective buyer. It was explained that the President himself had long cherished the hope that the estate should one day be acquired in perpetuity for all the nation, and that the house [of later date] might be converted

"into a museum for the display of forestry, landscaping and similar exhibits."

In view of this plea the prospective buyer withdrew, and a year later, through the owner's generosity, the former Bard estate was turned over to the public for the purposes outlined by Franklin D. Roosevelt.

Philadelphia, later the home of many great collections, was the birthplace of one of the first museums in the United States, founded by Charles Willson Peale (1741–1827), a noted portrait painter in his day and one of the very few members of his profession in the history of the world to achieve a goal of this sort.

Peale's first collecting venture, the assembling of a "Gallery of Portraits of distinguished Americans," was conventional enough, but in 1785 he branched out in a completely different direction. Having become much interested in natural history and in paleontology, he now, according to the description of his self-portrait given in the 1854 sale catalogue,

"commenced . . . the collection of a Museum of specimens in Natural History and the Arts, to embrace every object in nature or art which might be curious or instructive."

The first items in this ambitious collection were:

". . . some of the bones of the mammoth which he purchased, and a Paddle Fish presented by Robert Patterson."

Fascinated, as Jefferson was, by the subject of the mammoth, Peale later conducted extensive excavations in search of further evidence on this prehistoric creature, and in 1801 his labors were rewarded by the discovery of the first entire skeleton of a mastodon ever found.

His paints ignored as the museum project grew, Peale sailed abroad and hied from one European museum to another searching out their secrets, then came home and lectured on the subject. As the creator's intentions became more widely known, the Peale Collection was augmented by numerous gifts. The result was a characteristic hodgepodge which included, in addition to the portraits and natural history specimens, a group of wax figures representing the different tribes of North American Indians dressed in proper costume, a collection of Indian arms and utensils, other Indian and European curiosities, casts of ancient gems and statues—and some models of "machines." The museum was turned into something of a zoo as well when some of the animals—monkeys, a hyena, and a jackal—were brought in alive and kept for observation until they died natural deaths, whereupon they were duly stuffed and entered upon a career of permanent service.

Peale's huge self-portrait, now in the Pennsylvania Academy of Fine Arts, depicts the collector at the threshold of his exhibition hall and tells us that the paintings were hung in the same room with the natural history exhibits—"skied" above the cases containing the specimens. Nevertheless, the rudiments of specialization were evident within this miscellany. Peale himself compiled *A Scientific and Descriptive Catalogue* in which he described the exhibits under such headings as "Quadrupeds" (which included the American Indian exhibits), "Birds," "Fish," "Insects," and so on.

Although Peale first housed his collection in his own home at Third and Lombard Streets, he later moved it to the hall of the Philosophical Society and, later still (*c.* 1802), to the second floor of Independence Hall. After his death a suitable building was erected for it, but the sponsors failed financially and eventually the Peale collections were dispersed.

American museums in the early nineteenth century were still of a hesitant, hybrid sort. Assembled by their owners for profit, many sprang up and sputtered out like experimental lights in a prodigal laboratory. In New York City alone there were, in this period, several "museums" of varying degrees of importance. One was "The American Museum of John Scudder," founded in 1810 by an itinerant organ-grinder who, in his wanderings over the countryside, had been in the habit of collecting all the "curiosities" he could find. After the opening of his museum, Scudder took over the collection formed earlier by the Tammany Society under John Pintard, and his exhibits also included a collection of naval paintings. Although its owner charged the public twenty-five cents, the city rated The American Museum as a scientific institution and allowed Scudder to use the building rent free. Actually this museum—like so many of the English exhibits of the same period—was more of a pleasure haunt than an educational project, and music was provided in the evenings to attract additional customers.

A more specialized museum, also sponsored by one man and commercially conducted, was "Browere's Gallery of Busts and Statues." A sign-painter who had taken up sculpture and portrait painting, Browere declared that

"The object of this institution is to hand down to posterity the features and forms of American personages, as they actually were at the period of the execution of the likenesses by Mr. Browere."

Although many of the portrait busts were executed by the founder himself, the gallery was not entirely a one-man show since it also contained busts of Washington, Franklin, Paul Jones and Jefferson by the contemporary French sculptor, Houdon. There was also, in New York, "Peale's Museum and Gallery of the Fine Arts," opened in 1825 by Reuben Peale and containing, among its exhibits, some Egyptian mummies which may have been the first to be seen in this country. And finally came Phineas T. Barnum himself with "Barnum's American Museum," which, in 1841–42, absorbed both the Scudder and Reuben Peale collections. Its "five hundred thousand curiosities," including the Egyptian mummies, became the "wonder of the age" and attained, through the skill of master showmanship, a hitherto unprecedented popularity among institutions of the sort.

Meanwhile the discovery was spreading that it paid to collect and exhibit rarities of all kinds and, at a time when there were few public institutions for such divertissement, it was found by certain types of commercial establishments that collections of curiosities were bound to bring in the customers. The old-fashioned American barber shop, for example, like the eighteenth-century English coffee shop, was quite a museum, with pictures, Indian relics and foreign rarities; and the shop that could display the largest collection usually attracted the most enthusiastic and loyal clientele.

James Russell Lowell described one such place in detail—the barber shop in Cambridge, Massachusetts, which he had patronized as a boy. Of it he wrote in part, and with a faint overtone of nostalgia:

"The walls were covered with curious old Dutch prints, beaks of albatross and penguins, and whales' teeth fantastically engraved. Suspended over the fireplace, with the curling-tongs, were an Indian bow and arrows, and in the corners of the room stood New Zealand paddles and war-clubs, quaintly carved. The model of a ship in glass we variously estimated to be worth from a hundred to a thousand dollars . . . Among these wonders, the only sus-

Museum of the City of New York

AMERICAN MUSEUMS OF THE FIRST HALF OF THE 19TH CENTURY WERE A HYBRID LOT. *One of the last to survive was the collection of curiosities, Indian relics, cut glass, stuffed birds, paintings, prints, coins and miscellaneous oddments for many years displayed in the public room of the 5th Ward Museum Hotel, New York City, by Thomas Riley, proprietor. This lithograph of Major and Knapp, done for D. T. Valentine's Manual, was published in 1864 just before the sale of the collection at public auction.*

picious one was an Indian tomahawk, which had too much the peaceful look of a shingling hatchet . . ."

Apparently, even in a barber shop museum, there were items to raise a connoisseur eyebrow! Pictures of Frederick the Great, of Napoleon, and of famous sea battles constituted additional attractions, while a touch of nature was provided by a cageful of birds.

"Did any rarity enter the town," Lowell adds, "it gravitated naturally to these walls, to the very nail that waited to receive it."

Yet neither the barber nor his admiring customers could have known that all these treasures would one day be neglected, while the shaving mugs then in daily use would be highly prized by future collectors.

These were the romantic days of the New England whalers and clipper ships, hearty days which, to Americans, were as stimulating and revealing as the fifteenth-century voyages of discovery had been to Europeans. Every sea captain's home became a museum, chock-full of carved furniture and showy china from the Orient; of strangely shaped sea shells, dried starfish, sea horse skeletons, and whale bones; of Javanese slippers and Siamese costumes; of weapons and musical instruments and curious artifacts from Africa, South America, the far north, and the islands of the Pacific. Often the sea-going collector would occupy long months aboard ship by marking, with painstaking care, every item he was bringing home, detailing information as to its origin, meaning and date of acquisition—the "ship-shape" mind applied to cataloguing. Once home, shelves would be built, hooks and nails driven into the walls, whole rooms cleared for the exhibition of these treasures. A few such collections are still to be seen in their original state. Some have been gathered together to make museum exhibits of extraordinary interest, and notable among them is the one at Salem, Massachusetts, composed almost entirely of collections originally assembled by sailors and ship captains.

Inns, too, particularly in the seaport towns, were quick to make use of this form of attraction. To quote E. V. Mitchell:

"The inn which had no legend connected with it, and could not show a bed in which Washington, Lafayette, or some other bigwig had slept, sometimes had a collection of curiosities. . . . There is a description of such a place in 'Moby Dick,' a New Bedford whaling inn, the walls of which were hung with monstrous clubs and spears from the Cannibal Islands and rusty old whaling lances and harpoons, some of them storied weapons."

Just such an inn complete with the old-time exhibits and a proprietor who delights in telling tall tales about them, can at this writing be visited in Salem, Massachusetts; and doubtless there are others which, still open for business, have preserved their collections as picturesque reminders of the days when American traders sailed the seven seas and gathered souvenirs of every strange land they visited.

And did this vast common vogue affect modern connoisseurship to any appreciable extent? That it did can hardly be doubted, for not all the mass of stuff brought back by the seamen was trash, and more than one son, grandson, or great-grandson, inspired by the old Captain, became truly knowing in the arts of the Orient. Though the prodigal list of true museums, great art galleries, public libraries, zoological parks and botanical gardens flung across America today is mainly the result of efforts made by late nineteenth and twentieth-century collectors, the ground was broken by earlier men, by the Peales, the Pintards, and even the Barnums, the barber shop proprietors, the sea captains, and the innkeepers, who, until such time as there arose an organized movement for the creation of public institutions of this sort, provided a passable substitute in their quasi-museums.

It took time for people to realize that the lean furniture and utensils of colonial days possessed interest and beauty of their own. Such an idea would never have occurred to the pioneer housewife sitting at her spinning wheel or struggling with the heavy kettles and black spits in the smoke of her great fireplace. The barber who accumulated the weapons of savage tribes saw nothing quaint or historic in his own tools; and the clipper ship captain who brought back porcelain atrocities from the Orient probably never considered that his own "homely" tableware might some day claim the place of honor in another collector's cupboard. In certain cases, however, the native subject made its appeal relatively early, and particularly was this true in regard to anything concerning the dramatic founding of the nation itself.

What could be more basically original, more resoundingly dramatic than sets of autograph manuscripts in which the handwriting of every signer of the Declaration of Independence is represented? The origi-

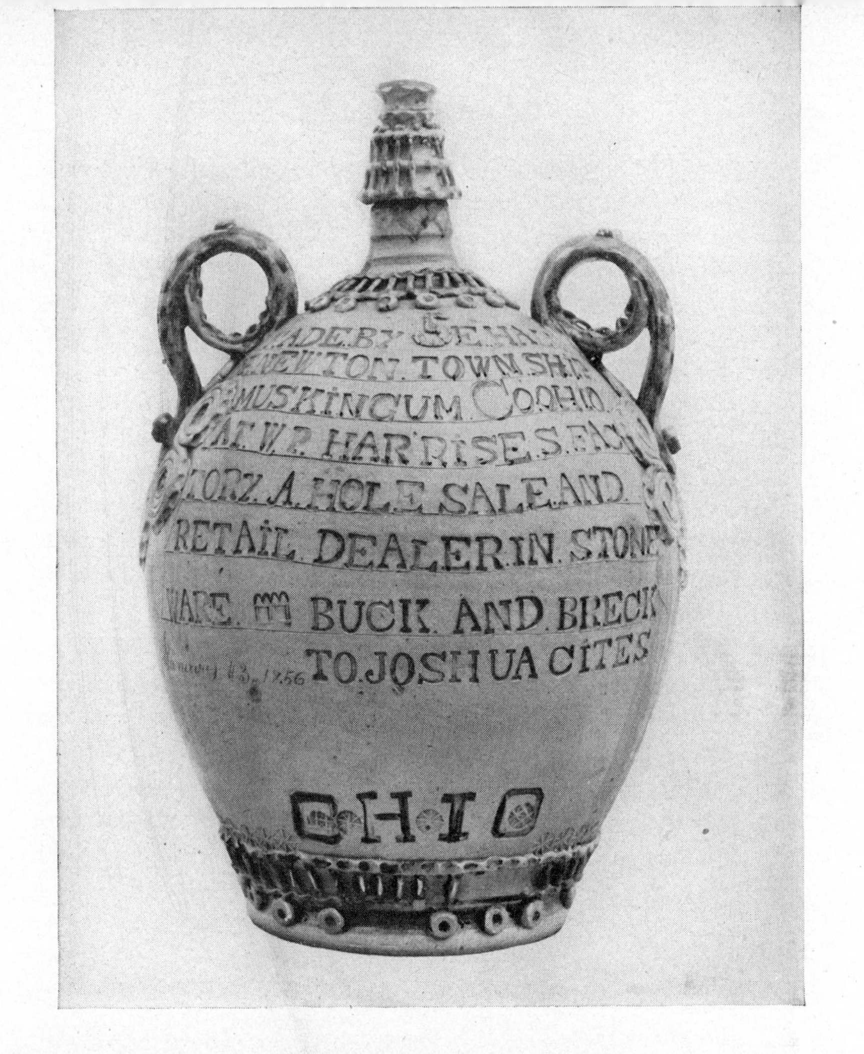

THE COLLECTOR'S ACCOLADE *is bestowed increasingly upon the simple objects of an earlier day.* ABOVE, *stoneware jug made in Newton, Ohio, 1856; from the collection of Charles Sawyer, Cincinnati.*

LEFT: *Pennsylvania slipware plate, 1818, with "Light Dragoon" sgraffito decoration; from the collection of Burford Lorimer, Philadelphia.*

Photos, courtesy New York Sun

nator of this distinctive American hobby was Dr. William Buell Sprague (1795–1876), the first great collector of autographs in this country. From boyhood, Sprague, who later became one of the most noted clergymen of his time, had cherished the plan of forming what is now known as a complete "Signer Set"; and soon after his graduation from Yale the opportunity of a lifetime came his way when, having been engaged as tutor to the children of Major Lawrence Lewis, nephew of George Washington, he went to live at "Woodlawn," about two miles from Mount Vernon. Sprague had not been at Woodlawn long when Bushrod Washington himself gave the young tutor permission to go through George Washington's correspondence selecting what letters he might want. The only condition was that Sprague should leave at Mount Vernon copies of the items he selected—but he was to be allowed to keep the originals. What would be the bid today for such an opportunity? (That curious sound you hear is made by autograph collectors licking their chops and sighing.) Sprague did quite well in his leisurely fashion, and of the forty thousand items which he is said to have possessed at the time of his death, fifteen hundred came from this single early haul.

The completing of Signer Sets always remained Dr. Sprague's chief enthusiasm, and not only did he succeed in gathering three sets himself (an achievement that would be impossible today) but he also inoculated many of his friends with an interest in this quest, even helping them along from time to time. One young disciple who profited thus by Dr. Sprague's help was the surgeon and gynecologist, Dr. Thomas Addis Emmet (1828–1919), whose passion for his own monumental autograph collection has already been noted. In the end Emmet outdid Sprague for he succeeded in forming not three but four complete Signer Sets, at a period when the project had become quite difficult.* Emmet dated his interest in the signers of the Declaration of Independence to a boyhood trip to Philadelphia when he had been taken, so he later believed, to Peale's Museum. The incident of that trip which impressed him most deeply was the visit to Independence Hall. There the child, an incipient collector, listened with wide-eyed attention to everything he was told about the men who had set their names to

* The rare Lynch autograph which is a feature of one of Emmet's Signer Sets was originally obtained by Sprague from the Mt. Vernon papers.

America's birth certificate, and long afterward he wrote concerning this occasion which proved to be a turning point in his life:

"This was my introduction to all with whom I was in after-life to become almost as well acquainted as if I had been their contemporary."

Having ten cents to spend during this fruitful trip, the youthful Emmet, after careful consideration, purchased a piece of continental currency—the first item in the Emmet Collection of American Paper Money, one of the largest of its kind ever formed.

Dr. Emmet was the outstanding American exponent of "Grangerizing" or the "extra-illustration" of books, so-called from Dr. James Granger, an English collector who, although he was not the first, became one of the most famous exponents of this hobby. Emmet's four Signer Sets (three of which are now in the New York Public Library) were all bound into books with prints, portraits and other illustrative material, a circumstance which increases the distinctive interest of each set, and he subjected some one hundred and fifty other works to a similar process, filling them with appropriate letters, documents and illustrative items of various sorts. He also accumulated over one hundred and fifty volumes of colonial newspapers, an invaluable achievement, as well as portraits (prints, drawings, clippings, and the like) of nearly thirty thousand persons involved in the history of the United States.

Emmet's extraordinary collection of Americana—manuscripts, books, newspapers, currency, prints—was built so well that students today continue to profit by his labors. Yet his highly personal feeling for his gathered treasure was exemplified not only in the emotional inscription appended to his Signer Set volumes, but also in the manner of his insistence that his name remain attached to his possessions after his final exit. In 1896, when doctors told him death was near, the amateur's first concern was that the collection should not be dispersed. With this in mind he sold it as soon as possible to John S. Kennedy, President of the Lenox Library, exacting the promise that the items should "be kept together and known as the Emmet Collection." And when later it appeared that the good doctor need not have parted with his beloved treasures in such haste (he survived the sale by twenty-three years to reach ninety-one), he wrote, in his long, chatty and illuminating autobiography, that his chief regret lay in his having neglected to identify his volumes of old newspapers as well as his books with his personal plate!

When Dr. Emmet was casting about for a permanent repository for his collection, the Lenox Library had already been in existence as a public institution for twenty-six years. As such it was one of the earliest examples in America of those great private collections which, though founded and built up exclusively for the personal enjoyment of wealthy amateurs apparently without any envisagement of potential usefulness to scholarship or to science, nevertheless came in the end to serve the public.

Early institutions founded with broad ends in view, museums like the Peale in Philadelphia and the Tammany in New York, often died young, largely because society was not yet ready for them. The Lenox Collection, which eventually became one of the cornerstones of the great New York Public Library, was originally the cherished avocation of James Lenox (1800–80), a man who, both in his manner of life and in his attitudes as a collector, was a transitional figure, standing midway between the serious-minded and modestly-fortuned gentry of the early Republic and the blustering tycoons of succeeding generations. Born to some wealth, Lenox retired from business at an early age to devote himself to investment, philanthropy and collecting, a pattern which was, in time, to become a fairly typical American phenomenon. Reserved and rather eccentric, a bachelor with religious inclinations, his first hobby was the collecting of Bibles. Later he became deeply interested in John Bunyan (his library eventually included every edition and translation of *Pilgrim's Progress*) and then it was Milton. Although never an accomplished connoisseur, Lenox learned as he went along, profiting so well by his errors that his collection of Bibles proved to be one of the greatest in the world, while his Milton collection exceeded even those of the British Museum and the Bodleian Library.

Whether or not Lenox had always intended to leave his library to the public, certainly he was not overly generous with it at first. For a while scholars who made application might obtain the use of specific volumes, which Lenox would deposit temporarily at the Astor Library for this purpose; but as time went on the collector, who was "always extremely nervous and fidgety about the safety of his treasures," would allow none but his personal friends to come to his house, and once he even refused permission to so well-fortified an applicant as the historian Prescott, when the latter requested permission to consult some of the unique source material in the Lenox Collection.

Like our old friend, Samuel Pepys, Lenox was an exceedingly tidy and methodical person, but since, aside from his consultations with agents in regard to actual purchases, he seems to have handled his immense collection entirely alone, it was impossible for him to achieve the sort of orderly arrangement that he must have thought proper. No one room could hold all his books, and he solved the problem in unique fashion. Using the numerous spare rooms of his large house for storage purposes, he would start at the back of one room and pile his items from floor to ceiling, advancing forward as new acquisitions made it necessary to do so. Sometimes he would cord the books up like wood. Always when the space in a single chamber was exhausted, he would lock the door behind him and begin on the next. And since books stored in this manner were obviously difficult of access, he would often buy duplicate copies for everyday use. Planning to have a definitive catalogue compiled as soon as his collection should be, as he considered, complete, he meanwhile entered each one of his accessions in a memorandum book or ticked them off in various catalogues with sufficient clarity for his own enlightenment. It was only when he realized that failing health would prevent the completion of his labors (and when the rooms in his house were at last overflowing) that he decided to entrust his books and his art objects to other hands.

The years of James Lenox's life spanned an era in his country's development during which collectors passed, with comparative rapidity, through many of the phases which had occurred in Europe over a much longer period.

In 1800 the majority of Americans were largely illiterate in matters of art, and collectors whose interests were of too serious a variety to be satisfied merely by exotica were still concentrating chiefly upon books and manuscripts. By the year of Lenox's death, however, America was in the heyday of her dilettante era. She had discovered the art of Europe, and had passed through alternate periods of deifying the Italianate, the French, the medieval. She had even discovered the Far East, particularly the art of Japan. American collectors, most of whom were now traveling the "Grand Tour" abroad, were beginning to envisage the foundation of home-town art museums on the basis of the Old Masters they were purchasing privately, while others, particularly New Englanders, were bringing back from the Orient fantastic numbers of Chinese and Japanese art objects and were laying the foundations, in Boston, for one of the greatest collections of Eastern art in the world.

There had even been, for a brief space between 1839 and 1853, an organized movement "for the Promotion of the Fine Arts in the United States," accompanied by a foreshadowing of twentieth-century methods of bringing art prices down to popular levels. Housed at first at the back of a New York City bookshop, the American Art-Union, as this organization was called, soon had many of New York's most distinguished citizens behind it—William Cullen Bryant served as its president for three years. It boasted, in its peak year, of a membership of eighteen thousand nine hundred and sixty art lovers from every part of the nation (including eight from California, who were of course listed with the members from foreign countries).

A nonprofit membership organization with minimum annual dues of five dollars, the Union, first known as the Apollo Club, purchased paintings, medals and sculpture by native or resident artists, and conducted an exhibition gallery at 497 Broadway. The gallery was open to the public and a thousand people often visited it in a single day. It was said that you could tell the hour by the type of person in the Art-Union gallery; and the "gentlemen" in charge of the project expressed genuine surprise that the common people who came in great numbers should behave so well. Why, more than one laboring man was actually seen to remove his hat!

Among American painters supported by the Art-Union while they were still comparatively unknown were George Inness and George Caleb Bingham. One of the latter's canvases, *Fur Traders Descending the Missouri,* which was acquired in 1845 by an Art-Union member from Alabama for the price of his annual dues, has recently been purchased by the Metropolitan Museum of Art for an amount that may be presumed to have been considerably higher. For each five dollars contributed, members were entitled to one original engraving from an American painting, published for this purpose by the Union, plus a share in the annual "distribution." The "distribution" was a great event, and the hall of the old Tabernacle where it was conducted was always crowded, not only by members but by others eager to participate in the excitement of the "drawing."

The Art-Union finally came to legal grief because it operated on the lottery principle, but before its untimely demise it had done much to enable people living far from the metropolises of the East to see their first original works of art, and in this way, also, it did much to foster the growth of collecting. One member, who had acquired a Cropsey landscape at the distribution of 1847, wrote back from the town of three thousand inhabitants in which he lived that

> ". . . the influence which is felt in this community from that single picture is such as to convince me that the value of the Art-Union to the Union at large can hardly be appreciated."

By 1864, James Jackson Jarves, whose famous synoptic collection of thirteenth to seventeenth century Italian paintings eventually found a home in the Trumbull Gallery at Yale University, could say,

> "It has become the mode to have taste. Private galleries in New York are becoming almost as common as private stables."

And with the establishment of the Fogg Museum at Cambridge in 1895 America had at last begun to train her own art "experts." At least one of these, Bernhard Berenson, was to achieve such world-wide prominence that, in 1891, when only twenty-six years of age, he would be called upon to expertize the paintings at England's Hampton Court, the first major assignment of a long and honored career. Whereas formerly any painting in an American collection was as likely to be misattributed as not, questions of authenticity now became important, and the new experts were in high demand for the recataloguing of older

---

A BED-ROCK AMERICAN SPECIALTY: Autographs of the "Signers." *1) Part of the only Lynch letter-signed known, this item endorsed in Washington's hand and labeled in the hand of the collector, Thomas Addis Emmet, gains further desirability because it also belonged to the originator of the "Signer-Set" vogue, Dr. William Buell Sprague, who obtained it while serving as tutor to the children of Washington's nephew, Major Lawrence Lewis. 2) Even a bill attains value in a collector's eye, if it carries "association." This one, from the Bella C. Landauer Collection of trade cards, is also an autograph collector's piece. The bill is in the hand of signer Francis Hopkinson, clothier, and achieves additional interest in that current prices of coatings and other materials are quoted on the reverse side.*

the most profound esteem, your Excellency's
obedient humble servt
Charles Town Thomas Lynch
July 5-1777

His Excellency
General Washington

The New York Public Library

The Hon: Thos Lynch
5th July-1777
Washington's endorsement.

The New York Public Library

LETTER FROM THOMAS LYNCH TO GEORGE WASHINGTON, JULY 5, 1777, *with Washington's own endorsement and Thomas Addis Emmet's label.*

TRADE CARD AND BILL OF FRANCIS HOPKINSON, 1769.

(See facing page.)

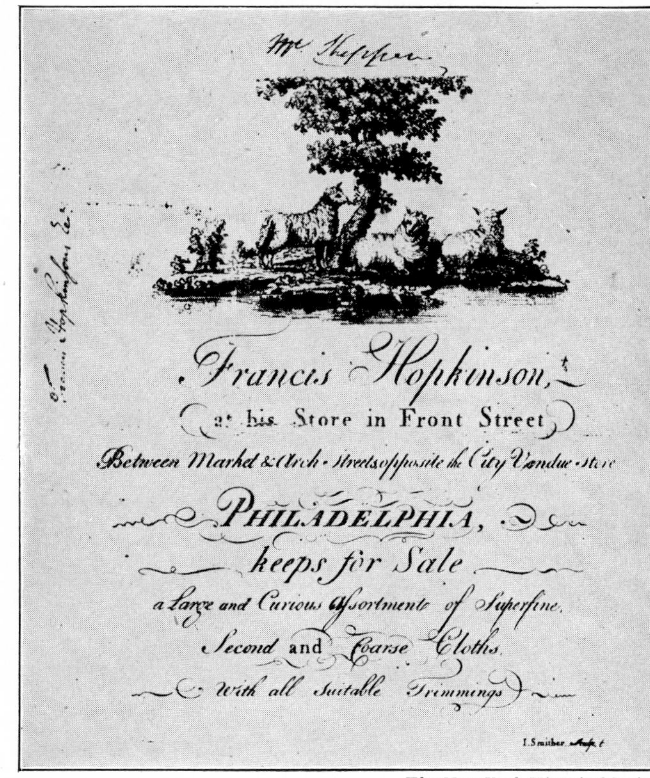

The New-York Historical Society

collections and the re-educating and guiding of suddenly self-conscious collectors. Many art-fanciers were content still to deal exclusively in the relatively safe traffic in old and established masters, but contemporary artists, particularly those of the romantic school, also had their followers. There were even a few incidents of the type that were to be repeated often in the future over abstractionist art, incidents like that of the Turner canvas which was sold upside down without, as one observer scornfully reported, its purchaser being any the wiser.

Art was not the only new field into which American collectors were now making enthusiastic forays. The vogue for antiques, product of nostalgia for the more lively era of the past, was in full cry by the early eighties as the comfortably ornate citizens of the Victorian age began to discover the charms of old native pewter, of quaintly uncomfortable old furniture, even of rude and primitively fashioned hardware. Association items, particularly those of a romantic sort—such things as Byron's plumed helmet, or a fragment of Dante's coffin—had been popular for some time. In this period, too, the specialist emerged; men like George Peabody with his important collection of musical instruments, Ernest Fenollosa with his epoch-marking collection of Japanese art, and Colonel Thomas Wentworth Higginson who formed a special collection of books dealing with the status of women.

Those painters and sculptors who were strongly under the influence of Italy purchased Italian works of art, and it was considered "the thing" for every artist to possess a collection, at least of articles of *virtu*. Many of the best-known figures of the day, writers, musicians, professors, were ardent dilettante collectors, and, with varying degrees of discrimination, women too were entering this now fashionable field.

As early as 1868 Julia Ward Howe was advocating the formation of art museums on a modest scale:

"The presence of twenty first-rate pictures in one of our great cities would save a great deal of going abroad, and help to form a sincere and intelligent standard of aesthetic judgment,"

she wrote, and her own home was filled with Old Masters, some genuine, some dubious.

A little later, under the able guidance of Charles Eliot Norton, Henry Adams and Bernhard Berenson, the irrepressible Mrs. Gardner, whose motto was *C'est mon plaisir,* was making of Fenway Court, her Boston palace, a terminal of European art treasure. She also gathered in many works of the two fashionable Anglicized American painters, Whistler and Sargent, although naturally enough she was, like most of her contemporaries, blind to the great talents of the unfashionable Homer and Ryder.

Despite rapid growth, modest American collections did not as a whole approximate in quality of connoisseurship those being formed in far greater numbers among the European middle classes, particularly in France. To some degree this is still true, and the reason is apparent. The older European tradition implies a serious and responsive approach to cultural fields; it has given to many of the continental peoples a deep-seated reverence for cultural objects and a natural familiarity with them which is even today lacking in most Americans. This contrast of course helps to explain the younger nation's relatively uneven collecting qualities which should become smoother as the nation advances into cultural maturity.

It is obvious that mimicry of the old European aristocracy was largely responsible for the fact that extensive collecting now became fashionable also among American merchant princes. And yet there were exceptions. Certainly some form of personal ambition was most often responsible for the apparently incongruous phenomenon of men turning from the collecting of mines, of railroads, of corporations, to the gathering of books and paintings, of porcelains and tapestries and French furniture; for though money became, at this time, power in the truest sense, even so it could not satisfy all a man's desires, nor achieve for him the complete and unqualified recognition of many of his fellows. Even in this country, so often accused of crass commercialism, there has been an unwillingness to concede that the ability to make money is the greatest of all abilities. In collecting, a man who has won "money-power" may find deep personal pleasure and a measure of release from the spiritual limitations of a strictly commercial career, while to this he may also add a certain sense of responsibility to the community whose facilities have enriched him, and he may try to discharge that responsibility by founding or improving some public institution with gifts from his own ample store.

Whatever the motive that drove him to enter cultural fields of collecting, it is important to remember that the tycoon's whole nature was keyed to dynamic ambition, and if and when he turned to collecting he could hardly avoid carrying over into this new venture the same driving desire for pre-eminence.

In this campaign most often dealers and experts constituted the general staff, for the tycoon found out soon enough how easily his solo judgment could cost a regiment of money. So caution developed and most of the new collectors played the game as safely as possible, buying only "old masters," which commanded fairly stable market prices, a fact of which the business sense approved. To insure against big dealer flimflamming, purchases were often made contingent to exchange at any time. Despite this precaution many of the millionaires were casualties of assault and battery, surrounded as they were by greedy advisers. Others fared better through greater luck, or shrewdness buttressed by some perceptive quality, and there were also those who entered the lists with a personal allotment of innate connoisseurship.

It is nevertheless true that most of these wealthy collectors were tarred with the same black spirit of ruthless acquisitiveness, with that fierce will-to-power, which were characteristics of the new industrial age in which they lived; and by Europeans even the best of them were accused of being "people of enormous wealth and little taste who accumulate masterpieces of art without appreciating them." It followed that without a sound foundation in connoisseurship the newcomers fell easy prey to fakers and charlatans, who organized wholesale manufacture of masterpieces and antiques for their benefit. Had the industrious Corot been quadruplets, he could never have produced the number of "Corots" sold. P. A. B. Widener "began by buying a few dozen Rembrandts, an adventure which . . . became a *cause célèbre*." Yet this sort of thing was not to continue indefinitely, and when the raw candidate evinced a capacity for taste and knowledge, improvement followed.

The accusation that the money bags of the New World were shamelessly robbing the "art loving" Europeans of their cultural treasure brings back familiar echoes, for young nations, turning to the old lands in their hunger for cultural objects, have almost always been disparaged and scolded for their temerity. When Alexander's rough soldiery, twenty-three hundred years ago, so eagerly snatched at the colorful pottery, precious plate and fine carpets and hangings long the pride of the East, those crude fellows, "who still smelled of goat," were lashed at witheringly by the suave aristocrats of conquered Persia. Later came the turn of the Greeks, and then it was they who railed at the Latin collectors who, touring the Hellenistic provinces, were compelled to employ Greek experts to advise them on their purchases. "An ape is still an ape, though adorned with jewels and gold," said the Greeks. In the early renaissance, Roman noblemen detested the rich bankers and wool merchants of Florence who were buying up the choicest antiquities unearthed in their ancient city. Later still, Roman and Florentine bitterly watched the departure of great numbers of Italian masterpieces to the "barbarian" French court. Italians then felt themselves despoiled by their inferiors, but the court of France, after first aping Italian ways in flattering fashion, became in time the most highly civilized in all Europe. And when France, holding, in her turn, the short end of the purse strings, saw upstart Englishmen marching off with art objects purchased wholesale in Paris, Gallic noses rose high in scorn for the unfeeling Nordics.

The tale is old, and though Americans have for some generations been the latest word for goat, there will probably be yet another people in the future to inherit this palm of ridicule. Generally it is the young, hungry nation, whose mass ambition has not yet been realized, which can move things about in the big league. Yet there were tasteless dilettanti as well as connoisseurs among European collectors long before there were collectors of either variety in America; and there were sincere amateurs and discriminating connoisseurs as well as vulgar show-offs even among the boisterous American "pillagers" of the late nineteenth and early twentieth centuries.

The classic example of this period is John Pierpont Morgan. In him there was embodied something more than the typical qualities of his fellow Titans—Vanderbilt, Frick, Whitney, Stillman, Havemeyer and the rest. This man, as a man, takes precedence over such questions as whether or not he loved and understood his books and works of art. Gigantic in business enterprise and Homeric in the collecting world, his personality alone became a force. There have been other American collectors more sympathetic, more generous, more admirable. But it is probably the Morgan personality, among them all, that will be remembered longest and with greatest contemplation—and this Morgan himself might easily have expected as his due. Those who knew him well tell us that his personality was commanding and faith-inspiring, reinforced by equally impressive physical attributes—a large frame, massive shoulders, piercing eyes, shaggy brows, a powerful, rugged

Museum of the City of New York

THE AMERICAN ART-UNION *thrived when California was still a foreign country. Above, distribution of prizes at the Tabernacle, New York, 1847. Sarany and Major lithograph.*

THE STOREROOM TECHNIQUE, *from which collections have barely recovered. The "Picture Gallery" in A. T. Stewart's marble palace, 5th Avenue and 34th Street, New York, in 1887.*

nose—backed by unusual mental vigor, decisiveness and extraordinary ability. "His manner was sometimes abrupt and dictatorial and he dealt in ultimatums," says one biographer; and a certain note of fascinated wonder, whether grudgingly or admiringly accorded, pervaded the writings of all those who, having had dealings with him as a collector or otherwise, recorded their reminiscences. In short, he has become a legend which, like most legends, includes some allegory.

Unlike most of his contemporaries, J. P. Morgan (1837–1913) had an excellent background for serious collecting. The son of a prominent international banker who himself had a considerable fortune, John Pierpont had access to those early cultural advantages which are so helpful to the connoisseur's development and which tend to gentle a man toward the world. Others in his position, men like James Lenox and the later Harry Elkins Widener, retired from the wars of business to the collecting sanctum. Not Morgan. This granite son, who so outmarched his enviably successful father, remained in the arena to the end. He became the world's greatest collector of corporations and directorships, and eventually attained such prominence in affairs of industry and finance that twice he was called upon to save from disaster the United States government itself.

His power was actually imperial, and he used it and fed upon it as truly as did emperors of Europe and Asia. Yet even though Morgan was first and foremost the hard, ruthless seeker of supremacy, it cannot be fairly said of him that his collecting in cultural fields was exclusively a synthetic by-product of his power-drive.

When only a child he had begun by soliciting autographs from Protestant-Episcopal bishops and other churchmen who visited the home of his grandfather, the Reverend John Pierpont; and this interest was encouraged by his father, Junius Spencer Morgan, who was himself a collector of autograph manuscripts. The boy's next preoccupation was with *objets d'art;* and set into certain windows of the present Morgan Library are pieces of stained glass which the youthful J. P. collected in his student days in Europe and which he is said to have carried about with him in a horsehair trunk—until breakage caused him to relinquish this typical collector's pleasure.

Both of these interests endured throughout Morgan's adult life, and in time he gathered about him not one but many outstanding collections of manuscripts, association books, Bibles, incunabula, ancient and medieval art, Old Masters, miniatures, drawings and etchings, tapestries, furniture, porcelains, watches, antique coins, medals and other objects in the collector's roster.

The mere cataloguing of each of these collections, for the purpose of which he engaged staffs of experts, required years of labor, and the catalogues, when completed, themselves constituted valuable histories of each subject. Morgan is reputed to have spent upwards of sixty million dollars on his treasures, and yet he never saw them all assembled, for no private house could have contained them. Many items were kept on loan at the Metropolitan Museum of Art in New York City, and at the Victoria and Albert Museum in London. He built the white marble library adjoining his New York residence for books and certain other items, but such a considerable portion of the collection remained in his English homes, on public exhibition in London, or in storage in Paris, that when, in the year before his death, he transferred these items to America, it was said that "the effect, practically, was to shift the art center of the world."

Whole collections were purchased at one swoop by the voracious giant, who once asked with characteristic grandiosity, "What is the use of bothering about one little piece when I might get them all?" He paid four hundred thousand dollars to obtain the entire manuscript collection of an Ethiopian Coptic monastery. He owned the world's only perfect copy of Sir Thomas Malory's *Morte d'Arthur* printed by Caxton; and his library contained hundreds of rare and beautiful Bibles. One of his specialties was the collecting of Walter Scott manuscripts, and the group of these in the present Morgan Library (which contains one purchased by Junius Spencer Morgan, and at least one added by J. P. Morgan, the second, as well as nineteen acquired by the first J. P.) is the most important in the world.

The list of unique items, of superlative collections, that once existed within the Morgan collection could be multiplied for pages. Yet to all this, from the point of view of your true collector, there was a single great disadvantage. Although Morgan himself took an active part in the formation of his collections, knew what he wanted, made, as in everything else, quick, sure decisions, and watched over his agents like a hawk, his was obviously the sort of collection which no one could really create alone. At the height of his collecting career he seldom attended auctions, and he turned over the actual purchasing of important items to dealers. In following this method, most collectors would say, he forfeited one of the greatest pleasures of collecting. On the whole, it is difficult to escape the conclusion that his passion for the pursuit, founded though it was upon sincere interests, became eventually a sort of impersonalized assertion of power. For this he paid the penalty (though it probably made not the slightest difference to his autocratic spirit) in ceasing to appear, in the eyes of most people, as a human being. Even when he lay dying in Rome, hordes of individuals with things to sell besieged his hotel, avid to reach into his miraculous pockets before it should be too late.

Yet there was another side to the picture, and it has been written of him that "in the presence of his collections, his books, children and grandchildren, he became a very human man." He was particularly fond of miniatures, for example, and one could tell "merely from the way he handled them . . . that they had a favored place in his heart." This question of his real attitude toward collecting remains a debatable one, since few outsiders can do more than theorize concerning the intangible elements that go to make up an uncommunicative man's most intimate thoughts and emotions. The best one can do is to mention certain external indications, and the opinions of qualified contemporaries.

Morgan's admiration of *il Magnifico,* and the pleasure he betrayed whenever anyone compared him to the great Italian, have been recorded by the majority of those who knew him. Yet he failed to achieve the true renaissance spirit, for his was more the temperament of the ancient Roman, a temperament from which he could not escape.

Shortly after his death an article appeared in the *Burlington Magazine* which seems to summarize the most considered opinions on Morgan's position as a collector. Declared the writer:

"In the world of art quite as much as in the world of finance, Mr. Morgan was above everything a man of action . . . He believed in military methods; he regarded rapidity and irrevocability of decision as more important than accuracy of judgment; he considered discipline more important than a nice discrimination. And in spite of many instances of failure it would be rash to say that for the end he had in view his choice of means was a wrong one . . . Having become the greatest financier of his age he determined to become its greatest collector, and he succeeded. He was a great collector; he was not a connoisseur. It was the conquest of the most precious objects of all ages and countries that tempted his active spirit. And this continual conquest . . . left him but little leisure for that prolonged contemplation of the intimate beauties of his spoils which is the delight of the connoisseur."

There follows, however, this reservation:

"Conquest was his joy, but who can tell how much the desire for conquest was inspired in him by an instinctive feeling for the esthetic needs of his country, and how much by the sheer delight in acquisition?"

Probably no such question will ever be asked concerning the activities of another voracious American collector, William Randolph Hearst. Supreme example of what Lewis Mumford calls the modern "department-store collector," this man succumbed to every one of the pitfalls which may so easily engulf the wealthy would-be connoisseur—personal ambition, lack of discrimination, ostentation, and emphasis on the symbolic values of mere size and quantity. Moneyed American collectors have often, in one way or another, given evidence of one or more of these faults, but the concentration Hearst represents is the nux vomica of bad collecting on the grand scale. A little ahead of his proper place, he is now brought to light because he symbolizes the pinnacle of nineteenth-century shortcomings rather than a significant milestone in the progressive development of American collecting. Hearst's collectomania embraced electric clocks, floor lamps or cigarette lighters as it did Old Masters. He never became a patron of contemporary art because, so it has been said, "living art cannot be torn from its roots and appropriated in the Hearstian manner as dead art can be." Nor was it, apparently, ever his intention to bequeath any part of his treasure to the public. Morgan had so intended, and even during his own lifetime had made vast sections of his collection publicly available; but as the Hearstian life grew feebler and most of his estates were put on the market, the Hearst trophies were converted back into cash assets—many of them sold, appropriately enough, in department stores.

Better results might have been expected from this son of a cultured mother, for Phebe Hearst was a woman of intellectual curiosity and artistic taste, who, in the latter part of her life, financed important archaeological expeditions and took an active interest in their progress. When her son was ten years old she took him abroad, and it was on this journey that "Willie" made his first recorded collections—of stamps and coins, of pictures of actors and actresses, beer steins, porcelain, and German comic pictures. Though he was forever collecting something from then on, he never showed any greater capacity for intelligent appreciation than is indicated in this childish hodgepodgery.

Before he was thirty, Hearst had embarked upon the collecting of art objects, but pretentiousness is the pattern that shows plain enough even through the flattering cloak of the "official" biography authorized by himself. Condensing and paraphrasing certain passages from the official account, two other biographers, Carlson and Bates, treat the Hearst Collection in sarcastic vein:

"The lord of the manor has the finest collection of armor in the world, having far outstripped his nearest competitors, Henry Ford and Andrew Mellon. He has also the finest collection of old silver, the finest collection of old furniture, the finest collection of stained glass, the finest collection of Gothic mantels, the finest collection of Mexican saddles. He has collected pottery and paintings and Indian rugs . . . he has collected tapestries and hangings and costumes, he has collected choir stalls and ceilings and fireplaces, he has collected mummies, he has collected Cardinal Richelieu's bed, he has collected—the Lord knows what he hasn't collected! Loot from all the world is gathered at San Simeon and the end is not yet.* . . . strewn along the valley for half a mile are packing boxes full of more treasures for which no appropriate place has yet been found. Underneath La Casa Grande is a two-acre store-room devoted to the same purpose. And in New York City, near Southern Boulevard and One Hundred and Forty-Third Street, is an entire block of Hearst warehouses, containing, among other acquisitions, a Spanish castle [monastery?] taken down stone by stone, each lettered and numbered, on its way to join some time the marvels of San Simeon. And then there are the Egyptian, Etruscan, Roman, Spanish and Italian pieces and the great English library still in the old Hearst home at Riverside Drive and Eighty-Sixth Street . . ."

The habit of buying European castles, churches or monuments for transportation overseas has been one of the causes for a blend of dismay and scorn meted out to certain American collectors by those nations shorn of valued historic relics, and in this practice, at least, Hearst was not alone in his doubtful glory.

Fortunately for American collecting, Hearst did not represent the

---

* The biography from which this passage is quoted was written in 1936, before the dispersal of the Hearst collection had begun.

master mold, and among America's collecting royalty a more typical development has expressed itself in the gradual growth of a capacity for genuine appreciation and in the eventual realization of a sense of social responsibility.

The first of these phases is perhaps most clearly exemplified in the experiences, over three generations, of Philadelphia's Widener family, the founder of which was Peter Arrell Brown Widener (1834–1915). A typical nineteenth-century nabob who, building up his fortunes from modest beginnings, succeeded in establishing one of America's plutocratic dynasties, Widener, unlike Morgan, started from no pinnacle, either financial or cultural. His first fifty thousand dollars were made selling mutton to the Federal troops located around Philadelphia during the Civil War. Next came a chain of meat stores, and an investment in those street railways which were to prove his true El Dorado. Like many of his contemporaries, he soon became a collector of corporations, and took a hand in forming many of the most powerful industrial organizations in the country. That he should also have become a collector of books, of art, and of objects of *virtu* was at first only typical; but in certain ways he was unusual among collectors of his type, for he made many of his own purchases, burning his fingers in the process but not burning them in vain. His early mistakes in judgment were carefully rectified in after years, when he weeded out the fakes. Eventually he succeeded in assembling two collections—of paintings, and Chinese porcelains—which came to be considered among the finest of their kind in America; and it is significant that his large and carefully selected library included, in addition to the usual expensive incunabula and rare books, many volumes chosen personally for the study of his art collections.

On the road to connoisseurship, P. A. B. even found guidance from Joseph, his son; and that the development would have been a progressive one within this family is shown by the fact that the mutton vendor's grandson, Harry Elkins Widener (1885–1912), had, at the time of his untimely death, given promise of becoming one of the most scholarly and enlightened book collectors ever to appear in this country. A product of the twentieth century, young Widener was typical of the considerable number of latter-generation scions of American dynastic families who turned their backs on mere giantism and tried to veer their wealth toward cultural and social purpose. Having actually decided to make book collecting his life work, he had trained himself for the pursuit as seriously as he might have for any other profession. Harry Widener loved his books and lived with them. His library was his bedroom, his study, and his workshop. He had the collector's desire for volumes in perfect condition, and also for association items, and he possessed many treasures which had formerly belonged to other great collectors. Yet it is to be emphasized that he was, as A. S. W. Rosenbach wrote of him:

> ". . . not merely a gatherer of rare and precious volumes, but a deep scholar, and an original and zealous investigator of the science of books."

In his short lifetime he rendered students such services as causing to be reprinted, for their especial benefit, certain of his more important items that were unique or difficult of access elsewhere. Bibliophiles everywhere accorded him unstinting admiration and affection, he is still considered to have been the youngest collector ever to form a truly significant library, and his tragic end came as a shock to a wide group of those who had felt he was destined to do much for bibliographical scholarship.

Ironically, it was his very devotion to book collecting which was, in a sense, responsible for his death, for he had been in London making purchases when he engaged passage on the *Titanic* expressly to be in New York for the third portion of the great Hoe sale.*

Two men, father and son, stand out as furnishing, perhaps, America's nearest approximation to the magnificent Medici. Unlike Morgan, most persistent pretender to that coveted distinction, William Thompson Walters (1820–94) and Henry Walters (1848–1931) were liberal patrons of contemporary artists as well as gatherers of ancient treasure; and the great collection they formed, now public property by gift of the son, has been called the best in the world for clinical research in the history of art.

The Walters' collecting methods were in large measure those common to the grandiose nineteenth century, but in the two men themselves the usual colossal acquisitiveness was tempered by a sincere amateurism; and while, in their own lives, they typified an era that is rapidly passing,

---

* The sale of the Robert Hoe Collection, 1911-1912, was the greatest event the book-collecting world had witnessed since the Roxburghe sale in England almost exactly a century before (1813). The Hoe sale attracted buyers from all over the world and realized nearly two million dollars.

their collection, long in the process of organization, appears to increase in educational and cultural value as study of the imposing contents progresses.

An Englishman by birth and trained as a mining engineer, Walters senior had come to the United States as a young man to study American mining methods, then, having decided to stay, finally made his home in Baltimore, Maryland. His career followed the general pattern of familiar nineteenth-century "progress": his early profession cast aside, he entered the produce commission business, made a small fortune, then switched to railroading, the great coin pot of the times. His climb upwards into the golden clouds of millionairedom was interrupted slightly by the Civil War. Yet this deflection turned him to collecting; for having decided for political reasons that it would be wise to live abroad for the duration, he migrated temporarily to Paris, and there, although he had always been interested in art, for the first time he came to know personally many of the French painters and sculptors of the day. From then on although he returned to America to live after the war, he rarely missed a Paris Exposition, and from each trip he brought home additional examples of the work of Delacroix, Corot, Millet, Barye and many others who were scarcely recognized when he began collecting them. In addition to painting and sculpture, William Walters collected Eastern ceramics and horses, and, in a manner reminiscent of many of the renaissance popes, was exceedingly fond of "trinkets of gold and enamel, of which he gathered a great number."

His son, to whom he bequeathed the art collection, seems also to have inherited his father's curious predilection for jewelry, and it is said that he daily changed the ring he wore, choosing from his large accumulation. Of father and son as collectors one biographer has written:

> ". . . to the elder Walters collecting was the polite avocation of a man of wealth, to the son it became a consuming passion."

However, the son did not by any means retire into the ivory tower of pure collectorship but took up the challenge of an expansion era, extending his operations as an active railroad man until, at the height of his career, he had become the richest individual in the South. Nevertheless, collecting from early youth was the constant theme of his life. Like his father, he traveled abroad a great deal, and painters and sculptors were among his closest friends. Habitually he lived in Europe at least three months of every year, devoting his attention to the expansion of his collection and frequently acquiring, in the manner of his day, entire other collections to add to his own mass. The largest transaction of this sort was made in 1902 when he wrote off a million dollars for the Don Marcello Massarenti collection of early Italian art and then chartered a trans-Atlantic vessel exclusively to transport the acquisition to Baltimore.

Inevitably the Walters Collection outgrew even two additional galleries built by the father, and in 1909 a new building was erected near by. An impressive structure, unusually large for a private museum, it was, however, not large enough to hold the continuous stream of treasure that poured into it. During William Thompson Walters' lifetime the public had been admitted at intervals to view the collection, and Henry continued this innovation. Yet the public saw no orderly array, for Walters was an accumulator who never accumulated a sense of order or arrangement. Indeed, until the collector's death in 1931 the Walters Gallery in this one respect was far behind the times, resembling the prints one sees of early and middle nineteenth-century exhibition halls. There were so many paintings that many of them could never be hung, while those displayed reached from floor to ceiling, like words on a printed page. Among the other exhibits a similar situation prevailed.

Walters, however, was no magpie collector. A definite plan governed his purchases, and quality of the highest sort distinguished his collection. When that collection passed by bequest to the people of Baltimore a board of trustees, composed of leading laymen as well as specialists, was appointed to organize and administer it; and the board's first annual report is revealing in its tone of breathless wonder, for despite the fame which the collection had previously attained, not one had realized how truly immense and potentially significant it was.

It is now known that there were in it over twenty-two thousand items, only about one-sixth of which can be properly shown even in the present remodeled gallery. From the days of Sumeria to the twentieth century every form and source of art are represented, and handsomely represented. In addition to such collector's items as illuminated manuscripts, incunabula and other rare books, there is a large art reference library. The paintings embrace every important school, and the sculpture includes ancient and modern works in marble, stone, alabaster, metal and wood. Greek and Roman antiquities are present in great numbers, and it is said that much of the Egyptian sculpture cannot be duplicated in any private collection in the world. Even the rare art of the early Indian civilizations of North and South America had been included. There are whole collections of textiles of every sort, of Oriental and Occidental ceramics, of lacquer, goldsmiths' and silversmiths' work, miniatures, watches, laces, jades, jewelry. The Byzantine and early Christian ivories, enamels and liturgical objects are thought to constitute the most important collection of these things ever gathered together by a single individual, and the Persian ceramics are conceded to be the best group of the sort anywhere.

After Mr. Walters' death, seven hundred paintings, water colors and drawings which had never been shown during his lifetime were found in the basement of the gallery, and among these were several "lost" works which experts had for years been attempting to trace. In that same basement—now famous as a kind of miraculous pitcher of art—were two hundred and forty-three packing cases which had never been opened. In them were some of the great treasures of Egyptian and Islamic art. In 1936, an object "so covered with the accumulation of dirt and paint . . . that it was impossible to tell what treasure was buried beneath" was taken out of this incredible storeroom. Careful probing, followed by equally careful cleaning, eventually disclosed a stone bracket and head—the finest example of thirteenth-century Gothic sculpture of which even this rich collection could boast. And in 1938, when two Roman bronze heads were, for the first time, installed in the gallery, they were described as having been "the result of certain 'excavations' " made at the gallery by one of the curators.

This new variety of treasure-hunt must have injected into the administration of the Walters' bequest much the same sort of suspense and excitement as had, on a larger scale, prevailed in renaissance Italy during the days of abbey-searchings and street-excavations. It also suggests, however, that Mr. Walters could himself hardly have known many of the individual items in his collection, a fact which opens him to the charge of mere "giantism." Yet of him it may be said, as it has been said of Mazarin, that it is of small moment whether or not he knew his collection intimately in its every detail: what matters is the total excellence of his creation—which speaks for itself and for him.

Among collections of art in America today, the Walters is ranked by some authorities second only to that in the Metropolitan Museum, and

Walters Art Gallery, Baltimore

From the 16th century to the present day, Limoges enamels have been included in most of the great eclectic collections. Painted enamel plate, "July," from a series of the Twelve Months, 1566, signed by Pierre Reymond.

BELOW: *Painted enamel plaque, "Temperance," signed by Jean II Pénicaud, of the famous Limoges family of enamelers, 16th century; ex. colls. Duke of Marlborough, J. P. Morgan, and others.*

Walters Art Gallery, Baltimore

in some of its sections second to none. The Morgan Collection, its only serious rival in scope and quality, has been largely dispersed—of all its former magnificence only the library can now be viewed as an entity. The Walters, on the other hand, has been transformed into a permanent source of public benefit, a trend which has prevailed in the modern age where great collections are concerned.

Obviously not all of the factors operating to produce this general result have been based upon pure and enlightened generosity: the age-old desire for a personal memorial is still with us, and there has also developed a new pressure known as the inheritance tax, an impersonal instrument which has caused a mighty wave of "public spiritedness" since, under its penalties, a valuable collection becomes a financial liability to one's heirs. Nevertheless, and for whatever reason, it remains a fact that more and more important collections are traveling the museum road, that many are now formed with an eventual public disposition in view, and that this has radically altered the nature of the collections themselves.

Nor is the pleasure taken out of collecting in this way. There was Henry E. Huntington (1850–1927), heir to the great railway fortune of his uncle, Collis P. Huntington. Henry was one man who, as a collector, combined the new conception of ultimate service with the grandly acquisitive techniques of the nineteenth century and who met with extraordinary success in achieving both personal satisfaction and public benefaction. Long and arduously occupied with business affairs, he did not begin to collect on a large scale until he was nearly sixty years old, but then, in twenty years of intensive and well-directed effort, he succeeded in forming one of the greatest libraries in the world.* If he enjoyed a sense of power in being able to acquire rarities to which few other men might aspire, at least the trait was not paramount in his case. Able to buy almost anything he wanted, he exercised taste and discrimination, and, as a collector, chose rather to apply the principles of specialization enunciated by Sir Joseph Banks: although he collected in at least three distinct fields—books, art, and botany—he selected certain phases of each subject on which to concentrate his effort and worked, in each, toward definitely conceived objectives.

* At the time of the collector's death this library contained 175,000 volumes, including 5,400 incunabula (the largest group in America), in addition to a large number of manuscripts.

In the field of botany he undertook to determine which of the world's plants of economic and ornamental value could be successfully grown in southern California where he lived, and to this end he gathered specimens from every continent, creating a collection as outstanding as the library. In art, he devoted his chief attention to the works of eighteenth-century English painters. (He was the purchaser, in 1921, of Gainsborough's *Blue Boy*, a purchase which achieved enormous fame chiefly because of the price—$750,000—the greatest ever paid up to that time for a single painting.) In the library, which represented his supreme collecting achievement, he had two specialties, incunabula and source material for the study of American and English history and literature; and as an index to his success it is to be noted that in the latter field the Huntington Library now ranks second only to the Bodleian and the British Museum.

As a book collector, Huntington passed through a rather interesting evolution. His first purchases were confined to excellent editions of his favorite authors, but few of these early acquisitions (like few of his early paintings) survived the specialized standards he later followed. The arts of bookmaking—fine printing, illustration, binding—also attracted him in the beginning, but he soon established a more scholarly goal, resolving "to concentrate upon the history and literature of the English-speaking peoples, and, at the same time, to restrict his purchases to first, early and rare editions and to manuscripts."

Once this goal had been determined upon, the collector worked toward it in business-like fashion. Typically, it became his custom to buy up entire collections, (in 1911 he paid a million dollars for the small but important Church Collection, one of the largest single book transactions on record); but his motive in doing so and his method of handling such vicarious collections once they were acquired marked a departure in collection building. In business affairs this man had been a successful exponent of the principle of consolidation, and he felt that the same principle might be advantageously applied to collecting. Yet his scheme had nothing to do with mere quantitative pyramiding. It was aimed, rather, at the building of complete series in his chosen subjects. Each new collection was carefully sifted and its items compared with the books already in his possession. Out-and-out duplicates were eliminated, for unlike certain other amateurs, Huntington was not obsessed by a desire to possess every possible copy of any particular rare book that happened to fall within his province. By selling these discarded but nevertheless valuable duplicates, Huntington eventually got back more than half a million dollars to devote to new purchases. Fifteen auctions were required for disposal of the Huntington duplicates, and other collectors, always eager to get their hands on these discards, considered this series of auctions the most important event in the book-collecting world since the Hoe sale. Volumes containing important "variations" were kept, however, and the work of collation done by his staff in this connection produced much valuable information of a bibliographical nature. The purchase of single items needed to fill in missing portions of each series or subject constituted the final step in this systematic method of building a truly complete collection.

Huntington understood the potential value that a collection thus intelligently formed might have for scholars and students. He was also, with Folger, one of the first collectors to appreciate the interest inherent in so-called "background" material, which, because of its apparent triviality, disappears much more rapidly than do more obvious items. Because he was a pioneer he was able to accumulate an amazing number of books of this sort—works on such subjects as theology, science, commerce, gardening, cookery, manners and conduct, costume, travel, and so on—which cast an essential light on everyday life and the social and intellectual influences that were at work during the periods covered by the main portion of his collecting. To repeat this feat today would be very nearly impossible, for the value of background material is now well-recognized, and competition among collectors is correspondingly keen.

Between 1919 and 1922, Huntington placed the various portions of his collection, as well as his California estate, in the hands of trustees for public use after his death. This munificent gift, made to America in perpetuity, included library, botanical gardens, and the art collection (now housed in the former Huntington house at San Marino). It was supplemented by an eight million dollar trust fund, the income of which was to be devoted not to the expansion of the collection but to fellowships for scholars engaged in historical research, to research work to be done by members of the library staff, and to the publication of the results of such original investigation. A new library building was erected on the Huntington estate and was opened to the public during the donor's own lifetime.

Because, in his first years of book purchasing, he had many times paid record sums for important items, Huntington was accused of being insanely, selfishly acquisitive, of raising prices so that no one else could compete with him. But he was neither insane nor particularly selfish. In after years, when the prices he had paid were in many cases exceeded, he seemed to care very little for the fact that his own appraisal of values had thereby been justified. The important thing to him, from the start, had been to build a good collection.

To your ardent amateur it might well appear that Huntington's method so consistently followed was, despite its remarkable and praiseworthy results, indicative of almost superhuman restraint, and yet it is quite possible for an unmistakable amateur to achieve similarly valuable results even while giving full rein to his less reasonable collector impulses. Of this Henry Clay Folger (1857–1930), founder of the Folger Shakespeare Library in Washington, D. C., gave an excellent demonstration. Long before Folger had accumulated a fortune he had begun collecting, and he once said that the most exciting moment in his life came when he made the successful bid (at an auction in 1889) which brought him his first original edition of Shakespeare—a Fourth Folio, for which he paid comparatively nothing, one hundred and seven dollars and fifty cents. He was to acquire much more valuable folios than this, but as is so often the case first love seems the freshest and fairest in retrospect.

For Folger, Shakespeareana dated back to college days, an interest precipitated, it appears, by Emerson's essay on the three-hundredth anniversary of the poet's birth, and from then on it was never absent from his heart. In 1885 he married Emily C. Jordan in one of those rare and fortunate alliances—a collecting partnership. Emily Folger had been a Shakespearean student before her marriage, and though Folger himself, a man of generous intellectual attainments, understood far better than have most wealthy amateurs, the nuances of his chosen subject, he drew increasingly upon his wife's special training and abilities for guidance and assistance. Her contribution would include the tracking down of obscure bibliographical details and the investigation of difficult allusions, and she was often called upon to help in decisions of purchase.

When the Folgers began collecting, nowhere in the world did there exist a library to which students of Shakespeare could go with the cer-

MR. WILLIAM
SHAKESPEARES
COMEDIES,
HISTORIES, &
TRAGEDIES.
Published according to the True Originall Copies.

LONDON
Printed by Isaac Iaggard, and Ed. Blount. 1623.

Courtesy, the Folger Shakespeare Library, Washington, D. C.

TITLE-PAGE OF SIBTHORP FIRST FOLIO, *sometimes called the Jaggard-Vincent First Folio, only contemporary presentation copy of a Shakespeare First Folio known; presented by William Jaggard, printer of the Folios, to his friend Augustine Vincent in 1623 (see inscription at top of page).*

tainty of finding, easily accessible, the mass of material necessary for the fullest and most unified investigation of their many-sided subject; and as the Folger fortune expanded, the couple felt that it might lie within their power to bring such a library into being. Many years passed, however, before outsiders became aware that Henry Clay Folger, high official of the Standard Oil Company of New York, had become a giant among American collectors, for the Folgers made their acquisitions as quietly as possible, giving little public indication of their desire to corner the Shakespeare market. They were well aware of the sort of intrigue and competition which had accompanied the formation of certain other large collections, and since many of the items they needed for the fulfillment of their purpose were either unique or exceedingly rare, a certain amount of secrecy became, in their case, a requisite to success.

Moreover, secrecy added to the zest of the game—and collecting was definitely a game to Folger, a game which he enjoyed tremendously. Like Huntington, with whom he was on terms of friendly rivalry after 1910 when the latter entered the book-collecting arena, Folger was a man with an idea, but he seems to have been far more deeply involved emotionally in his collection. Failure to acquire a desired item would send him into the depths of despair, and upon at least one occasion he desperately doubled, by cable, an already extremely high offer, in the vain hope of acquiring a particularly interesting copy of Shakespeare's First Folio. The details of this rather dramatic story have only recently been published in full. The Folio in question was one originally owned by the Bodleian Library, which had received it automatically and free of charge at the time of its publication in 1623. The subsequent history of the volume constitutes an interesting commentary on the evolution of a "collector's item." When, in 1663, the Bodleian received its copy of the Third Folio containing seven additional plays (all but one of which are now regarded as spurious), the first edition was looked upon as a more or less valueless duplicate. It was sold, and thereafter disappeared from view until 1905, when a Mr. W. G. Turbutt, whose son was a student at Oxford, discovered it in his family library and sent it to the Bodleian for examination and verification. By this time, of course, First Folios were looked upon with considerable awe—and commanded considerable sums. News of the discovery soon reached America, and Folger hastily cabled an offer of three thousand pounds. Tempted by the amount, but anxious to have this historic item remain in England,

Turbutt suggested that the Bodleian try to raise a subscription to meet the American's bid—and himself subscribed two hundred pounds. Unlike many of Folger's transactions, this affair achieved wide publicity and aroused considerable hostile feeling; but the collector's thirst for First Folios was such that nothing could sidetrack him. After a long period of suspense, during which he seemed to have a good chance of winning, Folger learned that the required amount had been raised in England—whereupon he increased his offer to five thousand pounds. When this proved of no avail, he declared himself willing to pay one thousand five hundred pounds for the privilege of keeping the volume in his library during his own lifetime, after which it should revert to the Bodleian, but this extraordinary offer was also refused, and for once Mr. Folger had to bow to defeat.

A similar tale, with a different ending, revolves about the only extant copy of a First Folio which contains a contemporary "presentation," the copy given on his deathbed by William Jaggard, Shakespeare's printer, to his friend the herald, Augustine Vincent, in 1623. Still in its original binding bearing Vincent's arms, and with pages "uncut," this unique prize for years lay unnoticed in the coach-house of the Sibthorp family, until a series of dramatic events blazoned its existence to the world. In 1899 Folger offered the then unprecedented sum of five thousand pounds. There were complications, however, and the owner refused to sell. This proved to be a clever move on his part, for once Folger had a bee in his bonnet it continued to buzz there, and three years later he acquired the "presentation" copy—for twice the original offer! He later called it "the most precious book in the world."

It so happens that First Folios were Folger's particular obsession, and his desire to obtain as many of these as possible seemed out of all proportion to the scholarly value of such an accumulation. That, at least, is the layman's point of view, a viewpoint shared by certain scholars who feel that these rare and important volumes should be more widely distributed geographically. Other specialists, however, justify the concentration on the grounds that the Folger Collection of nearly two hundred folio editions of Shakespeare's works (a total which includes Second, Third and Fourth as well as First Folios) "constitutes a splendid field for the study of textual variations, which have never been exhaustively considered."

In time, of course, some idea of the extent of the collection the Folgers were building had got abroad, and the English, naturally enough, resented the departure from their country of so much invaluable Shakespeare material. Efforts were made to induce Folger to set up his memorial at Stratford-on-Avon, but this he refused to do since it had always been an essential part of his plan that Americans should receive whatever cultural advantage might accrue from his lifelong effort.

Folger never saw his entire collection assembled, but he knew exactly what it contained, for he handled and examined every item of whatever nature before it was packed away for future use. Hoping to carry out his project within his own lifetime, he retired from business as early as 1923 in order to devote his entire attention to the collection's completion. In 1928, "quietly and without ostentation," he announced his gift to the nation, but secrecy had been maintained so long that some time elapsed before the importance of the gift was generally realized. Folger died before the beautiful building of the Shakespeare Memorial was completed, but his wife devotedly saw the project through to completion. Today at one end of the main reading room hangs a portrait of Henry Clay Folger; and with him there presides his wife. Students, glancing up from their work may pause a moment to remember two collectors who, loving their collection so dearly that they themselves wished always to remain with it (their very ashes are deposited behind the library), built it so that it should serve the weal of their fellow men; and in the room which houses it, supreme in the place of honor, the bust of Shakespeare, acknowledged by the living and the dead, surveys the scene, impassive, benign.

Although constituting public service of a very high order, the gifts of both the Huntington and the Folger collections remain, in one sense, personal memorials to the donors whose names they bear. That this is in the well-established tradition of giving and receiving only makes more significant the terms upon which the Andrew W. Mellon Collection of paintings and sculpture was turned over to the nation.

Mr. Mellon, who died in 1937, had been buying paintings for forty years and had brought together a relatively small but exceptionally fine collection. In 1935 he made the first public reference to the fact that he was intending to leave this treasure—which included about a hundred Old Masters, as well as the Dreyfus Collection of renaissance sculpture, and a separate collection of American portraits—to the people of the

United States.* He wrote to President Roosevelt a letter in which he set forth his proposed plan. That letter contained the following statement:

"Over a period of many years I have been acquiring important and rare paintings and sculpture with the idea that ultimately they would become the property of the people of the United States and be made available to them in a national art gallery to be maintained in the City of Washington for the purpose of encouraging and developing the study of the fine arts . . ."

Since one of the conditions of the offer was that the faith of the United States should be pledged to provide such funds as might be necessary for future operation and administration of the proposed gallery, the acceptance of the proposed gift was a matter for Congress to decide, and decide it did, in the affirmative, on March 16, 1937. There were repeated here, almost exactly, the circumstances which, in England, nearly a century earlier, had resulted in the birth of the British Museum.

In addition to the collection itself (roughly valued by Lord Duveen at fifty million dollars), the gift included an endowment fund for future purchases, and ten million dollars for the construction of a gallery in Washington. In the final analysis, however, it was not the large sum of money involved, but rather the freedom of action allowed the trustees by the donor that was extraordinary. Mellon made no stipulation that his collection be kept separate from future acquisitions, and instead of the expected request that the gallery be named after him he suggested that it be known impersonally as "The National Gallery of Art," so that other collectors, undeterred by the shadow of a rival's name, might be encouraged to deposit their own treasures within it. This far-sighted policy bore fruit even before the gallery was opened in 1941. In 1939 the important Kress Collection was donated. Next came the Widener Collection, final disposition of which had long been in doubt, and other gifts are rapidly following.

The only restriction placed upon the administration of the gallery

* This announcement came in the midst of the government's suit charging Mellon with falsification of his income tax returns. Upon hearing of the proposed gift, the Federal prosecutor intimated that Mellon was trying to create a situation whereby he would be exempted by special action from making the payment charged as due. However, it should be noted that Mellon had been negotiating for nearly ten years before this time to obtain the official sanction for an appropriate site in Washington on which to erect the gallery. Furthermore, the government's eventual acceptance of the gift did not affect the tax suit, which was still pending in 1937.

was that future gifts and purchases must be of a quality equal to that of the original collection. And, recognizing that standards change with the passing of time, Mellon even went so far as to grant the trustees permission to discard any of his items which, at some future date, might be considered inferior.

Quite possibly the trustees of the Smithsonian Institution, who were to be charged with the administration of the proposed gift, helped in arriving at these terms; but even so there is evidence that the conditions were quite in line with Mellon's own conception. As such they mark a new departure and an essentially modern one, best expressed, perhaps, in the moving inscription from Pericles on one of the National Gallery's massive interior pillars:

> *"For the whole earth is the*
> *Sepulchre of famous men and*
> *Their story is not graven*
> *Only on stone over their*
> *Native earth but lives on*
> *Far away without visible*
> *Symbol woven into the stuff*
> *Of other men's lives."*

Beyond the economic factors which turn large private collections to public purposes, modern thought, becoming ever more socialistic, tends to decry the very existence of such collections. The first point of attack is usually the wealthy collector himself, turned loose with his untrained vagaries to form a vast collection of cultural treasure basically the property of the community. Often called in question are both his sincerity and disinterestedness. It is pointed out that he may have a purely practical motive in gathering together valuable cultural stores. Certain collector's items, particularly works of art, constitute an international currency that is often as good as gold; and a large collection in generally acceptable fields may provide an excellent way of holding and diversifying wealth. It may be a sort of supplementary insurance policy against currency depreciation or other forms of financial fluctuation; and when its owner gives it away by bequest he may be chiefly impelled by a desire to avoid a tax raid upon his estate.

Even were such considerations to play no part in an individual case, it is said, the wealthy collector is likely to be simply a "culture-shopper," intent chiefly upon display for the enhancement of his own prestige; that he gauges art, as well as everything else, by quantitative standards. It has even been suggested that when such a man founds or patronizes a museum, he is merely buttressing his own position of power by imposing upon the people as a whole the standards of his social class. Motives such as these, it is then added, can hardly operate to produce ideal public institutions, which could almost certainly be better approximated by other means.

Surely it is obvious, so far as the first part of this argument is concerned, that not all wealthy collectors justifiably can be charged with an ulterior motivation. More complex, however, is the second phase of the discussion. Lewis Mumford, who is concerned to examine the broad significances of typical social phenomena, has declared that the metropolitan museum has its exact counterpart in the department store. Since, in both cases, the aim seems to be to gather the greatest possible number of articles together under a single roof, he considers both museum and department store as prime symbols of industrial-age acquisitiveness. He grants that genuine esthetic and scientific interests eventually develop within museums, then adds,

". . . but the trustees are more interested in abstract acquisition and honorific display than in matters of truth, taste and value. Physical size serves again as a substitute for organization . . . mechanical expansion is confused with significance."

Following his indictment, however, Mumford poses a question which embodies his suggestion for the future.

"Is there a single metropolitan museum of art or natural history in the world," he asks, "that could not profit enormously by being decentralized, with each unit reduced to a modicum of its present size, and completely reorganized?"

Sir Joseph Banks, in his day, inveighed against heterogeneous collecting, and suggested specialization as the intelligent course for individual collectors to follow in the future. In our time, Mumford goes further and, discussing public collections, advises decentralization plus a reorganization which shall look toward further specialization. Both in their similarities and in their differences these two statements provide an illuminating indication of progressive development, since one actually is only an extension of the idea embodied in the other—an extension itself made possible by altered social conditions and by a specific advance in the conceptions governing collectors.

While the completely heterogeneous collection is almost unknown in our day, many of our museums and libraries still suffer from the shortcomings of their founders, or from ill-conceived methods of organization. Nevertheless, we at least have many more such institutions, bad or good, than did men of the eighteenth century. The reforms advocated by Mumford and others are even now practiced by far-sighted curators and librarians—though the spread is slow. Until that day when similar ends shall be attainable by co-operative enterprise, streams of private gold or their equivalent in collected material will be required for the foundation and support of those great public institutions which, despite their failings, lend increase to the public's cultural opportunities. It is reasonable, then, that the contributions of rich men should be accepted as of value to the community, even though some are rascals. The gathering together, the harvesting of man's best labor is the important accomplishment of the moment, not arguing over hues of lily white.

Even today there are some privileged collectors whose views of potential public service go considerably beyond the expanded-collection conception of the museum. Members of this school visualize creating and using the collection as a direct educational tool in any of a number of highly specialized fields.

The use of collections for educative purposes is now widely practiced, but there is the interesting case of the lay collector who, through an infinite series of gradations, forms his collection for private purposes, then turns it into an educative instrument; while now and then one comes upon the individual who, from the outset, forms his collection primarily for instructive purposes. In this field two men may be chosen from the contemporary scene, though they stand apart from each other very nearly at opposite poles. One is Dr. Albert Coombs Barnes, the other Henry Ford.

What prompts a person to attempt the instruction of his fellows? Is it a simple or complex desire to share satisfying experiences, emotions, knowledge? Is it a form of exhibitionism, the assertion of an inferiority feeling? Is it nostalgia, the reincarnated Father setting before the Child a pattern to be followed? Or the child, undernourished in learning and spiritual values who, upon aging, wants the young to have a treasure house? Actually the combination of collecting and education at once conjures up the word science, yet though certain lay collectors are practically undistinguishable from the scientist in approach, this label is certainly not suitable to the case of Dr. Barnes.

Near Philadelphia at Merion this gentleman has established the Foundation bearing his name, and over it he presides in person. The doctor is as fine an eccentric as collectordom has ever produced. That his museum contains the finest collection of modern French painting in the world is, of course, no accident. More than thirty-five years of collecting and a reputed average of over a million dollars a year have helped to bring this about. Yet during this time the Doctor has had certain unpleasant experiences with the public and with museum officialdom, and so seriously has he nursed his wounds and fought his battles that it is now considered more difficult to enter his domain than to obtain admission to the Court of St. James. His temper and whimsy are unpredictable, and in all probability he is cursed more bitterly than any other collector in the world, for he has prevented countless amateurs from viewing many of the great examples of modern painting. What extenuating circumstances can successfully excuse a man who has thrust himself between a nice slice of Western culture and those serious students, artists and writers who have applied in vain for admission? Whether or not an eccentric should be permitted to stand guard, hand-culling prospective visitors by what seems to be the "method" of caprice is, however, beside the point, since the fact exists.

More relevant is another fact, that the same Dr. Barnes has also established under his roof a workshop for the training and education of aspiring young student artists. And here Dr. Barnes says, in effect, "Too many of you older people have found fault with my ways, with my pictures. Years ago you ridiculed them, and still today I can hear a murmur of dissent, so I'll turn my back upon you, but the youth who come to me in true meekness and piety I shall feed and nurture from my store."

In justice to Barnes and his project, as much of his background and story as can be retrieved from behind the wall of jealous secrecy should be told, though who is to have the last word, the collector or his critics, is still a question. Born of poor parents, Albert Coombs Barnes achieved education by means of scholarships won both in this country and abroad. His specialty was chemistry, and while a student at Heidelberg University he created silver vitellin, a compound now used extensively in medicine and from the sale of which, under the name of Argyrol, he eventually made his fortune. Among his early friends were a number of artists, including the American, William Glackens, and it is probably through these associations that Barnes' eyes were opened to modern art. At any rate, Glackens, an intense admirer of Renoir's work, is known to have advised the collector on some of his first purchases which date back at least as far as 1906.

From the start everything that Barnes did bore the mark of his distinctive personality—a personality which appears to include not only rebellion against the *status quo* but also a need for some definite and constructive expression of that rebellion. In his small chemical factory, for example, he chose to employ only Negroes, in whom he was, and is, much interested, as he later became interested from another point of view in African Negro sculpture; and for the benefit of his employees he would hang the walls of the factory with paintings from his rapidly growing collection. Once a week, in those days, either Barnes himself or someone he had engaged for the purpose would conduct a tour of the exhibits and give the workers a lecture on art.

Perhaps it was from this unusual social experiment that the chemist-collector evolved the idea of using his collection as a permanent workshop for the training and education of young artists. The Barnes Foundation was opened in 1927, and each year since a group of students, whom Barnes has selected from among many applicants, have here received free instruction of high order, with the collection itself an important adjunct. Particularly rich in the works of Renoir and Cézanne, nineteenth and twentieth century French painting is the specialized theme followed in the collection.

A devoted student of his subject, Barnes, with Violette De Mazia as collaborator, has written several interpretative books. He is no less interested in his students, and it is said that the brood returns his devotion with wholehearted gratitude. Many times he has taken groups of young people abroad to visit great museums, and several of the teachers at the school are former students whom he has "brought up."

Yet the doctor's prejudice is violently fixed against members of museum administration, and his manner of asserting this prejudice has been so offensive that, important as his collection admittedly is, few museum representatives will now seek permission to see it. From this situation there seems no escape. It is told that Homer Saint-Gaudens,

Director of the Carnegie International Exposition of Art, once approached Barnes to request the loan of some of the doctor's pictures for this world-famous show. According to the tale, Barnes' only reply was to shout, "You mind your business and I'll mind mine!" And when Walter Pach, the art historian, asked him (with other prominent collectors) to lend some of his paintings to the exhibition being planned for the New York World's Fair, he received a rather flighty telegram which suggested, among other things, that the sedate Mr. Pach "go fly a kite."

It has been pointed out, accusingly, that a high barricade surrounds the Foundation, that "savage" dogs and "massive" guards keep constant watch to ensure against unwanted visitors. The collector himself explains his irascible conduct on the grounds that his students work every day in the week and must have quiet and freedom from interruption—a manifestly incomplete explanation.

No such emotional complications disturb Henry Ford. A million people a year visit his collection of American industrial and domestic arts at Dearborn, Michigan, and that is exactly the trend of his desire. The Edison Institute and its vast museum, and Greenfield Village with its collection of old buildings and a complete re-creation of old-time American life are part and parcel of Ford's distinctive educational theories, and as such he wants them to have as wide an audience as possible. The merits of those theories need not be examined here, but if the important function played in it by the Ford Collection of Americana is to be understood the general scheme must at least be sketched.

The essential purpose of the entire project, based upon Mr. Ford's belief that ". . . the farther you look back, the farther you can look ahead," appears to be the building up of American ambition. Ford wishes to remind people how far and how fast Americans have come in technical progress over the past century or so, in the hope that once this has been vividly realized there will be greater belief in and more purposeful striving for a similar degree of future progress. But his scheme goes much farther than mere visual illustration, for it includes an entire school system in which the Village and the museum, with all that they contain, serve as campus and laboratory. It is his idea that such a school system should "emphasize the pioneer qualities of self-dependence and resourcefulness that carved this country out of the wilderness." To this end not only do the students at the Institute become familiar through observation with the various mechanical difficulties overcome by their ancestors, but they learn to carry on the old crafts, with the old tools, under the old conditions carefully simulated. As a final binding together of past, present and future, the system aims through its own organizational methods to instill in those who come under its influence Mr. Ford's strong conviction that the future progress of this country demands a far greater co-ordination between industry, agriculture and education than now exists.

Each of these ideas has played a part in determining the nature of the Ford Collection itself, really a group of collections held together by the thread of "Americanism." Ford has tried "to assemble a complete series of every article used or made in America from the days of the first settlers down to the present time." In some cases, as in the museum, the articles are displayed in series so as to illustrate the historical sequence. In other cases, as in the Village buildings, they are arranged in proper combination, in a period setting, so as to show how they would have looked in their own time. The theory behind this, in Mr. Ford's own words is that

". . . by looking at the things that people used and the way they lived, a better and truer impression can be gained in an hour than could be had in a month of reading,"

or, in the words of Charles Messer Stow,

". . . than can possibly be obtained from a formal exhibition of the articles in a museum."

There enters here, however, a particularly sad state of affairs, since Mr. Ford's misplaced zeal for spic-and-spanity has outraged the feelings at least of the specialists in antiques, who rightly rule that unessential refinishing is ruinous to the mint condition of fine old furniture. There are also many complaints that, in certain sections of the exhibition, objects have too often been thrown together without proper system. Had Mr. Ford been able to yield to capable professional advice a part of his pleasure in making all decisions, many mistakes in acquisition, arranging and restoring could have been avoided.

The collection is so enormous that many volumes would be required to describe it in detail, yet it is the fruition of the long-cherished ideas of one collector. It contains, among other things, a department devoted to the development of agriculture and showing all types of farm machinery, including the evolution of each from its most primitive to its most modern form; a department devoted to transportation, showing every medium that has been utilized in this country and including every form of horse-drawn vehicle, every form of bicycle, every type of railway locomotive, and (the personal touch) every step in the development of the Ford car. There is a department, truly astonishing, devoted to household arts. This one embraces a wide range of exhibits including (each in complete chronological series) furniture, glassware, crockery and china, clocks, stoves, candlesticks and lamps, pewter, britannia metal and silver, pictures, books, fabric decorations, dresses, suits, shoes and hats, toys, lighting equipment, tools and utensils, and so on and on until one runs out of gas.

Greenfield Village itself is a collection made up of old houses, stores, barns, sheds, shops, factories, warehouses, schools, meeting houses, post-offices and other buildings which have been brought to Dearborn from various parts of the United States. Each building in the Village has been painstakingly searched out for a specific purpose. Some, about to fall into decay, were salvaged just in time and have since been restored. And all, after having been given their proper location in the Village, are fitted with objects suited to their original functions and periods, and put into use once more.

Here, indeed, is a new type of collection and a new kind of collector, perhaps unique, perhaps prophetic; given a specialized idea within which an infinite variety is suggested, despite faults he aims to form a great museum-school of life having as its goal the fostering of a thoughtfully conceived educational project.

Part Three

HOW TO TELL A COLLECTOR FROM OTHER PEOPLE

"They have taken it into their hearts."

MI FEI

THE CASUAL OBSERVER, watching a collector as he pores over his "treasures," is often moved to inquire, "What can the fellow see in such things?" This is related to the familiar question, "What can so-and-so possibly see in that girl?" One answer serves both: John Jones is in love with his wife; George Bodelhop is in love with his collection. And just as love among human beings is far from being a simple emotion, so is the love of the collector for collecting a complex and varied experience, running the full gamut of those emotions we recognize in human love. In the ranks of the amateur (the word, of course, means lover) brought startlingly to life are parental love, love licit and illicit, and the contentment of successful matrimony. Here are to be found the impassioned, the impulsive, the jealous, the triumphant or the frustrated lover, even the home-wrecker and the suicide.

For centuries writers have retold, with malice or delight, the symptoms of man, the lover. The observer jots down his view of the familiar cascade as it falls into the pit of excruciating torture or leaps to the high reaches of joy; and for the audience there has ever been something comical about the lover's precarious situation, since people are inclined to be amused at other men who become intense (with gestures) or solemn (trance-like) over matters which have left the observer untouched. In this respect the audience usually treats the collector much as it treats the lover; yet for the lover other men have tenderness as well as derision, a tenderness born of an underlying sympathy and understanding; and were the collector better understood, he, too, might be regarded with greater warmth by his fellows.

All men are subject to biological love, but not all are subject to the earnest practice of collecting, and so it is important to realize that to most collectors the collection on its way to completion takes on a life and character of its own. To its creator it truly becomes a *living* thing, and it is then that its component parts, directed toward an orderly whole, also become the objects of the collector's very real affection. How that affection asserts itself will depend, of course, upon each collector, but to large or small degree the affection will always be there and will serve as a major mark of the true amateur.

The love of the collector for his chosen subject casts a pleasant aura about all that he says and does in this role. If your interest in this matter should cause you to browse through a half dozen books written by collectors on subjects as diverse as coins, antique rugs, sea shells, autographs, miniatures and china figurines, you would come to recognize a distinctive charm of style, a whimsical good-nature familiar to each, and a uniformly disarming tone of sincerity. No matter how uninterested you may originally have been, a collector with a gift for words can arouse eagerness to hear his tale. And conversely, another collector of your acquaintance may seem the most silent of men, a tongue-tied individual with no apparent interests, difficult to know or to befriend; but try mentioning something, anything, remotely connected with his collecting field and you will see the lamps in his eyes brighten. His tongue will be unloosed as though by magic, and he will take you into his heart for life.

It soon becomes obvious that the collector may experience an actual sensuous pleasure in possessing the objects of his pursuit, in seeing them, in touching them, in savoring their especial and distinctive physical qualities.

"You must learn to love the feel of old books; the smell of them must be unto you a delicious aroma,"

writes Barton Currie, and by this he means that if you have not experienced these sensations you do not know what it is to be a true collector. All collectors will understand this, but most would contend that far from having to learn to love the physical attributes of their treasures

The Metropolitan Museum of Art, Havemeyer Collection

"The Amateur." *Daumier drew and painted many versions of the collector, but this water color reveals the heart of the matter: his gaze falling perhaps inadvertently upon the Venus, the amateur is alone with his "family" in eloquent contentment.*

they could hardly avoid doing so if they tried. Richard de Bury, writing centuries ago, gave expression to this hunger when he spoke of the city that was then the book collector's Mecca:

"O Holy God of Gods in Sion, what a mighty stream of pleasure made glad our hearts whenever we had leisure to visit Paris, the Paradise of the world, and to linger there, where the days seemed ever few for the greatness of our love! There are delightful libraries, more aromatic than stores of spicery; there are luxuriant parks of all manners of volumes . . ."

As with lovers, the collector's attitude often embodies not only delight but reverence, and he is also inclined to be fiercely protective in the face of danger. There was once a Japanese collector, proud owner of a painting by Sesshiu (1420–1506), a master whom the Nipponese esteem much as we do Leonardo. When one day this amateur found himself in a burning building and realized that all escape was cut off, he slashed open his body with his sword, and the men who later recovered his half-consumed corpse found therein, quite unharmed, the priceless scroll. While the Westerner has always been reluctant to try a carving knife to his middle, he has been known to resort to the pedestrianism of rushing into a burning building, ignoring death and perhaps a few relatives, to rescue cherished items.

One school of psychiatry, led by the late Wilhelm Stekel, professes to see in the love motif the chief explanation for the typical reactions of the true collector. This theory is baldly literal. The emotions of such a collector, it is pointed out, are the emotions of a Don Juan engaged in forming a harem, and each item added to the collection-harem is a symbol of a new conquest seen "through a rosy veil of illusion." Although there is nothing imperative about accepting this theory, it is true that collectors themselves frequently admit to something of the sort.

The faithfulness with which many amateurs live with their collections may underline love and the affections strongly related to the possessive urge. Suppose a man of domineering nature is also a collector who has found a subject intensely to his liking, a subject charged with vivid meaning for him. In his collection he may find a pleasure beyond that which any human being would be capable of giving him. Quite possibly the wells of his affection seem already full. Suppose we assume that he is not unhappily married. Yet he is a man of stern convictions and very exacting. No person could succeed in pleasing him at all times under all circumstances. Do you see? The collection is *always* beautiful, perfect in tact, waiting without criticism, mysterious, alluringly silent, but with a certain eloquence. . . . So far there has been no report of a wife suing her husband's collection for alienation of affections, but more than one could show cause. And in such a baffling affair, the husband, strangely enough, has scored an unusually subtle victory. For what woman could stand the humiliation in open court of admitting marital defeat at the hands of mere "things," while The Collection sat in the witness chair, serene, imperturbable.

There have, however, been couples, like the Robertets of renaissance France, the Folgers of modern America, and, of course, the couples never in histories or newspapers, who convince us that when man and wife share a collecting passion the result is an ultimate in felicity.

Here is the story of one ideal collecting marriage, a tale of refreshing tranquillity, told by the most famous literary woman in Chinese history. Li Ch'ing-chao is speaking to us early in the twelfth century:

"When we were married in 1101, my husband was twenty-one, and was still a student at the National University. Both our families being poor, we lived a very frugal life. On the first and the fifteenth of every month, my husband had leave of absence from the University to come home. He would very often pawn his belongings to get 500 cash with which he would walk to the market at the Hsiang-kuo Monastery and pick up rubbings of ancient stone inscriptions. These, together with some fresh fruits and nuts, he would carry home and we would enjoy together the edibles and the ancient rubbings, forgetful of all the troubles in the world.

"In later years when my father-in-law became prime minister, and a number of influential friends were in a position to loan us rare books to copy, our interest in these antiquarian objects was greatly deepened and we often took great trouble and sometimes suffered privation in order to buy a rare manuscript, a fine painting, or an ancient bronze vessel. I remember once during the Ch'ung-ning Era (1105) we were offered a painting by Hsu Hsi for sale at the price of 200,000 cash. Although the son of a prime minister, my husband found it difficult to pay such a price. We kept the painting for two days and had to return it to the owner. For several days we could not overcome our sense of regret and disappointment.

"When my husband became prefect of two prefectures, he spent practically all his income on books and antiques. When a book was bought, he and I would always read it together, mending the text, repairing the manuscript, and writing the captions. And when a painting or a bronze vessel was brought home, we would also together open it, play with it, study its merits and criticize its defects. Every evening we studied together till one candle was burned up. In this way our collection of books surpassed all others in the country because of this loving care which my husband and I were able to give it.

"It was my good fortune to be endowed with a very good memory. Every evening after supper, we would sit together in the Kweilai Hall and make our own tea. We would wager against each other that such and such a quotation was to be found on a certain page in a certain chapter of a certain book. We must number the exact line, page, chapter and volume, and then check them from the book shelves. The winner was rewarded by drinking the first cup of tea. But when one of us did win, one was so happy that one's hand trembled with laughter and the tea would spill all over the floor. So the first cup was rarely drunk.

"We were resolved to grow old and die in such a little world of ours."

Eight hundred years have gone by since then, but the "little world" of this collector couple is still lovely and fresh.

Besides those words in collecting vocabulary such as *amateur* and *bibliophile* which evoke the emotion of love, there is another group of expressions which implies that the collector is a bitten, helpless victim. Barton Currie, famous editor and bibliophile, was once asked to identify the *first symptoms* of *"bibliomania."* His answer was one which, with appropriate variations, might have been given by any one of those who, like himself, have been willing sufferers from some form of collectionitis.

"It happens to you and you have it," Currie succinctly opened his description. "You are unaware of its approach. The germ is even more cunning and stealthy than the love germ. With love you have warnings and a tingling awareness, and the early symptoms are exalting. The first symptom of bibliomania, however, is much more subtle than love. It anesthetizes. It manifests itself by producing a form of somnambulism. You come out of a bookstore carrying a first edition of something or other. You cannot explain how or why you got it, or what you paid for it. But you have it; and when you arrive home with it you creep off to some secluded room to examine it. Then occurs the first little burning exaltation. Just a little glow to begin with, then by infinite gradations a consuming fire."

Later on when, having become a confirmed collector, such a man has gathered together many books, or many pieces of antique furniture, or a large assortment of pottery, that "consuming fire" is always with him and bursts forth whenever he sees or hears of, say, an association volume, a fine colonial chest-on-chest, or a Bennington pottery dog that he "needs" for his collection. He is in love with these things, yes, and possession of them, or the thought of possessing them exalts him. But he is also obsessed by them. He cannot do without them. He needs them as the opium eater needs his drug, and he is driven into strange paths by the compulsion of that need.

Dealers might well represent of all humans those least likely to be susceptible to the collecting dragnet. It is their business to tempt and to feed the appetites of their clients. In sober realism, the sensible dealer should himself avoid collecting for much the same motive of self-preservation as causes a good bartender to refrain from drinking while on duty: the dealer knows, from long observation, that should he once fall into the collecting ranks his profits are likely to be consumed by a growing unwillingness to sell. And yet they are not all immune. There is A. S. W. Rosenbach, for example. He is hardly headed for the poorhouse, and yet it is said that he manages to preserve inviolable his own private collection of books. He must be an unusually strong-minded individual.

One of the Duveens tells how, as an enthusiastic and incautious young man, he was first taught by a more hardened relative the dealer's first lesson in caution. The young novice had just unearthed a set of five beautiful Chinese porcelain vases that had once belonged to his renowned ancestor, the connoisseur Evrard Jabach. For these the Duveen family had been years searching, and the young man's delight in his discovery was such that he could not bear the thought of parting with the treasures. He pleaded with his uncle that they might be kept in the family—only these vases, just this once. He argued their strong sentimental value in addition to their rare loveliness. Pleas and arguments were alike unavailing. "No, no, my boy, I can't do that. It would break one of the strongest rules of the firm. Once I begin to compete against my own clients I'm a ruined man! I'm much too fond of beautiful things as it is, and if once I let myself go I'd never be able to stop."

Keppel tells of a London dealer in engravings and etchings who, upon inheriting a small fortune, "that day locked his door for the rest of his life and sat like a miser among the prints he no longer needed to sell," and Thorndike gives us the case of a Harvard librarian whose possessiveness made his profession a burden of frustration. If he can, a librarian who happens to be a collector at heart must also reconcile himself to the recurring disappearance of the books in his charge. In this the Harvard librarian was unable to find peace, for the continual circulation of volumes seems to have been well-nigh intolerable to him. Then one day a miracle of conjuncture occurred, and in his exultation he betrayed his true feelings. "Every book belonging to the library is here except one," he cried joyfully, "and I am going to get that one from Professor Child now!" Collectors alone, perhaps, could sympathize with this man's emotion.

The successful collector is among the happiest of men, but the frustrated collector, like the frustrated lover, is truly a pitiable object.

Never was there a more devoted and successful collector than Sir Robert Cotton, and it was a particularly malicious punishment, devised when he fell into political disfavor, which by order of the King of England kept him for months from entering his beloved library. One might as well have put him into solitary confinement on a diet of bread and water. Sir Robert took to his bed, no longer caring to live. His friends, seriously worried, pleaded with the king, but Charles I, an ardent collector himself, knew that his government had hit upon the most effective of all possible instruments of torture, and he showed no disposition to change weapons.

Only when it became apparent that Sir Robert was dying did the king finally relent, and then it was too late. Shortly before the end the great collector delivered himself of this final message, and if it bears the authentic purple stamp of melodrama, at least Cotton himself seems to have believed it. "Tell the Lord Privy Seal and the rest of the Council," he said, "that their so long detaining my books from me has been the cause of this mortal malady."

Fortunately few collecting stories end so tragically; yet collectors would vigorously maintain that the joy of Sir Robert's collection had afforded him more than made up for the unhappy dénouement—and here Cotton himself would probably have agreed.

One of the most interesting roles the collector plays, and in this he can be easily recognized, is that of Sherlock Holmes. Now he has cast off the gentle or violent ways of the lover. His eyes have narrowed to that calculating squint. He is on his way to track down the quarry, his conscience safe at home locked up in a cupboard.

He is a wary still-hunter, maintaining a "poker face" which even the hardened gambler could not better. If there are clues to be unraveled he works patiently, exhausting every possibility, persistent, single-minded, intent. His wits become sharpened by the challenge, and he develops an uncanny cunning. Yet such is the strength of his desire that he grasps at any straw, and is inclined to supplement the feats of his intellect with a superstitious belief in all sorts of signs, particularly in the run of his own "luck." In this, too, the gambler is recalled, which is not surprising, since collecting is the sort of game in which chance plays an important part.

It is, furthermore, a game filled with mystery, suspense and adventure, all of which the collector enjoys hugely. When a dealer leads him into the dark back room of his shop as though to disclose things which the ordinary man could never hope to see, or hints mysteriously of a glorious but somewhat shady past in the life of the object about to be divulged, the collector exults, as might a child permitted to gaze upon some hitherto forbidden fruit.

This love of mystery and surprise for the sheer excitement and dramatic effect is not dropped once the conquest has been sealed. A demonstration of this is to be found in a story long remembered by the officials of the National Gallery in London. These gentlemen once received a call from a rather shabbily dressed man whose face was unknown to the attendants. The stranger, who carried a picture case, asked to see the director. That would be impossible, he was told. He had better leave the case and it would be attended to in good time. But the fellow was persistent. He must see the director; nothing less would satisfy him; and so in desperation a brief interview was arranged.

Eying the case, the director curtly informed his visitor that the rules of the gallery forbade his examining paintings in the presence of the owner. The case would have to be left and its contents passed upon in proper order.

"You had better have just one look. I ask no more," insisted the stranger, and with that he began unbuckling the straps which bound his package.

Now thoroughly angry, the director stepped forward and refastened the first buckle while his visitor was undoing the second. This went on in a mild acceleration of furious silence, until the British official, abruptly recalling his dignity, froze in rigid disapproval. And then—suddenly the painting confronted him. Eyes helpless, the unfortunate director's expression must have been all that his guest had hoped, for the picture was

Terborch's famous masterpiece, *The Peace of Munich,* for which the National Gallery itself had once bid eagerly but unsuccessfully up to the limit of its available funds! The painting had been lost at the time to an unknown purchaser who had exceeded the gallery's offer by a thousand pounds, and all hope of acquiring it for years to come had vanished into thin air. Now, however, the shabby stranger who had insisted upon having his sport before disclosing his mission finally identified himself as the rival bidder, Sir Richard Wallace. In this droll way he had come to offer the Terborch as a gift to the National Gallery.

Once on the trail of a desired object, the experienced collector is not only shrewd, he is often unscrupulous. He has developed certain definite modes of behavior to be used in the presence of those who possess what he wants, and those methods are the surest and most characteristic marks of his kind. So stereotyped, indeed, is the pattern of his behavior in this regard, and so long has it been followed that one wonders how its transparency could fool any but the most naïve vendor. Yet collectors have persisted in following this pattern generation after generation, and it still proves reliable, bringing results.

Unless taken by surprise or so completely carried away by his desire that he forgets his role, the collector will pretend complete lack of interest in the very object he most craves to own. He will behave as though he did not see the bauble, or, if he deigns to look at it, it will be with the utmost casualness, as though it were too worthless to merit a second glance. He will make elaborate inquiries concerning every other picture, dish, chair or book in the place before he mentions the one thing upon which his concentration rests with an almost unbearable intensity.

Dr. Johnson, observing a group of his contemporaries at an auction sale, described their several reactions in the following words:

"One looks with longing eyes and gloomy countenance on that which he despairs to gain from a rich bidder,"

but another, more hopeful of success and therefore more cautious,

"keeps his eye with care from settling too long on that which he most earnestly desires; and another, with more art than virtue, depreciates that which he values most, in hope to have it at an easy rate."

The doctor might have been describing a group of collectors of any period and almost any nationality.

A favorite way of playing this game outside of the auction room is to select a group of items for which a lump sum is paid and then, at the last minute, to request that this mangy old firescreen or that dilapidated sofa (which, as the collector well knows, can be quite nicely restored) be thrown in to complete the lot.

Collectors have even been known to buy entire houses full of worthless junk in order to obtain a single valuable item without drawing the latter to the unsupecting owner's attention. Such was the case of the London banker who once purchased the ancestral home of a certain cheese merchant. The merchant had long wanted to build himself a new and more comfortable dwelling, so he was glad to be rid of the old house and flattered himself that he had "put over something pretty good." But the banker, who was a collector of illuminated manuscripts, happened to know that within the commonplace and uninteresting house reposed an ancient *Book of Hours* of exceptional rarity. Once this prize had been safely removed, he resold the building and the rest of its contents at a nice profit. Today that manuscript is a priceless treasure of the British Museum.

Collectors' wiles of this relatively mild sort may work on ordinary human beings who have not been forewarned, but seldom are they of any avail against another collector. Then is the time to trot out the most unscrupulous tricks of an elaborate repertoire, and a collector in a position of power is often the last word in out-and-out plundering of the sort typified by the ancient Romans. A word from such a collector is usually sufficient, and like Goering, he may know that when he visits a collection he need only express particular admiration for a certain work of art. The unfortunate owner will feel that he has no choice but to make his mighty guest a present of the object in question.

Even without power, the insistent collector can often find a way. Mi Fei, an eleventh-century Chinese collector of old writings and paintings, was once shown a calligraphy by Wang Hsi-chih, a great writer of the fourth century. The episode occurred on a boat, and the rarity touched the collector's heart so deeply that in his extremity he turned to the river for aid, threatening to jump overboard unless his friend, owner of the prize, handed it over to him. At first the friend was understandably reluctant to take this threat seriously, but Mi Fei went through the preliminary motions with such conviction that the victim (no longer a friend after this affair) became severely frightened, sufficiently so that he surrendered the disputed calligraphy.

Later, with delightful inconsistency, this same Mi Fei would write:

"When a man of today obtains such an old specimen it seems to him as important as life, which is ridiculous."

The deceptively well-controlled beings described by Dr. Johnson were collectors at a pre-sale exhibition, looking over the ground, still holding themselves in check. But let the bidding once begin and matters change complexion rapidly, for here is no battle of wolf against lamb, so often the case in private transaction, but wolf shoulder to wolf, and now it becomes a question of do or die, win or lose, the stakes to him who dares the most.

To be sure, the lambs are there, too, disinterested individuals who have come in search of an inexpensive chair or drape for the new house, curious people who have heard about auctions and want to see the wheels go round, and even that mild sort of collector who can take or leave with comparative equanimity—but the wolves are in full pack, the true collectors for whom this auction is an intensely serious business. Some of them are marked by the glitter in their eyes, the flush mounting to their cheeks, the tremble of their uplifted hands, by the expression of dismay or exultation when an item is finally "knocked down."

As the sale progresses the room becomes surcharged with excitement. Dramatic intensity is increased because this excitement is partially suppressed. And now is the time to beware, to steel oneself against impulsiveness, for the tension is highly contagious and demands *action.* More unsuspecting innocents have been bitten by the collecting bug at auctions than anywhere else. Indeed, auction-fever is a disease in itself, one of the numerous complications to which victims of collectomania are subject, and even the casual bystander can be swept off by this curious virus.

Closely allied to auction-fever is the somewhat milder catalogue-itis. A good part of the reading time of many a collector is devoted to the perusal of these inviting, tantalizing pamphlets which he consults often and carefully, noting prices and other items of especial interest, always on the lookout for unexpected windfalls. The collector's home is the natural objective of the catalogue, and the collecting of catalogues in itself not infrequently becomes an important (and at times valuable) specialty.

Collectors sometimes want an unobtainable object so badly that, failing all else, they will borrow it and with dogged bluntness neglect to return it, or, if this proves impossible, steal it outright. This is part of an ancient tribal technique, and though it is usually well suppressed, even collectors who have never yielded to the temptation will admit that at times they have had some pretty narrow squeaks.

Bibliophiles seem to be the most frequent offenders, perhaps because books are traditionally borrowable and, being small and many, are relatively easy to secrete and "forget." By contrast, the man who collects antique beds has little to fear from fellow enthusiasts. Book collectors have coined a special word, *biblioklept,* to fit the case, although similar activities have been known in other fields and the word or its counterpart has been applicable to a surprisingly large number of prominent and otherwise quite reputable citizens throughout time.

Ashurbanipal's bookplate inscription indicates that there were biblioklepts even in ancient Assyria. The Greek, Apellicon, was accused by Posidonius of borrowing old state documents and sending back copies, a technique that is scattered through the pages of East and West in many fields of collecting. Books in medieval monasteries were often chained to their stands to guard against theft, and in 1483 the Sorbonne purchased a number of books with a "conscience fund" contributed by a monk who, though he may have withstood the temptations of the flesh, fell before those of the book in his youth.

Boccaccio stole the precious manuscripts of Tacitus and Varro from the once great Abbey Library of Monte Cassino and, although he stoutly excused the theft by pointing out that he had found the library neglected and decaying, the door open, "grass growing through the windows, the books and benches piled high with dust," historians since have not been quite certain whether or not to believe this consummate story teller.

In the days before printing, the prevalence of bibliokleptry may well have been due chiefly to the scarcity and high value of manuscripts which fanned the book-lover's desire and made it difficult to satisfy. Long after the special circumstances which helped to produce this particular epidemic had passed, however, we still find collectors falling prey to temptation. Sir Robert Cotton caused a political scandal by his

CHRISTIE'S AUCTION ROOM.

AUCTIONS AND COLLECTING *have been united for more than twenty centuries and today they are more strongly coupled than ever. An early 19th-century scene at London's famous Christie's, bombed out in 1944. Aquatint after a Rowlandson drawing, 1808.*

habit of keeping historically important national documents in his own library, documents which had been loaned to him for specific purposes and which he afterward claimed had become his by right. Books and papers lent to Samuel Pepys "were not always punctually returned," and when the diarist wanted something very much in the way of a book he did not scruple to filch it. Usually, however, he employed more subtle methods. Like a salesman habitually padding his expense account, he would order a volume for his private library and have it put down to the Admiralty account. "I think I will let the King pay for this one," he would say.

Even clergymen of the highest degree of respectability, were they but collectors, have succumbed. The Reverend Thomas Prince "permanently borrowed from the libraries of Increase and Cotton Mather"; and of the Reverend Dr. William Buell Sprague, the contemporary diarist, Christopher C. Baldwin, wrote feelingly:

> "He has so much fury about him in collecting autographs that he would carry off everything that had a name attached to it. I am heartily glad he has gone out of New England, for he is so much esteemed wherever he goes that people let him into their garrets without any difficulty, and, being a Doctor of Divinity, they never think to look under his cloak to see how many precious old papers he bears off with him."

Sometimes one book-grabber will turn the tables on another. Napoleon, whose appetite for books was entirely genuine, once saw lying on the table of the Prussian king a copy of Montesquieu's work on the Roman Empire and noticed that it was full of marginal comments in the handwriting of Frederick the Great. Ordinarily the Little Corporal was far more scrupulous about books than he was about art objects, but the appeal of such an important association volume overwhelmed his conscience. A history of the Roman Empire which Frederick the Great had pored over and annotated seemed intended by fate surely for this latter-day Caesar. So Napoleon accepted Fate's dictum. Later, however, the Emperor's secretary loaned this highly treasured volume to Talleyrand, who, in his turn, "always had some pretext to avoid returning it."

Collector's thievery is not always committed with malice aforethought. A man may believe that his driving thirst for an unobtainable object will be satisfied, if only he can hold it in his possession for a time, so that by poring over it until he has become familiar with its every detail he will be able to keep it in his mind forever. . . . But days grow into weeks, and weeks into months, until at last he has forgotten, and even forgotten that he has forgotten (perhaps with a little self-help) that the treasure once belonged to someone else.

The prize once firmly secured, the collector's grip becomes one of dogged strength which neither hell nor high water can loosen. At this point no claims of friendship can melt him. His eyes are cool to the prospect of material profit, and even his vanity develops an armor against exploitation. Though calamity threaten, or the very jaws of death seize him where the cloth is slack, most often he will not let go.

In this tenaciousness women collectors have frequently proven themselves on a par with their brothers, particularly when the "brothers" were collecting rivals, although equality between the sexes is not always so well-balanced.

Even in the America of our time, with enormous numbers of good feminine collectors, comparatively few are outstanding. There have been some, of course. The name of Lillie Bliss is well known to American lovers of nineteenth-century French painting. There was Gertrude Vanderbilt Whitney, who founded the New York City museum bearing her name and pioneered in collecting contemporary American art. Amy Lowell was an ardent bibliophile and her Keats collection was important. Mrs. William D. Frishmuth of Philadelphia created a notable collection of musical instruments. Boston's Mrs. Jack Gardner, she who presided over Fenway Court, is still a legend in that city. And the names of many other contemporaries or near contemporaries are familiar to dealers and to fellow collectors in most special fields.

From the past of other nations a few names stand out indelibly—Hatshepsut of Egypt, Bel-Shalti-Nannar of Babylon, China's Li Ch'ing-chao, Isabella d'Este, the Duchess of Portland, Sweden's Queen Christina, the women of France in the years of elegance.

Yet which of these ladies can justly be called a feminine Ashurbanipal, Hui Tsung, Lorenzo de' Medici, Mazarin, Charles I, Hans Sloane or J. P. Morgan? Perhaps the crux of the matter lies in the fact that grand-scale collecting almost always calls for aggressive and material ambition to a degree uncharacteristic of women, aside from women's historic economic position. Those who came within hailing distance of the collecting giants were women who seemed to exhibit the masculine strain of a highly developed objective competitiveness, although this in no way detracts from the position of women as amateurs.

Demonstrating the tenaciousness of both men and women collectors and the lengths to which an amateur will go to obtain a desired item, a story is told about two intense bibliophiles, the one, Richard Heber, the other, Miss Richardson Currer, a lady who by good fortune happened to own a particularly rare and beautiful copy of the medieval *Book of St. Albans.*

Heber regarded Miss Currer with reasonable civility, yet when he came to call on her, the object of his affection (it need hardly be emphasized) was her handsomely illuminated manuscript. In eager haste and, it appears, with some lack of subtlety, he made this fact clear to his hostess, only to be met with uncompromising rebuff. No, Miss Currer repeated endlessly, she could not be induced to part with her *St. Albans.*

The unfortunate suitor tried all the wiles of the practiced bargainer, but the lady proved more than a match for him and would have none of his offers. Finally, in desperation, a brilliant maneuver occurred to Heber; he promptly asked the owner of the manuscript for her hand in marriage. To some spinsters this might have seemed overwhelming, but not to Miss Currer. When the smoke cleared, the indomitable maiden still clutched her book and Heber had to admit defeat. Miss Currer had not the slightest desire to share this or any of the other volumes in her splendid library with a husband whom she knew by reputation and experience to be as fanatical about books as she was herself. A true individualist, she is a good example of a female minority which can deny the strongest male argument.

Even the demands of royalty have been successfully defied by the determination of a confirmed amateur, as appears from the case of the late Kaiser Wilhelm of Germany and Frau Ermina Feist, another member of the same feminine minority. The Kaiser's methods of expanding the collections of the Berlin museums were notoriously highhanded. No provincial gallery, no church, no private collection was safe from his slightly indirect form of plunder. This amounted to a formula of admiring some object and then tactfully suggesting that he would welcome its transfer to one of the museums in the capital. In the case of private collectors the Kaiser might first send an important emissary to voice his Imperial Majesty's admiration for a special item, then follow with the suggestion that the Kaiser would be willing to take tea with the owner. The ultimate result of such a visit was a foregone conclusion; collectors felt that they had no choice but to comply, as to a royal command.

It was, however, quite otherwise with Frau Feist, a famous collector of her day, for she valued her Dresden china far above imperial favor and was neither terrified nor impressed by august attention. Nor was her feminine vanity permitted to betray her because of the implied compliment. Such an attitude was incredible to the Kaiser's emissary who simply refused to believe his ears and mentioned the names of several other important collectors who had been similarly "honored." Frau Feist listened attentively, but betrayed no interest in "collaboration." At last, according to Duveen who recounts the tale, the scandalized ambassador inquired whether she did not feel that the proposed visit was an act of graciousness for which she should be deeply grateful.

"Not at all," Ermina replied. "His Majesty has taken tea with so many collectors that I do not consider the honor worth *my* collection!" In more recent years Hermann Wilhelm Goering has followed a similar procedure, although with less polite pretense, in expanding his personal art collection. William D. Bayles writes, in his *Caesars in Goose Step,* "An official visit from Goering is a nightmare to any German town, because he comes only to plunder. The municipal council of a Franconian town he visited in 1938 sought to forestall his evident designs by presenting him with a beautifully illuminated medieval manuscript. 'I didn't come here for that,' barked Goering in the midst of the presentation address. 'Where is your collection of Cranach paintings?' Before he left the town, two prize Cranachs had been crated and placed on his special train. . . . Inspecting the new acquisitions in the Berlin German Museum, his eye fell upon a beautiful *Diana of the Chase* painting. 'Send that to the Official Gallery of the Reich Chief Master of the Hunt,' he ordered. Unable to find such a gallery, the museum authorities communicated with Goering's adjutant and were told the gallery was in Goering's home."

There are black periods in the lives of all men, and there are times when the amateur is faced by the choice either of giving up his collection or of enduring poverty or social or political ruin. Many collectors would, no doubt, force themselves to be sensible under such circumstances and make the necessary adjustment, hoping that at some future date they might be able to regain their treasures. On the other hand, collecting annals are full of tragic tales of men who have come to value their collections above anything else in life and who, confronted with the necessity of parting from them, no longer find life worth living.

"The major danger," said Arnold Bennett, "is the old danger of unconsciously losing one's perspective, of living in order to collect instead of collecting in order to live."

If forewarned of the impending doom, the collector, like the jealous lover, may even destroy the object of his affection rather than face the possibility of having it belong to another. Petronius dashed his cherished bowl to pieces so that Nero might not have it, though to do so meant death for himself as well. Verres allowed himself to be proscribed, although he might have saved himself by handing over his Corinthian bronzes. And many are the similar tales told of collectors in other lands. Sansom tells us, for example, how before committing suicide the Japanese collector, Matsunaga Danjō, a constable under the shogun Nobunaga (1534–82),

"smashed to atoms a precious tea-kettle rather than let it fall into the hands of a rival collector."

Among modern collectors economic misfortune has been the most common instrument of mental torture. Some collectors, faced by the necessity of selling their treasures in order to save themselves from financial ruin, have merely refrained from attending the sale, thus sparing themselves the intense pain of watching the dispersal. Were the collector to be present his emotions would be much like those of a condemned man who is first forced to witness the shooting of his wife and children. One amateur, who came manfully through the sale itself, afterward found that the deprivation was more than he could endure. He borrowed the necessary funds and laboriously began buying back from the dealers and collectors who had supplanted him in possession! For some poor wretches, however, no way out is available, and a number of these, among them a prominent English art connoisseur, have been known to commit suicide.

There are cases on record of collectors who, knowing they were about to die, have attempted to take with them some particularly cherished objects. There is an analogy here to the ancient and Eastern death sacrifice which requires the beloved and possessed—wife or concubine—to give up her life so that she may join her master in the world beyond and never belong to another on this earth. Chattels and material possessions were once similarly sacrificed, burned on the pyre or buried with the owner.

Man has not learned much about the dark, final step, and when the collector must go to his cheerless resting place he sometimes wants to carry along some warm and cherished companion. Long after the religious beliefs which led to such practices had died out, an unknown connoisseur of the French renaissance took with him to his grave eighteen antique bronze figurines which were later discovered and placed in the national collections of France. James Edward, an eighteenth-century English book collector, directed that his coffin should be made from the shelves of his library. And Harry Elkins Widener went to his death on the *Titanic* carrying in his pocket a particularly rare edition of Bacon's *Essays*, saying, just before the waters of the Atlantic engulfed them both, "Little Bacon goes with me."

Although there is on record at least one extraordinary case of murder planned and executed by a collector who could find no other means of achieving his ends, this is a trifle extreme for typical behavior. Yet the wish may exist, perhaps as impatience, if you will, that life lingers overlong with a certain rival.

Amateurs are never "detached" but always highly personal in their relationships with each other, which is one reason why they take pleasure in the discomfiture of a defeated rival and have developed, says Nobili,

> "a regular talent for flavoring bitter pills for deceived friends and comrades with troublesome innuendoes and smarting disclosures."

So it was said of Lord Hertford, founder of the Wallace Collection, that his chief joy in life was to learn that he had defeated some other great collector in the contest for a mutually desired treasure.

Even when there has been no actual battle between them, the successful collector longs to evoke the envy of his fellow-specialist before whom he is displaying his prize, and in order to accomplish this he will resort to subtle deceits and false exhibitions of modesty. "This is just a little piece I happened to pick up," he will remark casually of some particularly cherished and hard-won object, as though it were a matter of small importance, then wait with guarded eye for the harpoon to strike.

This sort of thing, however, becomes in the words of most collectors an engaging rather than an offensive quality; overtones of good-natured banter usually accompany such sallies and help to remove their sting. While the competitive angle remains strong, apparently malicious intent generally turns out to be nothing more than a sporting thrust, fully allowed for in the rules of the game: a sense of humor, a chuckle under the breath, more often than not save such encounters to the angels' side.

If further proof be needed that the "malicious" individualism of collectors has been somewhat exaggerated in literary reports, there is the fact that collectors frequently congregate among themselves. Perhaps you have never heard of the International Gourd Collectors' Society, the Clock Club, the Wedgwood Club, the National Doll and Toy Collectors' Club, the Antique Automobile Club of America, or the International Society of Collectors of Tin Soldiers—yet such organizations exist, and legions more.

A true collector would shun the most spectacular stage show in the world to attend the current meeting of his local hobby club and there listen, as critically and as absorbedly as any scientific specialist, to a paper on "Simon Willard and His Invention of the Clock Jack," or "The Evolution of Mechanical Dolls in Eighteenth-Century France." Here is one of the few places where difference in native tongue is no great barrier, since the medium of a beloved hobby becomes in itself a language easily understood by all. Differences of sex, profession and social status similarly fade away when button collectors or philatelists meet to mull over the fine points understood and cared for only by members of the same inner sanctum; and not only is this sort of thing a great pleasure to the amateurs concerned but also a profitable method of expanding each individual's knowledge of the subject at hand.

The correspondence columns of an extraordinary number of special publications and departments in scores upon scores of newspapers provide an additional means of communication. The enthusiasm for a special field which scholarship engenders thus tends to balance personal rivalry through mutual help, and collecting, though a highly individualistic activity, is certainly not without its co-operative aspects. It is even possible, upon occasion, for collectors to resolve their rivalries and help each other to success. An instance of this was given by two great bibliophiles, Huntington and Folger, at the time of the sale of the Britwell Collection when, exhibiting an extraordinary degree of forbearance and gallantry, they allowed a prize of particular rarity to be taken without a struggle by the estimable dean of book collectors of that time, William Augustus White. The prize at stake was the First Edition of Christopher Marlowe's *Hero and Leander* which, because it was unique, in magnificent condition, and because this poem contains the line, "Who ever loved that loved not at first sight," (a line quoted by Shakespeare in *As You Like It* in one of the few references the bard ever made to a contemporary author) had a tremendous importance to each of these great collectors. It will be remembered that while Huntington concentrated on English literature in general, Folger was strictly a Shakespeare specialist, and William Augustus White, a specialist in Elizabethan literature, is said to have had the greatest private collection in this field before Folger. In view of the latter's intense interest in "source and allusion" books (a field in which he was a pioneer) his sacrifice of the Marlowe was an act of almost superhuman abnegation, and it is good to know that Mr. White's family, recognizing this, allowed Folger to buy the treasure without competition after the older man's death in 1927.

In another field there were Dr. Thomas Addis Emmet and Theodorus Bailey Myers, boon companions although both were fanatical autograph enthusiasts. Emmet had the older collection, and early in their friendship Myers decided to specialize in subjects that would not conflict with the doctor's. The result was that the two men supplied each other with tips, swapped items, and enjoyed mutual benefit and pleasure from their long and close association. The end of their story held as pretty a sentiment as fiction could offer, for it came to pass that after both amateurs were gone, their two collections were placed side by side in the manuscript room of the New York Public Library, where they keep each other company to this day.

Not long ago we came upon a collecting book in which the name of a Philadelphia collector, John G. Johnson, was mentioned. Penciled in the margin next his name was the single devout comment, "A *true* collector!" —as one might exclaim, "A true artist!" or "A true saint!"

This was no mere hackneyed phrase, for collectors mean something quite definite when they use the term, and there are strict criteria by which the "true" collector may be distinguished from the inconsequential dabbler. These criteria have to do both with the collector's own attitudes and tastes and with his method of handling the collection itself. Concerning the details of these standards we shall have more to say in the next chapter, but some of the basic principles may be mentioned here.

The true collector, for instance, has nothing but scorn for the simple gatherer. He demands that any claimant to the golden title be sincerely and deeply concerned with his subject, that he be discerning and knowledgeable, as wise about what not to collect as he is about what to track down. A man who is not of this substance may, it is felt, be a collector of sorts, but he belongs to codeless *hoi polloi* rather than to the honored inner circle.

The true collector is only slightly less scornful of the wealthy dilettante who takes little or no part in the hunt himself, who instead puts all the searching and all the battling into the impersonal hands of an agent whose judgment must then prevail before the dilettante's lack of genuine knowledge. The true collector hardly envies such a man his unlimited purchasing power, for he feels that this power must, under these conditions, be exercised at the sacrifice of highly enjoyable suspense and well-merited triumph. The magnate can enter a sale room, see a table or painting he likes, and say, "I'll take it," but your true collector (in all sincerity) wonders what sport there can be in a transaction so quickly and easily consummated. The genuine trout fisherman never carries a stick of dynamite in his creel.

The outsider may be unaware that laws governing the formation and treatment of collections exist, but in almost any book written by a collector will be found sharp criticism of the would-be connoisseur who fails to conduct himself properly according to the letter of this law. How vehemently articulate collectors may be on this question was illustrated by a small tempest aired recently in one of our important national magazines. A feature entitled "Hobbies—America's Millions Express Their Ego in Profitless Fun," had just been published, and one of the hobbies discussed, inevitably, was stamp collecting.

To illustrate this particular topic the editors chose philately's most prominent exponent of the moment, Franklin Delano Roosevelt. Smilingly off guard, the President sat for the cameraman, but his mind must have been on other matters, for the picture shows two fatal mistakes which will probably dog his philatelic footsteps as long as any "true" stamp collector recalls the photograph. The disastrous view exhibited the President with two albums from his collection—and upon the open page of one he rested his elbow. In one hand he held a stamp, in the other a magnifying glass. To the ordinary observer the photograph looked like a run-of-the-mill publicity shot of only moderate interest. Not so to the stamp enthusiast. Immediately the mail began pouring in. Outraged philatelists fumed. For one thing, the President was holding a precious stamp between his fingers instead of protecting the treasure with tongs made exactly for that usage. "The merest tyro should have known better" than to commit this sacrilege.

"Fingers, no matter how clean they may seem," wrote one correspondent with just a suspicion of righteous sarcasm, "contain oil which dulls the color of the stamps."

Especially anguished were the cries of dismay which greeted Roosevelt's treatment of the album itself. How could he have permitted himself to defile the stamps on the open page by allowing his sleeve, cuff and wrist to rest upon them?

"As a graduate philatelist," wrote another devotee, "it is my privilege to take exception to President Roosevelt's method of fraternizing with this collection of rarities or otherwise. His handling of specimens, and the deliberate resting of his arm on the face of his stamps is unpardonable!"

How many political supporters were thus lost to the President? No one knows, but we may unquestionably assume that many unrelenting collectors would carry their bitterness to the polls.

Nor is this sort of thing a modern foible, limited to stamp collectors. The true collector of every age has felt that a collection worth forming at all merits respect and deserves treatment as careful as that one would accord an honored fellow being. As long ago as the eleventh century and as far away as China, our friend, Mi Fei, showed a similar consideration for his priceless collection of paintings and calligraphies. It so happened that the fame of this collection drew an unending stream of visitors to the collector's home, among them most of the greatest scholars of the day. There were, however, many persons who came inspired only by the sort of uninstructed curiosity which in our day brings thousands of sensation-seekers to the extreme modern art exhibitions. With such guests as these Mi Fei had no patience, for they neither understood nor properly respected his treasures. For this reason he divided his paintings into two series—one that might be shown to everyone, and one secretly reserved for connoisseurs.

"The reason why I kept a secret collection," he himself has told us, "was my fear that the people might touch the pictures with their fingers or brush them with their sleeves."

Our outraged philatelists might, then, have been understood by this careful Chinese, who continues with his explanation:

"Incidentally, such things happened, and I had to clean the pictures afterwards, but as the paper was quite thin, the pictures would not stand many cleanings. Anybody who touched a scroll out of curiosity brought it thus nearer to destruction."

In like manner, each of the rules set up by the modern collector has, for the most part, some good reason behind it.

Osvald Sirén, telling the story of this Chinese amateur, a thousand years dead, adds, "Nobody could make Mi Fei forget his strict principles as a collector," and, in proof, quotes further from Mi Fei's own writings:

"When Chancellor T'ang Chih-tung wanted to see my collection, I told him of my conditions. He agreed. I had two tables placed side by side and spread on them white paper and silk. I washed my hands and took out the scrolls myself from their respective cases and unrolled them for the visitor to see. He sat in front of the table with folded arms examining the scrolls with ease and care; when he said, 'Open,' I opened, and when he said, 'Roll,' I rolled. He sat there looking grand and dignified, while I ran about like a servant; and this I was willing to do in order to save my scrolls from being touched by his fingers or sleeves."

Mi Fei gave the ultimate description of the difference between a true collector and the man whom, for want of a better word, we may call dilettante.

"Yes, dilettanti * and students form two different classes of people," said Mi Fei. "To the latter may be counted those who are earnest in their love of painting, who have studied extensively . . . They have taken it into their hearts . . . What they collect is consequently of a high order. But those present-day people who possess wealth without a great love of painting, and whose am-

* Sirén's translations of the Chinese renders this word as "amateur," in the lay, rather than the collector's, sense. The distinction here intended is obviously that between dabbler and serious collector.

bition it is to pose as connoisseurs in the eyes or the ears of other people, may be called dilettanti. They place their pictures in silk bags and provide them with jade rollers as if they were the most wonderful treasures, but when they open them, one may break down with laughter!"

True collectors are those who gather paintings or books, furniture, glassware, stamps, coins, or whatever they will, not because they think that some form of collecting is expected of them, not as a perfunctory undertaking, but because they are "earnest in their love" of such things and have taken them "into their hearts." Collections formed in this spirit will be good collections, and the lives of their owners will be in many ways richer for their possession. The true collector can well afford to disregard the quips of the skeptics, for it is with him as though he had found an open sesame to happiness, and in his heart of hearts he can have only pity for those who, unlike himself, may be too blind to see the path into his enchantment.

WHAT MAKES A COLLECTION?

"So I became secretly persuaded that the value of a specialty was to learn it not in a specialized way but connectively, excursively, in its relation to the allness of things."

DONALD CULROSS PEATTIE

IN THE MADDENING WAY that dictionary-makers occasionally have of begging difficult questions, our friend Mr. Webster defines the noun "collection" as "that which is collected." True, he clarifies the matter somewhat when he adds that a collection is an "accumulation." But we have seen that the verb "to collect" may be applied to acts of accumulation as far apart in motive, in method and in result as the process mechanically performed by any physical organism when it gathers and stores chemical elements necessary for its own survival, and, at the other extreme, the conscious and at least partially volitional activity of the amateur who assembles a carefully selected series of paintings for the sheer pleasure of owning and having near him works of art he considers beautiful. Indeed, the range of activities covered by this single word is so wide that, before going on to examine in detail the make-up and characteristics of the so-called "true" collection, it may be helpful to review the distinctions between such a collection and various other types.

Let us, for the sake of convenience, think of collecting as something in the nature of a pyramid. At the broad base of the structure lie those activities which consist merely in the bringing together of a number of originally disjoined things: so stores of food may be collected, individuals may collect themselves into groups, a simpleton may collect pins, scraps of paper or bunches of lint, and, figuratively speaking, a fuddled man may collect his scattered wits. At the pyramid's narrow apex, high above the broad base, is perched that special kind of pursuit we have in mind when we say of a man that he collects Chinese jade, or illuminated manuscripts, or specimens of flowering plants from the Central Valley, and that he is an amateur, a true collector.

It is to be noted that from base to apex there is one common element, in that in each case some sort of assembling process has occurred. At the base of the pyramid no particular relationship is necessary between the individual items in the "collection," but when the term is used to define the creation of a hobbyist or scientist some such relationship is definitely implicit; that is, a system of selection is presumed to have been made in the course of the assembling process. Yet even this distinction is not in itself enough to fence off the "true" collection, for we often find selection and a unifying relationship between the individual parts of an accumulation existing at a very simple level, and selection often takes place below the level of potential mental selectivity. Thus a plant, far from being indiscriminate, "selects" only certain elements to gather up and store within its organism, while the bird who seizes upon bright stones in preference to all others is apparently exercising some form of instinctive choice. In the highest types of collecting, selection reaches its maximum, and here is evidence of man's maturity, for every true collector creates an ordered entity, endeavoring to give his collection form, meaning and value, in varying degree, within the limitations of his specialty and his own resourcefulness, and according to the capacity of his mentality and imagination.

By the restricted definition, then, an accumulation may not properly be called a collection when the assembled objects bear no intelligible relationship to each other. The man who piles his house high with junk of every description owns, in this sense, not a collection but a congeries.

Although a child busily engaged in gathering and piling up stones into as big a heap as possible may be forming a fugitive and rudimentary kind of collection, it is obvious that a much more sustained effort and far greater deliberation is demanded for the creation of a true collection. The serious collector, no matter what subject he pursues, digs deep into fields of knowledge related to his possessions, and even in the simplest ranks the true collector has curiously high standards of qualitative excellence and follows rigidly selective principles. Hence it is that an apparently insignificant collection may be as "true" and as good, from the collector's point of view, as a more obviously meaningful one.

The first two commandments of good collecting declare, in effect, that the objects contained in the accumulation should be so related that together they may be considered an entity, and that there should be an orderly arrangement which establishes this relationship of the parts to the whole and to each other.

Within this general framework, the specific rules which have been worked out for every collecting subject, no matter how trivial, provide additional standards of perfection which the good collector tries to meet; and so long as he abides by the rules which govern his particular pursuit, so long as he assembles and classifies a number of objects of a particular sort and endeavors to acquire the best specimens available, so long will he be forming a true and a good collection, whether his harvest consists of Old Masters or old whisky bottles.

No accurate compilation of all things collected is possible, but it may be of interest to record just a few of the things found among the gleanings of contemporary collectors—a faint suggestion of the adventurous variety of subjects covered; and it should be added that every one of the more unfamiliar items here listed claims a very real clan of devotees.

armor
ashtrays
antique automobiles
autographs
andirons

bandannas
bandboxes
toy banks
bells
bellpulls
bicycles
bird cages
birds' eggs
bookplates
bus tickets
buttons
butterflies
buggies

cats
canaries
early watering cans
canes
greeting cards
playing cards
chessmen
china
cigarette snuffers
cigarette lighters
clocks
coins
crime items
cuspidors
crutches
coffins

dolls
decoy ducks
drawings
dresses
dogs
daggers

fans
fish
flowers
furniture
fire engines
fossils
forceps

gags
garters
glassware
guns
golf tees
geologic specimens

handkerchiefs
hearses
hats
houses
hog kettles
holsters
hair

ink pots
ice skates
old insurance policies
cigar-store Indians

jewelry
jumping jacks
jam jars

knitting-needle holders
knickknacks
kites

leaves
lamps
lynching tokens
letter openers
laces
locks
labels

pins
pincushions
pipes
pottery
pestles
chamber pots
mountain peaks
phonograph records
paperweights
parrots
patent models

shoes
sculpture
snuffboxes
ship models
stoves
lead soldiers
samplers
stay-busks
fire screens
sugar lump souvenirs
stove plates
sea shells
saddles
streetcar transfers
signs
shaving mugs

textiles
tobacco items
thimbles
tapestries
typewriters
teeth (false and natural)
time tables
theater programs
toupees

And so on, *ad infinitum.*

It is natural enough that among collectibles we should think first of the noble things, the articles that man finds inspiring in themselves. Objects from the hands of the great, creations resulting from centuries of toil and search, the zenith of civilized effort speaking triumphantly in the language, say, of high art, the prized paintings, the sculpture, manuscripts, and those books closest to the author's hand—the collecting of these can readily be understood. And the historic objects, the numerous items associated in memory of famous names and events, the antiquities, the rare and the rich of money and the precious, the wrought gold, the gems, or the items of scientific interest, all these too go unchallenged. But when a collector is known to harbor a pile wherein value is difficult to recognize, then is the lay brow troubled and questions follow. Why does that man, who appears otherwise so sane, collect such trivia? How can he be absorbed in so childish a pastime?

Why, for instance, should a man like Stanley Baldwin collect owls? And why, on any week-end away from home, should he insist upon taking some of his defunct birds with him? Yet he is said habitually to have done just this, and similar conduct marks thousands of those who comprise collectordom. Here is something of the devotion that induced Julius Caesar to include mosaic tables in his campaign equipment, and Charles I to carry miniature copies of his favorite paintings wherever he went. But whereas a value set upon "beautiful" objects such as these can be generally appreciated, a similar devotion inspired by owls, alive or stuffed, seems to the innocent a matter of dark mystery.

Perhaps the average collector chooses his given subject in much the same way that people find friends and mates among those individuals whom chance has included in their small orbit. So a series of circumstances, coupled to personality peculiarities, has probably produced John's collection of cravat pins or Mabel's collection of telephone books. It may be that owls became Stanley Baldwin's inseparable companions in some such way as this: perhaps when Stanley was a small boy an owl seemed to him very wise, and perhaps young Stanley hoped to become very wise himself; through the prodding of Mother Superstition, the owl may have become a symbol to him. It might even have been that, for some reason or other, the bird's face reminded the child of his own; a few years later, perhaps, in the home of a local great man, he may have seen a stuffed owl; and when finally, as a promising young barrister, he was given his first stuffed owl by an admirer, what more natural than that he should have been convinced of its lucky omen. Why any man should become a collector, wanting, like Mr. Baldwin, to own not one but many owls, is another matter which we have discussed in another place. Once an avenue of interest has been opened, then owls, lead soldiers, or buttons assume ever-widening charms to their amateurs who find hidden resources in such homely objects, just as the seemingly commonplace person will, under the sympathetic warmth of friendship, gradually reveal unusual and unexpected qualities to his discoverer.

For many of the more unusual collecting interests the analyst, of course, has special explanations. Indeed, he finds hobbies of this sort easier to chart than more conventional ones, since, in collecting as elsewhere, when the beaten path is not followed the individual becomes a clearer figure. In so far as the oddity collector's status is concerned, however, he can be an amateur in as good standing as any other, depending upon his attitudes and his actions in following the rules.

To determine the characteristics of a true collection, we might start in the shanty-town of the pursuit with a visit to the string collectors who ply their occupation over a large part of the globe. It is obvious that when any and all bits of loose string are gathered and saved as a convenience and without regard to system one must refuse the name of "collection" to the pile that results. On the other hand, the man who boasts the "most varied collection of colored string in the world" (and there is such a man) is something of a collector, for he has concentrated on one particular phase of his subject—color—and has endeavored to complete a series in that category. A step beyond, we come upon a string fancier who chooses his items not only for varying colors but also for kinds of twists and plaits, for materials and size, geographic origin and period. So he might classify and arrange them for display, with labels giving their qualifications, even, perhaps, their history. In his case the general provisions of a true collection have been met, and a certain dignity found in this field which might otherwise be considered a suitable pasture for a vacuous mind obeying a sad compulsion.

Again, here is an individual (not by any means a fictitious character) whose collection is comprised of thousands of razors. He happens to be of fairly high development as a collector, since he bases his values not on quantity and simple unity of subject matter alone, but differentiates between his items, prizing most those special implements which, because they once belonged to famous persons, can be considered "association" pieces.

Although neither significance nor complexity are essential to a true collection, the collector himself, regardless of bystander opinion, usually finds something of both in his own creation. An Englishman named Hanks collects spiderwebs, and, with the true collector's emphasis on "condition," preserves each one carefully between two slabs of glass. Contrary to one's first impression, the appeal of such a subject can be multiple, for the items are not alone of potential beauty, but also difficult to obtain in a perfect state. The pleasure which this collector takes in the esthetic quality of his collection is supplemented by his sense of triumph in having met successfully a challenge to his skill and perseverance. In addition, he may, of course, be interested in spiderwebs from a naturalist's point of view, and if not, the chances are that time will find him knocking at that door, too, since the true collector's tendency is to learn as much as possible about his subject. Again, he may cherish the hope that such a collection will be unique, and if he has never heard of the similar collection displayed at a recent hobbyists' show in New York City, this hope may seem, for his purposes, fulfilled. All of these elements which are or may be of importance to him as a collector of spiderwebs—beauty, excellence of condition, a value set upon rarity or uniqueness—are among the characteristics of any standard, topflight collection.

At times, oddity in collecting appears within the confines of quite commonplace subjects. There must be thousands of people, ranging from fools to savants, who collect stones; but there are few contemporaries who, like a retired school teacher of Perry, New York, pursue that specialty which he has named "phantom mineralogy." Like the "curiosity" hunters of earlier centuries who sought for "signatures" on rock, this twentieth-century schoolman seeks pictures in stone, and he considers the prize of his collection to be a piece of Vermont marble on which can be discerned the figure of a swimming dog. In the terms of his own period this collector is not a scientist. His interest in the strange phenomena of nature is, nevertheless, the sort of curiosity from which began, centuries ago, the natural sciences. It is evidence, too, of man's perennial concern with those natural objects which, in one way or another, appear to be what they are not—pieces of wood which resemble animal forms, flowers that look like birds, butterflies with faces "painted" on their wings. The prehistoric Egyptian who gathered up stones that looked like baboons was a collector of this sort; and during the sixteenth and seventeenth centuries, "curiosities" in this category formed a major collecting hobby.

The kinds and degrees of collections to be found in the world approximate the variety in human personality. The animal kingdom was prevailed upon by Lord Walter Rothschild to yield up albino animals and birds, while the doors of N. C. Rothschild's English home welcomed a collection of thousands of fleas. So serious was this gentleman in his strange pursuit that he implored explorers to bring back specimens from their expeditions, and in time his house was satisfactorily arrayed with exhibits from all over the world. Unlike the American entomologist whose collection of lice may have been started because of a scientific interest in these unpleasant creatures, the flea fancier's interest was a queer form of amateurism, and he followed collector-rules with great scrupulousness; each item was immersed in spirits and preserved in an individual vial, carefully marked with its place of origin and with the name of the host (human or otherwise) upon whom it had been found!

Regardless of motive, over the earth's surface there is always a large army of normal, healthy, successful men and women who collect things usually associated with childhood, such as dolls, tin soldiers (this is H. G. Wells' hobby), jumping jacks, and tops. And these people, because they apply with intelligence the principles of good collecting, are able to find in their innocent subjects an intellectual stimulation that would dumbfound the uninitiate.

Some collecting hobbies belong definitely under the dark banner of the macabre; while trailing off in the distance is the borderland of aberration, that dismal territory whose inhabitants are the mentally unbalanced.

Yet normal people can be fascinated by crime, by violence, by death itself, a fact which is amply attested by the popularity of the murder-mystery tale, the magnet-like attraction of the street accident, or the world-wide interest always called forth by news of some horrendous butchery or spectacular disaster. The Cleveland Health Museum recently reported that three out of five boys and girls, writing out their comments on a current exhibition, had begun by saying: "I like the skeleton." A typical explanation amplified: "I like the skeleton. He was very ugly. I liked the bone faces they had on. The skeleton was very dead looking." Here seems to be a clue to the degree that death attracts the uninhibited young, and the adult by implication. At the scene of every airplane crackup or train wreck, at public hangings, at every lynching bee, there will be some—perhaps hundreds—who snatch for grisly mementoes, and one type of morbid souvenir hunter makes a practice of gathering as many such tokens as possible, even forming collections of them. Physicians and psychologists are aware of many curious collecting habits of this sort which are practiced in varying degrees of complexity; and there also exists a no man's land in which no rigid barrier may be discerned between an insane and a relatively sane preoccupation with the morbid and the gruesome.

Certain macabre collections have a definite interest over and beyond their immediate morbid associations, so that it would be difficult to

---

THE CHILDREN HAVE GONE, *but in their place a host of collectors have taken up the playthings of many lands. Curiously strong is the nostalgia evoked by those furnishings of childhood known to our forefathers. When pennies were big, and young Americans were schooled in thrift,* toy banks *found a ready market. Over 600 varieties were made between 1860 and 1885. The vogue is new.* Toy soldiers *are seriously collected in numerous countries. Most ancient and popular of toys now collected are* dolls. *Among businessmen and kings, queens, housewives and radio entertainers, a good doll will always find a home, from Egypt to Chicago.*

Nos. 1-5, Andrew Emerine Collection, Fostoria, Ohio. 6-11, Eleanor Hudson Welch Collection, Still River, Mass. 12, Janet P. Johl Collection, Groton, Conn.

Banks: 1) *Monkey and Coconut;* 2) *Red Riding Hood;* 3) *Merry-Go-Round;* 4) *Circus;* 5) *Liberty Bells.* Dolls: 6) *Late 17th-century, named for Anne Hutchinson;* 7) *Coronation, George VI, 1937;* 8) *French* Jumeau, c. *1870;* 9) *New England homespun, said to have witnessed Battle of Concord;* 10) *Parian;* 11) *Rubber, 1851;* 12) *Hopi Indian* Katchina. (See facing page.)

determine to what degree the morbid appeal is of prime importance and how far it may be incidental or even fortuitous. At one extreme could stand Laurence Hutton's unique collection of death masks preserved at Princeton University under the title of "Portraits in Plaster." This collection has decided value for those interested in recreating personalities of the past and was undoubtedly formed with such an end in view. One would have to know more about the little girl who systematically collected from newspaper obituaries the "ages at which people die" before one could venture upon an explanation of this cheerless occupation of childhood; but the man who made a collection of tombstones may have had any one of a number of reasonably cheerful motives for his principal interest, just as the man who collected death warrants for Salem witches was quite conceivably inspired by historical curiosity.

In Kansas City a collection of handcuffs has a nicely legitimate historical interest, with the earliest exhibit dating back to 1620. This collection, furthermore, was formed with proper attention to rules of procedure. To qualify for admission, all cuffs must have gripped the wrists of a genuine murderer, that is, they had to be association items. This rule in itself suggests something concerning the nature of the collector's basic interest, however, and it is sufficient to note that the item he doted upon most was a pair of handcuffs with which the Negro criminal who wore them had beaten his guard to death.

The most conventional collector sometimes succumbs to the seductions of the gruesome. Not so long ago the English scientist, Arnold W. Oxford, wrote a charming little volume entitled, *Notes from a Collector's Catalogue—Collecting Things in a Small Way.* Among the hobbies which he described from his own repertoire were such comparatively innocuous pastimes as the gathering of early English cookery books, carved knitting-needle holders, and stay-busks inscribed with hearts, rings, birds and other pleasantly sentimental decorations. Yet this same apparently gentle person devoted an entire chapter—also out of his personal history—to the collecting of crime items, a chapter which centered about the particularly callous English methods of dealing with criminals prior to the nineteenth century. Items in his collection included a talisman against hanging, a public whipper's bill dated 1767, some of the medals formerly issued as mementoes of notorious murderers, and a hangman's receipt for his fee. The choicest item (the history of which he describes in considerable detail) was a piece of the tanned skin of the criminal, Burke, witness to the fact that before 1813 a hanged man whose body was not redeemed by relatives might look up from hell to see sections of his especially prepared epidermis being eagerly bought by the souvenir gatherers of his day. One might skip to the conclusion that our collector was no more than a morbid souvenir hunter; but actually he deserves higher ranking, since he went about his pursuit in a businesslike way, systematically selecting his items from one well-defined period of history, studying and recording their origins and significances, and creating from them a collection of considerable interest.

With the exception of the child's collection of death dates, we have so far noted only the tangible items in the collector's potential harvest. There remains, however, the entirely distinct class of nonmaterials. The very act of gathering and remembering facts, a practice which might be called universal, is a kind of collecting, and all true collectors indulge in it as a byway to their main occupation. The stories, the legends, the bits of information concerning the objects in a collection—all these are, in a sense, added to the store itself by any amateur or connoisseur.

Although the collecting of intangibles is most often a corollary to more orthodox forms of collecting, there are many people who as collectors concentrate entirely upon the sort of item which cannot be exhibited on a cabinet shelf. At least one man is known to have read through the entire encyclopedia, attempting to cram his memory with the facts therein contained. When, at effective moments, he pulls forth items from his store, he is displaying them no less than if he were a fancier of early American glass tenderly lifting down a piece of prized "amethyst" to show it off.

Some collections of nonmaterial items may actually be translated into tangible form. The man who collects "mental quirks and lapses of celebrities" has many of his items in letter form, letters written to him in answer to his appeal for relevant data, and eventually his collection will be displayed in a book under some such title as *Absent Moments in the Lives of Significant People.* Data on, say, Siamese twins or centenarians (both actual hobbies) can be gathered from newspaper clippings, photographs or souvenirs. The hobbyist assembles and keeps these things along with transcriptions of the odd bits of information disclosed by his search, and mounts his material in an album or otherwise displays it. But though display is here introduced through visible items, such a man is primarily collecting facts of a particular sort rather than clippings, letters or photographs.

In the handling of his collection, the gatherer of intangibles follows methods identical with those employed in other forms of collecting. One New York workman, whose mind runs to figures, collects distances. When his day's work is done he dons a pedometer and starts out for some predetermined destination, and in his pocket is another recorder—his notebook—the repository of the information he gathers. He measures everything, and his items run something like this: "Walked from Home to World's Fair (9 miles) 2 hours, 45 minutes"; or "Walked from Home to Empire State Building (7½ miles) 2 hours." City spots are of interest to him in proportion to their uncommonness. In his notebook he has written where one may find New York's oldest grave, its oldest tree, its most ancient house; where to go to see the last surviving gas lamp, and a hayloft in the heart of the metropolis; which is the shortest street, and the location of a spot where six thoroughfares meet. He visited the World's Fair until he had been in every building, until he had sat at every bar, until he had been in every free moving picture show, and he recorded the number of each. He even put down the number of pairs of socks ruined in this ordeal. Although driven, perhaps, by some relentless compulsion, there is surely something of the collector in this man, the sort of collector who delights especially in classification and whose goal is the "complete" series.

Indianapolis is the home of a man whose hobby is collecting odd names. On the face of it, this sounds like a limited occupation, and it is hard to see how one could do much to organize the results of one's research on such a subject. However, the gentleman in question has been busy with his pursuit since 1895, and by 1939 he had accumulated one thousand seven hundred items—all entered on cards and carefully classified according to subject, that is, people with names representing colors, occupations, birds, flowers, nationalities and many more (a type of classification, by the way, exactly like that used by many stamp collectors). "Peatsch" and "Bertsch" are a couple of his "trees." "Pflasterer" is one of his "occupations." Two of his shortest items belong to a Mrs. Ek and a Mr. Ge. And there are long ones, of course, like Pappageorgekooplos. Here is a good instance of the scientific root struggling in profitless soil, of the collector whose collection is for him sufficiently amusing or interesting in itself and who, enjoying such mental exercise as the cultivation of his hobby affords, does not demand that his tree put forth fruit for others than himself. On the other hand, another possibly more serious collector, H. L. Mencken, who has approached a similar subject from the scientific point of view, has been able to make his interest in strange given names valuable to students of language, and to himself in dividends from books and articles.

Occasionally the collector of ideas and symbolic abstractions may be impelled to his pursuit by the need to find an outlet for unrealizable desires—as, if we care to believe the psychoanalysts, the collector of certain types of "symbolic" objects finds in them an expression for his individual frustration. An example of apparent simplicity is the lad on Long Island who collects the names of railway lines and the numbers on railroad engines. It has been suggested that this child, who admits a wishful preference for mountains rather than the sea, longs to travel on the trains which daily pass his home; that he is really collecting the places to which those trains go and of which, in real life, he can only dream. Something of a similar nature enters into vast numbers of those stamp collections whose makers focus their attention upon the ships, planes, or foreign scenes portrayed on their items.

At least one adult collector of picture post cards has analyzed his own hobby in terms much like those used by the psychologist to explain the child's interest in train names. "What I really collect is places, not cards," says this man, who adds that he is helping to preserve a record of the scenes represented in his collection since certain features of any specific scene are in time likely to be altered, after which they can be remembered or reconstructed only by means of pictures. Thus our post card amateur catches a ride, for a little distance, on the train of scholarly endeavor, lending, thereby, added significance to his humble collection. And since he is an Englishman whose collection was in the making long before 1939, he has, if he has been able to preserve his pictorial record of places, performed a service even more valuable than he himself expected it to be.

General collections were once far more common than they are today, for the intensive use of specialization among collectors has paralleled the similar development, also relatively late, in the various fields of scholarship and science. As knowledge increases the chosen field becomes broader, until no one man could cultivate it all. True, in collecting the indiscriminate will probably always exist; but in an era of growing enlightenment and adulthood the magpies are recruited chiefly either from the ranks of children and simpletons, or from the abnormal misers and hoarders, although we must include those who are adult except in their childish collecting habits.

Wanting his collection to have meaning and to be, as nearly as possible, complete, the collector comes to realize in the very process of collecting that it might easily be a lifetime job, for example, to try to gather one good example of every sort of penny bank ever made, or to complete a series in a single rare pattern of glassware. So as one part of his collection begins to take shape and to command his special interest, he is prone to pare away other parts.

A child collects natural history specimens. He catches butterflies and mounts them. Moths and other insects fall prey to his net. He presses flowers and makes a herbarium; leaves and ferns are included. A shelf of stones in his room will glady receive a snake skin or a snail shell. Perhaps all this is a passing fancy, destined to blow away on the wind of his adolescence; but perhaps his early interest continues and develops, and he begins really to study his specimens. Then he learns that there are more than 450,000 known species of insects in the world, that at least 80,000 species of butterflies and moths have been described and that more than 9,000 of these are to be found in America north of Mexico. Figures of rival immensity will stagger him in the other categories of his collection as well. How hopeless a task to continue an unlimited gathering! Butterflies alone, or moths, or stones will keep him busy for a long time to come. And so, if he does not give up, he will select that phase of his hobby which interests him most, and he will give the rest of his specimens away, or swap them, or they will rest under attic dust until some day his own little Willy finds them. The child now grown has become a specialist, a true collector, who, if circumstances had been slightly different, might have turned into a scientist like the young collector whose name was Darwin.

There is one purely physical reason for specializing and it is to be found in the realistic consideration of *Lebensraum.* The collector will not have room in his house for an unlimited number of objects, and while it is true that the specialized collection is not necessarily small, at least it is easier to control than a heterogeneous accumulation to which anything of passing interest may be added under the sway of temptation.

Moreover, few collectors will have money enough to pay for an endless number and variety of acquisitions, unless the hobby be of a sort which entails very little expense. Even when funds are no object, however, the modern collector will probably limit his activities if for no other reason than that otherwise his collection would command scant consideration among the elite. Even the so-called "eclectic" (who is usually wealthy—a Morgan, a Walters, a Marquess of Hertford) is actually a specialist within certain broad but well-defined limits. He may form a collection which includes such various classes as paintings, sculpture, porcelains, jewelry, furniture, books and manuscripts, but with them he will not mingle a miscellany of match-clips, post cards, sea shells, sticks and stones, for in almost every case he collects only objects of accepted intrinsic value, and those possessed of a promised esthetic, historic or scientific interest. Furthermore, he usually subdivides such an "eclectic" collection into a number of distinct groups, so that the whole becomes a collection of collections, with each of its component parts devoted to a single subject. Thus within the remarkable Walters collection of paintings, there is one of the best collections of Italian primitives in America.

The everyday collector, man of moderate means, is, perforce, less likely to spread himself. He it is who most often becomes a specialist among specialists, and one important reason is that he can circumvent the power of money through the very distinction achievable in his own niche.

One of the major reasons for a limited field is the possibility of achieving a complete series. Of equal importance to the true collector is the historical interest of his items, the gathering of facts concerning their origin and previous uses, and the understanding of those qualities which determine their excellences or shortcomings. If he becomes a specialist, he may, like one philatelist, have so much to say about a single stamp that two books are required to publish the information; or be like Dr. Charles Francis Brown who combed the world for his collection of one thousand five hundred lamps which illustrate the history of lighting from prehistoric to modern times, and who states that one volume apiece would barely suffice to explain his items.

The collecting world is full of those who prey upon unsuspecting or ill-informed acquisitors, and the collector who has failed to make himself at least something of an authority is a lamb among those wolves—the fakers, the forgers, the unscrupulous vendors—to whom a later chapter of this book is devoted. But if he concentrates, perhaps, on early American or eighteenth-century furniture, he will learn to recognize the marks of authenticity, the shapes, the woods, the "points" that are to be expected. The more he studies his specialty, the less likely he is either to be fooled by those individuals who set out to capitalize on his weakness or to be betrayed by impulse.

There are endless divisions whereby a collector may specialize, but here is a notion of the way of it: subject, period, class, object, or material, size, shape or color, and on down the scale to minutiae never dreamed of by the non-collector. Nor is this the end, for within the framework of each of these relative generalities, the collector may develop innumerable subspecialties, each an outgrowth of his original choice.

Is he steeped in ships, or chess, wines, or tea, the history of a particular locality, or some such subject as the evolution of writing? Very well, for him the world will be an amateur's cornucopia and he will find items of immense variety everywhere ready for the plucking. Thus the ship lover is obviously drawn to models of every kind of craft or of vessels famous in history; but he may also collect drawings, paintings, etchings and prints having to do with maritime history. Books dealing with his subject will fall within his province, and so will souvenirs of the sea. He may collect sailors' uniforms, anchors, flags, or those curious objects which sailors used to make during long voyages. He may find nectar in log books, bills of lading, or autograph letters and documents. Probably he will not attempt all of these things, but, God help him, he may.

On the wings of his favorite brew the western tea fancier travels, literally or figuratively, to China and Japan, picking up as he goes color prints that portray various aspects of the tea ceremony. Among the libraries of the world he wanders, studies the habits and customs of tea drinkers everywhere, and gathers "everything anyone has ever known or printed about tea." He discovers the fine points about tea caddies and tea cosies, teacups, teapots, tea bowls, tea glasses and teaspoons, tea tables and tea chests. A special collection of antique furniture, silver, porcelain, or curios may be assembled in which each item will have some association with tea.

"Parisians collect wines as others collect postage stamps," wrote G. Selmer Fougner of the good old days; and in more limited numbers men of other nationalities have done likewise. It was an Englishman, George Saintsbury, who, in his *Notes on a Cellar-Book,* wrote a minor classic on this subject; and while Saintsbury's interest, if one is to judge by this work, was focused largely upon the gustatory qualities of various vintages, he tells us that an important part of his hobby was the study of "wine and its fellows" in their "innumerable and world-ranging associations, in life and literature, in history and society." Interest of this sort often leads the wine specialist far from the bottle and its liquid contents. He may be fascinated by the histories of communities which produce the best wines; by the origins and development of different grapes, the methods of culture, or the processes and tools used in creating his chosen nectar. Containers and recipes, beverage promotion literature, "protocol," and legal regulation all fall within his province. Literature which touches upon his subject becomes essential to him, and lo, there is yet another book collector among us—a specialist, of course. So the amateur of wines may come to possess, in addition to his beautiful cellar, whole collections not only of books but of bottles, casks, drinking glasses, pictures, maps, even advertisements, menus or revenue stamps, all related to his central theme.

Many collectors, however, are content with the simpler task of assembling one specific kind of object. In early New York, they say, General Vandamme had sixty thousand pipes. Or it may be pitchers, boot-

---

SOME CATEGORIES OF THE SPECIALIST. *1) Many collectors concentrate on* object and material; *American pressed-glass footwear (opposite), sometimes known as "early Woolworth." 2)* Size, material and national origin: *miniature silver whisky still, fully hallmarked, a unique work of the famous 17th-century English silversmith, George Middleton. 3) The* association *appeal is universal, and when it is joined by a fine material, well-designed and executed, plus good condition, a great item may emerge. Longfellow's midnight rider is, surprisingly perhaps, the same Paul Revere who turned out this elegantly fashioned tea set. The story of the set, which bears the patriot silversmith's mark (bottom of pot) is told in the inscription: "To Edmund Hartt Constructor of the Frigate BOSTON. Presented by a number of his fellow citizens, as a memorial of their sense of his Ability, Zeal and Fidelity in the completion of that Ornament of the AMERICAN NAVY, 1799."*

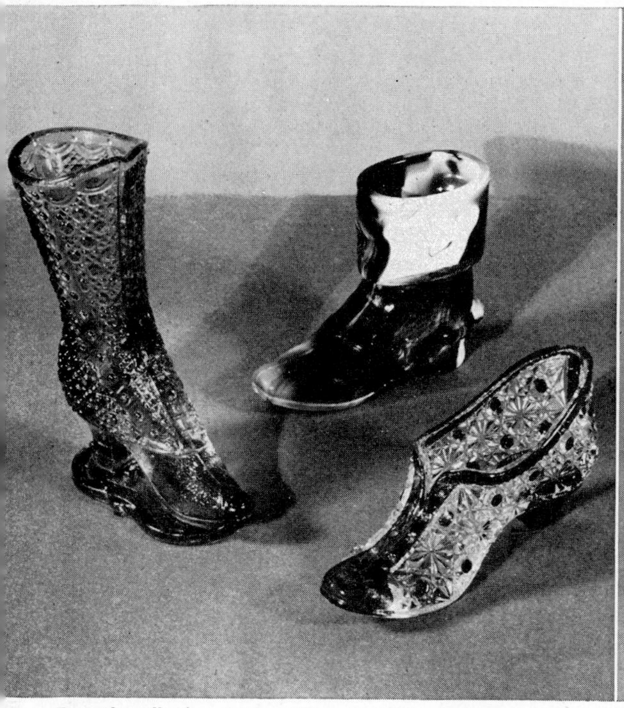

From the collection of Mrs. William R. Butler, Pelham, N. Y.

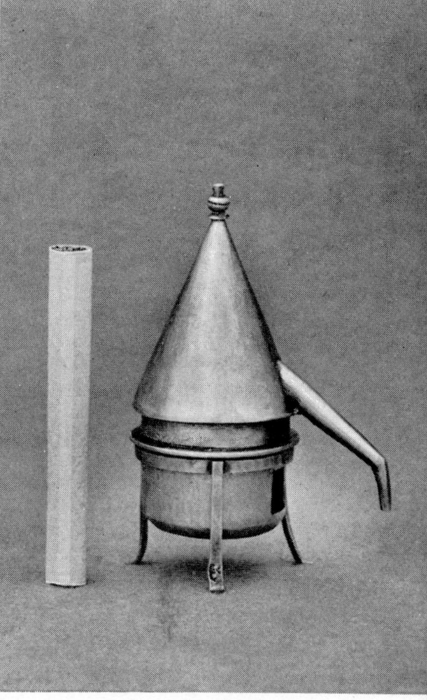

From the collection of Mr. & Mrs. Joseph M. May, New York

(*See facing page.*)

Museum of Fine Arts, Boston

jacks, paperweights or glass slippers. Within the confines of some larger specialty, "object" collections may be merely subspecialties, as when an antique collector assembles a series of chairs, another of candlesticks, and still another of doorstops, all falling within some particular period in history. On the other hand, the object collection can be a fully developed specialty in its own right, with numerous subdivisions. So a pipe collector may want oriental pipes only, or be inclined toward those made of some specific material or those characteristic of a single period or a single land.

Another type of specialty depends chiefly upon size for its focus, and this, too, can be the narrowing down of a wider category or the expansion of one originally restricted. The book collector may decide to concentrate only upon miniature or upon oversized volumes. More often the size itself constitutes the original appeal and in many cases it remains the chief criterion of this sort of collection.

"Books are the most dangerous things to collect, unless one collects with a method," writes A. W. Oxford; and book collectors, in sheer self-protection, have developed a fantastic number of specialties. Perhaps most obvious is specialization by subject. A book collector may harvest only old cookbooks, or children's books, bibles, books on sports, fifteenth- and sixteenth-century books on lacemaking, illustrated books on fans, books on tobacco, early Italian disquisitions on philology, old law books, old books on the early navigators of the Mediterranean—in short, books on any obscure or commonplace subject, mentionable and unmentionable.

Yet subject is only one avenue of approach here. Some book collectors specialize in the works of a particular author, others in the volumes issued from one of the famous early presses—Aldine books, Caxton books, Pynson books. Some specialize in fine bindings, others in illustrated volumes. They want the jeweled and carved ivory bindings of the tenth, eleventh and twelfth centuries, or early Gothic bindings in carved wood. They want mosaic bindings and armorial bindings, Grolier bindings and Maioli bindings. They want illustrations by Cruikshank or Picasso. Many specialize in first editions, old or new; or in the association items, volumes that have belonged to famous or admired individuals, annotated books, or presentation books, as the collectors of musical instruments sometimes want the very instruments which the maestri used. Some bookmen collect sale catalogues, and some pamphlets. Many correlate one or more of these specialties about a particular subject, author, or period. And then there are the "extra-illustrators" or "Grangerizers" (so-called from a famous follower of this hobby) who, by adding pictures and autograph letters to their books, sometimes turn a single volume into ten ponderous tomes.

Stamp collecting is eminently suited to be a specialist's bailiwick. To many people a stamp is an annoying necessity, something seldom at hand when most urgently needed, but to the collector a stamp may represent an entire universe, as his specialties prove. Your garden variety of stamp collector is likely to concentrate on a single subject, country or period; yet that is but the first step down a path tortuous with possibilities. Here, for example, is Colonel Charles Robert Morris who assembles and classifies his stamps in accordance with the subjects portrayed on the postal paper. Following a well-established method of library classification he begins with nine main divisions, which are:

General
Human Beings
Human Activities
Human Creations
Nature
Transportation
Scenery
Intellect
Miscellaneous

Each of these he divides into smaller classifications. For example, under *Human Beings* he lists:

Rulers
Political
Professional
Arts and Letters
Military and Naval
Science and Invention
Exploration and Discovery
Social Workers
Miscellaneous

Continuing with this process, he further subdivides *Professionals* (to take but one of his groups) into:

Theological
Medical
Legal

And the *Theological* category includes:

Ministers and Priests
Saints
Madonnas
Monks
Nuns

Be assured that there are stamps for all of these headings. His full classification code includes, under the 9 main heads, 48 subheads; and under these, 107 sub-subheads; and under these, a further division of 47 sub-sub-subheads; and under these, 21 sub-sub-sub-subheads—*making a total of 184 actual subjects,* not including the subdivisions of *Rulers* under the main head *Human Beings,* because Colonel Morris divides *Rulers* by *Countries,* thus making possible as many more sub-subheads as there are stamp-issuing nations. Within this maze of subject matter there are topics for all sorts of specialists, for those who are interested in autographs, or airplanes, horses, architecture, agriculture, symbolism or mythology, since one may form "topical stamp collections" illustrative of all these subjects and a great many more.

Suppose, however, that a collector specializes by country—in United States stamps. To him subject is of less interest than many other special considerations. Yet he, too, may find in his collection an outlet for non-philatelic predilections. Thus if he likes adventure and romance he may choose to acquire only stamps issued by the Confederacy, and he need not be overly imaginative to sense the full quota of drama in his eloquent items—stamps stuck to the envelopes with molasses or sewed on because no glue was available, envelopes turned inside out and used twice because of the scarcity of paper, or perhaps, if he is lucky, an envelope bearing General Lee's autograph.

If at heart the collector of United States items is also an historian, he may want the stamps of the local posts—those stamps which preceded the first Federal issue in 1847 and which were not entirely suppressed until 1894. Or he may become interested in Match and Medicine stamps —revenue stamps issued from private dies between 1862 and 1883 and known among philatelists as "M and M's." Both these hobbies will challenge his ingenuity and perhaps his purse, for examples are quite often rare. If his resources are limited, however, he can choose a more modern development and specialize in Air Post stamps which date, in the United States, from 1918. Within this field he may further specialize in envelopes ("covers" in the stamp collector's jargon) that have been flown, a fact provable by special markings. Or, as in every other field, he may concentrate upon the association item, like the collectors who search only for stamps having some bearing upon the career of Charles A. Lindbergh.

Specialists in "covers," "cancellations" and "postmarks" are legion, and each may develop some particular phase of his particular field. Covers portray the use of stamps in different periods, and in many instances provide revealing sidelights on the historical background. Among cover specialties, for instance, there are government post cards, private post cards, wrappers for circulars and printed matter, even fragments of parcel post packages to be gathered, each forming a minute specialty in its own right. First-day mailings (envelopes mailed on the first day the stamp was issued, and postmarked from the place where the issue was first put on sale) enjoy wide popularity today. Some collectors build cover collections around some chosen subject; for example, a series relating to all the wars in which the United States has been involved. Free and franked covers constitute still another specialty, and some of these include the appeal of the association item, since they may bear the autographed franks of presidents, presidents' widows and other distinguished persons. For other philatelists there is a fascination in old envelopes with curious return cards, known as "illuminated and fancy illustrated covers."

Just as there are aeronautic cover specialists, so there are naval specialists, for many American naval vessels have post offices on board. Cancellations of letters mailed aboard ship often show the port of call, and the naval post specialist may be interested in obtaining as wide a variety of ports as possible; or again he may choose to build a series consisting of at least one "cancel" from each ship in the United States fleet. Similarly, landlubbers among philatelists often specialize in town cancellations, the aim again being to acquire cancellations of geographic versatility. To achieve his purpose such a collector inserts a self-addressed post card or envelope in another envelope addressed to the postmaster in the desired town, and includes a money order and a letter requesting the postmaster to mail back the enclosure properly stamped and canceled. It sounds a bit dull and simple enough, but listen to what one authority on this hobby, Desmond D. Jagyi, has to say:

"Collecting cancellations is more interesting and cheaper than collecting stamps, although in a sense all cancellation collectors are 'stamp collectors.' However, there is a difference. . . . An empty space in an album [stamp album] can usually be filled, if the collector possesses the money necessary to purchase the item. In collecting cancellations, rich and poor are more or less equal. Skill counts, not money, which, in this case, means very little as compared with alertness and knowledge. Your ability to coax the mail clerk into giving you a certain type of cancel and your luck in receiving a nice clear distinct cancel or postmark make the hobby interesting."

Which proves not only that there is no disputing tastes, but also that even the humblest collector can find an important degree of personal satisfaction in his specialty.

Cancellation collecting is, however, capable of being developed into a field of unimaginable complexity and may include subspecialties and sub-sub-subspecialties. Among these are the precanceled stamps (known in the family as "precancels") which are stamps issued under special conditions or by special permit and canceled at a local post office before being used. A whole set of rules governs their collection, and specialists find endless variations to pursue within this apparently quite limited territory. The typical evolution of a collector-specialist is described by one precancel amateur, Stephen D. Rich, when he says:

"We all start as general collectors. Most of us soon limit ourselves to U. S. precancels, and then center on one issue, one state, one city, or one type of precanceling interest."

Nor is this all. There are, for example, precancel collectors who further specialize in "Bureau Print Precancels" (government-issued for use in a particular post office). And when such a specialist has acquired one fine copy of each Bureau Print, he can try for those items which he calls "block" and "coil" pairs, or for the further subdivisions known as "line" pairs, "gap" pairs, and "line-gap" pairs.

Even as the general cancellation collector feels himself superior in many ways to the general stamp collector, so the precancel collector believes himself to be in a better position than the general cancellation collector. This sort of fellow can make from a single denomination—say a two-cent stamp—an entire collection by gathering one example from every post office which has precanceled it! He says that his advantage over the general cancellation collector lies in the fact that most of the cancellations he obtains are "really legible and usually fairly well-centered on the stamp." Now it so happens that these are considerations of the utmost importance to any good stamp collector, whatever his specialty, but the precancellist is so enamored of his particular field that he is inclined to dismiss every other phase of philately as being "merely accumulated wall paper."

Stamp collectors specialize also in a category so apparently humdrum as metered mail; or in slogan postmarks packed with terse command and information—"Air Mail Saves Time," "Mail Early for Christmas," "Address Your Mail to Street and Number." Or at the other extreme they pay learned respect to highly intricate and technical subjects such as "The Plating of United States Stamps" or "Color Research in Philately," and turn out treatises as scientifically worded as a chemistry book and as difficult for the lay mind to fathom as an Einsteinian ocean.

Each of the stamp specialties has its local, national or international organization in which the brothers may gather with others who speak their own special language. To illustrate, there are, in addition to the many general stamp collectors' clubs, a Precancel Catalog Association and a Precancel Stamp Society, a Bureau Issues Association, an American Air Mail Society and an International Air Mail Society, a Universal Ship Cancellation Society, an International Slogan Postmark Society, and many more of the same highly specialized nature. There are even organizations, like the Netherlands Collector Philately Club of the United States, which require applicants to pass an examination before being admitted to membership.

As the scientist must organize his material and manipulate his specimens with the utmost care, so some collector-rules have to do with the arrangement and handling of items, for the amateur believes that an object worth collecting at all is worthy of a high degree of respect. The purpose of certain other rules of collecting, also as in science, is to establish a method of procedure that will eliminate error and make it possible to achieve interpretable results. And the system of "points" which regulates any given hobby has the additional practical importance of fixing uniform standards of quality and recognizable criteria of value for the entire field. In its reasons for being and in its effects, then, this system is not very different from the laws, written and unwritten, which govern most competitive activities from sports to international trade.

To follow the rules often involves acquiring special knowledge (quite aside from the collector's normal curiosity about his items) and requires of the amateur that he seek out certain details as zealously as any student preparing for his doctorate; but with the amateur, as with the student, this emphasis on minutiae can and sometimes does over-

Lillian Smith Albert Collection, Hightstown, N. J.

Notable for beauty and historical interest are these Washington Inauguration Buttons. Those with eagles, dated March 4, 1789, were made for his first inauguration; those inscribed "Long Live the President" are thought to have been for his second.

BASEBALL, BATS AND DIAMOND, *Waterbury, Conn.*

HEART, *Waterbury, Conn.*

LINCOLN HEAD

ELEPHANT, *Waterbury, Conn.*

Philatelic Research Laboratories, Inc.

Between 1847 and 1869 American postmasters and postal clerks were privileged to adopt any canceling device they chose and carved out a wealth of individual designs. All examples above on U. S. 1861 stamps.

shadow the broader aspects of the subject involved. As the bibliophile, Barton Currie, has said of his kind,

"Once we have the formula we abide by it with a fanaticism compared with which the faith of the worshipers of Mohammed is a feeble exhibition."

To begin with the field of autograph collecting. Here we find at the outset two distinct types of collectors: 1—those who seek items with some claim to literary or historic significance (manuscripts, letters and signed documents) and who rank with bibliophiles and art collectors in the potential value of their contributions; 2—those who are interested in detached signatures (usually, though not always, of contemporary celebrities) and who are little more than souvenir hunters.

The "serious" autograph collector has only scorn for members of the second group, to whom he applies, with considerable justice, epithets such as "scourge of the heroes of the front page," "autograph hound," "fiend" and "pest." Yet it must be admitted that even the signature hunters follow certain rudimentary principles. In the nineteen-thirties they had an "Autograph Guild" and through this society they worked out the best methods of bagging their prey. When they can be obtained, autographed pictures, books, programs and so on are preferred by these hobbyists to plain cards or album sheets, and the careful collector in this field tries to have his own name included in the inscription so that the authenticity of his item may be demonstrated.

Such trivial distinctions as these are, however, a poor substitute for the fine points, based largely upon significance and authenticity, pursued by the true autograph collector. To him a detached signature is the lowliest item in his possible harvest, desirable only when nothing better is available to complete a series. This gentleman recognizes at least five separate classes of autographs, and for each he has a cryptic symbol. These are, in order of value:

MS.—*manuscript*—a copy of a book, poem, play etc. in the handwriting of the author;

A.L.S.—*autograph letter signed*—an entire letter in the handwriting of the person who signed it;

L.S.—*letter signed*—which means that the body of the letter is in the handwriting of some other person than the signer;

A.D.S.—*autograph document signed*—a legal, commercial or historical document entirely in the handwriting of the signer;

D.S.—*document signed*—a document which, like the "letter signed," contains only the signature of the person in whom the collector is interested.

Even the L.S. and the D.S. are more highly valued by the good collector than a detached signature, for the latter is of interest only as a sample of handwriting, whereas letters and documents usually contain some information relevant to the history of the person or subject around which the collection is being built.

"How many people have clipped signatures from old letters and documents under the mistaken notion that they are collecting autographs," A. E. Newton once wrote in dismay at the ignorance of the clipper. To a bibliophile such conduct is little short of sacrilege, particularly if a book is so vandalized, for a valuable association item is thus destroyed. Nor is it in accordance with the autograph collector's Hoyle to clip signatures, although such signatures already clipped may be accepted if they happen to supply the only available examples of their kind. There are a dozen or so known signatures of Thomas Lynch, Jr. (one of the two "rarest" signers of the Declaration of Independence) which two of his nieces once cut from some of his books. Good autograph collectors would be much happier had those signatures been left in their original positions, but *faute de mieux* builders of "Signer Sets" today are very glad indeed to get their hands on one of them.

The building of sets is one of the most popular specialties of the autograph collector. A "set" is a series of autographs all having to do with some central theme—the Declaration of Independence, for example. The set-builder may seek examples of the handwritings of all the Presidents of the United States, of all members of all the cabinets from Washington's day to our own, or any such series as his ingenuity can contrive. In doing this, however, he is not content with just any specimen which happens to fit into his scheme.

Completeness is only one criterion, even to the set-builder; and rarity, while it sends the price of an item sky-high and makes it desirable from a competitive point of view, can only partially compensate the collector for lack of significance. Of course, even the connoisseur has his human weaknesses. He may succumb to the attractions of mere rarity at times, or renounce his stricter principles in order to complete a set; but basically he wants his items to be of a sort that will cast an unusual or intimate light upon the subject of his study, and his first principle is relevance. In this latter connection, the collector of "Signer" autographs values most a letter written during the actual year of the signing of the Declaration, particularly if the letter makes some reference to that document; and next most desirable in his eyes is a letter dated during one of the Revolutionary years.

Personal preferences aside, definite principles of this sort when agreed upon throughout a collecting field make it easier for the collector to judge of the desirability of any item; but even specialists—often still in the process of determining what the laws of their field are to be—do not always manage to agree on the finer points. Two autograph collectors, one American and one English, once carried on an amusing feud in the pages of their successive books on such questions as the merits or demerits of "extra-illustration" and the proper method of handling and arranging items. It was a very polite little feud, but deadly intention lurked behind each pointed sally, and, reading between the lines, one could not escape the conviction that the disputants, for all their urbanity and gentle humor, were as bent upon proving their respective points as a pair of rival attorneys in a *cause célèbre.*

"Chairs have points to those who know, same as horses," writes C. R. Clifford, and so have old glass, coins, rugs, books, etchings and pewter. To express such points a set of words has grown up in each collecting field and these words constitute a unique and extraordinary terminology. On stamp collecting alone one book includes in its glossary at least ninety terms that are either entirely incomprehensible to the layman or require explanation because they are used by philatelists in some special sense; and there is a *Glossary of Terms Compiled for the Philatelic Congress of Great Britain* (London, 1933) which contains about five hundred such special definitions.

Book collecting is a subject fairly familiar to us all, and most people think they know the meaning of "first edition"; but how many, outside of publishers, dealers and collectors, understand the differences between an "edition," an "impression," an "issue" and a "state"?

Actually, an "edition" consists of all the copies of a book printed from one setting of type. When the type is reset, a second, or third, or fourth edition has been issued. But there may be several printings from the same type at different times, and these are called first, second or third "impressions." Under such circumstances, "first impression" and "first edition" are synonymous terms, but there may be a second impression of a first edition. An "issue" consists of all the copies of an edition which have been put on the market at the same time; and there may be several issues of the same edition, as well as several impressions. The issues are distinguished from each other by individual corrections of misprints, or changes in text or make-up made without a complete resetting of the type, and separate issues are often further distinguished from each other by different bindings. When corrections are made without a complete resetting of type, but all copies are put on the market simultaneously, an edition of a book is said to exist in several "states" rather than issues. Each of these distinctions is of tremendous importance to the specializing book collector, who must check each prospective item for specific and often minute points before he can be sure that it is "right." No wonder he sometimes has that faraway look in his eye.

The collecting of first editions might seem to be a simple enough procedure, but actually it presents innumerable complications. For example, a popular variation on the hobby is known as "following the flag." A first-edition collector who follows the flag desires that first edition of an author's work which was *first published in the author's native land,* even though the true first edition may have been published elsewhere. Thus the first English edition of Galsworthy's *The Forsyte Saga* may command a higher price than the true first edition, because the latter was published in the United States. Similarly the first American edition of Mark Twain's *Huckleberry Finn,* dated 1885, is considered far more valuable than the English edition which preceded it by several days and which bears the date 1884. Nor is this all, for there were two first American editions issued simultaneously in different colored bindings. The blue-bound edition, issued for subscription sale, is rarer than the green-bound trade edition, and commands a premium of about three hundred per cent.

All other things being equal, however, the *earliest date line* in a book is of paramount importance. Some famous books now widely collected went to press during the last week in December of a particular year, but the entire first edition was not printed during that week. The publishers, wishing to make the book sound more up to date, changed the date on the remaining copies to fit the New Year. There may have been only a few hours difference between the printing of one copy bearing the date 1865 and another dated 1866, yet collectors today (reversing the criterion of value that governed the original publisher) will pay a small fortune for the earlier copy and let the latter go begging.

Minute *variations in text* often have a similar effect upon the value of a book. One of the most famous cases concerns the first edition of the Authorized Version of the Bible, printed in London in 1611. There were two issues in that year, now known as the "HE" and the "SHE" because of a single error in the Book of Ruth (III, 5) which was corrected in the second printing. The first version read, "He went into the citie . . ." and this was later changed to "She went into the citie. . . ." The change of this one word enables collectors to tell the difference between the first and second issues, and the "HE" Bible is therefore worth a great deal more than the "SHE." In the same way, Gray's famous *Elegy* was first published as having been *Wrote in a Country Church Yard.* A second issue, printed in the same year, changed the word "wrote" to "written," and that grammatical change for the better today worsens the second issue by several thousand dollars compared to the value of the first.

A *suppressed "first state"* of a first edition is likely to become particularly rare and hence to command a high price; while a "presentation copy" of a first edition (one bearing a dedicatory inscription) is desirable for reasons of sentiment. Books originally published in parts present special problems:

> "There is no written word that will help you accurately to establish all the points that all the Dickens firsts in original parts should possess," writes Barton Currie. "After half a century of research, there is still a wide difference of opinion . . . I have listened to some wranglings on this subject that verged on violence."

In the first place (to take one of the simpler points) such books, which were issued serially between paper covers, should not be rebound. We once acquired—in all innocence and great excitement—a first edition of Dickens' *Dombey and Son,* handsomely bound in leather and with all the individual title pages and advertisements which the parts had contained carefully deleted! We cherished the book for years, and still do (as an object lesson), but today we know that no self-respecting collector would look at it twice.

This is because of the importance of *mint condition.* A book in "mint condition" is one that remains exactly as it was on the day of publication. If it has been in any way doctored, restored, altered or damaged, if even so much as a missing blank end-paper has been inserted, a volume cannot be said to meet this specification. A. E. Newton tells us of books published in parts that:

"In order to take high rank it is necessary that each part should be clean and perfect and should have the correct imprint and date; it should have the proper number of illustrations by the right artist; and these plates must be original and not re-etched, and almost every plate has certain peculiarities which will mislead the unwary. But this is not all. Each part carried certain announcements and advertisements. These must be carefully looked to, for they are of the utmost value in determining whether it be an early or a later issue of the first edition. An advertisement of 'Rowland and Son's Toilet Preparations' where 'Simpson's Pills' should be, might lead to painful discussion."

Size is another question of importance to collectors of certain types of books, and the implications of this point go far beyond the mere fact of a volume's being of miniature or oversized proportions. The serious book collector, when he comes to consider size, measures his volumes to the sixteenth of an inch, and a tiny variation may make all the difference between a "right" and a "wrong" item. Some books were issued both in "large paper" and in "small paper" editions; and when, as was usually the case, the former was intended for special subscribers, the "large paper" issue has become the scarcer of the two and hence the most valuable.

Even a variation in the *color of end papers* may make a difference; while the *kind of binding* and its condition often has to be taken into consideration. It is important to know, for instance, that before the eighteen-thirties books were bound in boards, after that in cloth. The color of the binding, the blocking, printing or stamping on the cover and spine, the kind and condition of the labels, are all carefully studied by the serious collector. In some cases it is even important whether the binding be rough or smooth; and often it is essential that the original dust covers should have been preserved. "In original boards uncut" is a frequently seen piece of book-collector's jargon; the last word in the phrase meaning, not as the layman might suppose that the book is uncut in the sense of being unopened (of having the pages unseparated one from another), but rather that the outer edges of the leaves have not been trimmed at any time since leaving the printer.

Huntington Library, San Marino, Cal.

The "Palmer-Nash" copy (above) is unique in being the only known First Edition of Pilgrim's Progress *containing the portrait frontispiece of Bunyan, the Dreamer, and the only copy of any edition in which "Vanity" rather than "Destruction" appears as the name of the city from which Pilgrim can be seen fleeing.*

Collecting "association volumes" is another hobby popular among bibliophiles, and here too several different categories are recognized. In addition to first-edition "presentation copies" a collector may be interested in any volume that has been annotated by the author or by some famous former owner, or in those which, having once belonged to famous persons, still contain the distinguishing autograph or bookplate. One of the supplementary attractions of collecting association volumes lies in the fact that each such item is of necessity a *unique* one.

Modern publishers have often capitalized upon the book collector's desire for signed copies as well as upon his desire for first editions. Thus it has become common practice to issue "signed and limited" first editions (often on rag paper) along with or just before the "first trade" editions of authors popular among collectors. In some cases there have been four first editions:

1—an American edition, signed and limited
2—an American trade edition
3—an English edition, signed and limited
4—an English trade edition

Under such circumstances the baffled collector, uncertain which will eventually be considered the most desirable, sometimes rushes to secure all four. After a few such experiences, however, he is likely to feel that he is caught in a shell game and may back away to look for another specialty.

The study and collection of stamps is another pursuit of incredible complexity when seriously pursued. There are nearly a score of elements which the philatelist may find himself required to consider, including such things as:

size

shape—whether a stamp is square, round, rectangular or "bisect," and if the latter, whether the stamp has been cut diagonally, vertically or horizontally.

the type of paper upon which a stamp has been printed—whether laid, wove, granite, silk and so on.

the watermarks used on the paper—there are five kinds of these.

the color of ink used—including the shade-variations of a single issue.

the type of impression or method of printing by which the stamp was produced—whether engraving, typography process, lithography, embossed printing, or typeset.

the kind of gum used

the scheme used to separate the stamps—whether perforation or roulette, including the five possible variations of each.

whether the stamps were overprinted or surcharged—an "overprint" is something printed or impressed upon a stamp after the stamp was completed, and the term is used by philatelists to denote some inscription that does not alter the face value of the stamp; a "surcharge," to be distinguished from the simple overprint, indicates an overprint which either alters or confirms the face value of a stamp.

whether the stamp contains control marks, burlage, or grill—"burlage" is a fine network pattern composed either of waves or of dots, as originally issued; the "grill" is a pattern of small square dots (usually arranged in a square or rectangle but in some instances covering the whole stamp) embossed upon some of the issues of the United States and certain other countries in order to break down the fiber of the paper and so make it difficult to remove the cancellation.

These are but a few of the questions to be studied, and there are, furthermore, numerous ramifications to each of them. Take separation, for example. There are, to begin with, "imperforated" stamps and "perforated" stamps. Among the latter there are five different kinds of holes to be found: the round (this is the most common); the square; the "hyphen" or rectangular; the "lozenge" or diamond; and the "bastard," "pin" or "sewing-machine." And occasionally still another way of dividing stamps known as the "roulette" method is employed, by which rows of pierced dots or short consecutive cuts are made without actually removing any of the paper. There are five different kinds of roulette cuts, too, and the serious collector must familiarize himself with these as well as with the five kinds of perforations. The size of the holes in perforations may vary greatly, as may the distances between them. The philatelist counts the number of holes contained in a length of two centimeters, and this is called the "gauge of perforation." Far from being merely an arbitrary pursuit, the study of these features helps the collector to distinguish between rare and common specimens, between original and reprinted stamps, and between genuine and spurious ones.

Various minor features—such as *the differences between new en-*

graved plates, re-engraved plates and retouched plates—are of interest to specialists. And in order to study the many fine points involved in their hobby, stamp collectors employ a battery of special instruments such as magnifying glasses, watermark detectors, gauges, and so on. Other instruments—such as the tongs for holding the stamp—are for the purpose of protecting the specimens from damage, since *condition* is important to the philatelist, just as it is to the bibliophile. A "good" stamp must be clean and legible, so the collector must take care not to allow a specimen to become torn, bent or discolored; and before he will accept an item in the first place, the true philatelist will examine it to be sure that it is not "off-center," "straight-edged," or too heavily canceled.

Another exacting field centers about antiques of various sorts. Here the points to be considered in each subject reach the ultimate in subtlety, while the antique collector's vocabulary is such as to give the uninitiate the most abject feeling of inferiority.

Kenneth L. Roberts once satirized this subject in an article entitled *Antiquamania.* The following passage, concerning collectors of furniture, might be applied with suitable modification to any class of antiquephile:

"One must know whether it is more desirable for the molding on a chest of drawers to consist of a cyma reversa and a wide fillet, or of a quarter-round, a fillet, a cove and a fillet. One should even be able to argue in favor of having the moldings consist of a fillet, a cove, an astragal, a fillet and a small cove. One should have a comprehensive grasp of what it is that an astragal does to the base moldings, if any; and if one lacks that comprehensive grasp, one should be able to simulate comprehension with such assurance as to confound any other person who thinks that he knows all about it."

As in the case of the stamp collector, these distinctions (not greatly exaggerated by Mr. Roberts) serve definite purposes. They have to do with esthetic appeal and with authenticity, with rarity and with value; in short, with "rightness." A proper understanding of them adds greatly to the collector's enjoyment of his hobby as well as to the quality of his collection; and the antique collector's jargon has such peculiar charm that one can relish the words even without knowing what they signify.

If you collect furniture you must first of all learn to recognize the various *kinds of wood* used in which countries, at what periods and for what purposes: oak, walnut or mahogany, ash, maple, cherry, beech, elm, pine or red cedar, satinwood, ringwood, sycamore, harewood, ebony or yew, citron, coramandel, holly tree, sandalwood, zebra wood, Brazil wood or *bois du roi*—the very names are promising. When you have mastered this subject, however, you have scarcely begun. You must also make a study of *veneers* and learn the differences between "oyster," "crotch" and "burl" veneers. Nor is it enough to know that a certain piece contains *inlay* work. Is it "intarsia" or "marquetry"?

Again, a chair, a bed, a chest, a table does not just have *feet.* It may have "ball" or "bun" feet; "trumpet" or "inverted cup" feet; "colt's hoof" feet; "scroll" feet; "spade" or "club" feet; "claw" feet; "ball-and-claw" feet; "pad" feet; "vase-form" feet; or "periwinkle" feet. Nor are its *legs* mere props. They are "cabriole" or "bandy" legs; "turned" legs; "Marlborough" legs; "trumpet" legs. And in some kinds of furniture the legs have "ears" as well as "knees" and "feet." Queen Anne furniture is distinguished for its "club feet" and "bandy legs"—and is beautiful nonetheless. And, like the backs that lean against them, chair *backs* can be complicated, for there are "ladder" backs, "shield" backs, "oval" backs, "vase-splat" or "fiddle-splat" backs and many others.

What are acanthus ornaments, shells, wreathes, medallions, torches, cabochons, the Greek fret, and the Vitruvian scroll sometimes known as the Chinese wave? They come under *decorations* in furniture collecting. *Brasses* constitute an important identification for some types of furniture—pear-shaped drops, keyhole escutcheons, back-plates, loop handles, and H-hinges—and "complete with original brasses" is as common a phrase in the literature of old furniture as "in original boards uncut" is in the literature of book collecting.

As a leg is not just a leg for a' that, nor a foot a foot, so each type of furniture is of many different kinds. A chest of drawers may be a highboy, a lowboy, a chest-on-chest or a commode. It may have a straight front, a "swell" front, or a "serpentine" front. And a chair may be all manner of things. It may be a "Farthingale" seat (made without arms to leave room for the hoops of a farthingale or hoop skirt). It may be a "Ponteuse" of the sort upon which the French courtiers used to sit facing the back so that their elegantly embroidered coattails might not be hidden from view. A Ponteuse has a little cushioned shelf at the back, and the courtier rested his arms on this while playing cards. A chair may be a "love seat," a "courting chair" or a "Darby and Joan settee"; or it may be, less romantically, merely a "conversation seat." It may be a "Forty-wink" or a "Sleepy-hollow" or a "slipper" chair. And if it is Early American, it may be a "Governor Carver," an "Elder Brewster," a "Boston" or a "Windsor." But the distinctions do not stop with the names. A Windsor chair, for instance, is, to begin with, either straight or a rocker; and then it may be a "low-back," a "hoop-back," a "loop-back," a "fan-back," a "comb-back," or a "double-comb-back."

Names indicating similar distinctions prevail among all antiques, and in each case the name indicates to the collector a wealth of special information concerning the origin, uses, period and so on of a particular object. Thus a drinking glass may be plain-footed, folded-footed, dome-footed, or domed-and-folded-footed. Its bowl may be "drawn" (that is, with the bowl and stem drawn from a single piece of glass), bell-shaped, ovoid, straight-sided, waist-formed, bell, straight-sided rectangular, ogee (with an S-shaped profile), lipped-ogee or double-ogee. The shape of the bowl helps the collector to date the glass properly, as does the type of stem—baluster, plain, air-twist, opaque white twist, color, cut, and "tear-glass" (so-called from the bubbles of air imprisoned within the stem). And so it goes on, into a whirlpool of fine distinctions.

There are principles to be followed in dating works of art and craftsmanship, in attributing them to the proper masters or designers. Standards for judging quality in pottery, porcelain, engraved gems or silverware are based partly upon esthetic criteria, partly upon considerations of genuineness, rarity or condition. And rules for the proper care of each type of object are established with a view to ensuring the maximum preservation of collectibles.

"Fine medals and coins should be tenderly treated," writes Gardner Teall. "Each should be kept protected from abrasion. It is vandalism to subject a medal or coin to an unskilled scouring or scraping."

Here speaks not the specious splitter of hairs but a collector who seeks immortality for the objects he loves.

Nor is there anything new or regional about points in collecting. The Romans had their minute criteria for judging the quality and value of murrhines, Corinthian bronzes and citrus wood tables. In seventeenth-century England, Sir Thomas Roe, writing to the Countess of Bedford, said:

"Four things are required in medals—truth, antiquity, beauty, story or poetry."

In old China, Mi Fei advised collectors on the best ways to mount, clean and protect fragile old paintings, and instructed them in methods of dating pictures by the grade or type of silk upon which they were painted —as, in certain cases, the Westerner tells by the type of panel or canvas used. And in modern Japan a collector of match-papers (among the Japanese this hobby is as highly developed as is philately in this country) may spend years classifying and studying the papers issued in a single province.

DETERMINING VALUES IN THE COLLECTION

"It is perhaps a more fortunate destiny to be born with a taste for collecting shells than to be born a millionaire."

ROBERT LOUIS STEVENSON

THE WORD "value" like the word "collecting" is a versatile term. It signifies the one or more considerations which render a thing useful or desirable. It is the estimation of the worth of an object in comparison to the worth of other objects. It may have to do with market price, and on the other hand it may have to do with excellence or significance quite apart from money. As far as collectors are concerned, it may be and often is based upon such specialized considerations as the "need" to complete a collection, or the desire to create a series of related objects any one of the individual items in which might be valueless unless viewed as links in that series.

The general standards of value by which all collections or items in collections are judged are for the most part basically alike in various parts of the world and even among people at various stages of development. Thus a primitive, whether collector or not, may value an object for any of the following reasons individually or in combination: usefulness; durability; rarity, which makes the object difficult to acquire; evidence of skill; because possession of the object brings the owner social recognition; because of association with the memory of a venerated ancestor, an admired hero, or a holy place.

Civilized man judges things in much the same way, although in his case some of the primitive values have been transmuted. In making a collection he places less emphasis upon physical utility and durability, frequently collecting things which are of no practical use to him, as well as those which he knows to be exceedingly fragile. On the other hand, utility from the point of view of intellectual interest or *significance* is highly regarded; and although the collector usually ignores potential durability, he emphasizes *condition*: objects which have endured the buffets of time and have survived relatively intact are preferred to damaged items, which are acceptable only when perfect examples are very rare or nonexistent. Like the primitive, the average civilized man prizes *rarity*, and in his case it is not only because rare items are difficult to obtain but also because they are usually expensive. However, the reason for the value is basically the same: to own such things is one means of earning a reputation for cleverness.

The amateur values many things because they seem to him to have *esthetic qualities*, a condition which often involves the incorporation of some creative skill; and he cherishes objects possessed of a personal or historic *association* (to which he sometimes gives the name of *antiquity*). Moreover, he wants his possessions to be the best of their kind available, and in establishing this criterion of value he takes into consideration *quality* and *authenticity*. Alone among all these considerations, the question of authenticity is one which probably did not come into being until the collecting custom was sufficiently developed to be worth exploiting, and even this criterion to our certain knowledge has been in existence for several thousand years.

Within these broad divisions, some of which make for value in the eyes of the non-collector also, the collector in each field concerns himself with many specific criteria which emerge as the result of his special study or which are due to his desire to be unique, to be consistent, or to create a complete entity.

The law of supply and demand decrees that rarity, quite apart from any other consideration, will create value just so long as the rare object is desired by a sufficient number of people; and because that value exists, some people prize rarity for itself alone. This, we have seen, is not always due solely to monetary considerations, for rarities are often desired quite as much for the prestige which ownership of them brings as for monetary worth: when cotton was rare and silk common, the

Emperor of China wore garments of cotton because these set him apart from the common herd; and so it often is with collectors.

Sometimes rarity is but one of the factors in a compound standard of value. We are told that Lorenzo de' Medici disapproved of printing partly because he considered its products inferior to the flowing script of the manuscript writers and partly because the new process threatened to turn hitherto rare books into commonplaces; and old manuscript books still command a high price because they are rare as well as because of their beauty. Again, modern collectors treasure the early "soft-paste" Sèvres porcelain (manufactured between 1753 and 1804) far more than they do the later "hard-paste" pieces, partly because the soft-paste examples are older, partly because they are actually finer, and partly because, due to the destruction in 1804 of the secret formula by which they were made, the early pieces are rarer and will become progressively more so.

On the other hand, rarity by itself may overshadow all other standards of value in making a collector's item desirable, and this results in some strange contradictions. It is frequently the early editions of the obscurest and least significant work of a collected author rather than those of his masterpieces that will command the highest prices, since these obscure pieces, little valued in their own time, have become difficult to find. The 1828 edition of Hawthorne's *Fanshawe* in original boards uncut brings more than a comparable edition of *The House of Seven Gables* or *The Scarlet Letter;* and a first edition of Shelley's *Address to the Irish People* is more eagerly snapped up than early editions of his poems. A four-drachma coin of the time of Alexander the Great brings less than ten dollars in our time because there are many such coins still in existence, but a five-dollar American gold piece dated 1822 is worth a hundred times its face value because of its rarity.

Under certain conditions even autograph collectors neglect significance in favor of rarity. The scarcest and hence the highest-priced item in a "Presidential Cabinet Set" is the signature of one Titian J. Coffee who was not even a regular cabinet member but served *ad interim* as Attorney General under Lincoln. As early as 1925, a Warren G. Harding holograph (a letter written and signed in his own hand) was worth far more than that of any other president, not even excluding George Washington, for the simple reason that such a specimen was almost impossible to find. Of the fifty-six signers of the Declaration of Independence, among whom were some of the greatest names in American revolutionary history, the two whose signatures command the most fantastic sums are Thomas Lynch, Jr., who died at the age of thirty having done little to distinguish himself besides signing the famous document, and Button Gwinnett, the Georgia politician who was killed in a duel.

One of the oddest contradictions growing out of this emphasis on rarity is the interest sometimes taken in "errors" or imperfections. The Roman murrhine collector looked for "freakish accidentalities" in the material of which his cups and bowls were fashioned; and Samuel Johnson, in one of his more uncharitable moods, made the most of what must always seem to outsiders an unfathomable absurdity. In Number 56 of *The Idler* the sharp-tongued doctor had this to say of certain eighteenth-century specialists who bore an uncanny resemblance to the Roman murrhine collectors in this respect:

"The novice is often surprised to see what minute and unimportant discriminations increase or diminish value. An irregular contortion of a turbinated shell, which common eyes pass unregarded, will ten times treble its price in the imagination of philosophers. . . . Among shells that please by their variety of colors, if one can be found accidentally deformed by a cloudy spot, it is boasted as the pride of the collection."

So the book collector prizes a volume rendered unique or uncommon by the accidental intrusion of a misprint or textual variation, by a misbinding or a page put in upside down, and a man like the late A. E. Newton could speak lovingly of a copy of *She Stoops to Conquer* that had "all the errors just as they should be." It is to be noted, however, that those errors are usually valued only when they were a feature of the original edition, almost never if they are the result of subsequent tampering—since in the first case they provide important clues for identifying the early edition, whereas in the second they detract from "mint condition."

The knowledgeable stamp collector will have nothing to do with specimens exhibiting certain normal imperfections of production (off-center printing, for example), but actual errors of printing which tend to make a stamp rare or unique are highly valued. Of this sort are upside-down printings, errors in color, minor defects in the engraver's plate, lack of perforation between two stamps when the division marks should be there, and accidental printing defects a few examples of which have slipped by unnoticed before being corrected. This produces some curiously paradoxical expressions—"a good unused error," for example. Writing of Bureau Print Precancels, a specialist in this field declares proudly, "We also have three well-known and interesting errors: Alhol (for Athol), Sppingfield (for Springfield), and Mikwaukee (for Milwaukee)."

The smallest bit of paper in the world worth so much money—the British Guiana one-cent black-on-magenta issued in 1856—attained its supreme status partly because it was printed in the wrong color, partly because it is, so far as is known, the only specimen of its kind still in existence, and partly because of the intensely competitive circumstances under which it was once sold. The story which has developed in connection with this stamp provides an excellent demonstration of how one sort of value in a collector's item may grow.

In 1856, the little city of Georgetown in British Guiana ran short of stamps and had to print an emergency issue to be used until a new shipment should arrive from England. The printer who did the job used the wrong color ink for the one-centers of the set, and although most of these were withdrawn as soon as the mistake was noticed, a few had escaped into circulation. Sixteen years later a Georgetown boy, L. Vernon Vaughan, found one of the 1856 stamps on an old envelope in the family attic and sold it to a local dealer for six shillings. Eventually this dealer unloaded his stock, including the then little-known error, for about six hundred dollars; and the purchaser, realizing something of the significance of the one-cent Guiana magenta, resold this single item to the famous collector, Count Ferrari, for seven hundred dollars. When, after the First World War, the Ferrari Collection was put up for sale, a battle royal was waged over this stamp, by this time realized to be unique. The King of England was one of the competitors, but victory went to an American, Arthur B. Hind, whose agent paid thirty-two thousand five hundred dollars for it. By the time the commissions and taxes had been added, the stamp had cost its new owner several thousand dollars more, and for years his widow held it for an "asking" price of fifty thousand dollars. No wonder its original discoverer was slightly breathless when he wrote, in 1934, to the *London Daily Mail:*

"It is strange to think that this precious British Guiana one-cent magenta once belonged to me. Sixty-one years ago I unearthed it and sold it for six shillings. Now it is shown in a glass case all by itself when on exhibition, with a bodyguard of detectives to look after it."

In 1938 it was rumored that an unnamed collector, considering the purchase of this stamp, had hesitated because of some difficulty in tracing its earliest history on the basis of government records, but in 1940 the stamp was sold (supposedly to an Australian who veiled the transaction in secrecy) for a reputed price of forty thousand dollars, and the famous morsel of paper was then accompanied by a certificate of genuineness issued by Great Britain's Royal Philatelic Society. It is to be noted that if doubt had been convincingly cast upon the authenticity of the item the end of the story might have been a drop in value as spectacular as the rise had been; although it is just possible that the stamp's history, its association with two of the most famous philatelists in stamp-collecting annals, and its quality of being unique whether genuine or not, might have kept afloat at least part of its dollar value.

A different sort of variation was responsible for one of the most valuable "covers" in existence. This item, an envelope with two 1847 Mauritius stamps on it, was also at one time in the Hind collection. Postage stamps were still an innovation in 1847, when a printing was ordered for invitations to a ball to be given by the wife of the governor of Mauritius. The local watchmaker who engraved the issue put "post office" on his plate instead of "post paid" as had been intended, and only a very few stamps of the issue were made in this form.

Another famous and now valuable error occurred in the case of the first American air mail stamp. An unknown number of sheets of one hundred stamps each were accidentally printed with the picture of the airplane inverted, and all but one of these sheets were destroyed in the postoffice as soon as the error was discovered. One sheet, however, reached a substation in Washington, D. C., and was bought by a young man named William F. Robey. Robey paid the correct price—twenty-four dollars—for the pane. Then, noticing the error, he pointed it out to the mail clerk who offered to exchange the sheet for him, but Robey was too wise to surrender his prize. Three days later he had disposed of the "errors" to a Philadelphia dealer for twelve thousand dollars; and not long after that the dealer resold the sheet to Colonel E. H. R. Green (a famous philatelist whose specialty was erroneous issues) for twenty thousand, nearly a thousand times the face value, and this in the case of an issue just fresh off the press! By 1938 a single fine example of this stamp was worth five thousand dollars and a block of four might bring as much as fifteen thousand.

WHEN RARITY OVERTAKES ANTIQUITY. LEFT: *United States half dime, 1802, which may bring as much as $1,000.* RIGHT: *Marcus Aurelius Roman silver denarius,* A.D. *167, which can be purchased today for less than $1.00.*

Stack's and The Numismatic Review

Philatelic Research Laboratories, Inc.

1

H. L. Lindquist Publications

3

POSTAGE FOUR PENCE
CAPE OF GOOD HOPE

Harmer, Rooke & Company

2

4

H. L. Lindquist Publications

SOME VALUABLE ERRORS. (*1*) *Only known used 24-cent invert block of the U. S. 1869 general issue stamp. Said to have brought as much as $25,000.* (*2*) *One of the "classic" errors of stampdom, the "Cape Wood-Block" 4-penny red, Cape of Good Hope, 1861.* (*3*) *The famous "inverted center" 1918 U. S. 24¢ air mail stamp.* (*4*) *The storied British Guiana 1¢ black-on-magenta 1856 stamp.* (*See p. 375.*)

As book publishers take first-edition collectors into consideration in making their plans, so the United States government on one occasion catered to the philatelist's interest in the unusual by purposely producing a few sheets of a regular issue without gum or perforation. Such sheets immediately become valuable; and because they are usually presented to favored individuals, many collectors consider the practice unfair. Complaints may still be heard about a somewhat more justifiable incident which occurred as long ago as the eighteen-nineties, when the government released several imperforate sheets to a dealer as a reward for his having built a difficult-to-assemble collection of early American stamps.

A more recent affair of this sort has twice come perilously close to causing a national scandal. Early in the Franklin D. Roosevelt administration, Postmaster General Farley made a practice of purchasing a few sheets of each new stamp-issue before the sheets had been either gummed or perforated, and these he would autograph and present to some of his friends in government service. Not being a collector himself, he said later, the Postmaster General was unaware of the full implication of this practice and considered the gifts as being in the nature of souvenirs rather than of monetary significance. Stamp collectors were fully aware of what was happening but had no objection until the occurrence in quick succession of two untoward incidents.

One day, just to see what would happen, a collector from Norfolk, Virginia, wrote to Farley and, sending the regular purchase price, asked if he might have a similar sheet. Much to his astonishment the request was granted, whereupon he went to New York to have his prize appraised by experts. Twenty thousand dollars was the verdict. In the second incident, a subordinate officer of the Interior Department prevailed upon Harold Ickes (one of the original recipients) to give him a few copies of the special stamps and then proceeded to offer them for sale to the highest bidder at the regular meeting of a local stamp club. Stamp collectors all over the country were up in arms and the attendant publicity threatened to be exceedingly unpleasant for everyone who had ever received one of Mr. Farley's innocent gifts as well as for the gentleman himself. However, Mr. Ickes managed to get his stamps back before they had been sold (the vendor had not been offered as much as he thought he should get and was holding on for a higher price); while Farley solved his end of the problem by offering similar ungummed, imperforate sheets (minus the autograph) for public sale. Under these circumstances, the stamps were no longer exceedingly rare items, but shoals of collectors, still under the spell, in short order snapped up two million dollars worth.

Age is often an important factor in producing rarity, but rarity is only one of the reasons why old things have such an especial appeal for so many collectors. Antiquity is often worshiped for itself, for man likes to think of himself in relation to enduring time, to feel that while he may not be immortal as an individual at least he is part of a stream of life that never dies. In this sense, anything that is old becomes an association item—associated with the life and accomplishments of humanity; but if, in addition, an object is related to some specific hero it takes on further value. If a Shakespeare letter were to be discovered today, we are told by an experienced dealer, many collectors would not consider five hundred thousand dollars too much to pay for it. In this particular case the high value which a Shakespeare holograph might assume would be partly a question of uniqueness, since no such letter is known to be extant, but age and association would also have a great deal to do with it. Sociologists call this phenomenon "historic sentimentalism," and historic sentimentalism has always played a prominent part in setting collectors' values.

A collector reminds us of the old saw that one should keep a thing seven years before throwing it away, then adds: "Seven times seven and there is a collector after it." In many fields there is a definite cycle leading up to this result. You may furnish your home in the modern manner for reasons of fashion, perhaps, or because to do so is to follow the line of least resistance, or again because you genuinely prefer the contemporary style. But the members of the next generation will be preoccupied with newer styles. What went immediately before is likely to seem crude or gaudy or just plain old-fashioned. The outmoded furnishings of their parents are discarded, sold, perhaps, or even destroyed. Of that which survives much will deteriorate from lack of care, and eventually excellent examples of the period will be difficult to find. Nevertheless in time they will be ardently sought, and not only because of their comparative scarcity but also because of a lively interest in them. The antagonistic reactions of the second generation, generally a result of desire for change, will be mellowed in the third and fourth when people begin to look back on the "good old days" as on a golden age, or as a very quaint period indeed, so that things which for a while had seemed ugly will seem "amusing" and appealing instead.

Closest to our time are the "Victorian" items which have passed through just such a cycle. The heavy mahogany furniture, the haircloth sofas, the ebonized tables with bouquets of flowers and mother-of-pearl, the "whatnots" with their miscellaneous array of knickknacks, the ornate mirrors, the wax flowers and artificial birds under glass, the tasseled covers and lamp shades with which our grandmothers' homes were filled came later to be regarded with horror. As they were originally used they were actually a confusing conglomeration of dust-catchers which, by most standards of mature taste, would always remain mildly horrific. Yet they have come back into favor as antiques and collectibles suitable for display and for use, in moderation, since they are characteristic of a period that has already become historic and imbued with a degree of romance. They are no longer merely furnishings and ornaments, for they have become symbols.

How long has there existed an active and conscious interest in the antique? The Sumerians and the Babylonians had it, and so did the ancient Chinese. It manifests itself even among the primitives, in Borneo, in Samoa, and among the Kula of New Guinea. It plays a valuable part in the creation of historical and social record, but because worship of antiquity can become a cult in itself, a modern object of equal or greater beauty than an antique is often discarded as valueless merely because of its modernity. For centuries controversy has raged over the relative merits of beauty and age in collectibles; and it will probably always remain a moot question to be decided in each case by the individual upon the basis of his own particular interests. Fortunately there have always been followers of both schools so that some objects are collected and preserved for their beauty alone, just as others are collected primarily because they are old or historically significant.

In talking of collecting values there is a temptation to think chiefly in terms of high or low figures; what will such and such an item bring on the open market? Yet the money value in terms of collecting is not at all the heart of consideration for most collectors.

There is the book man, for example, who spends no more than ten cents per volume and yet who really loves his dime tomes. When such a collector prowls through the stacks in a secondhand shop he may, it is true, be on the lookout for "treasure trove," some item which, having miraculously escaped attention, will turn out to be a rarity that could command a high price. But if he is a realist, he will understand that the chances of his happening upon such an item are, in a collectible-conscious era, slim indeed, and he does not count much upon the possibility. Instead he chooses a subject which interests him, then centers his purchases around it and values his books for their relevancy to his collection rather than for their price in dollars and cents. The same thing can, of course, often be said of collectors who spend a great deal on individual items. Some of these amateurs would not resell at any price and are interested in the monetary value of items only in so far as the existence of such a value tends to substantiate the validity of their own judgment.

Art collectors and collectors of "art objects" and antiques may be swayed primarily by esthetic considerations although, more often than they are usually willing to admit, other questions play an important part in establishing even their standards of "beauty." Little though the collector may be aware of it, it is often true that such factors as rarity, antiquity or authenticity may be the basic criteria by which a man judges whether or not an object is to be considered beautiful. So an untrained person in casually inspecting a painting whose authorship is unknown to him will probably remain unimpressed. If something about it should appeal to him personally, he may murmur, "Not bad," and still fail to go into ecstasies over it. But let someone tell him that it is by a famous master and his attitude mysteriously changes. Here is a name of prestige and from that name the picture itself develops an aura of importance.

Conversely, something highly valued may tumble in his estimation once the props have been removed.

"While I was convinced that my enameled glasses were made by Baron Stiegel they were, I thought, beautiful," writes Joseph Hergesheimer. ". . . I spoke, in their connection, of the charm of primitive art.—But when I recognized that Baron Stiegel had not made the glasses in question, they immediately, in my eyes, became ugly."

This question of authenticity is a curious one. It can, as everyone knows, make all the difference between a valuable object in terms of money and one that commands no price at all. And this may be, indeed quite often is, entirely apart from any attributes of beauty or intrinsic interest that the unauthenticated object may possess in its own right.

FASHIONS: SOME ARE CONSTANT, SOME RECURRENT. *Time increases the beauty of the well-designed wooden chair, hand-wrought by a master craftsman.*

Victorian furnishings are labeled "monstrosities" by most connoisseurs, but, partly as a reaction to functional design, the style has become a mid-20th-century pet.

Few collectors today are attracted by the chemist-brew of plastics, but synthetics, beautiful and durable, will yield a harvest to future generations.

RIGHT: *Museum of Fine Arts, Boston*

Queen Anne walnut side chair with drake feet, c. 1740, Philadelphia. From the M. & M. Karolik Collection.

Museum of the City of New York

Victorian armchair of rosewood, by John Henry Belter, c. 1860, New York.

Bakelite Corporation

Modern chair of laminated wood and heat-pressed Bakelite, *by Alvar Aalto.*

Even museums rarely buy paintings solely on the strength of beauty, and no more do the majority of private collectors. It is true that they want the works of a certain master because that master's works are, in the main, known to be great; yet both museums and collectors will sometimes be content with inferior examples if only such examples can be proven genuine, and will reject a known copy even though it may be practically indistinguishable from the original.

One might say that, would a man but be honest about it, two paintings (or two glass pots) which look exactly alike to him must give him equal pleasure; and in one sense—the purely visual sense—this can be true. In another sense, however, it is an entirely false assumption; for once the collector knows which painting or pot is genuine and which is not, he may actually *feel* quite differently about them. The original seems to stand for all of the master's work, for the individual style which that master created (and upon which the copyist is entirely dependent), as well as for the great gift of his uniqueness. In short, the work becomes dæmonic and through it the collector feels that he stands face to face with the artist himself. The copy, on the other hand, or the item "in the manner of," is derivative, and once it has been recognized as a copy the dæmonic quality is lacking: its stolen perfection represents nothing more than a mirrored figure, and one cannot commune with a man in a mirror.

Occasionally there is a collector whose true interest lies in beauty alone. He will care little for the origin of an object so long as the object itself measures up to his standards of esthetic perfection. Michelangelo once fashioned the figure of a Sleeping Cupid. This statue, deeply imbued with the classic spirit, fell into the hands of a dealer, Baldassare del Milanese, who, wise in the ways of his collector-customers, kept the figure buried in earth for a while so that it would assume the aspect of antiquity, then sold it for two hundred crowns as an old piece to Cardinal San Giorgio. When the Cardinal discovered how he had been tricked, he ragingly insisted that the fraud, Milanese, take back the Cupid and refund the purchase price. Meanwhile Isabella d'Este had seen the statue and had recognized it as a surpassing fine work of art. Avid though she was, like the rest of her contemporaries, for antiquities, her love of beauty was universal, capable of encompassing new as well as old, and she moved heaven and earth to obtain Michelangelo's *Sleeping Cupid.* It came into her possession at last and remained, as long as she lived, one of the great prides of her collection. Vasari, commenting on this incident, tells us that San Giorgio

> ". . . incurred no small ridicule and even censure in the matter, he not having been able to appreciate the merit of the work; for this consisted in its absolute perfection, wherein, if a modern work be equal to the ancient, wherefore not value it as highly? For is it not a mere vanity to think more of the name than the fact? *But men who regard the appearance more than the reality, are to be found in all times.*"

On behalf of San Giorgio, however, and of other collectors in his position, it should be remembered that he had been fooled about the statue which had been palmed off on him as an antique, whereas Isabella had known exactly what she was buying.

In many instances the collector's insistence upon the genuine is based upon excellent esthetic reasons of which the uninformed outsider is unaware. Sheffield Plate provides an example of this. Genuine Sheffield was made by rolling silver over copper and was originally called "copper rolled-plate." Later it was discovered that silver could be deposited on copper by electroplating; and still later electroplated articles were made by using a nickel or white-metal base instead of copper. Genuine Sheffield Plate was produced by running silver and copper sheets cold through the rollers until those sheets were inseparably joined and pressed out to the required thinness, after which the metal was cut and shaped by hand hammering; whereas in electroplated ware the baser metal form is already shaped by machine before being coated with silver. All this is elementary to the Sheffield amateur; and he also knows that because electroplating does not wear well unless done on nickel, the latter metal is usually used as a base in this process, although neither nickel nor white metal can bring out the true beauty of silver as does a copper base. So it appears that the Sheffield collector's preference for the genuine article is not after all purely arbitrary.

In similar fashion there will be qualities of beauty and significance possessed by an authentic piece of Chinese porcelain which cannot be duplicated in any imitation, and the connoisseur who appreciates these qualities is quite justified in his insistence on having the genuine and nothing else.

It is apparent that there are two distinct aspects to the problem: "What constitutes value in a collectible?" One concerns the subjective value that the collector himself perceives in such an object. The other, more concrete, has to do with the comparative prices paid in the open market. However, if enough people respond to the same subjective values, that fact will influence the monetary value, since demand will be increased and comparative scarcity will result.

Some collectibles may be said to possess an intrinsic importance, a value based not only on preciousness of material but also upon widely accepted standards of beauty, historic interest, association, or scientific significance. Such objects will almost always command a price so long as the standards upon which their value is based remains valid. Under certain conditions, however, the value of a collected object may alter, for better or for worse, overnight; and at any given moment that change in value may bear no obvious relationship to intrinsic standards of any kind.

The element of chance plays a larger part in effecting such variations than one might suppose. Even the temper of the people at a particular auction may, for example, make an enormous difference:

> "I have seen a lithograph sell for eighty-five dollars," writes Clifford, "and the identical same subject (Currier and Ives' *Thanksgiving Day*) in just as good condition, with a larger and more competitive audience, go for eight hundred dollars."

And since collectors, like other people, are often inclined to be impressed by high prices, such a price once paid may have a favorable effect upon the market value of all similar items, even though it was originally due only to the effect of some fortuitous circumstance.

The same process operates in reverse, for ill-informed collectors, like uninstructed consumers, frequently accept expensiveness as a valid criterion of quality or desirability without taking the trouble to investigate the actual merits of the object concerned. James Lenox, the nineteenth-century American book collector who did much of his purchasing from foreign catalogues, once ordered a tract priced at one hundred and fifteen francs. By the time his order was received, the dealer had discovered a typographical error in the catalogue: the correct price was only fifteen francs. Now Mr. Lenox was a highly valued and regular customer and so the dealer refunded the difference when he forwarded the tract to New York. To his amazement he received the pamphlet back by return post. Lenox had based his judgment of the value of the item upon price alone which, he thought, indicated rarity; a mere fifteen-franc item, he had concluded, must certainly be without importance—and this is a simple example of a multitudinous happening.

Discrepancies between prices paid and the relative significance of the items concerned are sometimes brought about by the accident of having present at a particular sale or active in the field at a particular moment more specialists in one subject than in another, for, as Dr. Johnson said, although "the collector is attracted by rarity, he is seduced by example and inflamed by competition."

Accidents of publicity (to say nothing of intentional propaganda) have also been responsible for certain cases of contradictory values. Of the two rare Declaration signers, specimens of Thomas Lynch's autograph are believed to be even less numerous than those of Button Gwinnett, but Gwinnett's rarity has been more loudly trumpeted than Lynch's, just as Paul Revere (thanks to Longfellow) long ago outdistanced his fellow rider, William Dawes, in the public fancy. Because Gwinnett is more widely known as a rarity his autographs bring by far the higher prices of the two.

Rarity, as we have seen, is one of the chief distillers of value in collectors' items, but changes in degree of rarity may come about with dismaying suddenness; and in the case of objects valued for their rarity alone rather than for intrinsic interest, the discovery of new sources of supply may break down an accepted scale of values in short order. Thus should someone unexpectedly come upon a dozen Button Gwinnett autographs in an old trunk, Mr. Gwinnett's handwriting would no longer be regarded in the light of the record price of fifty-one thousand dollars paid for it in 1927 (in this case for a letter not even in his hand but merely signed by him in company with five other notables). It is wise, therefore, not to count too much on rarity alone, although its importance is manifest.

Rarity is often, though not always, produced by the passage of time, but if to age one adds the ingredient of fragility rarity is almost certain to result. Old coins are durable and hence the mere fact that they are old may not mean that they are also rare; but glass and china break easily and so the older a specimen is the greater its probable rarity. Since newsprint decays quickly, the same principle applies to old newspapers—but not to the oldest, which were printed on rag paper and so outlive their descendants. On the other hand, newspapers are among

Courtesy, The New York Sun

Lacy Glass. *American 19th-century historical cup plates, from the collection of Albert C. Marble, Worcester, Massachusetts.*

From collection of Mrs. A. K. Hostetter, Lancaster, Pennsylvania

Stiegel Glass, *American 18th-century. Twirled fluted blue creamer; and deep purple flask, diamond daisy pattern.*

the trivia of their own day and like all such things are quickly disposed of, so that age in their case (as with many similarly disregarded commonplaces) may indicate rarity quite aside from the effects of fragility. The man who collects early automobiles will find the automatic action of time increasing the value of his collection for exactly the same reason —the specimens he owns may be among the few of their kind to have escaped the junk heap. Again, an increase in rarity and hence in value is sometimes produced suddenly by a natural or a man-made catastrophe. War, fire, earthquake and flood—each in its turn may reduce the available supply of certain prized collectibles, and with the passage of time an increasing number of such catastrophes is likely to overtake most of the objects treasured by man. No better example could be found than the rarity of early Chinese paintings, a direct result of a fantastic series of these disasters continued over the centuries.

Whatever the reason or combination of reasons, the effect of time upon rarity and value is sometimes staggering. While Shakespeare's First Folios jumped in value from five dollars to ten times that many thousand in about three hundred years, it was toward the end of that period, as the folios grew rarer and the demand for them increased, that the value of these books was augmented twelvefold in little more than half a century. In 1847 James Lenox paid two thousand five hundred dollars for a copy of the Gutenberg Bible, but since his day collectors have given fifty thousand dollars, one hundred and six thousand dollars, even one hundred and twenty thousand dollars for similar ones. In 1848 the Boston Athenaeum purchased four hundred and fifty-five books and about seven hundred and fifty pamphlets from George Washington's library. Three thousand eight hundred dollars was then the price for the lot; but in 1936 a famous dealer paid nine thousand eight hundred dollars for a single volume from that same collection. And when James H. Manning paid out four thousand six hundred dollars for a Gwinnett "D.S." in 1912, he was branded as insane, but ten years later that same document (a will to which Gwinnett had appended his name) brought twenty-two thousand five hundred dollars.

Much of this sort of rise in value is due to the prevalence of fashions in collecting. The game of collecting sets of autographs of the signers of the Declaration of Independence, for instance, has lent many of these signatures undue value. There are about forty such completed sets now in existence, and one authority tells us that unless some of these are broken up or a new source of supply for some of the rarer signatures is discovered, it will be impossible ever to complete any more sets; yet some amateurs continue hopefully to gather a nucleus, just in case.

Fashions in collecting are sometimes artfully fostered by dealers. By skillful publicity a painter or a designer of furniture or glass or jewelry may be built up to become the star of a passing hour. And in all collecting fields there are perfectly natural cycles of taste, changes of popular interest. These changes in themselves cause tremendous fluctuations in market value, and trying to guess the next favorite calls for a combination of luck and knowingness—one should have the abilities of a skillful stock market plunger. When it was formed, Horace Walpole's "memorable curiosity shop" was a highly fashionable collection, but in 1842, when it came up for sale, the majority of things it contained were of a sort no longer in vogue among collectors. Walpole's pride as a connoisseur would have been sorely tried had he witnessed the skimpy prices his treasures brought; yet in another fifty years those same items, fashionable once more, would have caused bidding spirited enough to make Horace preen his feathers.

Since values based upon fashion alone are far from constant, the wise collector with a limited purse and no immediate interest in turnover often seeks out some temporarily unpopular subject which happens to appeal to him. When it was the fashion for book collectors to specialize in fine old bindings or in books printed by certain famous presses, at the height of the vogue such items became too expensive for the man in moderate circumstances. Today, on the other hand, many of the very volumes once so greatly in demand are comparatively easy to obtain; and for one who takes pleasure in the physical beauty of books, the collecting of these specimens is none the less enjoyable for being unfashionable. In the same way, Cruikshank prints were once all the rage among collectors, but later few people were interested in them; wherefore the man who collected them still had found a zestful and relatively inexpensive pursuit, the while he might be gambling upon the future return to favor of his specialty. So *millefiori* paperweights, once extremely popular, fell neglected, and are now in vogue again. The collector who was fascinated by this "glass of the thousand flowers" and who collected it in its Cinderella days now finds himself at the top of the heap.

Fashions in collecting, like fashions in dress, are often induced by contemporary events or stimulated by individuals much in the public eye. The shogun Yoritomo in thirteenth-century Japan set the first vogue for Kato Shirozemon's pottery: it became known that the shogun considered this native ware of especial worth when he instituted the custom of rewarding each individual who had done him a service by presenting him with a Shirozemon tea jar filled with the newest luxury imported from China—powdered tea; and collectors rushed to the band wagon to start a fashion that still lives on. A notable London exhibition of pewter in 1904 was responsible for the sudden craze for this product which swept collectors in England and America off their feet at the beginning of our own century. Soon there were so many amateurs of this hitherto little considered alloy that books were being written about it, societies of pewter collectors were being formed, and prices soared. The vogue later suffered a slight decline, but the field has become a solid and enduring one.

It is true in all fields of collecting that values based upon intrinsic qualities endure upon a reasonable scale, and if they be temporarily eclipsed by fashionable impedimenta, they will nevertheless emerge whole again. We could do no better than to close this chapter with a quotation from an eminent authority, Dr. Arthur Upham Pope, who, though he happens here to be discussing the particularly specialized field of oriental rugs, gives voice to a principle that may profitably be followed by every good collector:

"Rugs are to be judged primarily by their intrinsic beauty. They were created for the purpose of being beautiful. Rarity, historical association and fashion are largely irrelevant. Of these, fashion as usual has had too much to say, and there has been much imitative buying, much buying of mere names and types, of general neglect of the great artistic merit of some of the less advertised kinds. The austerely beautiful Dragon carpets were no better than poor relations until given social rank by the Metropolitan exhibition of 1910. The Vase carpets, the most virile and magnificent of all Persian weaves, went begging in the New York market thirty years ago. Now the few that were then available have gone into great collections and no more are to be had. All of this means that the alert and discerning few who had the independence and judgment to make acquisitions on the basis of sheer beauty have reaped a great harvest, and the undiscriminating many who follow only fashion pay high prices for inferior examples."

THE CHASE AND THE LUCK

"Though you may never have shot or hunted, when you begin to collect you begin to understand the pleasures of the chase: the searching in likely places; the spotting of the game; the keen, patient following-up; and the kill."

SIR JAMES YOXALL

THE TRUE COLLECTOR is a transformed hunter. Although his hands are seldom bloodstained, his intense concentration, like the hunter's, is pointed toward the objective of getting a full bag. There is the same patient following of clues, the same wile and guile, the matching of wits and the pitting of strengths, the tense expectation as the pursuit nears its conclusion, the deep exultation following a triumph. Like the hunter, the collector studies his prey and develops his own flair (a word which he applies symbolically, but which still means the ability to smell out the quarry). And like the hunter, he sometimes relishes the sport leading up to the kill as much if not more than the kill itself.

"One of the real pleasures of collecting stamps," writes a philatelist, "is not in the having but in the locating and the getting,"

while a bibliophile declares,

"My sport is book-hunting. I look upon it as a game, a game requiring some skill, some money, and luck."

Collectors who find their keenest satisfaction in the hunt itself have been known to lose interest in a completed collection which is then put away or sold and a new one begun. Characteristically, love of the chase is deep-seated in every collector. Watch one at work, if you can. Observe him, wily as a fox, clever as a cat with a mouse, sparring for position. Note the expression of his eye when he feels himself upon the brink of victory. It might be the glint in the eye of a savage about to spring upon his victim. Witness his exultation as, literally or figuratively, he brandishes his prize. It is an exultation no less than that of the hungry tracker holding aloft his first meal in three days. More subtle, perhaps, but not essentially different.

The joy of the chase can, like its counterpart the primitive hunting instinct, be turned into useful and productive channels in the new environment. It was partly by means of the hunt that early man developed his intelligence; and similarly the modern collector grows in skill and discernment as he practices his avocation. Against the difficulties encountered he sharpens his wits and through experience develops clearness of vision. As a disciplined code is necessary to the hunter even when on pleasure bent, so it is to the collector, and he becomes increasingly selective, learning to choose between those objects which are (by any of the various standards of his field) worth hunting and those which are not. In the end, his satisfaction in a successful foray may coincide with a high type of creative pleasure, with the most exacting cultural demands.

The "big-game" collectors have often traveled as far, endured as much grueling suspense, and faced almost as many dangers in quest of a rare object as any "bring-'em-back-alive" trapper of jungle beasts.

There was James F. Ballard (1854–1931), the American businessman whose valuable rug collection became world famous. Ballard began his career unexcitingly enough as a midwestern drug clerk, and though in time he rose to high financial success, never had he intended to wander far from the beaten track of his first half-century—until his chance encounter with a particularly entrancing oriental rug. He was over fifty years of age when, during a routine business trip to New York, he saw his charmer, was deeply captivated, and won her—with a check. Once she was in his possession he found himself, as so often happens, desiring a harem. James F. Ballard, the drug merchant, was transformed into an amateur whose studies then began in earnest, taking him into the most vigorous research.

It so happened that he had fallen into one of the most difficult of all collecting hobbies:

"The specialist needs to know everything that can be known on the subject [of oriental rugs], a prodigious task," writes Arthur Upham Pope.

Starting from scratch, Ballard made of himself one of the foremost rug experts in the world. Truly good oriental rugs, the early ones that interest collectors, are relatively scarce and widely scattered, and James Ballard thrice circled the globe in search of his specimens. He crossed the ocean thirty-six times and traveled more than four hundred sixty thousand miles on his various quests, traversing forty thousand of them on the trail of a single Indo-Persian Ispahan, a particularly rare item. Incidentally, he at last found it by chance in the Bombay home of one of his Persian acquaintances who had invited him to tea.

Once this indefatigable hunter had taken up the trail of a specific item nothing was allowed to stand in his way, not war, famine or fire and certainly not discouragement. More than once this midwestern businessman stood face to face with death—but he always got his rug. In 1923 Ballard was intent upon locating a lost specimen of the famous Seljuk Turk "bird rug" woven about 1550. Dealers in London and Paris told him he was wasting his time. They had searched for that very rug for years, and had failed to turn up even a clue. So Ballard headed East accompanied by a friend who was also a rug expert. In 1923 Greece and Turkey were at war, a particularly merciless and bloody conflict, and no man "in his right mind" would have attempted to cross the scene of battle. Ballard went.

At Thrace he and his companion were taken off the train and placed under arrest—suspicion naturally fell upon anyone "looking for a rug" in that hellhole. Yet the two men made the most of their predicament. Striking up a conversation with the young Greek officer who had been ordered to guard them, they told him of their mission. As he listened to the description of the long-sought rug the officer's face lighted with unexpected interest. Courteously he heard his prisoners through, then dumbfounded them by remarking casually that he knew the rug well. That evening the young officer agreed secretly to conduct the foreigners to a dilapidated shop behind the walls of Adrianople—and there, without the shadow of a doubt, was the lost bird rug.

Under ordinary circumstances this would have been the happy end of the trail. As things were, however, the finding of the rug was only part of the battle. There remained the delicate problem of getting it out of the country. Finally released from custody, Ballard and his friend went on to Constantinople—and arrived on the night that twenty thousand Turks from Stambul invaded the Greek quarter to avenge the

The Metropolitan Museum of Art

SELJUK TURK "BIRD" RUG, *late 16th-17th century.*

In search of this once lost rarity, James F. Ballard, former Mid-Western drug clerk, risked his life, but found the rug and added it to one of the finest rug collections known.

capture of Smyrna. It was a night of murderous rioting, and some of the guests in Ballard's hotel were killed. However, clutching the precious bundle, the two Americans managed to escape, and, hearing of a ship soon to sail from Smyrna, they headed there, only to arrive in the midst of an even bloodier massacre. Perhaps the proverbial collector's luck protected them, for despite the fact that nearly a third of the city's population of four hundred fifty thousand lost their lives in this final holocaust, our friends and their rug reached the boat in safety. As they sailed away they could see great tongues of flame licking skyward. The city of Smyrna had been fired.

Shipwreck, piracy and the Terrible Turk have played a part in more than one collecting adventure. So, too, has the intrigue consequent to those fierce rivalries that so often spring up among collectors, rivalries which may assume national importance. Particularly interesting from the collector's point of view is the story of what happened to Joseph Haydn's skull long after the composer himself ceased to inhabit it. Scientific interest, associative value, prestige, and faking all played a part in the wanderings of this relic, wanderings which began with a grave robbery and ended, in 1938, with a maneuver in power-politics.

Items associated with Joseph Haydn have been widely collected, but the world's most important repositories of these treasures are the British Museum, the *Reale Academia Luigi Cherubini* in Florence, Italy, the Society of the Friends of Music in Vienna, and the collection of the Esterhazy family (Haydn's lifelong patrons), formerly in the ancestral home at Eisenstadt but recently moved to Budapest. It was between the two last-named collections that the feud over the skull raged.

When Haydn died in 1809 there was a fashionable theory abroad in Europe that the examination of a man's skull would show the source of his talents. It was for this reason that on the night of the great man's burial (so goes the tale) two Viennese officials opened the grave and absconded with the head of the genius. The loss was not discovered until Prince Esterhazy some years later transported Haydn's remains to the parish church at Eisenstadt. Their villainy exposed, the scientific thieves confessed and promised to make restitution. They lived up to their agreement with, in the words of Olin Downes, "another head from their collection." Still later, however, one of them bequeathed Haydn's true skull to the Viennese Friends of Music, and despite repeated demands and even law suits initiated by the Esterhazys the Society kept it for many years on public exhibition with the rest of the Haydn treasures.

After the First World War, when the Burgenland district (including the village of Eisenstadt) was awarded by plebiscite to Austria, Prince Esterhazy, an ardent Hungarian, left the place which had been his family's home for generations and moved to Budapest. He built an imposing mausoleum intended for Haydn's body but left it empty—against the return of the disputed skull; and empty it remained until shortly after the Austro-German *anschluss,* at which time, reputedly as part of the Third Reich's policy of appeasing Hungary, the relic was restored to Prince Esterhazy.

Adventure of a more glamorous sort attended the collecting of ancient Greek relics by Europeans from the seventeenth through the early nineteenth centuries. Few people today in considering the fragmentary Arundelian Marbles of England, for example, have any conception of the energies marshalled to gather them. Their history is compounded of human frailty and natural and political obstacles and is typical of what may happen to the big-game collector when his interests conflict with those of a rival.

Sir Thomas Roe, His Britannic Majesty's Ambassador to Turkey from 1621 to 1628, was quite tranquil in fulfilling his official duties and adding to his private collection of antique medals and coins. His difficulties began when he consented to act as the Earl of Arundel's agent in the collection of antiquities. And those difficulties were picayune compared to the storms which raged about the Ambassador's head after he had accepted a similar commission from Arundel's competitor, the Duke of Buckingham. Roe entered upon his first commission lightly enough, and although, after preparatory conferences with various officials in 1621, he had regretfully to report to Arundel that there was no use searching for Greek manuscripts, since "the last French ambassador had the last gleanings," he added optimistically:

"Concerning antiquities in marble, there are many in divers parts, but especially at Delphos, unesteemed here; and I doubt not, easy to be procured for the charge of digging and fetching. . . . It is supposed that many statues are buried . . . and that if leave were obtained, would come to light. . . ."

Two years later Roe's optimism is somewhat tarnished in the light of experience. Prices for antiquities are high, he finds, because of competition from French and Italian collectors. Local and international political factors complicate his task. Searchers for antiques are suspected of being spies; and when that is not the case, there is the problem of official corruption to be dealt with, for a good statue will usually go to the highest briber. In Asia Minor, however, there are innumerable marble pillars, statues and tombstones with Greek inscriptions to be had secretly and with the help of gratuities, while closer at hand, "I may also light of some pieces of marble by stealth." Here were difficulties enough, and as a collector himself Roe should have known better than to attempt to please two greedy amateurs at the same time; yet off his guard, that was the task he eventually undertook.

Naïvely enough he seemed to believe that he could divide the spoils evenly between his two powerful clients to their mutual satisfaction; but Arundel at least would have nothing to do with such an arrangement and to "assist" the Ambassador, sent out a personal agent, a Mr. Petty, who proceeded to double cross Roe in order to procure all the treasures for Arundel, to Roe's great embarrassment and Buckingham's irritation. The varying aims of the two agents demonstrates the conflict in values sometimes held between different collectors. In this case Roe, the perfectionist, did not deeply understand the broad significance of his field. He had never perceived much value in mere antiquity but had felt that a statue, in order to be desirable, should be in good condition as well. Thus he speaks scornfully of one figure of a woman brought to him for consideration. Hand, nose and lip were gone and she was "so deformed that she makes me remember an hospital." Petty, on the other hand, was a more experienced antiquarian, and he endeavored to explain why some of the cruelly battered stones were nevertheless worth preserving. Unconvinced, and embittered by his trials, Roe declared some years later,

"I could have laden ships with such things as Mr. Petty digs; but good things undefaced are rare, or rather not to be found."

Nevertheless he accorded Petty a grudging admiration for the tireless manner in which the latter hunted down his quarry:

"There was never man so fitted to an employment," Roe wrote to Arundel in 1626, "that encounters all accidents with so unwearied patience [Petty had just recovered a whole shipload of marbles wrecked and sunk off the coast of Asia]; eats with Greeks on their worst days; lies with fishermen on planks, at the best; is all things to all men, that he may obtain his ends, which are your Lordship's service."

And Roe himself is spurred on to sharper search by the desire to outdo his relentlessly efficient rival:

"I have sent three servants together to Tassos, Cavalla, Philippi, and all the coast of Thrace; followed Mr. Petty to Pergamo, and Troy; am digging in Asia,"

he cried frantically upon one occasion; and he repeats the ever-recurring plaint that if only Arundel and Buckingham would agree to co-operate, his task would be easier by far.

Eventually Roe employed a capable agent of his own, and began to feel more hopeful. Dispatching to Venice (where Arundel spent much of his time) the marbles he had already succeeded in gathering, he sat back and waited. As good a hunter as the indefatigable Mr. Petty, the new agent traveled to every corner of Greece, and as fast as he unearthed new treasure he buried it in the sand for safekeeping or left it with the Greeks until he could return from his continued explorations. Things were looking up for Roe—and then suddenly his agent died before the task was completed, leaving only some illegible papers to show where the finds had been secreted.

A century and a half later, many of the dramatic elements of this tale were repeated in the course of Lord Elgin's quest for Greek marbles—only now it was the collector himself who was Ambassador to the Porte and who, being on the spot, spurred his agents on to the chase. One of those agents, a reincarnation of Petty named Hunt, traveled the whole area in search of antiquities. Another, Battista Lusieri, gave the best part of his life to the Elgin collection. Italian by birth and artist by profession, he had been engaged originally to make drawings of the ancient monuments, but he remained on as his Lordship's agent long after the Ambassador's own departure, and he died in Athens years afterward. His devotion was largely in vain, for all his valuable drawings were shipwrecked on their way to Italy.

As Arundel had been confronted by the victorious French ambassador of the old manuscripts, so now Elgin's chief rival was another French ambassador, the Comte de Choiseul-Gouffier. This, the Napoleonic period, witnessed a great resurgence of interest in archaeology, and more than ever European nations were vying for the possession of relics. Elgin was hoping to form a collection that would equal or better the work done by French savants in Egypt, but what he could accomplish depended to a large extent upon the relative fortunes at any given moment of the French and British armies and navies. When the French seemed to be winning, not even bribes could move the Turkish officials—if the bribes were English. In the end it was largely the British victories in Egypt that made possible the export to England of the Elgin Collection.

Political intrigue was but one of the difficulties. Traveling through Greece in 1802, sometimes spending half a day at a stretch on horseback over rough mountain roads, Lord and Lady Elgin were shaken by earthquake, alarmed by the plague. Lost trails, tents rendered almost unbearable by smoke, fleas, and excessive heat attended the couple. Robbers by land and pirates by sea were encountered, but Lord and Lady saw it through.

To solve the problem of shipping heavy marbles in vessels then available required the utmost ingenuity, and one of the Elgin ships, the *Mentor,* sank with its cargo and was laboriously salvaged. Lady Elgin herself tackled the task of getting some of the most unwieldy pieces aboard ship, and still infectious over the years is the note of delightful triumph in a series of femininely bubbling letters to her husband. When Lord Elgin was away from Athens for a week (May 19–26, 1802), she reported with glee how she had put to work her feminine wiles to secure the shipment of certain cases that were considered too large for the *Mutine,* then in port:

"In the morning I sent a *very civil* message to Capt. Hoste saying I was sorry to hear he was so ill and if there was anything I could send him it would give me great pleasure," she began. "I then coaxed over the Lieutenant to prevale upon the Captain to take the Three large cases you saw in the Magazine. I told him they were seven feet long, he gave me little hopes as it was impossible to put anything above three feet long in the hold. I then found it necessary to use my persuasive powers . . . *Female* eloquence as *usual* succeeded, the Capt. sent me a very polite answer, and by peep of day I sent him down the 3 cases."

The next day the lady hunter pressed her efforts still further:

". . . having got them safely off my Hands, I next set to work to see if I could not contrive to get away something *more.* What say you to Dot? This is a Holliday nobody will work, but I have offered *Backcheses* [tips]. Lusieri is all astonishment at me, he says he never saw anybody so keen as me . . ."

By eleven that night she reports:

"Now for some news that will please you. I have got another large case packed up this Day, a long piece of the Baso Relievo from ye Temple of Minerva, I forget the *proper term,* so I have by *my* management *got on board* 4 immense long heavy packages, and tomorrow the Horse's head etc. etc. is to be carefully packed up and sent on board; this is *all* that is ready for going . . . The *two* last Cases is *intirely* my doing, and I feel proud, Elgin!"

The day before Elgin's return his tireless lady seeks to accomplish the one thing she knows will please him most.

"But in hopes that I shall be the *first* to tell you what I have done for you— Know that besides the 5 cases I have already told you of I have prevailed on Capt. Hoste to take *Three* more, two are already on board, and the third will be taken when he returns from Corinth. How I have faged to get all this done, do you love me better for it, Elgin? . . . And *how* I have pushed Lusieri to get Cases made for these last three large packages!"

Finally her successes challenge the supremacy of the dignified ambassador himself.

"I beg you will shew delight (Lay aside the Deplomatic Character) to Capt. Hoste for taking so much on board," she writes. "I am now *satisfied* of what I always thought; which is how much *more* Women can do if they set about it, than Men. I will lay any bet had you been here you would not have got half so much on board."

She tells him of further plans for getting things down from the Acropolis, and then drops a postscript caution:

"Mind, Elgin, you do not drop this letter out of your pocket."

All collecting adventures, however, do not fall to the big-game hunters. Adventure can live as well at the stamp collector's table as he wields his magnifying glass or in the quiet cabinet of the china fancier, for it is not by any means exclusively dependent upon physical encounters, and intrinsically it makes no difference that the little man may acquire his find, not behind the darkened walls of a war-torn foreign city after numerous perils but in an obscure shop in his home town. The thrill of the record collector, for example, who, going through piles of awful platters in a secondhand store, suddenly comes upon an original Caruso, may well equal Ballard's when the elusive "bird" rug was so unexpectedly revealed to him one night in Thrace.

Every amateur in any field who uses his imagination to recreate the history of his treasures experiences adventure in still another sense, for he lives it vicariously in their life stories. A lamp that lighted the home of a pioneer, or an ancient flintlock that fired at Indians from behind a stockade, a snuff-box buried for safekeeping by some fleeing nobleman at the time of the French Revolution and dug up long afterward, a coin that has traversed the long road of time and space between ancient Greece and modern America—these are eloquent of adventure.

Even a child can find vicarious adventure in the postage stamp. Suppose that his album contains a "cover" from Niuafooa Island in the South Pacific, a cover bearing the curious cachet, "Tin Can Mail." Investigating, he will learn that no ship can anchor at this remote South Sea island, and so when mail is to be delivered or taken off the island, a tin can attached to line is thrown from a vessel far offshore, and through the sharky waters a native swimmer acts as mailman. He would be a dull youngster indeed who did not in some measure imaginatively participate in the adventurous undertaking implied. Or perhaps, rummaging through the family attic, he comes upon an old Pony Express envelope recalling those exciting days when Buffalo Bill rode the mails across the plains. As he grows older, if stamps remain his interest, he will come to realize that the difficulties involved in transporting the mails across an expanding America, before the construction of the first transcontinental railway, constitute one of the most interesting phases of philatelic study from the historic point of view.

There can be adventure in attending a country auction. Perhaps you have bid in an old sea chest and opening it you find a packet of letters, brown at the edges but still legible, by means of which you can reconstruct in part the story of the man who once sailed all seas with the chest now yours. Such adventures befall many sedentary collectors. The son of a Boston lighthouse keeper was exploring the ruins of an old house on Middle Brewster Island in Boston harbor recently, when he came upon a rotting leather jacket. Rummaging in the pocket he pulled out a tattered yellow sheet of paper. In old-fashioned characters was a ballad entitled *The Lighthouse Tragedy*. The lightkeeper's son was more than casually interested when an expert told him that his discovery was a copy of a ballad written by Benjamin Franklin when the latter was fourteen years old. Mentioned in the *Autobiography*, no copy of the poem had been known in a hundred and seventy-five years. To come upon such a find in such a manner is adventure of high order.

Collecting can and often does begin without conscious intent; but once actually engaged in the hunt the tyro will find a number of different methods available, his choice depending upon his personal needs and preferences.

Occasionally he will be content (and find it feasible) to rely solely upon the receipt of gifts; but even so he must find a way to make known his desires—he must, in other words, set traps—and to this extent he follows the chase sitting down. So on birthdays and anniversaries, when his friends and relatives are good enough to inquire of him his desire, he will say: "Well, if you really want to know, I'm collecting old bottles (or shaving mugs or etchings by so-and-so) and I saw one in a window the other day. . . ." Before long most of his friends, delighted to have found a permanent solution to the troublesome gift problem, will have become his agents, each searching, with the approach of the year's gift days, for just one more item for George's blessed collection.

This procedure alone of course is not for most collectors, although it may prove useful in supplementing other efforts. If there is little or no money available for the hobby, the collector may rely upon finding items—like the milkman who collects amusing or unusual notes left in bottles by customers.

The "finding" collector may map out a plan of action as carefully as an expedition leader, testing hunting grounds for quality and techniques for effectiveness. He may follow this method not because he is impecunious but because, as part of his philosophy of collecting, he has set up a definite rule against the relatively "easy" method of purchase. It becomes a matter of professional pride that the formation of his collection should depend entirely upon his own ingenuity and perspicacity, unfortified by the use of money. He challenges himself to accomplish the harder task, and when he succeeds in creating something valuable, the very limitations he has set for himself return good dividends, for he has built alone and by the sweat of his brow. Even when he permits himself a nominal expenditure, like the autograph collector who assembled a fifty-thousand-dollar album by regularly and painstakingly going through the junkman's sack in search of letters, bills, documents (anything bearing a signature that might one day be important) he remains a "finder" nevertheless.

Closely allied to the gift and finding techniques—because it, too, represents a way of getting something for nothing—is that of actively soliciting items. This is a favorite method among autograph hounds who are usually most adept as trailers and trappers.

Numerous are the ways by which autograph collectors, if they are sufficiently clever, may catch their victims unaware. A favorite technique of long standing is to write a letter which demands an answer, preferably the sort of letter which, because of its provocative nature, can be counted upon to arouse the quarry to action. Often unscrupulously employed, this method has been found most effective.

Take the case of William Riddle, a nineteenth-century Englishman who acquired many valuable "autograph letters signed" by using this technique. Each letter that he wrote in pursuit of his hobby contained a question aimed straight at the mark, and he always neglected to mention the fact that what he really wanted was not an answer to his question *per se* but an interesting A. L. S. for his collection. When he desired John Stuart Mill's signature, he wrote inquiring about a specific phase of political economy. To Charles Dickens he submitted a child's manuscript story and asked the novelist's opinion of it. Of Ruskin he inquired how a man could know whether or not it was his true vocation to become a lecturer. From Richard Cobden he requested some reference sources on Cobden's life history. In each case he received a prompt reply. Ruskin succumbed to this letter ruse more than once, but perhaps the cleverest trap ever set for him was by a man who, knowing that the author had a particular aversion to a certain religious sect, wrote in the name of the sect, asking for a contribution toward a new church building. Ruskin answered immediately in scathing words that later brought a very good price in the autograph market.

Not all collectors of contemporary signatures are tricksters. Some, on the contrary, employ a disarming frankness. They treat the prey with consideration, stating their requests openly and enclosing postage for the hoped-for reply. Their method is really the wiser of the two, for when it succeeds it will in all likelihood bring in an item of very real personal interest. When Robert Louis Stevenson was living in Samoa, a collector who wrote to ask him for an autograph letter not only enclosed postage but went to the trouble of sending Samoan stamps. Stevenson was so touched by this extra measure of consideration that he, in turn, took especial pains to compose something better than the usual perfunctory lines. And one Samuel Simpson of Liverpool, who phrased a similar request to Robert Southey on the flattering grounds that without the poet's signature his series of autographs of distinguished writers "must remain forever incomplete," bagged the following unique prize, a bit of doggerel composed especially for the occasion:

> *"Inasmuch as you, Sam, a descendant of Sim,*
> *For collecting handwritings have taken a whim,*
> *And to me, Robert Southey, petition have made,*
> *In a civil and nicely-penned letter—postpaid—*
> *That I to your album so gracious would be*
> *As to fill up a page there appointed for me,*
> *Five couplets I send you, by aid of the Nine—*
> *They will cost you in postage a penny a line:*
> *At Keswick, October the sixth, they were done,*
> *One thousand eight hundred and twenty and one."*

Another technique, and one more generally employed in all fields, is that of trading or swapping. It is a friendly method and like finding or soliciting, has special advantages for the slim in purse; but even collectors who could well afford to buy anything they wanted short of the moon have sometimes resorted to it. Charles I of England swapped the Holbein Windsor drawings for a Raphael owned by the Earl of Pembroke. Richelieu was a confirmed swapper of books. And the late King George V of England is reputed to have sent Clara Bow, the original American "It" girl, three stamps from his collection for one of hers that he wanted.

Our Chinese friend, Mi Fei, had something delicate to say about swapping when he declared that scholars prefer to exchange paintings and manuscripts among themselves because that is a more "refined way" than purchase. Such, however, is hardly the motive which impels most Occidental collectors to trade items. With them the method is either a matter of convenience or of sport, of solving the problem of getting something new to replace something no longer desirable without spending any more money. To locate the owner of something desired adds zest to the hunt. It puts one on one's mettle to obtain in fair exchange, at least in one's opinion of the moment, as good as or better than one gives. Some people actually enjoy the whole procedure involved in making a successful trade, and, like the old-fashioned American horse coper, would of choice refuse to deal in cash. It seems to them a relatively simple matter to set a money price upon an object or to check such a price against the standard market value. It is considerably more difficult, they feel, to pit one object against another, to maneuver your adversary into wanting to hand over to you what he has that you want.

Among children, swapping is a ready favorite, and the young ones frequently collect duplicates expressly for such use. Although the method has its limitations for the adult and is seldom the only technique of expansion employed, it is nevertheless firmly planted as a means of acquisition and enjoyment, as every collector's magazine, with its "Swappers' Column," testifies.

Seizure by force is another technique of acquisition which we have already had occasion to discuss at some length. Plunder, outright or disguised, comes under this head—a method which victorious nations and powerful individuals have always used. Not infrequently, pictures, books and *objets d'art* that have been stolen from galleries, libraries and museums are bought by collectors who are fully aware of how their purchases were obtained by the vendors. These are the collecting "fences," the illegal purchasers, and their numbers include some surprisingly reputable names.

Many genuinely impeccable citizens who have never actually stolen an item in their lives admit to the insistence of the temptation. Others cheerfully acknowledge occasional falls from grace. One, who preferred to remain anonymous, once wrote a delightful article entitled, *The Criminal Confessions of a Collector.* This gentleman, who can now be identified as Dr. Walter Prichard Eaton of Yale University, owned an old New England farmhouse that he wanted to restore and furnish in proper period style. A lover of antiques, he watched with what amounted to physical and spiritual agony the havoc being wrought all about him by the ignorance and neglect of his neighbors. A farmer would buy a fine old paneled house for the beams, say, then rip everything else to pieces, including the precious paneling which once gone was irreplaceable. Fire and exposure accounted for many losses to which this amateur was a dismayed witness. Often he saw the remains of fine old furniture that had been thrown into the woodpile to make room for the latest horrors out of Grand Rapids. And when the gentleman could bear the destruction no longer he made up his mind to become a detective—and a marauder.

His "criminal" career had begun and thenceforward he made a practice of breaking into abandoned houses and taking whatever he could find that was good—mantels, paneling, hinges, cranes, doors, chairs, tables, anything that was old and fine:

"I consider myself a sort of Society for the Preservation of New England Antiquities—or any others that come my way," he declared. "Some people have described certain of my activities by a shorter and uglier term. But they are jealous. They envy me my house . . . and they envy me my courage to take what I want when I see it . . . I have crawled and poked amid the rubbish and brambles in old cellar holes. I have followed old roads marked on the map where no traveled road now exists, and have been rewarded by broken car-springs, bent wishbones, punctured tires—and a corner cupboard! I have acquired hand-wrought hardware from a farmer's pig pen—he had used the original front door of his ancient dwelling for one side of the pen—and once I drove twenty-one miles over the worst road in New England to get a latch I had heard of. I had to pay two dollars for it, too. Somebody was living in the house."

Usually somebody does live in the house; but just because a collector may buy the majority of his items, it does not follow that he is any the less a hunter. From the wealthy man perusing the reports and cables of his agents, to the prowler of little shops, every true collector remains constantly on the alert for clues. He may have a regular espionage system to aid him—tipsters whose whole business in life is to ferret out the game—but whether or not he can afford such assistance, he trains himself to recognize every lead.

The greatest prize in the Folger Library—the unique 1594 copy of *Titus Andronicus*—was acquired because of Mr. Folger's own watchfulness and knowledge of his subject. No copy of this edition had been seen in many years and none was believed to be extant. Then, in 1904, a copy was discovered in a private library in Sweden. Inconspicuously, the New York *Sun* published a short notice of the find, and the Folger eye happened upon it. The book sounded genuine enough and the collector lost no time in cabling a London dealer to send an expert courier on the trail. The following week two dealers in great excitement, and somewhat overoptimistically, informed Folger that they would soon be in a position to offer him a copy of the long-lost *Titus Andronicus*—1594. Their client smiled, for he himself had beaten them to the kill.

The buyers hunt in many places—in the specialty shops, at auctions

THE MOST LAMENTABLE ROMAINE

Tragedie of Titus Andronicus:

As it was Plaide by the Right Honourable the Earle of *Darbie*, Earle of *Pembrooke*, and Earle of *Suffex* their Seruants.

LONDON,
Printed by Iohn Danter, and are
to be ſold by *Edward White & Thomas Millington*,
at the little North doore of Paules at the
ſigne of the Gunne.
1594.

Title-page of the unique 1594 First Quarto of Shakespeare's Titus Andronicus, *prized above the First Folios.*

and in private homes, in "thrift" shops and out-and-out junk stores, in charity institutions where the discards of their ancestors have been deposited, at Police Department sales and lost-and-found disposals. They develop an uncanny flair for buried treasure, and a capacity for guile in dissembling their true interest in such matters that would do credit to the cat innocently looking out the window while its mind was on the canary. Like all members of the tribe (from the youngest swapper without five cents, to the oldest and wealthiest habitué of the great sales) purchasing collectors enjoy testing their own skill; and since the measure of their success is based at least partially upon monetary standards of value, they take an enormous pride in being able to acquire an item for far less than its true worth. The acme of this talent is to be found in "junk snupping" defined by no less a person than the elder Mrs. Theodore Roosevelt as,

"The art of finding quaint and valuable things in junk heaps, and the ability to get them cheap."

Walking the streets of Florence, one day, the renaissance amateur, Niccolò Niccoli, passed an urchin about whose neck there hung a grimy cameo. The novice might not have noticed it, but the connoisseur's hunting eye fastened on the gem like the greyhound to the rabbit. A second later he had the child by the arm and was fingering the fine carving, so beautiful that it might have been the work of the great Polycletus himself. Niccolò's heart pounded with excitement; yet he was bland enough when he stopped at the boy's home and purchased the cameo for a few ducats. Later he sold it reluctantly for two hundred to Cardinal Scarampi, a fiery collector who forced the sale upon spying the prize among Niccolò's possessions. The next owner of this precious *calcedonio* was no less a connoisseur than Pope Paul II; and when finally it entered the collection of Lorenzo de' Medici, Niccolò's chance discovery was valued at fifteen hundred gold florins.

The immortal collector, Cardinal Mazarin, came by chance upon a bauble which his own trained eye turned, in effect, into the foundation stone of his vast fortune. While still a young, obscure and relatively impecunious papal nuncio traveling back and forth between Rome and Paris on church affairs, Mazarin stopped one day at Montserrat. There a provincial priest happened to mention a chaplet he had found while digging in his garden. The circumstances were interesting, said the priest, but the chaplet itself was of no value, a mere trinket made of glass. Mazarin asked if he might see it. "A pretty thing," he remarked casually, after a brief examination. "I think I might enjoy owning it. Would you take a few crowns for it?" Thinking himself in luck, the priest agreed with considerable alacrity. And Mazarin—who knew that the "glass" stones actually were emeralds, sapphires and diamonds—walked off with a piece that he later disposed of for the equivalent of some two hundred and ninety-one thousand six hundred dollars.

It is not always the potential profit in treasure trove that is of greatest importance to your dyed-in-the-wool collector, however. Often enough it is the pure joy of discovery that he most relishes. So Harry Elkins Widener, who, being the heir to a great fortune, might well have been content to conduct his search for rare books through the regular channels of trade, sometimes went fishing for the sake of the heightened sport he found in more remote streams. He was once discovered on his hands and knees under a table in a bookstore going through a pile of dusty books that had not been touched in years. Suddenly he pulled a copy of Swinburne out of the debris, and there came over his face that luminously happy smile of the collector who has just made a big catch—the volume was a first-edition presentation copy, treasure trove of the first water. "This is better than working in a gold mine!" he exclaimed.

Although a prize may flop into anyone's lap, in the long run there is no substitute for the specialist's knowledge. The textile amateur, for example, knows that antique furniture which has been frequently re-covered is likely to conceal some fine old fabric under the commonplace upper coverings: he has only to strip it down for examination and he may happen on a prize. Similarly the autograph collector learns that people often hid deeds and other valuable papers in the backs of picture frames where they may still, upon lucky occasion, be found; and he who loves Currier and Ives prints knows that before these prints became collector's items they were sometimes used for padding behing bright new chromos, as we might employ a discarded calendar picture for a similar purpose. The bibliophile has heard that old bookbinders often took leaves out of any handy volume and used them as inner reinforcements for the bindings of new books. He knows that one of the rarest specimens of Caxton's printing—an Indulgence—was discovered so used inside the binding of an old book, and he may have heard of other treasures found by collectors upon careful examination of these inner binding papers. Despite their mutilated condition, these book-fragments are often valuable, since, secure in their hiding places, they may have become the only bits of the original work which have survived.

The merest accident often leads to the discovery of treasure trove, and such accidents occur in every part of the world, both in war and in peace.

A subway is dug in Rome—and two antique Roman statues in good condition appear.

Bombs are dropped from a plane in Libya in 1940 and the ruins of a temple in which Cleopatra may have worshiped are brought to light; while two years later American soldiers digging for road gravel near Paestum stumble upon a stone-age burial ground replete with relics, perhaps the oldest archaeological find of its kind yet to be made in Italy.

A man in New Mexico cleans out a well—and finds a bucketful of old Spanish coins and jewelry, by weight alone worth nine thousand dollars. They are thought to have been part of the famous collection once owned by J. S. Candelario, an Indian trader who lived on the place, but how they got into the well remains a mystery.

In Paris some workmen are in the midst of demolishing an old building in the *rue Mouffetard,* when they uncover a cache containing three thousand six hundred twenty-franc gold pieces of the time of Louis XV. A document found with the coins shows that these were hidden in 1756 by the royal secretary, Claude Nivelle. Collectors pay from eighteen to twenty-five dollars apiece for the best specimens when the coins are put up at auction and the workmen divide the profits with Nivelle's heirs.

Excavators preparing for the construction of a department store in White Plains, New York, reveal a section of tunnel thought to have been used as a hideaway by General Howe and his officers just before the Battle of White Plains. Bearing out the theory is the nature of the Revolutionary relics scattered throughout the tunnel.

And far away in Ethiopia, a Coptic monastery's entire collection of manuscripts is thrown into an unused well for safekeeping during an Arab invasion of the country. The Sheik who later retrieves these manuscripts sells them to J. P. Morgan for four hundred thousand dollars.

It is not always or even most often by excavation that treasure trove is discovered. Dr. Williamson, Morgan's expert on miniatures and jewelry, once dropped a frame containing a valuable miniature. To his horror he saw it split as it struck the floor, but when he stooped to pick it up he realized that it was not broken. The impact of the fall had touched a secret spring in the upper half of the case which now turned out to be a double frame. Within the upper section, thus disclosed for the first time, lay a second miniature in a better state of preservation (because of its long protection from the light) than the first, already so highly prized.

Toward the end of the nineteenth century the ancient Castle of Teylingen in Holland was destroyed by fire. As much of the furniture as could be saved was thereafter sold at auction, and fifteen dealers who had connived with each other to secure the items cheaply, held a post-sale "knockout" to divide up the loot. While they were busy about their shady affairs a child, playing with a dilapidated casket that lay ignored upon the ground, touched a hidden spring in the box. There was a click, and a secret drawer sprang out. One of the rainbow's two feet stood in that drawer, and the boy plunged his hands into glowing colors and played with the bright stuff that had been revealed. His performance was not long unobserved. Babbling with excitement and mutual congratulations his elders had soon pushed him aside and were crowding over the ancient casket. Those diamonds and rubies, all those precious stones, were the famous long-lost jewels of Teylingen which the imprisoned Jacqueline of Bavaria, Countess of Holland and Zeeland (who died in 1437) had successfully concealed from her oppressors so long ago. They made the fifteen dealers richer by a sum never publicly disclosed but estimated at well over half a million dollars when dollars were big and fat.

The emotions, too, have played stellar roles in revealing collection riches; and while some emotions are more to be recommended from most points of view, in all fairness to the truth it must be admitted that anger has now and again brought unexpected happiness in this particular connection. In an English country house there was once a desk with a recalcitrant drawer which stubbornly resisted being pulled out all the way. Naturally this was inconvenient, but members of the household finally agreed that the desk must have been built with a stud placed in the drawer for this express purpose and so they usually ignored it altogether. Then one day someone wanted to reach a paper which had slid toward the back. His patience finally exhausted, he pulled lustily. To his astonishment there came a noise of breaking glass, whereupon the hitherto stubborn drawer willingly came forward, a reformed character. It was removed, and in the dark reaches was found a handsome miniature, intact except for its glass. Inquiry revealed that it was a valuable heirloom which, when it had disappeared a generation before, had been presumed stolen.

In the winter of 1899 Dr. George A. Reisner was directing a series of archaeological excavations in Tebtunis, Egypt. Things were going poorly for the doctor. Gloom spread through the camp, for no matter how valiantly the workmen might dig they could turn up nothing but mummified crocodiles. A few of these were interesting, but enough was enough and no more were needed or wanted. It so happens that, in order to prevent stealing, Arabs who work for such expeditions are usually paid separately for each valuable item they unearth. Dr. Reisner finally refused to pay for any more bandaged crocodiles, but still the beasts appeared. The leader's annoyance was matched by that of his workmen who now found themselves deprived of the usual gratuities. Finally, in an unsphinxlike rage, one of the Arabs picked up his latest find and dashed it to the ground. The mummy flew apart as he had expected, but his ill temper turned to delight when the wreckage revealed quantities of the very stuff—old papyrus covered with strange pictures—for which his eccentric employer always stood ready to pay the best price!

Confronted with this discovery, Dr. Reisner proceeded to break up all the scorned crocodiles with great care, for he soon realized that papyri, discarded by the ancients, had been used as wrapping paper for the inner layers of all these animal mummies, and today the documents thus recovered are included in the fine collection of the University of California.

Most specimens of early English pewter now in collections have been found in wells, in drains, in old blocked-up cupboards or between the floors of ancient dwellings. The old Pewterers Company, forbade its members to mend any broken pieces on the theory that it was better for the trade that new ones should be made and sold rather than used ones preserved. Unable to find craftsmen who would repair their damaged pewter dishes, tankards and candlesticks, the owners threw them into obscure holes and corners from which, now and again, they still reappear.

The factors responsible for lost or hidden treasure are often as dramatic as the circumstances attending the rediscovery. Sometimes an old and half-forgotten tragedy is shrouded in the history, as with the fragments of beautiful Orvieto chinaware cast down into a well upon order of a local priest who, applying rudimentary principles of hygiene, thought to check the spread of plague by forcing the populace to discard its dishes. Centuries later a modern inhabitant of this Italian hill town was cleaning out his well and came upon the shattered remains of once lovely pieces. He took the trouble to restore them and today his family does a thriving business manufacturing copies of the ware with its quaint medieval designs in emerald green or orange yellow on white.

Romance as well as tragedy lay behind the disappearance of Gainsborough's famous portrait of Mrs. Graham, a canvas which now belongs to the Edinburgh Gallery. As the tale has it, the lady died soon after her portrait had been completed and her husband, finding that constant sight of her likeness reminded him too poignantly of his loss, had the painting walled up. Perhaps intentionally, perhaps through neglect, he failed to tell anyone what he had done; and for a generation's time the existence of the Graham portrait was forgotten. When a new owner took over the property many years afterward, he ordered a wall torn out to increase the length of one of the rooms—and there hung the lost Gainsborough, now considered one of the artist's best works.

The annals of book collecting and philately vie with each other in the number of miraculous tales of rediscovery. An English dealer buys a pile of unsorted music at a sale. Most of it he gives away, but he keeps a few sheets for himself. Looking through these one evening he discovers a quarto pamphlet tucked away between two pieces of music. He is startled to find that it is a copy in original wrappers of the *Posthumous Fragments of Margaret Nicholson,* edited by Fitzvictor. Being an initiate, he knows that Fitzvictor was one of Shelley's pen names, and that Shelley propagandist pamphlets are extremely rare. Later he is able to dispose of this haphazard find for one thousand two hundred and ten pounds.

In Derby, England, lives a barber who has inherited along with his barber shop a small stack of books. The barber's wife is taken sick, and in order to entertain her, her husband brings home one of the books from the shop. It is a copy of *Pilgrim's Progress,* but that of course means nothing to the barber. Then the family doctor pays a call and happens to glance at the bedside literature. Reaching for the volume he sees that it is a first edition, in good condition except for the lack of two pages. "Send that book to Sotheby's in London and get them to tell you its worth," he urges the barber, adding that he is sure it must be quite valuable. But the barber snorts derisively. How could his impoverished family have owned anything of value? At last, under pressure, he consents, but he feels very sheepish indeed about the whole affair. With the book he sends an illiterate and apologetic letter, explaining that a foolish friend has suggested the volume may be worth something but adding that he himself is sure it cannot be. If he is right, Sotheby's have his permission to throw the thing away. Sotheby's, however, send back word that this copy of *Pilgrim's Progress* should be worth at least nine hundred pounds, and that if the owner is willing they will put it up for sale at their next auction. The barber's reply to this communication is, naturally enough, somewhat incoherent, and heaven alone can understand his words when he hears that his "worthless" book has brought twenty-five hundred pounds, more money than he has seen in a lifetime of shaving and snipping.

Mr. George Dexter, Boston collector, travels abroad and picks up a book at a private sale of an old French library in Brussels. It is a small volume printed in Amsterdam in 1648 and still bound in the original vellum. Its frivolous text has no particular interest for the collector, who is, however, attracted to the book by an engraving which forms the frontispiece. Then his wife notices that the front flyleaves are pasted together, and Dexter remembers that this was a trick frequently resorted to during the French Revolution. A gentleman in those days knowing that he was about to be executed would, if he possessed volumes with valuable autographs and was unable to communicate with exiled members of his family, paste the flyleaves together with flour paste and hope that relatives would later stumble upon the treasure: it was his last slim hope of providing for them. Recalling this fact, Dexter carefully pries apart the two pages, sees a signature and a cryptogram. The signature reads "Louis Soleil, 1684," and the cryptogram, later deciphered, declares, "If you know who was called Soleil, you know who signed this book." Dubious, as a good collector must be, Dexter has the signature examined at the *Bibliothèque Nationale.* It proves to be genuine. A bit of personal history comes to the fore. It is recalled that "Soleil" was the name given Louis XIV by Madame de Maintenon, the lady whom he married at Christmas, 1683, after the death of the empress and shortly before Dexter's little book was inscribed. A well-known firm excitedly offers an enormous sum. "We know of no other book signed 'Soleil,' " they say, but Dexter, ever the true amateur, refuses to part with his unique association item.

A dealer recently offered a certain law firm five hundred dollars, sight unseen, for a single sack of the firm's old letters which were about to be discarded. Why? Perhaps he had heard of the janitor who once brought another dealer some hundreds of United States and Canadian stamps, including a number of rarities, which had come from some miscellaneous junk and waste paper found in an old business house. When the dealer instituted a search for the rest of the papers, he learned that they had already been shipped to a New Jersey plant for repulping and had been mixed up in a three-car shipment including a quantity of waste paper from other sources. In order to obtain the privilege of searching for the letters he wanted, the dealer then had to buy the entire shipment, but he gambled that the venture would prove worth the money and time required, bought the three carloads of paper and recovered fifteen thousand dollars worth of stamps.

Or perhaps the dealer who was so anxious to obtain the law firm's sack of old letters had in mind the Philadelphia man whose business it was to buy scrap paper. This man once saw a pile of old letters, books and papers on the floor of an office being vacated by a banking firm. He offered fifteen dollars for the rubbish and his offer was accepted. For some reason he decided to sort over the papers before disposing of them in his usual fashion. Treasure trove lay hidden in his rubbish pile, treasure in the shape of a number of autographs of famous men, some old unused stamps

---

BEAUTY AND VALUE. *Qualities of beauty and significance are prime criteria of value for some. This vase (opposite) is decorated with cartouches depicting the Hundred Antiques or Precious Things,* famille noire *enamels. Engraved gems and seals have been prized collectors' items from early times (opposite page), and from the renaissance until the fateful Poniatowksi Sale in 1839 they ranked high among fashionable collectibles throughout Europe. Faking on a wide scale resulted, and when every item in the famed Poniatowski Collection was proved spurious, the field fell to ruin, nor has it yet recovered. From top down: 1) Graeco-Roman intaglio, Syrian garnet, signed Gaius [artist]; ex Chesterfield, Bessborough and Marlborough colls. 2) Intaglio, early 5th cent.* B.C.*, scaraboid, mottled chalcedony, inscribed "I am [the seal] of Hermotimos" [owner]; ex Evans coll. 3) Intaglio, late 1st cent.* B.C.*, sard, inscribed Popilius Albanus [owner]; ex Tyszkiewicz coll. 4) Intaglio, late 5th cent.* B.C.*, scaraboid, yellow jasper mottled red, signed Dexamenos [artist]; ex Evans coll. 5) Graeco-Roman cameo, sardonyx, signed Tryphon [artist]; ex Arundel and Marlborough colls. 6) Hellenistic intaglio, black jasper; ex Ludovisi and Tyszkiewicz colls.*

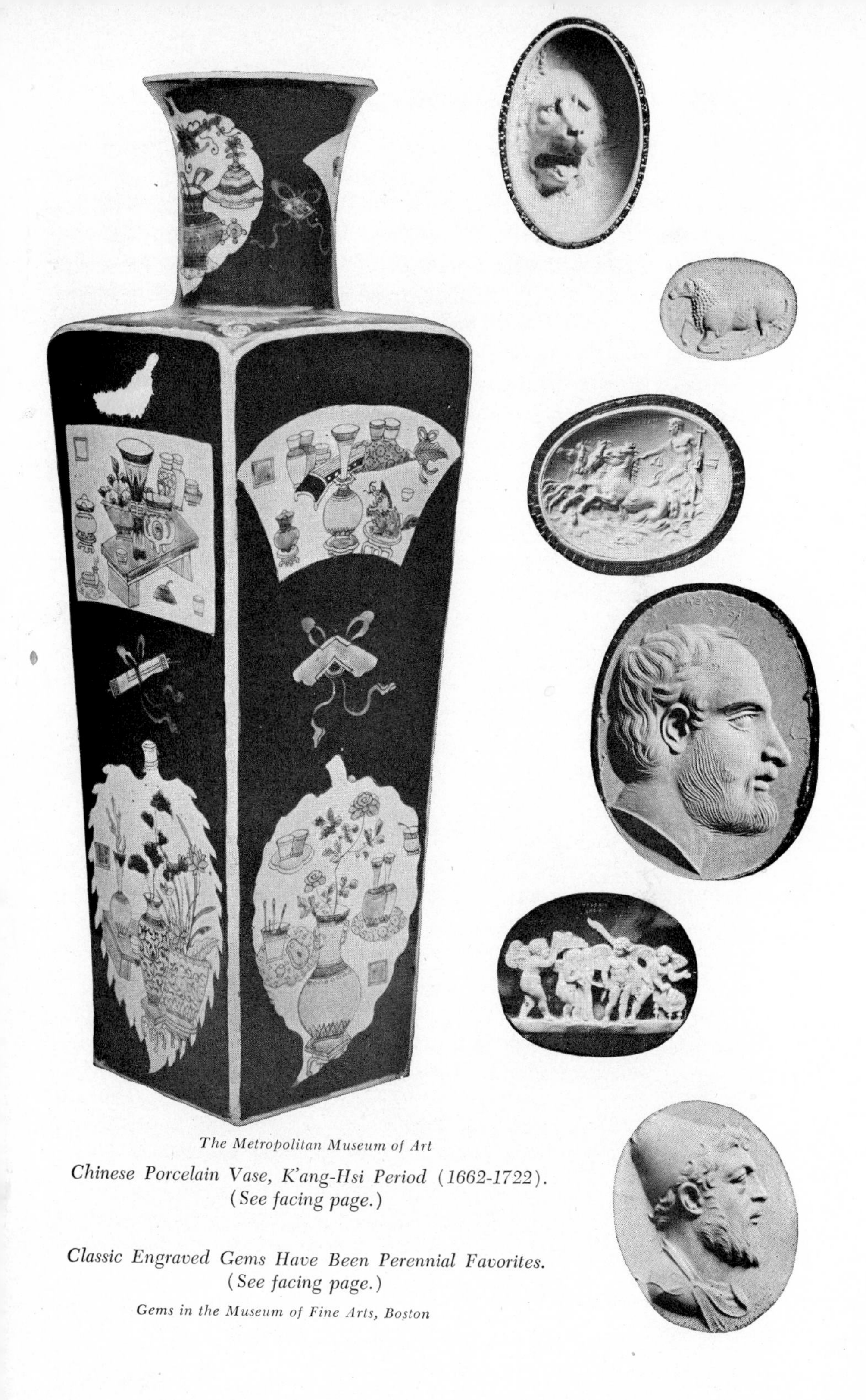

The Metropolitan Museum of Art

Chinese Porcelain Vase, K'ang-Hsi Period (1662-1722).
(See facing page.)

Classic Engraved Gems Have Been Perennial Favorites.
(See facing page.)

Gems in the Museum of Fine Arts, Boston

and hundreds of canceled ones. The stamps alone turned out to be worth more than seventy-five thousand dollars.

Less fortunate is the stamp collector who threw away four unknown "errors" now estimated to be worth seven hundred and fifty dollars each. They were found not long ago by a Massachusetts garbage man who happened to show them to a boy who was interested in stamps. The boy knew enough to suspect their value. He got in touch with dealers, and these stamps which once lived precariously in a garbage can are now favored property of one of the foremost American stamp collectors, a Du Pont official.

A seedy looking fellow who could well have used a bit of treasure trove once brought a batch of old books into a shop, and parted with them for the price of a good meal. The dealer, who had given about three cents apiece for the items in the lot, had not examined them. He knew they would be good for ten, fifteen, twenty-five cents apiece to sentimentalists who purchase any book which happens to look a bit battered and worn. Sorting the items, his eye lit upon a pamphlet in brown paper wrappers. Entitled *Prose Romances. No. I. Containing The Murders in the Rue Morgue,* published in Philadelphia in 1843, it was a first edition (at that time only three or four "firsts" of this Poe masterpiece were known to be extant, although more have turned up since) and the dealer very tenderly laid it aside. Within a few days this find had changed hands, and a famous collector had parted with twenty thousand dollars in order to obtain it. What the twenty thousand would have done for the indigent who sold the little pamphlet for a penny or two no one could ever learn, since he had lacked the magic password to open the door of a new world. With the books under his arm he was unaware that Lady Luck walked with him in the street, and when he left the shop he was more alone than he knew.

Obviously the dealer or collector who knows his subject well has a tremendous advantage over the uninformed owner of a desirable item. The successful hunt for treasure trove frequently depends upon this fact, and the collector bent upon his game of getting the best for as little as possible seldom feels bound to consider the ethics of the case. If he must do battle for possession against another collector, he will pay to the limits of his purse's endurance; but when it comes to pitting his knowledge against a stranger's innocence he can put Machiavelli himself to shame and be proud of it.

Not all the greediness is on one side, however, nor all the dubious conduct. In sections of the country that have been awakened to the potential value of antiques, the "simple" folk will not hesitate to gouge overeager collectors who come knocking at the door, and it so happens that the items in a true antique shop may often be bought at prices no higher and sometimes lower than at the "stocked" farmhouse run by canny natives. Yet even in such cases the odds are on the side of the knowing collector. When all is said and done, it is fair enough that knowledge should command something of a premium, but should the innocent and perhaps the needy be "outsmarted"? This is a matter for the individual and his inner council to decide. Some have humanitarian codes, and there are, believe it or not, even dealers among them.

The collector knows that once he admits to a craving for a certain object the price will generally go up, up even beyond its actual worth, for barter and trade are the same the world over and always have been. When the sculptor, Cristoforo Romano, wrote to Isabella d'Este to tell her about a crystal cup mounted on a stand of silver-gilt and enamel which he was sure she would want for her collection, he advised her not to let the maker know that her interest in the cup was other than casual. Else, said Romano, the man would be sure to clap another fifty ducats on to a price that was already sufficiently high. Yet, given a sense of honor and fairness on both sides, it should be possible for the collector to obtain his prize without robbing the man who has made or preserved it for him. And sometimes this compromise is successfully effected. We should like, therefore, to close this chapter with the pleasant tale of an English antique dealer and a country couple who had no reason to complain of his treatment of them.

Thomas Rohan, the dealer, and his wife were on one of their periodical tours of the back country. They had stopped at a farmhouse and were talking to the owners. The house, they learned, had been recently inherited, and the young couple who now lived in it were anxious to modernize it—a familiar story. Already most of the old "rubbishy" furniture had been discarded and was being replaced with the English equivalent of Grand Rapids. Rohan pricked up his ears and began to look about. The first thing he saw was a battered old settee tucked away in the corner of the covered veranda. The piece was finely shaped and beautifully carved and the dealer inquired about it.

"That's one of the old things we were speaking of," was the reply.

"It's terribly shabby and we didn't want it in the house. There are two chairs like it in the attic, but the settee was too big to put up there so we've just stuck it here temporarily. We're going to get rid of it as soon as we can."

Rohan asked if he might see the chairs. He explained that he might be willing to buy them. Quite earnestly his young hosts protested. It would not be worth his time, they insisted; the chairs were in terrible shape, actually falling to pieces, worse, even, than the settee.

"If you don't mind," it was the dealer's turn to insist, and finally the two chairs were brought down from the attic and set alongside the larger piece. To a connoisseur the result was breath-taking. Dilapidated the furniture certainly was, but Rohan visualized the three pieces restored: together they formed a matching Chippendale set—a rare prize—and it would be no trick at all to put them into condition.

And what did this English dealer then do? Offer the young couple the few shillings he knew they would protest as too much? Not at all. He proposed a decent price. "I'll give you eighty pounds for the three—if you care to sell."

The farm woman was incredulous. "He doesn't mean it, does he?" she asked Mrs. Rohan. Reassured that the offer was no joke, the young people accepted what to them was a miracle, and they were profuse in their thanks to Rohan for his "generosity." All the things they could buy for their house with eighty pounds!

He laughed it off. "I am not a philanthropist," he assured them with refreshing frankness. "I shall make a fair profit on the set." And he did, very soon afterward.

Part Four

BUYER, BEWARE!

"Beware, ye innocents—there are dangers abroad . . ."

IN THE FOREST of *Collectiana,* where Little Red Riding Hood and her brothers go with baskets to gather up so many fascinating things, the wolves still infest the wood and do a thriving business. Although there are many simon pure items to be picked up quite easily, even when these are at their very brightest the collector is in danger and should be extremely wary; for as soon as the watching wolves see collectors pursuing a new favorite, they scamper back to their lairs, work like mad for a while, then scramble into innocent disguises and stand forth idly dangling the forgery.

When a clamor is set up for certain rarities so that these become rarer still, prices jump and the path of the exploiter is forthwith made easier by the fact that expensiveness is in itself one of the chief criteria of value to the snob collector who, furthermore, is often without ability to distinguish the choice from the rank. Battening upon the ignorance of his clients, the artful charlatan is quick to seize his opportunity and usually succeeds in lining his pockets exceedingly well before his knavery is discovered.

Something of this sort has existed in human society as far back as there has been sufficient demand to induce men to risk the prevailing penalty, and it is even possible that forgers of antique art may have flourished among the cave dwellers eighteen thousand years ago, as Will Durant rather whimsically suggests. However, leaving the cave man to his cave, we can find provable cases of fraudulent imitation in very early times that quite neatly fit the familiar modern pattern.

In Greece of the eighth century before Christ, parvenu merchants were pushing their way into power and trying to climb into high social places in a manner not exactly unknown to our own society. The acquisition of wealth was important then, and display of the symbols of wealth no less so. It was for this reason that every well-to-do householder of that time wished to own quantities of valuable vases which might be exhibited upon public occasions, much as an early American industrialist might desire a collection of Old Masters or a solid gold table service. During that period in ancient Greece, Corinthian potters first began to sign their handiwork, and though at first glance these two phenomena may seem completely unrelated, quite the opposite is true. Signatures served not only to advertise Corinthian products but did duty as trademarks also, and trademarks had become necessary because as the fine Corinthian ware grew more and more popular copyists in other cities began to offer their imitations as the genuine product. In time, because of the mass fashion in buying, this sort of cheating affected other products, until in many cities statues as well as painted vases were being signed or marked by both artist and manufacturer.

In imperial Rome, fakers lived under conditions tailored to their measure. In that period, when almost every Roman collected some sort of art object whether he knew anything about it or not, the sharpers often ignored the originals entirely and passed off their own productions, simply appending the signature of whatever master was most in demand at the moment. According to Phaedrus, in the time of Tiberius Caesar (42 B.C.–A.D. 37):

> ". . . sculptors carved the name of Praxiteles [*fl.* 340 B.C.] on their marbles and the name of Myron [*fl.* 450 B.C.] on everything they wrought in silver."

Little wonder then, since antique Greek works were universally admired and commanded a far better market than native ones, that Roman collectors who wanted to be sure of getting originals often employed experts to advise them.

Even China, the knowing and polite, has produced many fakers energetic enough to capitalize upon a collecting demand; and long ago one brazen Chinese in good standing invaded the royal sanctum in order thus to victimize an Empress. This villain, a clever trickster named Chang I-chih, was the favorite of the Empress Wu-hou (684–705). Suggesting one day that the paintings in the imperial collection were badly in need of repair, Chang convinced the good lady that he should oversee the operation. Removing the paintings, he took them to one of those master counterfeiters to be found "in all climes." After a suitable interval, when the beautifully "restored" collection was returned to the palace, only three men—Chang I-chih, his professional accomplice, and one other—knew that skillful copies reposed in the imperial cabinets. Chang and his painter-friend fattened their purses well on this transaction, but the third man—an unnamed prince who had purchased the stolen originals—lived in a frenzy of fear lest his act should be discovered. Eventually guilt so oppressed him that there was only one way out and he burned all the irreplaceable treasures.

The Italian renaissance, with its hunger for classical antiquities, like China, Greece and Rome had its share of forgers and also a chorus of roguish dealers willing to peddle their products. Not all of the copies made at this time were produced with fraudulent intention, for the renaissance artists went consciously to the classicists for their schooling, but neither could the artists always control the marketing of their works once removed from the studio.

As the legitimate artist needs an agent to market his works, so the fraud generally has his. Behind almost every successful creator of fakes in history has stood an artful dodger ready to handle the business end of a most promising partnership. It should at once be emphasized that the majority of dealers in collectibles are quite honest and no more likely to employ intentional fraud than the majority of other business men. On the other hand, art objects, books and the like offer easier temptation to dishonesty than most commercial wares, and the dealers who set out to exploit the foibles and weaknesses of the collector go far beyond the mere marketing of spurious goods.

In 1776 there was published in France an illuminating little volume which lights our scene well. Entitled *Confession publique du brocanteur* (The Public Confession of a Dealer) its theme is timeless. It was written at the quantitative high-mark of collecting in France, when genuine connoisseurship had fallen off and the careless public was an easy target for charlatans. The danger, then as always, lay not only in actual forgery. Wall Street practices such as "rigging" or "cornering" the market were not the inventions of New York City slickers. Our *brocanteur* relates how he and his companions went about "rigging" the prices on mediocre works of art, and how they managed to depreciate the value of good items temporarily for later gain. To accomplish the first goal, several dealers would get together before a sale and agree to put up the bidding on certain paintings or objects of art which one or more of them wanted particularly to unload. And reversing this process, if members of the collusive group happened to spot a valuable painting at a sale, two of them might stand near the prize, examine it, and then exclaim in voices so pitched that no one could fail to overhear: "Too bad it's only a copy!"

Such a remark from an expert could be counted on to scare off the customers. One of the confederates would get the picture at a fraction of its value and, at a future sale, make a killing from which he would pay a commission to other members of the group.

The American moguls of the last century and the beginning of our own were glorious dupes in the field of art, and the market became so fertile for the manufacture of fakes that an entire industry flourished in this field. According to Edmond Haraucourt, one-time director of the Musée Cluny in Paris, certain European cities even developed their own *faking specialties,* and set up studios, factories, even schools in which the art of turning out Rembrandts or Corots was mastered. In 1908, Sir Purdon Clarke declared that the astounding total of twenty-seven thousand paintings signed "Corot" had, *up to that time,* passed through the New York customs house; and Samuel Swift, writing in *Harper's Weekly* that same year, remarked:

"Deceptions like this are a source of profit to dishonest dealers, and they enable a certain number of industrious painters in Paris and New York to make a modest but comfortable living. Even Brooklyn has, or had, its salaried art forger, who, for a fixed sum, . . . turned out a stream of monotonous imitations of Diaz, Corot, Inness, Wyant, Homer Martin and other important and salable paintings. For a man to be worth to his employer forty dollars a week, at this obscure and nameless toil, year in and year out, implies an unfailing market for his daubs. And he is, or was, only one of an army of subterranean art workers here and abroad."

Americans have learned a good deal since those earlier days when any collector on this side of the Atlantic was a splendid answer to a crooked prayer, but the superlative faker can still reap well in any part of the world.

The art market is not the only collecting field spotted with gold bricks. Let anything be collected by enough people willing to pay

COLLECTOR: "It's ancient—very?—and worn by a Greek?—and his name is inside?"
(*Harper's Weekly*, 1877. *The Bettmann Archive.*)

The less "knowledgeable" collectors of Thomas Nast's day inspired the cartoonist to lash them with ridicule.

sizable prices and one may expect to find imitations. Even sacred relics were faked in medieval times when they were universally desired; and just as artists have not all been above using their ability to fraudulent ends, so then there were monks and nuns willing to traffic in the popular symbols of their faith. In 1352, according to Burckhardt, "a cunning Neapolitan abbess" sent to Florence a spurious arm of the patroness of the Cathedral, Santa Reparata, made of wood and plaster. Naïve rather than cunning we should call this lady, who did not succeed in fooling the intelligent Florentines; yet the existence of quantities of duplicate "relics" treasured in religious houses throughout medieval Europe points to the prevalence of many more clever fakers in this field than she.

In the sixteenth, seventeenth and eighteenth centuries "curiosities" were the rage, and to fill the demand for the strange and uncommon these things were artificially produced in great quantities. A certain botanist is known to have transformed a dead rat into the likeness of a "dragon" and to have exhibited it as a genuine discovery. "Basilisks" were mythical creatures variously thought to resemble serpents, lizards or dragons and to be possessed of the breath that kills; and although no one had ever actually seen one, basilisks, accepted as authentic, were common items in the curiosity exhibits of the period. Even more common were the specimens of "unicorn" horn without which no such collection was considered complete. Mermaids "made of the head and shoulders of a monkey neatly attached to the headless body of a fish" were not unheard of: as late as 1835 one of these synthetic creatures was exhibited in the Museum of Practical Science at Edinburgh.

Curiosities are still faked, although not so often as they once were, since the demand for them today is less and the profits to be derived from this field are consequently insignificant. The shrunken human heads collected as trophy-fetishes by the Jibaro Indians are occasionally found in civilized collections ranging in seriousness of purpose from the anthropological to the simple curiosity collection; and side by side with the heads, one may sometimes see an entire shrunken body or Indian "mummy"—but since the Indians never make such mummies, every exhibit of this sort is necessarily a fake.

One of the simplest and yet shrewdest stunts ever perpetrated by a modern faker was, however, based upon the common attraction for collecting gruesome souvenirs. When William Palmer, notorious English poisoner, was hanged at Rugeley in Staffordshire toward the middle of the last century, eighty thousand people are said to have flocked from all parts of the British Isles to watch his demise. Since the public had often bought souvenir pieces of rope at past performances, the hangman, who was something of an impresario, began to think in terms of enough rope for his man and his audience besides. To take care of the crowds he purchased in advance a huge rope stock, cut it into souvenir lengths, and after the hanging passed these out for sale as bits of the real McCoy. The crowd quickly took the entire issue, and the hangman made a modest fortune, enough, in fact, so that thereafter he was free to live and let live.

Ever since William Henry Ireland, at the end of the eighteenth century, pulled the wool over the eyes of the entire literary world with his sensational "discovery" of a batch of Shakespeare manuscripts (including an entire "unknown" play), charlatans gifted with imagination as well as ambition have been trying to equal or surpass his dubious accomplishment. Because Shakespeare is the literary idol of the English-speaking world, and because no single sheet of manuscript in his handwriting is known to exist, the stakes would be of the highest; but for the same reason, successful faking approaches the impossible, since any collector in his right mind would check and double-check and check again before accepting such a Shakespeare "discovery" as authentic.

The optimism and ingenuity of the faker, however, are boundless, and now and then he expects to meet a collector *not* in his right mind. An attempt to cash in on the handwriting of the Bard was made as recently as 1926 by one H. C. Rogers who described himself as a workman and "occasional gardener" of Langley, Buckinghamshire, England. According to his story, Rogers had happened upon a faded map in the false bottom of an old chest, and on this map in orthodox pirate-tale manner a significant cross appeared. Conveniently the chest also contained a letter dated August 14, 1818, addressed to a "Brother Sumner" by one "Brother Thomas of the Plymouth Brethren Community." A group of Shakespeare manuscripts, this document stated, had been buried on a specified date, at the exact spot marked on the map, and this, the explanation continued, had been done to keep this important material from falling into the hands of a forger such as Ireland, who was still alive.

The story seemed plausible enough, and when Rogers, digging at the place indicated, came upon a casket containing the very papers described, he had collectors all over the world in a furor. There were grave doubts, of course, but every detail seemed to check under investigation, and it appeared unlikely that a mere gardener would have been well enough informed to work out a plot so complicated, if plot it was. Plans were made to bring Rogers and his manuscripts to America for a further examination; and then an alert genealogist pointed out that Elizabeth Hall, Shakespeare's granddaughter (through whose descendants Rogers claimed to have inherited the false-bottomed chest), had died childless. Those who persisted in believing in Rogers' sincerity, however, raised an interesting question. May he not, they asked, have stumbled upon a set of Ireland's old forgeries, planted years before by the ingenious Ireland himself?

Not many collectors are as naïvely trusting as Michel Chasles, that extraordinary professor of mathematics who, outside his own vocation, seems to have fulfilled in the extreme the proverbial reputation of professors for absent-mindedness. Chasles was a noted and highly respected mathematician. He was also an ardent autograph collector, made-to-order for one Vrain Lucas who came to him one day with the tempting tale of a magnificent autograph collection, formerly the property of a Comte de Boisjourdain. According to Lucas, the nobleman had been lost at sea in 1790, but his collection had been rescued, and now, fifty years later, he, Lucas, was authorized to dispose of it. Chasles, so he said, might have the first opportunity to select items from it, if he so desired, and Chasles' answer seems to have been a series of Gallic squeals of delight. Among the items which he then proceeded to buy were autograph letters from such redoubtables as Cleopatra, Julius Caesar, Ovid, Plutarch, and Charlemagne, *all written in modern French,* on paper which, although it looked old and worn, was afterward discovered to be watermarked "Angoulême."

Chasles might have enjoyed his treasures in innocent peace, and Lucas might have continued to ply his trade unmolested (he later confessed to having manufactured more than twenty-five thousand spurious autographs during his scandalous career), had not the professor one day ventured to publish out of his collection a letter from Pascal to Sir Isaac Newton—a choice morsel in which Pascal claimed that he, not Newton, had first discovered the law of gravity. Publication of this letter caused quite a stir in learned circles, and Chasles himself wrote a scholarly paper on the subject which was much discussed. No one suspected anything wrong until Sir David Brewster, after a bit of figuring on a slip of paper, rather brusquely pointed out that at the date of the letter Newton was all of eight years old. Matters grew worse until the affair finally came to court, and poor Chasles was exposed before the world in all his extraordinary bemusement.*

Often enough the collector is deceived by the simple procedure of calling an object something which it is not, for there will always be some who believe whatever they are told. This is dangerous business, however, unless the salesman selects his victim with proper care. Recently a well-known American architect, whose wife is a sculptress, told us the following tale. Upon entering an antique shop the architect's collecting eye came to rest upon a piece of pottery, a bowl rather roughly fashioned to which he was strangely drawn. "That," said the dealer, "is a particularly fine piece—Archaic Greek," and, naming an impressive price, he lifted the bowl from the shelf and handed it to his customer for a closer inspection. To the architect there was a hauntingly familiar quality about the piece, although he could not at first place it. Curious but still uncertain, he left without comment. The next day his wife strolled into the shop, examined the bowl and inquired its origin. Upon receiving the same explanation, the lady struggled to check her emotion for here was a man charging that her own student days went back twenty-five hundred years. As laughter finally overcame her, the discomfited dealer's curiosity rose to ask the source of so much joyousness.

"Antiquity aside, this bowl never even saw modern Greece," she replied, "because I made it myself a good many years ago."

"Madam, that is impossible," the dealer cried hopefully, gathering his unraveling aplomb.

Whereupon the lady turned the disputed piece over and pointed to a mark. "My signature," she said.

Usually the business of faking requires skills beyond that of merely hooking the fish. As Ben Jonson put it:

"It is an art to have so much judgment as to apparel a lie well, to give it a good dressing."

* This incredible story, famous in collecting annals, appears to be thoroughly documented by French court records. The authors wish to state, however, that they have not had access to the original sources.

The faker must know how to practice that art from start to finish, and he must be able to practice it so well that big fish as well as small fry will take his lure. Sir James Yoxall once wrote a fanciful description of an expert faker, probably a composite portrait, which gives some idea of the varied abilities of these light-fingered gentry:

". . . Himself he knew how to crackle new ivories by boiling them like eggs; how to cook new pictures in the oven; how to smoke new prints; how to green new bronzes with nitrate of potassium. It was so amusing to see the things age in a minute. He would bring a new earthenware dish out of the oven, burning hot, and plunge it into iced oil; result, contraction, chill-chilblains, so to speak —and the glaze all cracked into the wrinkles of premature age. And then he would rub the surface upon a dirty paving-stone, till signs of wear and tear appeared that might outwit anybody. As for pictures, it was easy to find an old canvas or an old panel for a faker; it was when the painter's work was over that the real science and art began. First of all a wash of varnish that had been colored with sepia; next, on the more raised portions, rubbings with liquorice-juice to attract the flies. He could even imitate fly marks with India ink. A few drops of salty water left on the canvas would produce mouldiness and mildew. A needle deftly used would cover the picture with a network of cracks. He knew how to transfer the marks of plain old silver to new goblets more imposing to view. And in quite a few minutes, by the use of nitric acid, powdered sandstone, a file, blows with a hammer, and whacks with a stick he would transform a new wooden chair into an old one, upon which a great-grandfather of the purchaser might have sat, you would think."

Fakers in every field have their own tricks, based upon an exhaustive knowledge of the proper attributes of originals. The painting faker must, if he is to imitate the work of a particular master, make a study of the artist's brushwork, of his typical palette, his style of composition, and a dozen or so other more or less abstruse matters. If the fraud is intended for the knowledgeable market, everything must be in order. The stretcher and canvas must be old, and of the type in use during the artist's lifetime; the paint must be of the right chemical composition, if such paint can still be found or made; and so on.

But should the prospective client be known as ignorant, so that it will do merely to make the painting look superficially antique, ordinary house paint may be used—is, in fact, particularly desirable, since it contains earths and dryers which cause it to harden in a few days and give a surface which the innocent cannot distinguish from one that is fifty to a hundred years old. Equally important are the next steps, the toning with a film of varnish into which a small amount of color has been added, the recoating with shellac and then with a thin film of glue—a combination which dries very hard and shrinks unevenly in drying, so that in the end the new painting will be covered with just the sort of network of cracks suitable to old varnish.

The furniture faker in plying his trade may shoot a modern reproduction full of spurious wormholes, paste a page from some old periodical (*Gleason's Periodical,* say, or the *American Gazette*) over the bottom of a drawer in a "treated" highboy to give it that authentic touch; or carry the legitimate process of restoration to such illegitimate extremes as creating one whole chair out of the separate fragments of several badly damaged ones. In order to manufacture a convincing reproduction, he may use old wood from railroad ties, ancient docks, windmills, even wood from old sunken ships; or he may bury new wood for a time in manure and mud to "age" it.

Other fields are as complex in their requirements—and as easily manipulated by the skillful. Plain old china can be used as a base for fake painting and glazing to produce a far more valuable example of the ceramist's art. Pewter has "touch marks," and silver, "hallmarks," which may be transferred by means of an expert operation. And book "presentation copies" may be effectively forged when the faker is thoroughly learned in the intimate details of his subject's life and manner of writing, so that the autograph inscription which is added to the title page may sound, as well as look, convincing.

The pirates of respectability and old age have even invaded the kindergarten. Edmond Haraucourt describes the marketing system once used by a Barcelona firm which manufactured "medieval" toys—little tin soldiers costumed in the fashion of the sixteenth century. At the factory itself a simple acid treatment was used to create the illusion of age. What followed, however, constituted an elaborate conspiracy. Agents from the factory would deposit their wares with the lock-keepers along the banks of the Loire, the Seine, or the Marne, wherever the tourist trade was known to be heavy. The lock-keepers, fully in cahoots, would then give the toys to their children to play with; and when tourists came along, the children, in accordance with their instructions, would explain how Papa had found the curious little soldiers in the river mud when he last dragged the lock. Usually the tourists, jumping at the bait, would offer to buy the "old" toys for a sum that seemed to them craftily small; and Papa would receive a handsome commission from the factory in Barcelona.

One of the most ingenious faking methods ever devised was that reported by Andrew Lang who, writing of antique engraved gems, tells how

". . . the gem-cutter will take a real gold ring, with an unimportant subject on the stone, and will on the original stone make an intaglio of an important subject; make a turkey swallow the trinket, kill the turkey, and produce the fresh intaglio with all the marks of age which attrition in the crop of a bird can produce."

Even the stamp market has its fraudulent issues, and students of postal paper have often found enough material for entire treatises in the counterfeits of a single period, such as the American Confederacy. In characteristic orderly fashion the philatelist classifies each type of fraudulent issue under a name of its own, for the simple word "counterfeit" cannot cover all the tricks of which the sharper in this field is capable. Thus a "bogus stamp" is one that has been printed and sold to collectors as coming from a country which is either nonexistent, or which has never had postal issues; a "fake stamp" is one that has been doctored to give it a fictitious value, or one that has been issued without government authorization; a "counterfeit stamp" is one printed from an original engraved plate that has been re-engraved without authorization, or from a newly engraved plate copying the original; and a "forged stamp" is one in which some part of a good stamp has been fraudulently changed to enhance its value. Then there are the "reprints" which are sometimes legitimately issued from original plates, but which are not authorized for use as postage: when sold as reprints (for the benefit of collectors who desire copies of out-of-print issues) they are quite in order, but fakers often take advantage of them and dispose of them as rare originals.

The faking and forging of stamps is a highly demanding enterprise in skill and requires considerable knowledge of the rules of the game as well as an expert's technique. "Doctoring" may be accomplished by cleaning, repairing, grafting, coloring or reprinting. A heavy and disfiguring postmark or cancellation may be removed (since stamp collectors value clearly visible surfaces). In fact, the entire design may be lifted off, leaving only the watermarked and perforated paper on which the design of a valuable stamp may then be drawn. Such valuable stamp "errors" as the *tête-bêche* (in which two stamps, still unseparated from each other, are printed in reverse position, one right side up and the other upside down) may be created by the ticklish process of rubbing down the upper surface of one of a pair until it is only half its normal thickness, then taking a third stamp, rubbing it down from behind, cementing the two together in proper position, and finally putting the whole creation through a press. It is obvious that a "bogus stamp" could fool no one but a fool or a novice among philatelists—and equally obvious that it would take a tempered expert to distinguish some of the more subtle frauds in this field.

One famous collector has said that the skill of the faker is such that eighty per cent of all dealers and collectors can be fooled by it at times; and, even more uncompromisingly, J. H. Duveen declares that a dealer or collector who claims never to have been duped is, in all probability, either lying or ignorant.

Evrard Jabach was a great connoisseur, but he had in his collection at least one fraudulent painting, a Titian *Tarquin and Lucrèce,* which is now recognized as a mediocre copy and is consigned to an obscure corner of the Louvre, although the museum authorities themselves once accepted it as genuine.

J. P. Morgan had access to the best expert advice that money could buy, and he was shrewd enough to realize that he needed such advice. Nevertheless, misrepresentations occasionally gained places of honor among his treasures. One Morgan "mistake" was the famous Guzman rock-crystal cross, an old reliquary which, despite its extraordinary beauty, did not seem quite "right" to the expert, Dr. George C. Williamson. Unearthed by a Paris dealer some months after Morgan had incautiously let it be known that he was looking for something particularly valuable in rock crystal, this cross was profoundly enjoyed by the financier. Once doubt had been cast upon its authenticity, however, he empowered Williamson to investigate it. After a sleuth-hunt of international proportions the truth was finally tracked down, and the dealer who had made the sale confessed to a swindle. Confronted with certain damaging facts, he admitted that he had found the cross—genuinely old, but with its magnificent gold-enamel work set in ebony, not in crystal—and that, in order to meet Morgan's desire for "something in crystal," he had engaged a master workman to fake a new setting in the required material.

In part to avoid falling into such traps, the good collectors work hard to become connoisseurs. And it is because of the difficulty of the task, and the importance set upon its successful performance, that "expertizing" has become a profitable profession. Every collecting field involving items of value has its experts, and in each case extraordinarily elaborate techniques have been worked out for the detection of fraud.

Some time ago an organization known as the Philatelic Research Laboratories, Inc., was set up for the purpose of determining or disproving the validity of claims regarding perforations, watermarks, texture of paper, character of ink, and other "physical fundamentals" of great concern to the serious stamp specialist. The laboratory's equipment—some of it especially constructed for the purpose—includes such highly technical tools as an arc lamp with infra-red filters and plates, a quartz lamp with ultra-violet light, a photo-electric spectrophotometer, monocular and binocular microscopes, a polarized microscope, and a comparison microscope of the sort used in ballistic investigation. Pressed into service are applications of photo-micrography, chemistry, physics, and other branches of science. One of the principles here used in the detection of philatelic fraud is the same employed in looking for new facts about the planets. Technically fortified, it is relatively easy to prove, for instance, that a stamp showing no trace of cancellation and purporting to be a "mint" specimen has actually been used and canceled, but so skillfully washed that the cancellation bars are not visible even through a powerful microscope.

Similar principles are applied in testing the authenticity of books, manuscripts, engravings and paintings. Painting sleuths have worked out techniques ranging all the way from the simple "pin test" (whereby a pin stuck into a lump of white paint on the canvas indicates, by the amount of resistance it encounters, the relative age of the pigment) to the highly developed method evolved by the French chemist, Bayle, involving the use of X-ray, ultra-violet ray, the microscope, and an instrument called the chromoscope which Bayle invented for this specific purpose.

In some fields, of which painting is one, the expert must supplement these scientific tests by the exercise of a more subjective sort of diagnosis. As Frank Jewett Mather expresses it:

"The connoisseur knows his art as the tea-taster knows his tea. A wide experience accurately remembered is the whole thing."

But, he continues, and here he is speaking chiefly of the professional expert who must determine questions of period, authenticity and authorship, often for the benefit of clients who pay him a fee for his services:

"It would be highly impolitic for the connoisseur, who must have the air of a greater authority than can ever be his, to betray the instinctive character of his judgments. Since he cannot say frankly, 'This is the way it feels to me,' for purposes of exposition and demonstration he alleges all sorts of *materialia*, which while confirming, have not really influenced his judgment. Thus we write about morphological ear marks, costume, patina, linear characteristics, color schemes, and cite the evidence of the X-ray and eke of the ray of ultraviolet hue; of chemical analysis or microscopic observation . . . The connoisseur does this, not to mislead his public, but to avoid misleading himself."

"Expert" testimony in the collecting world often reads like a rather technical detective story, full of suspense, false starts, elusive clues, and the triumphant solution. The expert should possess a vast and varied fund of information, an eye keen to perceive every detail of the object he examines, and a mind alert to many exceedingly clever ruses. Speaking of the man whose business it is to unmask fraudulent antiques, Haraucourt declares that he should combine the qualities of an historian, a psychologist and a logician. It is no wonder that he sometimes falls short of perfection.

Many experts who enjoy a widespread confidence in their talents also fall short in their use of methods ranging from the questionable to downright fraudulence. It is an open secret among collectors and artists that for years there has existed in this country and in Europe a thriving business open to experts in the "authentication" of questionable items. An "Old Master" is produced by someone from nowhere in particular; perhaps it has been "discovered" in a junk shop or in the house of a poor man, and it cannot be sold for a big-name price until its genuineness has first been vouched for by one or two so-called experts. As is the case with alienists whose expert testimony can be hired in a court of law, for or against, at so much per yard of testimony, so, if the painting should merit anything approaching reasonable doubt, the affidavits of certain art experts can readily be had, for cash. To the honest expert, however, no small part of his enjoyment is found in the genuine sleuthing his profession involves, and he says that "those who have never practiced this kind of work have no idea what a pleasure it is to unmask a false piece."

Like collecting itself, expertizing becomes a sport, a hunt, and an exercise in intelligence and ingenuity; for, according to a famous French authority, the "perfect crime" in fake collectibles is nonexistent: always a small technical error, a misconception of custom or an anachronism is there to reveal the truth to the master-mind capable of detecting it. Yet this statement is difficult to uphold, for there are many "crimes" so nearly perfect as to meet, for practical purposes, every requirement of success. When fakers are good enough, they can often out-expert the experts, and it is not only the private collector who falls victim to the skill of these backstage gentry: the museums of the world also bear ample testimony to their ability both as manufacturers and as salesmen.

When Sir James Yoxall, the famous English connoisseur, "sat on" the management of the South Kensington Museum as a member of the Select Committee of the House of Commons, he learned about a certain Palissy platter for which the museum had paid heavily. When purchased, the platter, stained with "age," had been broken and then artistically mended with two strips of canvas cemented across the back. After it had been on exhibition for several months the English damp had loosened these strips, so that it became necessary to remove them and replace them more firmly. While this was being attended, there was discovered beneath the artful canvas strips the imprint of a modern French maker of facsimiles. The museum authorities had to admit that the proper price for such a platter, new and unbroken, would have been much closer to ten pounds than to the two hundred they had paid for it.

The work of a nineteenth-century Italian, Giovanni Bastianini, was purchased by most of the museums in Europe as superlative renaissance work. The son of a poor peasant, Bastianini had shown a great and genuine talent even as a child, and between his work and that of the renaissance masters there actually was an innate resemblance. This artist might have had a legitimate and successful career of his own, had he not fallen under the influence of a corrupt antique vendor who employed the naïve young sculptor, at the rate of two *lire* a day, to create pieces in the old style. These were original works, not copies, but so convincing in artistry and manner that they were disposed of at high prices as "excavations" or "discoveries."

Bastianini's most famous creation was probably the portrait head purporting to be that of Savonarola's friend Beniveni, for which the Louvre paid thirty thousand francs when francs were solid money. According to one of the several versions of this story, only when a noted Florentine art collector, Dr. Foresi, brought several of his own genuine antiques to show to the director of the Louvre was the truth divulged about the Beniveni head. The director ventured to doubt the authenticity of some of Foresi's items, whereupon the collector shouted angrily that the museum had best look to its own laurels—that Beniveni head, for instance, of which they were all so proud, was, to his certain knowledge, a blatant fake! A great scandal ensued, and despite the Louvre's anguished efforts to hush up the affair, it became necessary to conduct an investigation. Bastianini himself was summoned, and in considerable bewilderment declared that he had indeed made the head. Still the experts refused to believe. It was impossible, they maintained, for any modern, much less this obscure peasant, to create a renaissance piece so perfect in style and conception, so exquisitely right in every detail. Bastianini had to produce the very-much-alive cigarmaker whom he had used as a model, as well as a great deal of additional evidence, before the Louvre authorities would admit their error.

Alceo Dossena (1878–1937), who executed "renaissance" works in the twentieth century, claimed to have worked in good faith (at least he had had photographs of his productions taken in his own studio) and only to have realized what was happening when he saw a photograph of a

---

VALUES IN FAKES AND COPIES. *Master fakers, like Bastianini and Dossena, do not make exact copies but work in the style of certain masters and periods. Compare the genuine Florentine carving (above, left) from the Kaiser Friedrich Museum, Berlin, with the adjoining marble bust, purchased for the Detroit Museum but later exchanged. Acknowledged copies by great artists, however, are always valuable. The Rubens copy (below, left) from Vienna's Art History Museum, preserves the memory of a lost Titian original. And Josiah Wedgwood's copies of the famous Portland Vase have become collectors' items.*

PORTRAIT OF A WOMAN, *by Desiderio da Settignano.*

MODERN "RENAISSANCE," *artist unknown.*

ISABELLA D'ESTE, *by Rubens, after Titian.*

The Metropolitan Museum of Art

WEDGWOOD COPY OF THE PORTLAND VASE.

(*See facing page.*)

"newly discovered Donatello" which he recognized as his own handiwork. For many years, two dealers, one in Venice and one in Rome, handled his output; and it is believed that, quite aside from the European sales, more than a million dollars worth of Dossena-renaissance sculpture was disposed of in America between 1920 and 1927. The Boston Museum of Art is said to have paid one hundred thousand dollars to the Italian dealer, Volpi, for a "tomb of Catharina de Sabello," supposedly a Mino da Fiesole work; but it escaped buying the two life-sized flanking angels which Volpi had also intended for it. Dossena and his dealers were finally uncovered because of an investigation attending the purchase of a "Greek Athena" (for one hundred and twenty thousand dollars, reputedly) by the Cleveland Museum—a statue that had been endorsed by leading archaeologists both in this country and abroad: the work was a bit unusual, they admitted, but might well have been the product of some provincial school. Miss Helen Frick contributed to the unmasking of this crooked ring after she had become suspicious of a "Donatello," a "Vecchietta" and a "Simone Martini" in the Frick Collection. Incidentally, she later made a point of collecting photographs of all the known Dossena fakes so that other collectors might be forewarned.

Once attributed to Dossena but now thought to be an older product was the "Mino da Fiesole" marble bust purchased in the nineteen-twenties by Edsel Ford for a reputed one hundred and twenty-five thousand dollars and presented by him to the Detroit Museum. This bust, "planted" in a Florentine palace, had been authenticated by no less than three eminent experts, one a former director of the *Museo Nazionale* in Florence, another considered the greatest connoisseur of Italian sculpture in the world. Dr. W. R. Valentiner, a genuine authority and one of those who approved the purchase, later discovered the error, readily and sensibly admitted it, and effected a satisfactory exchange for the museum with the dealer responsible for the sale.

Incidentally, some time before, one of the same trio of experts, Wilhelm von Bode, had authenticated a "Leonardo" bust of *Flora* that had been offered to the Kaiser Friedrich Museum in Berlin. When a photograph of the *Flora* was published in England, an obscure English sculptor saw it and claimed the work as his own. Again, "Impossible!" was the verdict from the experts. "Very well," said the English sculptor, "but if you will chisel into the base, you will find that I used scraps of

English newspapers for filler." Forced to test the truth of this statement, they chiseled away—and brought forth pages of the *London Times* from the "Leonardo" bust!

Upon occasion the long list of similar experiences has made honest experts overcautious. Forgeries in Egyptian antiquities, for example, became so common and so convincing in the nineteenth century (they were being manufactured wholesale to meet the demands of archaeologists and tourist collectors), that when Mesopotamian cuneiform tablets were first found in the valley of the Nile, experts all over the world poohed at the discovery. The tablets could not possibly be genuine, it was said, until German scholars with their inevitable thoroughness, decided to decipher some of them. Then it was found that these "forgeries" were not only genuine but were unique and highly important correspondence which had passed between the Pharaohs Amenhotep III and Iknaton and the kings and governors of Babylon, Tyre, Jerusalem and other Syrian and Mesopotamian lands a hundred years before the birth of Moses. Today these "fake" tablets are famous as the Tell el-Amarna letters and are the source of much of our detailed knowledge of the period in which they were written.

In turning the page on this section, it might be well to remember that while honest expertizing has its areas of confusion, it is most often an invaluable aid to the community at large, safeguarding public and private museums, collectors, and other buyers, and may be considered as the inevitable supreme court. For the collector there are costly steps to be saved under expert guidance. It is partly with this in mind that a number of museums have begun exhibiting fakes alongside genuine articles. In January, 1937, the Metropolitan Museum of Art performed a valuable and courageous act when it brought all its Greek and Roman fakes out into the open and placed them on display as an educational feature. Concise explanatory notes revealed in what respects each of the fakes was at fault, although Miss Gisela Richter, curator of the classical department, cautioned that:

> ". . . the fakes are getting cleverer and cleverer all the time . . . It takes a real artist in his own right to make a good forgery. The good forger is an artist who is also an archaeologist."

This frank attitude on the part of museum authorities is manifestly superior to the kind of "pride" exhibited, in the case of the Beniveni head, by the Louvre only a few decades ago. As the authorities and professional experts disclose those frauds which are the masterpieces of their kind, lesser collectors will lose some of their reluctance to reveal their own mistakes; and the consequent pooling of knowledge will make the path of the faker far more difficult.

When copies are made for legitimate purposes it is customary, for obvious reasons, to add some distinguishing mark. The following story indicates that although a great deal may be at stake, it is possible for the best of experts to be defeated.

This tale concerns a magnificent silver reliquary, the *Chef de St. Martin,* which came upon the market at the time of the Combes Law in France, by which all ecclesiastical treasures were to be converted into state property. At that time many members of the clergy felt that it was preferable to dispose of church treasures than to allow them to fall into the hands of the Republican government. Duveen Brothers, the English firm, bid for the *St. Martin* and their offer was accepted, with a condition: the priest who owned the reliquary would sell only if it were agreed that he should receive a perfect copy in its place. Commissioned for the task was a man with the promising sobriquet of "The Chelsea Wizard." Now the Chelsea Wizard was as great an artist in the imitation of fine old silver work as Bastianini was in his field; and thus it happened that when the copy was received no one could distinguish one from the other except by the fact that the original contained the relics and had been marked by affixing to it a small piece of paper. In fact, the resemblance was so amazing that the Duveens bet each other that none among them could honestly say which reliquary was which.

In the course of carrying out the test, the relics and the paper marker were shifted several times. And then fate intervened, for the game was interrupted and when the contestants returned several hours later their wager had become a disastrous reality: no one could remember with certainty whether the marker had last been put upon the original or the copy! The Wizard was sent for, but even the master craftsman could find no key to the puzzle. A feverish council ended in the decision to ignore the matter. One reliquary containing the relics was delivered to Mr. Morgan who had ordered it, and the other was sent to the priest, who could not believe that he had not received his original back, and perhaps he was right. The tale might have ended here had not someone in league with the devil suggested to the priest that he repeat the transaction with another firm; and this was done not once but several times so successfully that "selling the real head of St. Martin" became quite an industry. Each time a collector bought one of the reliquaries he was pledged to strict secrecy, on political grounds. But eventually one amateur confided in another, and when it appeared that each of them had bought a *Chef de St. Martin,* the truth came out.

The case of the master being fooled by his own copy is not extraordinary. Nearly a hundred years ago there was an Englishman named Harris who made a business of supplying facsimile pages to be added to old books from which one or two pages were missing. This is often done quite openly, and scrupulous dealers will tell their customers when books have been so doctored. When the volumes change hands, however, the fact is sometimes forgotten, and usually no one is any the wiser since, if the job has been well done, it may be practically impossible to detect it. It is said of Harris that he once executed such an order for a celebrated collector, and that five years later, when his customer brought the book in again, the copyist could not identify his own pages but had to go to his records to see which they were.

Bastianini was such a past master at his work and prize pupil of his rascally employer, Freppa, that in the end he could hoodwink Fagin. Working at home nights, the sculptor finally devised a method of augmenting his meager salary at Freppa's expense: he would carve a small "antique," then arrange matters with a peasant neighbor, who would undertake to present the new work at the store, saying that he had just found the *antichità* in his field and thought Freppa might be interested. Many times Freppa, the double-dealer, falling into his own trap, bought these works at a far higher price than he would have paid Bastianini for them had he known they were his.

A still more curious reversal of roles occurred in the case of George Geminder of Astoria, Long Island, a legitimate copyist of stringed instruments who lived in the second half of the nineteenth century. Geminder made instruments of all sorts, but his specialty was the reproduction of the historic works of such masters as Stradivarius, Guarnerius and Amati. These reproductions—always sold for exactly what they were and marked as such—had earned for their maker an enviable reputation in this country, and he decided to take some of them to Vienna, where an exhibition of the work of modern violin-makers from all over the world was being held. Imagine his distress when his colleagues, after examining his work, all but drove him from their midst. "These 'Geminder' instruments," they cried, "are too impossibly good! Don't expect us to believe that *you* made them. What do you mean by trying to palm off genuine antique masterworks as your own?" And nothing would convince them otherwise.

Not all copies, of course, are produced for fraudulent purposes. Painters sometimes make copies of their own works, and if the deed is not duly recorded this may prove a source of great embarrassment to experts of a later day, confronted with the necessity of establishing the status of a pair of nearly identical canvases. In certain fields, copies are frequently executed to a client's order when, as in the case of certain kinds of early American furniture today or of Greek sculpture in Roman times, the individual cannot afford or finds it impossible to procure the original. And eventually, as the copies themselves become old, they may, if they are good, acquire a value of their own, even when the circumstances under which they were originally created are perfectly well known. If the copyist himself was a great artist, this almost inevitably will be so. According to Vasari, Michelangelo, who was a collector as well as a creator of art,

". . . copied plates from the hands of many old masters in such sort that the copies could not be distinguished from the originals, for Michelangelo had tinged and given the former an appearance of age with smoke and other things, so that he had made them look old, and when they were compared with the original no difference could be perceived. All this he did that he might give his own copies in the place of the old works which he desired to possess from the hands of their authors, admiring in them the excellence of art and seeking to surpass them when engaged in the execution of his own works."

Today these copies executed by Michelangelo might well be valued more than the originals, combining as they do the appeal of twofold greatness.

That master ceramist, Josiah Wedgwood (1730–95), once devoted an entire year to copying the famous Portland Vase. Fifty of these facsimiles were issued at the time and sold to subscribers at fifty guineas apiece, and Wedgwood himself is said to have considered this work his finest achievement. The copies were so much admired that others have since been made from the same molds, but, typically enough, collectors place the highest value on the "authenticated early copies." One thousand dollars was paid for one toward the end of the last century; and in postscript it should be added that it was the existence of the Wedgwood facsimile that made possible the restoration of the great original when, in 1845, the latter was smashed to bits in the British Museum by a maniac.

But what of those far more numerous cases in which the copy has been executed not by a master but by some obscure though competent craftsman? Granted the craftsman would be incapable of the original creative conception, it is quite possible for him to duplicate the master's *technique;* and this fact gives rise to those numerous controversies regarding authenticity which so often strike the layman as absurd. When, and it has happened many times in the history of collecting, a twin of some highly valued work of art long considered authentic suddenly turns up, to establish which is the original may become of the utmost importance to the museum or the collector involved.

If, however, no one has ever known the identity of the original artist, so that the value set upon the piece has always depended solely upon its intrinsic merits then a recognized copy of superlative quality may be highly valued on the basis of that quality. If it seems impossible to identify the original, the search may be abandoned more willingly than if a Rembrandt or a Velasquez were at stake. The "St. Martin" reliquary is a case in point. When the facts of this comedy of errors were revealed, J. P. Morgan (who had made the first purchase and who, therefore, had a fifty-fifty chance of possessing the original) was approached by the French government to which, by the law of the land, the original rightfully belonged. After explaining that he had purchased the reliquary in good faith, being unaware of its history, Mr. Morgan then offered his piece to the Louvre as a gift. This offer was gratefully accepted, although everyone realized that it would be impossible ever to establish whether or not this particular "St. Martin" was the original or one of the copies.

Fakes may also come to be valued in accordance with a principle similar to that which causes book collectors or stamp collectors to value "errors." There are stamp specialists, for instance, who place great value on philatelic forgeries, if those forgeries are ones that have "got by"—i.e., passed through the mails. Or association may play its part in lending value to fakes—certain fakes become attractive because of their dramatic history. The notorious catalogue of the "Fortsas Sale" is today a collector's item among bibliophiles. Bastianini's sculpture is collected today both on its own merits and because of its history. And William Henry Ireland's forged Shakespeare manuscripts were in such demand in his own lifetime, even after their unmasking, that he himself conducted a profitable business making forged copies of his own original forgeries. Today, however, collectors interested in the Ireland papers want "the original forgeries, not his double and triple fabrications," because it was the originals that played a part in the amusing drama of his grandiose and so nearly successful deception.

Old Sheffield plate was itself a counterfeit of Queen Anne and Georgian silver, and now that the Sheffield process has been lost and the original plate has attained great value in its own right, old Sheffield is plentifully (if surreptitiously) imitated. Even more complicated is the case of the sixteenth-century Japanese potter, Shonzui. Shonzui went to China to study the methods and designs of the Chinese craftsmen, and when later he set up his own factory at home, he produced such excellent imitations of Chinese ware that, so Durant recounts, "the Chinese potters of the eighteenth century did their best to imitate these for export under Shonzui's counterfeited name."

Recently an American forger, arraigned for counterfeiting the money of his government, advanced the ingenious defense that his engraving was so fine that it had an intrinsic value, and he suggested that some day his fake bills would command a price far above their face denomination. Quite possibly he may have been right. Stranger things than that have happened in the unpredictable world of collecting. There was the man who, in his impecunious youth, forged a letter from Major André to General Washington and sold it for six hundred and fifty dollars. Behind this misdeed there lay, apparently, an incipient collecting interest, an interest which continued to grow long after the youth had become successful in business and removed from the pressure which had urged him to resort to cruder methods of making money. One day this respectable citizen heard of an André letter about to be included in an English sale of autographs; and since André autographs had remained his hobby in altered form, he cabled an unlimited bid. The reader, of course, has guessed correctly that when the letter arrived it proved to be our friend's own forgery come home to roost at thrice the price for which originally he had sold it.

Under ordinary circumstances, very little publicity attends the revelation of a hoax, for the collector, priding himself on his discrimination, hates to confess that he has been victimized. There are thousands of collectors in the world who own fakes. Some would want the hide of dealers or friends who dared tell them so. Some know but refuse to believe. Some know and, smoldering silently, resolve not to get caught another time, for the fake is also a challenge, and the very fact that there are stiff fences to be taken in the hunt adds zest, puts a premium upon good judgment, and makes success still more desirable.

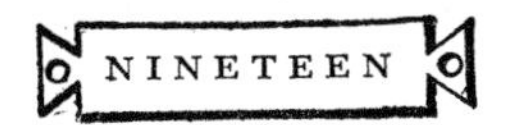

THE DARK BORDERLANDS OF COLLECTING

> *"Look here, upon this picture, and on this,*
> *The counterfeit presentment of two brothers."*
>
> SHAKESPEARE

THE INSTINCT to survive has led us not only in the path of virtue but also into dismal dead-ends; for, starting from scratch, the instinct becomes subtly altered by the combined circumstances which make up the life of individual or nation. Then its purpose to ensure man's progress toward maturity and enlightenment sometimes becomes twisted toward chaos and destruction.

As a diversion from books and art, let us look for a moment at polygamy, a form of collecting which constitutes a *bona fide* example for this point. In early and primitive societies, the collecting of wives fulfilled a definite economic-security function, and later it served as a satisfactory symbol of wealth and prestige. When carried over into more advanced societies, however, polygamy has often though not always degenerated into a pernicious form of collecting having such highly undesirable results that society eventually casts it away.

This was pointedly true in Turkey where large-scale polygamy endured until the beginning of the twentieth century and had become a special privilege of the very wealthy, with the ruler as the head man. Although the poor Turk could rarely afford more than one spouse, the Sultan could write his own ticket, and Abd ul-Hamid II, deposed in 1909, had three hundred and seventy wives. Among the harem inmates themselves and even more disastrously among their children virulent rivalries inevitably arose, so that the reigning Sultan almost always lived in terror of sudden death. In order to protect himself from the ambitious designs of his many sons he often threw all but one into incredible dungeons where, for the rest of their miserable lives, they survived under conditions impossible for most beasts to endure. To take care of the women, the eunuch system evolved with all its horrors of child-kidnaping, torture, degeneracy, and power-intrigue. The women themselves, mentally clipped and deprived of normal life, became poor excuses for human beings, with the exception of the few who were more talented and ambitious than the rest and they usually increased the number of corpses in the Bosporus.

These scandalous and inhuman conditions were the unfruitful end-development, in one society, of the original gathering of wifely numbers for entirely practical purposes (as where men were the warriors and women the laborers). Just so, in certain individuals, there has been a twisting of the customary tendency to lay by a reserve supply of food or money against future need. In these people there exists a chronic and intense fear, or else the natural impulse to provide for their own security is warped through some form of shock so that the prudent saver becomes the obsessed hoarder; and then the method usually defeats its practical (though not necessarily its psychological) end. When, for example, the newspapers inform us that a seemingly poverty-stricken creature has been found dead in an unheated tenement room with forty thousand dollars in a mattress, we may be reasonably certain that the victim chose to suffer hunger, cold or disease rather than touch savings which represented to him the security, or power, for which he had an abnormal craving and which, paradoxically, he was never to attain except perhaps within his own distressed mind.

There seems here to be a relationship to the collector who chooses to perish of starvation rather than sell his collection. One remembers a certain stamp collector who jeopardized not only his own life but his wife's also in favor of his precious albums. Until he reached the age of fifty this man had been in the habit of spending about seventy-five dollars a week on his collection, being to all appearances a perfectly normal person enjoying the pursuit of a hobby well within his means. When he lost his job, however, and was unable to find another, he stood revealed as the victim of an obsession, for although his stamps were worth thousands of dollars he refused to use them to raise money.

Oriental Harem, *18th-century British version. From George Henry Millar's* The New and Universal System of Geography, *London, 1782.*

When his wife and he were on the point of starvation, he did consent to *mortgage* the collection, but the sale of even a part was not considered. At last he found a job in a bank at thirteen dollars a week, and his pride could bear the shock of this demotion more easily than his heart could bear the thought of relinquishing his stamps. Even when his wife became ill and was in dire need of medical care and special food, this extreme amateur was unable to alter his course; and when his affairs had improved slightly, although neither he nor his wife were yet able to afford proper nourishment, he scraped pennies to reduce the mortgage on his beloved collection.

A collector in this condition is like the sorcerer's apprentice in Dukas' scherzo. His collection, in the role of the broom, has run away with him. A spell is upon him, and there can be no end to his unreasonable behavior until the sorcerer—death, or perhaps a psychiatrist—comes to lift it. Yet there is a difference between this blighted sort of amateur and the money-miser. As a rule the miser's hoard is for him nothing more than the symbol of, or the potential means to, security and power, a potential which he dares not touch for fear of exhausting it. If his bills, his coins or his savings account were suddenly to be demonetized, the miser would no longer value them, although the shock of his security-deprivation might kill him. To the normal amateur, on the other hand, the collection is in a sense his *alter ego*, and it (not its potential purchasing power) has become the recipient of his deepest affection and concern.

On the borderline between the off-balance true collector and the miser is the man who gathers and hoards not money but junk—old newspapers, cast-off clothing, bits of wire and pipe, broken umbrellas and battered kitchen pots, in fact anything that can be found in ashcans and dumps. One junk hoarder described by William James filled his home with barrels and shelves piled high with every imaginable sort of trash, and when there was no more room he stretched wires from the ceiling in order to suspend therefrom the items in his oddly assorted and ever-growing collection. Another, who specialized in gathering and keeping newspapers (without, however, any regard for their historical significance) had piled his large house from floor to ceiling with these, leaving only a few narrow alleys between the piles for his own living requirements. Such people, who are usually hermits as well, represent a type of abnormality that is continually reported with wonder. Yet there is undoubtedly a psychological explanation for the overdevelopment of the acquisitive instinct which they betray,* just as there may be in the case of the insane person who follows a similar pattern.

Many of the "collecting manias" or "peculiar" hobbies, as distinguished from more normal collecting pursuits, are explainable as growing out of specific compulsions or repressions. Here we find the fetish collectors, gatherers of objects holding a symbolic meaning or subconscious value; and because the collections thus formed are, in one sense, specialized, their psychological significance is seldom apparent to the layman. One might mention in this connection the wealthy New York woman who buys from two hundred and fifty to three hundred pairs of new shoes annually and houses them in specially built rooms; the Russian countess who paid fabulous sums for bedpans that once belonged to historical personages; the innocent old Scotchman who collected thousands of horseshoes, living quite happily in ignorance of their Freudian significance. More obvious are the frank collections of erotica in numerous fields, including books and art.

Although, as in all comparative classifications, there are gradations which automatically touch the borderline making some cases difficult if not impossible to analyze completely, it is by and large true that collecting manias—less closely related to true collecting than they appear—may vanish should the repressions causing them be lifted, whereas the true collector's love for his items and his field usually remains unshaken to the grave.

As in every large family, the *genus collectianus* occasionally produces unworthy, weak or perverse members. Among the black sheep are some souvenir hunters who, although they apply one specific and collector-like rule to their pursuit, should in the main be listed as false collectors. These are the pilferers—candid thieves who pillage hotel, dining car and steamship of linen, ashtrays and silver. Their rule is that items not gained by their own "adroitness" do not count. In their peculiar code their depredations do not constitute stealing (a distasteful word); yet they cost hotels and restaurants alone tens of thousands of dollars yearly. This horde of petty thieves should be viewed as composed of persons with an urge to steal who find their outlet in this so-called form

* Thus it may be an overt expression of the Freudian "anal character."

of collecting. Rarely if ever prosecuted, they pass off their peccadillos as fun, finding a thrill in outlawry without penalty. In fact, this pastime has become so popular and is so widely accepted as a "sport" that many individuals indulge in it who would be outraged if challenged in the name of law and order.

And what of that uncontrollable impulse to steal, kleptomania, which in some of its aspects seems very much like a runaway collector urge? Actually it is quite a different thing. Kleptomania used to be interpreted simply as an abnormal degree of acquisitiveness; but psychiatry now recognizes the complexity and infinite variations of this condition, viewing it as but one symptom common to a number of differing psychic or mental difficulties. Far from being an aberrational form of the collecting urge, kleptomania is a manifestation which has as its goal not the acquisition of the objects themselves but the satisfaction of some repressed urge, a repression which, in some cases, is symbolized by the object taken, in others by the act of stealing itself, since that act may supply a substitute solution for some inadmissible inner conflict.

To the collector one of the cardinal drives is the desire to complete a series. Thwarted in his hope, the average collector takes defeat in a reasonable manner. However, in an extremist this objective sometimes becomes a sheer obsession, in which case anything can happen, even the commission of a major crime.

A fifteen-year-old schoolboy, a few years ago, attempted to hold up a well-known stamp dealer to obtain a rare Mauritius stamp valued at twenty thousand dollars. The lad was not typically a juvenile delinquent. On the contrary, he had always been well-behaved and conscientious both at home and at school, a good student unusually well-informed in history, geography and art. Much of this knowledge had been derived from several years preoccupation with a fine stamp collection, and the history of that collection casts an illuminating light on the young amateur's eventual fall from grace. The nucleus of the collection had been a gift from the boy's father which at first aroused little interest. When it was realized, however, that nearly every youngster in the neighborhood was collecting postage stamps, the albums took on a certain aura, and the imitative tendency natural to children went to work.

In the beginning the young collector was content to add to his gift through the usual channels of soaking stamps off envelopes or swapping duplicates with his playmates. But in due course the competitive instinct made itself felt, so that the boy began to strive for a collection that should be not only "good" but "the best." By this time a genuine interest and knowledge had developed. He now became a specialist and his small allowance was no longer sufficient to cover the cost of the items he "needed," so he worked during vacations. The collection improved until only one item—the "penny orange" Mauritius—was missing from the prize series. So long as he lived, the boy brooded, he would never be able to earn enough to buy this blue-ribbon stamp. Then one day, obviously goaded by an abnormal desire to excel, he abruptly decided to get that stamp by force. How simple it would be, if only he could manage to be a bit tough for an hour or two. And so he set out with a gun for the dealer's shop. . . . Fortunately the gun was not loaded, the robbery failed, and the judge who tried the case was an understanding human who knew something about stamps and gave the youth a suspended sentence.

Three-quarters of a century before, however, there was a Spanish bibliophile who was not forgiven. The Bluebeard of all collectors, he forfeited his life for rare or unique books, brushing aside as quite incidental to the value of choice volumes the lives of other men as well as his own. Don Vincente was a monk who had had access, for many years, to the valuable library of the monastery at Poblet near Tarragona. Always a book lover, the more he worked with the monastery treasures the more passionate grew his attachment to them, until at last he lost all moral sense in his desire to have the finest for his own. His opportunity came with the political upheavals that wracked Spain in the eighteen-forties. No one then had time or inclination to maintain a rigid check on monastery collections, and Don Vincente, after taking what he wanted, temporarily disappeared. When next heard of, he had set himself up as the proprietor of a bookshop in Barcelona and had become a frequenter of local book auctions. One day he started out with quickened step and unusual anticipation, for the collection about to go on the block was known to contain a long-desired item of importance—a work of Lamberto Palmart, published in 1482. It was thought to be the only one of its kind then extant, and now at last. . . . But someone else was there, equally tenacious. In a fever the two men bid for the prize, and each knew that the loser would lose forever. At last Don Vincente reached his limit, and the Palmart went to Augustino Paxtot. When his anguish had paused for a moment, there was for Vincente no generous handshaking. Instead, he rushed from the room cursing and threatening his victorious opponent.

A few days later, Paxtot perished in a mysterious fire which destroyed his home. Because of his violence on the day of the sale, suspicion was immediately directed toward Vincente, and it could hardly surprise anyone that the police, rushing to his shop, should have found there the disputed volume; but what followed was enough to baffle the wisest, except, perhaps, one familiar with collectors. Confronted with the evidence, Vincente did not bother to deny his guilt; he only begged the police to be careful of the precious book. At the subsequent trial it was proven that this ferocious bibliophile had made away not only with Paxtot but with not less than eleven earlier victims. In each case murder had been done to get hold of some coveted book. During the trial Vincente's calm remained Olympian until, in an effort to clear him of the final murder by throwing doubt on the assumption that the copy found in his client's shop had belonged to Paxtot, Vincente's lawyer revealed that, only a few days before, *another copy of the supposedly unique Palmart had been found* in Paris. At this the ex-monk promptly became hysterical, and for days thereafter, whether he was alone in his cell or confronting the court, he could be heard moaning, "Alas! Alas! My copy is not unique!" This attitude was no pose, for when his time came to ascend the scaffold, Vincente displayed the same concentration upon a single interest: possessive bibliophile to the end he asked, in the face of death, that his collection be kept intact, and instructed that it should be given to the Barcelona library.

Although collectors normally revel in display, there are a few who seem to find greatest satisfaction in hiding their possessions. A clear instance of this compulsion appears in the case of the seventeenth-century French numismatist, Basin de Limeville. This gentleman was a member of a good Huguenot family of Blois, well educated, in comfortable circumstances, and "not unintelligent." He devoted most of his time to the creation of a collection of medals, but his purchase of a fine specimen was the signal for mourning among other connoisseurs. When a medal came into his possession it disappeared into a locked cabinet especially constructed for the purpose. Behind its iron door no other human being ever penetrated during the Sieur de Limeville's lifetime, and after his death no one could work the intricate lock which had been so constructed that only the owner and the locksmith (also deceased) ever knew its secret. When entry was finally forced by cutting a hole through the wall of the room, the cabinet was seen to contain a curious hoard that might well have delighted a Freudian. Among the decades' accumulation of cobwebs were six watches, a strongbox containing wooden rollers of all sizes and kinds wrapped in paper, and a large number of scissors and napkins. The money was on the floor under the napkins and scraps of paper, and the precious medals were all heaped inside a filthy old sack!

Occasionally among collectors secrecy goes hand in hand with the impulse to steal, and this may be quite apart from the ordinary sequence in which stealing produces a sense of guilt followed by secrecy. Here, for example, is a bizarre case wherein the "collector" and the kleptomaniac seem to cross trails and become united, pointing once again to the infinite number of combinations possible. Even the wood rat trait is indicated in this man, a "specialist" in silverware and kitchen utensils, who stole items from his own dining room and kitchen to increase his secret hoard, which he kept in a back shed. So that the suspicions of his family might not be aroused, this extraordinary individual became involved in an endless chain of stealing and replacing, yet despite the inconvenience he kept up the game for many years.

Although this procedure could hardly be called shrewd, there are numerous cases on record of presumably reputable and successful (i.e., moneyed) citizens who, although not willing to risk the actual stealing, have at least been eager to connive in theft to obtain for themselves some valuable and famous object, fully aware that the ownership of stolen goods enjoins secrecy forever. In order to compensate the thief for the risk he runs, large sums must be paid for such items; and the buyer's position could not possibly be worse, for should he find that a fake has been delivered to him, how can he complain to the authorities? Yet there are always collectors willing to chance a crooked gamble.

Sometimes the theft can be successfully rationalized (as in the case of the *Chef de St. Martin* reliquary) but often enough no war or political upheaval exists to provide the excuse. The *Mona Lisa* is said to have been sold six times shortly after its theft from the Louvre, and each client, of course, fondly believed that he was getting the original. Sometimes (it happened in the case of the *Mona Lisa* to more than one rich American) before the theft is undertaken, a collector will be approached most tactfully, and behind a very convincing front, with the suggestion that arrangements are complete to "remove" such and such a masterpiece. Would he care to become the new owner? If it should become necessary, the first step can be passed off as a joke; but should the collector agree to the plot, details are entered into, and the collector is advised to contain his soul in patience. If a multiple sale is planned by the gang, as many victims as possible are corralled before the actual theft is carried out. This can be done with relative ease, since secrecy is important to the would-be owner. Afterward, public announcement of the theft is proof enough that the deal is half consummated.

More often no theft is perpetrated at all, for a knowledge of psychology and clever handling can make possible the disposal of a facsimile as a "stolen" original without arousing the suspicions of the purchaser. It is said that the men who stole the *Mona Lisa* tried first to sell it without the risk of actually taking the original, but their prime American client was unusually talkative for a man in his position. The museum authorities, hearing of the affair, promptly denied the theft, and the angry collector almost exposed the criminals despite his own part in the shady business. Corrupt Paris journalists then came to the rescue by keeping the rumor of theft alive and the collector did not carry the matter any farther; but it was seen that the picture would have to be stolen, and stolen with much fanfare, if the same trick was to be worked again.*

Prior to this the same gang for three years had been selling fake articles "stolen" from the Louvre; and before that they had long conducted a successful business in "stolen" Murillos in South America. In the case of the Louvre treasures, they would show their clients a forged, official-looking document—an intra-museum memorandum marked "confidential"—in which it was explained that such and such an object had disappeared and that, in order to avoid a scandal, a copy had been temporarily substituted. In the South American business, the gang habitually chose victims a considerable distance from the museum or church to be "looted." Each picture delivered was accompanied by a fake newspaper clipping describing the "theft," and the criminals relied

* The first sale was made in 1910, the others in 1911. Later the story persisted in Paris that the picture taken in 1911 (and later recovered) was itself a copy that had been substituted for the original after the "hushed up" theft in 1910!

on the chance that should the customer visit the city and see "his" painting, he would believe it to be a copy.

Frequently a game was played in South America, and perhaps still is, which was quite without risk for the gamesters. The collector too smart for ordinary methods would be personally conducted to the museum or church and with his own eyes be allowed to watch a conspirator "bribe" the guard to leave the scene or turn away, whereupon the client could march up alone to the picture and mark its back in some way known only to himself. Upon delivery of the painting he would then feel confident that he could identify a sheep from a goat. He did not know that the attendant had *previously* been bribed, and that he, the customer, had actually marked a copy at the back of the original. If he returned later and saw the painting in its familiar setting, he too assumed that a copy had now been substituted for the stolen "original" which he had at home.

But what appeal for the collector can these stolen goods have? By his very method of obtaining them he relinquishes two of the greatest pleasures known to his kind—the pleasure of display, and the pleasure of boasting about the object. The solution appears to rest chiefly on two fundamentals, of which the first is apt to hold more universal significance: 1—prestige resulting from ownership of an object of great fame, even without outside acknowledgment (the owner knows that he possesses a potent secret); 2—an unprincipled man actually falls in love with an object which can never become his by legitimate means. The purchaser of a stolen masterpiece might say, "Here is something that every collector in the world would give his eyeteeth to own—and I alone possess it. No one knows of this but my accomplices. Nevertheless, every time I meet a rival collector I can rejoice secretly in a victory which gives me unquestioned superiority over him."

When the secretiveness is not the result of a feeling of guilt, when the collector merely prefers not to display or to share his possession in any way, his attitude is sometimes described as the enjoyment of privacy in ownership. This attitude, which may constitute a somewhat more direct approach to the assertion of power and importance, occasionally crops up in the most unexpected places. We are told, for example, that when the elder J. P. Morgan purchased the manuscript of Abraham Lincoln's unpublished poem, *The Bear Hunt,* which was one of only three or four extant examples of Lincoln verse and hence of great interest to students and bibliophiles, he paid a sizable premium to retain the publication rights. Having thus acquired mastery, so long as he lived and despite numerous entreaties he would never consent to publication.

Very occasionally a man may actually create a valuable and useful collection at the same time that he is flooding and confusing the market with illegitimate items, and a crime of this sort is of the greatest concern to other collectors, since the last person they would suspect is a highly proficient and honored member of their own tribe.

The archetype, the classic Jekyll-and-Hyde example of collectordom, was the late Thomas J. Wise (1859–1937), bibliophile and excellent bibliographer, publisher of first editions, dealer (in secret), pirate and forger. Wise, who began collecting books at seventeen, apparently had a tremendous drive to achieve wealth and fame, power and prestige and the satisfaction of having associated with the great in his chosen field. All of these things (with the possible exception of the last) he could have had, and, as a matter of fact, did have entirely and quite legitimately through natural ability and persistence. Yet he jeopardized this fair prospect by resorting to fraud to supplement an already bursting bank account, and, as he thought, to strengthen his enviable reputation. In the first of these objectives he succeeded, but the reputation so painstakingly built up over half a century came toppling down about his head three years before he died, leaving him a lonely and bewildered old man. It seems clearly indicated that Wise suffered from a deep-set feeling of social and economic insecurity, for no reasonable assurance was enough for him. Yet there must have been, in the corkscrew paths which he followed as a faker, considerable satisfaction for him. Year after year he was able to deceive the best scholastic brains on both sides of the Atlantic, and yet he was the creator of a collection for which the British Museum was glad to pay more than a quarter of a million dollars even after his sins had been exposed.

Born into the quiet despair of the impecunious middle class, Wise's entire career was dominated by the desire to achieve importance and recognition through every channel open to him. He went into business and became highly successful, but there the satisfactions he sought were insufficient, and when he had made a fortune he retired to devote himself to collecting and bibliography. Profit remained a motive with him always, but in his later years he seemed to be ashamed of this fact and disguised it effectively. More important to him, perhaps, was the wish to be looked up to as friend and confidant of the great and as an authority in the world of books and letters. Also it seems that he liked to see himself pictured as a princely giver of gifts, although actually he had acquired so much that he could well afford the munificent gesture.

He set about becoming a crony of the great by forcing himself on the outstanding literary figures of his time, among them Browning and Swinburne, and later boasted of the most casual association or meeting as evidence of an estimable friendship. Nevertheless, Wise indeed became an authority on Elizabethan and nineteenth-century books, pamphlets and other collectors' items. As a member of the highly respectable Browning and Shelley Societies, in charge of certain reprints from first editions, he gained valuable typographical and bibliographical experience. He worked with F. J. Furnivall, the famous philologist and editor, and with Edmund Gosse on the complete edition of Swinburne's works. His own collection of Browning letters was consulted by the most eminent students of the poet, and some of these letters eventually were published in a special volume edited by Thurman Hood who, for this express purpose, was granted a Guggenheim Fellowship. According to Wilfred Partington, Wise was one of the "very few great collectors —and he was one of the greatest" to have compiled the catalogue for his own collection, a most exacting bibliographical task to which he was entirely equal. He became editor of a column on "Recent Book Prices" in the English *Bookman,* and as a consultant to collectors who relied upon him "alike for his knowledge and for his boasted intolerance of anything second-rate, shoddy or spurious," his reputation spread from England to America. Nor did his scholarship remain unrewarded, for an honorary Master of Arts was forthcoming from Oxford and he was elected to membership in that most exclusive of all book collectors' societies, the Roxburghe Club, as well as to the presidency of the Bibliographical Society.

On this ground of real achievement there was no hoax, no trickery. Yet today there is something which hovers about this great collector's name like an albatross to curse it. For Wise had early embarked upon the publishing of "first editions," and, more surreptitiously, upon the sale of books to collectors. His book-dealing (which was, after all, no crime except against his avowedly nonprofessional standing) was almost always carried on anonymously through a third party—he wished to be known as a member of the *élite*, as a collector and bibliographer, rather than as a salesman. Although this part of his life resulted in some shady performances (for which one of his accomplices once threatened to expose him), still it did not strike at the heart of collecting.

Quite different was his publishing, conducted on three different levels—one legitimate and calculated to enhance his reputation as scholar and benefactor, the other two of progressive illegitimacy and villainy. His system was to borrow or, if necessary, purchase, original and hitherto unpublished manuscripts—verse, prose or letters—the work of some famous and collectible author. These he would print inexpensively in a "limited" edition which, because it was also a first edition, would immediately become quite valuable. So far so good, and for this constructive enterprise on the part of one of their own kind the world of collectors and bibliographers could rightfully be grateful. Occasionally, to a man of letters whose friendship was desired, Wise would present a copy of one of these privately printed works and, with its attendant publicity, the gift would help boost the sale of the work, thus serving a double purpose. A judicious hint or two in the *Bookman* column which he edited could also be made invaluable to the well-concealed profit motive. And still no overt crime was committed. Sometimes, however, a borrowed or newly discovered work or series of letters would be printed without proper authorization, and this practice, resulting also in valuable and authentic first editions, constituted the crime of piracy; although for some reason—Wise was a man of utmost shrewdness—the malefaction escaped airing.

More serious and equally successful was the crime of forgery. His method here was to take certain small but collectibly valuable pamphlets already published, and to reprint them, inserting false imprints and dates earlier than any known. These he would announce as "new discoveries" of first editions of exceptional rarity—and his devious manipulations resulted in his achieving from their sale an enormous profit as well as the much-desired reputation for being a collector of exceptional ability in making valuable discoveries.

It was a fat game while it lasted and it lasted the better part of Wise's lifetime; but it came bitterly a cropper when in 1933 two young men decided to make *An Enquiry Into the Nature of Certain Nineteenth*

Century Pamphlets. The results of their "Enquiry," published in 1934, caused a furor in the literary world that had not been equaled since the days of William Henry Ireland, and left Thomas J. Wise sputtering and speechless—a forlorn end to a brilliant collecting career, despite the subsequent acknowledgment by the British Museum that Wise's own Ashley Library was an exceptionally fine accomplishment.

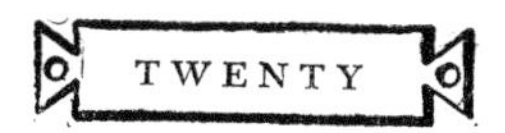

SOME AMENITIES

"I have found that all people in the world who are dull in their conversation and hateful to look at in their faces are those who have no hobbies."

YUAN CHUNGLANG
16th century

A GOOD COLLECTION is like a well-balanced symphony orchestra—each item must pass searching inquiry as to its validity for inclusion, its *raison d'être,* and must harmonize with all other parts to form an integrated unity. In this regard no virtuoso piece is a match for the final purpose, the ensemble, and the complete collection is endowed with a distinct personality of its own, the possessor of an especial and perhaps unique beauty or significance.

To the making of such a collection one may give one's self completely, finding therein not only an outlet for emotion, intellect and energy, not only replenishment, but growth as well. To the extent that the collector has brought into being that distinctive beauty or meaning which belong only to *his* particular collection, his pleasure is truly like that of any other creator. In some the pleasure may be as simple an emotion as that of the child who has successfully constructed a house of blocks. In others it may be as taxing and rewarding a satisfaction as the architect's who surveys at last his completed masterpiece. Whether simple or complex, however, there is always to be found the particularly keen pleasure of creating, and the library of an A. E. Newton bears in its own way the mark of its maker as surely as does a Rembrandt painting or a Shakespeare sonnet.

Yet since even a true amateur or a great connoisseur is not the originator of the individual objects he selects, enjoys and orchestrates, there is a limit to the creative aspect of his pursuit, and some collectors may be inclined to regret their comparatively passive role. "If only I, myself, had conceived and executed this marvelous painting, this handsome bowl, this exquisite bit of tapestry," such a man might say, "how much deeper the satisfaction, how much more pervasive the pleasure it would surely give me since appreciation alone gives so much." This is a vain and foolish regret which most amateurs are too wise to harbor; for to the collector, in his very role as a member of the audience, belongs the highly desirable privilege of pure enjoyment.

One has only to step behind the scenes for a moment to become aware that the creator's nose is so deep in work that to enjoy his own or other men's creations with the freedom and pleasure of the amateur is quite impossible. The writer's time to read is limited, and when he reads it is likely that he is constantly making mental notes and comparisons. With intense enjoyment the painter stops now and then to gaze at a masterpiece—but he must hurry back to the studio, where there are certain problems. . . . As for their own work, query the creators on how many among them linger in pleasure over a completed task: most often they turn their backs at once, striving for something closer to the goal; their pleasure lies in the act of creating, the amateur's in leisurely contemplation of the finished product. Comparatively, the amateur then is the carefree man. He need not chase after the rainbow. With the hearty gusto of the vintage bibber he can linger over his rare and fine example for a lifetime without ever a pang of the creator's probing to cloud the cup. In words appropriate to any reasonably successful collector, Mather has written of the art amateur:

> "It is the high privilege of the true collector to domesticate beauty, to crown the ardor of pursuit with the serener rapture of possession. In the realm of esthetics he is the ideally married man."

From the robot collector to the gifted connoisseur is a long step; as long, let us say in rough comparison, as that between the bricklayer and the architect. The true collector is a person of developed potentials who uses his native talent through his perception, intuition, integrity, and an abiding love. The more pedestrian collector finds sufficient satisfaction in merely obeying his urge to accumulate. Another relishes most the process of classifying his items, or finds his greatest triumph in completing a series. Within its limits this makes a good game—long, zestful, and reasonably objective—and it is precisely this quality of objectivity that proves to be one of the great amenities. Because of it, collecting can be counted upon as a therapeutic agent, offering release from the demands of the inner self, demands of worry, attention to troublous or monotonous details of life and the distress of loneliness.

While some devote their best energies to collecting, finding in it the greatest satisfaction life has to offer, other men, busy, successful in business or the professions, discover in collecting a soothing diversion, an interesting relaxation from their careers. Here is a new world with a different set of values, another language, a relief after the day's work. Beyond such diversion and refreshment many ask little more of collecting. For them it is possible to neglect the collection without suffering the pangs of a deprived lover.

For some, collecting approaches the impersonal systematic preserve of science where one may gratefully forget the emotional plight of man in the contemporary picture, or lose sight of conditions too familiar, too saturated with the personalities of one's environment. Used thus, a collection may be more than mere relaxation. It may be an escape, but the sort of escape which permits one to return to the horsepower world strengthened and heartened. Too, there is valuable security in having always at hand an absorbing interest to which one can turn. It is told of a defeated presidential candidate, John W. Davis, that the morning after election he turned up in his favorite old bookstore and browsed contentedly for his collection. "By and large," said the dealer, "he was better off." Another man, grief-stricken over the death of his young son, turned back for distraction to one of his own boyhood hobbies—a collection of clippings concerning the odd pastimes of other people—and found not only consolation but the idea for a new and highly successful career. This was Dave Elman, whose radio program, "Hobby Lobby," became one of the most popular on the American networks.

"Diverting" and "relaxing" would not, however, be appropriate terms to use in describing the amenities of the collectors furious and impassioned. Indeed they are as contemptuous strangers to such ideas. As serious as duelists, they abhor the implied softness of the word "hobby." Although as collectors they must at times suffer anguish and despair, the peaks of their joy are correspondingly high. This sort of intensity has good and bad points, but in at least one case it has saved a collector's life. The story concerns one John Allan (1777–1863), a New York connoisseur of books, engravings and coins, whose formidable testiness and great collecting accomplishments caused him to be held in awe by friends and competitors alike. Once seriously ill with quinsy, his life was despaired of—until his physician hit upon the following audacious ruse. Gathering a number of fellow collectors, the doctor gave them their instructions and herded the worthies through the sickroom door. There they stood a short distance from Allan as though awaiting his demise; and while they waited, their voices low but carefully toned to include the patient, they argued how they would divide up his treasures when he was gone. The act was of short duration. Enraged beyond endurance, and with a rising sun spreading rapidly over each pallid cheek, the sick man sat bolt upright in his bed and shouted so long and furiously at his "false" friends that the stubborn abscess in his throat broke, as the wily doctor had hoped, and John Allan lived to enjoy his precious possessions a while longer.

Even in our day few medicos are skillful enough to use a dying man's collection instead of a lancet, but the general health of the community is nevertheless benefited by the practice of collecting, and as this fact becomes increasingly recognized the hobby is used as a therapeutic agency with increasing frequency. Educators now often employ collecting to reawaken self-confidence and stimulate ambition, particularly in the case of children who for one reason or another have failed to make a satisfactory group adjustment. The invalid who collects literature on mountaineering or the blind man who collects airplane models are typical instances of extreme need, and although in such cases as these the substitute activity can hardly bring complete satisfaction, it is nevertheless a compensation that serves in large measure to lessen almost intolerable situations.

In a somewhat different class are those whose fight is basically against emotional impedimenta, yet here too a suitable collection often supplies a passable solution. There is the authentic case of a minister's son who, resenting strict early discipline, saved newspaper clippings in which the escapades of ministers' sons and the misdoings of ministers themselves were described. In this mildly amusing way the young man found innocent outlet for a rebellion that might otherwise have led him down the proverbial path of such sons.

Many educators advocate encouraging children to collect not only for psychological and social reasons, but also because they have found that collecting stimulates study, helps to train memory and observation, focuses and holds interest, and encourages disciplined habits of thought. Bankers have likewise urged their employees to collect stamps for the less altruistic reason that trained philatelists find it easier to recognize counterfeit money!

The serious collector poking into the specific and general backgrounds of an item uncovers many fascinating sidelights of history and resurrects, through the objects he seeks to understand, endless human-interest stories of the past, in the process revealing those intimate facets of everyday life so much more illuminating than battle dates and king lists.

The subject of fan collecting might at first appear a frivolous unpromising enterprise, and yet. . . . Should you collect fans, before long you would be boning up on the ceremonials and beliefs of the ancient Chinese, Egyptians, Phoenicians, Greeks and Romans, for the fan played an important part in the lives of these peoples. You would, for instance, discover that your favorite article is considered the Emblem of Life by many Oriental races, that it was once the royal symbol of China, that long ago it was used to hasten the coming of the God of Love and to ward off the Evil Eye, and in the light of this discovery the playful fan takes on a profound dimension. You will journey through the sixteenth century, traveling with your items from East to West on the crest of the Age of Discovery, amused by the pleasure and tactics of coy European belles in this coquettish novelty just introduced from the Orient. There was, for example, the "peep-hole" fan, its purpose to allow court ladies to appear entirely modest without thereby relinquishing a single spicy detail of the latest risqué theater piece. Many famous painters—Rubens, Greuze, Boucher, Watteau and Fragonard among them—launched their careers by decorating the fan. Years can be spent in fascinating research on fans that were issued in commemoration of important events (much as postage stamps are today), and on others that were used by politicians to satirize current happenings or even to promote revolutions. No matter what your special interest, there will always be the heart-warming pastime of searching out past owners; fetching up with tales of intrigue and lacy romance; and, with the pretty bauble you hold in your hand to serve as passport, those lives and incidents again come to life.

For most mortals there is pleasure enough in the art of lifting a drinking glass; but when the toast is raised, the specialist's mind is very apt to wander off in speculation about the family tree of the glass he holds. Though the subject is fairly simple, it leads back to a study of artifact evolution, and soon one becomes partner to the intriguing knowledge that even the most elegant vessel of this sort is finally a descendant of some crude natural product—a gourd, a coconut, a buffalo horn or an ostrich egg—which our forebears manipulated to serve their thirsty gullets. This pellucid hobby has led more than one collector into halls of scholarship in American or English history, social or political, far from the original contract of simple collecting. It is yours to discover that vessels of a certain footless type were "coaching glasses," used to serve travelers when they stopped at some relay inn to change carriages in days when travel was work. But why, you pause to ask, why were not ordinary glasses good enough? Reading on, the answer appears. Because carriage changes were hasty intermissions to long journeys, the inn servants were in the habit of legging it madly to the travelers, balancing aloft huge trays of those inverted glasses, the special shape having been contrived to minimize accident. Coaching glasses are comparatively rare today, but it matters little. The drinking glass specialist is bound to happen upon the information if not upon one of the glasses, and his will be the sedentary temperate pleasure that comes from ability to see into the past, recreating detailed scenes of old-fashioned conviviality—and perhaps the fun of telling someone else about it.

Nor is that all, for the trail leads further still. It may find you delving into the romantic adventures of rebellious Englishmen such as those portrayed through Jacobite drinking glasses. In this way you can discover how, in 1701 when the Stuarts by Act of Parliament were forever excluded from the throne of England, subterranean clubs were formed; and how the members of these clubs, sympathizers of the current "Pretender," would, when they drank a toast, hold their glasses above a bowl of water to show that they were drinking to their "King over the water" (in France, where the exiled pretenders lived). Treason and gritty courage, idealism and political maneuvering, will be revealed, and you will even be able to judge the characters of the individuals for whom

The Metropolitan Museum of Art

French fan, c. 1700-1750, Vernis Martin on ivory. 19th-century sun-shaped Chinese fan. 18th-century English engraved wine glass, inscribed with complete Jacobite anthem; ex. coll. Mrs. Palmer Douglas of Hawick, Scotland.

each of your items was first fashioned, since the activities of the Jacobite clubs had to be carried on *sub rosa,* and a timid member would have the Stuart emblems and Jacobite mottoes engraved only upon the underside of the foot of his glass, but a less fearful man would have them emblazoned boldly and in full sight on the side of the glass itself.

Most of the fields of human knowledge are called upon by the collector, and none seems to promise handsomer dividends in amusement and enlightenment than an occasional excursion into the origin of names.

On such a holiday the porcelain fancier discovers that the complicated history of his luxurious favorite's name goes back to the highly inelegant porker or pig, since *porcelain* was first so-called from the resemblance its polished surface bore to the "porcelain" or cowrie shell, which in turn had received its name (through the Italian *porcella*) because the curved upper surface resembled a pig's back. In Scotland, as any amateur will inform you, chinaware is still occasionally spoken of as "pigs," while the word *china* itself derives from the circumstance that porcelain was first brought into Europe from the Orient.

Similarly the chintz collector's favored material derives from the animal kingdom, being related philologically to the cheeta or spotted hunting leopard. As he will point out, the word *chint* (plural *chints*) was first applied to the printed cottons of India and was an adaptation of the Hindu word *cint* (from the Sanskrit, *chitra*) meaning spotted or variegated.

As for silver, the collector will find that *salver* has the same origin as the word *salvage,* to save—a surprising relationship explained by the fact that a salver in the Middle Ages was the dish upon which the food left over from a nobleman's table was saved so that it might be distributed among the poor people waiting outside.

In this manner, collectors stray from philology to history to sociology to medieval romance. The acquisition of items, then, is but one part of the collector's concern, and the items themselves, far from being the terminus are often the embarkation point toward a lifetime of fresh intellectual vistas.

By definition, the true collector does not usually consider the practical potentialities of the objects he collects, but this does not mean that he may not put them to work. It is obvious that the antique collector may use many of his items at home without being less the amateur; and the genuine bibliophile may create a specialized library which serves in his work without loss of amateur standing. In all the infinite shadings from this point to unequivocal commercialism, one will find that it *is* possible for the amateur to have his cake and eat it too. He can remain faithful to the code (which includes an honest attitude, a matter of constant inner integrity) and even make money through his collection, not, of course, by trafficking in it or by speculating in collectibles.

There are many who derive a more or less steady income from the public exhibition of the unusual collections they have created. The zeal of the amateur in this is of the same order as the missionary's in his educative work—he wants to open the eyes of the many to the delights of his faith, and the money of course is a necessary adjunct to the lives of most mortals. Exhibiting the collection often leads to a career of writing and lecturing, sometimes with such good results that no other means of livelihood is required. The late G. Selmer Fougner wrote a daily newspaper column and many books and articles all based upon his hobby of collecting wines and liquors. Much of the material he used came from his special library gathered over the years from almost every country in the world. Similarly, collectors in many other fields from antiques to philately daily make capital of their specialized knowledge through writing; while some professional writers whose collecting is secondary find in it material for entire novels. Michael Sadleir did this when he wrote a tale of Victorian night-life, *Fanny By Gaslight,* an offshoot of his collection of "not so prudish" periodicals, fly sheets and small books once sold in the London of that period.

Collectors become editors of collecting periodicals and newspaper columns. They are often museum curators and consulting specialists; and their collecting habits have been the helmsmen leading to these careers. To produce such results a collection need be neither expensive nor pretentious, as Mrs. Bella C. Landauer's various collections attest. Composed of "scraps of old paper," these are all now in museums or libraries; and of the Landauer Trade Card Collection at the New York Historical Society she herself has long been curator.

Collections which cost practically nothing can be the most prolific payers of dividends. A reference book since 1897 known and used the world over, *Jane's Fighting Ships,* which runs to some five hundred pages and sells for a stiff price, was the result of an English boy's collection of photographs, diagrams, facts and figures concerning warships.

Harry E. Twohy of California has been content, nay quite happy with automobiles no less than twenty-five years old which can be reconditioned for use. This collector, who treats his curious items as a stable of blooded steeds, embarked upon his hobby as a completely disinterested amateur; but the ancient conveyances he gathered soon were in great demand as "props" for period motion pictures, automobile shows and other events—with results highly beneficial to the collector's exchequer.

In the old tradition of "museums" in barber shops, coffee houses and inns is Bill Hardy's "Gay Nineties" collection of shaving mugs, wooden phonograph records, gold-trimmed spittoons, barroom nudes and other relics of that droll era, all used to embellish his New York City restaurant. In addition to the customers on pleasure bent, the exhibit attracts outsiders of every sort from milliners to museum workers, who go to Bill Hardy's to do research and who tarry, we suppose, to revive the inner man.

Sometimes the collection shoulders out a business never well liked by the owner and takes its place on a professional footing. If the results could always be as hypnotically attractive as the case of "Ye Olde Curiosity Shop" on Colman Dock in Seattle, Washington, perhaps more collector men would drop businesses that never warmed their hearts and let, if it must, the amateur standing go. About half a century ago "Daddy" Standley had a grocery store in Denver. Besides the sacks of flour, the apples, slabs of bacon and harness around the place, people had trouble staying clear of such items as whales' teeth, petrified bullfrogs, and Chinese beheading swords. Of course Daddy was a collector. After a while things got so bad that his customers could no longer find the groceries, and so the grocery store was shut fast and Daddy moved out West where he became a highly successful and internationally known dealer in curiosities.

Perhaps there is a theme for a psychologist's thesis in the relation between grocers and the collecting temperament, for the incidence rate appears to be very nearly as high as it is for physicians. In a Vermont town of under ten thousand people there lives a man whose collecting propensities are almost terrifyingly ravenous. Here is the collector of nearly everything, including jobs and titles:

BUSINESS CARDS OF A "MERCHANT EXTRAORDINARY"

J. E. BUSHNELL

Grocer	Lumber
Real Estate	Gravel, Rock and Loam
Curios	Apartments
Antiques	Summer Camps

92-112 ELLIOT STREET — BRATTLEBORO, VT.

JASON E. BUSHNELL

THE YANKEE TRADER

GREEN GROCER & MERCHANT EXTRAORDINARY

Health Officer and Coroner
Brattleboro Chairman of Vermont Sesquicentennial Committee
Chairman Chamber of Commerce Civics Committee
Member Vermont State Retail Grocers Ass'n
Member National Retail Grocers Ass'n
Member National Geographic Society
Member Independent Grocers Ass'n
Notary Public — Multiple Hobbies

94 ELLIOT ST. — BRATTLEBORO, VT.

BUSHNELL'S MUSEUM

**Curios—Oddities—Antiques—Fossils—Sea Shells
Indian Relics—Minerals—Money—Eggs—Old
Documents of Vermont—Antique Tools and Utensils
of New England—Old Guns and Pistols
Many thousands of Interesting, Odd and Curious things**

There may be other museums, but none like this.

J. E. BUSHNELL 102 Elliot St. Brattleboro, Vt.

JASON E. BUSHNELL

(EX-)

Selectman, Police Commissioner, Tree Warden, Manager of the Town Farm, Member of Board of Civil Authority, Member of Public Works Board, Member of Civil Works Board, Member Liquor Commission, Overseer of Poor, Sec.-Treas. Windham County Code Authority, Member of Red Cross Disaster Relief Committee, Chairman of Windham County Boy Scouts of America, In Charge of Unemployed Relief and Chamber of Commerce Milk Depot, Chamber of Commerce Welfare Relief, President Brattleboro Chamber of Commerce, President Vermont Retail Grocers Ass'n and Director Vermont State Retail Grocers Association.

94 ELLIOT STREET BRATTLEBORO, VT.

This man runs a profitable grocery business. Adjoining, and much closer to his heart is his "museum." A visitor finds that the museum is part second-hand store and part warehouse collection; and the owner proves to be part Barnum (with the shrewd Barnum eye) and part true amateur. A general collector in the good old seventeenth-century sense, almost every business or undertaking he has ever touched has yielded up items. This grocer-gravel-merchant-real-estate-agent has a notable group of historic weights and measures much in demand at fairs and antique shows; a large assortment of ancient books, good, bad and worse; cases of geologic exhibits; antiques of all sorts gleaned from scores of New England attics and cellars; a dozen specialized collections including a valuable one of old hats, truly startling in style and dimension; assorted weapons, wooden legs, Indian arrowheads, old spectacles, and autograph letters. There is a back room of exhibits which, because of their gruesome or otherwise dubious character are displayed only at his discretion. True, this man is a dealer, for you can buy many of the things in his "museum." But the fact that, as a hard-headed Yankee, he manages to wring considerable dividends from his hobby cannot bar him from the list of dyed-in-the-wool collectors. He talks like a collector. He acts like a collector. And should your eye happen to covet one of his particular personal prizes, a part of one of his true collections, it would do little good to offer him the moon for it, although the occasion might provide a diverting battle between the man's business sense and his amateur possessiveness.

Occasionally a collection becomes simply bread-and-butter, and then the enjoyment of collecting affords a little jam, as an extra dividend. Such is the well-known "Bettmann Archive," the owner of which was once curator of the rare book department of the State Art Library in Berlin. With a large photographic collection under his care, he received frequent requests for exhibition material to illustrate such subjects as the history of book-reading, paper-making, or surgery. Because the library's collection had been compiled by art experts who cared very little for "story" interest, the curator discovered that it was almost impossible to use the collection in this fashion, and yet he felt that "far clearer, less equivocal facts concerning various phases of human history could often be gleaned from old illustrations than from any text." He bought a camera and began to create a collection of his own which he brought with him when, in 1935, he came to America. Today he has indexed and cross-indexed more than thirty thousand photographs from old books, prints, etchings and paintings which can be used by book publishers, advertising agencies and other organizations to illustrate more than six hundred different phases of human activity.

In a different category are those who approach collecting as an escape from frustration or death, and who have found not only consolation but a life's career thereby. Forced to give up his cherished ambition to follow the stage, Albert Davis became a show card painter who collected theatrical photographs, programs and lithographs as a hobby. Before he died he had gathered over one hundred and fifty thousand items in one of the finest collections of its sort; and for forty years these items, which were useful as source material and for reproduction purposes, earned his living.

Somewhat similar is the case of Dave Elman, previously mentioned as the collector of hobbyists who fashioned a radio program from his collection. Not all of Mr. Elman's "items" as displayed on this program are collectors, but many of them have been, including such prize exhibits as the woman with a cabinet containing forty thousand wishbones, the man who watches over five thousand telephone books, and the girl who specializes in postscripts because she believes that they are the most important part of any letter. Even as a boy incurably a collector of the usual juvenilia—stamps, matchbooks, bottle caps and cigarette souvenir pictures—at one period Elman compiled a scrapbook of information concerning the odd hobbies of other people; and it was this collection, revived as a distraction upon the occasion of his son's death, which led him directly into the unique form of airwave entertainment which made his fortune.

Elman's wide audience furnishes the key to the question, "Is it easy to put the collection to work?" The answer is yes, providing one happens to collect something of current interest or if business sense dictates the choice of subject. Most of the numerous collectors in any community literally swarm about displays of their own pet subject. Moreover, in the public at large are thousands of collectors-in-embryo, people who respond to the novel or startling and who, although not active in accumulating such things for themselves, will crowd about exhibits of an unusual nature, drawn by a mysterious but compelling fascination. On Cape Ann in Massachusetts there lives a man who collects Boston newspapers. He is not a "serious" collector, yet he has managed to turn his accumulation of some two hundred thousand items to good account (good, that is, for his purposes). Using only his collection, he has built and furnished a house, complete with piano, strong enough to withstand New England winters. The house itself and everything in it has been constructed of newspapers rolled and glued together in a clever process he invented, and the "Paper House" draws a considerable and lucrative tourist trade.

For a quick haul, however, the businessman's profit appears picayune by comparison to that made when explorers and scientists take over, angling for collectors' money. Philatelists play a major role here, and envelopes with canceled stamps carried on unique air flights or scientific expeditions have returned remarkable revenue. Collectors are so anxious to get these items that they pay a sizable premium for the privilege. Envelopes which rode the Graf Zeppelin on its first transatlantic flight fetched a dollar apiece, and Dr. Hugo von Eckner himself stated that none of the big ship's experimental flights would have been possible without the support of philatelists. Piccard's first stratosphere flight was financed by a special issue of stamps. In this fashion nearly six hundred thousand dollars were realized for Amundsen's flight over the North Pole. And Byrd's first expedition to Little America was partially paid for in this way. Tens of thousands of collectors bought three-cent stamps and paid a fifty-cent fee for the transportation of self-addressed envelopes to Little America where these were postmarked and mailed back to them. Had a similar system prevailed in the days of Livingstone, it is unlikely that the explorer could ever so thoroughly have lost himself, for stamp enthusiasts, exacting as they are, would have insisted upon knowing where he was every step of the way.

As the function of collecting is observed to broaden impressively, its history and present and future status begin to assume the proportions of an heroic community monument, for it should not be forgotten that, regardless of original motive, the collector has done much to make the history of civilizations and cultures available to us by his persistent preservation of the world's records, physical relics and minutiae. Science is not organized to carry out this huge job in all its details; the time, interest and perseverance to trace the last question on some obscure subject to its lair belong to a thousand thousand collectors. By virtue of his curious passion, the collector sees the fascination that lurks in the merest trivia, embraces the small along with the great, and leaves it to posterity to choose between them.

Writing of the endless avenues open to Parisian collectors toward the end of the eighteenth century, Louis Sebastien Mercier declared:

"The most painful research will fail to find every treasure hidden in every branch of the sciences and art . . . Every searcher in whatever line will find an inexhaustible fund of things to look at: medals, books, pictures, antiques, shells, prints may each become the sole occupation of a lifetime . . . Death often opens these richly furnished cupboards, these unknown and hidden repositories. On breaking the seals, the inventory taken astonishes and amazes the spectator; one has difficulty in imagining how a man can have had sufficient leisure to amass so many things; but time, money, patience, and above all, infatuation have gone to the composition of these great collections."

And when the cupboards are open, what then? Mercier speaks first of coins. With the related medals these constitute one of the oldest items in the collector's harvest, and from them the historian derives an enormous amount of information—dynasty dates, historic deeds of forgotten heroes, location of vanished cities, descriptions of costumes and of the peoples who wore them, information concerning trade and economics and many other things. Books and statuary, and, in modern times, paintings, prints and postage stamps play a more obvious role of this sort, while actually there is nothing preserved by collectors, not even matchclips with advertising slogans, without potential historical value.

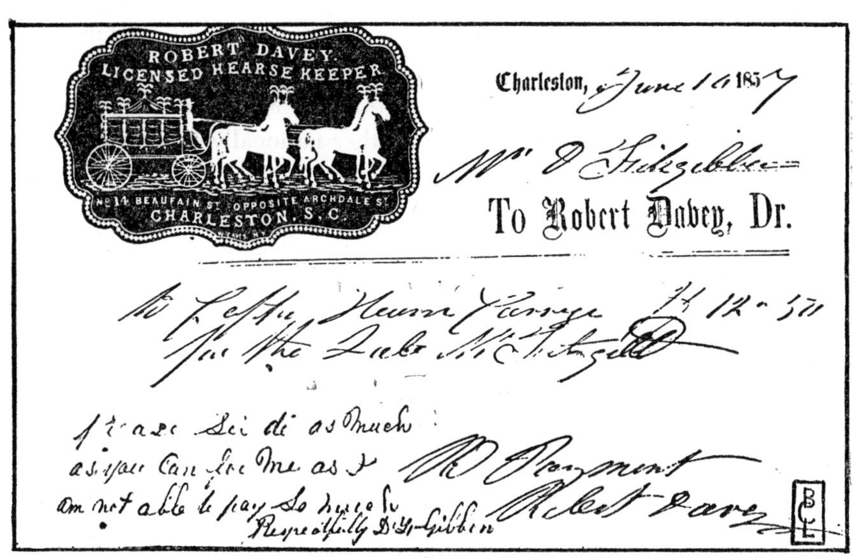

ROBERT DAVEY.
LICENSED HEARSE KEEPER.
No 14 BEAUFAIN ST OPPOSITE ARCHDALE ST
CHARLESTON, S. C.

Charleston, June 16 1857

Mr D Fitzgibbon

To Robert Davey, Dr.

Please Sir do as much as you can for me as I am not able to pay so much Sir

Respectfully D Fitzgibbon

Robert Davey

Courtesy, New York Historical Society, New York
From the Bella C. Landauer Collection of Trade Cards

HEARSE KEEPER'S BILL, *Charleston, S. C., 1857. Note from client pleads, "Please Sir do as much as you can for me as I am not able to pay so much."*

The Cluny Museum in Paris possesses a valuable and fascinating collection of old boots and shoes formed years ago by a French etcher. From these one can learn how the people of an older time shod themselves, what materials they used, methods of manufacture, styles, needs of the time and standards of comfort. And that American shoe manufacturer who today is gathering contemporary footgear may well be creating a collection eventually as museum-worthy. For it is a fact that a great number of private specialized collections come to roost finally in public institutions where they benefit particularly the student, the writer, the designer and others for whom specialized material is a necessity.

Among the great historical treasures of England today is the collection of one hundred and fourteen volumes of sea-manuscripts in the Pepysian Library, many of which were gathered by the diarist in the routine course of his work as Admiralty Secretary. Sir Hans Sloane owned a collection of letters and notes written by most of the important physicians of his day. Now in the British Museum, these must, according to one biographer, "always be one of the main sources of medical history in England from the time of Charles II to that of George II." Turning to one of a thousand good examples from our own time, there is Joseph Broadman's five-hundred-thousand-item war library as an outstanding instance of a collection which, begun solely for a personal reason, has achieved such importance within the lifetime of its maker that twenty-five colleges and universities and two other nationally famous institutions have expressed the hope of inheriting it.

The principles leading to specialization in collecting are readily recognized, but the query arises, what is the public to gain when, as frequently happens, a collector splits his subject into parts almost microscopic?

First we might say that the specialist is the scientist of the collecting field. Studying his subject more closely than can the eclectic, he unearths and preserves the sort of minute but revealing information that goes into the furbishing of historical patterns. When he relates this information and illustrates it with a complete series of objects, he is making a small but important contribution to the sum of our knowledge, and in this his resemblance to the laboratory worker and the scholar is clear: the isolated scientist working on segments of his field brings his work to a common pool through meetings and publication, and so often does the collecting specialist. When the latter's concern centers in a bygone day, his collection of one-time commonplaces may demand the most painstaking research, and we have seen how as a corollary to hunting down the objects themselves he will trace every available fact concerning their derivations, uses and methods of manufacture, thereby not infrequently preparing nutritive tidbits which scholarship is not above accepting.

The person who collects tea caddies tells us that the eighteenth century reckoned tea a luxury so precious that it was to be kept locked up in a special box, and for this reason the old caddies were beautifully made and decorated. He points out that the expensiveness of the brew led to the development of a new tea-serving ceremony. And through his investigations he discovers a few long-forgotten tales still further to illumine the life of that fastidious century.

American cattlemen of the pioneer era used handwrought branding irons. In pursuit of these, a contemporary collector has amassed biographical material concerning men of our virgin grasslands from which an absorbing book has been written. Had this material not been unearthed by the toiling amateur, it might have disappeared, although it constitutes an important part of American history.

The gatherer of old spittoons refurbishes an obscure corner of the American scene when he relates, from his collector's store of peculiar knowledge, that our early churches often had elaborate twenty-inchers, set in the aisles at the pew ends, and that, as Shackleton says, "it was good form and a matter of distinction to use a spittoon four or five pews ahead, with no interruption to the preacher by the slightest movement of the listener's head!" Alas for one more early American technique lost, a skill now vanished but marked down for memory by a collector.

The early naturalist did not consider everyday trees and flowers worth describing, because, thought he, everyone knew about them; and the old-time collectors were likewise interested chiefly in the rare and the exotic, or in things considered to be masterpieces of their kind. Yet from the commonplace objects of everyday life the clearest picture of any period is reconstructed. Even though ably written descriptions may still exist, how can they convey an idea of strange or outmoded products of the past so well as the articles themselves? It is here that the collector who finds no object too insignificant to be preserved plays an important role in completing the record. Such collections when they survive may become unique, and invaluable to scholarship. Nor is it only the inhabitant of the ivory tower who profits from the preservation of this sort of background material. The reading public benefits by indirect education when the novelist, biographer or scenario writer uses such material to lend authenticity to his productions. The craftsman has wider sources of inspiration upon which to draw when he can examine the collected works of his predecessors. In this way by direct access to the designs of the past such amenities of everyday life as apparel and home decoration are also enriched.

Perhaps the most famous example in our time of this principle of accretion is the collection formed by Franklin Delano Roosevelt simply by never throwing away any document or correspondence received at the White House, however trivial. Mr. Roosevelt is a born collector, and like Pepys he has a special interest in things maritime because of his own early connection with the navy. His private library includes, in addition to many volumes on naval history, a collection of old views, ship-models, contemporary naval manuscripts, paintings and relevant autographs. But the major collection, housed in a museum of its own at Hyde Park and owned by the nation, is of quite a different sort. In fact, better qualified than the Vermont grocer, Mr. Roosevelt might well say, "There may be other museums but none like this." The common citizen, the ordinary officeholder who had from early youth saved everything from Christmas cards to crank letters, from post cards requesting his autograph to important official communications, would surely be set down as queer or inordinately vain. Yet the idea is entirely sound. It is not only that the Hyde Park Library contains hundreds of clearly important letters and papers of the sort that must remain closed to public scrutiny for many years to come. These would be preserved under any circumstances. It is the preservation of trivia that is unusual.

First there is the correspondence of a nation never before in history so pen-in-handed, correspondence addressed to that nation's chief during some of the most amazing years man has yet known. Tens of thousands of Christmas cards in extraordinary variety against the day when this form of greeting may have become obsolete or so changed as to be scarcely recognizable. Letters from children, from housewives, from unemployed workmen, discussing the everyday problems of an everyday

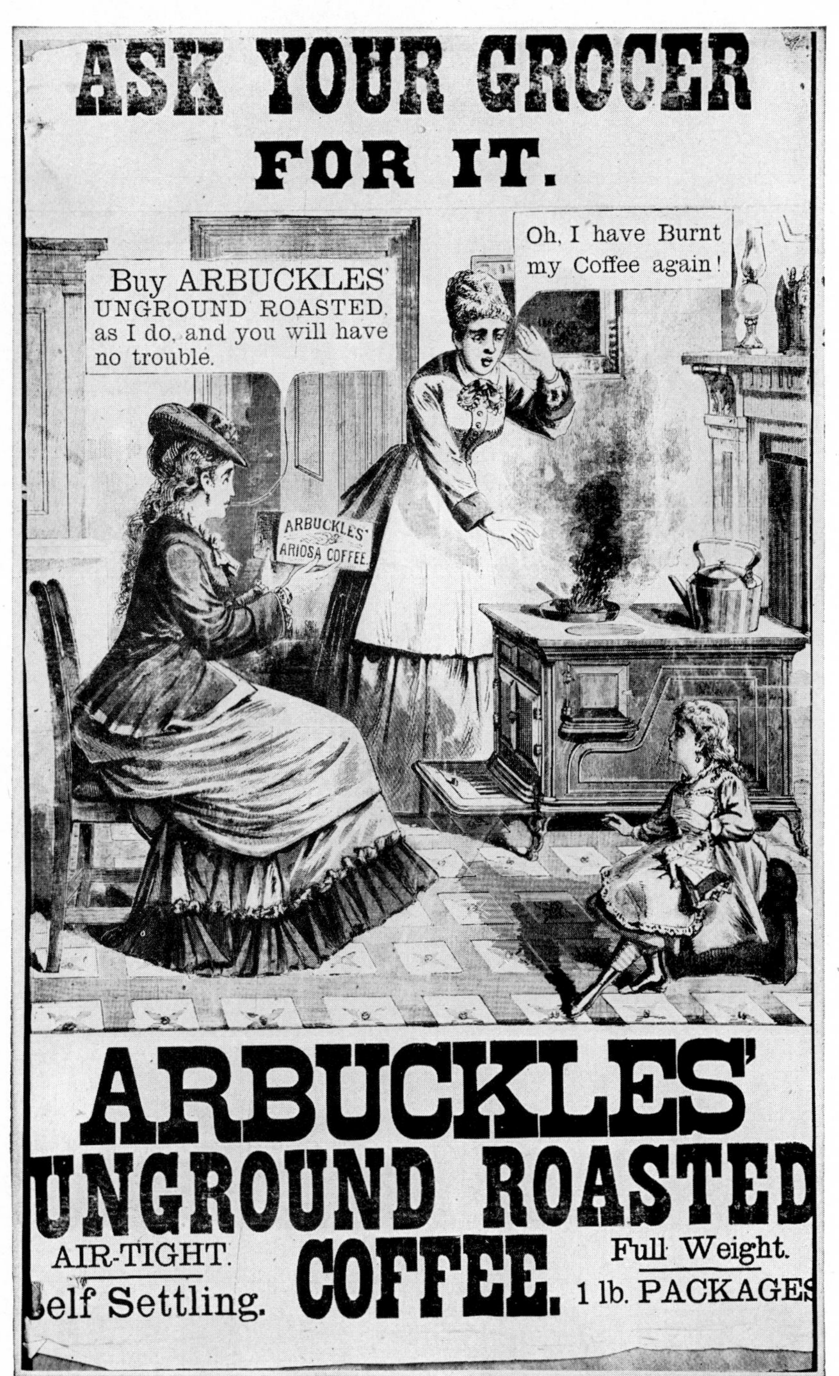

From the Bella C. Landauer Collection of Trade Cards.
Courtesy, New-York Historical Society, New York City

From such "trash" as this advertisement-broadside of the 1870's come collections of surprising value and interest, as today's ephemera become tomorrow's source materials.

life—letters that may some day prove as valuable as the Paston Letters of fifteenth-century England. There is even an "Oddities" room in which items illustrating typical forms of humorous expression and queer quirks of today's Americans can be found. The collection as a whole provides an amazing cross-section of American and world history—social, political, psychological—addressed to a dominant historical figure at a crossroad of international destiny. Dramatic? Intensely so. Information on methods of communication, the types of letterheads in use, telegrams, cablegrams, radiograms, and printed on them the rates and regulations in force in our time. Regional speech peculiarities revealed in letters; curses, forms of blessing and courtesy caught and retained for future examination. Pamphlets and circulars, every copy of which would normally be thrown into wastepaper baskets and forever lost.

Of course it is not always the trivia that collectors save from destruction. The world's oldest printed book, the *Diamond Sutra* printed on the eleventh of May in A.D. 868, and the first known folded book (earlier ones were rolled), both were found by an archaeologist in 1907 in a Chinese Turkestan cave-temple where they had been deposited centuries before by priest collectors. Devoted amateurs performed yeoman service throughout the troubled history of Chinese painting. The Roman collectors were instrumental in the preservation of much Greek art. Bibliophiles and antiquephiles of the renaissance performed a similar service in their time both for ancient art and ancient literature. During the English Reformation period, collectors like Archbishop Cranmer and Sir Robert Cotton recovered many priceless medieval manuscripts from the suppressed religious houses, scripts otherwise sold for their parchment and gold leaf.

This record of honorable service is one of the brightest gifts collecting brings to man. From the record, collectors could fashion a telling answer to those detractors who flatly accuse them of crimes of selfishness. Many amateurs are well aware of their mission of preservation, and the following words of two English bibliophiles—one working in the "darkness" of medieval times, the other echoing the same faith in the nineteenth century—are posted as testimony in the name of all good collectors:

"We are not only rendering service to God in preparing volumes of new books," wrote Richard de Bury in 1473, "but also exercising an office of sacred piety when we treat books carefully, and again when we restore them to their proper places and commend them to inviolable custody."

"It is a good thing to read books, and it need not be a bad thing to write them," declared Frederick Locker-Lampson some four centuries later, "but it is a pious thing to preserve those that have been some time written."

In the history of the world's collected items lie cradled the heartbeats of a million little men and the rise and fall of great nations. In truth, here is one source for the history of the world itself. Look at a single example. As a trophy, thousands of years ago, the majestic *Lion of Babylon*, fastened to a bright chariot of war, journeyed from the land of the Hittites who had created it to the land of the Tower of Babel. It lived through the final conquest and destruction of that warring city whose name it now bears. It endured in stifled silence the dust and debris which covered it layer upon layer over the centuries, while Assyria and Egypt disappeared from the earth as political powers, while the greatness of Rome flared and faded, and Christ and Mohammed rose to change the religious faiths of entire peoples, while barbarian tribes emerged from the northern forests unwittingly to begin the creation of "Western Civilization." Through all this the *Lion* survived and was restored to the sun again toward the end of the nineteenth century by German scientists, descendants of those young barbarians. Today, in the reconstructed ruins of the ancient city which once proudly proclaimed its capture, the *Lion of Babylon* again surveys the scene. A millennium, barely noticed, rolls off that imperious back; and, considering its potential life-span, its view of man and the world may have just begun.

Many items now reposing in museums and private collections have led lives even more eventful, and though their records have rarely survived intact, some men, however haltingly, manage to interpret their meaning. The stone age arrowheads and statuettes of prehistoric man, and the bronze age "hoards" of tools and weapons which moderns have dug out of the earth in many parts of the world; the gold-and-beaded headdress of Queen Shub-ad of Ur who died a thousand years before the birth of Abraham, and whose reconstructed possessions now form a part of the University of Pennsylvania collection; the lifelike stone portraits of twenty-sixth-century B.C. King Gudea of Lagash, which had journeyed as far as the Louvre at last recording; the scarabs, amulets and other relics of old Egypt which now peer out from the cabinet shelves of collectors everywhere; the *faïence* ornaments and seals of India's Mohenjo-daro; the thin-waisted pottery women and vase-recorded bullfighters of old Crete; the carved oracle bones of China's An Yang, and the golden jewels of the South American Incas—what have these not seen, what could they not tell us of people long since vanished? Though forever silent, these ancient sentinels are revered most for the mystery of that silence.

From a closer bond the relics of old Greece and Rome speak to us with compelling eloquence. In the Vatican there is a statue of Demosthenes which once held a place of honor in Cicero's collection, and a *Meleager* which Caesar cherished. Not only centuries, but men whose names we still know and honor, talk to us directly through the living durable veins of hewn stone. In the same way, no dry chronicle could link alien worlds so humanly as do the remnants of certain Hindu libraries founded by Mogul princes in the sixteenth and seventeenth centuries of our era, remnants which survived the destruction and looting of a nineteenth-century mutiny to enter the fund of Western connoisseurs. Collectors know the import of kindred migrations of cultural objects, and other men who pause in museums before these traveled venerables sense the profound story of man and his works.

Michelangelo's *Slaves*, passing without interruption from the master's hands through those of a series of great amateurs—Robert Strozzi, Francis I, Anne de Montmorency, Cardinal Richelieu and Richelieu the Duke-Marshal—is officially owned by the Louvre, although one of the bandit Nazi collectors, Hitler, Goering, Goebbels or Himmler, may have "borrowed" it. While Italy's day of renaissance glory flowered and fell, a new country, France, had risen from comparative "barbarity" to world leadership, only to crumple and sink within a few centuries under the heel of a conqueror, then rise again; yet war's destruction aside, the Angelo marble lives on, prized by friend and foe.

This matter of noting the lineage of an item, the handing down from one collector to another, is a source of ponderable interest. The collector turns toward his predecessors and asks, what manner of men were they who once owned this treasure, how did they live and die, what sort of collectors were they, how illustrious? Did not Morgan, for example, as he sat four-square before the great tapestry, *The Triumph of Christ*, sometimes think of Cardinal Mazarin? Folger treasured most highly those Shakespeare volumes, however commonplace in themselves, which bore on their flyleaves the signatures of literary masters of later centuries, who for inspiration had turned the pages until they were thumb-worn. And with or without important names to conjure with, collectors yet unborn will surely experience the compelling bond, stronger than cousinship, as they study items in the ownership lineage of classic collectibles.

Although preservation has always been one of the most important services rendered by collectors, in certain instances the amateur in the role of patron has contributed further by fostering contemporary creative talent. The collector playing the part of Angel of Mercy to the artist has been, particularly in recent years of heightened social consciousness, the object of much criticism and some homage. In time it is quite possible that circumstances may eliminate the need for the patron, but until this comes about it seems likely that the behavior of amateurs will be little changed by scoldings, that they will continue to go their way as stubbornly as ever.

While it is widely understood that many of the greatest artistic treasures of the Italian and French renaissance were executed to fill the orders of collectors, perhaps it is less realized that even the days of Akbar, Mogul Emperor of India, offered such inducements to painters, and that this Eastern ruler spread the vogue for collecting contemporary works so successfully that by the end of his reign there were one hundred masters at Delhi and at least a thousand amateurs. Peter Paul Rubens said of the Earl of Arundel, who collected contemporary paintings as well as antique marbles, "I regard the Earl in the light of an evangelist in the world of art, and as the great supporter of our profession." In our day, too, many artists would have starved physically and spiritually without the support of collectors; although the charge is sometimes made that collectors are too prone to back unknown men.

Undoubtedly it often takes courage to collect contemporary art—courage and the ability to develop one's own judgment, as well as the willingness to rely upon that judgment once formed; for whenever new trends appear, whenever creative men strike out and away from familiar methods, the conservative pack cries in protest, howling down not only the innovators themselves but those who give their works credence. There were only a few dogged collectors who believed in the laughing-stock of the nineteenth-century art world, Paul Cézanne, and in the Impressionists. The critics, all of them, bayed their derision. Only the faithful adherence of a handful of brave amateurs helped some of those painters to go on to great success and eventual world acclaim. Certainly

Walters Art Gallery, Baltimore

LE BIBLE HISTORIALE, PETRUS COMESTOR, *c.* 1380.

Collectors preserved this fine 14th-century French manuscript in unbroken lineage from 1410. Once watched over by the greatest of medieval bibliophiles, John, Duc de Berry, whose famous librarian, Flamel, inscribed it with the duke's name, its flyleaves bear the names of ten successive owners up to 1785. Later secured by the Earl of Ashburnham and by Henry Yates Thompson, it rests now in the Walters Collection.

there is more to support of this kind than financial backing, vital as money is. Something highly important happens to an artist when he has behind him deep-felt and genuine enthusiasm of the sort the amateur is capable of giving. To be able to buy bread is much, but to receive the faith of those who know something about one's art and its goals supplies to the artist that life-giving warmth sometimes needed to nurse the creative spark. And throughout the ages collectors have supplied that warmth to painters, sculptors, medalists, craftsmen and creators of every variety.

The story of the birth and development of museums and libraries and the collector's vital contribution in this field unfolds in a continuous line from the dawn of civilization into the depths of the future. In Europe there is hardly a great public library or museum which was not originally the private collection of king or nobleman, or which did not draw heavily in its earliest days upon the surviving collections of priests, statesmen and bankers, scientists, antiquarians and citizen amateurs. The collector's work as "guardian of past and present" is on view in every museum in the world. Even in America, which has had no cumulative history of royal collections to build upon, the number of museums and libraries owing their genesis to a robust army of collectors is appreciable, while every institution of the sort in the land is constantly fed from the same source.

While the importance of this phase of collecting cannot be overemphasized, there is space here only to indicate the origin and growth of a few famous institutions and to trace the ownership of a handful of items. The French *Bibliothèque Nationale* should be cited because it is one of the earliest libraries still in existence. In the fourteenth century John II gathered together the first of its books, and to these were added over the years ever larger libraries of succeeding princes and their families. The *Louvre,* greatest pile of art in the world, at first comprised collections of royalty and nobility exclusively. Centuries in the making, these were suddenly nationalized at the time of the French Revolution. The names of illustrious collectors are encountered repeatedly in the library of the *Sorbonne,* whose first gifts were from private collectors and whose shelves were later to be enriched by Richelieu's books. Mazarin's volumes are in the library named for him. Peiresc's medals are in the Abbey of Sainte Geneviève, and the coins and natural history specimens collected by Gaston, Duke of Orléans, after passing through the hands of Colbert and others, became important foundation exhibits for museums devoted to those subjects.

Wherever one chances to look on the continent this pattern is dominant. The museums of Dresden, also among the oldest still extant, originated in "curiosity" collections formed by the Electors of Saxony. Munich's *Glyptothek*, which though young enough is yet the oldest such structure in Germany (erected 1816–30), houses the Greek and Roman sculpture collected by Ludwig I of Bavaria while he was Crown Prince. And the great *Kaiser-Friedrich Museum* in Berlin which, under the guidance of Wilhelm von Bode, one of the ablest of museum directors, was rivaled only by London's National Gallery in the completeness of its historical representation of European schools of painting, was built upon a nucleus of many famous private collections, including the Giustiniani purchased at Paris in 1815, the English Solly collection purchased in 1821, the Suermondt collection purchased in 1874, a selection of paintings from the various royal collections, and many others.

In The Hague the *Mauritshuis* with its notable picture gallery contains the collections formed by the princes of Orange, among them that of the Stadtholder William V. And the *Ryks Museum* in Amsterdam, foremost in a country rich in great museums, has absorbed numerous collections formed by individuals, including the collection founded by Burgomaster Jan Stix, friend and patron of Rembrandt; while one of its most distinguished works, Rembrandt's *Night Watch*, came from the Trippenhuis Gallery which housed paintings brought from The Hague by Louis Bonaparte when he was king of Holland. Many of these had been originally in the house of Orange collections, shattered during the Napoleonic wars.

The museums of Vienna still display the armor, coins and other antiquities gathered by the Emperor Ferdinand II. To at least five royal collectors—the Emperor Charles V, and Kings Philip II, IV and V and Ferdinand VII of Spain—Madrid's *Prado* owes its great assemblage of paintings, the *Royal Palace* the world's best collection of tapestries, and the *National Palace* its historic collections of arms and armor, metalwork and embroideries. It was Ferdinand who, in 1818, gathered together into one incomparable collection the masterpieces from all the royal palaces except the Escorial, and to this were later added items taken from the Catholic convents. Despite loss by State seizure at various times in European countries, the Roman Catholic Church in its totality must itself be reckoned as an important reservoir of cultural deposits, and in this sense it should be ranked with museums, since its hoard of high art, of fabrics, of worked gold and of jewels must equal that of at least fifty such institutions. Similarly the temples of other religions, particularly in the Orient, have contributed much to the preservation of the public heritage.

The long history of the amateur in Italy is signalized by the *Uffizi Gallery,* one of the largest and finest in any country, which contains the magnificent collection of paintings created by the Medici, plus many later additions from churches, monasteries and private collections. The *Vatican* has half a dozen separate museums originated by collecting Popes of the renaissance. The Florentine library known as the *Magliabecchiana,* said still to be a model for other more modern institutions, was founded by an early specialist in fine editions, the bibliophile Antonio Magliabecchi; while in Rome, the leading museum of the Jesuit College was based on the collection of Athanasius Kircher who, in the seventeenth century, bequeathed his antiquities to the college.

In England the story was much the same. Oxford's *Ashmolean Museum* of "artificial and natural curiosities" was, it will be remembered, the creation of the Tradescants over two generations, supplemented by the contribution of Elias Ashmole. And the *British Museum* got off to a rumbling start through the prodigal service of many collectors, Sir Hans Sloane leading the way with his immense natural history collections, to which were added the manuscripts gathered earlier by Sir Robert Cotton, the Harleian manuscripts, the library of King George II, and a number of other collections; and this great institution has since been built up continuously "by the munificence of open-handed collectors." What, again, was the origin of London's *National Gallery*? Thirty-eight paintings from the Angerstein Collection. Both the *Tate Gallery* and the *Wallace Collection* were founded by the gentlemen whose names they bear, while the *John Rylands Library* in Manchester, one of the richest in Europe, was the creation of a great bibliophile, the Second Earl Spencer, although it owes its name to the fact that it was presented to the city by the widow of a wealthy merchant who had purchased the library as a memorial to her husband.

This type of evolution holds true of every sort of museum. Based upon the palace collections of King Christian V of Denmark and his son, Frederick IV, the great museum at Copenhagen became famous in the nineteenth century for its contributions to the advancement of archaeology. Still preserved in Florence is Andrea Cesalpini's sixteenth-century herbarium, while the museum at Bologna contains the original collection of the early naturalist, Ulisse Aldrovandi, examples which could be multiplied by the score; and in England we can even trace the origin of a zoo to a private collector, one Mr. Cross, who a century ago gave his animals as a nucleus for the *Surrey Zoological Gardens.*

Many of the earliest American museums were founded by collectors, and if none of these pioneer ventures has survived it is because the foundations built hastily by individuals were pitifully fragile as compared to the collection building that had been going on in Europe for centuries before community museums were thought of. By the time America was ready for the establishment of truly successful and permanent museums, the nineteenth century was half spent and museums were being founded in a new way, not merely by the haphazard piling up of inherited accumulations, but through purposeful planning.

So it was that in America the oldest art gallery still extant was to be established in connection with a great Eastern university; and the first incorporated public art museum, the gallery of the *Wadsworth Atheneum* at Hartford, Connecticut, was to be founded not by a single collector but by popular subscription, in 1844, "for the preservation and exhibition of works of art, instruction in the fine arts, and to provide headquarters for its affiliated organizations"—which were the Hartford Young Men's Institute and the Connecticut Historical Society. During this period such was the pattern most often followed in America, and also in England, France and Germany, with wealthy non-collectors as well as communities or scientific and other specialized organizations frequently providing the necessary funds.

It had been fitfully true even of the first public museum in this hemisphere, now the *Charleston Museum,* which in 1773 had grown out of the Library Society of Charles-Town's program "to collect materials for a full and accurate natural history of the province of South Carolina." Nevertheless it was with the acquisition of the collections of Colonel John Trumbull that the *Yale Gallery of Fine Arts* was launched in 1831, while the *Wadsworth Atheneum* was materially and typically expanded, nearly three-quarters of a century after its foundation, by the addition of the *Colt Memorial* housing the collection of firearms gathered by Colonel Samuel Colt, and by the *Junius Spencer Morgan Memorial Art*

'ational Gallery of Art, Washington, D. C.

THE MAZARIN TAPESTRY, *Brussels School, c. 1500. Widener Collection.*
Flemish Gothic tapestry, "The Triumph of Christ," which bears the name of the illustrious Cardinal who once owned it. Last collectors who gathered it up were Morgan and Widener.

Gallery erected in 1908 by J. P. Morgan in memory of his father, a native of Hartford.

There are hundreds of libraries and museums which owe their origin solely to private collectors—from Austin, Texas, where the *John Henry Wrenn Library* is the pride of the State university, to Providence, Rhode Island, where the *John Carter Brown Library* lends fame to Brown University; and from Sarasota, Florida, with its *John and Mabel Ringling Museum of Art,* to Sacramento, California, whose *E. B. Crocker Art Gallery* is still housed in the private museum erected between 1870 and 1873 by Judge Crocker to accommodate the art objects he collected in Europe (with his remodeled private home now in use as an annex).

Laurence Vail Coleman, in his illuminating work, *The Museum in America,* uses a curious and significant term to describe present-day private collections which are sometimes open to the public. He calls them private or *larval museums,* and explains the term as follows:

". . . private museums are 'larval' because there is every likelihood of their developing into public institutions, as others of their kind have done in the past."

For an idea of the true contribution of American collectors to the museum field, however, one should thumb through the *American Art Annual,* an impressive publication which has been in existence since 1898. Time after time in describing the origin of community galleries the phrase is repeated, "to collect, preserve, and exhibit works of art and to afford instruction." From the Annual it becomes strikingly apparent how heavily most American institutions have drawn upon the donations of completed private collections. A typical entry in a recent issue is the one which describes the contents of the *City Art Museum* in St. Louis, founded in 1879 as the St. Louis Museum of Fine Arts. Among other possessions of this museum, according to the Annual, are: The Daniel Catlin Memorial Collection of Paintings; The James F. Ballard Collection of Oriental Rugs; The Frank Spiekerman Collection of Miniatures; The William K. Bixby Collection of American Paintings; and The Samuel C. Davis Collection of Chinese Ceramics.

What is true of art museums is equally true of natural history museums, historical museums and libraries; while in still other ways collectors give impetus to the community effort, as witnessed by the organizing in 1922 of the Detroit Historical Society (its museum opened six years later) to carry forward the work of Clarence M. Burton in collecting original printed records of pioneer life in Michigan and the Northwest.

Multiply the St. Louis entry many thousandfold, and it will readily be seen that, even without such major individual contributions as the *National Gallery* in Washington, D. C., the *Morgan Library* in New York City, the *Folger Memorial* and the *Huntington Library* across the continent from each other, the American community owes more of a debt to its native collectors than could ever be calculated in any material medium.

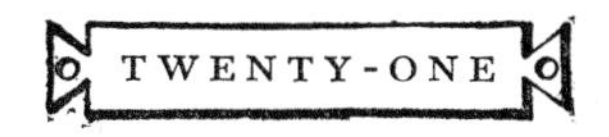

THE THRESHOLD OF TOMORROW

"The finest of all, Credula, is reserved to the future."

DEMPTER

THE CONTEMPORARY who seeks to anticipate collecting trends must bear in mind consequences of two world wars.

It is a truism that always in the past the lost-and-found columns of collectordom have been largely compounded of war casualties. Because certain items possess definite commercial worth, and because under the red light of battle many collectibles are viewed as trophies, they become particularly vulnerable in wartime, when property rights are brushed aside by the invader. During the course of hostilities, soldiers and even civilians may revert to the infant morality of "finders, keepers." Some hold their loot and pass it on to their children in symbol of adventurous days. Some sell to buzzard dealers or in turn become victims of other thieves. Others, like the forgetful crow, soon lose their pickings. It seldom turns out that the original owner ever sees his treasures again, and in any case transactions involving stolen articles are likely to be, for some time thereafter, either careless or clandestine. Long and carefully kept catalogue records are broken in consequence, and then, for those items not destroyed in the process, a rudderless voyage is begun.

Gaze for a moment at the China of 1860 when French and British troops, marching into Pekin to compel an overdue ratification of a treaty, halted at the outskirts of the city beside the old Summer Palace. "To depict all the splendors of this palace," wrote an eyewitness, the Count d'Hérisson, "I should need to dissolve specimens of all known precious stones in liquid gold for ink, and to dip into it a diamond pen tipped with the fantasies of an Oriental poet." Actually, gathered there were centuries of treasure, not only in art and jewels of the East but also in countless gifts of Western merchants who, ever since the days of the Portuguese navigators, had been calling intermittently at the Dragon Court. Small wonder that the "visiting" troops rushed in like lawless urchins attacking an overloaded Christmas tree. Some among them recognized the opportunity that was theirs, and they crammed their pockets or makeshift bags with fine porcelains and jeweled boxes, gem-bestudded cloth of gold and other fine and valuable fabrics from the Near East, brought long before in caravans. They stuffed in golden plates, carved ivories and jade, and fine examples of the clock and watch-makers' art—gifts to the Emperor from earlier Western visitors.

The commanding French general made off with a magnificent string of black pearls which later he presented to the Empress Eugénie, receiving for his thoughtfulness a coveted title. Many of those objects taken by the knowing looters are still with us. Some have found their way back to China, only to be swept off by the invading Japanese. One or two may be in your local museum, waiting for the next turn of the wheel. Many, like the enormous diamond which vanished from the top of a great golden pagoda under the eyes of two sentries posted there to guard it, have disappeared into the unknown. But the miserable fate that overtook thousands of other items is notorious. Neither beauty nor historic sentiment could penetrate the bird-brain exuberance of the foreign soldiery during two days of orgiastic pillaging. To light their pipes, to start their cooking fires, the troops used priceless manuscripts and books of which no other copies existed in the world. They masqueraded by firelight in magnificent garments of silk and brocade from the wardrobe of the Empress and her mandarins, then humorously trampled the precious stuff in the mud. Their camp re-echoed to a hellish noise as they played, all at once, the thousands of musical clocks and mechanical toys, those most popular gifts from Western favor-seekers, which had made the Pekin Summer Palace a kind of Oriental Pinocchio's house. In the bitter end, overburdened with loot, the departing hoodlums dropped under the wheels of their wagons countless objects of great value, including many masterpieces of Oriental arts and crafts whose lives and travels were thus brought to an end.

Brutish as the stupidity of this incident was, it does not stand alone except, perhaps, in the number and value of objects involved. Here is another little tale, far from the splendor of the East, close to the plain pine of Puritan America, a tale which concerns the war-propelled wanderings of a homely book so highly valued that men could not rest until it was found again. When the British occupied Boston at the beginning of the American Revolution they converted the Old South Church into a cavalry riding school. Before leaving for New York the soldiers had discovered, stored in the church tower, the collection of the famous bibliophile, the Reverend Thomas Prince, and they took along with them as souvenirs many books and papers, including original documents, invaluable records of Colonial history. Most unfortunate of all was the disappearance of Pilgrim Father William Bradford's unpublished manuscript, *History of Plimoth Plantation.* In this had been told, as in no other work, the story of Plymouth Colony up to 1646, recorded by an eyewitness; and many a good scholar would later have bartered his bride for an inkling of its whereabouts.

Twenty years after the Revolution a fragment of Governor Bradford's letter-book was turned up in a grocer's shop in Halifax, and since it was of the original Prince Collection, new promise quickened the search. The promise fell short of fulfillment, however, and hope finally flickered. Yet half a century later an American historian, leafing through a new history of the Protestant Episcopal Church in America, stumbled upon an exciting clue. Here, he felt certain, were passages quoted from Bradford's lost work; passages taken, apparently, from an unnamed manuscript belonging to the Diocese Library in London, England. The surmise proved correct. By what devious paths had the manuscript come into the library of the Bishop of London? Through whose hands had it passed since its theft by an unknown soldier? No matter. Forty-two years after its rediscovery, a gift from the London Bishopric to the State of Massachusetts, it was sailing home.

During the early stages of the Spanish Civil War there took place what might be called a national drafting of valuable cultural objects, accomplished through a house-to-house census, for the purpose of guarding them as fully as possible against destruction. This seems to have been the first total effort of its kind ever made by any government, although partial steps, affecting museums chiefly, had been taken elsewhere before.

Although it was a wise precaution which saved many treasures from disaster, there were besides other results totally unexpected. Formed by the Loyalists for "the requisition and protection of the artistic patrimony" of Spain, the committee or *Junta* set up for this purpose discovered or uncovered in the course of its work three Greco paintings, eight manuscript volumes of religious plays by Calderon de la Barca, and, most illuminating for those interested in collectors and their mysterious ways, the fourteenth-century *Codex* of Gonzalo Berceo which had been stolen a number of years before from the National Library. At the time of its disappearance it was thought that the valuable manuscript had been smuggled into France. Now, however, the thief caught red-handed with the loot in his house proved to be a wealthy and supposedly impeccable Spanish citizen, one of the best known dilettantes of Madrid!

Incidents born of war are more significant for collecting than, at first glance, they might appear. In a country where certain items formerly were plentiful, they may suddenly become scarce and hence more desirable through the obvious uses of plunder, protective removal or enforced sale. Elsewhere, war conditions inject new blood into collectordom, as individuals who never collected before plunge into the tide of a new pursuit; and while this is advantageous as insurance for the salvage of items, on the debit side war is far too kind to the faker and forger who trade upon the mysterious disappearances of renowned or valuable pieces.

The shifting fortunes of war cause a tidal wave that reaches even distant lands, bringing new fashions in collecting that sometimes remain for generations; while among the nations—and this, too, is important—new leaders emerge, culturally enriched by fresh deposits of foreign treasure. Indeed, in seeking causes for the growth and the shifting of global collecting centers, it is reasonable to assume that war and commerce are the two factors chiefly responsible. Looking solely to our own century, it will be remembered how the commercial hand made possible, in the book-collecting world, the swing of balance from England to America through the purchases of Morgan, Huntington, Folger and others, while the gyrations caused by World War I bid fair to give us the balance in many other fields as well.

Our time witnesses a period in which entire populations have been uprooted, impoverished, exiled by the most bestial of military-political struggles. Practically every factor which contributes to the breakdown of established order, in the collector's world as elsewhere, has been churning convulsively to tally the greatest mass turnover of possessions known to any single generation; and while the story will continue to unfold for decades, the wanderings of collected items recorded even now give some idea of the storm's impact.

In 1936, the heart of Spain's cultural heritage embarked upon an ordeal during which many Spaniards were, ironically enough, to get their first glimpse of a Greco, a Velasquez, a Goya, or one of the marvelous tapestries from the royal collection. The Prado had been considered a sure haven; but when, one November night, it was bombed, everything it contained was moved only a short distance away to vaults somewhat less vulnerable in the Bank of Spain. And then began the hard work of evacuation.

As this progressed, Valencia became the new art center of the nation: in this provisional capital exhibitions were staged designed to inculcate in the hearts of the people an appreciation for beauties that, it was said, would soon belong to them forever. Workmen and soldiers were to learn for what reasons old books, say, are more to be valued than a stuffed bear. . . . But a year later Valencia, too, had to be abandoned, and once more Spanish art took to the roads. It went to Catalonia, and after temporary storage in private houses was placed in the castle at Perelada. By now the outside world was aroused. Rumor, ever prosperous in wartime, was exaggerating the number of losses suffered in each new bombardment, in each imperfect rescue. An international committee was formed—to its credit, a successful one—for the salvage of the treasures, and it was agreed to use the palace of the League of Nations in Geneva until the danger should have passed.

Yet before the complicated project could be effected, still another catastrophe—the firing of the castle at Perelada—threatened to destroy at once all that was gathered there. Again the greatest masterpieces were saved, but many of them, waiting shipment, were hurried into a talc mine. Small wonder that some of the paintings were later found to be damaged and flaking. To say that it was a heavy task can give little notion of the weight of responsibility borne by the men who were trying to save something deeper than crated tokens; but at last the convoy got under way.

Packed into the long slow chain of lorries were some thirteen hundred pictures, many of the world's finest tapestries, choice medieval armor, manuscripts, books, objects of art and historic relics. The roads were teeming with desperate human beings in flight, roads constantly exposed to bombing and machine-gunning from the air. Despite all this the French border was reached in time. The journey was now taken up by rail in sealed and guarded cars; and though the war itself was to go on for many months, this accomplishment brought some solace to Europe and the Americas where it was known that, for a time at least, the Bible of St. Louis, the great Grecos from the church of Illescas, the fabulous tapestries of the National Palace (more than fifteen hundred of these), the masterpieces of the Prado, were to live.

In the summer of 1939 a selection of the Spanish treasures—many of which had come, centuries before, from the far-flung reaches of Empire, from Antwerp and Brussels, from Milan, Naples and Sicily, from Vienna and Augsburg—graced for a few months the walls of the Municipal Museum in Geneva in a gesture of recompense to the French committeemen who had dipped into their own pockets to pay for the rescue. And then everything was returned to Spain. The completeness of the story (to the satisfaction of Western man, whose interest in this considerable monument of his civilization is easy to understand) does not find a counterpart in the abortive flight of the treasures of Holland and Belgium before the Nazi machine at the outset of World War II, while the story of French belongings during the same tragic period is yet another tale reserved for the future.

Indeed, the successful return trip from wartime journeys is notable in few instances. By a curious turn of fate one occurred when certain valuable manuscripts taken from the Vatican by Napoleon were returned by his conquerors, not to the Papal Library but to the University of Heidelberg from which, nearly two hundred years before, they had been seized by Maximilian of Bavaria and presented by this prince to Pope Gregory. When, in 1815, the Louvre was forced to disgorge after the Napoleonic orgy of looting, more than five thousand items were returned to their owners. A hundred years later the makers of the Treaty of Versailles confirmed the principle that historical material belongs wherever possible to the land of its birth and saw to it that Austria restored to Italy many objects taken or "borrowed" during the nineteeth century.

The skein of our day, however, which Hitler has snarled, will be a long time unraveling. Most incidents will be harder to solve than one case of Polish loot in which the ritual vessels, episcopal regalia, pictures and statues snatched by the Nazis from Cracow and the great cathedral at

Warsaw were shipped to Spain in the autumn of 1940 as a palpable bribe. The Spanish Catholics who received this "gift" served immediate notice that they would consider themselves only temporary trustees. Far less likely to find their way home are the countless unrenowned items stripped from conquered Holland, Belgium and France by the favorite Hitlerian method of gradual confiscation effected through large-scale "buying" with marked-down marks.

The collector in the ridden country is a man twice broken, and items scattered in this fashion will be extremely difficult if not impossible to trace. Yet it is a doubly safe prediction that after a century has passed many of the prominent lost will be found again. And what of items and collections surreptitiously carried out of war-torn nations to ensure bread and butter for their owners? Thousands of items were brought out of Europe and China in the nineteen-thirties before hostilities began in the easily predictable Global War, and the race grew painful as the nets closed. From all this it is not difficult to foresee that in the postwar years the collectors' market will be flooded with great and small refugee pieces, many genuine, many fraudulent.

For the past fifty years the building of the American cultural heap has been part of the unconscious role of the private collector. During World War II this country became a haven for refugee collections, and many of these will remain through purchase. Those from Europe in large measure merely augment a type of riches we already possessed; but from China the war has brought us treasures we might never otherwise have seen or owned. Bronzes, jades and other relics of profound beauty and antiquity, as well as Oriental libraries that had been the sacred possessions of single families for centuries, have poured by the thousands into our homes, our universities and our public institutions, so that it is said a scholar of Chinese history and philosophy will henceforth go to Washington rather than to Peiping, as even now a Shakespearean scholar might go to our Folger Memorial even in preference to the British Museum.

Although certain key collections (such as the three thousand rarities officially entrusted to us for safekeeping by the Peiping National Library) are slated for return after the danger has passed, they will remain with us for reference purposes. By the invention of microfilm the international exchange of film copies and their multiple deposit in world centers is now possible if not yet carried out, so that the catastrophes of attempted cultural extermination or natural disaster may never again wreak total havoc.

If the past is any criterion of the future, we can be sure that many things we now hold valuable will be scorned by our descendants, while in certain of today's commonplaces, now unperceived, there rests a hidden heart of gold which may be esthetic or historic or simply worth unexpected dollars.

When Japanese printmakers began to depict the *Ukiyo* or "Floating World" of Japanese cities, their gaily colored portrayals of everyday life were to conservative Japanese art lovers much as calendar art is to us. The prints of Utamaro, Hokusai and Hiroshige were hawked through the streets for a few "cash" until, in the latter half of the nineteenth century, Western collectors stumbled upon them and found them good. The Japanese collector could not understand the Westerner's sudden craze for these cheap prints which spoke only of the most familiar aspects of life rather than of traditional subjects of lofty significance. And yet to the newcomer a world that for two hundred years had been carefully guarded from Occidental view was revealed for the first time in the despised *ukiyoe*.

Seen through the lens of novelty the charm of the prints was immediately apparent, and because that charm was real and not a fortuitous nubbin of novelty alone, what might have been merely a fad has withstood the rubbing and scraping of a century; and now, of course, the Japanese amateur, no longer contemptuous of these colored woodcuts, has learned to treasure them.

Referring to the arms, costumes and utensils from abroad which in his day were popular collectors' items, Dr. Johnson had this to say:

WHEN THE PEOPLE'S ART GATHERS PRESTIGE. *Good examples of Japanese color prints, which sold originally for a fraction of a cent apiece, now create brisk competition.—Considered American folk art, the 7,500 subjects published by Currier and Ives during nearly seventy-five years have become important collectors' items. An originator of the vogue is Harry T. Peters, whose strong appetite for prints of various kinds has, according to his estimate, garnered some 40,000. In 1923 he purchased the print shown opposite for $10. In 1928, in the James Sale, a second print of this subject, despite its lack of historical or esthetic qualities, reached $3,000, highest price yet paid for a Currier and Ives at public auction. Rarity is the answer.*

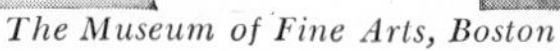
The Museum of Fine Arts, Boston

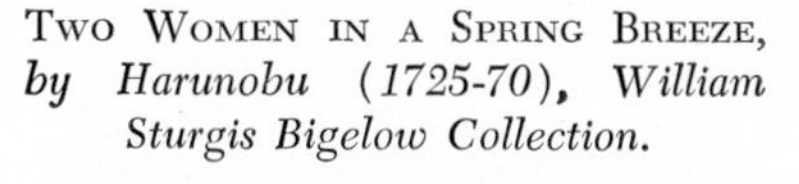
TWO WOMEN IN A SPRING BREEZE, *by Harunobu (1725-70), William Sturgis Bigelow Collection.*

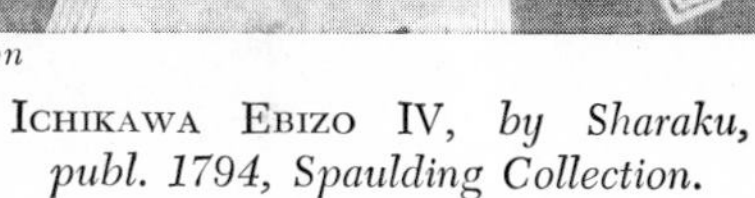
ICHIKAWA EBIZO IV, *by Sharaku, publ. 1794, Spaulding Collection.*

THE LIFE OF A HUNTER—A TIGHT FIX, *Currier & Ives lithograph, 1861* (*see facing page*).

Harry T. Peters Collection, New York

". . . nor can it be always safely determined which should be rejected or retained; for they may sometimes unexpectedly contribute to the illustration of history, and to the knowledge of the natural commodities of the country, or of the genius and customs of its inhabitants."

Similar reservations should be applied to all contemporary judgments. Although the collector's wide haul and his study of commonplace things is now and then the object of derision, it is rather the deriders who are misguided, for they forget that the values and standards of any age must submit to severe alterations in perspective of the future. Joseph Green Cogswell, first librarian of the Astor Library in New York City, gives the right touch in a letter written in 1854:

"The readers," he declared, ". . . read excellent books, except the young fry, who employ all the hours they are out of school reading the trashy, as Scott, Cooper, Dickens . . ."

Or there is English furniture, with its three main periods of oak, walnut and mahogany. The products of the mahogany age, which comprised the works of those master designers, Chippendale, Hepplewhite and Sheraton, are now, a century and a half later, the most widely prized. Yet there was a time when these too were "modern" and by connoisseurs considered crass in comparison to the sturdy oak of an earlier day. William Cobbett, on October 25, 1825, could write:

"I went to a sale at a farm . . . held by a man . . . in whose family the lease had been, I hear, a great number of years . . . Everything about this farm-house was formerly the scene of plain manners and plentiful living. Oak clothes-chests, oak bedsteads, oak chests of drawers, and oak tables to eat on, long, strong, and well supplied with joint stools. Some of these things were many hundreds of years old. But all appeared to be in a state of decay and nearly of disuse . . . and, which was worst of all, there was a parlour. Aye, and a carpet and bell-pull, too! . . . and there was the mahogany table, and the fine chairs, and the fine glass, and all as bare-faced upstart as any stock-jobber in the kingdom can boast of . . ."

There are contemporary collectors who similarly scorn all furniture this side of the Victorian; yet even Grand Rapids furniture some day may achieve glorification (though there are few who deem this worth sitting up for), while it is a certainty already in process that many pieces of our functional steel and chrome-plated furniture will be in museums, a handsome red rope forbidding the tourists, eager, as tourists will be, to try their buttocks to the master chairs.

Within our lifetime Cinderella changes have taken place in numerous instances, and even as we have long collected (and paid high prices for) the earthy objects of early American days—cobblers' stools, pickle jars, mustache cups, bootjacks, and many other things—so a smaller number have already begun to collect the first typewriters, automobiles, phonographs, radio sets and other products of the machine age.

Perhaps it is because objects fall into disuse faster in our day than ever before that the possibilities for collectors are endless. A type or two of old-fashioned gas ranges, certainly never considered objects of especial interest by those who used them, may some day be as highly valued as the tile stoves retrieved from faded Dutch and German kitchens. What would you think, for example, of a steam radiator as a favored item of your collection? You may smile a bit wryly, but some of those heating irons have a decided dignity and decorative value. No longer are the tall organ-like ones made, and after a pause for the contempt of familiarity to vanish, when air conditioning has become universal it would not be surprising to discover a radiator in a garden corner being used as a background for flowers. They may even call it an example of organic sculpture. At any rate, you may be sure that radiators will be finding their way about long after the thumping and leaking, the wheezing and whistling have been forgotten.

Of iron also are the hitching posts, once the commonest of conveniences but collected now. Granted, it might be more difficult to pick up today's traffic lights or fire hydrants, but assuredly in this too more than one collector will some day succeed. Iron footscrapers, those adornments of yesterday's doorstep, are today included in collectors' cabinets. Is there reason to doubt that tomorrow's cabinets will contain the grace-

---

AMERICANA—YESTERDAY AND TOMORROW. *Of household objects ordinary to us, what will be collected tomorrow? The coffee mill is without "quality" or respectable age, yet already museums and collectors reach for it. The Franklin stove is comparatively handsome, but potbellied stoves also are prized. In their day of popular use such items were regarded as we regard radiators and kitchen utensils; yet there is good reason to assume that, with the age of synthetics advancing, aluminum percolators and plain iron piping will become as obsolete as the old stone jug. Certainly this age of science will be responsible for outmoding materials and utilitarian objects with unparalleled speed.*

Old "stone" jug.

Wiggins Old Tavern, Northampton, Mass.

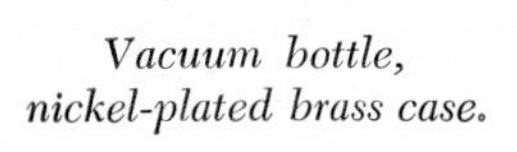

*Vacuum bottle,
nickel-plated brass case.*

Coffee grinder, c. 1865

New-York Historical Society

Aluminum percolator.

From the Rigby Kitchen.

*Brass-trimmed cast-iron
Franklin stove, c. 1800.*

*Verona radiator, once used
in Morgan and Gould houses.*

Courtesy American Radiator Corporation

fully curved chrome faucets now presiding over kitchen sinks? If penny banks are prized items, why may not letter-scales or stapling machines be so in the future? If medicine bottles and wine kegs of bygone centuries are cherished by the modern collector, why may not corresponding objects of our own day be similarly valued by our children's children?

Handsome and large as life, standing in front of a feed and harness store in New Milford, Connecticut, there is the wooden figure of a white horse. That old-time carved display was no more intended as a work of art than were the Cigar Store Indians or the thousands of manikins which today inhabit store windows. Yet for some the sight of that white horse is a heart-warming experience, and it requires little imagination to see it as museum material, since its innate charm already offers the symbol of a vanishing age. Not so very long ago there were almost as many Cigar Store Indians in the United States as live ones, and while both species have dwindled, the wooden braves who took up their posts on the sidewalks of our cities and towns glumly holding in one hand a bunch of cigars and in the other a tomahawk have now found staunch champions in collectors and museum curators. Some indeed wear brave price tags of fifteen hundred, two thousand dollars, or more.

If time, rolling on, swiftly changes man and his ways, it leaves many of the objects man has created suspended in a time-space where human beings no longer dwell. Once these objects were part of a workaday world. Today, because they live on they have become the monoliths, the heroic symbols of a bygone day. In the long pull it is even possible that the commonplace object may outstrip the many honored items of the day in actual value, chiefly because of the factor of rarity. No informed individual would toss out a painting by contemporary Picasso, say, no matter how poor the example. On the other hand, relatively few persons make any effort to save things akin to the daily newspaper or, during our wars, bulletins and pamphlets prodigally sown by governments and other agencies. It is not suggested that every man forthwith turn his home into a warehouse, but the possibility remains that a newspaper containing the first offering of some tomorrow's Milton *may* eventually command a larger sum than the Picasso, while a surviving series of those come-and-gone pamphlets which supplies an important missing link in the chain of history's recording can also achieve considerable value.

In Little Chelsea, England, there once lived a hermitlike bibliophile who responded to the exquisite name of Narcissus Luttrell (1657–1732).

Narcissus was a specialist who collected the fugitive political tracts forever being peddled through the streets in his day. As a collector he exercised no critical discretion but bought up everything in his field he could find, marking each piece meticulously with price and date of purchase, and binding masterpieces indiscriminately with trash. A century after his death most of Luttrell's gatherings were in the hands of two other collectors and one of these was Richard Heber, whose friend, Sir Walter Scott, found the tracts of inestimable value in editing the works of Dryden. In the Luttrell Collection he discovered not only the earliest editions of some of the best English poetry (much of it scorned or ignored at publication) but also the only editions of other works never preservable as pure literature but casting an important light on the life of their times. Today, the woman from Topeka, Kansas, who collects magazine illustrations in which the work of more than seven hundred artists is represented may similarly be preserving some unnoticed "firsts," and regardless of this possibility she is, at the very least, adding to a graphic record many ephemera of contemporary life useful to later historians.

Far more clearly than his predecessors, the modern collector realizes that today's trivia may possess extraordinary interest if gathered together into well-organized collections and preserved for future study; and in this fact there should lie encouragement for the collector who strives to meet the goal of significance on a slim budget.

A full collection of family photographs if properly dated and documented will more vividly than textbooks fix habits and customs long after the family is forgotten. No better example of this could be found than the call issued early in 1943 by the curator of Cornell University's Collection of Regional History:

"Take a look at the old papers and yellowed letters in the attic or packed away in the old family trunk, and if you no longer want them send them to us."

Why? To help make better history books, the appeal explained. In this manner the collector of stamp slogans may know that he is providing future students and writers with valuable touches of local color; while the collector of playbills and theater programs preserves for the interested perusal of future scholars not only the theatrical record of his day but also all the sidelights on *mores* which the critical commentary, the advertisements and the program jokes provide.

Already falling within the list of historical curiosities are the pioneer examples of typewriters, and they will surely be added to collections of brushes, styluses and quills as an essential part of any exhibit designed in the future to show the evolution of the written word. Similarly, looking toward the day when the trolley car shall be as extinct as are the horsecar and the stagecoach, the Rochester Museum, in 1941, salted one away. There is, however, another type of contemporary commonplace of almost equal potential significance and even more widespread popularity.

Where were you on the night of December 5, 1938? If you do not remember you were probably not one of the serious collectors among the swarms of souvenir-hunters who rallied to the last run on the celebrated New York City Sixth Avenue Elevated Railway. In that festive mob, there were many serious collectors, and they sought out the potbellied stoves which were for so many winters the warm hearts of the waiting rooms. They grabbed up the thirty-three lion heads that had decorated some of the stations, the scales which had been used to weigh coins in the days when gold money was plentiful (only three were discovered), and the old-fashioned ticket choppers in use before the modern turnstile and also relatively rare, while of course many eager hands sought the hundreds of signs and early editions of the "Interborough System" maps.

The first washing machine holds a place of honor in that section of Henry Ford's Dearborn Museum which is given over to "household arts"—a prime example of the new piece creeping into the rear ranks of the museum procession in which it one day will be a venerable leader. As a further indication of the extent to which the modern has become impressed by the drama of his generation's role in history we turn to our politicians, who have made with characteristic American impulsiveness numerous gestures of generosity toward future taxpayers by selecting samples of our culture which they consider typical and important. These mementoes they encase in cornerstones or "time capsules" (a characteristic phrase, glibly and disarmingly coined for such occasions) which are intended to be dug up centuries hence to the amazed delight of our descendants.

In 1939 one was made expressly for the year 6939, and here is what the glad future will find: a seven-foot torpedo-shaped copper alloy tube containing ten million words on one thousand feet of microfilm, one thousand pictures, and one hundred items intended to represent a comprehensive section of life in our time and ranging in significance from a woman's hat and a man's pipe to a sheet of swing music, a symphony by Sibelius, and a copy of a Picasso painting. Included also are a rag-paper copy of the Bible, samples of United States money, a deck of cards, a golf ball, samples of materials such as glass-wool and artificial leather, and, written on permanent paper in nonfading ink, special messages by Albert Einstein, Thomas Mann, and Dr. Robert A. Millikan. Truly, if all these items remain as permanent as was hoped, things will be made easy for historians five thousand years hence; yet one cannot but wonder whether, if such enthusiastic foresight should become universal, the community will not eventually embalm itself as a total exhibit for the omnipotent future.

The treasure-house period in Western collecting was predicated upon individual power of birthright, military and political, and, in more recent centuries, largely upon the power of money. As an adjunct to the process of collecting and to its pleasures the effect of money is at once obvious, and it is equally obvious that the obverse side, poverty or the bare subsistence level, has never been conducive to this pastime. In approaching true collecting, some tranquillity of mind is essential, some decent leisure removed from abjectness and warmed at least partially by an atmosphere friendly to enterprise and initiative. The poverty-stricken modern, like early man, has been chiefly engrossed in solving the threadbare physical problems of existence. Perhaps it is supposed by some that the children of poverty would be the very ones most likely to keep eye and hand open for the gathering up of stray objects, and in part that supposition is true enough, but eye and hand must obey the calls of hunger before turning to the demands of curiosity or esthetic appreciation.

This important aspect of the pattern of our age appears now to be altering, a fact which will materially affect the future of collecting. For some years it has been apparent that our entire social-economic competitive system, in which money has been the dominating power, is shifting; and just as the development of agriculture once opened a new age to the roaming tribes of a prehistoric era, so this change in the basis of an entire social system can, if it progresses, permit the development of a more mature society in which new and enlightened values may come

Atget Photo, from the collection of Berenice Abbott

POVERTY AND COLLECTING *are usually uncongenial, but the Parisian* chiffonier's *array of toy animals and dolls testifies for the spirit. Atget, documentary photographer whose prints today are rarities, recorded this and hundreds of Paris landmarks now departed.*

to the fore. Already in the making, these changes are on view in their historical frame. Wanted or not, good or evil, in one form or another the planned society is making its appearance around the world. It tends to provide such things as unemployment insurance and old-age pensions or their equivalent in enforced savings. It tends through high taxes to whittle down, where they still exist, the great fortunes and to make it more difficult to amass new ones. And as the inventiveness of the modern mind makes possible cheap mass production in more and more fields, it seems quite likely that, for the first time in the history of any complex civilization, all the material things that might be essential to a reasonable living standard can be regularly and inexpensively assured to the vast majority of people. So far as collecting is concerned, this means that more people than ever before will be free, mentally and physically, to pursue their natural inclinations along nonutilitarian lines.

In collecting or out, however, the change does not mean that man will ever be completely divorced from competition. Competition, because it is a factor deeply situated and a vital human asset, will continue to live on in one form or another. On the other hand, with an increasing emphasis on group living and thinking, and with relative physical and emotional security available to most people, the dominance of the money base in competition might possibly tend to lose its meaning and to recede toward extinction. In collecting the competitive stress will lie more and more in the direction of scholarly, scientific and social achievement, while pure amateurism and simple hobby-riding will move toward flood tide.

In the demolition of the treasure-house pattern the iron that has been splitting it apart in the United States and England is forged of higher and higher taxes, and of these the inheritance tax has been the most deadly. There have been other factors, of course, such as the economic torpedoing of 1929, but taxes have worked the true destruction. Just how effective the process has been is illustrated in the following passage from P. A. B. Widener, 2nd's *Without Drums*. Inheritor of one of the heavily starched princely collections which were mured within the exclusion of private mansions, Mr. Widener refers to the fact that the nation has at last received as a gift the art collection created by members of his family over several generations:

"The days of America's privately owned treasure houses are over. They are gone with the wind as inevitably as the great Southern plantations of before the Civil War . . . Such a gift is more than a mere disposition of beloved treasures. It signifies the end of private art collections in the grand style . . . Few can any longer afford to buy a half-million-dollar Rembrandt or Van Dyck merely for their own personal pleasure, far less a gallery of them. Today there is a general and salutary leveling of extravagance to safeguard this great heritage of ours, America."

The public, however, does not always receive as gifts the large collections now being broken down; very often the process has moved too swiftly, catching unprepared even those individuals who had intended eventually to bequeath their collections to the community. During the depression of 1929 and the years following, many huge fortunes that had seemed as solid as the Rock of Ages were dangerously cracked. Income and corporation taxes were being levied at increasingly high rates, but the inheritance tax was a special sword at the throat of most men of wealth. Even among the smaller estates it has often happened over the last few years that heirs have been unable to afford the high inheritance tax against evaluations on art, and the big collections were anathema; sell them, give them away if you could, but be not caught dead with them or your estate would be a plucked crow.

Alas, then, for purity of purpose. Behind the public-spirited offers to communities over the country during these times, many a man has secretly quaked in his shoes fearing that his "magnanimous gesture" would not be accepted by city or state. Nor has it always been clear sailing to give treasures away. Although many such offers have been accepted gratefully enough, others have been turned down, either because the collections offered did not meet the higher standards of certain museums, or because maintenance is expensive and city and state have had to consider their own shortened revenues.

Until recent years some fields of collecting have been entirely in the *élite* class, a forbidding distance above the reach of the average purse, hence associated solely with museums and millionaires in the public mind. The education and general attitude of the average middle class citizen in America also helped to make his relationship to certain aspects of his cultural heritage unfamiliar and awkward.

The public could collect postage stamps by the pound and even modern first editions. The public could collect buttons and birds' nests. But the public could not afford to touch incunabula, Old Masters or

Chinese porcelains, and being realistic the public rarely made the attempt. In the heyday of high prices and great fortunes, dealers in the more "select" fields of collectors' wares rarely looked beyond the small coterie of their regular customers.

Department stores were among the first to sense a stirring in public interest in art and a few of them toyed with art departments. Popularized museum shows such as the Van Gogh exhibition of 1935–36 scored phenomenal attendances. "Modern art" instead of creeping along began to hurl its influence into household furnishings, into architecture and popular literature. It became "the thing" to be familiar with big-name painters, to converse about them knowingly for a few minutes. The man in the street and his wife were becoming reconciled to the idea that art was not as bad as it had been painted.

The grotesque gargantua of our collecting era, the man of many warehouses and palaces, was William Randolph Hearst. The demolition of his vast accumulations began in the late nineteen-thirties with orthodox auctions in England and America. Conventional auction sales, however, could never dispose of Mr. Hearst's possessions in the remainder of the life-span allotted to him, so more forceful means were improvised. First at Marshall Field's in Chicago in December, 1939, then a few months later in a St. Louis and in a Seattle department store portions of the collection were offered publicly. These ventures attracted large crowds and resulted in a surprising number of sales. They were followed, early in 1941, by a genuine "blockbuster" dropped on the collecting front, when a larger portion of the Hearst collection was installed in two New York department stores at bargain prices ranging from thirty-five cents to hundreds of thousands of dollars.

This project bulged with interesting possibilities. To the public it was part carnival, part shocking, but the entire community knew about it. Had the stores taken on a white elephant? Would the public buy? And if it did, would not ruin grip the antique and art markets? These were some of the questions asked, as conservative heads shook forebodingly. What actually happened was a surprise even to the promoters of an experiment which, despite its Barnumesque features, proved to be something of an epochal innovation.

Prior to the sale itself, one hundred thousand engraved invitations found their way into the homes of society and suburbanites, members of patriotic organizations, foreign ambassadors *and* the department store charge-account customers. The hundred thousand "elect" were invited to three formal nights of preview. Many came out of curiosity to see the Hearst Collection, many to view first-night celebrities. All were staggered by thousands upon thousands of *objets d'art,* each with odd-price tag affixed, arrayed over a hundred thousand square feet of merchandising space that had recently been cleared of boys' clothing and infants' wear. The range of items was fantastic (Mr. Hearst had collected in five hundred and four categories). Tiny Egyptian scarabs and little carved cats "from the tomb of Cleopatra" were scattered about, along with the seventy paneled rooms taken from English, Dutch and French castles. Even the famous Spanish monastery, packed away in The Bronx, was represented by mounted photographs and enticing descriptions, with a titled guide of immaculate foreign accent to polish off potential customers.

Nine months after the emporium opened its doors to culture, Dr. Armand Hammer could announce that buyers of the Hearst and other collections taken over in that period included an estimated thirty thousand persons who had never before collected. Indeed the experiment succeeded on such a scale that its repercussions will permanently mark the collecting world, and it therefore deserves fairly extensive examination. Because of its miscellaneous nature (permitting the use of the familiar "loss-leader" principle in selling), and because of the fame and fabulous reputation of its creator, the Hearst Collection turned out to be the ideal proving ground for popularization. Significantly enough, although the public flocked to plebeian Gimbels where the bulk of the collection was displayed, customers barely trickled to the showroom at the swankier Saks-Fifth-Avenue store where a selected group of paintings had been set up according to more conventional gallery methods. This venture, therefore, was soon discontinued, but the Gimbel galleries burgeoned and flourished like Iowa corn. The psychology behind these contrasting conditions was successfully penetrated through the newspaper advertisements which, with all our admiration, are quoted below.

The depression begun in 1929 also seriously threatened the telegraph millions of Clarence H. Mackay, and just four months after the opening of the Hearst sale Gimbels took over four thousand items from the Mackay Collection. Again the public was tempted by such opportunities as an eighteenth-century sword for exactly one dollar and

A BOY'S POCKETS *often hold his collection. The attraction of bright metal objects rates high and, when available, articles touching the imagination, such as Indian arrowheads, are eagerly included. From pockets of Joseph Andre, 10-year-old collector-swapper of Jackson Heights, N. Y., photographed by his father.*

The goddess of love with price tag attached ($9,875.00). This happened when the Hearst "warehouse" collection and the department store came to terms.

LIFE Magazine

ninety-eight cents or, if they preferred, such tidbits as an Indo-Persian rug from the Lahore Palace for nineteen thousand five hundred dollars. Joining the American troupe at this time, a steady stream of British collections began finding its way to this abattoir of collections, not without occasional submarine losses. Included were items originally owned by such of the exalted-sounding as the Duke of Portland, Lord Robert Cavendish, the Honorable Mrs. Fortescue, the Duke of Devonshire, the Earl of Kinnoull and Leopold de Rothschild. Sales were still vigorous when, six months later, the store put up "five million dollars worth of art" from the collection of Warner S. McCall, elderly St. Louis utilities man, who had already given enough of his collection to the City Art Museum of St. Louis to fill an entire wing, and who was indirectly quoted as saying that the remainder was being turned over for sale to facilitate settlement of his estate after his death.

bargains IN DEL SARTOS AND BROADLOOM bargains IN NATTIERS AND GAS STOVES

October 18, 1942

When full-page notices like this began appearing in the New York newspapers, people of taste shuddered. They shuddered even more at the humiliating vulgarity of Turners offered "from $6.75 to $298.50" (these were five hundred sketchbook water colors and they were sold within a few hours), a del Sarto for $7,980, or four matched fifteenth-century tapestries at $199,894! The point of course was that the very shrewd advertisements were aimed not at the connoisseur who would have come if he wanted to, regardless. They were meant, rather, to break down the traditional hush-hush that had always frightened the plain citizen—and in this they succeeded. Here is a choice example of the first step; there is no squeamishness about attacking the collections of the late Professor Leslie Verne Case, the late William Edward Glyn and others:

"Are the pieces usable? Of course! Send a scarab along with your Christmas card to ward off evil. Have your scarab set in a magnificent gold ring. Use that tiny oil lamp for a paper weight. Wear the amulets on your charm bracelet. Wear that necklace of Egyptian emerald beads with a black mat dress. . . . You may use Gimbel's Easy Payment Plan on purchases of $23 of over."

This campaign was a mammoth of earthiness tearing at the roots of a discreet system to liquidate an empire. Mrs. Klotz of The Bronx, they swear, in answering one of these genial advertisements, wrote in for "a Benvenuto Cellini bowl to go with a blue dining room"; and of course hundreds of people did buy single pieces out of vanity or curiosity, as souvenirs or "to show the neighbors." To offset Mrs. Klotz there was the woman from St. Louis who intended to buy her young son a suit but got off the elevator at the wrong floor and there yielded to her offspring's prolonged entreaty for a three-hundred-and-four-dollar Lincoln autograph. While more than usually expensive, this chance encounter is of the sort which often starts a collecting career.

However, it seems only just to report that all the stuff advertised and found within the galleries of department stores is not necessarily the equivalent of pure gold. Indeed, the potential buyer is quite apt to be faced by an assortment of goats, blatant or otherwise, which, mixed in with items from good collections, would make respectable dealers shudder. For example, in one such store-gallery the authors once noted a paneled room priced at a song, while on near-by walls hung paintings at two hundred and ninety-eight dollars, or higher, suitable for souvenirs to be given away with a package of tea. Even a price tag of $298.00 is no guarantee of money's worth, and nothing but connoisseurship or its equivalent in expert advice can serve to separate the sheep from the goats. It should be held in mind, then, that because of sheer physical dimensions department stores can accommodate more goats than can the smaller establishments.

Actually there was more than sensationalism in the huge advertisements which continued to appear and which, for sheer canniness, were curious masterpieces worth noting. Take this, for example:

"Gimbels is selling acres of art to museums and millionaires—but Gimbels is also selling acres of art to Flatbush, Montclair, Peoria and points west.

"Who *does* buy art? Everybody! You don't have to be the Countess G . . . to cherish an exquisite little Ch'ien-lung jade Kuan-Yin. You don't have to have a family tree going back to William the Conqueror's great-uncle to prize a gadroon-bordered Georgian silver soup tureen. You don't need a Mayflower ancestor to linger over a pine hutch table. You don't even need a fat check book, because we'll extend your payments for your treasure over months if you like, just as we should if you bought a refrigerator. You can live in Flatbush and love Reynolds. You can live in Montclair and worship Ingres. You can live in Peoria and have a passion for Hitchcock chairs. You can pay $50 for your apartment and put your dollars instead into the possession of one perfect, slender Sheraton table. Or you can pay $3 for a blue glaze faïence Egyptian scarab. You can ride the 7th Avenue subway and carry home a pair of dainty ear-rings that belonged to Martha Washington. You can live in Racine or Galesburg or Tucson or Butte or Denver or Sacramento. Where you live and what you do and how much money you have has nothing to do with your love for incunabula, your interest in Byzantine madonnas, your devotion to Corot.

"... We're a plain store for plain people. We don't have any chi-chi, we don't have any frozen-faced footmen. Plain ordinary people want waterless cookers, window ventilators, new hats. We have them. Plain ordinary people love hand-blown early Jersey glass, old wrought iron, portraits by Gainsborough, rooms from the Duke of Hamilton's palace, 17th century Dutch flower tiles. We have them. It's all as simple as that. . . .

". . . Have you always wanted one piece of genuine old Wedgwood, but thought it was forever beyond you? Come find one here—browse around to your heart's content. Have you always wanted an ancestral portrait? We have some—and who's to care (or to know) whether it isn't your grandfather's aunt? Would it thrill you to cherish a bit of brocade that had paid glittering homage to the brilliant beauty of its wearer at Louis XV's court? We have it. Do you want to touch, every day of your life, a silky satinwood table that Hepplewhite made? We have it . . ."

Few who read that advertisement knew just what a Ch'ien-lung Kuan-Yin was, jade or otherwise, but there was a subtle element of flattery in assuming that they did. Equally breezy was the suggestion concerning the ancestral portrait—"who's to care, or to know . . ."—a suggestion in past years very often proffered with exquisite discretion behind two closed doors. Particularly significant were the last three sentences:

"Beautiful precious old things aren't only for museums and art galleries and great hushed private collections. Artists never made them for museums and art galleries. They made them to be worn, to be used, to be looked at, to be appreciated, to be loved."

In the genuine realization of this fact America will at last find the means, individual genius aside, for a creative and appreciative era comparable to that of the Italian renaissance.

How can the new era affect the vast public in small cities and towns, in suburban and rural districts? How have the widening collecting horizons benefited them and what are their future prospects? Mail-order catalogues are old standbys in several collecting fields. In stamps, for example, one Denver firm alone sells seventy million items a year through its catalogues; and the book business by mail is enormous. But mail-order art is a recent development, again a result of the notorious 'thirties.

In 1934 an enterprising young man launched the first mail-order business in prints based upon low prices and big volume. He induced one famous American artist to increase the number of prints taken from a lithographic stone from one hundred to "two hundred and fifty" —on the plea of bringing ART to the average home—and reduced the price of the prints from forty-eight dollars each to five. Then he rounded up a coterie of other well-known painters and lithographers and etchers and went into business. There were protests from established gallery men about "cheap practices," "cutting prices," and so on, but today the first art gallery to be founded on the principle of mass turnover is reputedly the largest in the world. From it more than forty clerks send out three million pieces of literature a year, and orders have come from the Australian bush, the Alaskan forest and the African veldt, as well as from American farms, suburban rectories, and small-town business men.

The advertisements used by this gallery are calculated to remove the last vestige of apprehension from the mind of the newcomer who thinks he might like to take a flyer into modern art but who is not quite sure of his ground. "Your money back on demand within thirty days" is the principle used hitherto by cigarette and toothpaste manufacturers but now followed when a print is ordered by mail; and although some buyers are content with a single print to hang above the living room sofa, many become enamored of their first purchase and, upon re-examining the catalogue, are unable to resist its descriptions and illustrations, decide to buy more—and become collectors.

The same principle has since been followed by another firm in the field of small sculpture. Groups of artists have even banded together, advertising low prices for a "popular" market. And in 1938, just about one hundred years after the establishment of the ill-fated American Art-Union, a group known as the Collectors of American Art was founded in New York City "to encourage the production and distribution of Fine Art in America." Curiously enough it was without any prior knowledge of the old Art-Union's history that the Collectors adopted an almost identical method—the five-dollar membership fee and the annual "distribution by the wheel"—while its parent organization, Contemporary Arts, employs the "budget" or installment plan, thus enabling cafeteria bus boys, stenographers and impecunious old ladies to indulge a collecting desire that would otherwise have been stillborn or starved out of existence.

The trend is everywhere the same—new buyers and new collectors, thousands of them, in "ten easy payments" if necessary. Crass and cheap though it may sometimes seem, here is another step in the extension of opportunity and the eventual spread of appreciation and cultural enjoyment to the fallow millions.

In the era lying ahead the average citizen may be expected to become more familiar with his own and other cultures and to inherit even the collecting mantle of the tycoons. Certain items, because of their rarity or high desirability, will still fall to the more wealthy for a long time to come, but with comparative enlightenment even the rich will veer toward smaller specialized collections as, sooner or later, changing taste marks the indiscriminate massing of possessions as crude and ostentatious.

Increasingly the larger collectors will co-operate with museums and libraries or, with some community project in mind, will build accordingly. The widening community sense is demonstrated in yet another direction through the resurgence of the true "patron" collector, men and women who, like Albert Bender of San Francisco and Gertrude Vanderbilt Whitney, are concerned with the living source of art as well as with its material embodiment, and whose wish it is to assist in making the cultural benefits of fine collections as widely available as possible. In dedicating the Whitney Museum of American Art, since her death inherited by the Metropolitan, Mrs. Whitney said:

"In making this gift to you, the American public, my chief desire is that you should share with me the joy which I have received from these works of art."

A type of community benefaction that may be multiplied by new collectors is well expressed through the contribution of Dr. Albert A. Berg who, in 1940, systematically set about enriching the collection of the New York Public Library. First he presented to that institution an exceptional library of three thousand five hundred books representing over forty years of selection by his bibliophile brother and himself. Six months later he added the twenty-thousand-volume William T. H. Howe Collection, paying two million dollars for it and turning it over immediately. This gift was followed by another, a joint contribution with Owen D. Young (made at Berg's instigation) of Young's internationally famous collection of rare books, manuscripts and other literary treasures.

A generation ago it would not have occurred to a rich businessman such as Thomas J. Watson, instead of amassing an impressive collection of his own, to form several collections of paintings by international contemporaries and to exhibit these at regular intervals in offices and factories or to send them out on museum tours of the entire country. The search for motivation might prove that Mr. Watson's collecting was largely prompted by a sort of advertising or "good will" policy for business purposes. Even so, the forces that induced him to employ this method will affect others; his collecting itself is directly effective, and the influence of his example will also make itself felt. In fact, there are indications that industry will underwrite a large proportion of art "collecting" for an indeterminate period, as this course fits into the personal convictions of executives and into the advertising schedules. Perhaps Watson's method of circulating art is an approach to the day when we shall have lending libraries of art in every community as now we have of books; or we may have government-sponsored loan exhibitions somewhat comparable to the government "stampmobiles" which of late years have been touring the remoter districts for the benefit of rural philatelists.

Just how far government should enter into the affairs of the people in a democracy is a matter for the people themselves to decide and, though it is still a moot question in the United States, in continental democracies government Fine Arts departments have long existed without interfering with free enterprise. Even without this step, however, the role which our government has begun to play in the field of basic collecting is significant.

Begun as a "make work" project, government patronage of the arts in this country soon expanded into a vast collecting endeavor which scooped up not only the results of contemporary creative effort but also many long neglected deposits in every field of the past from folk-music to lacemaking. Small galleries for the display of local arts and crafts were set up in communities whose inhabitants never before had entered a museum. Regional art exhibitions were held, and purchase prizes provided nuclei for permanent community collections, while centralized and traveling exhibitions served for the first time to familiarize one part of the country with the artistic products of the others.

From the beginning of the Work Projects Administration's art program to October, 1941, five hundred and fifty-four exhibitions representing two thousand individual showings were circulated at new community art centers, and in a typical month close to four hundred and seventy-five thousand people attended three hundred and thirteen of these exhibitions. The program even stepped into certain well-established museums and assisted them forward along new roads; as witness its activities in co-operation with the Walker Foundation in Minneapolis. Here an outstanding private collection, begun in the eighteen-seventies by T. B. Walker and housed as a public collection in his own home from 1875 to 1927 (when the Walker Art Galleries were built), became, in 1940, the "Walker Art Center—A Museum in the Modern Manner." Its new program, aided and abetted by government funds, then became the up-to-date one of "presenting art of all ages by educational exhibits."

Through the American Guide Book Series of the WPA, forgotten and dusty archives were combed for significant stories and facts in every state in the Union. Collected, collated and printed, many of these crumbling cells of the body of our national heritage were reconstructed and saved. In the same way a photographic record was made of numerous historic relics and obsolescent landmarks such as covered bridges and windmills which, in a few more years, would probably have disappeared. Through the government-sponsored Index of American Design, by means of nearly twenty-one thousand drawings, permanent records were made of old and new folk-art and of vanished and vanishing crafts from every part of the nation. Unemployed experts and researchers were set to work digging out and recording regional dialects, music, and the sort of local history which, in the normal course of events, is passed on orally and hence precariously.

All this was accompanied by a widespread handcraft movement in newly formed adult education schools, a movement which was bound to arouse collecting interest in many who had never given a thought to old wood-carving, for example, or to handmade pottery, until they had tinkered with such things themselves, working from the old designs. The WPA and its subsidiaries may have passed into history with the opprobrious term "boondoggling," but during its decade of existence this agency aroused in its cultural aspects a widespread consciousness of the part that government can play in making the arts widely available. Because of the magnitude of the effort and the accompanying results, that consciousness will not soon die, and for the future a permanent role now seems clearly indicated for what was at first a mere improvisation. It is obvious that no private agency could possibly organize and complete a task so huge, and in the possibility of such completeness there lies a value to the nation equally obvious.

It is even possible that in the future certain phases of collecting may be placed under a definite though limited national control. Granted that it would be a grotesque imposition for the government to say to all private collectors, "This and that you may not purchase," or "You must arrange your collection according to Section 543, Code 17-A." Good sense forbid! Yet he would be thoughtless indeed who saw ahead no added restrictions upon that unqualified freedom of action which, although it does not actually exist, appears to so many as the be-all and end-all of democracy. The social ethics involved in the unrestricted piling up of money and property by individuals is a subject primarily removed from the domain of this book. Relevant, however, are the effects which unbridled exercise of individual rights may have upon collecting in relation to long-term community rights.

For several hundred years the only constraint upon an individual's collecting activities has been the limit of his ability to gain money and power. Of the treasures, *often unique and irreplaceable,* in any cultural arena he might select, any man has had the right to buy as much as he could afford. What became of those treasures, once they were his, has been considered his own business and his alone.

The Metropolitan Museum of Art

Cleveland Museum of Art

Colorless glass goblet, engraved with arms of Pennsylvania and said to have been presented to Governor Thomas Mifflin, 1791; from the New Bremen, Maryland, factory of John Frederick Amelung. Embroidered panel made and signed by Abigail Parkman, 1758.

The future of privately owned objects depends of necessity upon the uncertain fortunes of the chance owner. Homes containing valuable collections are usually insured, yet they are seldom as secure as state property against fire and theft, while even insurance cannot restore lost heritage. An owner forced to sell can seldom select the purchaser who replaces him or insure an item against falling into incompetent hands. Who is going to care for the items? Is he expert, or even remotely qualified? And there is the danger from whims and eccentricities of individual collectors. Under present conditions, for instance, there is no legal restraint to prevent an owner from destroying, perhaps spitefully, priceless works. Such things have actually occurred. Collectors have even ordered that prized items be buried with them, and at least one owner of a great contemporary collection has vowed that he would destroy it rather than allow it to come into the possession of others. The same man would be called to strict account by the state were he to deface a dollar bill or mutilate a penny; and it might well be argued that the community can hardly afford to take a greater gamble on the survival of irreplaceable symbols of its culture.

It is true that the conditions which have made possible the dredging by individuals of great chunks of the public heritage are rapidly changing; yet there is no ultimate solution merely in reduced incomes, for it would still be possible for certain touchstones of a nation or an entire civilization—relics epitomizing the accomplishments of a town or of half the globe—to be withheld from the public view for generations or forever. There is no simple answer available; and yet an appeal might well be made for the same form in the building of a great national collection as we have seen the private collector, in so far as he is able, apply to his own collection. For reason's sake it would be hard to deny the parent vein of logic: that the entire population should have the greatest and most perfect collection that the combined efforts of the nation might assemble, and that the doors of that collection should never bar scholars, students or the public at large.

It is reasonable to assume that the future will witness a combining of certain key parts of existing collections necessary to make master groups, if for no other reason than that the ultimate in the logic of collecting demands, when conditions permit, that the parts be joined together to make whole each collecting field and then to correlate all the collections. This is nothing less than the ultimate step in cataloguing—a vast job of indexing and cross-indexing, a census of national artifacts.

No less should be expected in an age of science (which demands in all fields as complete a listing of data as possible), and no less should be demanded of education. This would mean a census of cultural objects and data, and here would be something of great value which, if properly presented, might be undertaken as the logical step preceding the establishment of an interwoven national collection of collections. A census is hardly a threat to one-hundred per cent individualism. Aside from our periodical census of people with its accompanying descriptions, the printed cards in the Library of Congress which are available to every library in the country constitute in effect a census of every book printed here; and a similar centralized record service could well be set up in other fields. The two hundred and ninety-five thousand prints in the photographic record of paintings from American and European collections made by Miss Helen Frick is a good start in this direction, even though it is probably incomplete.* Were such censuses to be taken by the government they would, as demonstrated by the recent experience of Spain, be of indisputable service in time of disaster, making possible a national assumption of guardianship over the country's most valuable possessions. The service to education in normal times would be equally indisputable, for the census should make available all existing data in any given field.

In the event that legislation should ever be considered for the foundation of a cultural master collection, questions would fly much quicker than right answers. Who should be the arbiters of what such a collection should contain? Where should it be centered and how distributed? Should carefully selected commissions be appointed to earmark items of unquestioned historical and artistic significance within or after the owner's lifetime? How and by whom would payment be made for the items chosen? Might not the owner, proving to be adequate custodian, be permitted to keep his items if he desired, providing only that he would agree to lend them at certain intervals to national exhibitions?

Although laws providing for the purchase by the state of certain extraordinary items might force a few owners to sell, the existence of the national census would tend to render this extreme measure un-

---

* Said to be "fairly complete" for American collections.

necessary. As an alternative, the owners might be under legal obligation only to meet the specifications for adequate care, and to join with their fellow collectors in a reasonable sharing of their major possessions—an obligation that would generally be deemed an honor, since only objects of considerable importance would be so marked out. In this way the owners of great or chronologically important items could have their cake, and yet the public could occasionally eat of it, while the mass of private collectors would not be affected at all. Legislation affecting cultural touchstones, far from being dictatorial or an invasion of rights, might be considered in accord with the same logic that today provides zoning and building laws for our towns and cities.

To which items should the community have prior rights over the individual? Surely the most noteworthy paintings of the master artists of the Western world should in some way be made accessible to public view, although this would not necessarily entail public ownership. Items which are unique in forming the chain of continuity in the study of any given field come within the range of historical "musts" and should eventually be included in the public property. The importance of completing the chain for scholarship and the unborn centuries is incomparably more important than the desire of any individual. If several million Chicagoans would like to look upon the lamp that betrayed Mrs. O'Leary's cow, surely the most suitable of the city's public museums should possess that lamp (did it actually exist), for it has entered into the lives of the people as legend and their pleasure is in viewing an important symbol of their city's history.

While it may be argued that with the availability of colored reproductions and much descriptive matter it is hardly essential to insist upon wide distribution of original items, this is refuted on the grounds that personal experience, at least for the layman, is far superior to mere hearsay. The child who all through life can remember being held high to glimpse for a moment a great President is the possessor of a far more vivid and inspiring experience than is the beholder of a photograph of the man. There is unquestioned magic when people gaze, with their own eyes, upon the touchstones of our world—the Liberty Bell, a Gutenberg Bible or a Shakespeare First Folio, the Magna Charta, Lincoln's cape, Botticelli's *Venus Rising From the Sea*—and it is not beyond the modern world's ability to enrich with that magic the lives of individuals everywhere.

The collection units once established, whether through actual assembly in certain key spots or even through a correlation of the census listings, arrangements for their systematic distribution could be effectively handled through a central Bureau of Arts and Sciences. In this way the parts and series of the national collection could be rotated throughout the country in district museums during several months of the year; and eventually there could be international exchange tours. In outlying districts a holiday system might be employed, staggered to permit everyone access to the exhibitions. Though admittedly complex, it is not too formidable a task for a central agency to synchronize exhibitions with local educational programs. Modern man is not unresourceful. He has solved intricate traffic problems of transport systems; why should he not be able to do as well with his cultural hoard?

It is true that the world owes an immense and permanent debt to private collectors for the countless items which they have preserved and which have eventually become public property; and it is all the more to be emphasized how much recognition and gratitude is due those who have relinquished to the public trust, within their own lifetimes and without pressure, key masterpieces and other landmarks of man's progress, foregoing in the process that deep personal satisfaction in ownership known fully only to other collectors. A man of that select company continues to collect with the same zeal, but his perception of the broader humanistic values frowns upon an exclusion act pertaining to the stream of public heritage.

It would, of course, be folly to count on this spirit and this perception in all collectors; and yet once established the precedent would soon become accepted practice. As English bidders for years have generally refrained from competing with the British Museum, so the national collection would automatically be given first choice at auctions and sales, and to the local museums would go key historical documents of the community and key association items of favorite native sons. Today Ralph Waldo Emerson's writing chair and the bed Henry Thoreau made for himself are both rightfully public property in Concord, Massachusetts; and it would inflict no injustice and little hardship on collectors were similar items taken over and paid for with permission, or willed to the community upon death. So it would become firmly fixed in the public conscience that the communal heritage should, like the Sequoia Forest, be secured to the people for as long as it may endure.

Not so long ago one could, with good cause, have charged that relinquishing touchstones to the museums would be virtually to embalm them. Museums have long been known for their tomblike negation of the simple enthusiasm and curiosity of the layman; but this truth diminishes with every passing year. Affected violently by economic and social changes, the museums of the nation too have been undergoing considerable alteration, and it is of interest that the nature of the change swings the cycle of their evolution back to the direction of its beginnings—with decided improvements.

In ancient Athens there were a number of "Museums" or institutions of learning, and all of them were dedicated to the Muses and to the cultural pursuits which they symbolized. Although they represented the first use of the word *museum,* its meaning was then more closely equivalent to that of the modern university than it was to our present usage. Plato's Academy was known as the *Museion;* and Theophrastus, in honor of his great teacher, Aristotle, established a *museion* which was actually a school of literature and art. The Alexandrian Museum more closely approximated our definition, since the famous library and other collections were important sections of that institute for the advanced sciences.

The word next settled into the doldrums. Its changes were slow and uncertain. By the sixteenth and seventeenth centuries "museum" was the term used to describe an important private collection of any sort, but not until well along in the latter century (1683) did it come to mean

"a building used for storing and exhibiting objects illustrative of antiquities, natural history, fine and industrial art, etc."

A hundred years later (1760) "museum" was still being used vaguely to denote

"a building or apartment dedicated to the pursuit of learning or the arts; a study; a library."

At the opening of the twentieth century, David Murray, writing of *Museums—Their History and Their Use,* declared,

"A museum, as now understood, is a collection of the monuments of antiquity or of other objects interesting to the scholar and the man of science, arranged and displayed in accordance with scientific method."

But what of the layman? It is a far cry from any of these definitions to that given recently by a leading contemporary museum director, Francis Henry Taylor, who expressed the new concept of the museum as *"the free and living university of the common man."*

Until quite recently museums as we know them were operated for the benefit of small minorities. At the beginning of the nineteenth century only about two hundred persons a year visited the art collections of Berlin. Visitors to Vienna's art collections were long obliged to give the attendants extremely high tips. Up until the 1917 revolution visitors to Russian collections were symbolically supposed to remove their hats, and only those attired in white ties and tails were admitted into the Imperial Hermitage at St. Petersburg.

It must not be assumed that the shift from glorified mausoleum to "free and living university" is as yet complete. The change is not an easy one. Hard-shelled scholars on the one hand and insatiable acquisitors on the other have been running the show for so long that from almost every point of view museum methods must be radically altered before the contents can be fully and successfully utilized. Subdued at the outset by the forbidding character, the cold formality of ordinary museum architecture, baffled by the inaccessibility of the curators, half bulldozed, half annoyed, by the frigid uniformed guards who have been his chief media of public contact, the layman more often than not has been too much awed or, because of superficial education, too uninterested to enter freely these so-called "public" institutions.

Something of this situation is now being realized, and increasingly positive action is being taken by progressive curators. This, however, is only the beginning, and it will require universal cutting away of dry rot, a humanizing, fraternizing, a mingling of everyday life and the eagerness of children introduced where once timid whispers were interred. But slow as it may be, when finally it has crystallized, the new attitude of educators and curators will bring about an incalculably important change in the entire national outlook. Once given suitable encouragement and assistance, the community is certain to emerge from its sulphur-and-molasses approach to the museum, developing instead a built-in-from-youth acceptance and appreciation of civilization's gifts, gifts to stir the mind to greater accomplishments, gifts which properly used and understood cannot fail to fortify and multiply the creative faculties of a talented young country.

Art History Museum, Vienna

Museum of Modern Art, New York

Not as naive as our contemporary "primitives," recently in vogue, Lucas Cranach, the elder, has been popular for four hundred years. His Portrait of Three Young Women *is shown with Juan Gris' abstraction,* The Chessboard (1917). ~ *Collectors often have the opportunity of meeting the challenge of fine originators in the arts and crafts, and of rediscovering that the old and the new are not always incompatible.*

In 1930 new public museums were being established in this country at the rate of one each fortnight, according to the *Handbook of American Museums;* and seventy to eighty per cent were located in communities of less than one hundred thousand inhabitants.

In 1910 there had been not more than six hundred museums in the entire land. In 1939, the most recent year for which figures are available, there were twenty-five hundred, blanketing the various fields of history and science, art and industry. Included in the figure were seventy-two state museums of all kinds, double the number of thirty years earlier; six hundred and forty "historic house" museums as compared to twenty in 1910; and seventy-two "trailside" museums, a new variety born of the automobile age (the first one was recorded in 1921). Even more revealing than the number of such institutions is the figure Coleman gives us when he states that an estimated fifty million persons visited museums in the United States in 1938.

During this period, after thirty years of scoffing, the public fell in love with the modern masters in the field of art, undergoing a sort of cheap cultural jag, superficial but nevertheless indicating a significant mass longing. At the same time, interest in scientific and industrial displays increased. This was accompanied by a schoolroom approach to "realism." The boys and girls, progeny of post-World War disillusionment, quite naturally wanted reasons for everything. Understanding this problem, some teachers began experimenting with the application of art to everyday life—to architecture, to furniture, to clothing and decoration.

The forward looking directors of a few museums were encouraged to experiment in their own bailiwicks which, as some of them had long realized, provided one of the most promising of all fields for visual and experiential education, although it had hardly ever been cultivated from that point of view. Programs were set up in co-operation with the schools, and in some places special museums geared to the interests and absorptive powers of the young were established, while elsewhere a few live museums like the Toledo created special children's departments. Guided tours in the old manner were largely discarded in favor of actual project work, and here and there the youngsters were even given the opportunity and responsibility of holding the reins of curatorship. All this was accompanied by an extensive growth in specially adapted literature, making it possible to utilize the museum experiences in classroom or home work.

The development of the adult education movement has been more gradual because the effort to do something about adults is relatively a new phenomenon. In the schools the so-called "progressive" movement has emphasized the value of concrete and first-hand experience; therefore it is understandable that it should have found ways rich or poor of using the wealth of material in museums. The situation for adulthood, on the other hand, could be epitomized by the conventional attitude that a college degree is the end of the road called education. What a man might thereafter obtain of knowledge and understanding, from books, from museums, from experience, was—and still is largely—incidental; for while the general public worshiped the college degree, it could not understand it as a beginning rather than as an end.

Little guidance, therefore, has been available for the man or woman eager for more light. Today that situation is slowly changing. In this country, libraries have been far ahead of museums in recognizing that laymen as well as scholars, scientists and other trained specialists are amenable to and eager for a continuing extension of knowledge, a broadening of outlook, an enrichment of their appreciative capacities.

The circulating library, the library bulletin, the reader's guide, the information desk, the newspaper and periodical room, the popular exhibits geared to events and interests of the day, are an old story in most of our public libraries. The fact that museums are now beginning to catch up with the libraries is at least partially due to that by now familiar tradition-breaker, the financial depression: with wealthy trustees no longer able to sustain the museums singlehanded, these institutions must depend more and more upon the taxpayer. Recent reports do not disguise the fact that this is one important reason for contriving new ways to arouse public interest and attendance—a realistic motive for discarding the ivory-tower, public-be-damned attitude which has for so long prevailed.

Once again it can be said that the motive counts less than the results; and these can be seen in changing methods of display calculated to make exhibits less a quantitative show than a selective pleasure to mind and eye. They are evident in the use of informative labels which often tell the story of an exhibition around the room. They are discernible in bulletins and catalogues, attractively illustrated, which adhere to the demands of a reasonable scholarship while reaching without formality, even with unaccustomed geniality, toward the larger audience. They can be seen also in the use of more comfortable seating facilities, and in increasing demonstrations of the interplay of the fine arts. So a concert and an exhibition presented in conjunction to feature the art and spirit of a particular period draw the museum closer to the role of a community center.

As the educational role of the museum advances, there is also to be noted a tendency toward the establishment of smaller and more specialized units. In many museums evening hours have been adopted to make the institutions' facilities available to a broader section of the public; and for similar practical and psychological reasons admission charges are being abolished by institutions belonging to the public. Everything considered, the day may come when museums will be almost as attractive to the general public as screen and radio, theater and concert hall; and if John Doe is reluctant to come to the monument, then the wonders of the place will be taken to him. Although interrupted by conditions of war, television has already performed this feat experimentally, and some day it may be expected to deliver museum riches to every living room.

There is one final factor. The increase in popular leisure which appears inevitable for the future will need imperatively more enlightenment and more avocations. While transition into this state of affairs has been interrupted by world chaos, the march sooner or later will be resumed, for it is part of a cycle which can take in its stride a lost generation or two and still march forward without dismay. When that time comes, let us hope, there will be prepared for all the citizenry a sound and comprehensive educational program in the use of leisure. The results would include a new flame of intellectual curiosity and esthetic appreciation. For collecting, this will usher in an expanding era notably of new collectors, higher standards and increasing specialization, and more assuredly than ever before it will be manifest that the collector and his harvest shall never die.

ACKNOWLEDGMENTS

THE AUTHORS wish to express their appreciation to all those who so promptly and courteously responded to requests for photographs, and to those who in other ways have helped in the production of this book.

We are particularly grateful to G. H. Edgell, Director, Museum of Fine Arts, Boston; Miss Dorothy E. Miner, Librarian and Keeper of Manuscripts, and Acting Director of Decorative Arts, Walters Art Gallery, Baltimore, Maryland; James G. McManaway, Assistant Director, Folger Shakespeare Library, Washington, D. C.; A. G. Wenley, Director, Freer Gallery of Art, Washington, D. C.; W. R. Valentiner, Director, Detroit Institute of Arts; Ambrose Lansing, Curator of the Department of Egyptian Art, Metropolitan Museum of Art; Miss Grace M. Mayer, Curator of Prints, Museum of the City of New York; Charles Messer Stow, Antiques Editor of the New York *Sun;* N. H. M. McOstrich, British Information Services, New York; and Mrs. John Lisle, The University Museum, Philadelphia, all of whom supplied valuable information in regard to photographs used or were helpful in the search. Also to Andrew Emerine of Fostoria, Ohio; Mrs. Lillian Smith Albert of Hightstown, N. J.; and Mrs. Austin H. Welch of Still River, Massachusetts, for allowing us to examine many photographs of items from their respective collections.

Our sincere gratitude is extended to Dr. Hu Shih for the translation from Li Ch'ing-chao's charming *Second Preface* to the twelfth-century *Catalogue of Bronze and Stone Inscriptions* by her husband, Chao Ming-ch'eng.

We should like to pay special tribute to the excellent and ever-helpful staffs of the various departments of The New York Public Library, particularly to Miss Romana Javitz, Superintendent of the Picture Collection, and to her staff; and to John Gault and Benjamin Schwartz of the Photographic Service. Also to the staff of the Library of the Metropolitan Museum of Art, and to Miss Alice D. Franklin of that museum's Reference Collection of Photographs.

For reading certain sections of the manuscript, we thank Dr. Marion E. Kenworthy; Mr. Y. Souren; and Mrs. Ruth Thompson Grandin, who, during more than one Vermont summer, as the manuscript grew, endured all with wondrous forbearance and good friendship. And finally, we are appreciative of the very capable editorial help of Miss Tay Hohoff, New York Editor of J. B. Lippincott Company.

Thanks are due to the following publishers and authors for permission to use quotations from the books and articles listed:

American Association of Museums, Washington, D. C. *The Museum in America,* 3 vols., by Laurence Vail Coleman. 1939.

D. Appleton-Century Company, New York. *Japan: A Short Cultural History,* by G. B. Sansom. 1931.

The Burlington Magazine, London. Editorial on J. P. Morgan, unsigned. 1913.

University of Chicago Press, Chicago. *Ancient Records of Egypt,* Vol. II, by James Henry Breasted. 1906. *They Wrote on Clay,* by Edward Chiera. 1938.

The Club of Odd Volumes, Boston. *Thomas Jefferson in 1814—Being an account of a visit to Monticello, Virginia* (Diary of Francis Calley Gray—notes and introduction by Henry S. Rowe and T. Jefferson Coolidge, Jr.). 1924.

Doubleday, Doran and Company, Garden City, L. I. *Antiquamania,* by Kenneth Roberts. 1928.

E. P. Dutton and Company, New York. *Secrets of an Art Dealer,* by James Henry Duveen. 1938.

Walter Prichard Eaton. "Criminal Confessions of a Collector," anonymous article, *Saturday Evening Post,* April 19, 1924.

Faber and Faber, London. *The Pompadour,* by Margaret Trouncer. 1937.

Harper and Brothers, New York. *Caesars in Goosestep,* by William D. Bayles. 1940. *Meditations of an Autograph Collector,* by Adrian H. Joline. 1902.

Hu Shih. "Woman's Place in Chinese History," article, *The Week in China,* Peiping. February 7, 1931.

J. B. Lippincott Company, Philadelphia. *The Stamp Collector's Round Table,* edited by Foster W. Loso. 1937.

Little, Brown and Company, Boston. *Fishers of Books,* by Barton Currie. 1931. *The Late George Apley,* by J. P. Marquand. 1938.

Little, Brown and Company, and The Atlantic Monthly Press, Boston. *The Amenities of Book Collecting,* by A. E. Newton. 1918.

The Macmillan Company, New York and London. *The Life of the Ancient East,* by James Baikie. 1923. *Greek Life and Thought from the Death of Alexander to the Roman Conquest,* by J. P. Mahaffy. 1896.

Robert M. McBride and Company, New York. *Collecting Antiques for the Home,* edited by Henry H. Saylor. 1938.

The Medici Society, London. *A History of Early Chinese Painting,* Vol. II, by Osvald Sirén. 1933.

The Museum Journal, University of Pennsylvania, Philadelphia. "The Excavations at Ur, 1931-32," by C. Leonard Woolley. 1933.

Oxford University Press, New York. *The Civilization of the Renaissance in Italy,* by Jacob Christoph Burckhardt, translated by S. G. C. Middlemore. 1937. *Horace Walpole,* by Austin Dobson. 1927.

Stanley Paul and Company, London. *More About Collecting,* by Sir James Yoxall. 1913.

Princeton University Press, Princeton. *Concerning Beauty,* by Frank Jewett Mather, Jr. 1935.

G. P. Putnam's Sons, New York. *Without Drums,* by P. A. B. Widener, 2nd. 1940.

George Routledge and Sons, Ltd., London. *The Picture of Paris,* by Louis Sebastien Mercier, translated by Wilfrid and Emilie Jackson. 1929.

Charles Scribner's Sons, New York. *Ur of the Chaldees,* by C. Leonard Woolley. 1930.

Simon and Schuster, Inc., New York. *The Story of Civilization: Our Oriental Heritage,* by Will Durant. 1935.

Stackpole Sons, Harrisburg, Pa. *The American Village,* by Edwin V. Mitchell. 1938.

The Viking Press, Inc., New York. *Hearst—Lord of San Simeon,* by Oliver Carlson and Ernest S. Bates. 1936.

BIBLIOGRAPHY

BOOKS

ALLEE, WARDER CLYDE
Animal Life and Social Growth, Williams and Wilkins Co., Baltimore, 1932.

ALLEN, A. H. BURLTON
Pleasure and Instinct, Harcourt, Brace & Co., New York, 1930; K. Paul, Trench, Trubner & Co., Ltd., London, 1930.

ALVERDES, FRIEDRICH
Social Life in the Animal World, Harcourt, Brace & Co., New York, 1927.

AUNGERVILLE, RICHARD (RICHARD DE BURY)
The Philobiblon (1385), ed. and trans., Ernest C. Thomas. Kegan Paul, Trench & Co., London, 1888.

BAIKIE, JAMES
The Life of the Ancient East, A. & C. Black, Ltd., London, 1923; The Macmillan Co., New York, 1923; *The Sea-Kings of Crete,* 3rd ed., A. & C. Black, Ltd., London, 1920.

BEAGLEHOLE, ERNEST
Property: A Study in Social Psychology, G. Allen and Unwin, Ltd., London, 1931; The Macmillan Co., New York, 1932.

BELLOC, HILAIRE
Richelieu, J. B. Lippincott Co., Philadelphia, 1929.

BONNAFFÉ, EDMOND
Les Collectionneurs de l'Ancienne France, Auguste Aubry, Paris, 1873; *Les Collectionneurs de l'Ancienne Rome,* Auguste Aubry, Paris, 1867; *Dictionnaire des Amateurs Français au XVIIe Siècle,* A. Quantin, Paris, 1884; *Recherches sur les Collections des Richelieu,* E. Plon et Cie., Paris, 1883.

BOULE, MARCELLIN, ET PIVETEAU, JEAN
Les Fossiles, Masson et Cie., Paris, 1935.

BREASTED, JAMES HENRY
Ancient Records of Egypt, University of Chicago Press, Chicago, 1906; *The Conquest of Civilization,* Harper & Brothers, New York, 1926; *The Development of Religion and Thought in Ancient Egypt,* Charles Scribner's Sons, New York, 1912; *A History of Egypt,* Charles Scribner's Sons, New York, 1912.

BRILL, A. A.
Psychoanalysis, W. B. Saunders Co., Philadelphia, 2nd ed., 1923.

BROOKS, VAN WYCK
New England: Indian Summer 1865–1915, E. P. Dutton & Co., Inc., New York, 1940.

BROWN, F. MARTIN
America's Yesterday, J. B. Lippincott Co., Philadelphia, 1937.

BUDGE, E. A. WALLIS
The Literature of the Ancient Egyptians, J. M. Dent & Sons, Ltd., London, 1914.

BURCKHARDT, JACOB C.
The Civilization of the Renaissance in Italy, trans. S. G. C. Middlemore, The Phaidon Press, Vienna, 1937; Oxford University Press, New York.

BURTON, WILLIAM
A General History of Porcelain, Cassell & Co., Ltd., London, New York, 1921.

EDITED
Cambridge History of India, Cambridge (England), At the University Press, 1937.

CAPART, JEAN
Thebes, The Dial Press, New York, 1926.

CARLSON, OLIVER, and BATES, ERNEST S.
Hearst—Lord of San Simeon, The Viking Press, New York, 1936.

CARTER, HOWARD, and MACE, A. C.
The Tomb of Tut.Ankh.Amen, Cassell & Co., Ltd., London. Vol. I, 1923; Vol. 2, 1927; Vol. 3, 1933.

CARTWRIGHT, JULIA (JULIA M. C. ADY)
Isabella d'Este, E. P. Dutton & Co., New York, 1926 (reprint).

CASSON, STANLEY
Progress of Archaeology, Whittlesey House, New York (London), 1934.

CHANCELLOR, E. BERESFORD
The XVIIIth Century in London, B. T. Batsford, Ltd., London, 1920; *Life in Regency and Early Victorian Times,* B. T. Batsford, Ltd., London, 1926; *The Pleasure Haunts of London During Four Centuries,* Houghton Mifflin Co., Boston & New York, 1925; Constable & Co., Ltd., London, 1925.

CHARLES-ROUX, F.
Bonaparte: Governor of Egypt, trans. E. W. Dickes, Methuen & Co., Ltd., London, 1937.

CHIERA, EDWARD
They Wrote on Clay, ed. George G. Cameron, University of Chicago Press, Chicago, 1938.

CHILDE, VERE GORDON
New Light on the Most Ancient East, D. Appleton-Century Co., Inc., New York, 1934; K. Paul, Trench, Trubner & Co., Ltd., London, 1934.

CLAY, FELIX
The Origin of the Sense of Beauty, Smith, Elder & Co., London, 1908.

CLEMENT DE RIS, L.
Les Amateurs d'Autrefois, E. Plon et Cie., Paris, 1877.

CLIFFORD, C. R.
The Junk Snupper, The Macmillan Co., New York, 1927.

COLEMAN, LAURENCE VAIL
The Museum in America, 3 vols., The American Association of Museums, Washington, D. C., 1939.

COLLINS, A. FREDERICK
Collecting Stamps for Fun and Profit, D. Appleton-Century Co., New York, 1936.

CONSTABLE, W. G.
Art History and Connoisseurship, Cambridge (England), At the University Press, 1938.

CORTISSOZ, ROYAL
Art and Common Sense, Charles Scribner's Sons, New York, 1913.

COSNAC, GABRIEL-JULES, COMTE DE
Les Richesses du Palais Mazarin, Librairie Renouard, Paris, 1885.

CURRIE, BARTON
Fishers of Books, Little, Brown & Co., Boston, 1931.

DARWIN, CHARLES
The Formation of Vegetable Mould Through the Action of Worms, with Observation on Their Habits, D. Appleton & Co., New York, authorized edition, 1896.

DEXTER, GEORGE B.
The Lure of Amateur Collecting, Little, Brown & Co., Boston, 1923.

EDITED
Dictionary of American Biography, ed. Dumas Malone, under the auspices of The American Council of Learned Societies, Charles Scribner's Sons, New York, 1932.

EDITED
Dictionary of National Biography, Oxford University Press, London, 1921-22 (reprint).

DOBSON, AUSTIN
Horace Walpole, Oxford University Press, London, 1927 (reprint).

DUNBAR, GEORGE
History of India, Ivor Nicholson & Watson, Ltd., London, 1936.

DURANT, WILL
The Story of Civilization—Part I, Our Oriental Heritage, Simon & Schuster, New York, 1935.

DUROST, WALTER NELSON
Children's Collecting Activity Related to Social Factors, Bureau of Publications, Teachers College, Columbia University, New York, 1932.

DUVEEN, JAMES HENRY
Art Treasures and Intrigue, Doubleday, Doran & Co., Inc., New York, 1935; *Secrets of an Art Dealer,* E. P. Dutton & Co., Inc., New York, 1938.

EDWARDS, EDWARD
Free Town Libraries, in Britain, France, Germany, America, Their Formation, Management and History; Together with Brief Notices of Book-Collectors, and of the Respective Places of Deposit of Their Surviving Collections, Trubner & Co., London, 1869; *Lives of the Founders of the British Museum,* Trubner & Co., London, 1870; J. W. Bouton & Co., New York, 1870.

EMMET, THOMAS ADDIS
Incidents of My Life, G. P. Putnam's Sons, New York, 1911.

EDITED
Encyclopedia Britannica, New York and London, 11th Edition, 1910; 14th Edition, 1929.

EDITED
The Encyclopedia of Contemporary Biography of New York, Atlantic Publishing & Engraving Co., New York, 1882.

ERMAN, ADOLF
Life In Ancient Egypt, trans. H. M. Tirard, The Macmillan Company, New York and London, 1894.

EVELYN, JOHN
Diary—4 vols., ed. and with preface by H. B. Wheatley, Bickers and Son, London, 1906.

FEDERN, KARL
Richelieu, Frederick A. Stokes Co., Inc., New York, 1928.

FITZGERALD, C. P.
China, The Cresset Press, London, 1935; D. Appleton-Century Co., New York & London, 1938.

FLETCHER, WILLIAM YOUNGER
English Book Collectors, Kegan Paul, Trench, Trubner & Co., Ltd., London, 1902.

FRIEDLÄNDER, LUDWIG
Roman Life and Manners Under the Early Empire, 7th ed., enl. and rev., 4 vols., George Routledge & Sons, Ltd., London; E. P. Dutton & Co., New York, 1910-13.

FROBENIUS, LEO
The Childhood of Man, trans. A. H. Keane, J. B. Lippincott Co., Philadelphia, 1909.

FUNCK-BRENTANO, FRANTZ
The Renaissance, trans. F. C. Fletcher, The Centenary Press, London, 1936.

GARRATT, GEOFFREY T. (editor)
The Legacy of India, Oxford, At the Clarendon Press, 1937.

GILES, HERBERT
A Chinese Biographical Dictionary, Bernard Quaritch, London, 1898.

GLOTZ, GUSTAVE
The Aegean Civilization, Alfred A. Knopf, Inc., New York, 1925; *Ancient Greece at Work,* Alfred A. Knopf, Inc., New York, 1926.

GOLDENWEISER, ALEXANDER
Anthropology, F. S. Crofts & Co., New York, 1937.

GRANISS, RUTH SHEPARD
See LEHMANN-HAUPT, HELLMUT.

GRANT, HAMIL
Napoleon and the Artists, Grant Richards, Ltd., London, 1917.

GRAY, FRANCIS CALLEY
Thomas Jefferson in 1814—Being an account of a visit to Monticello, Virginia (Diary). Notes and introduction by Henry S. Rowe and T. Jefferson Coolidge, Jr., The Club of Odd Volumes, Boston, (publ.) 1924.

HACKETT, FRANCIS
Francis, The First, Doubleday, Doran & Co., Inc., New York, 1935.

HAMMERTON, SIR JOHN, and BARNES, HARRY ELMER
Illustrated World History, William H. Wise & Co., New York, 1938.

HANUM, PRINCESS DJAVIDAN
Harem Life, The Dial Press, New York, 1933.

HARAUCOURT, EDMOND
Medieval Manners Illustrated at the Cluny Museum, Larousse, Paris, 1927.

HASKINS, CARYL P.
Of Ants and Men, Prentice-Hall, Inc., New York, 1939.

HASKINS, CHARLES HOMER
Studies in the History of Medieval Science, Harvard University Press, Cambridge, 1924.

HAZLITT, WILLIAM CAREW
The Book-Collector, John Grant, London, 1904.

HEARN, LAFCADIO
Japan — An Interpretation, The Macmillan Company, New York, 1905.

HELLMAN, GEORGE S.
Lanes of Memory, Alfred A. Knopf, Inc., New York, 1927.

HIRTH, FRIEDRICH
The Ancient History of China, Columbia University Press, New York, 1923 (reprint).

HOBHOUSE, L. T.
The Historical Evolution of Property, in Fact and in Idea, (Chap. in "Property–Its Duties and Rights," essays by various writers), The Macmillan Company, New York, 1922.

HOWE, WINIFRED E.
A History of the Metropolitan Museum of Art, Metropolitan Museum of Art, New York, 1913.

HYDE, JOHN A. LLOYD
Oriental Lowestoft, Charles Scribner's Sons, New York, 1936.

JAMES, WILLIAM
The Principles of Psychology, Henry Holt & Co., New York, 1893.

JASTROW, MORRIS
The Civilization of Babylonia and Assyria, J. B. Lippincott Co., Philadelphia, 1915.

JOLINE, ADRIAN H.
Rambles in Autograph Land, G. P. Putnam's Sons, New York, 1913; *Meditations of an Autograph Collector,* Harper & Brothers, New York, 1902.

JOSEPHSON, MATTHEW
The Robber Barons, Harcourt, Brace & Co., New York, 1934.

KARDINER, ABRAM
The Individual and His Society, Columbia University Press, New York, 1939.

KARSTEN, RAFAEL
The Head-Hunters of Western Amazonas, Helsingfors, 1935.

KENT, HENRY W.
Van Braam Houckgeest, An Early American Collector, American Antiquarian Society, Worcester, 1931.

KEPPEL, FREDERICK
The Golden Age of Engraving, The Baker and Taylor Company, New York, 1910.

LAMPLAND, RUTH (editor)
Hobbies For Everybody, Harper & Brothers, New York, 1934.

LANCIANI, RODOLFO
The Golden Days of the Renaissance in Rome, Houghton Mifflin & Co., Boston, 1906.

LEHMANN-HAUPT, HELLMUT; GRANISS, RUTH S.; and WROTH, LAWRENCE C.
The Book in America, R. R. Bowker Co., New York, 1939.

LINTON, RALPH
The Study of Man, D. Appleton-Century Co., New York, 1936.

LOSO, FOSTER W. (editor)
The Stamp Collector's Round Table, J. B. Lippincott Co., Philadelphia, 1937.

LOTH, DAVID
Lorenzo the Magnificent, Brentano's, New York, 1929.

LOWIE, ROBERT H.
An Introduction to Cultural Anthropology, Farrar & Rinehart, Inc., New York, 1934.

LUNDBERG, FERDINAND
America's 60 Families, Vanguard Press, New York, 1937.

LUQUET, G. H.
The Art and Religion of Fossil Man, trans. J. Townsend Russell, Jr., Yale University Press, New Haven, 1930; Oxford University Press, London, 1930.

LYDENBERG, HARRY M.
History of the New York Public Library, New York Public Library, New York, 1923.

LYNCH, BOHUN
Collecting—An Essay, Harper & Brothers, New York, 1928.

MACCURDY, GEORGE G.
Human Origins, D. Appleton & Co., New York, 1926.

M'VICKAR, JOHN
A Domestic Narrative of the Life of Samuel Bard, A. Paul, New York, 1822.

MADIGAN, THOMAS F.
Word Shadows of the Great, Frederick A. Stokes Co., New York, 1930.

MAHAFFY, J. P.
Social Life in Greece from Homer to Menander, The Macmillan Company, London, 1925 (reprint); *Greek Life and Thought from the Death of Alexander to the Roman Conquest,* The Macmillan Company, London, 1896; *The Greek World Under Roman Sway,* The Macmillan Company, London, 1890.

MAIR, JOHN
The Fourth Forger—William Ireland and the Shakespeare Papers, Cobden-Sanderson, Ltd., London, 1938; The Macmillan Company, New York, 1939.

MALINOWSKI, BRONISLAW
Argonauts of the Western Pacific, E. P. Dutton & Co., New York, 1922.

MARIÉJOL, JEAN H.
A Daughter of the Medicis—The Romantic Story of Margaret of Valois, trans. John Peile, Harper & Brothers, New York, 1929.

MARQUAND, JOHN P.
The Late George Apley—A Novel in the Form of a Memoir, Little, Brown & Co., Boston, 1938.

MASPÉRO, GASTON
Life in Ancient Egypt and Assyria, D. Appleton & Co., New York, 1895; *Manual of Egyptian Archaeology,* trans. and enl. by Agnes S. John (reprint from 6th English edition, 1913), G. P. Putnam's Sons, New York, 1926.

MATHER, FRANK JEWETT, JR.
Concerning Beauty, Princeton University Press, Princeton, 1935.

MAYER, JOSEPHINE, and PRIDEAUX, TOM
Never to Die—The Egyptians in Their Own Words, The Viking Press, New York, 1938.

MEAD, MARGARET
Cooperation and Competition Among Primitive Peoples, McGraw-Hill Book Company, New York, 1937.

MERCIER, LOUIS SEBASTIEN
The Picture of Paris; Before and After the Revolution, trans. and with introd. by Wilfrid & Emilie Jackson, includes extracts from: *Picture of Paris,* 12 vols., pub. 1781-88; *The New Paris,* pub. after Revolution, George Routledge & Sons, Ltd., London, 1929.

MITCHELL, EDWIN V.
The American Village—Illustrated with material from the Henry Ford collections in Greenfield Village, Michigan, Stackpole Sons, Harrisburg, Pa., 1938.

MITCHELL, SAMUEL L.
Discourse on Thomas Jefferson—More Especially As a Promoter of Natural and Physical Science, G. & C. Carvill, New York, 1826.

MUMFORD, LEWIS
The Culture of Cities, Harcourt, Brace & Co., New York, 1938.

MÜNTZ, EUGÈNE
Les collections des Médicis au XVe Siècle, Jules Rouam, Paris, 1888.

MURCHISON, CARL (editor)
Handbook of Social Psychology, Clark University Press, Worcester, 1935.

MURRAY, DAVID
Museums—Their History and Their Use, James McLehose & Sons, Glasgow. 1904.

EDITED
Handbook of American Museums, The American Association of Museums, Washington, 1932.

MYER, ISAAC
Scarabs, Otto Harrassowitz, Leipzig, 1894; E. W. Dayton Co., New York, 1894.

NEWTON, A. EDWARD
The Amenities of Book-Collecting, Little, Brown & Co., and The Atlantic Monthly Press, Boston, 1918.

NOBILI, RICCARDO
The Gentle Art of Faking, J. B. Lippincott Co., Philadelphia, 1922.

OLDER, MRS. FREMONT
William Randolph Hearst—American, D. Appleton-Century Co., Inc., New York, 1936.

ORLIAC, JEHANNE d'
Francis I—Prince of the Renaissance, trans. Elisabeth Abbott, J. B. Lippincott Co., Philadelphia, 1932.

OSBORNE, DUFFIELD
Engraved Gems, Henry Holt & Co., New York, 1912.

OXFORD, ARNOLD WHITAKER
Collecting Things in a Small Way—Notes From a Collector's Catalogue, J. and E. Bumpus, Ltd., London, 1909.

PARTINGTON, WILFRED
Forging Ahead: The True Story of the Upward Progress of Thomas James Wise, G. P. Putnam's Sons, New York, 1939.

PASCHANG, JOHN L.
The Popes and the Revival of Learning, Catholic University of America, Washington, 1927.

PEATTIE, DONALD CULROSS
Flowering Earth, G. P. Putnam's Sons, New York, 1939.

PENZER, N. M.
The Harem, George G. Harrap & Co., Ltd., London, 1936.

PERKINS, JAMES BRECK
Richelieu, G. P. Putnam's Sons, New York, 1900.

PHILLIPS, CHARLES J.
Stamp Collecting, H. L. Lindquist, New York, 1936.

PLUTARCH
Plutarch's Lives—The Translation Called Dryden's, corrected from the Greek and revised by A. H. Clough, Little, Brown & Co., Boston, 1882.

PONSONBY, ARTHUR
Samuel Pepys, The Book League of America, New York, 1929.

PUTNAM, SAMUEL
Marguerite of Navarre, Coward-McCann, Inc., New York, 1935.

RIGGS, ARTHUR STANLEY
The Romance of Human Progress, The Bobbs-Merrill Co., Indianapolis, 1938.

RIVERS, W. H. R.
Instinct and the Unconscious, 2nd ed. Cambridge (England), At the University Press, 1922.

ROBIE, VIRGINIA
The Quest of the Quaint, Little, Brown & Co., Boston, 1916.

ROBINSON, FREDERICK S.
The Connoisseur, Longmans, Green & Co., New York, 1897.

ROE, SIR THOMAS
The Negotiations of Sir Thomas Roe in his Embassy to the Ottoman Porte, from the Year 1621 to 1628 Inclusive, Samuel Richardson, London, 1740.

ROHAN, THOMAS
In Search of the Antique, Mills & Boon, Ltd., London, 1927; *Old Beautiful,* The Dial Press, New York, 1931.

ROSE, J. HOLLAND
Bonaparte and the Conquest of Italy, Chapter XVIII in Volume 8 of *The Cambridge Modern History,* Cambridge (Eng.), At the University Press, 1904.

ROSENBACH, A. S. W.
Books and Bidders, Little, Brown & Co., Boston, 1927; *A Book Hunter's Holiday,* Houghton Mifflin Co., Boston, 1936.

ROSS, JAMES BRUCE
A Study of Twelfth-Century Interest in the Antiquities of Rome in *Medieval and*

Historiographical Essays in Honor of James Westfall Thompson, ed. James Lea Cate and Eugene N. Anderson, University of Chicago Press, Chicago, 1938.

RUSSELL, C. E.
Charlemagne, First of the Moderns, Houghton Mifflin & Co., Boston, 1930.

SAINTSBURY, GEORGE
Notes on a Cellar-Book, The Macmillan Company, New York, 1933.

SANSOM, G. B.
Japan, D. Appleton-Century Co., New York, 1931.

SATTERLEE, HERBERT L.
J. Pierpont Morgan—An Intimate Portrait, The Macmillan Company, New York, 1939.

SAYCE, R. U.
Primitive Arts and Crafts, Cambridge (Eng.), At the University Press, 1933.

SAYLOR, HENRY H. (editor)
Collecting Antiques for the Home, Robert M. McBride & Co., New York, 1938.

SCHMIDT, ROBERT
Porcelain As an Art and a Mirror of Fashion, trans. W. A. Thorpe, George G. Harrap & Co., London, 1932.

SEELY, GRACE HART
Diane the Huntress—The Life and Times of Diane de Poitiers, D. Appleton-Century Co., New York, 1936.

SHACKLETON, ROBERT, and ELIZABETH
The Charm of the Antique, Hearst's International Library Company, New York, 1913.

SHELLEY, HENRY C.
The Art of the Wallace Collection, L. C. Page & Co., Boston, 1913; *The British Museum,* Sir Isaac Pitman & Sons., Ltd., London, 1911.

SICHEL, EDITH
Women and Men of the French Renaissance, J. B. Lippincott Co., Philadelphia, 1901.

SIMONDS, WILLIAM ADAMS
Henry Ford and Greenfield Village, Frederick A. Stokes Co., New York, 1938.

SIRÉN, OSVALD
A History of Early Chinese Painting, The Medici Society, London, 1933; *A History of Later Chinese Painting,* The Medici Society, London, 1938.

STEVENS, HENRY, of Vermont
Recollections of Mr. James Lenox of New York and the Formation of His Library, Henry Stevens & Son, London, 1886.

SUETONIUS
Lives of the First Twelve Caesars, trans. Alexander Thomson, G. G. & J. Robinson, London, 1746.

SYMONDS, JOHN ADDINGTON
Renaissance in Italy: The Revival of Learning, Smith, Elder & Co., London, 1907.

TEALL, GARDNER
The Pleasures of Collecting, The Century Co., New York, 1920.

THOMAS, WILLIAM I.
Primitive Behavior, Chapter XIII, The McGraw-Hill Book Co., New York, 1937.

THOMPSON, JAMES WESTFALL
Byways in Bookland, The Book Arts Club of the University of California, Berkeley, 1935.

THOMPSON, JAMES WESTFALL, and others
The Medieval Library, University of Chicago Press, Chicago, 1939.

THORNDIKE, EDWARD L.
Educational Psychology, Teachers College, Columbia University, New York, 1930.

TROUNCER, MARGARET
The Pompadour, Faber & Faber, London, 1937.

TYLOR, EDWARD B.
Primitive Culture, Henry Holt & Co., New York, 1874.

VAN DYKE, PAUL
Catherine de Médicis, Charles Scribner's Sons, New York, 1927.

VASARI, GIORGIO
"Michelangolo Buonarroti" in *Lives of Seventy of the Most Eminent Painters,*

Sculptors and Architects, ed. E. H. & E. W. Blashfield & A. A. Hopkins, Charles Scribner's Sons, New York, 1909.

VEBLEN, THORSTEIN
The Theory of the Leisure Class, The Viking Press, New York, 1935 (reprint).

WEALE, B. L. PUTNAM (pseud. of B. L. SIMPSON)
Indiscreet Letters from Peking, Dodd, Mead and Co., New York, 1907.

WEIGALL, A. E. P. B.
The Life and Times of Marc Antony, G. P. Putnam's Sons, New York, 1931.

WELLS, H. G.; HUXLEY, JULIAN S.; and WELLS, G. P.
The Science of Life, Doubleday, Doran & Co., New York, 1931.

WERNER, MORRIS R.
Barnum, Harcourt, Brace & Co., New York, 1923.

WEST, HERBERT FAULKNER
Modern Book Collecting for the Impecunius Amateur, Little, Brown & Co., Boston, 1936.

WESTERMARCK, EDWARD
The History of Human Marriage, Vol. III, 5th ed. rewr., Allerton Book Co., New York, 1922.

WILLIAMSON, GEORGE CHARLES
Stories of an Expert, Herbert Jenkins, Ltd., London, 1925.

WINKLER, JOHN K.
Morgan the Magnificent, The Vanguard Press, New York, 1930.

WISSLER, CLARK
The American Indian, Oxford University Press, New York, 1922.

WOOLLEY, C. LEONARD
The Sumerians, The Clarendon Press, Oxford, 1928; *Ur of the Chaldees*, Charles Scribner's Sons, New York, 1930; *The Development of Sumerian Art*, Faber & Faber, London, 1935.

YOXALL, SIR JAMES
The ABC About Collecting, 4th ed., E. P. Dutton & Co., New York, 1923; *More About Collecting*, S. Paul and Co., London, 1913; George W. Jacobs & Co., Philadelphia.

CATALOGUES AND SPECIAL PUBLICATIONS

AINÉ, DUCHESNE
"Musée Français. Recueil des plus Beaux Tableaux, Statues, et Bas-Reliefs qui existaient au Louvre avant 1815," (343 line engravings, with descriptive text in French and English; gives history of items, including restoration of those taken by Napoleon), 4 vols. imperial folio, A. et W. Galignani, Paris; J. O. Robinson, London, 1829-30.

BOLTON, ARTHUR T.
"Description of the House and Museum —The Residence of Sir John Soane," ed. from the original description of the Founder, 1835. Soane Museum Publication, No. 1, London, 1920; "Pitzhanger Manor," Soane Museum Publication, No. 4, London.

BONNAFFÉ, EDMOND
"Inventaire des meubles de Catherine de Médicis en 1589," Auguste Aubry, Paris, 1874.

BRECK, JOSEPH, and ROGERS, MEYRIC R.
"The Pierpont Morgan Wing," Metropolitan Museum of Art, New York, 1929.

CHALON, RENIER HUBERT GHISLAIN
"Catalogue d'une très-riche mais peu nombreuse collection De Livres provenant de la Bibliothèque de feu M.-le Comte J.-N.-A. de Fortsas," Mons, 1840.

COX, TRENCHARD
"A Short Illustrated History of the Wallace Collection," printed for the Trustees of the Wallace Collection, London, 1936.

DIMOCK, GEORGE E.
"Henry C. Folger – A Biographical Sketch," in memorial volume, Privately Printed, New Haven, 1931.

HARCOURT-SMITH, SIMON
"A Catalogue of Various Clocks, Watches, Automata, and other miscellaneous objects of European Workmanship Dating from the XVIIIth and early XIXth centuries, in the Palace Museum and the Wu Ying Tien, Peiping," The Palace Museum, Peiping, 1933.

HÉRISSON, COUNT D'
"The Loot of the Imperial Summer Palace at Pekin," extracts translated from *Journal d'un interprète en Chine,* Nouvelle édition, Paris, 1901, in Smithsonian Institution, Annual Report, Washington, 1899-1900.

EDITED
"Histoire des collections de peintures au Musée du Louvre," Musées Nationaux, Palais du Louvre, Paris, 1930.

HOBHOUSE, L. T., WHEELER, G. C., and GINSBERG, M.
"The Material Culture and Social Institutions of the Simpler Peoples," No. 3 of the Monographs on Sociology, The London School of Economics and Political Science, University of London, 1930 (reprint).

JEFFERSON, THOMAS
"Classified List of Manuscripts, Books, Correspondence, etc., of Thomas Jefferson, Offered by Purchase to the United States by Sarah N. Randolph," includes "Bound Catalogue of His Library," U. S. Government Printing Office, Washington, 1889.

LIANG CHI-CHAO
"Archaeology in China," in Annual Report of the Smithsonian Institution, Washington, 1927.

LOW, THEODORE L.
"The Museum As a Social Instrument," Published at The Metropolitan Museum of Art, New York, for The American Association of Museums, 1942.

MCCALL, GEORGE HENRY
"The Joseph Widener Collection–Tapestries at Lynnewood Hall, Elkins Park, Pennsylvania–with Historical Introduction and Descriptive Notes," Privately Printed, Philadelphia, 1932.

UNSIGNED
"Andrew W. Mellon's Art Gift to the Nation," The Smithsonian Institution: Annual Report of the Board of Regents, for year ending June 30, 1937, Washington, 1937.

UNSIGNED
"An Almanac for the Year 1930–The Sixtieth in the History of the Museum," (includes dates of museum history from all nations), Metropolitan Museum of Art, New York, 1930.

UNSIGNED
"Annual Reports of the Trustees," Metropolitan Museum of Art, New York, 1871-1938.

UNSIGNED
"A Brief Record of Development, 1870–1937," Metropolitan Museum of Art, New York, 1937.

UNSIGNED
"Handbook of the Benjamin Altman Collection," Metropolitan Museum of Art, New York, April, 1915.

UNSIGNED
"Guide to the Loan Exhibition of the J. Pierpont Morgan Collection," Metropolitan Museum of Art, New York, 1914.

UNSIGNED
"The Pierpont Morgan Wing," Metropolitan Museum of Art, New York, 1918.

UNSIGNED
"The Metropolitan Museum of Art–A Review of Fifty Years' Development," Metropolitan Museum of Art, New York, 1923.

MIERS, SIR HENRY ALEXANDER
"A Report on the Public Museums of the British Isles–To the Carnegie United Kingdom Trustees," T. & A. Constable, Ltd., Edinburgh, 1928.

PARRIAUX, L.
"Anet et le château de Diane de Poitiers," Anet, France.

UNSIGNED
"Peale's Museum Gallery of Oil Paintings," sale catalogue, M. Thomas & Sons, Philadelphia, October 6, 1854.

PEALE, C. W. and BEAUVOIS A. N. F. J.
"A Scientific and Descriptive Catalogue of Peale's Museum," Samuel H. Smith, Philadelphia, 1796.

PETRIE, W. M. FLINDERS
"Abydos—Part II, 1903," p. 27; and plate IX, numbers 194, 195, 196, 24th Memoir of the Egypt Exploration Fund, London, 1903.

ROSENBACH, A. S. W.
"Henry Clay Folger As a Collector," in memorial volume, Privately Printed, New Haven, 1931; "A Catalogue of the Books and Manuscripts of Robert Louis Stevenson in the Library of the Late Harry Elkins Widener—With a Memoir," Privately Printed, Philadelphia, 1913.

SCHAD, ROBERT O.
"Henry Edwards Huntington – The Founder and the Library," 4th printing rev., Henry E. Huntington Library and Art Gallery, San Marino, 1937.

SIDGWICK, FRANK
"Bibliotheca Pepysiana—A Descriptive Catalogue of the Library of Samuel Pepys," Part II, General Introduction, Sidgwick and Jackson, Ltd., London, 1914-23.

SLADE, WILLIAM ADAMS
"The Significance of the Shakespeare Memorial," in Henry Clay Folger memorial volume, Privately Printed, New Haven, 1931.

EDITED
"Descriptive Sociology—Ancient Egyptians," Div. I, No. 11 of the Herbert Spencer Trusteeship Compilation, Williams and Norgate, Ltd., London, 1925.

STARR, FREDERICK
"Japanese Collectors and What They Collect," The Bookfellows, Chicago, 1921.

TRADESCANT, JOHN
"Museum Tradescantium or A Collection of Rarities Preserved at South Lambeth neer London by John Tradescant, London," Printed by John Grismond, and are to be sold by Nathanael Brooke at the Angel in Cornhill, M.DC.LVI (1656).

WALPOLE, HORACE
"The Duchess of Portland's Museum," introd. W. S. Lewis, The Grolier Club, New York, 1936.

UNSIGNED
"Handbook of the Collection," Walters Art Gallery, Baltimore, 1936.

UNSIGNED
"Annual Reports of the Trustees," Walters Art Gallery, Baltimore, 1933-41.

MAGAZINE AND NEWSPAPER ARTICLES
(a partial list)

ALEXANDER, JACK
"Cellini to Hearst to Klotz," *Saturday Evening Post*, Philadelphia, Nov. 1, 1941.

ARNOLD, FRANK A.
"Collecting Crooked Sticks," *The Countryside and Suburban Magazine*, Boston, August, 1915.

UNSIGNED
"Albert Coombs Barnes," *Art Digest*, New York, April 15, 1935.

UNSIGNED
"Albert Coombs Barnes," *News Week*, April 25, 1936.

UNSIGNED
"A Few More Masterpieces Immured in Barnes Collection," *News Week*, September 12, 1936.

UNSIGNED
"75th Cézanne," *Time*, New York, September 14, 1936.

BARSTOW, NINA
"The Forgeries of Bastianini," *Magazine of Art*, Vol. 9, London, 1886.

BENNETT, ARNOLD
"Collecting," *Woman's Home Companion*, New York, May, 1924.

BENSON, E. F.
"The Joy of the Chase," Fine Arts and Antiques Supplement to *The Spectator*, London, April 20, 1929.

BLUMENTHAL, H. M.
"Antiquedotes," *Saturday Evening Post*, Philadelphia, Sept. 17, 1932.

BROOKS, PHILIP
"Notes on Rare Books," (Berg Collection), *New York Times Book Review*, New York, June 22, 1941.

BROWN, BARNUM
"Is This the Earliest Known Fossil Collected By Man?", *Natural History*, Vol. XXVI, No. 5, New York, 1926.

BURK, CAROLINE FREAR
"The Collecting Instinct," Pedagogical Seminary, Vol. VII, Worcester, 1900.

CALDWELL, KATHERINE FIELD
"The American Art Patron," (Albert Bender), *Magazine of Art*, Washington, August, 1938.

CARLTON, W. N. C.
"Henry Edwards Huntington," *The American Collector*, Vol. 4, Metuchen, N. J., 1927.

CARPENTER, WARWICK S.
"Mr. Gray's Horseless Carriages," *Country Life*, New York, January, 1935.

CARTWRIGHT, JULIA (JULIA M. C. ADY)
"The Lost Cupid of Michelangelo," *Magazine of Art*, Vol. 9, London, 1886.

CASSON, STANLEY
"The Popularity of Greek Archaic Art," *Magazine of Art*, Washington, May, 1937.

UNSIGNED
"Collecting: Impulse Ranges from Relaxation to Big Business," *Literary Digest*, New York, February 27, 1937.

COTTON, ALBERT LOUIS
"Association Books," *Contemporary Review*, London, October, 1922.

CRAWFORD, O. G. S.
"The Dialectical Process in the History of Science," *Sociological Review*, London, April-July, 1932.

UNSIGNED
"The Criminal Confessions of a Collector," *Saturday Evening Post*, Philadelphia, April 19, 1924.

CUSHING, CHARLES P.
"Costly Blunders That Make Valuable Stamps," *Colliers*, New York, January 10, 1925.

DECKER, KARL
"How and Why the Mona Lisa was Stolen," *Saturday Evening Post*, Philadelphia, June 25, 1932.

DEVREE, HOWARD
"The Museum As a Human Thing," *New York Times Magazine*, New York, May 5, 1940.

UNSIGNED
On Alceo Dossena, *Art News*, New York, December 1, 1928.

UNSIGNED
On Alceo Dossena, *Art and Archaeology*, Washington, June, 1929.

UNSIGNED
On Alceo Dossena, *Art Digest*, New York, May 15, 1931; June 1, 1931.

DOWNES, OLIN
"Five New Haydn Symphonies," *New York Times*, New York, February 5, 1939.

DUCACHET, HENRY W.
"A Biographical Memoir of Samuel Bard," *American Medical Recorder*, Vol. 4, Philadelphia, 1821.

DUVEEN, JAMES HENRY
"The Rise and Fall of Old Masters," *Windsor Magazine*, London, November, 1936.

EARLY, STEPHEN (FOR FRANKLIN DELANO ROOSEVELT)
Correspondence with "Father Divine," *re* disposition of former Bard estate pub. *New York Times*, New York, August 17, 1939.

UNSIGNED
"Fleet of Antique Cars is Big Money Maker," *Popular Science Monthly*, New York, February, 1935.

FAVIER, ADOLPH (BISHOP OF PEKIN)
"An Answer to Charges of Looting," *The Independent*, New York, December, 1901.

FLOWER, DESMOND
"Napoleon As Bibliophile," *Book-Collector's Quarterly*, London, January-March, 1932.

FRIEDEMANN, MAX
"Cleptomania: The Analytic and Forensic Aspects," trans. Clara Willard, *Psychoanalytic Review*, New York, October, 1930 (originally publ. in German, 1928).

GARMAN, C. W.
"Collecting As an Educational Factor," *General Science Quarterly* (now *Science Education*), Salem, Mass., March, 1929.

GRUNDY, C. REGINALD
"American Collectors," *Connoisseur*, London, November, 1926

HALL, WILBUR
"His Hobby Is Collecting Branding Irons," *Sunset Magazine*, San Francisco, April, 1935.

HARAUCOURT, EDMOND
"Recognizing the Fraudulent Antique," *House and Garden*, New York, October, 1927; "Making and Launching Frauds," *House and Garden*, New York, November, 1927; "When Experts Go Astray," *House and Garden*, New York, December, 1927.

HARRINGTON, JOHN W.
"Postal Carditis and Some Allied Manias," *American Magazine*, New York, March, 1906.

HERGESHEIMER, JOSEPH
"Of Ultimate Antiques," *Saturday Evening Post*, Philadelphia, December 22, 1928.

UNSIGNED
"Hobbies," *Life*, New York, January 2, 1939.

UNSIGNED
"Letters to the Editor," (*re* above) *Life*, New York, January 23, 1939.

HOFFMAN, JOSEPH
"The Hobby of Kids and Kings," (Stamp Collecting), *World Review*, Mt. Morris, Ill., March 5, 1928.

HOUGH, DOROTHY WHITEHEAD
"Hobbies and Collections," *Child Welfare Magazine* (now *National Parent-Teacher*), New York, February, 1930.

HUMPHREYS, A. L.
"Elias Ashmole," *The Berks, Bucks, and Oxon Archaeological Journal*, Reading (England), Spring, 1924.

HU SHIH
"Woman's Place in Chinese History," *The Week in China*, pub. by *The Leader*, Peiping, February 7, 1931.

JEWELL, EDWARD ALDEN
"Hearst Collection Put on Exhibition," *New York Times*, New York, January 28, 1941; "Melange: Hearst's Collection Put On Sale," *New York Times*, New York, February 2, 1941.

JOHNSON, SAMUEL
The Idler, London, May 12, 1759; *The Rambler*, London, December 29, 1750.

JOHNSON, THOMAS M.
"Strange Things People Collect," *Popular Science Monthly*, New York, August, 1934.

JONES, E. ALFRED
"Pepys As an Art Collector and Critic," *The National Review*, Vol. 76, London, 1920.

UNSIGNED
"King George and Other Famous Stamp Fans," *Literary Digest*, New York, September 22, 1928.

UNSIGNED
"Kings and Queens as Collectors," *The Antique Collector,* London, May, 1937.

LANG, ANDREW
"An Exhibition of Fakes," *The Independent,* New York, October 17, 1901; "The Humors of Collecting," *The Independent,* New York, June 16, 1910.

LAW, MARGARET LATHROP
"Collectors' Pitfalls," *Saturday Evening Post,* Philadelphia, December 19, 1925.

LESUEUR, FRÉDÉRIC
"Menars, le château, les jardins et les collections de Mme. de Pompadour et du Marquis de Marigny," *Société des Sciences et Lettres de Loir-et-Cher,* Vol. 21, Blois, 1912.

LE SUFFLEUR, DAVID
"Louis XIV Collectionneur," *Revue de Paris,* Paris, March 1, 1927.

LITTLEHALES, H.
"A Medieval Autograph Book," *The Connoisseur,* London, August, 1925.

LYDENBERG, HARRY M.
"The Collector's Progress," *Journal of Adult Education,* New York, April, 1940.

MCCARDLE, CARL W.
"The Terrible-Tempered Dr. Barnes," *Saturday Evening Post,* Philadelphia, March 21, 28, April 4, 11, 1942.

MACFARLANE, HAROLD
"Napoleon versus Wellington—The Comparative Value of Relics," *The Connoisseur,* Vol. 8, London, 1904.

MADAN, FALCONER
"The Ashmolean Museum," *The Berks, Bucks, and Oxon Archaeological Journal,* Reading (England), October, 1897.

UNSIGNED
Reports on Andrew W. Mellon Collection, *New York Times,* New York.
January 3, 4, 7, 10, 1937
February 11, 1937
August 27, 1937
January 14, 19, 1938; *New York Times Magazine,* New York, February 28, 1937.

UNSIGNED
"A Million Dollar Hobby Everyone Can Ride," *Popular Mechanics Magazine,* Chicago, October, 1934.

MONTAIGLON, ANATOLE DE
"Diane de Poitiers et son goût dans les arts," *Gazette des Beaux Arts,* Paris, April, 1878.

UNSIGNED
"Mr. John Pierpont Morgan," *The Burlington Magazine,* London, May, 1913.

MORISON, SAMUEL ELIOT
"F. D. R., Librarian," *Reader's Digest,* Pleasantville, N. Y., June, 1939, reprint from *American Magazine.*

MORRIS, FRANK D.
"Stamp Stampede," *Colliers,* New York, July 30, 1938.

MUDGE, E. LEIGH
"Girls' Collections," Pedagogical Seminary, Worcester, September, 1918.

MUNRO, THOMAS
"Art and World Citizenship," *Magazine of Art,* Washington, October, 1938.

UNSIGNED
"New Traps for Picture Fakers," *Literary Digest,* New York, April 26, 1924.

NICHOLSON, ARNOLD
"Slightly Off Center," (stamps), *Saturday Evening Post,* Philadelphia, October 27, 1934.

O'DONNELL, JACK
"The Hobby of Kids and Kings," (stamp collecting), *Saturday Evening Post,* Philadelphia, November 14, 1925.

OSBORNE, DUFFIELD
"Collectors and Collecting," *The Independent,* New York, November 21, 1912.

OWEN, JENNIE SMALL
"Collecting Hobbyists," *Scribner's Magazine,* New York, January, 1936.

OWL, GREY (GREY OWL)
"My Animal Guests at Ajawaan," *Reader's Digest,* Pleasantville, N. Y., January, 1940.

PATTON, JOHN S.
"Thomas Jefferson's Contributions to Natural History," *Natural History,* New York, April-May, 1919.

PELLIOT, PAUL, editor
"T'oung Pao—Archives concernant l'histoire, les langues, la géographie et l'ethnographie de l'Asie orientale," Series II, Vol. XXVI, E. J. Brill, Leyden, 1929.

PHILES, GEORGE P.
"Bibliographical Hoaxing—Count de Fortsas' Library," *The Philobiblion,* New York, April, 1863.

PICAUD, M. A.
"Le collectionnisme chez les animaux et chez l'homme," *Société Dauphinoise d'Ethnologie et d'Anthropologie,* Grenoble, April and July, 1903.

PRICE, CLAIR
"A Full-Length Portrait of Pepys," *New York Times Magazine,* New York, January 29, 1939; "Stirring Odyssey of Spanish Art," *New York Times Magazine,* New York, May 28, 1939.

REID, GILBERT
"The Ethics of Loot," *The Forum,* New York, July, 1901.

REINACH, M. SALOMON
"Le Musée de l'Empereur Auguste," *Revue d'Anthropologie,* Series 3, Vol. IV, Paris, 1889.

REY, PATRICIA
"Morgan House of Treasures," *New York Times Magazine,* New York, May 21, 1939.

ROBERTS, EDITH D.
"Book Collector, Italian, Seventeenth Century," *Colophon,* New Series, Vol. I, New York, February, 1936.

ROBERTS, KENNETH L.
"Antiquamania," *Saturday Evening Post,* Philadelphia, March 14, 1925; "Collectors' Wives," *Saturday Evening Post,* Philadelphia, January 25, 1930.

ROBINSON, A. MARY F.
"Diane de Poictiers," *Magazine of Art,* Vol. 9, London, 1886.

SALAMANCA, LUCY
"America Honors Shakespeare the Poet," *re* Henry Clay Folger bequest, *New York Times Magazine,* New York, August 24, 1930.

SALESKA, MARILYN
"Fox Teeth," in "What Is Your Hobby?", Children's Day section of *Woman's Day,* New York, April, 1939.

SARGENT, GEORGE H.
"H. C. Folger—Shakespeare Collection," *New York Times,* New York, April 22, 1928.

SCHOEN, EUGENE
"Industrial Design: A New Profession," *Magazine of Art,* Washington, August, 1938.

SHACKLETON, ELIZABETH
"Fads and Fancies of Collectors," *Saturday Evening Post,* Philadelphia, August 9, 1924.

UNSIGNED
Reports on history and prices of Shakespeare First Folios, *New York Times,* New York.
September 25, 1927
March 13, 14, 1929
April 3, 1938.

SLATER, WILLARD
"Why Japan Collects Western Art," *International Studio,* New York and London, April, 1922.

SMITH, A. R.
"Lord Elgin and His Collection," *Journal of Hellenic Studies,* Vol. 36, Part 2, London, 1916.

SMITH, E. H.
"Art and Useful Art," *Saturday Evening Post,* Philadelphia, May 17, 1924.

SMITH, ROBERT H.
Review of analysis of Shakespeare folios in the United States, *New York Times,* New York, May 8, 1927.

UNSIGNED
"Festive Crowd Strips Train of Souvenirs," *World-Telegram,* New York, December 5, 1938.

UNSIGNED
"Souvenirs of the 'El' Prized," *New York Times Magazine,* New York, February 5, 1939.

STILES, KENT B.
"High Price for Block American Rarity of 1869 Joins the Collection of E. B. Martin," *New York Times,* New York, December 18, 1938; "More Tests for

Stamps," *New York Times,* New York, May 14, 1939.

STOW, CHARLES MESSER
"Henry Ford—Historian," *The Antiquarian,* New York, April, 1929; "Henry Ford, Rebuilder of Tradition," *The Antiquarian,* New York, April, 1930.

SWIFT, SAMUEL
"A Deal in Pictures," *Harper's Weekly,* New York, June 6, 1908.

THOMPSON, LAWRANCE
"Notes on Some Collectors in Colonial Massachusetts," *Colophon,* New Series, New York, October, 1936.

UNSIGNED
"Treasures Laid Up," (autographs), *The Nation,* London, October 2, 1920.

VALE, EDMUND
"The Postcard Fancy," *The Spectator,* London, August 13, 1937.

WALEY, ARTHUR D.
"The Rarity of Ancient Chinese Paintings," *Burlington Magazine,* London, April, 1917.

WANG KUO-WEI
"Archaeology in the Sung Dynasty," trans. C. H. Liu, *China Journal,* Shanghai, May, 1927.

WATTS, ARRETTA L.
"Around the World for Rugs," *The World Today,* London, April, 1930.

WHARTON, ANNE HOLLINGSWORTH
"Charles Willson Peale," *Scribner's Magazine,* New York, June, 1923.

WHITLEY, M. T.
"Children's Interest in Collecting," *Journal of Educational Psychology,* Baltimore, April, 1929.

UNSIGNED
"Mrs. H. P. Whitney, Sculptor, Is Dead," *New York Times,* New York, April 18, 1942.

WINN, MARY DAY
"Don Juan As a Collector," *North American Review,* New York, March, 1932.

WITTELS, FRITZ
"Some Remarks on Kleptomania," *Journal of Nervous and Mental Disease,* New York, March, 1929.

WITTY, PAUL H. and LEHMAN, HARVEY C.
"Further Studies of Children's Interest in Collecting," *Journal of Educational Psychology,* Baltimore, February, 1930; "Sex Differences: Collecting Interests," *Journal of Educational Psychology,* Baltimore, March, 1931.

WOOLF, S. J.
"The Rich Gift Mellon Bestows on the Nation," *New York Times Magazine,* New York, February 28, 1937.

WOOLLEY, C. LEONARD
"The Excavations at Ur, 1925-6," *The Antiquaries Journal,* London, October, 1926; "The Excavations at Ur, 1926-7," *The Antiquaries Journal,* London, 1927; "Excavations at Ur, 1931-2," *The University of Pennsylvania Museum Journal,* Vol. 23, No. 3, Philadelphia, 1933.

WRIGHT, DUDLEY
"Elias Ashmole," *The Freemason,* London.

YOUNG, JAMES C.
"Search for Shakespeare Manuscripts Is Never Ending," *New York Times Magazine,* New York, February 21, 1926.

INDEX

(Italic entries indicate titles of books and works of art. For an indexed guide to the illustrations, see front of book.)